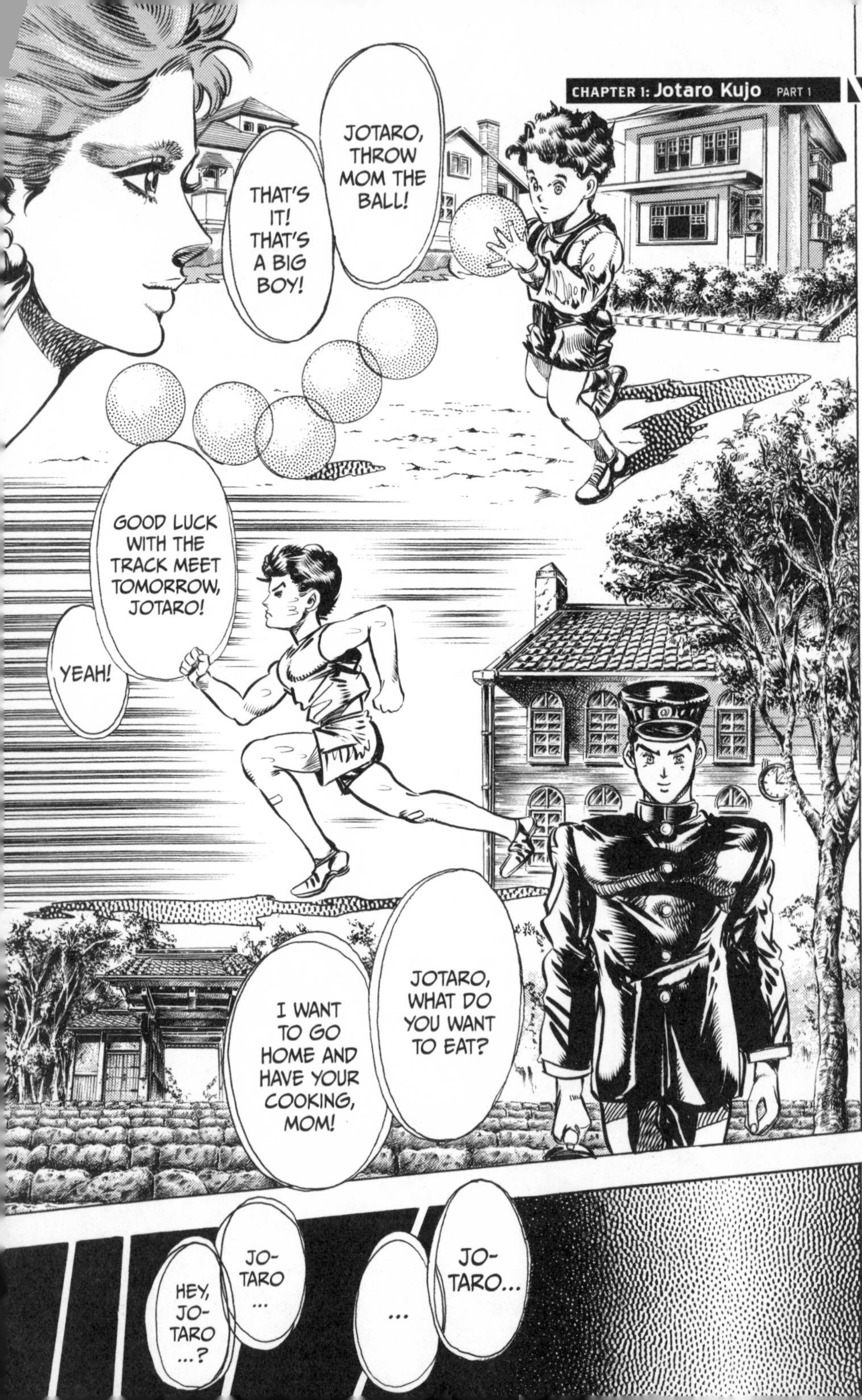
JOTARO, THROW MOM THE BALL!
THAT'S IT! THAT'S A BIG BOY!
GOOD LUCK WITH THE TRACK MEET TOMORROW, JOTARO!
YEAH!
JOTARO, WHAT DO YOU WANT TO EAT?
I WANT TO GO HOME AND HAVE YOUR COOKING, MOM!
JO-TARO...
...
JO-TARO ...
HEY, JO-TARO ...?

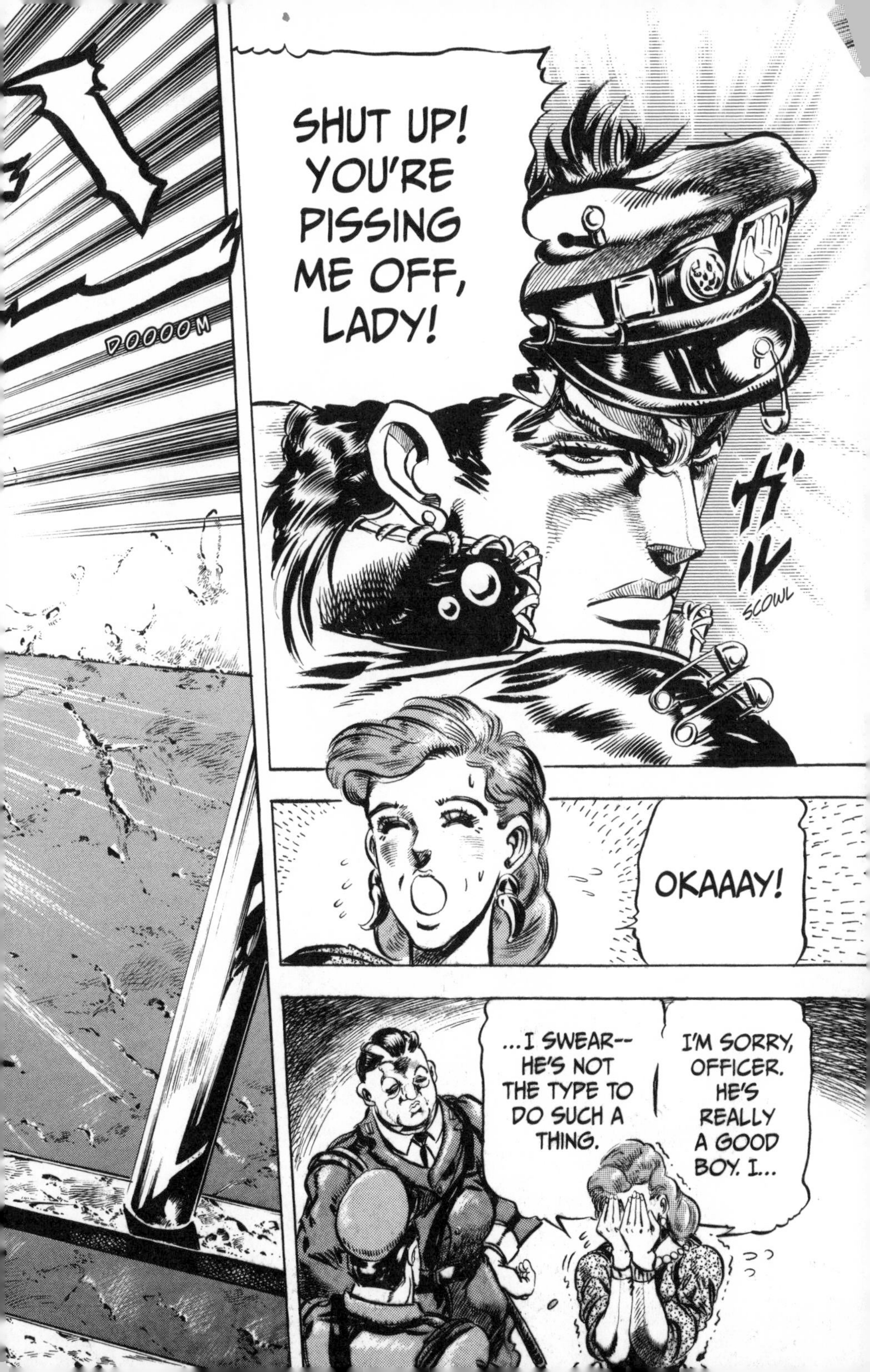
SHUT UP! YOU'RE PISSING ME OFF, LADY!
SCOWL
OKAAAY!
I'M SORRY, OFFICER. HE'S REALLY A GOOD BOY. I...
...I SWEAR-- HE'S NOT THE TYPE TO DO SUCH A THING.
DOOOOM

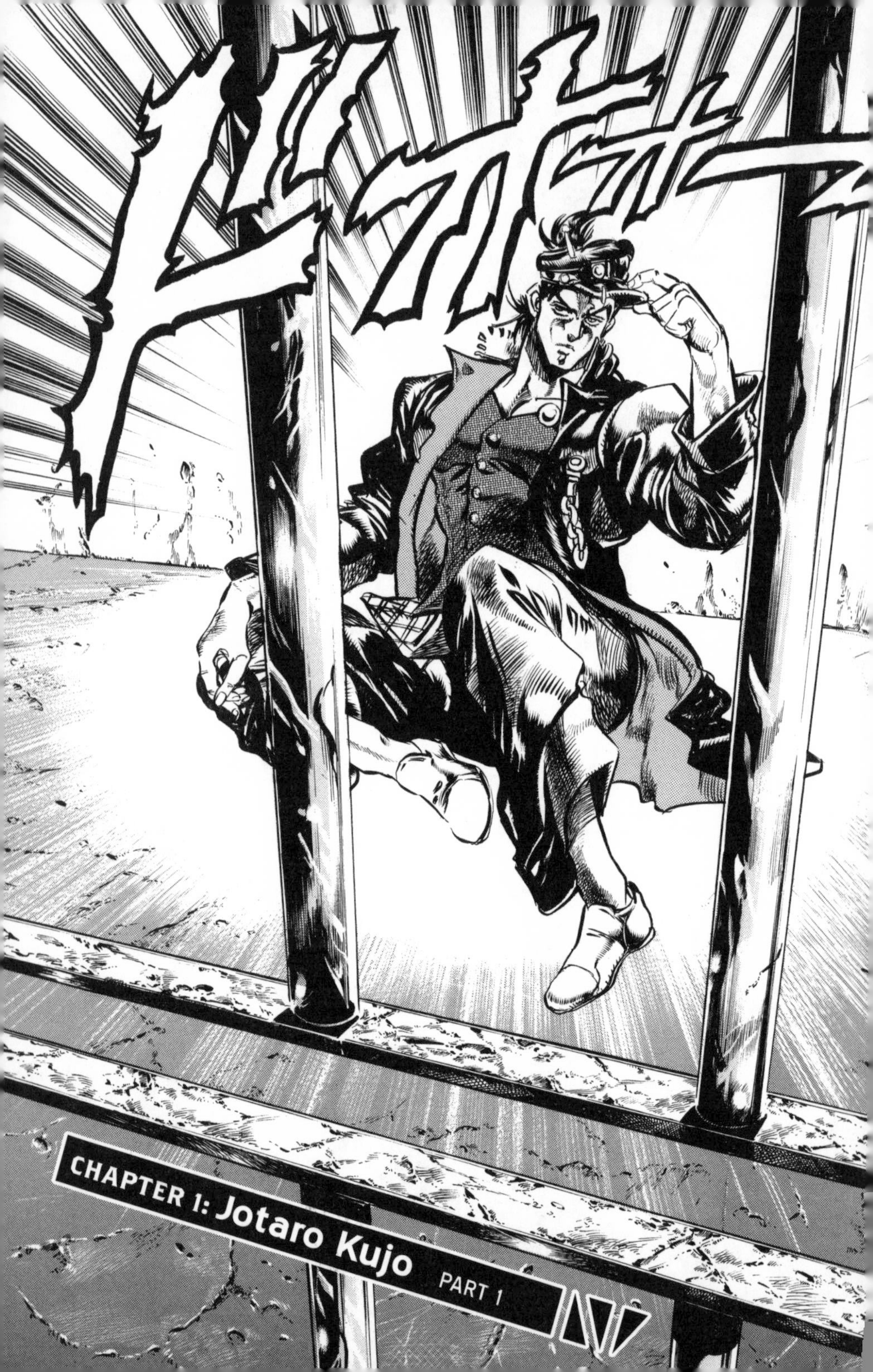
CHAPTER 1: Jotaro Kujo PART 1

PART 3

STARDUST CRUSADERS

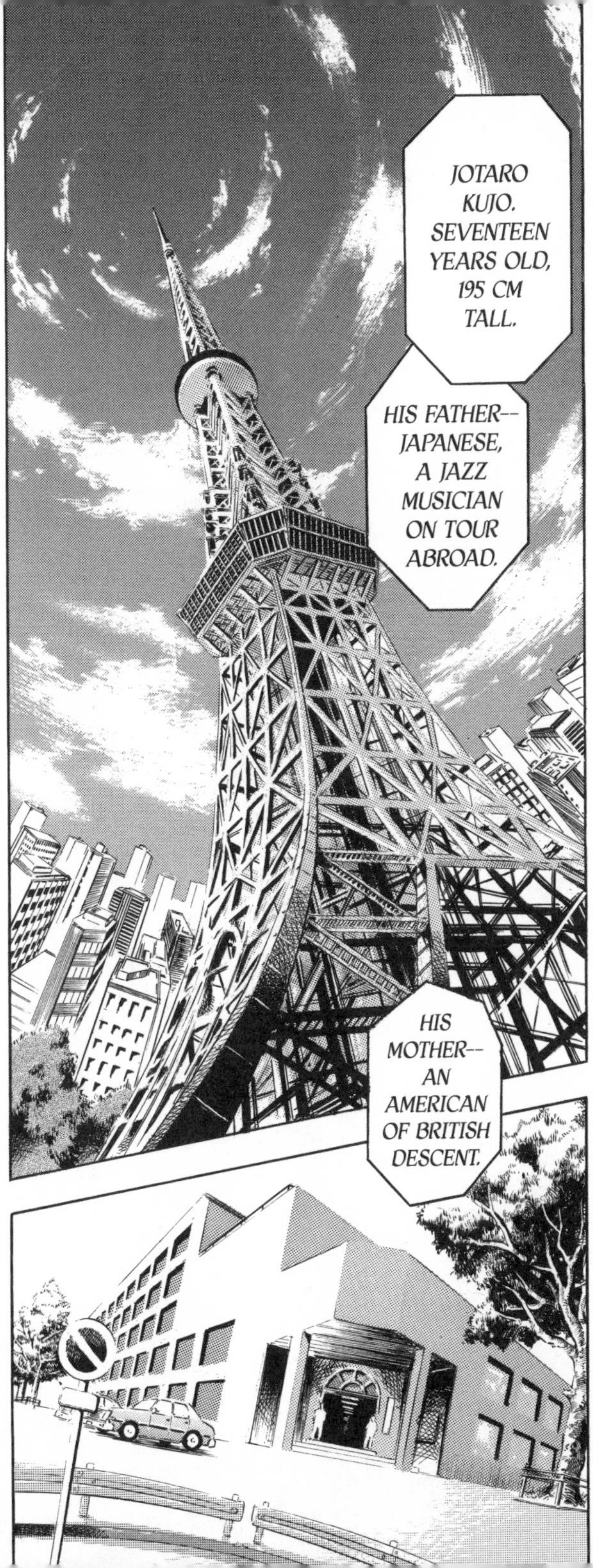
JOTARO KUJO. SEVENTEEN YEARS OLD, 195 CM TALL.
HIS FATHER--JAPANESE, A JAZZ MUSICIAN ON TOUR ABROAD.
HIS MOTHER--AN AMERICAN OF BRITISH DESCENT.

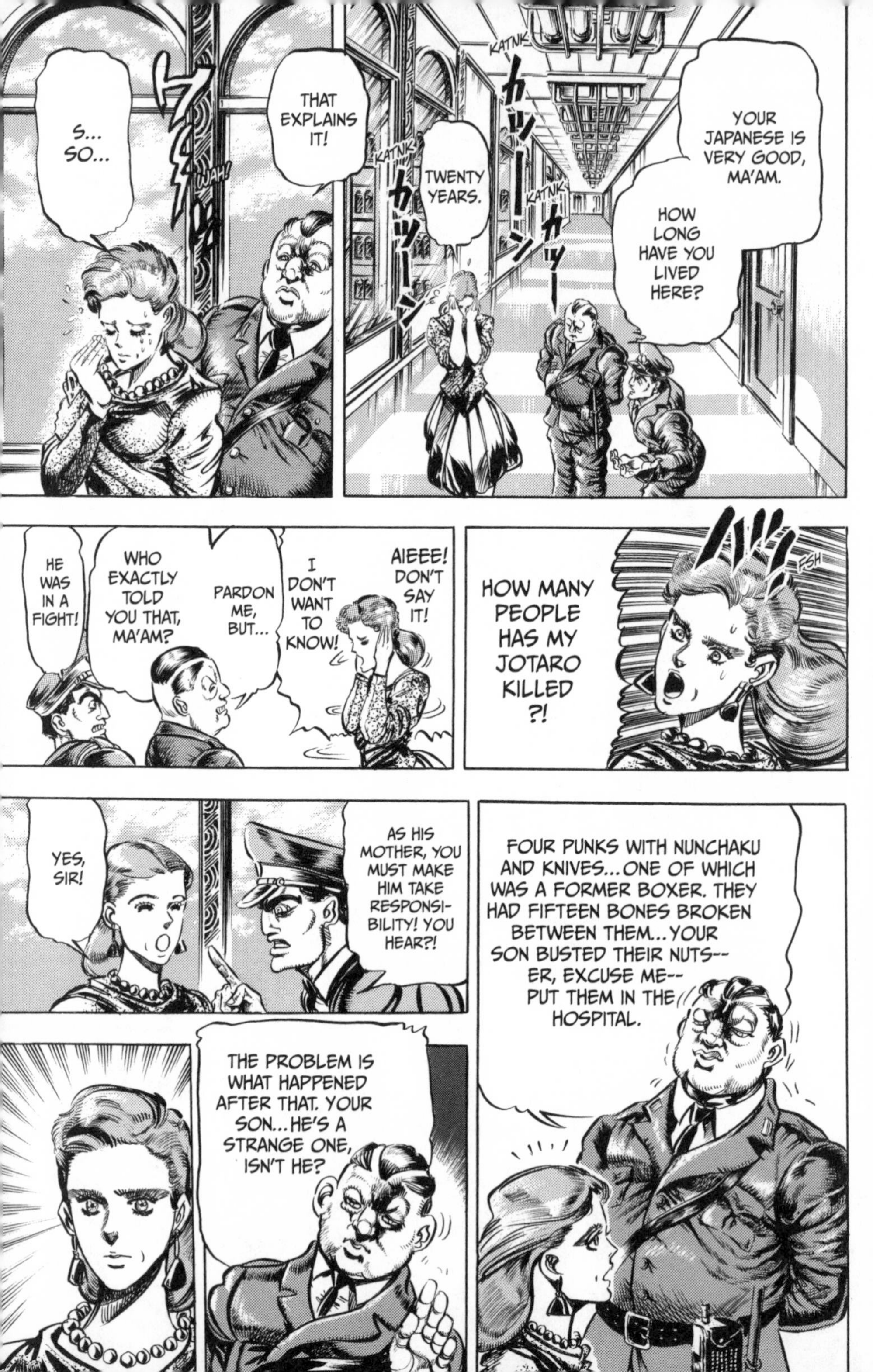
KATNK
YOUR JAPANESE IS VERY GOOD, MA'AM.
HOW LONG HAVE YOU LIVED HERE?
KATNK
KATNK
TWENTY YEARS.
THAT EXPLAINS IT!
WAH!
S... SO...
FSH
HOW MANY PEOPLE HAS MY JOTARO KILLED?!
AIEEE! DON'T SAY IT!
I DON'T WANT TO KNOW!
PARDON ME, BUT...
WHO EXACTLY TOLD YOU THAT, MA'AM?
HE WAS IN A FIGHT!
FOUR PUNKS WITH NUNCHAKU AND KNIVES...ONE OF WHICH WAS A FORMER BOXER. THEY HAD FIFTEEN BONES BROKEN BETWEEN THEM...YOUR SON BUSTED THEIR NUTS-- ER, EXCUSE ME-- PUT THEM IN THE HOSPITAL.
AS HIS MOTHER, YOU MUST MAKE HIM TAKE RESPONSI-BILITY! YOU HEAR?!
YES, SIR!
THE PROBLEM IS WHAT HAPPENED AFTER THAT. YOUR SON...HE'S A STRANGE ONE, ISN'T HE?

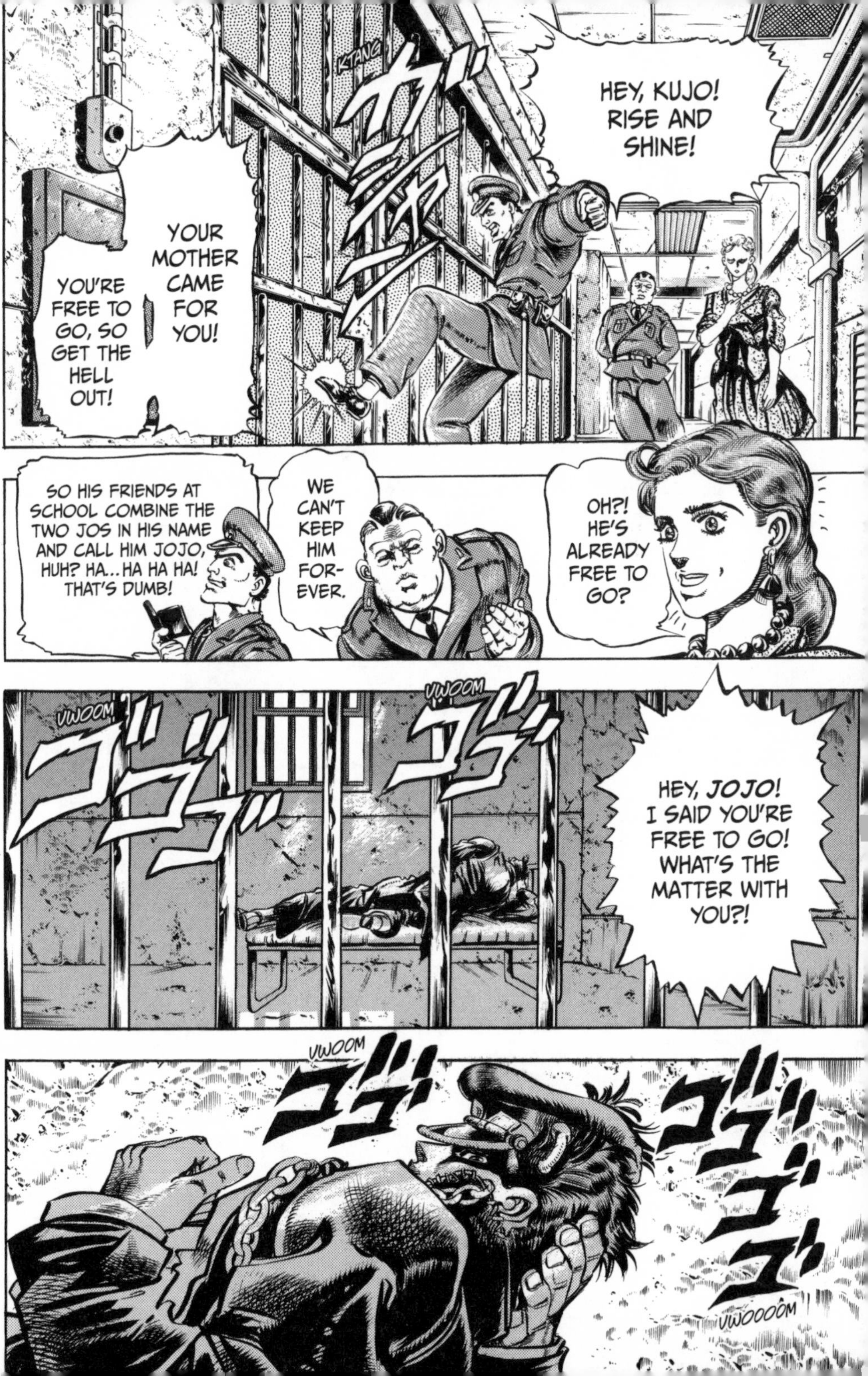
HEY, KUJO! RISE AND SHINE!
KTANG
YOUR MOTHER CAME FOR YOU!
YOU'RE FREE TO GO, SO GET THE HELL OUT!
OH?! HE'S ALREADY FREE TO GO?
WE CAN'T KEEP HIM FOR-EVER.
SO HIS FRIENDS AT SCHOOL COMBINE THE TWO JOS IN HIS NAME AND CALL HIM JOJO, HUH? HA...HA HA HA! THAT'S DUMB!
HEY, JOJO! I SAID YOU'RE FREE TO GO! WHAT'S THE MATTER WITH YOU?!
VWOOM
VWOOM
VWOOM
VWOOOOM

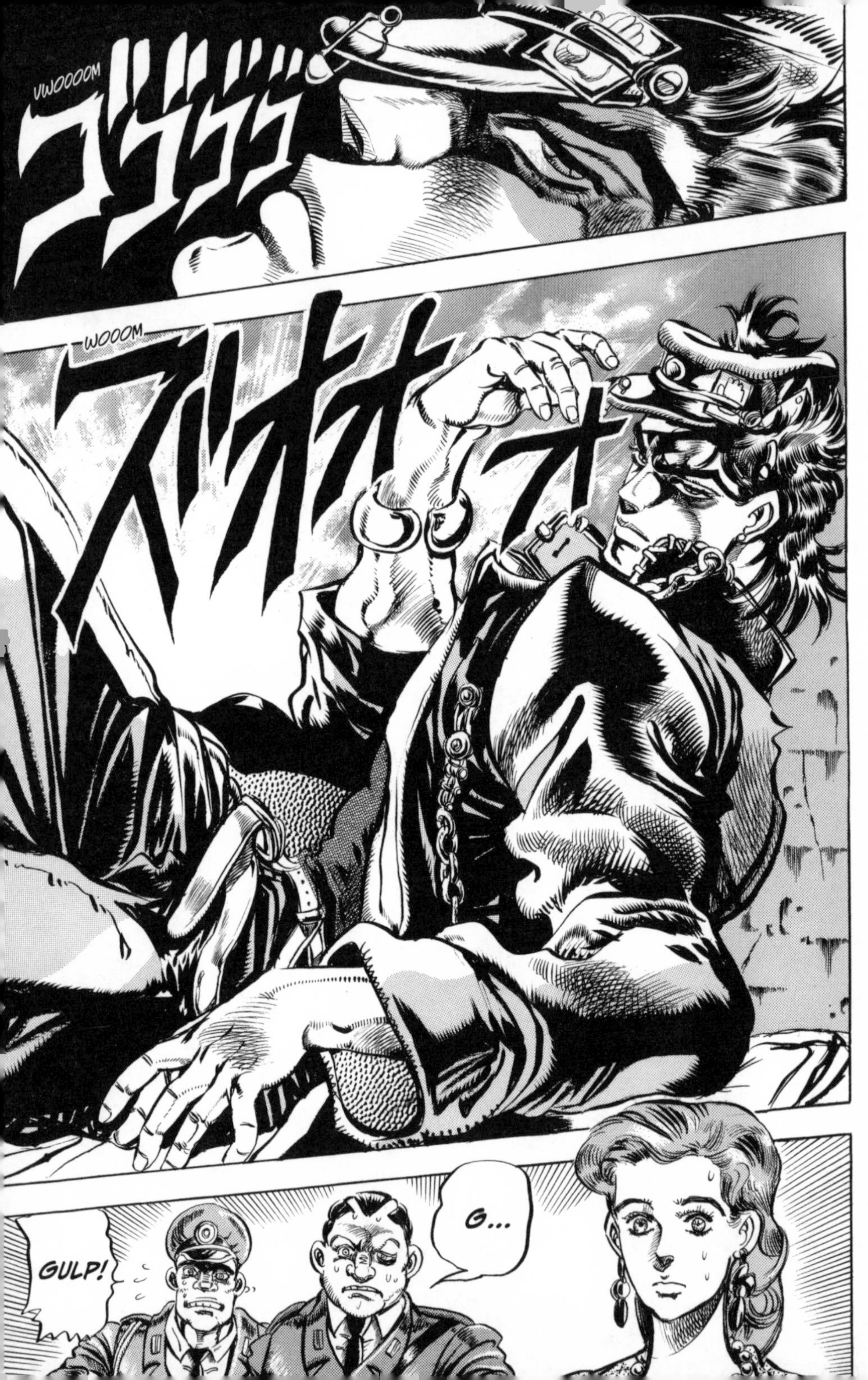
VWOOOOM
WOOOM
G...
GULP!

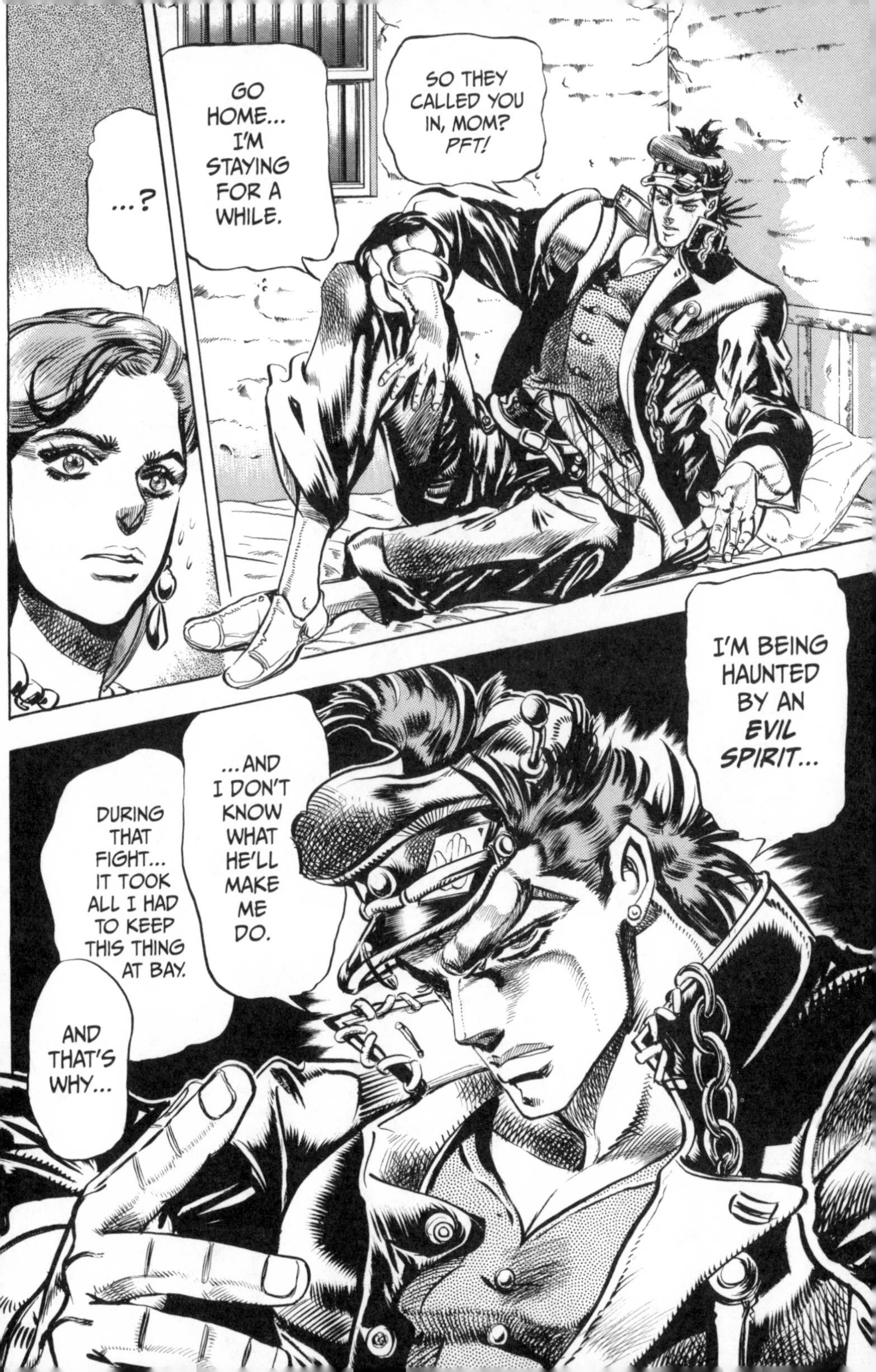
SO THEY CALLED YOU IN, MOM? PFT!
GO HOME... I'M STAYING FOR A WHILE.
...?
I'M BEING HAUNTED BY AN EVIL SPIRIT...
...AND I DON'T KNOW WHAT HE'LL MAKE ME DO.
DURING THAT FIGHT... IT TOOK ALL I HAD TO KEEP THIS THING AT BAY.
AND THAT'S WHY...

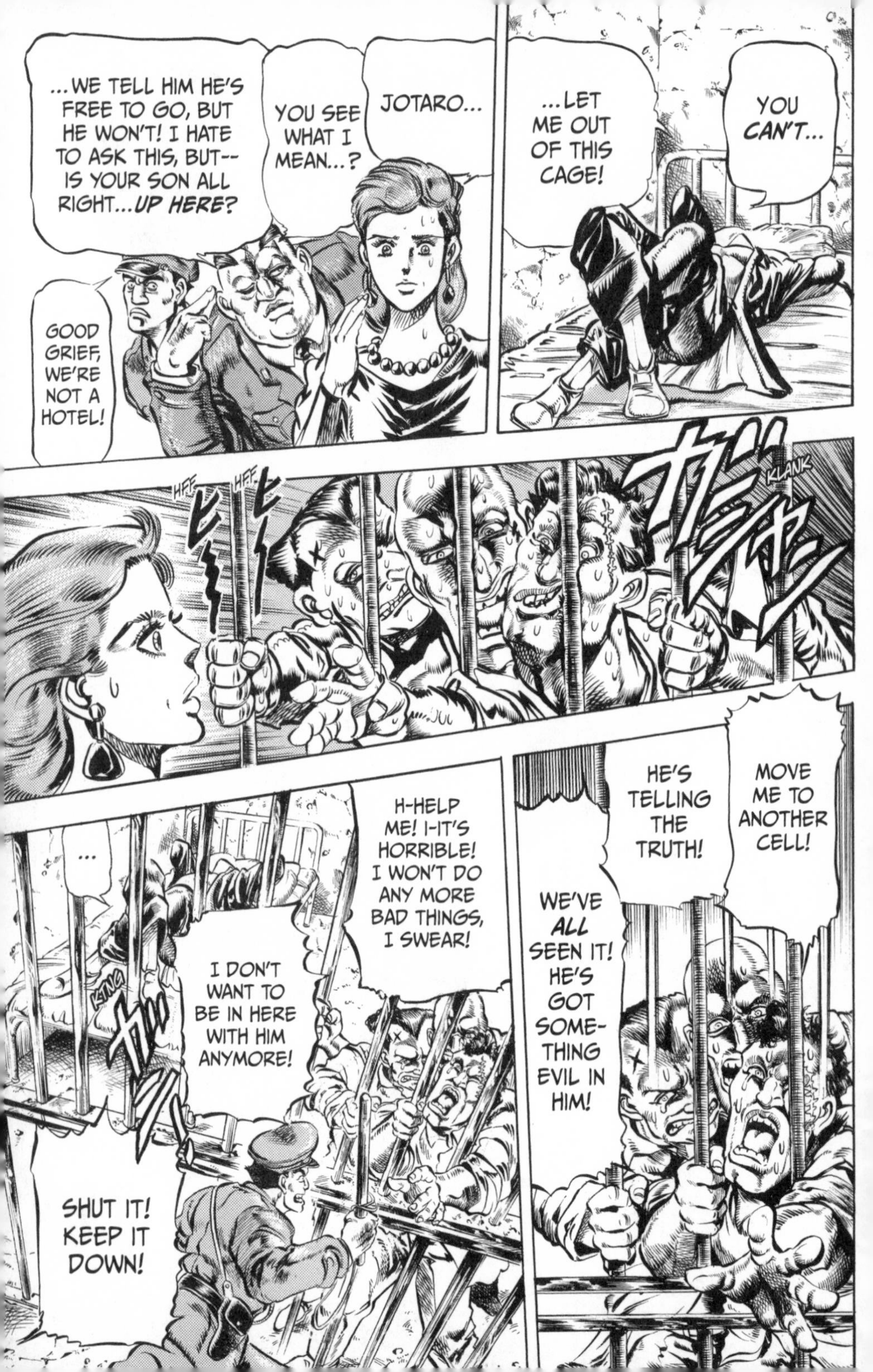
YOU *CAN'T*...
...LET ME OUT OF THIS CAGE!
JOTARO...
YOU SEE WHAT I MEAN...?
...WE TELL HIM HE'S FREE TO GO, BUT HE WON'T! I HATE TO ASK THIS, BUT-- IS YOUR SON ALL RIGHT...*UP HERE*?
GOOD GRIEF, WE'RE NOT A HOTEL!
KLANK
HFF
HFF
MOVE ME TO ANOTHER CELL!
HE'S TELLING THE TRUTH!
WE'VE *ALL* SEEN IT! HE'S GOT SOME-THING EVIL IN HIM!
H-HELP ME! I-IT'S HORRIBLE! I WON'T DO ANY MORE BAD THINGS, I SWEAR!
...
I DON'T WANT TO BE IN HERE WITH HIM ANYMORE!
SHUT IT! KEEP IT DOWN!

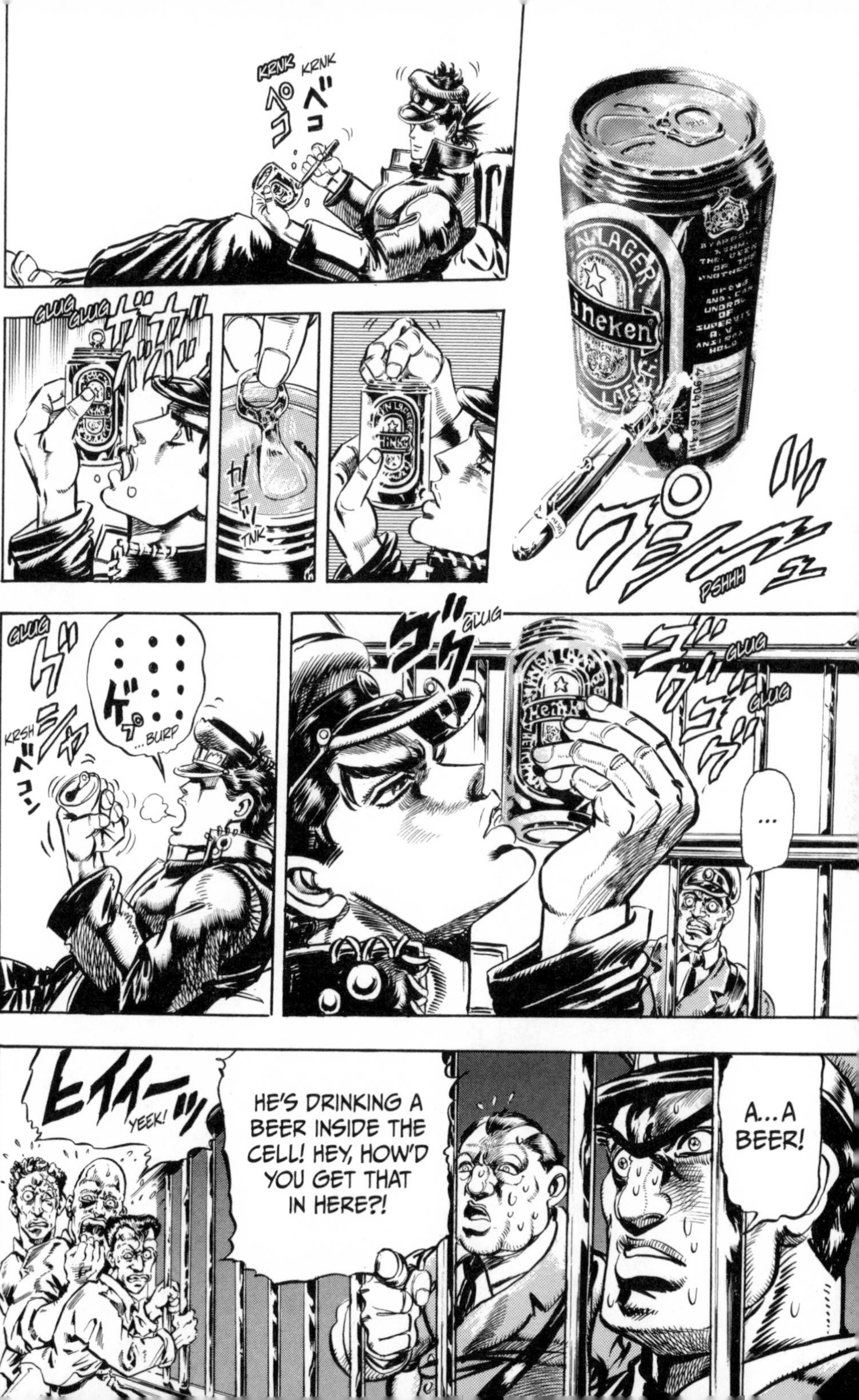
PSHHH
KRNK
KRNK
TNK
GLUG
GLUG
GLUG
GLUG
GLUG
...
GLUG
KRSH
...BURP
A...A BEER!
HE'S DRINKING A BEER INSIDE THE CELL! HEY, HOW'D YOU GET THAT IN HERE?!
YEEK!

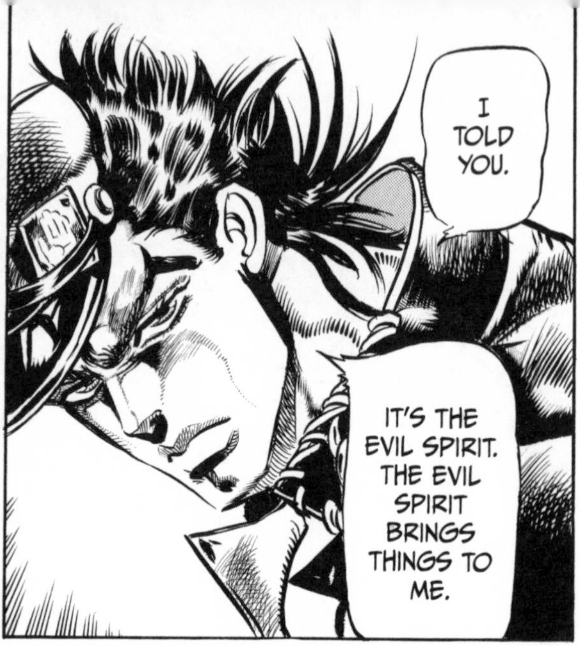
I TOLD YOU.
IT'S THE EVIL SPIRIT. THE EVIL SPIRIT BRINGS THINGS TO ME.

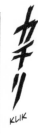

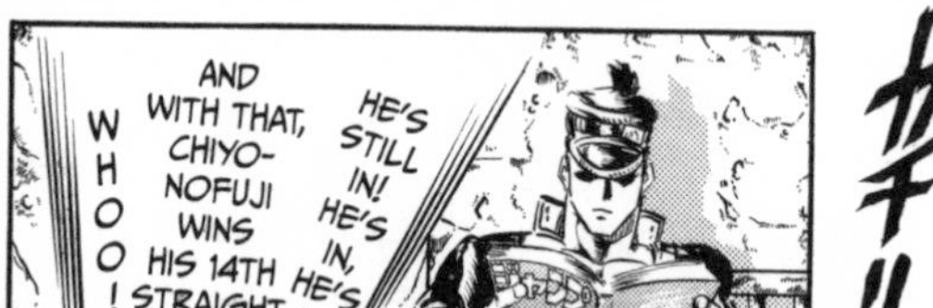
カチリ
KLIK
HE'S STILL IN! HE'S IN, HE'S IN!
AND WITH THAT, CHIYO-NOFUJI WINS HIS 14TH STRAIGHT MATCH.
WHOOO!

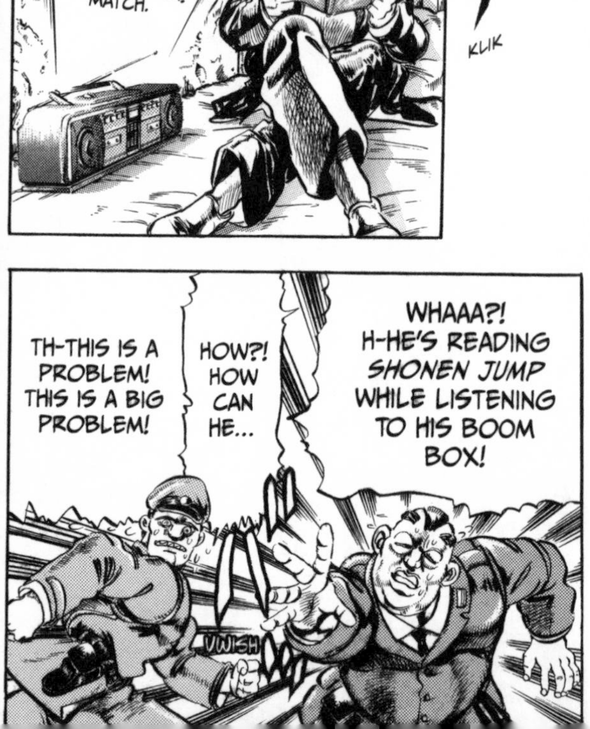
WHAAA?! H-HE'S READING *SHONEN JUMP* WHILE LISTENING TO HIS BOOM BOX!
HOW?! HOW CAN HE...
TH-THIS IS A PROBLEM! THIS IS A BIG PROBLEM!
VWISH

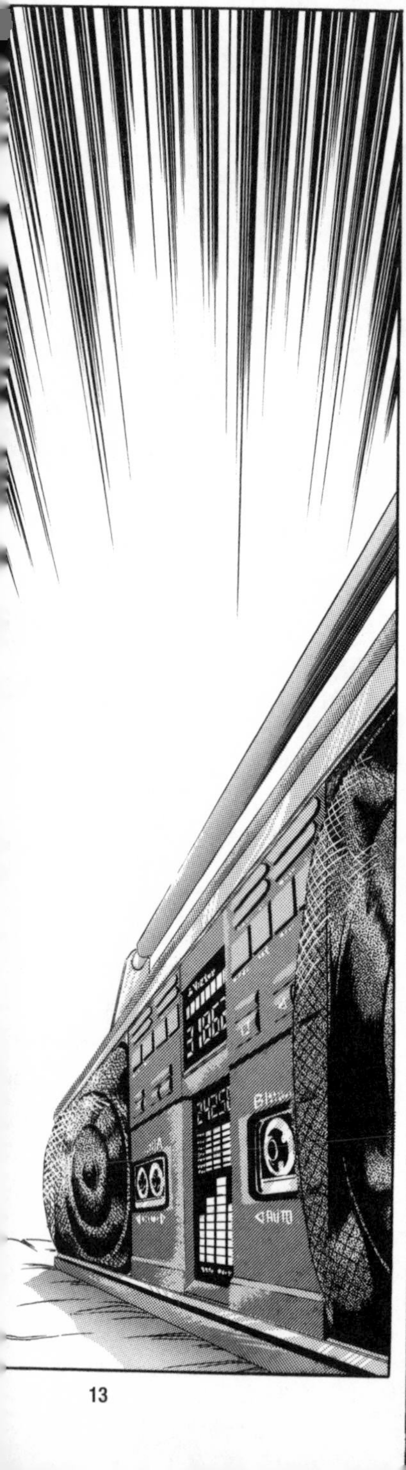

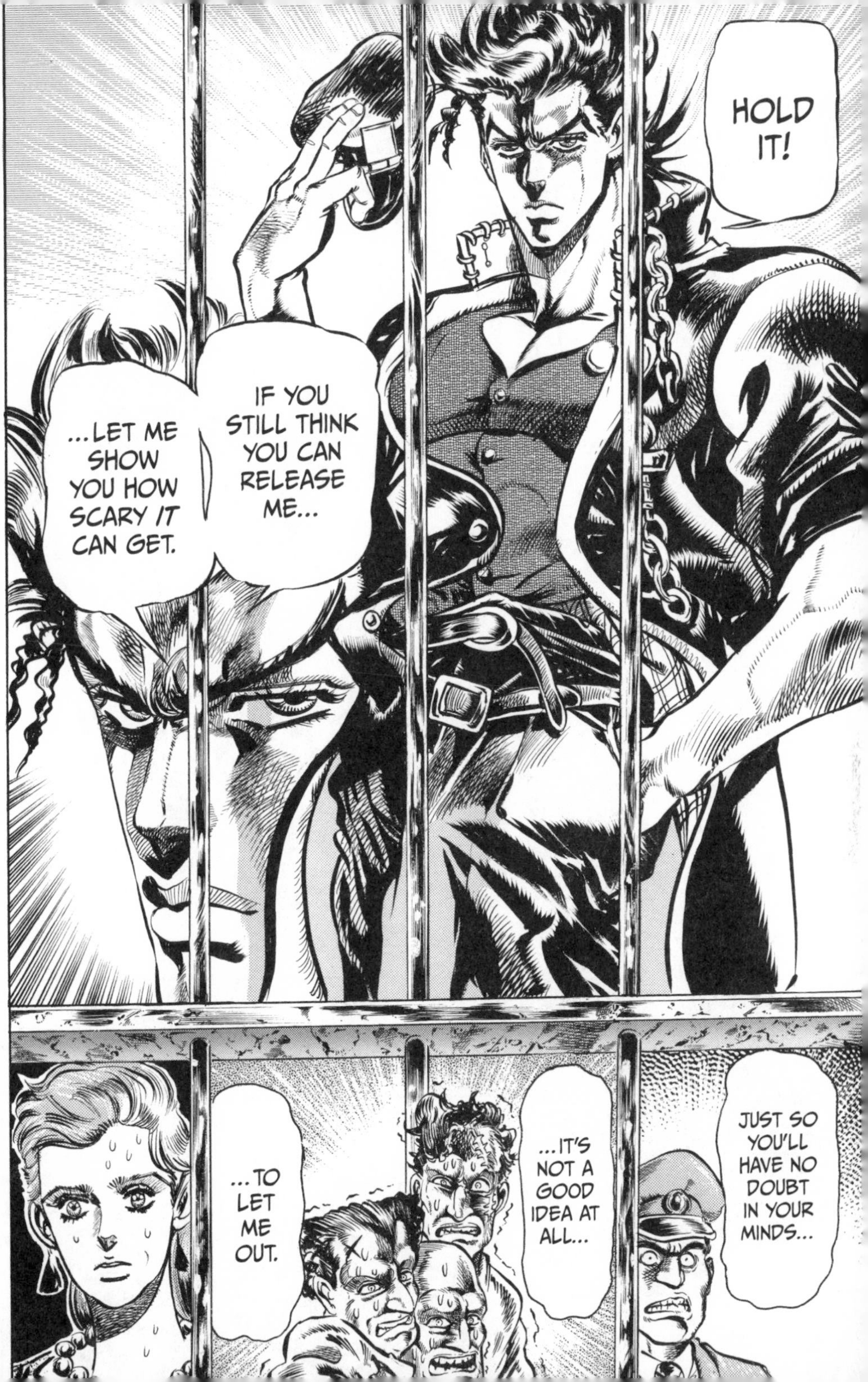
HOLD IT!
IF YOU STILL THINK YOU CAN RELEASE ME...
...LET ME SHOW YOU HOW SCARY IT CAN GET.
JUST SO YOU'LL HAVE NO DOUBT IN YOUR MINDS...
...IT'S NOT A GOOD IDEA AT ALL...
...TO LET ME OUT.

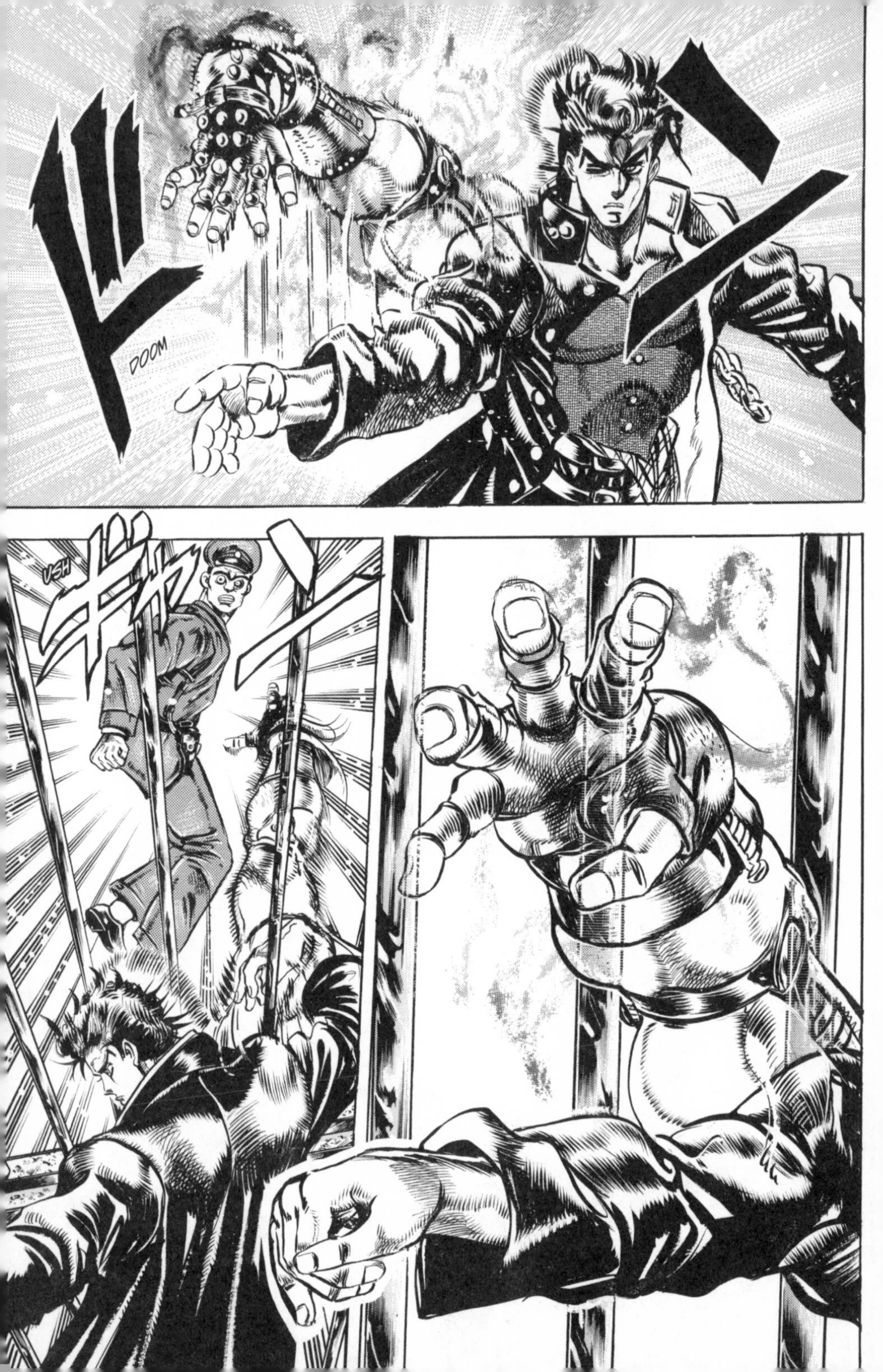
DOOM
USH

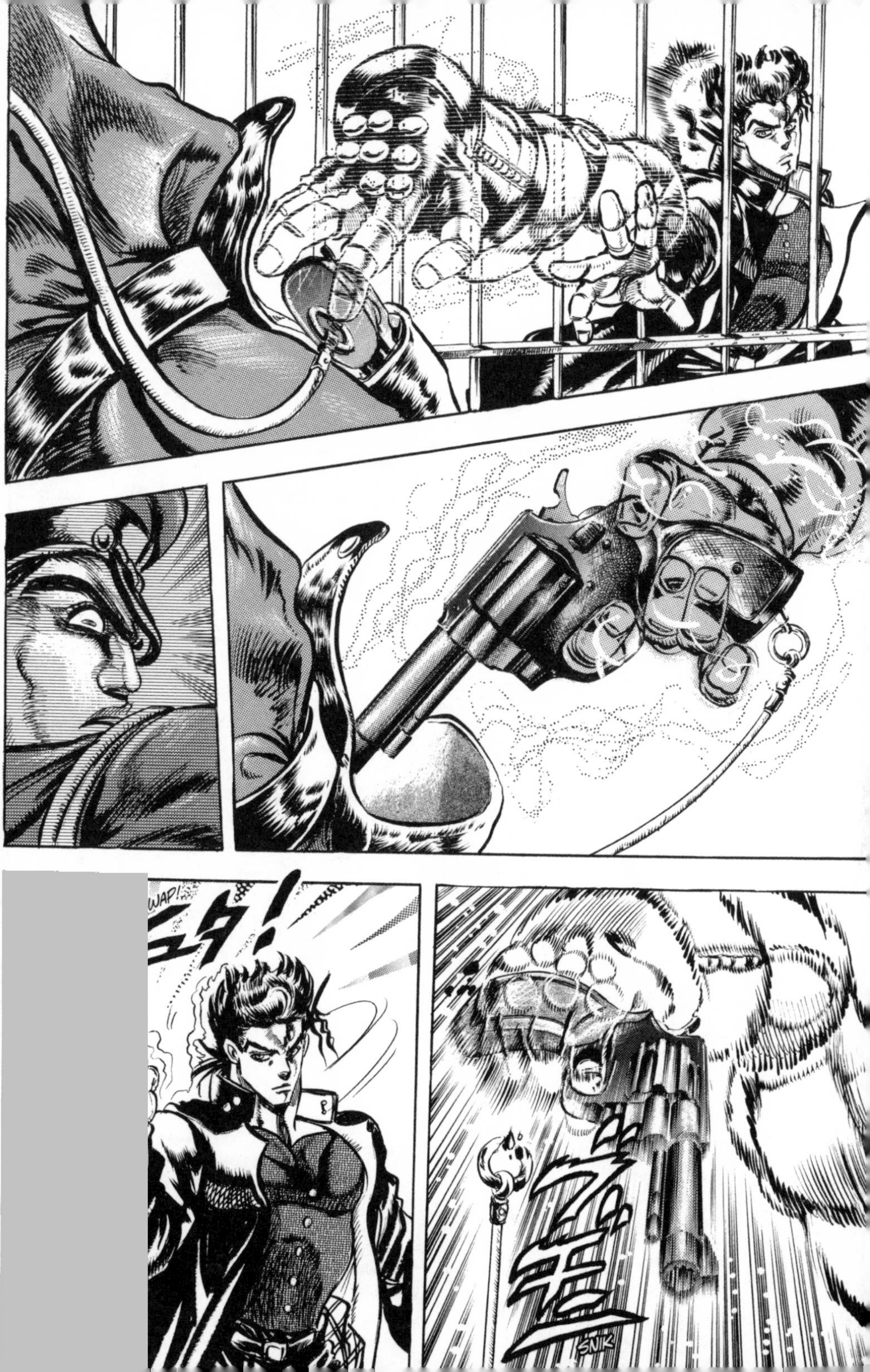
SNIK
WAP!

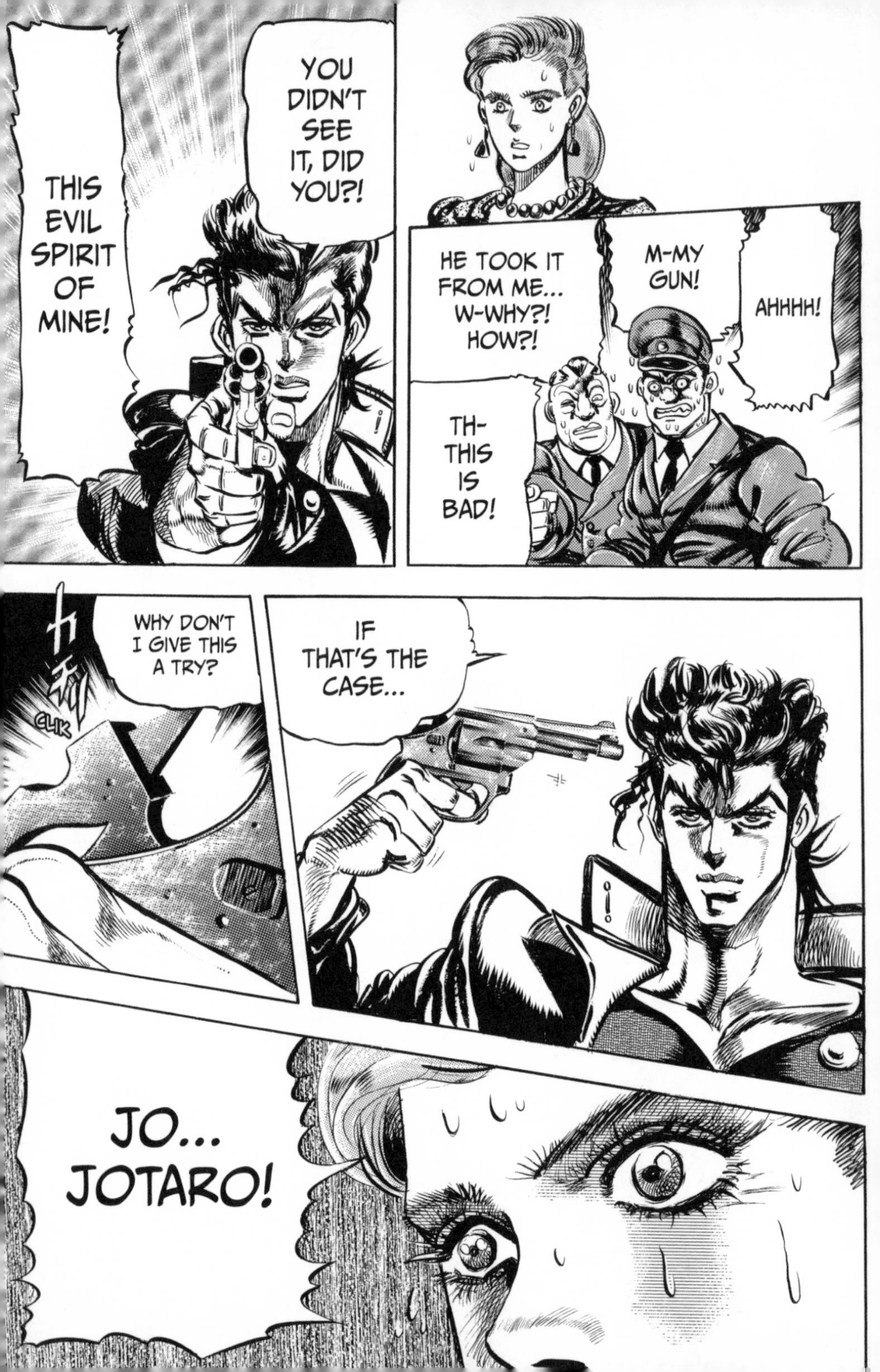
AHHHH!
M-MY GUN!
HE TOOK IT FROM ME... W-WHY?! HOW?!
TH- THIS IS BAD!
YOU DIDN'T SEE IT, DID YOU?!
THIS EVIL SPIRIT OF MINE!
IF THAT'S THE CASE...
WHY DON'T I GIVE THIS A TRY?
カチ
CLIK
JO... JOTARO!

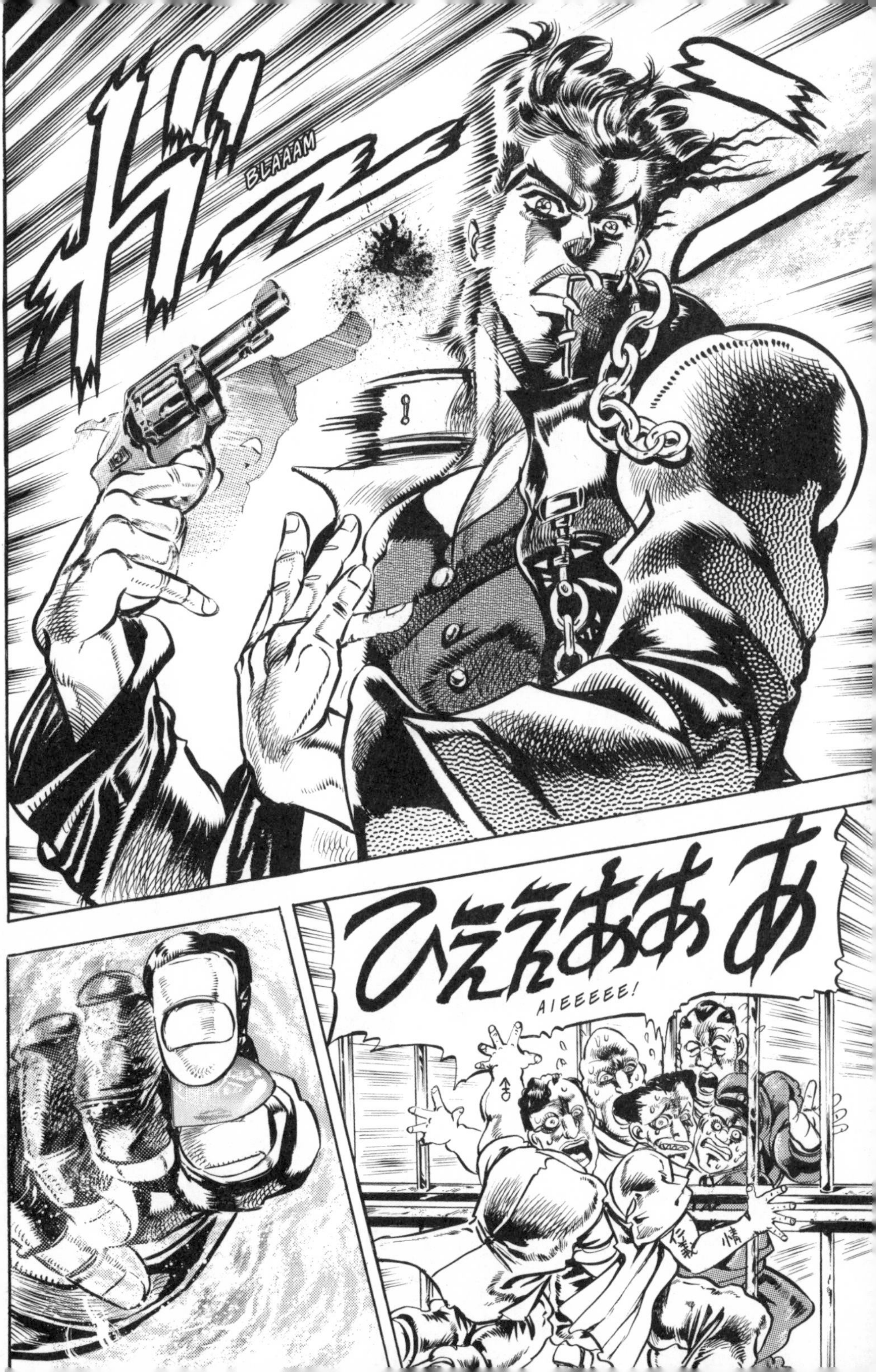
BLAAAM
ひええあああ
AIEEEEE!

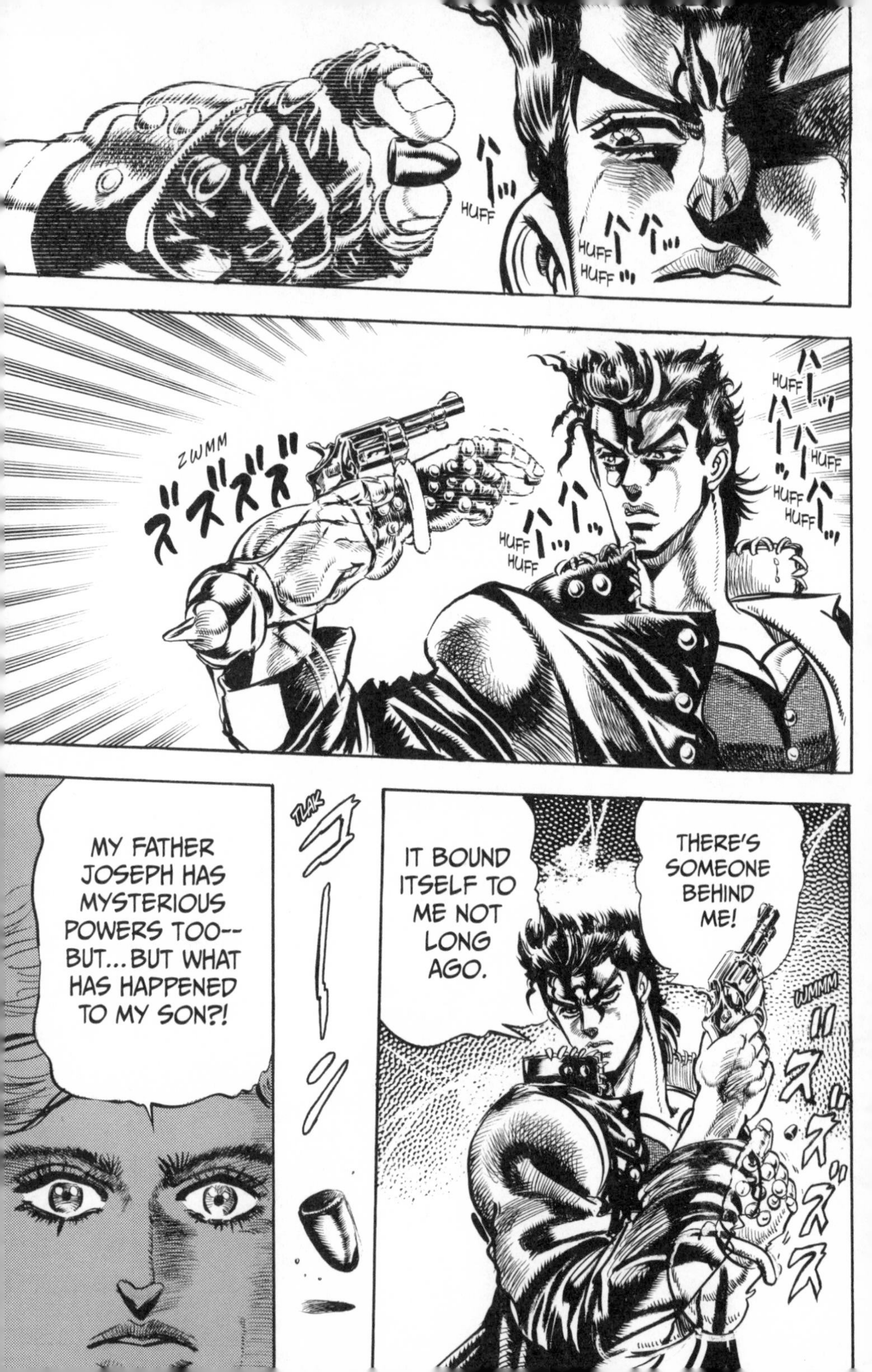
HUFF
HUFF HUFF
HUFF HUFF
HUFF HUFF
HUFF HUFF
ZWMM
THERE'S SOMEONE BEHIND ME!
IT BOUND ITSELF TO ME NOT LONG AGO.
WMMM
TLAK
MY FATHER JOSEPH HAS MYSTERIOUS POWERS TOO-- BUT...BUT WHAT HAS HAPPENED TO MY SON?!

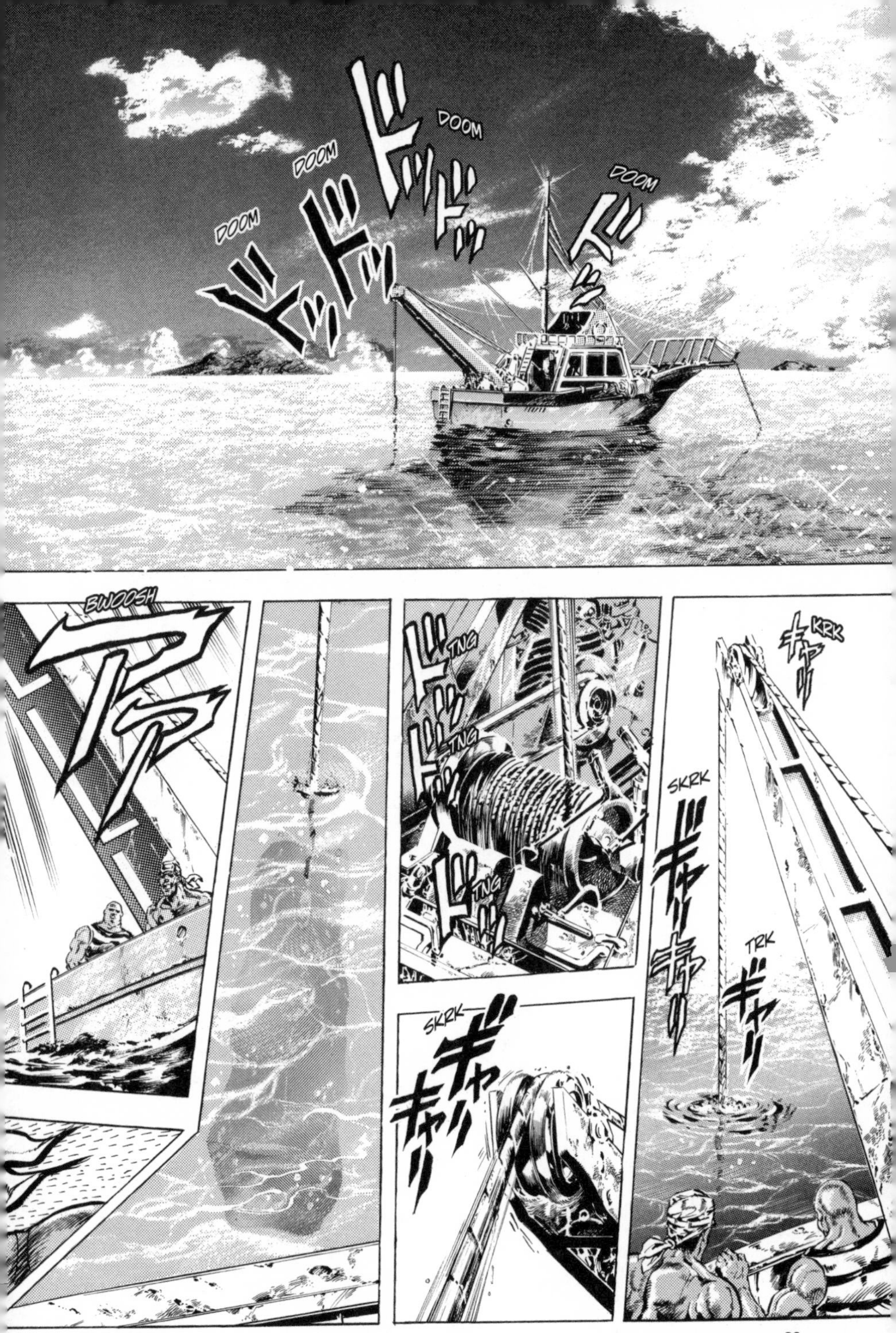
DOOM
DOOM
DOOM
DOOM
KRK
SKRK
TRK
TNG
TNG
TNG
SKRK
BWOOSH

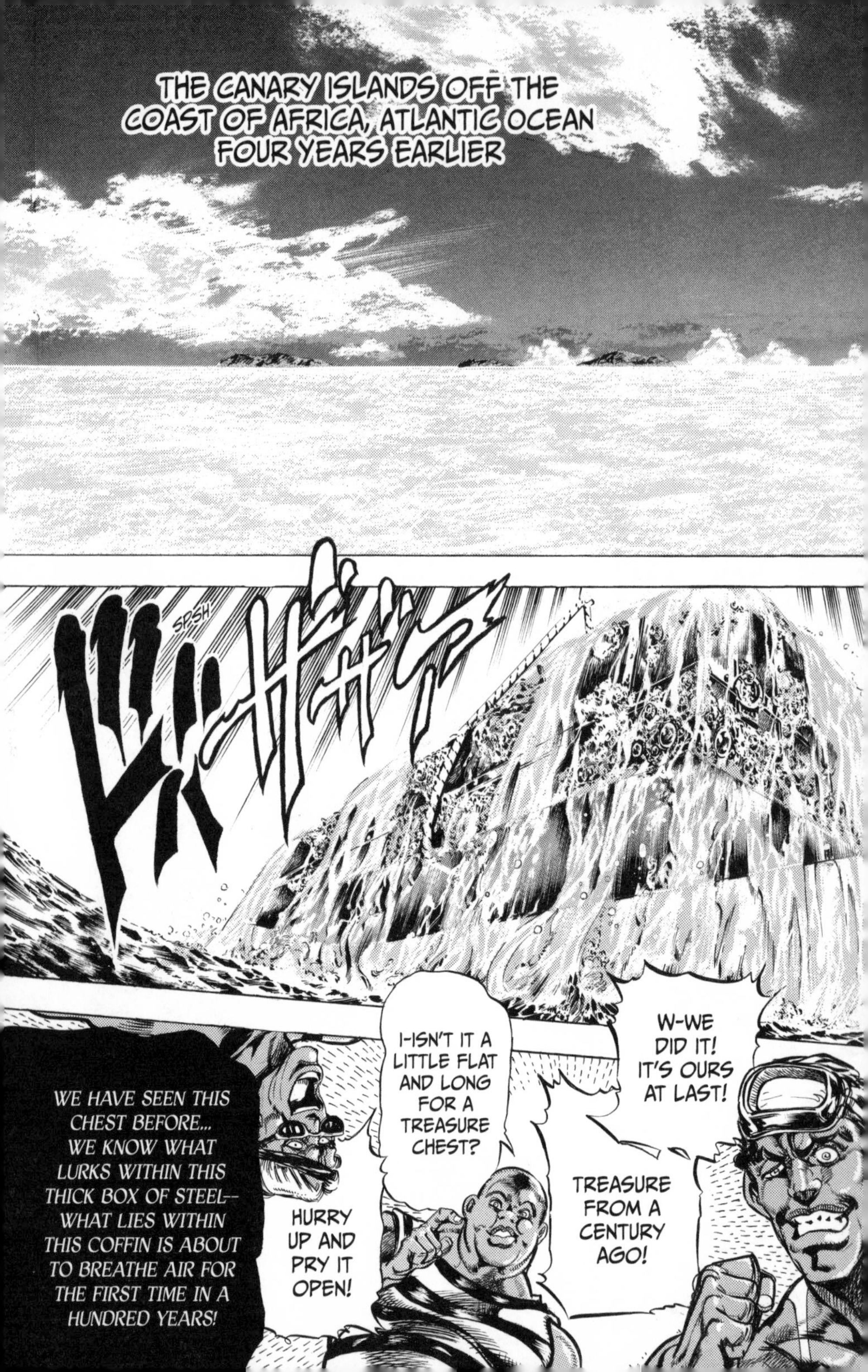
THE CANARY ISLANDS OFF THE COAST OF AFRICA, ATLANTIC OCEAN FOUR YEARS EARLIER
SPSH
W-WE DID IT! IT'S OURS AT LAST!
TREASURE FROM A CENTURY AGO!
I-ISN'T IT A LITTLE FLAT AND LONG FOR A TREASURE CHEST?
HURRY UP AND PRY IT OPEN!
WE HAVE SEEN THIS CHEST BEFORE... WE KNOW WHAT LURKS WITHIN THIS THICK BOX OF STEEL-- WHAT LIES WITHIN THIS COFFIN IS ABOUT TO BREATHE AIR FOR THE FIRST TIME IN A HUNDRED YEARS!

THE STAR 17

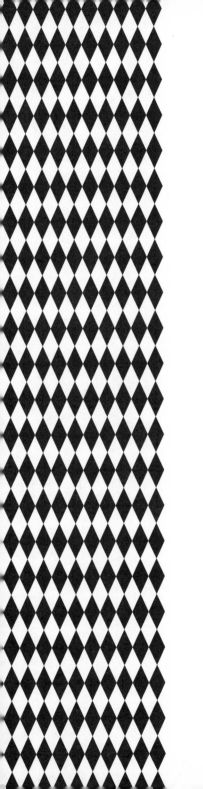

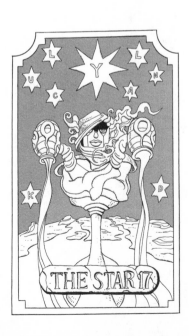

CHAPTER 2: Jotaro Kujo PART 2

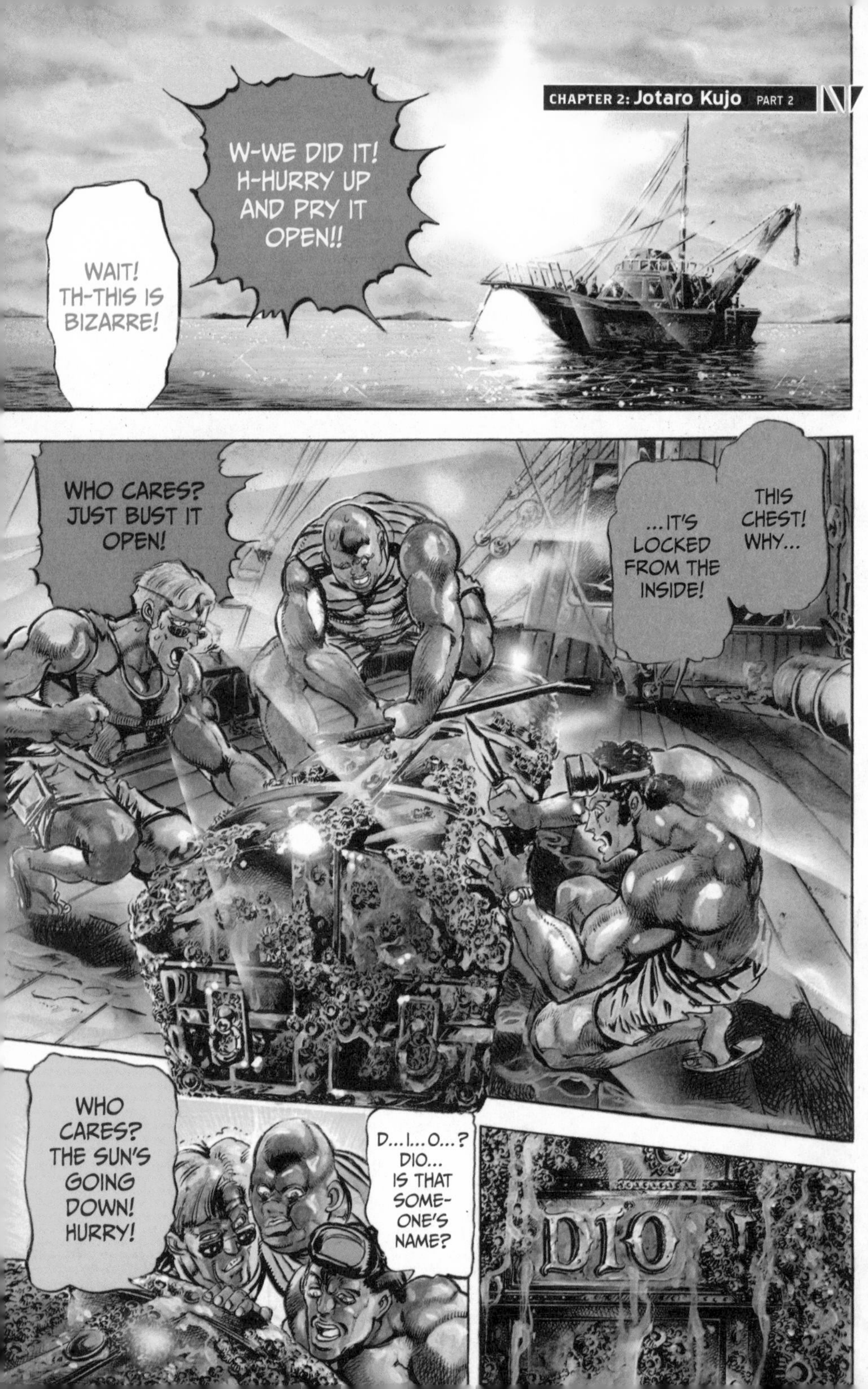
W-WE DID IT! H-HURRY UP AND PRY IT OPEN!!
WAIT! TH-THIS IS BIZARRE!
THIS CHEST! WHY...
...IT'S LOCKED FROM THE INSIDE!
WHO CARES? JUST BUST IT OPEN!
DIO
D...I...O...? DIO... IS THAT SOME-ONE'S NAME?
WHO CARES? THE SUN'S GOING DOWN! HURRY!

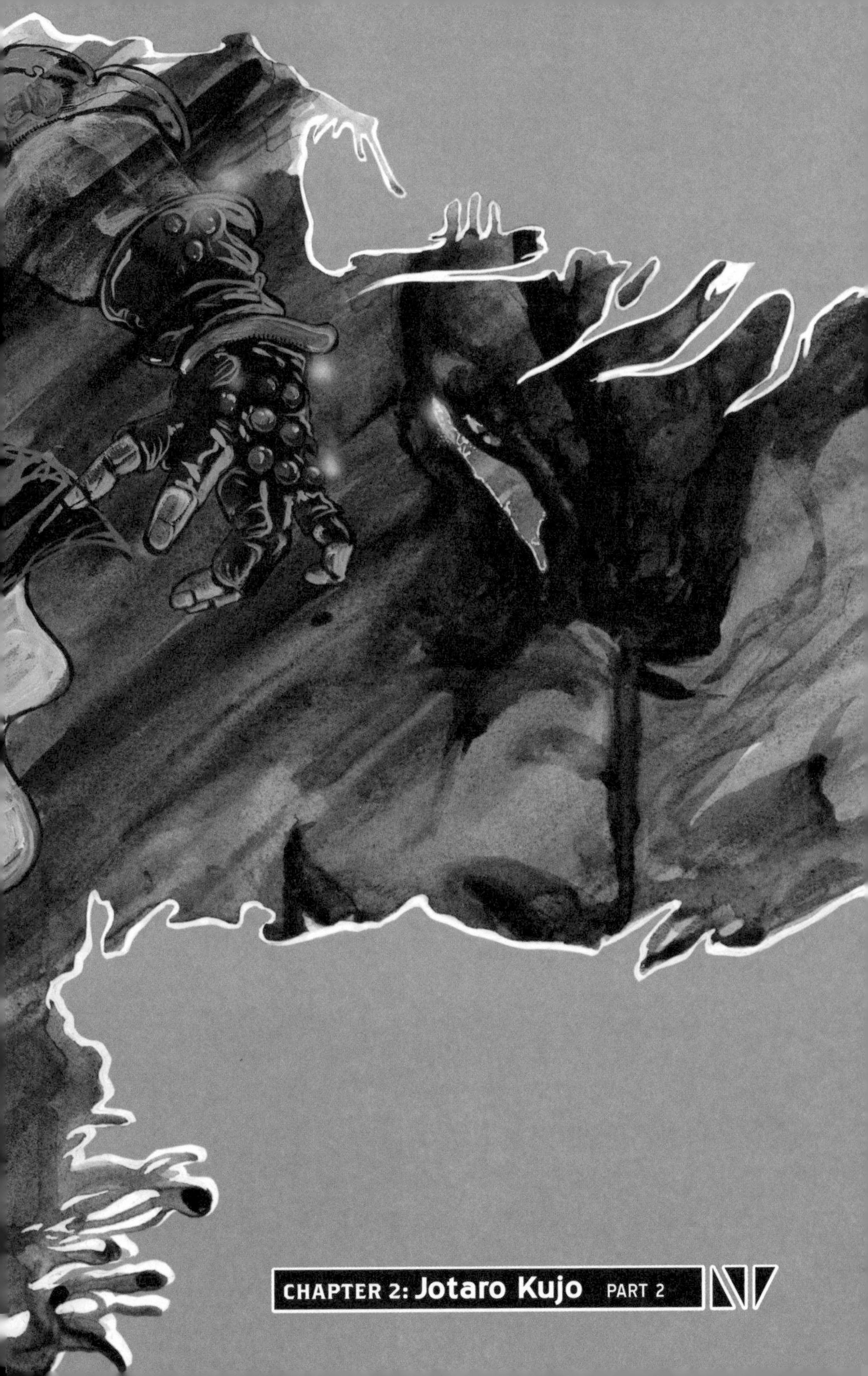

CHAPTER 2: Jotaro Kujo PART 2

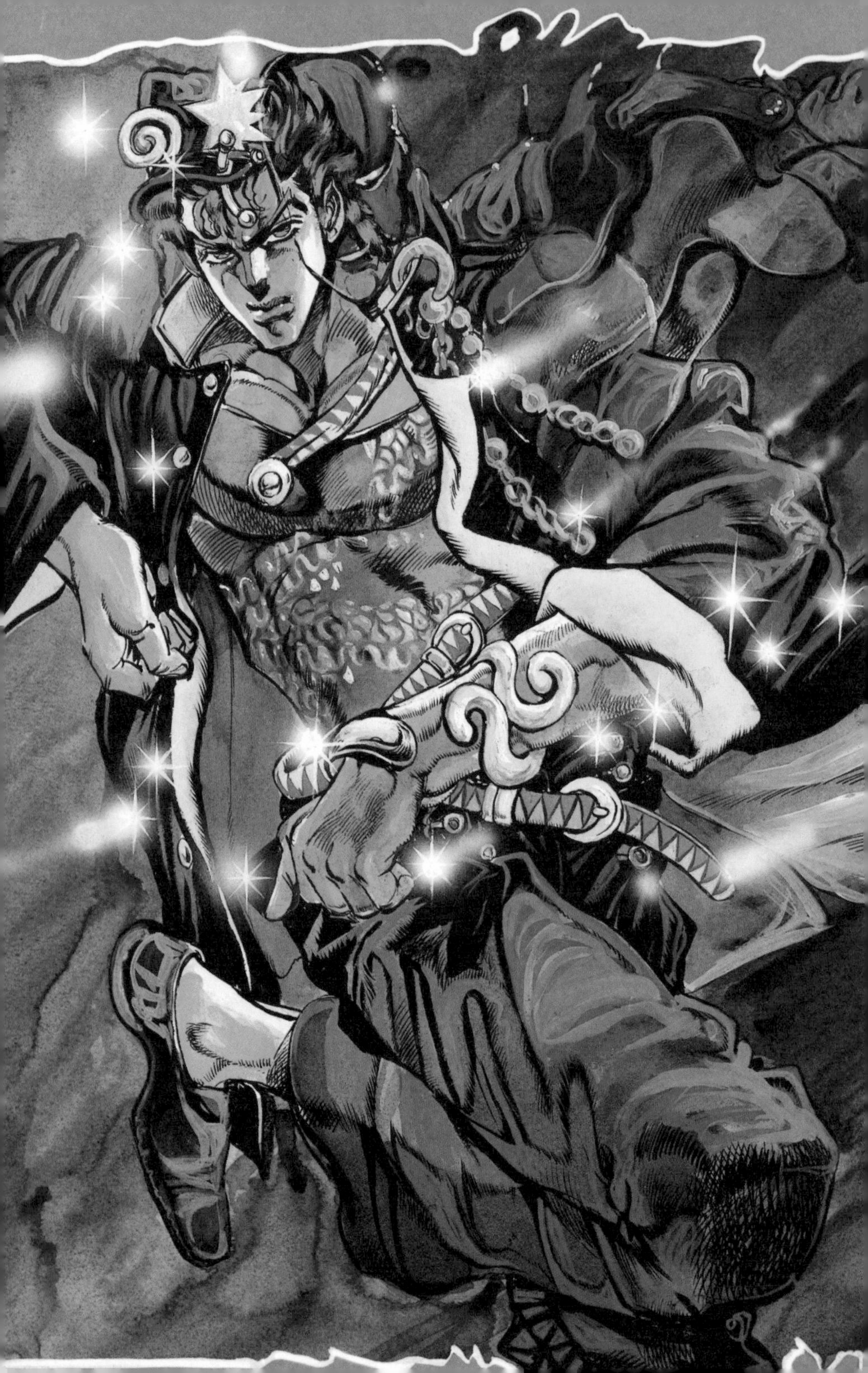

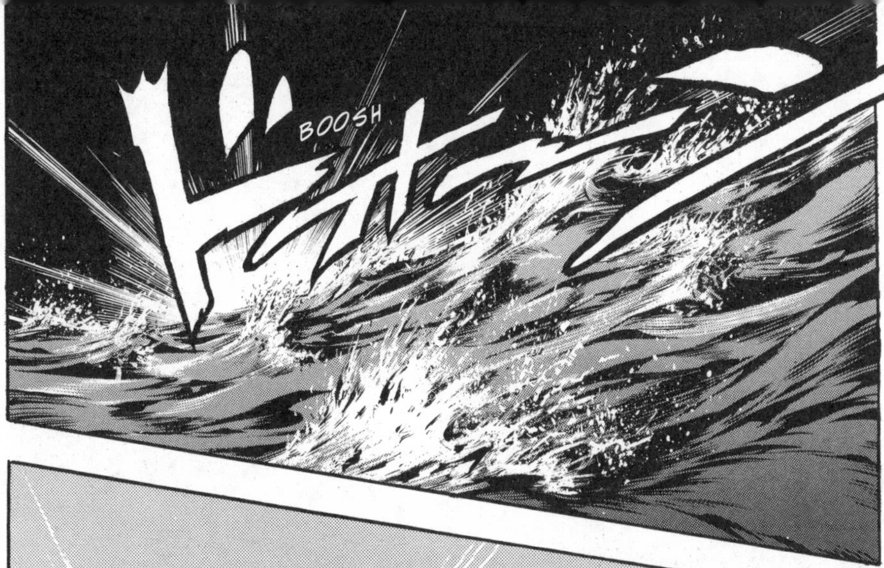
BOOSH

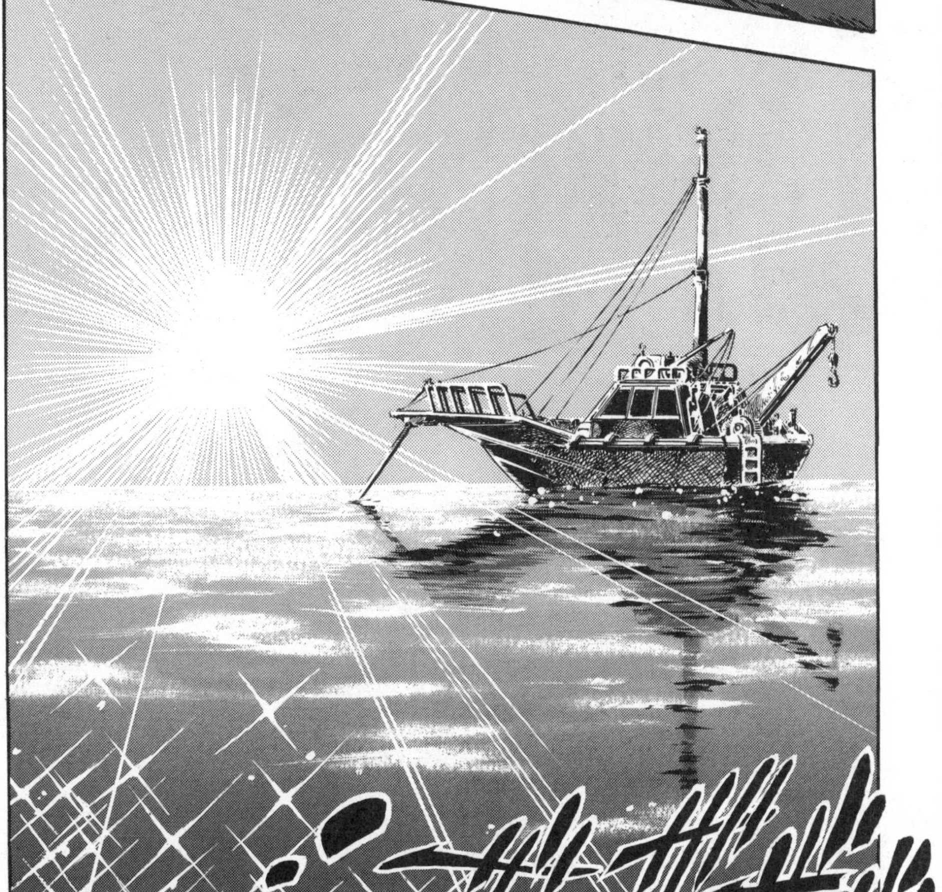
SHAAASH

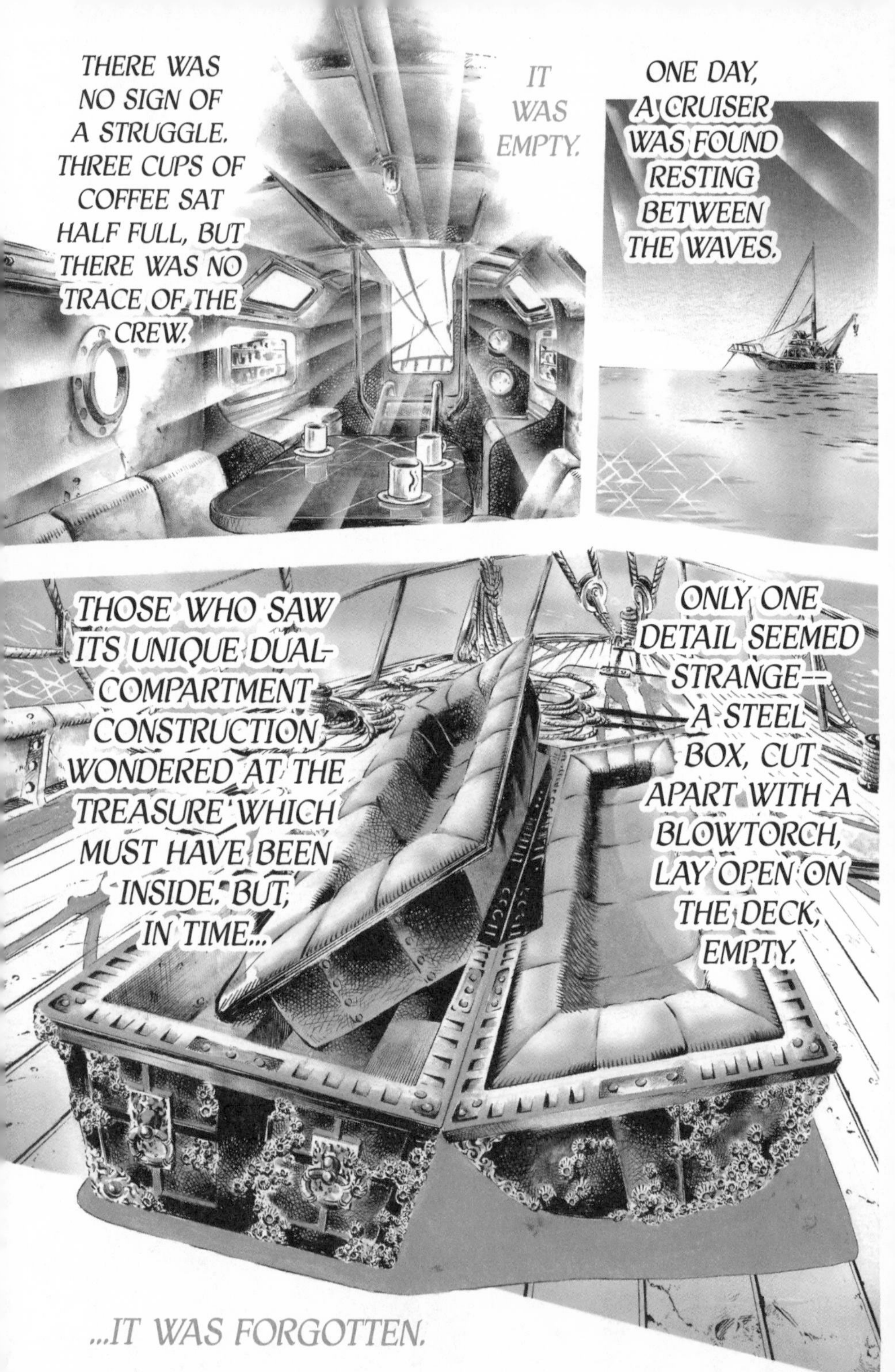
ONE DAY, A CRUISER WAS FOUND RESTING BETWEEN THE WAVES.
IT WAS EMPTY.
THERE WAS NO SIGN OF A STRUGGLE. THREE CUPS OF COFFEE SAT HALF FULL, BUT THERE WAS NO TRACE OF THE CREW.
ONLY ONE DETAIL SEEMED STRANGE-- A STEEL BOX, CUT APART WITH A BLOWTORCH, LAY OPEN ON THE DECK, EMPTY.
THOSE WHO SAW ITS UNIQUE DUAL-COMPARTMENT CONSTRUCTION WONDERED AT THE TREASURE WHICH MUST HAVE BEEN INSIDE. BUT, IN TIME...
...IT WAS FORGOTTEN.

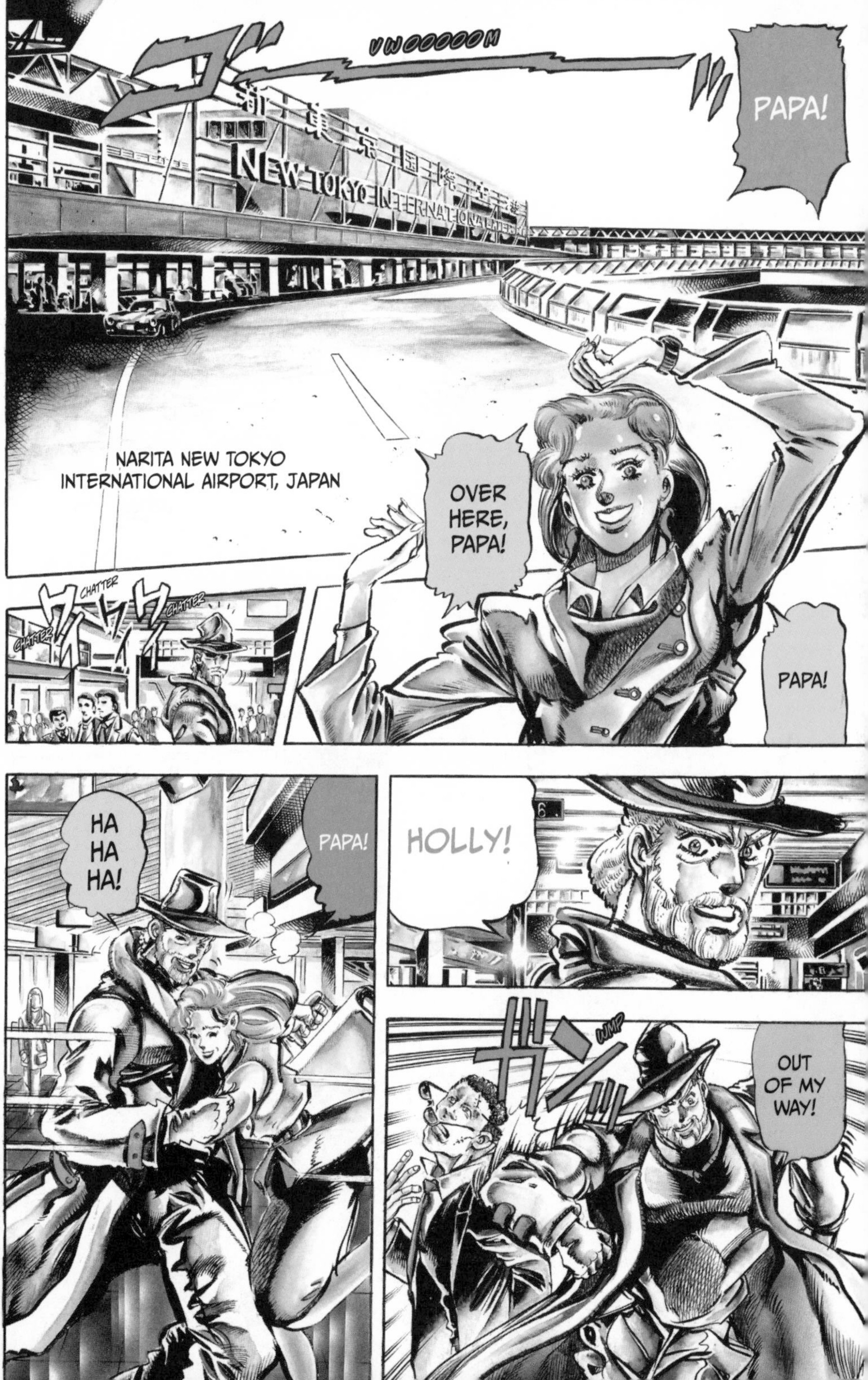
VWOOOOOOM
PAPA!
NEW TOKYO INTERNATIONAL
NARITA NEW TOKYO INTERNATIONAL AIRPORT, JAPAN
OVER HERE, PAPA!
PAPA!
CHATTER
CHATTER
CHATTER
HOLLY!
WUMP
OUT OF MY WAY!
PAPA!
HA HA HA!

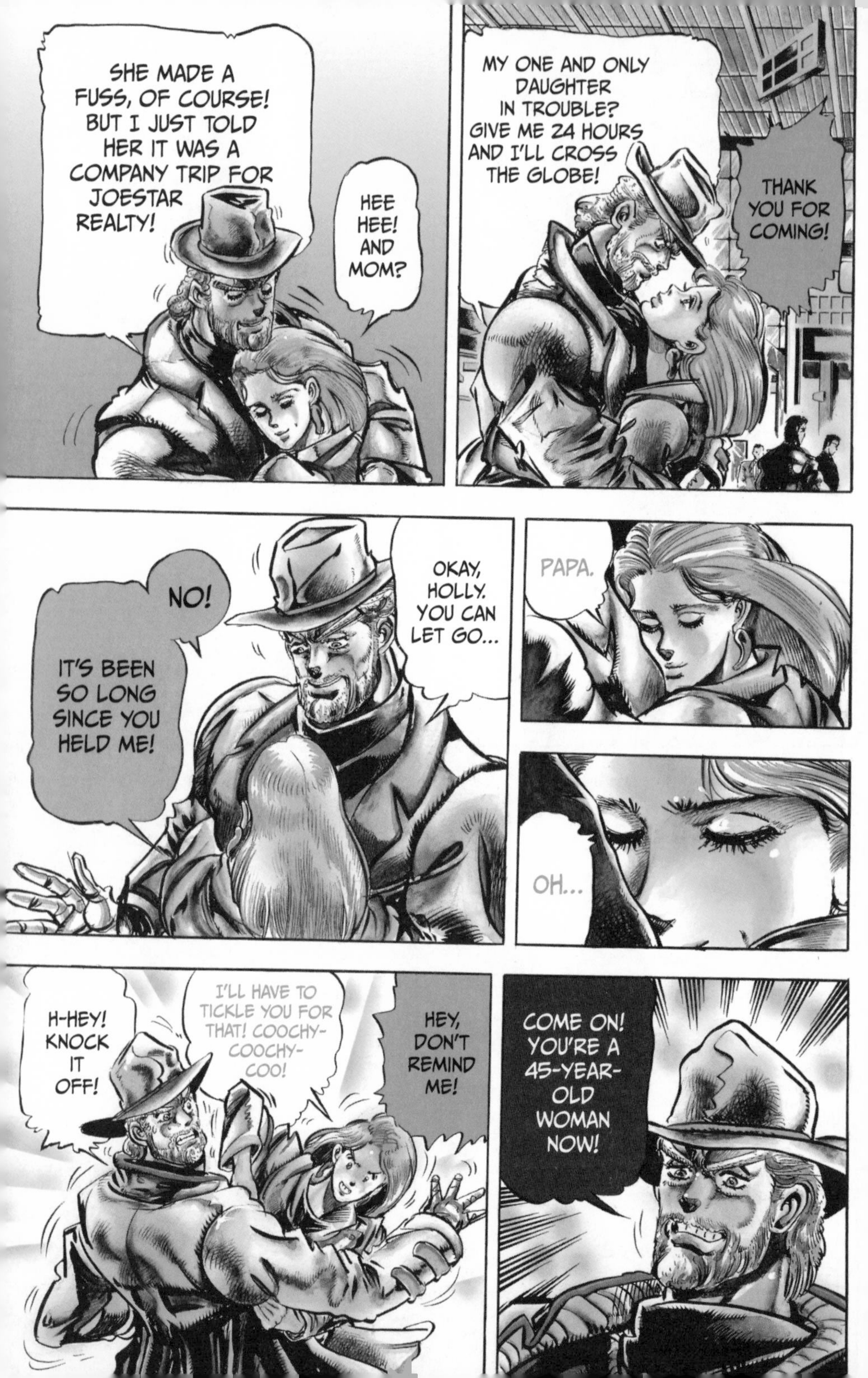
THANK YOU FOR COMING!
MY ONE AND ONLY DAUGHTER IN TROUBLE? GIVE ME 24 HOURS AND I'LL CROSS THE GLOBE!
HEE HEE! AND MOM?
SHE MADE A FUSS, OF COURSE! BUT I JUST TOLD HER IT WAS A COMPANY TRIP FOR JOESTAR REALTY!
PAPA.
OH...
OKAY, HOLLY. YOU CAN LET GO...
NO!
IT'S BEEN SO LONG SINCE YOU HELD ME!
COME ON! YOU'RE A 45-YEAR-OLD WOMAN NOW!
HEY, DON'T REMIND ME!
I'LL HAVE TO TICKLE YOU FOR THAT! COOCHY-COOCHY-COO!
H-HEY! KNOCK IT OFF!

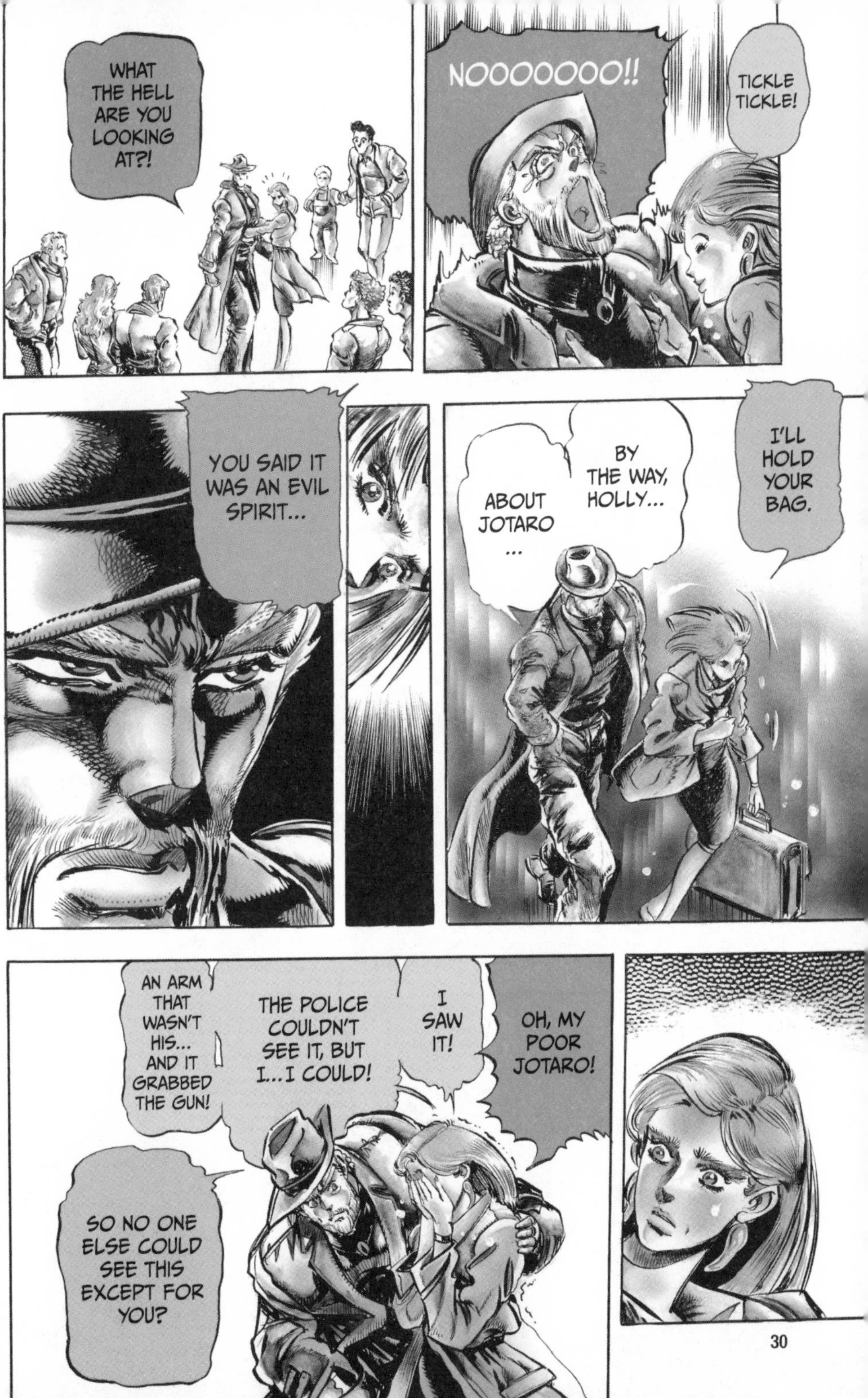
TICKLE TICKLE!
NOOOOOOO!!
WHAT THE HELL ARE YOU LOOKING AT?!
I'LL HOLD YOUR BAG.
BY THE WAY, HOLLY...
ABOUT JOTARO ...
YOU SAID IT WAS AN EVIL SPIRIT...
OH, MY POOR JOTARO!
I SAW IT!
THE POLICE COULDN'T SEE IT, BUT I...I COULD!
AN ARM THAT WASN'T HIS... AND IT GRABBED THE GUN!
SO NO ONE ELSE COULD SEE THIS EXCEPT FOR YOU?

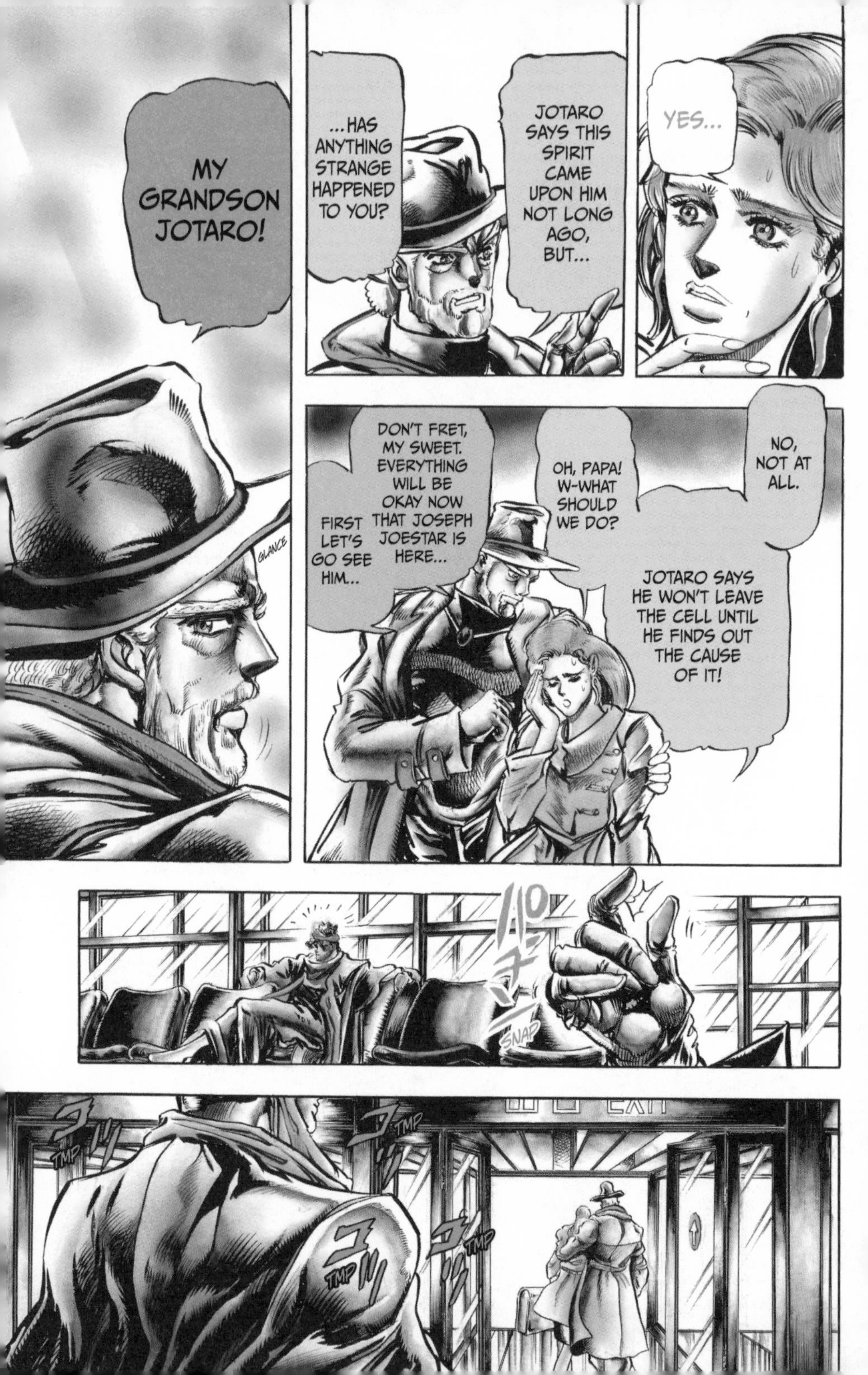
YES...
JOTARO SAYS THIS SPIRIT CAME UPON HIM NOT LONG AGO, BUT...
...HAS ANYTHING STRANGE HAPPENED TO YOU?
NO, NOT AT ALL.
JOTARO SAYS HE WON'T LEAVE THE CELL UNTIL HE FINDS OUT THE CAUSE OF IT!
OH, PAPA! W-WHAT SHOULD WE DO?
DON'T FRET, MY SWEET. EVERYTHING WILL BE OKAY NOW THAT JOSEPH JOESTAR IS HERE...
FIRST LET'S GO SEE HIM...
GLANCE
MY GRANDSON JOTARO!
SNAP
TMP
TMP
TMP
TMP

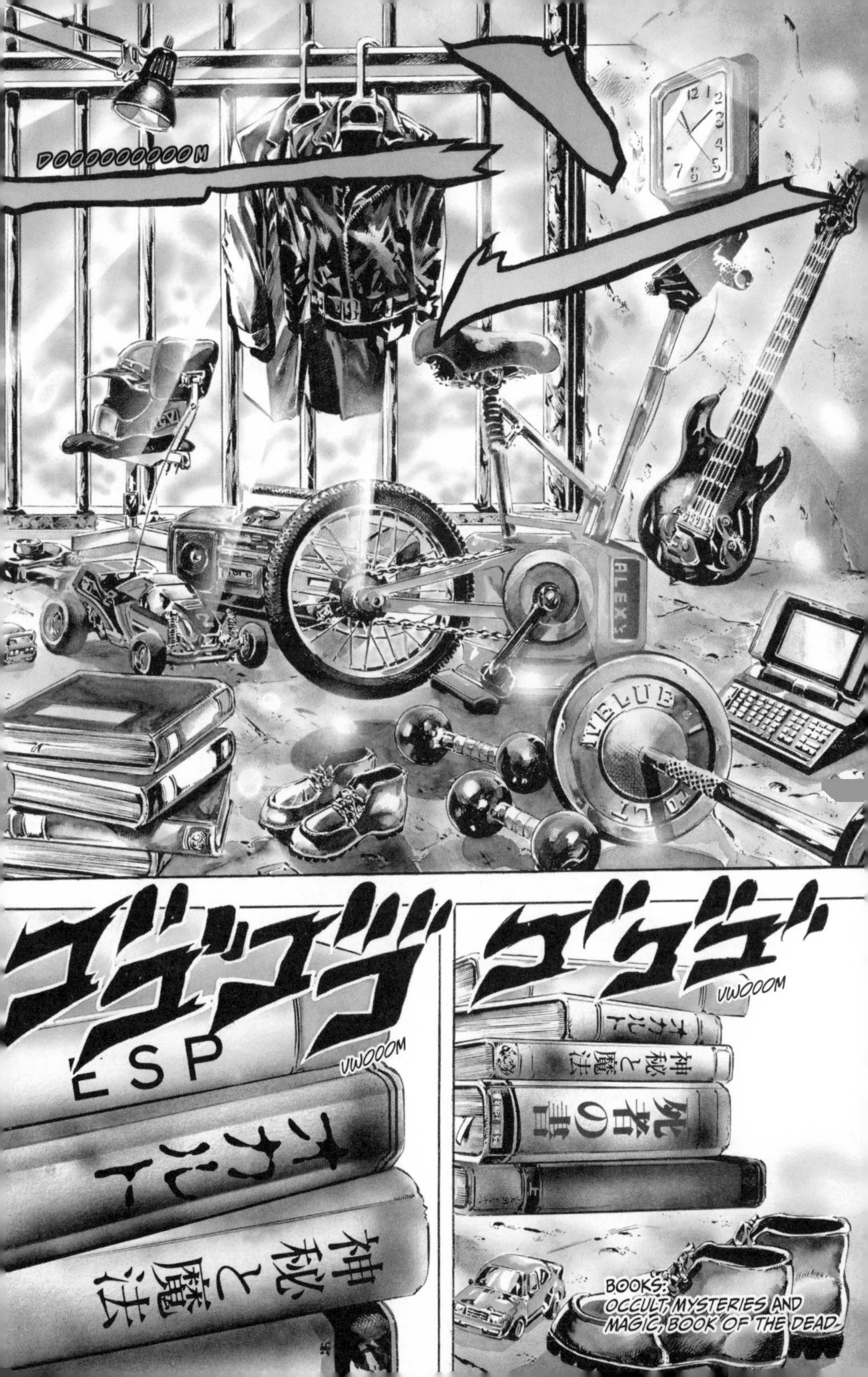
DOOOOOOOOOOM
ALEX
ゴゴゴ
VWOOOM
オカルト
神秘と魔法
死者の書
BOOKS: OCCULT, MYSTERIES AND MAGIC, BOOK OF THE DEAD
ゴゴゴ
ESP
VWOOOM
オカルト
神秘と魔法

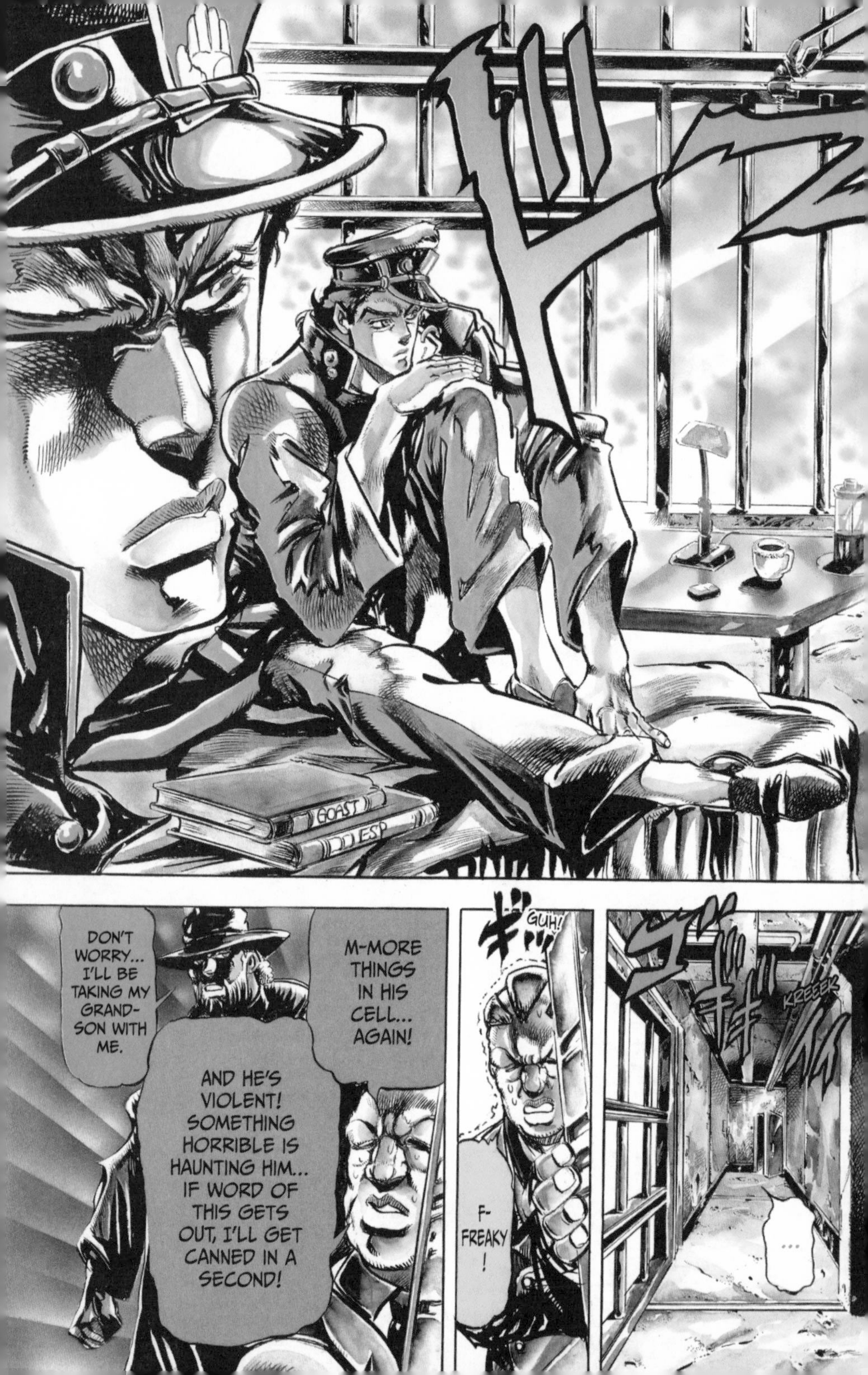
GOAST
ESP
KREEEK
...
GUH!
F-FREAKY!
M-MORE THINGS IN HIS CELL... AGAIN!
DON'T WORRY... I'LL BE TAKING MY GRAND-SON WITH ME.
AND HE'S VIOLENT! SOMETHING HORRIBLE IS HAUNTING HIM... IF WORD OF THIS GETS OUT, I'LL GET CANNED IN A SECOND!

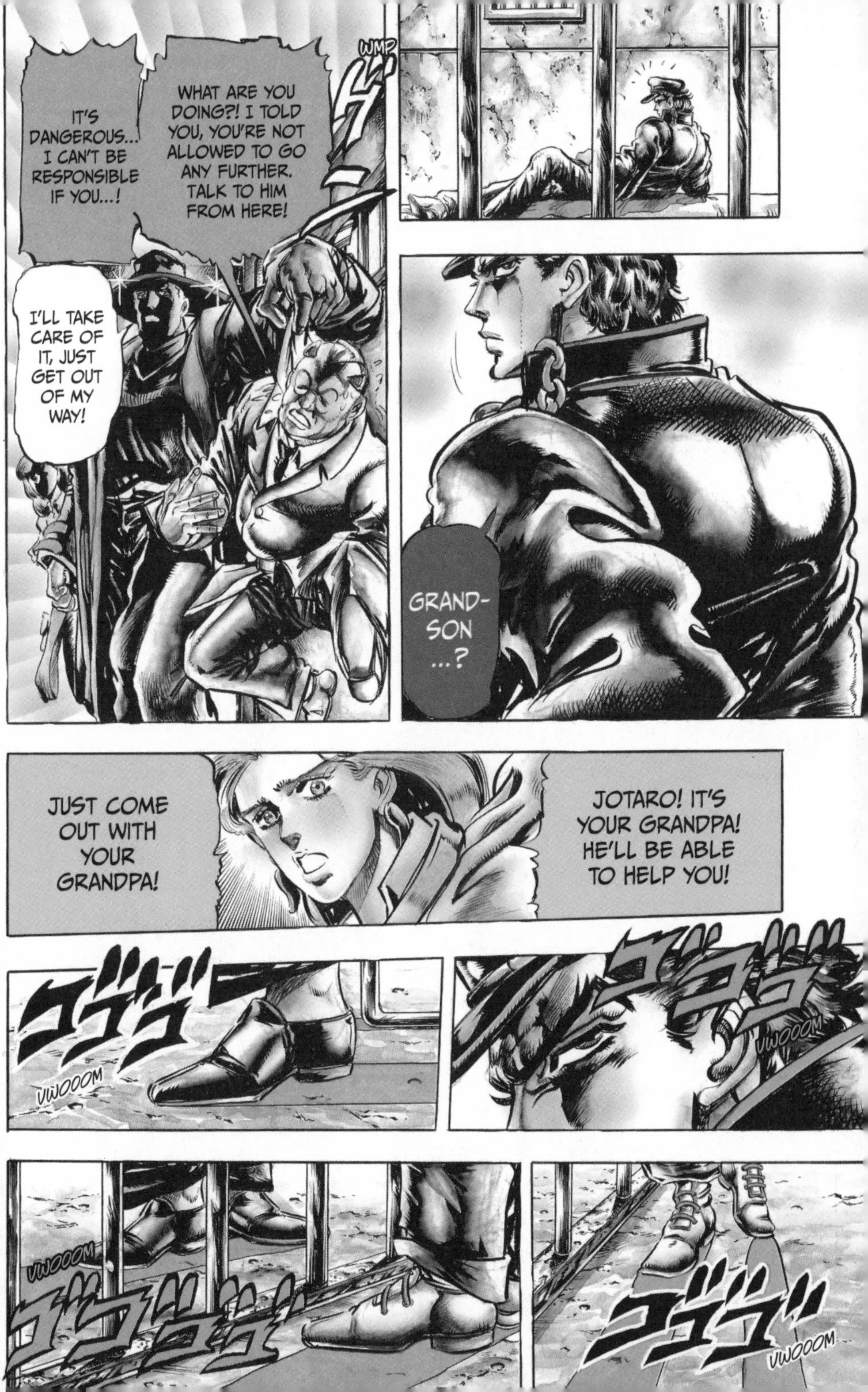
GRAND-SON ...?
WMP
WHAT ARE YOU DOING?! I TOLD YOU, YOU'RE NOT ALLOWED TO GO ANY FURTHER. TALK TO HIM FROM HERE!
IT'S DANGEROUS... I CAN'T BE RESPONSIBLE IF YOU...!
I'LL TAKE CARE OF IT, JUST GET OUT OF MY WAY!
JOTARO! IT'S YOUR GRANDPA! HE'LL BE ABLE TO HELP YOU!
JUST COME OUT WITH YOUR GRANDPA!
VWOOOM
VWOOOM
VWOOOM
VWOOOM

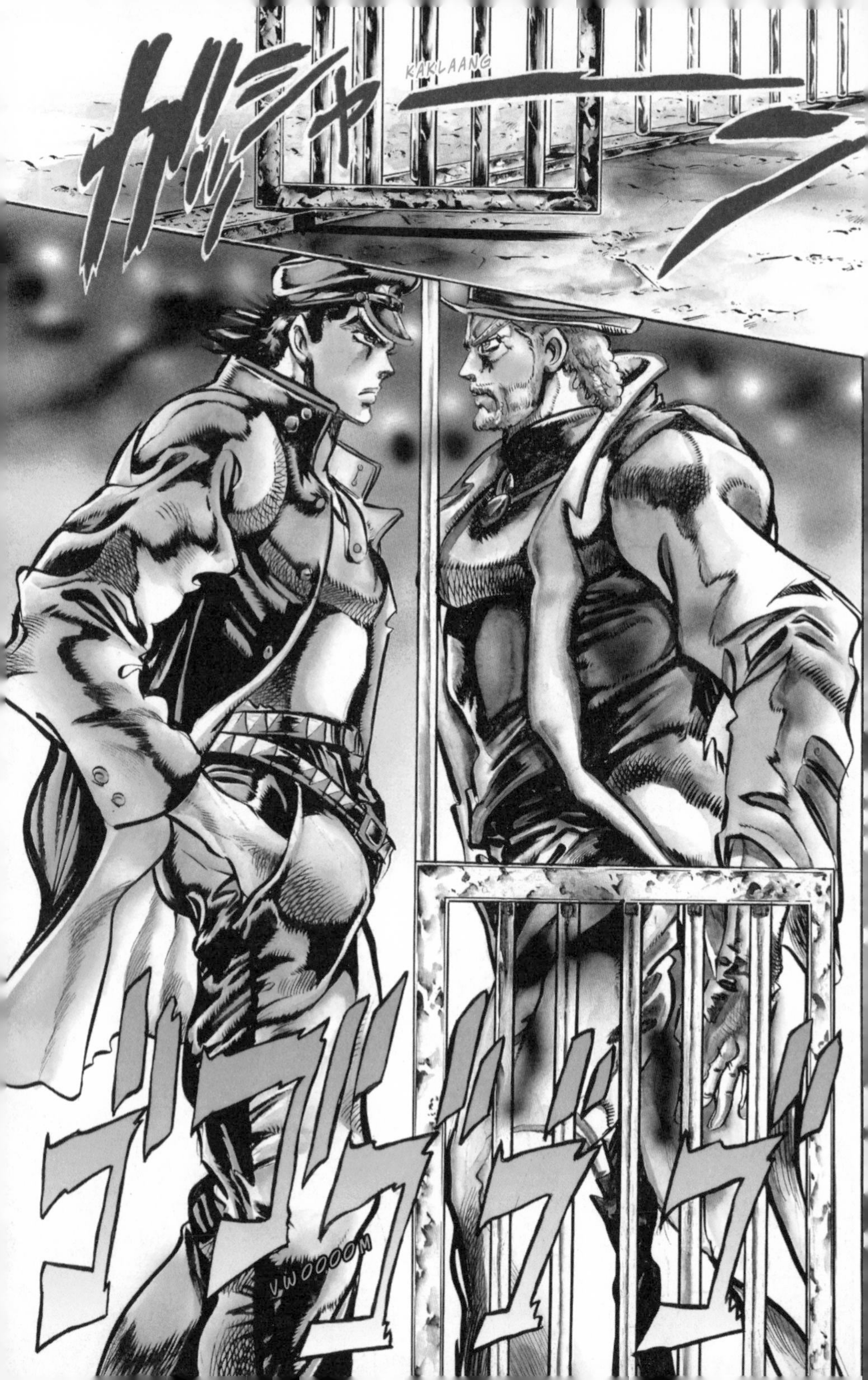
KAKLAANG
VWOOOOM

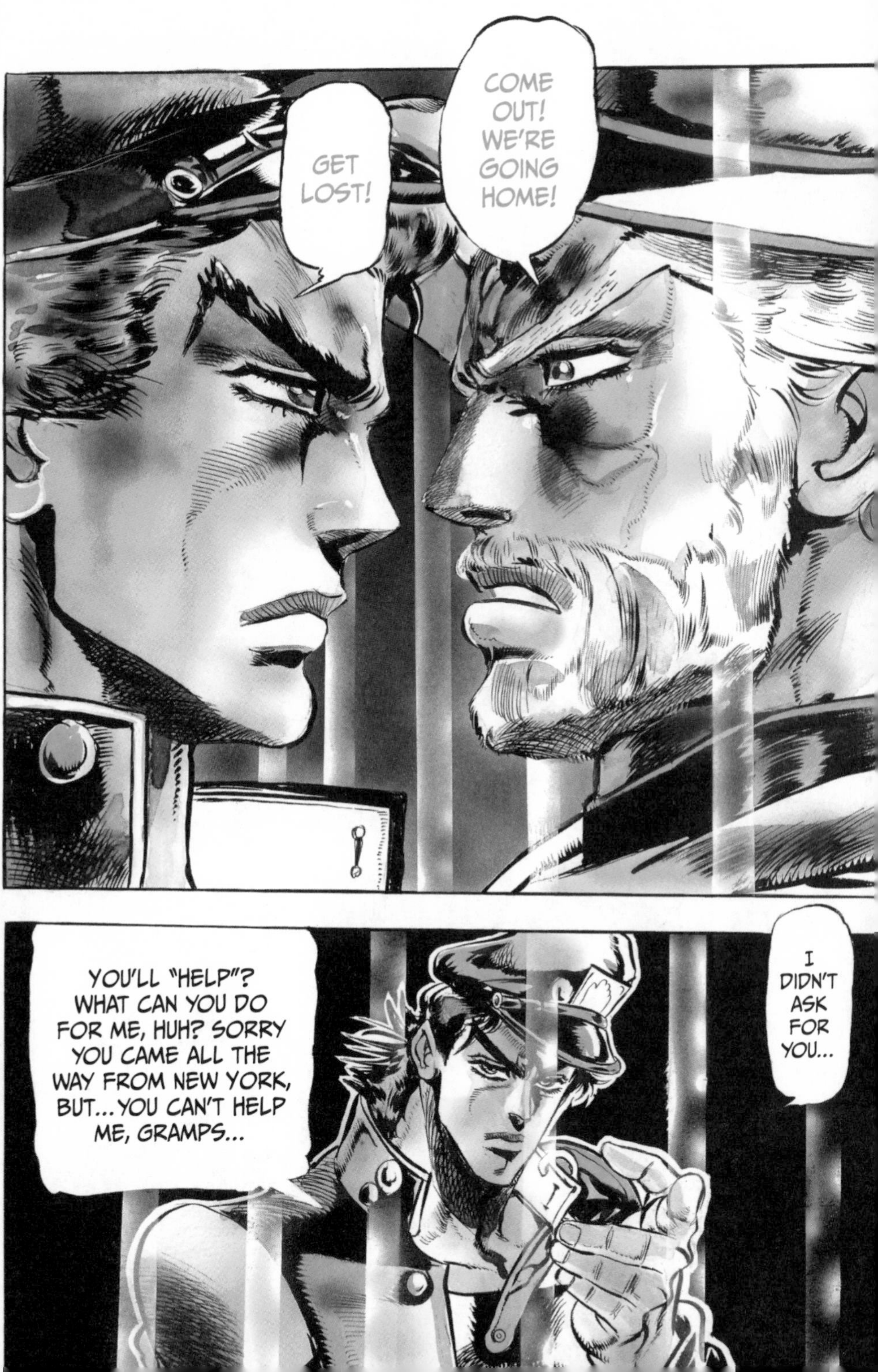
COME OUT! WE'RE GOING HOME!
GET LOST!
I DIDN'T ASK FOR YOU...
YOU'LL "HELP"? WHAT CAN YOU DO FOR ME, HUH? SORRY YOU CAME ALL THE WAY FROM NEW YORK, BUT...YOU CAN'T HELP ME, GRAMPS...

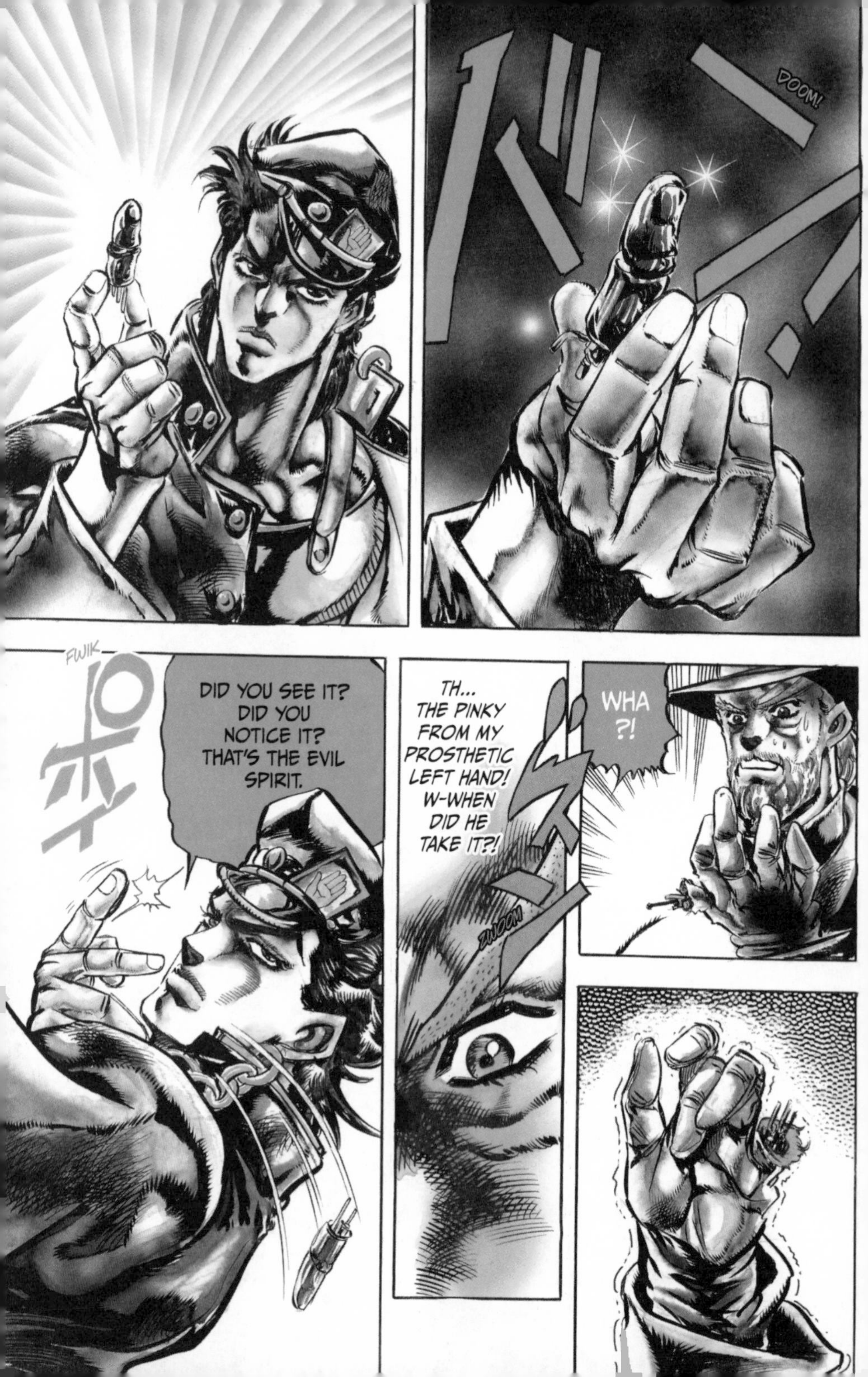
DOOM!
WHA ?!
TH... THE PINKY FROM MY PROSTHETIC LEFT HAND! W-WHEN DID HE TAKE IT?!
ZWOOM
FWIK
DID YOU SEE IT? DID YOU NOTICE IT? THAT'S THE EVIL SPIRIT.

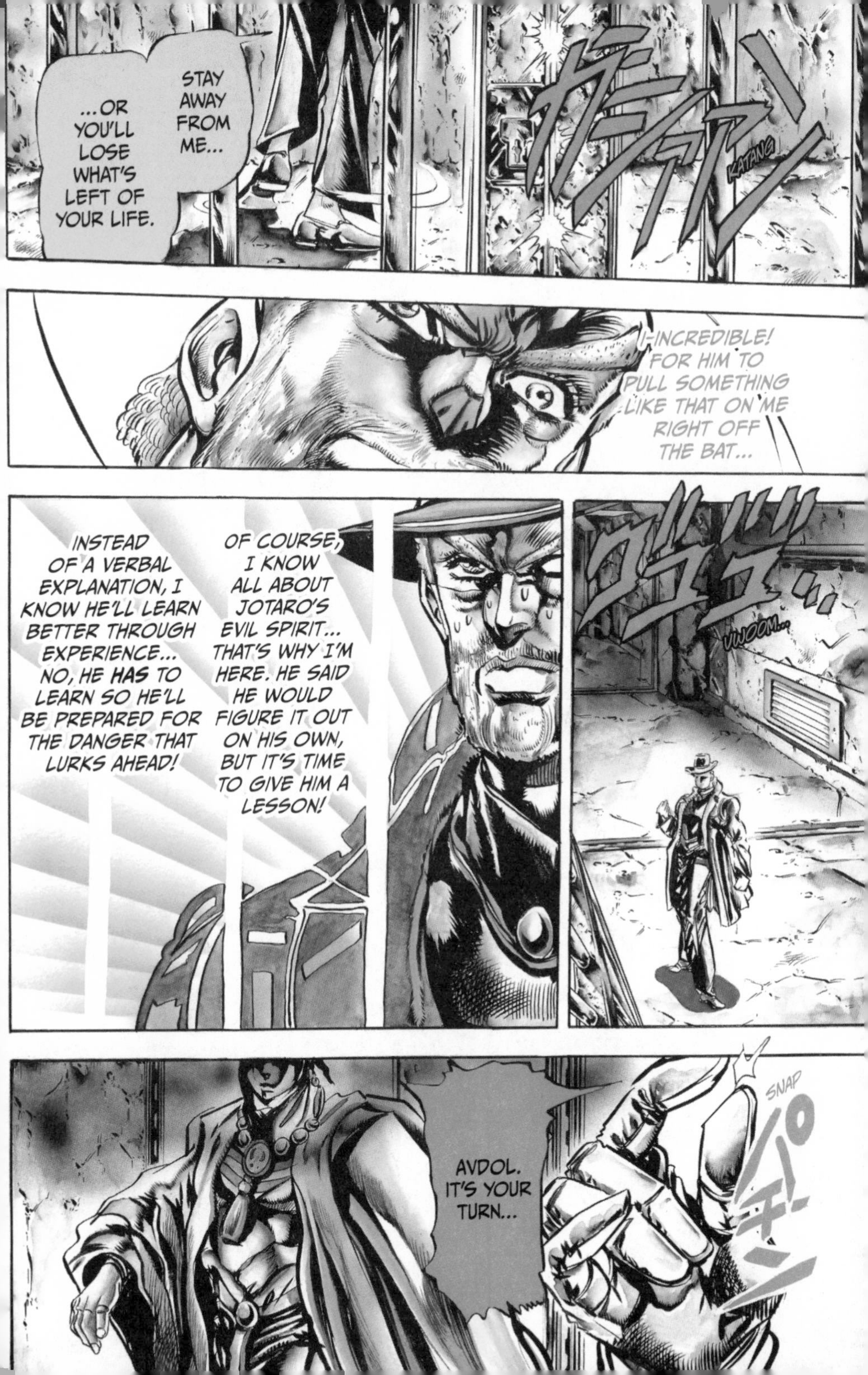
KATANG
STAY AWAY FROM ME...
...OR YOU'LL LOSE WHAT'S LEFT OF YOUR LIFE.
I-INCREDIBLE! FOR HIM TO PULL SOMETHING LIKE THAT ON ME RIGHT OFF THE BAT...
VWOOM...
OF COURSE, I KNOW ALL ABOUT JOTARO'S EVIL SPIRIT... THAT'S WHY I'M HERE. HE SAID HE WOULD FIGURE IT OUT ON HIS OWN, BUT IT'S TIME TO GIVE HIM A LESSON!
INSTEAD OF A VERBAL EXPLANATION, I KNOW HE'LL LEARN BETTER THROUGH EXPERIENCE... NO, HE HAS TO LEARN SO HE'LL BE PREPARED FOR THE DANGER THAT LURKS AHEAD!
SNAP
AVDOL. IT'S YOUR TURN...

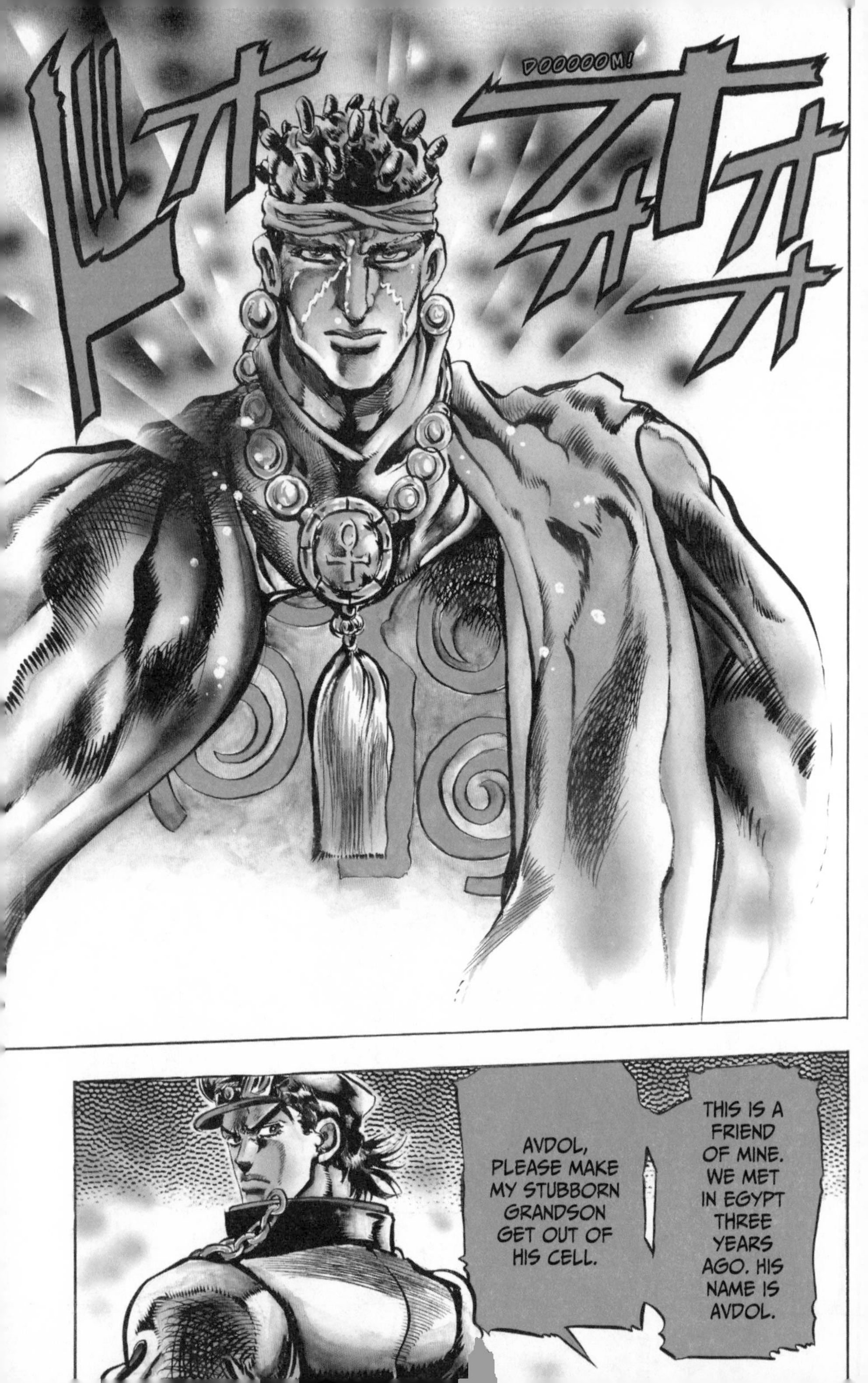
DOOOOOM!
THIS IS A FRIEND OF MINE. WE MET IN EGYPT THREE YEARS AGO. HIS NAME IS AVDOL.
AVDOL, PLEASE MAKE MY STUBBORN GRANDSON GET OUT OF HIS CELL.

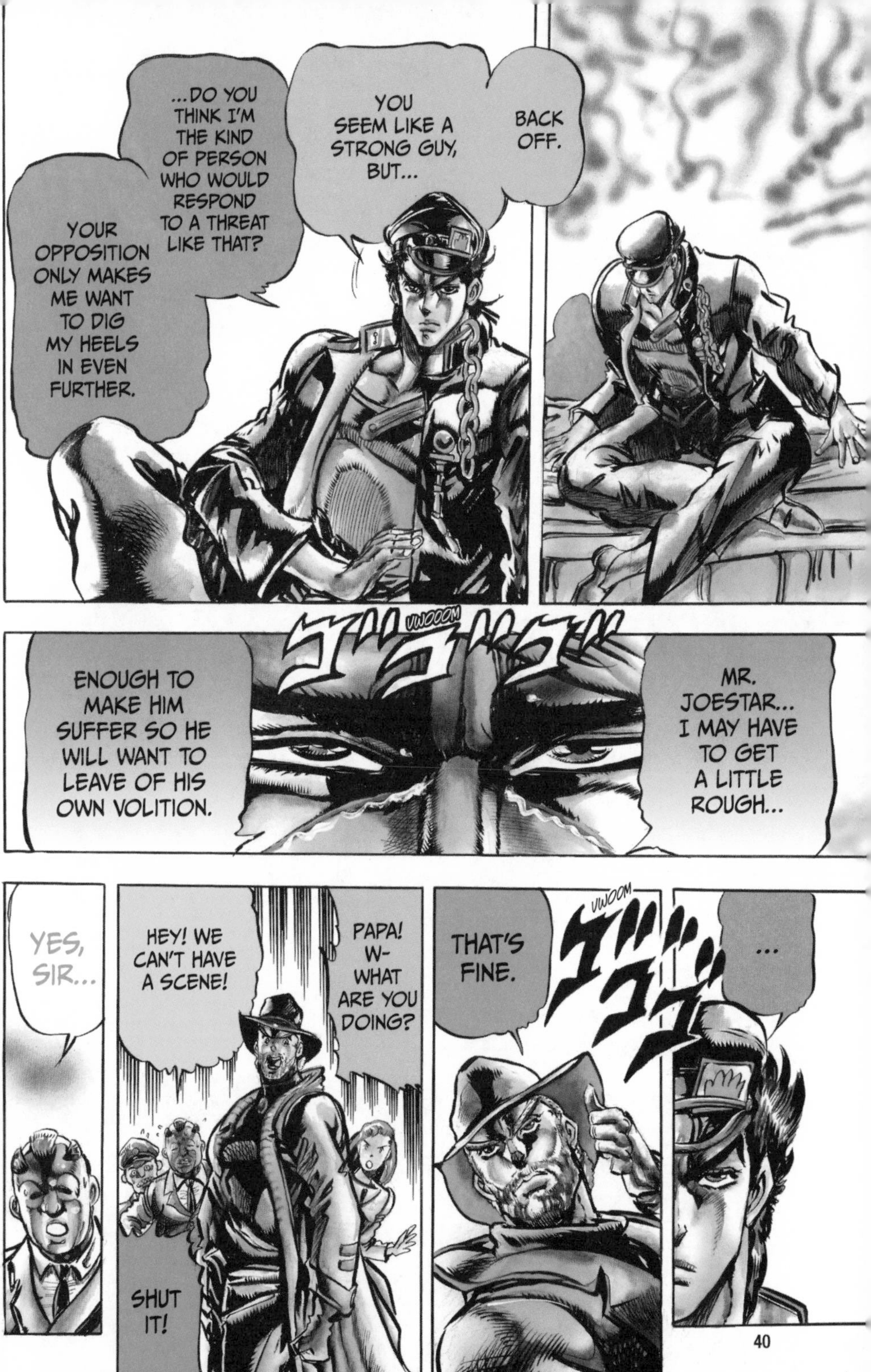
YOU SEEM LIKE A STRONG GUY, BUT...
BACK OFF.
...DO YOU THINK I'M THE KIND OF PERSON WHO WOULD RESPOND TO A THREAT LIKE THAT?
YOUR OPPOSITION ONLY MAKES ME WANT TO DIG MY HEELS IN EVEN FURTHER.
MR. JOESTAR... I MAY HAVE TO GET A LITTLE ROUGH...
VWOOOM
ENOUGH TO MAKE HIM SUFFER SO HE WILL WANT TO LEAVE OF HIS OWN VOLITION.
...
VWOOM
THAT'S FINE.
PAPA! W- WHAT ARE YOU DOING?
HEY! WE CAN'T HAVE A SCENE!
SHUT IT!
YES, SIR...

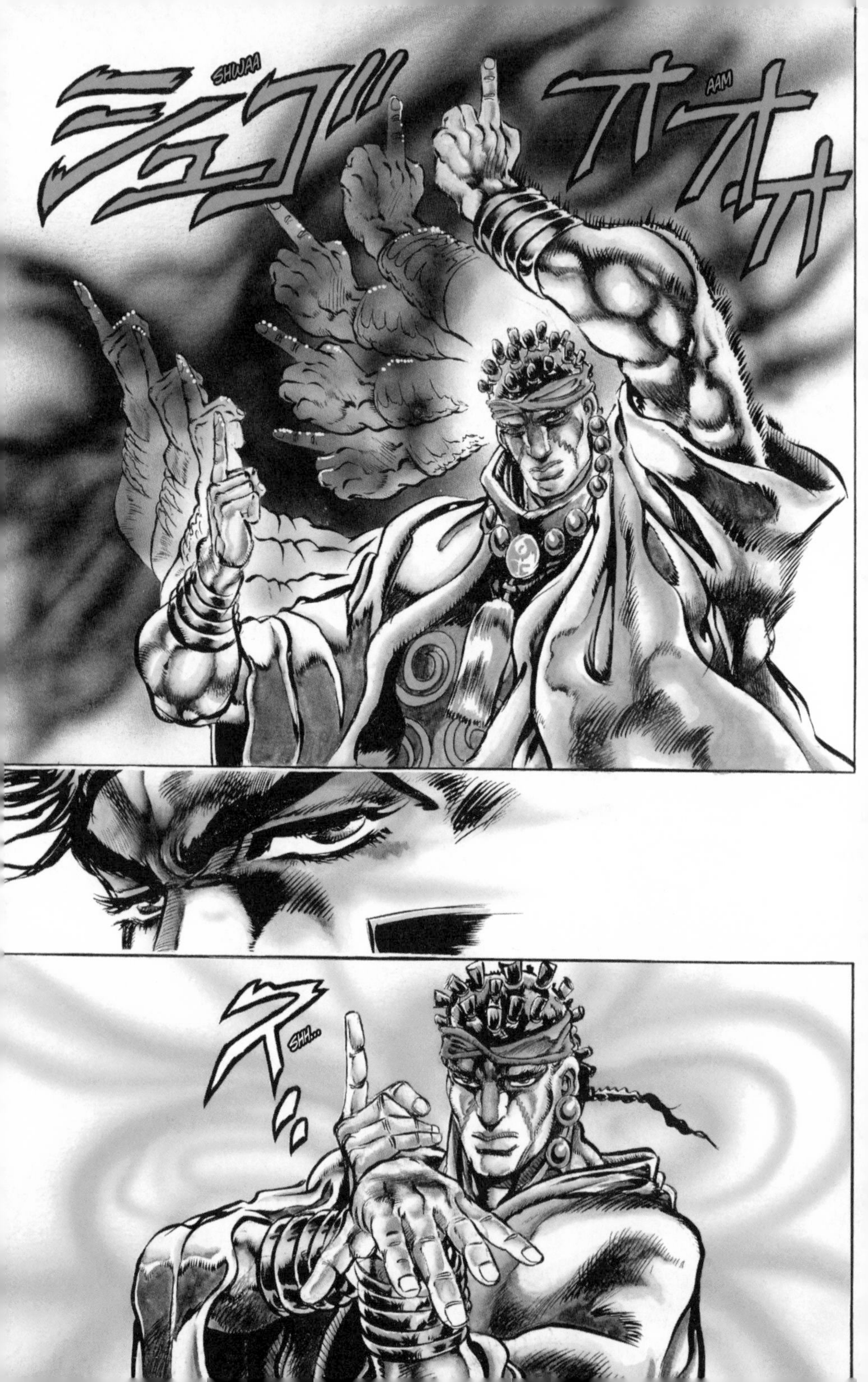
SHWAA
AAM
SHH...

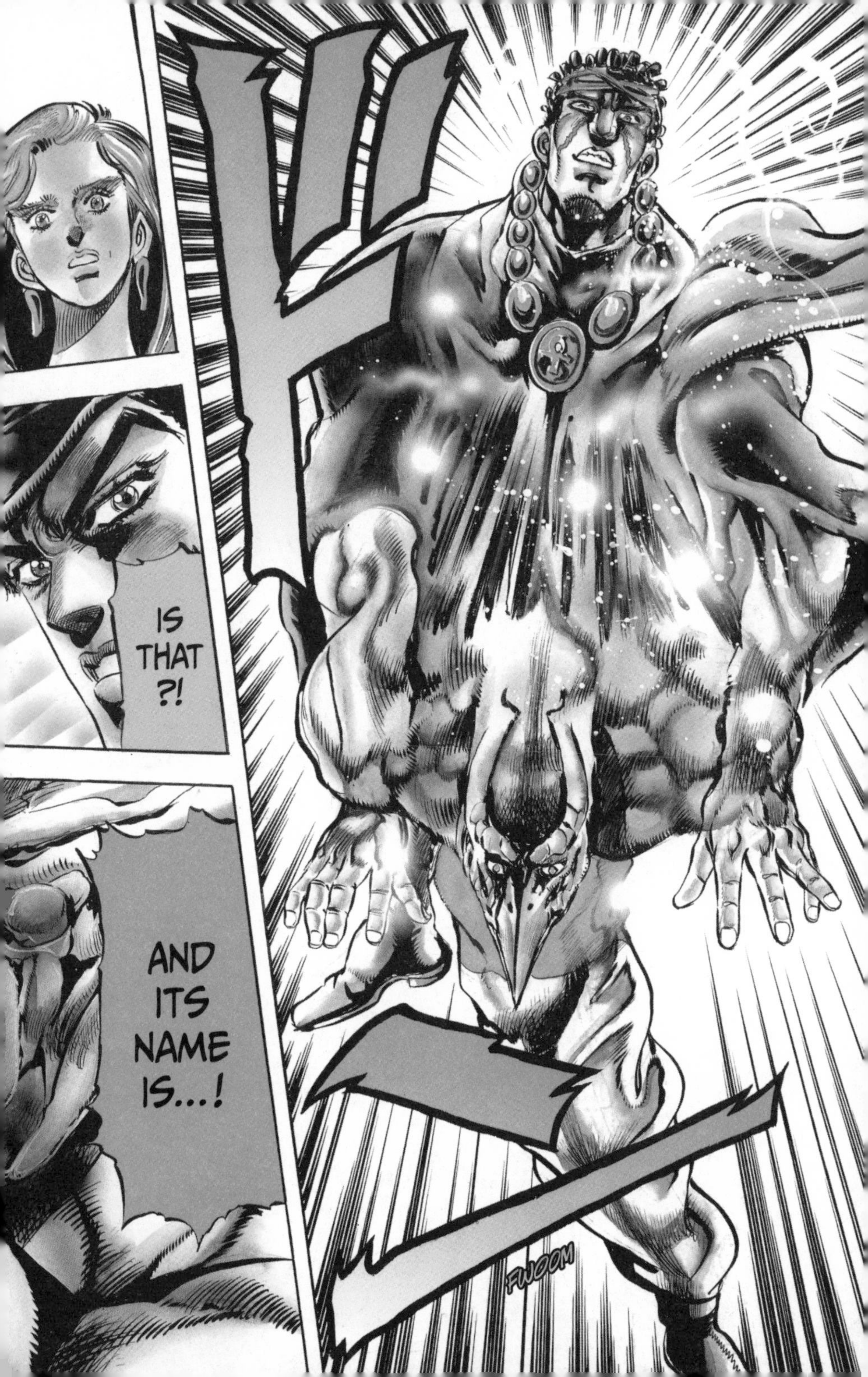
FWOOM
IS THAT ?!
AND ITS NAME IS...!

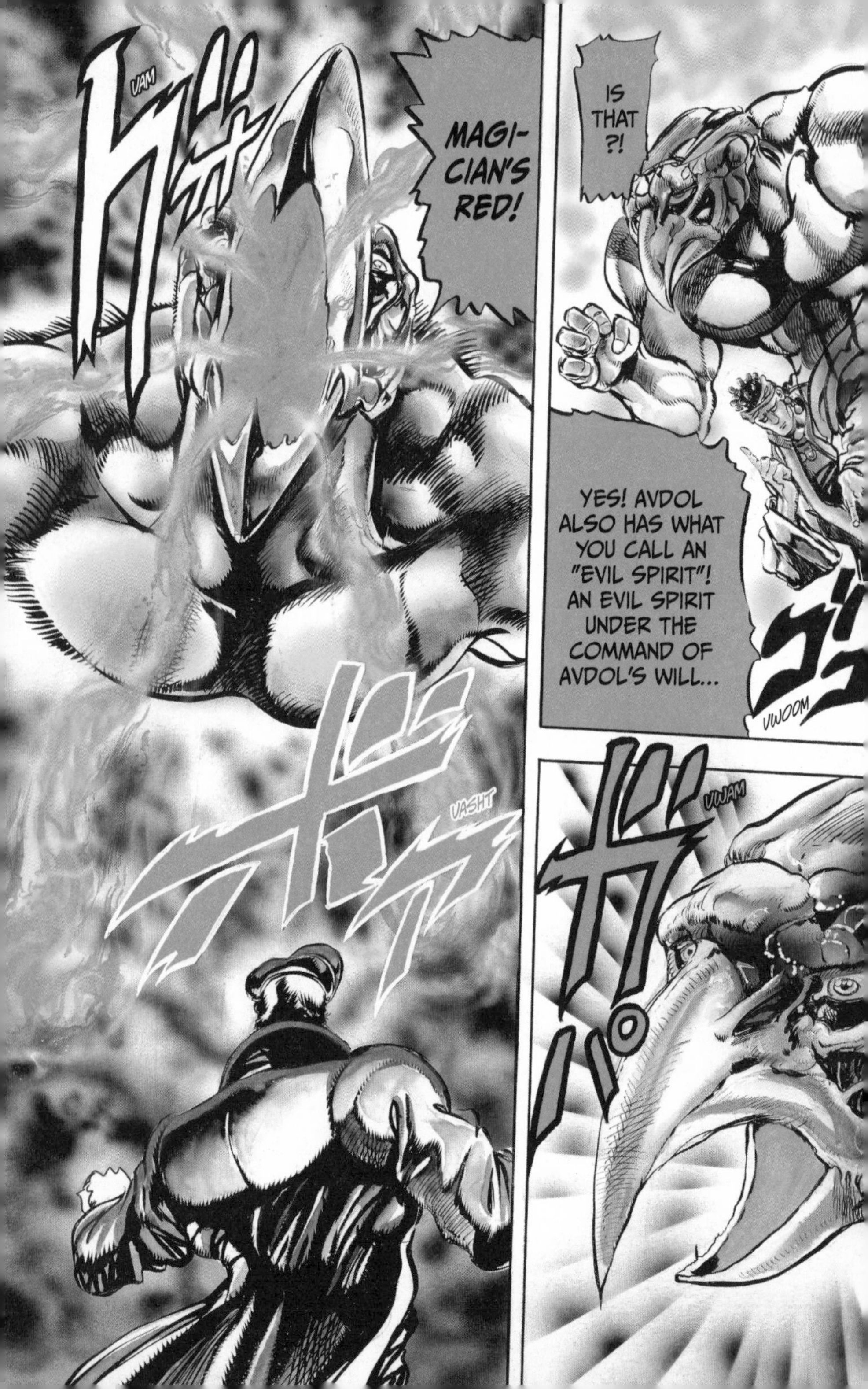
IS THAT?!
YES! AVDOL ALSO HAS WHAT YOU CALL AN "EVIL SPIRIT"! AN EVIL SPIRIT UNDER THE COMMAND OF AVDOL'S WILL...
VWOOM
UWAM
UAM
MAGI-CIAN'S RED!
VASHT

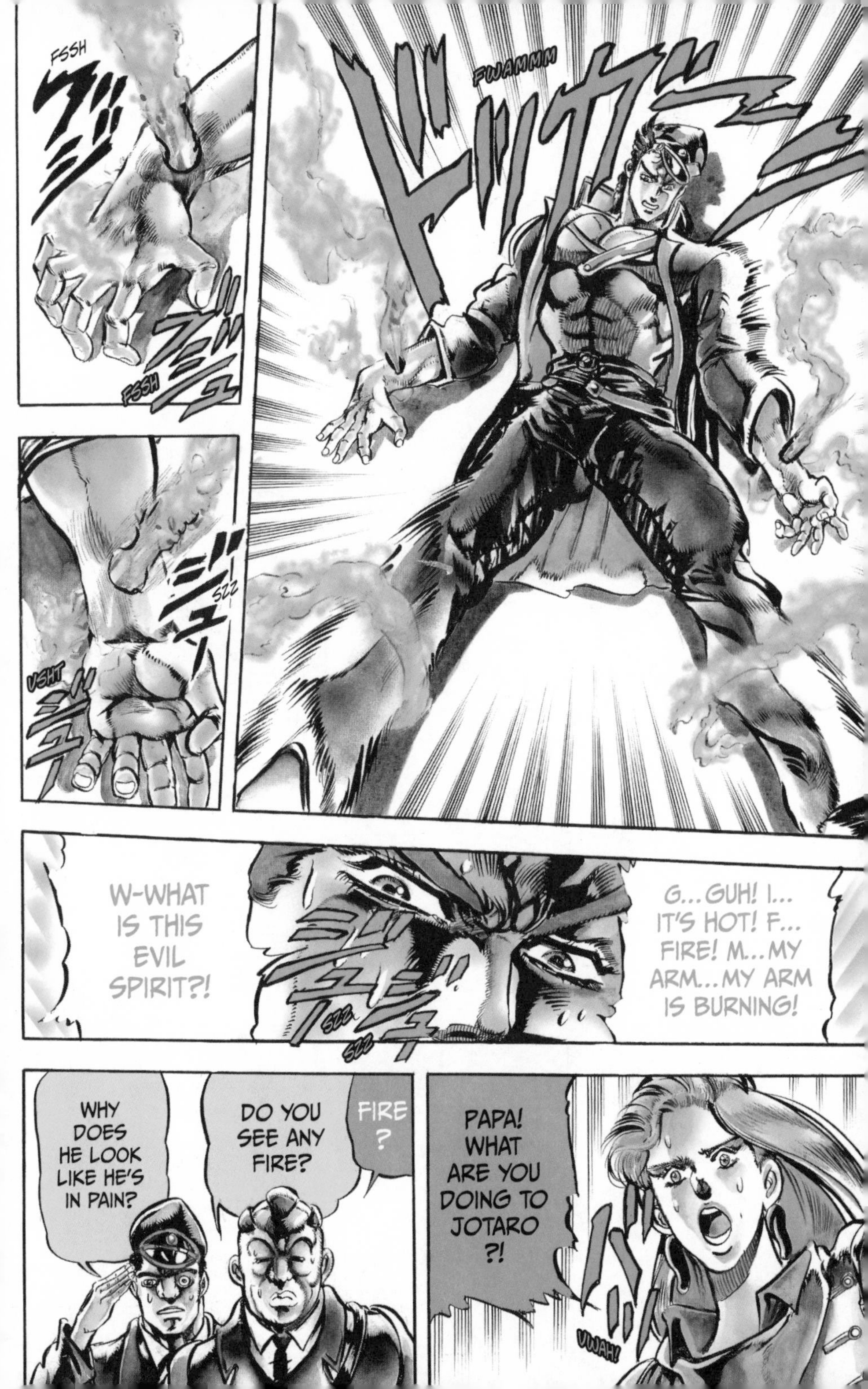
FWAMMM
FSSH
FSSH
SZZ
USHT
G...GUH! I... IT'S HOT! F... FIRE! M...MY ARM...MY ARM IS BURNING!
W-WHAT IS THIS EVIL SPIRIT?!
SZZ
SZZ
PAPA! WHAT ARE YOU DOING TO JOTARO ?!
UWAH!
FIRE ?
DO YOU SEE ANY FIRE?
WHY DOES HE LOOK LIKE HE'S IN PAIN?

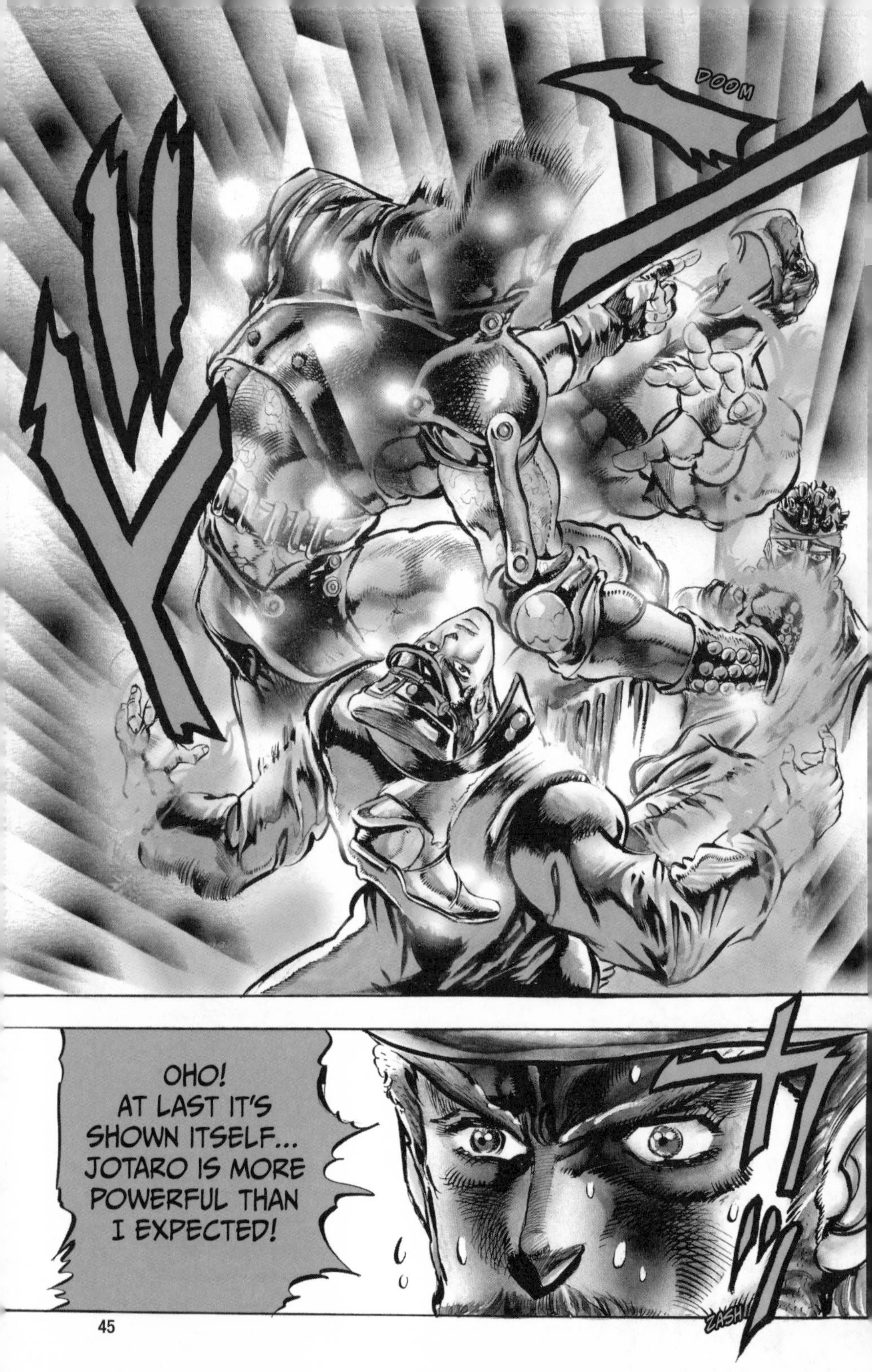
DOOM
OHO!
AT LAST IT'S SHOWN ITSELF... JOTARO IS MORE POWERFUL THAN I EXPECTED!
ZASH

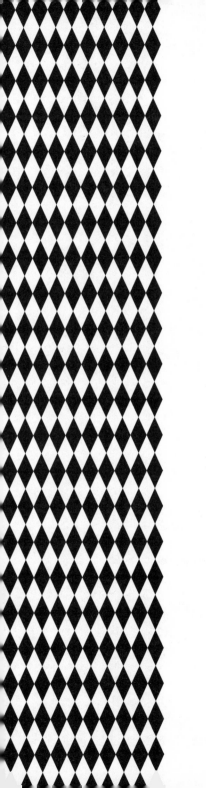

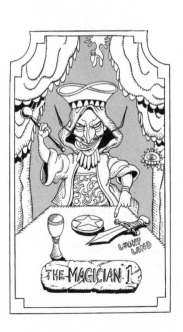

THE MAGICIAN 1

LUCKY LAND

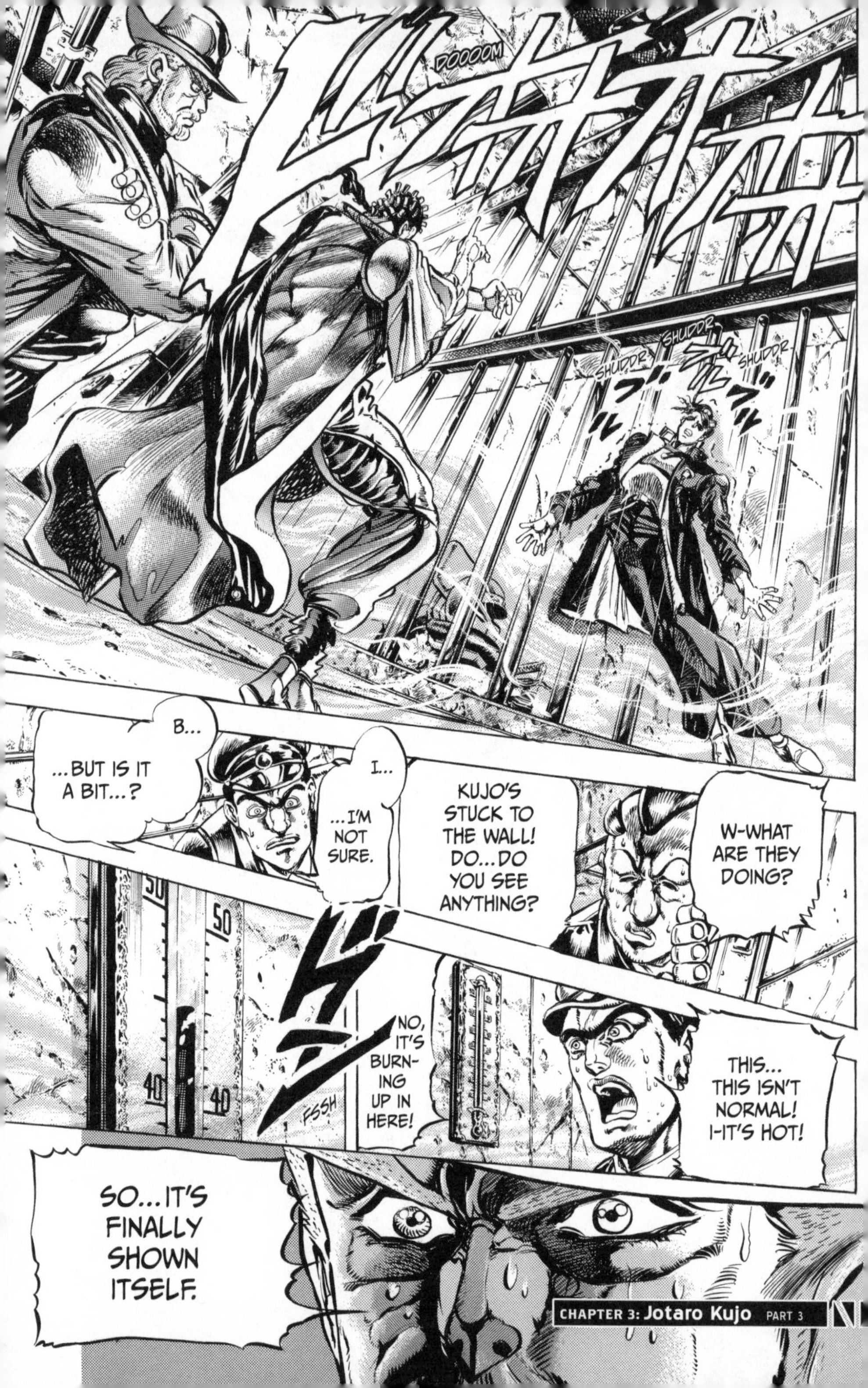
DOOOOM
SHUDDR
SHUDDR
SHUDDR
W-WHAT ARE THEY DOING?
KUJO'S STUCK TO THE WALL! DO...DO YOU SEE ANYTHING?
I... ...I'M NOT SURE.
B... ...BUT IS IT A BIT...?
THIS... THIS ISN'T NORMAL! I-IT'S HOT!
NO, IT'S BURNING UP IN HERE!
FSSH
SO...IT'S FINALLY SHOWN ITSELF.
CHAPTER 3: Jotaro Kujo PART 3

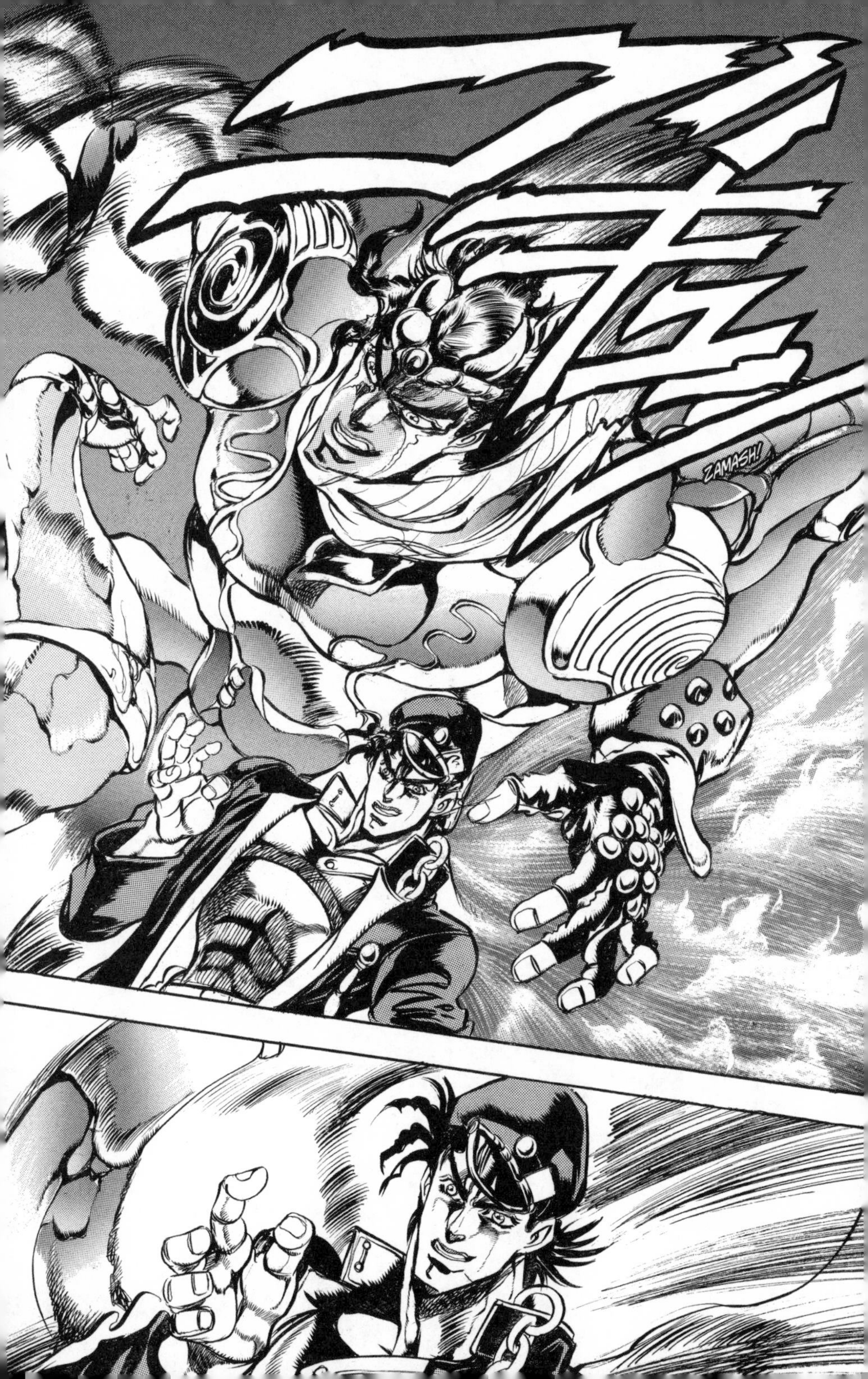
ZAMASH!

CHAPTER 3: Jotaro Kujo PART 3

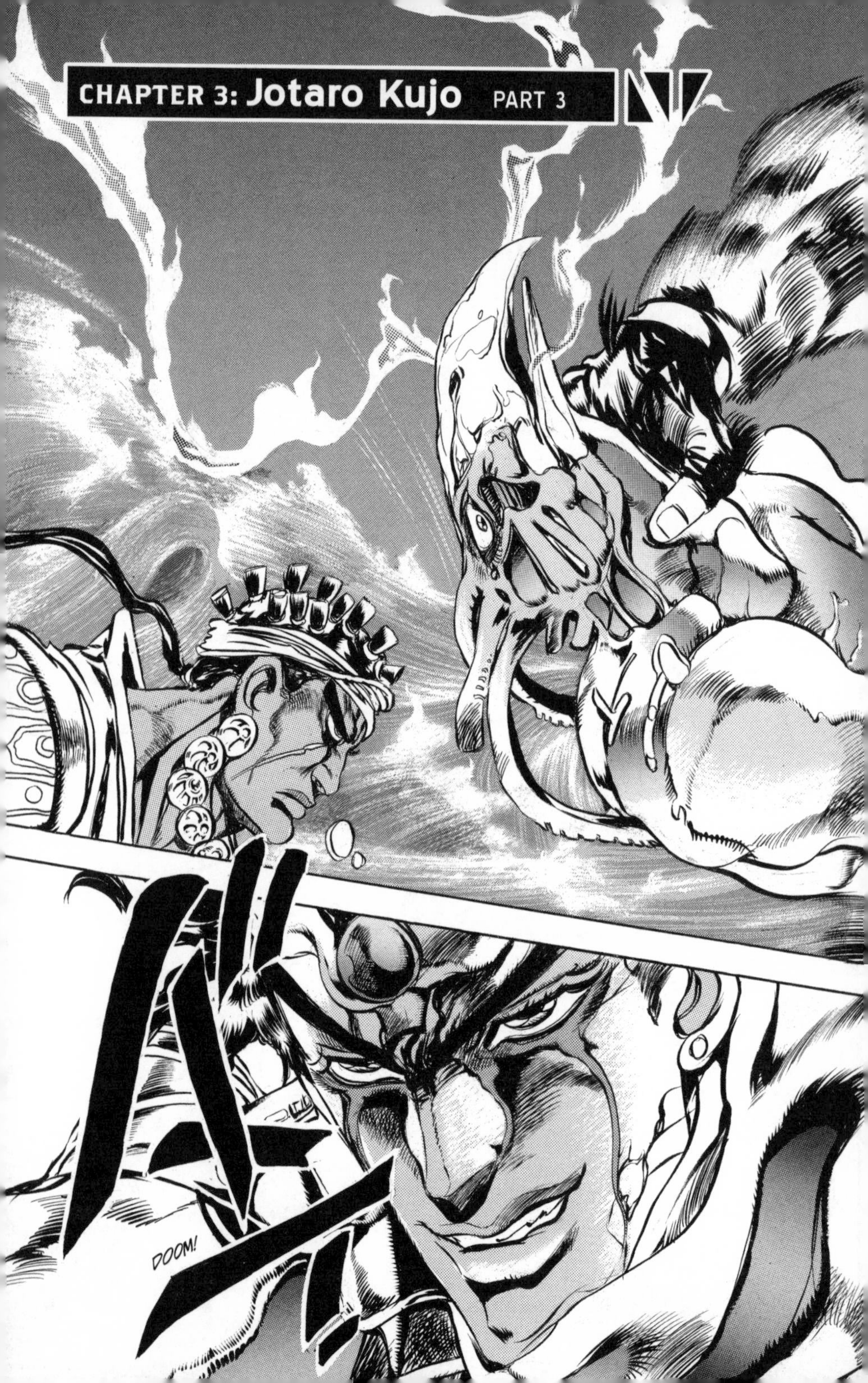
DOOM!

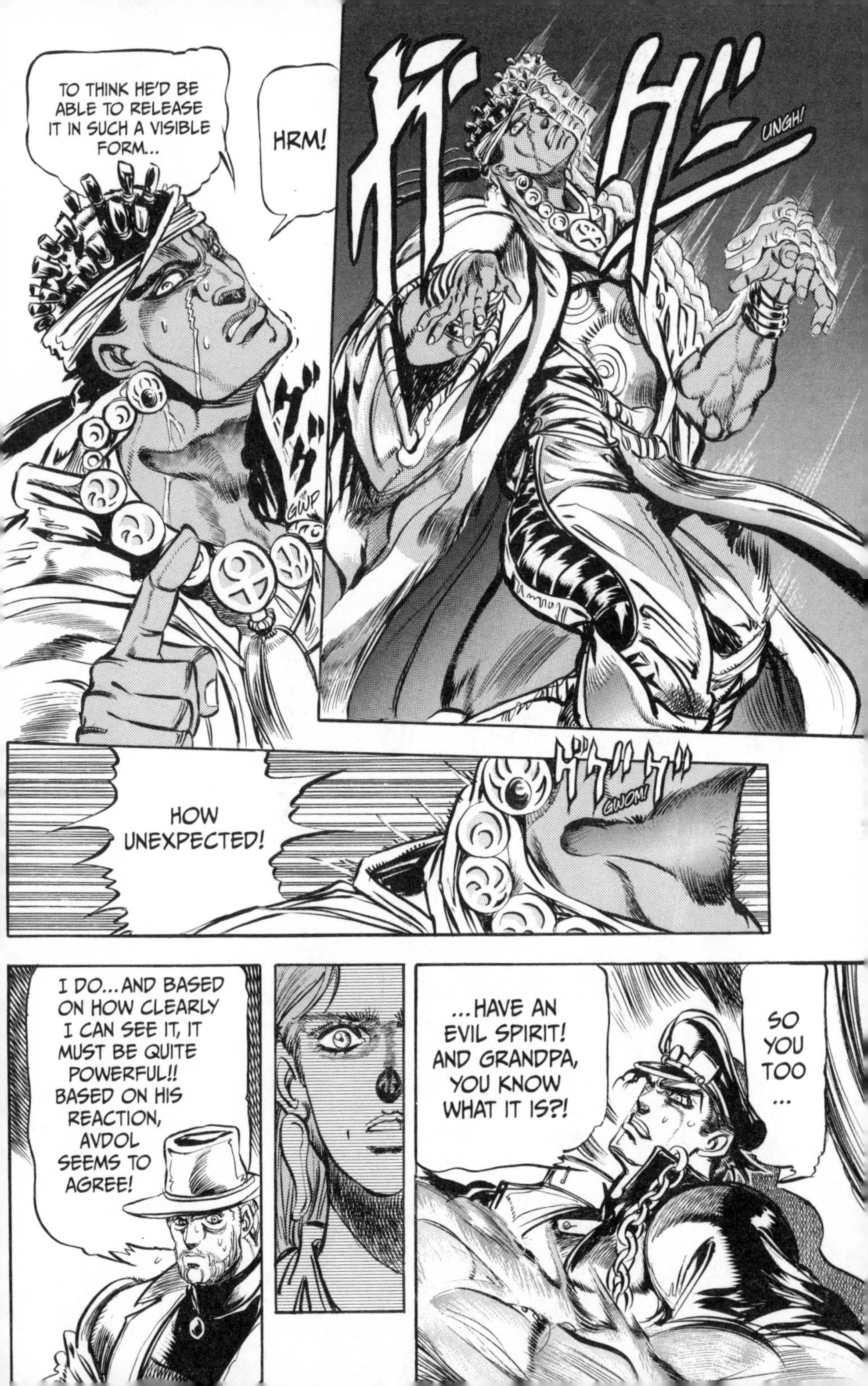
UNGH!
HRM!
TO THINK HE'D BE ABLE TO RELEASE IT IN SUCH A VISIBLE FORM...
GWP
GWOM!
HOW UNEXPECTED!
SO YOU TOO ...
...HAVE AN EVIL SPIRIT! AND GRANDPA, YOU KNOW WHAT IT IS?!
I DO...AND BASED ON HOW CLEARLY I CAN SEE IT, IT MUST BE QUITE POWERFUL!! BASED ON HIS REACTION, AVDOL SEEMS TO AGREE!

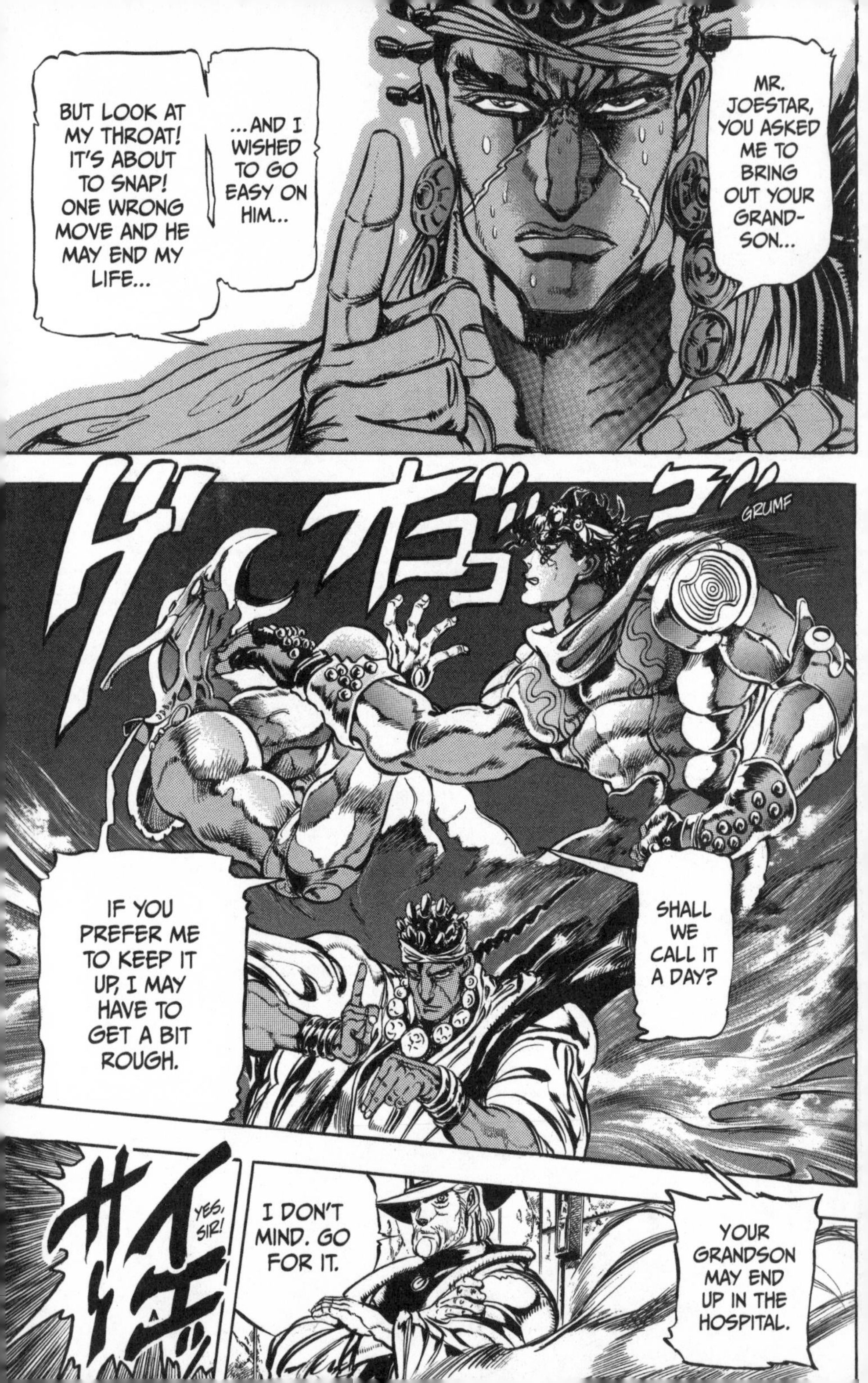
MR. JOESTAR, YOU ASKED ME TO BRING OUT YOUR GRANDSON...
...AND I WISHED TO GO EASY ON HIM...
BUT LOOK AT MY THROAT! IT'S ABOUT TO SNAP! ONE WRONG MOVE AND HE MAY END MY LIFE...
GRUMF
SHALL WE CALL IT A DAY?
IF YOU PREFER ME TO KEEP IT UP, I MAY HAVE TO GET A BIT ROUGH.
YOUR GRANDSON MAY END UP IN THE HOSPITAL.
I DON'T MIND. GO FOR IT.
YES, SIR!

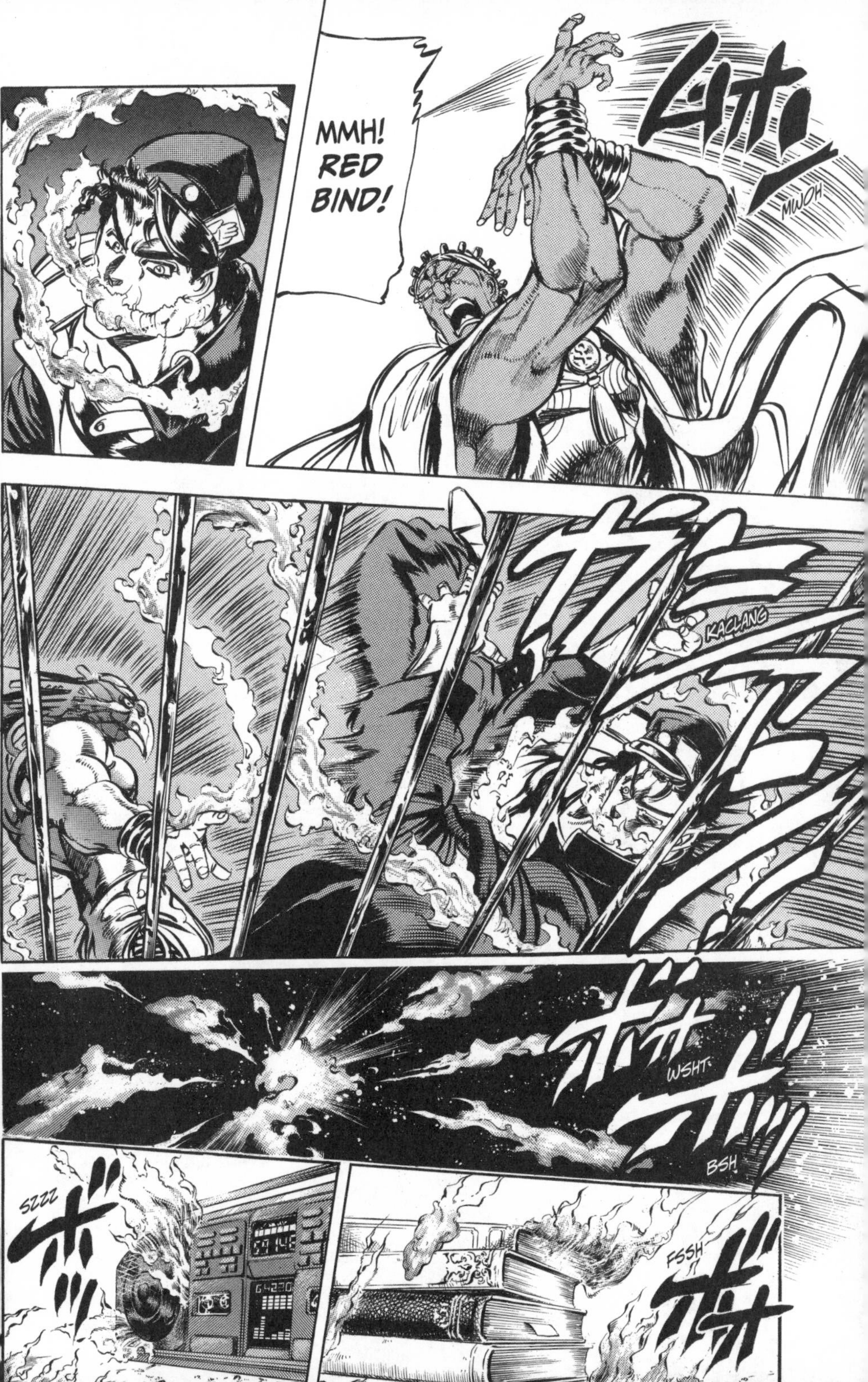
MMH! RED BIND!
MWOH
KACLANG
WSHT
BSH
FSSH
SZZZ

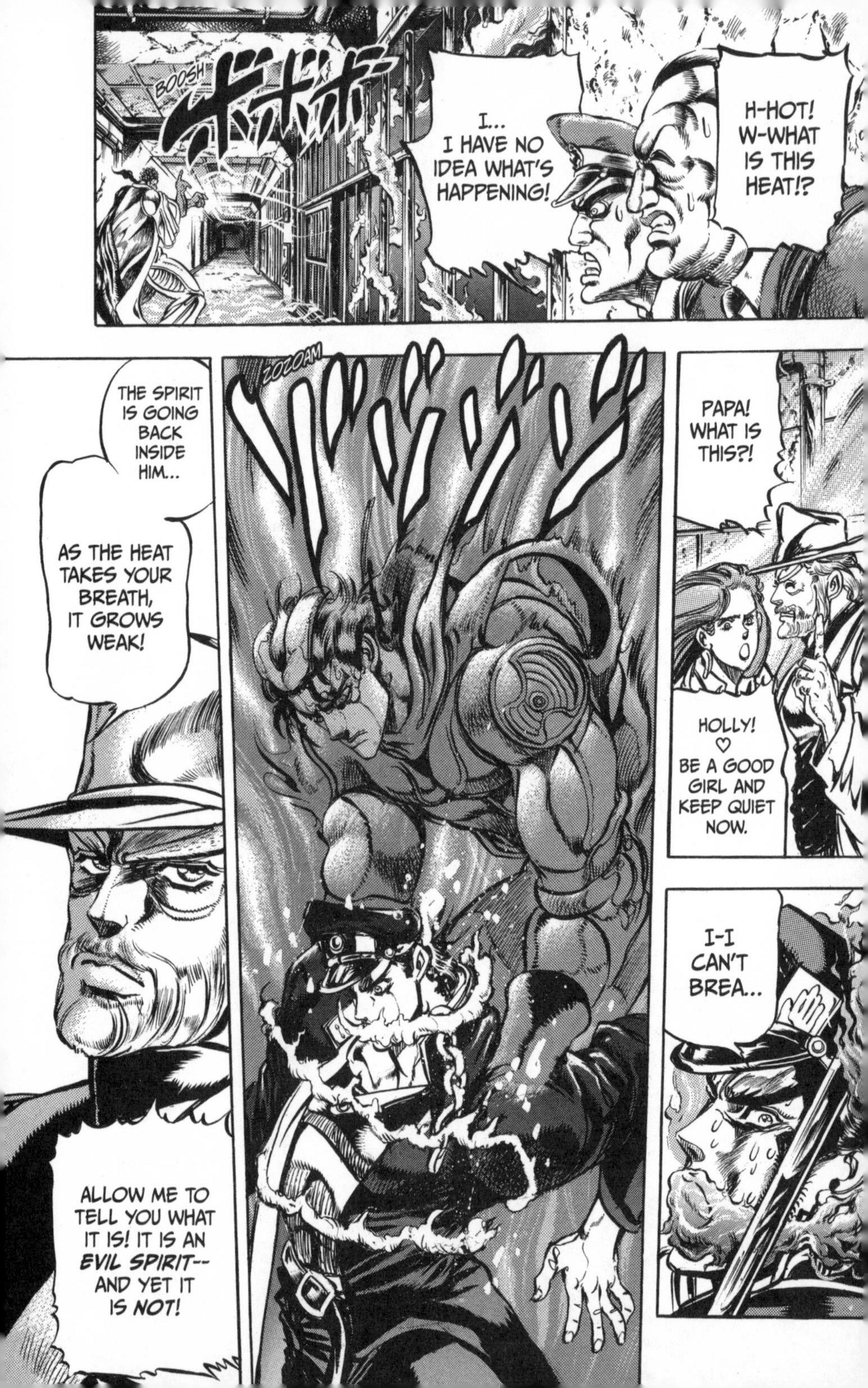
H-HOT! W-WHAT IS THIS HEAT!?
I... I HAVE NO IDEA WHAT'S HAPPENING!
BOOSH
PAPA! WHAT IS THIS?!
HOLLY! ♡ BE A GOOD GIRL AND KEEP QUIET NOW.
I-I CAN'T BREA...
ZOZOAM
THE SPIRIT IS GOING BACK INSIDE HIM...
AS THE HEAT TAKES YOUR BREATH, IT GROWS WEAK!
ALLOW ME TO TELL YOU WHAT IT IS! IT IS AN *EVIL SPIRIT*-- AND YET IT IS *NOT*!

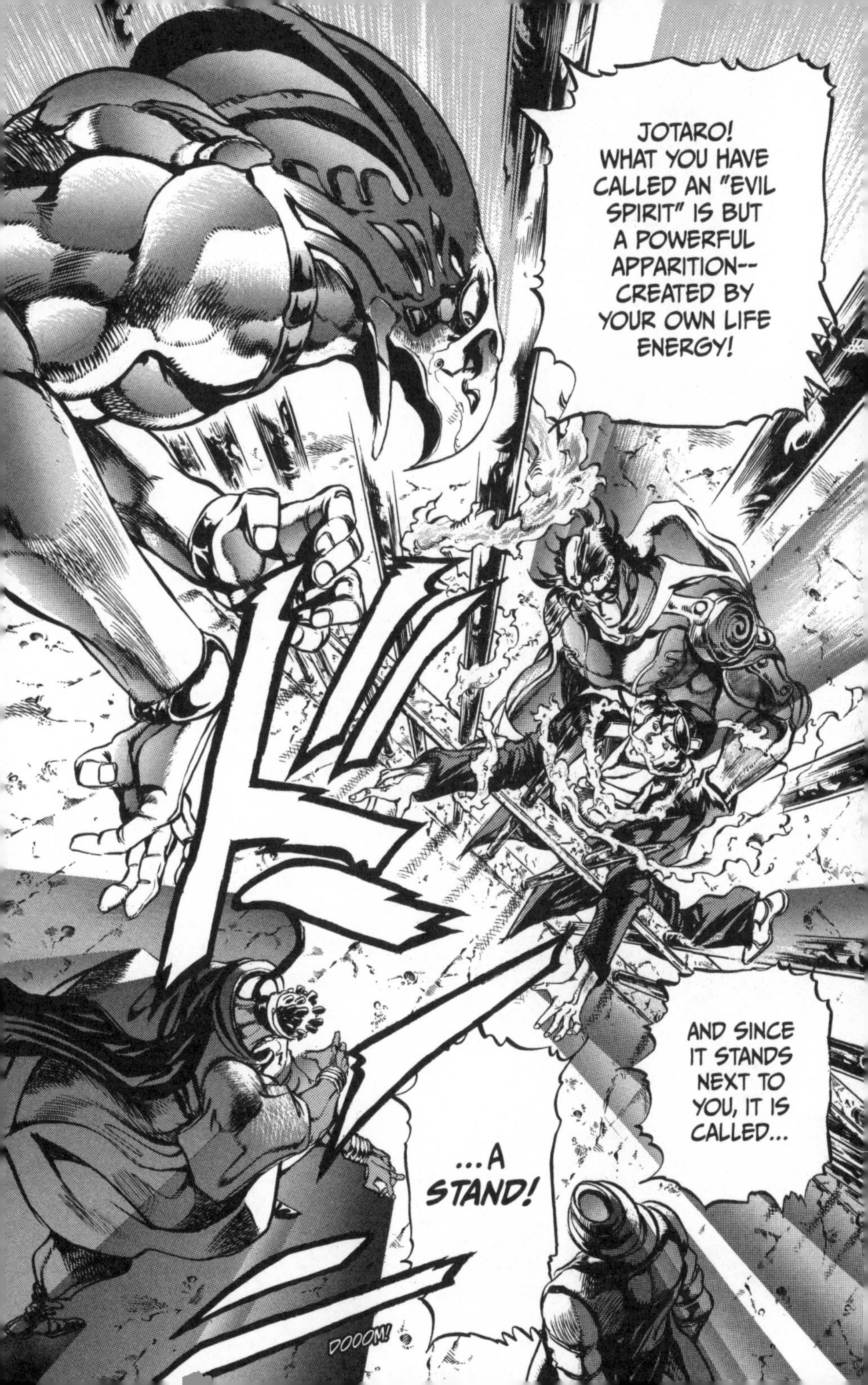
JOTARO! WHAT YOU HAVE CALLED AN "EVIL SPIRIT" IS BUT A POWERFUL APPARITION-- CREATED BY YOUR OWN LIFE ENERGY!
AND SINCE IT STANDS NEXT TO YOU, IT IS CALLED...
...A STAND!
DOOOM!

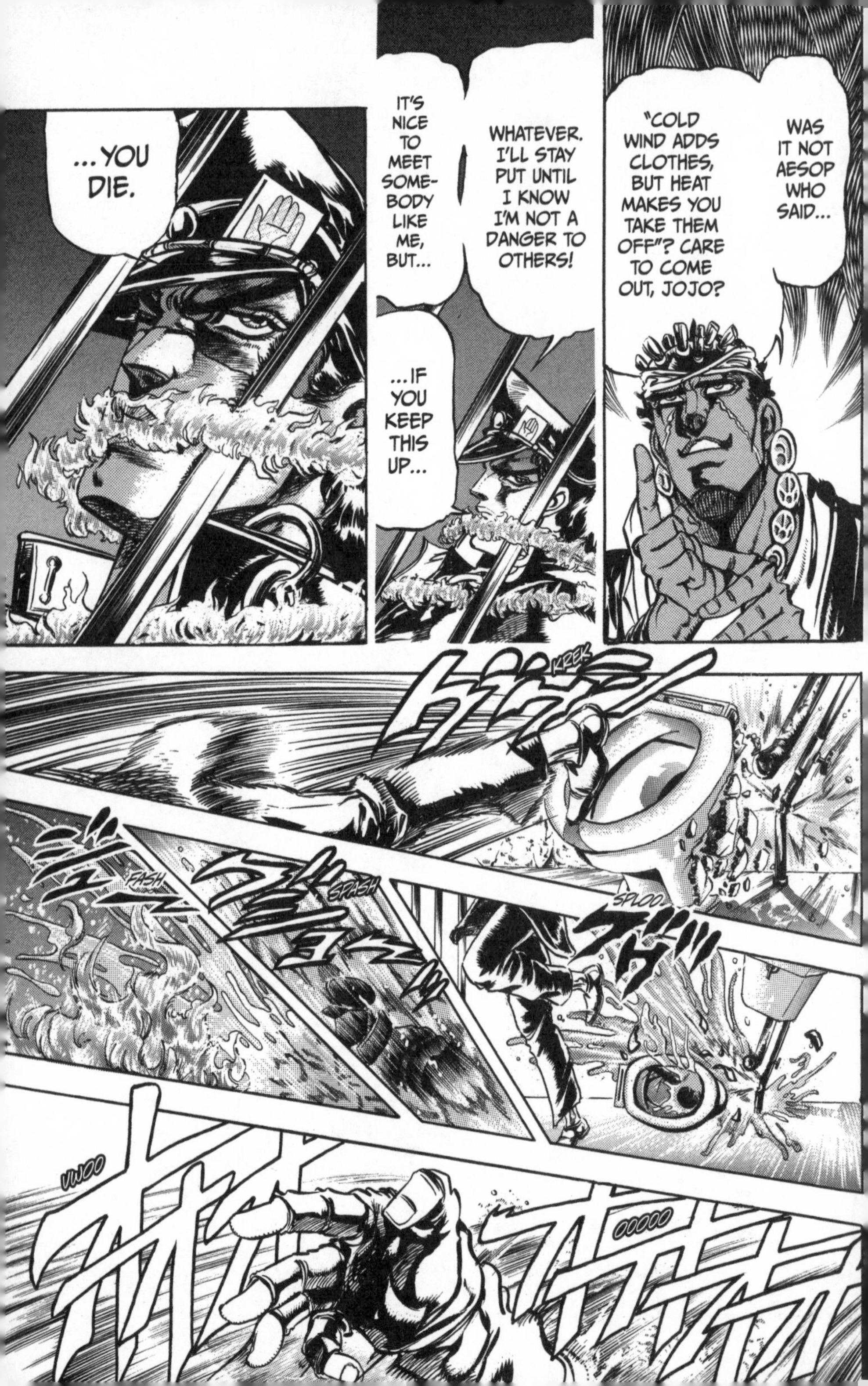
WAS IT NOT AESOP WHO SAID...
"COLD WIND ADDS CLOTHES, BUT HEAT MAKES YOU TAKE THEM OFF"? CARE TO COME OUT, JOJO?
WHATEVER. I'LL STAY PUT UNTIL I KNOW I'M NOT A DANGER TO OTHERS!
IT'S NICE TO MEET SOMEBODY LIKE ME, BUT...
...IF YOU KEEP THIS UP...
...YOU DIE.
KREK
SPLOO
SPASH
FASH
OOOOO
UWOO

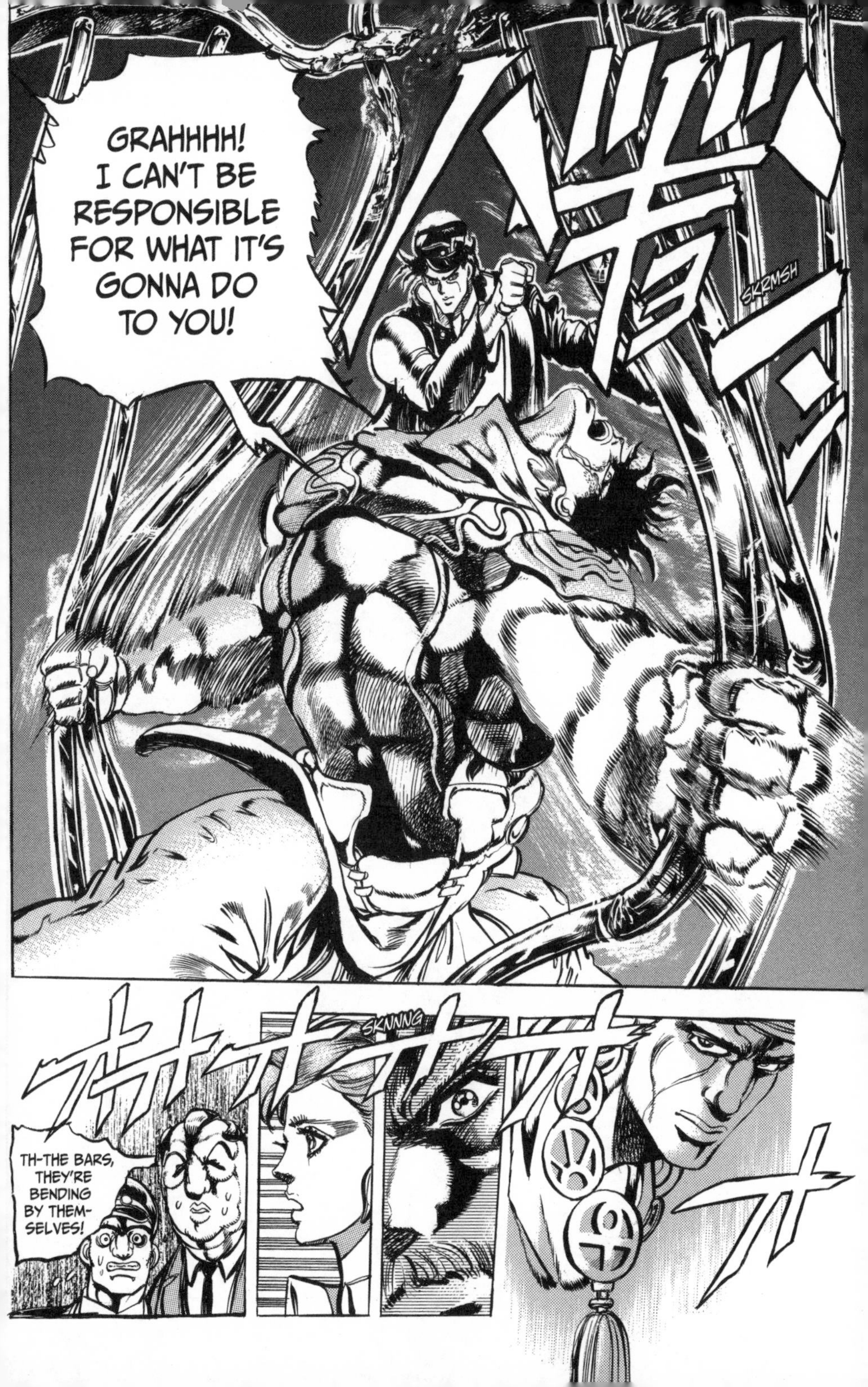

GRAHHHH! I CAN'T BE RESPONSIBLE FOR WHAT IT'S GONNA DO TO YOU!
SKRMSH
SKNNNG
TH-THE BARS, THEY'RE BENDING BY THEM-SELVES!

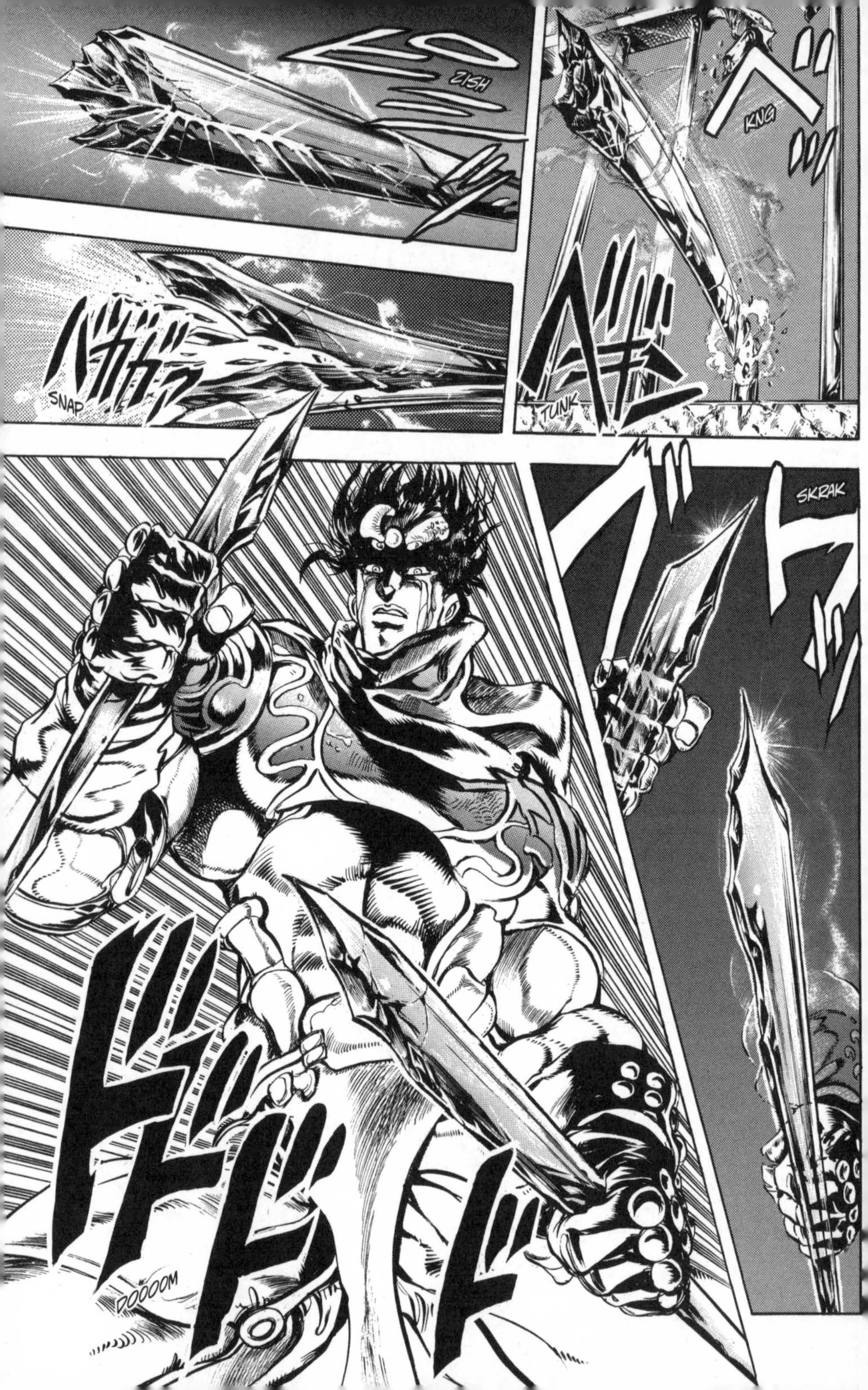
KNG
TUNK
ZISH
SNAP
SKRAK
DOOOOM

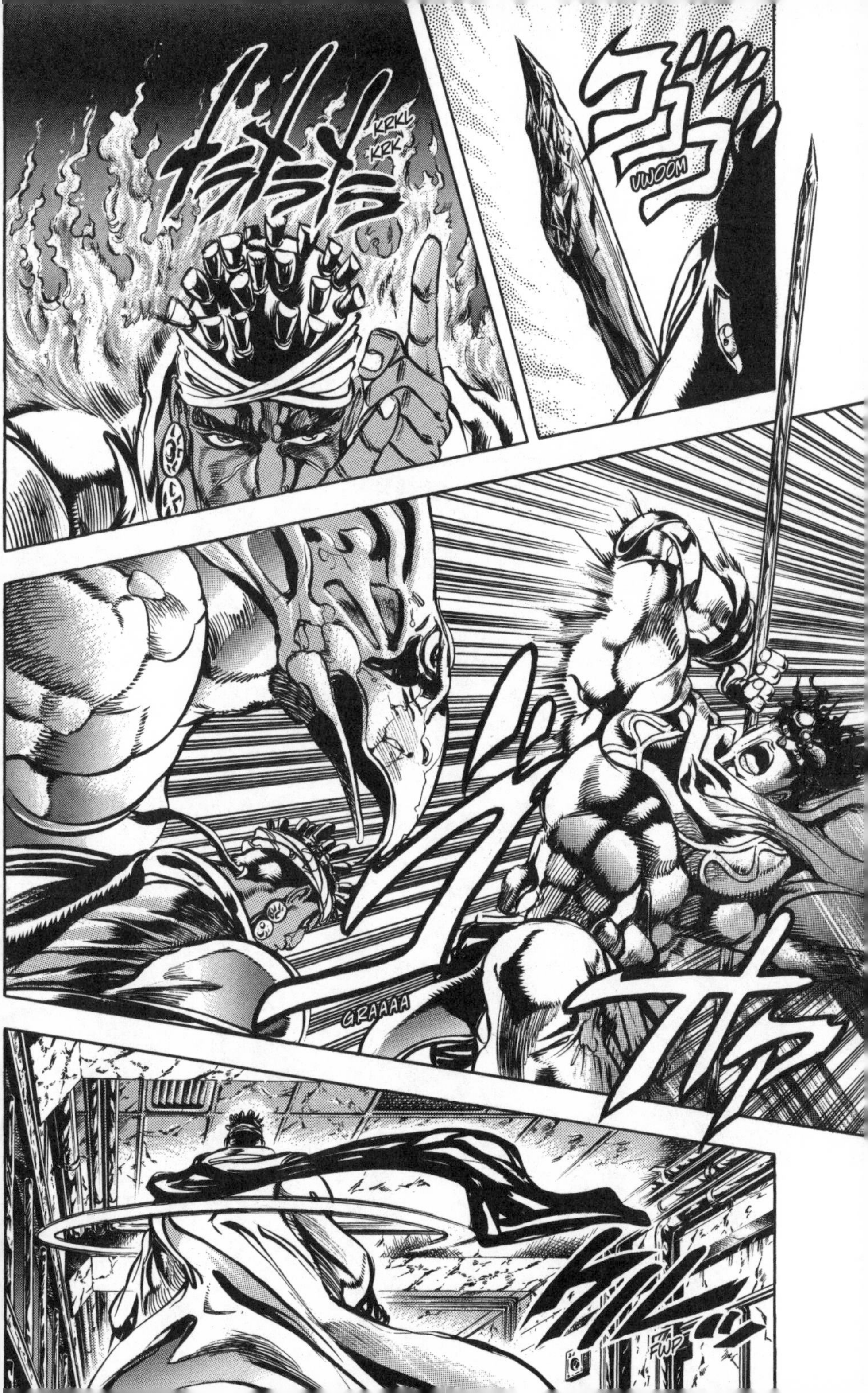
VWOOM
KRKL KRK
GRAAAA
FWP

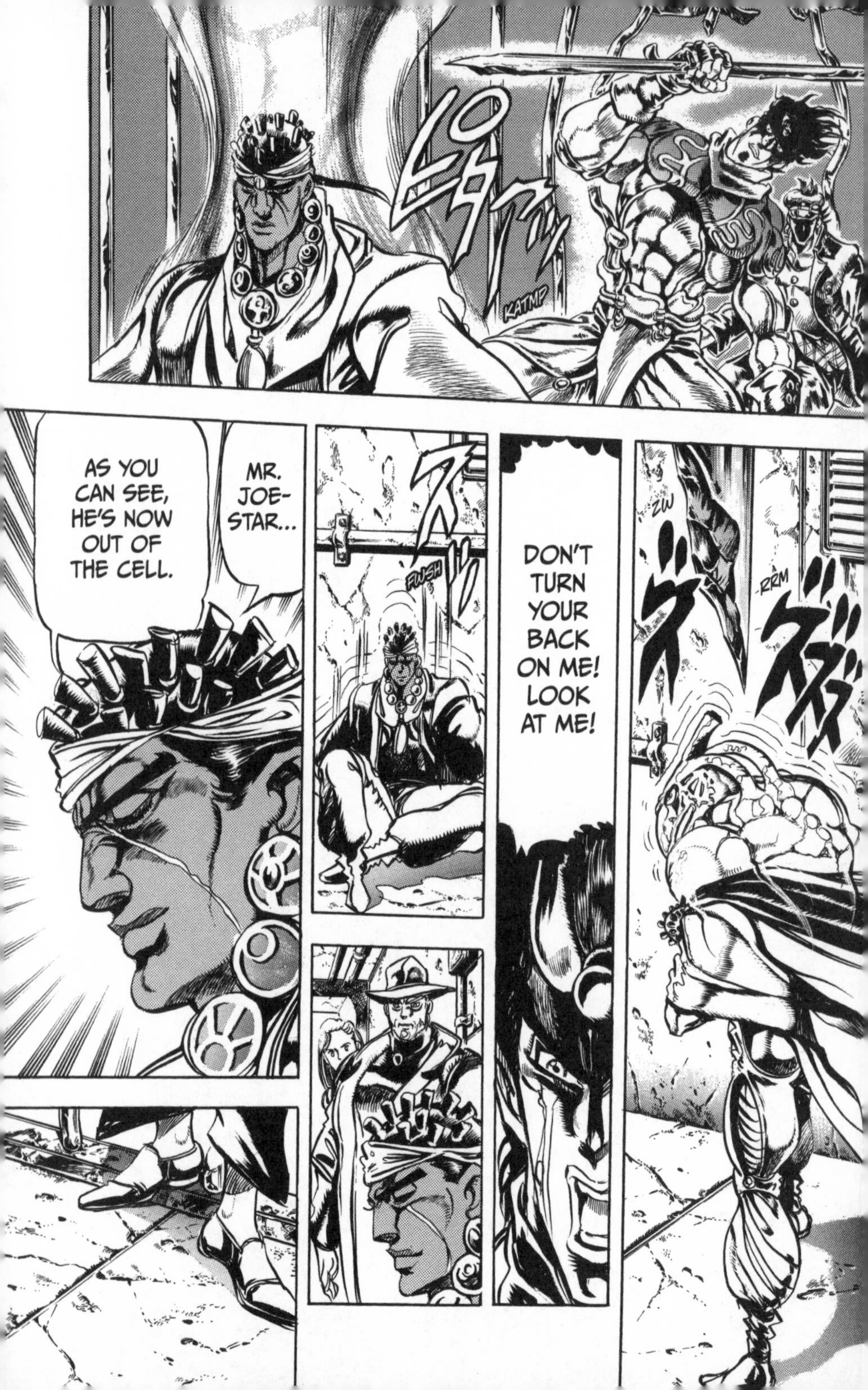
KATMP
ZW
RRM
DON'T TURN YOUR BACK ON ME! LOOK AT ME!
FWSH
MR. JOE-STAR...
AS YOU CAN SEE, HE'S NOW OUT OF THE CELL.

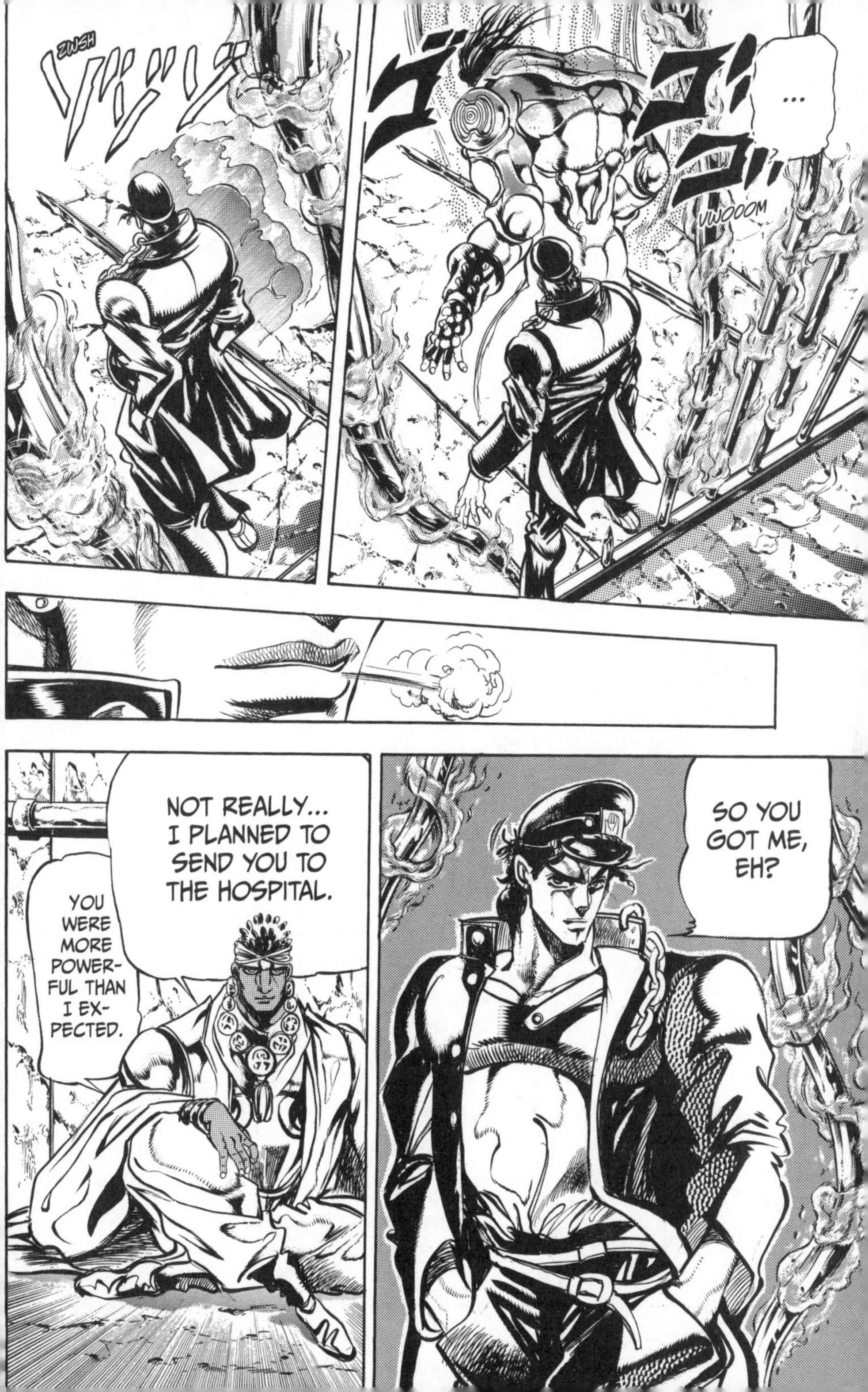
...
VWOOOM
ZWSH
SO YOU GOT ME, EH?
NOT REALLY... I PLANNED TO SEND YOU TO THE HOSPITAL.
YOU WERE MORE POWER-FUL THAN I EX-PECTED.

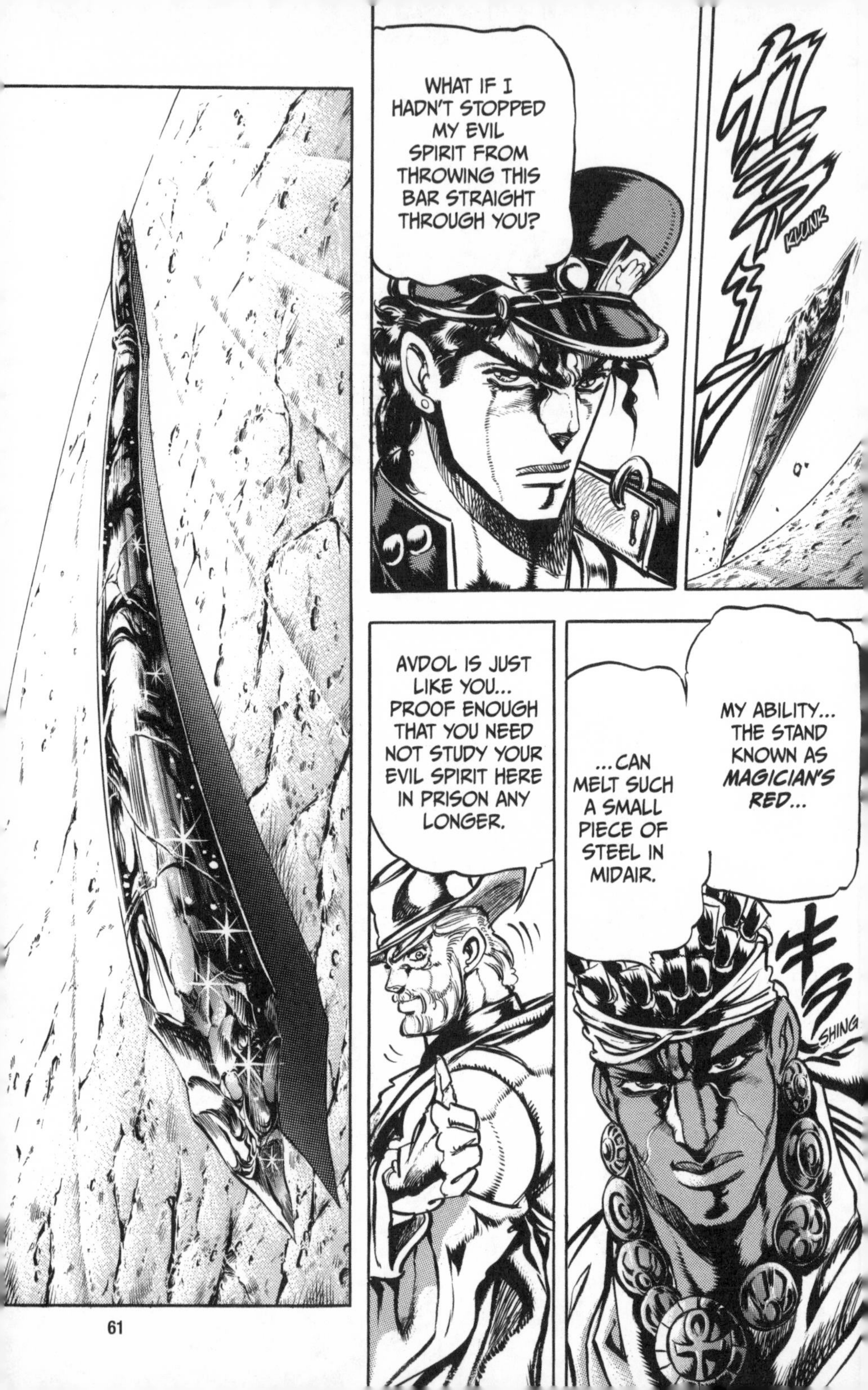
KLUNK
WHAT IF I HADN'T STOPPED MY EVIL SPIRIT FROM THROWING THIS BAR STRAIGHT THROUGH YOU?
MY ABILITY... THE STAND KNOWN AS MAGICIAN'S RED...
...CAN MELT SUCH A SMALL PIECE OF STEEL IN MIDAIR.
SHING
AVDOL IS JUST LIKE YOU... PROOF ENOUGH THAT YOU NEED NOT STUDY YOUR EVIL SPIRIT HERE IN PRISON ANY LONGER.

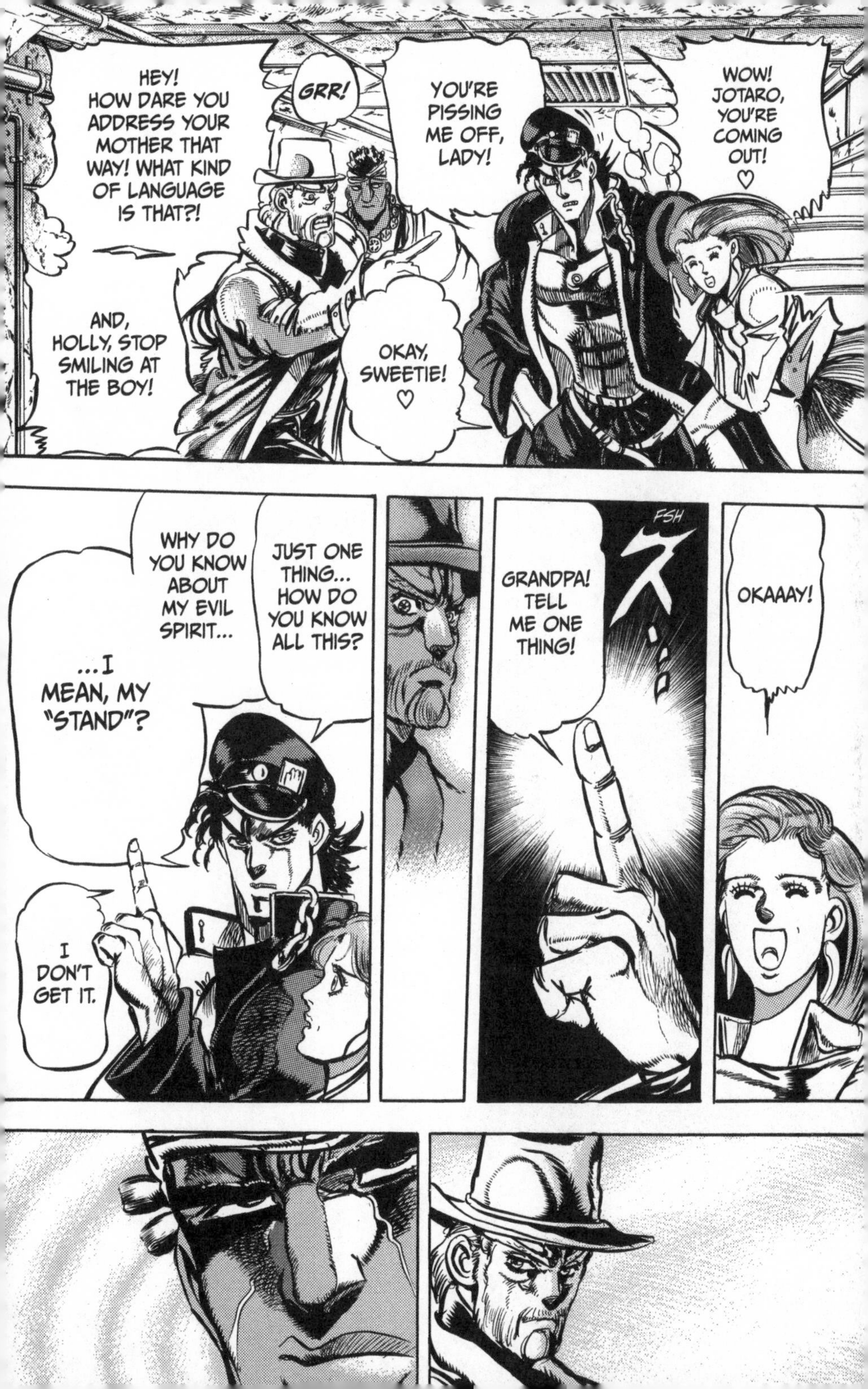
WOW! JOTARO, YOU'RE COMING OUT! ♡
YOU'RE PISSING ME OFF, LADY!
GRR!
HEY! HOW DARE YOU ADDRESS YOUR MOTHER THAT WAY! WHAT KIND OF LANGUAGE IS THAT?!
OKAY, SWEETIE! ♡
AND, HOLLY, STOP SMILING AT THE BOY!
OKAAAY!
FSH
GRANDPA! TELL ME ONE THING!
JUST ONE THING... HOW DO YOU KNOW ALL THIS?
WHY DO YOU KNOW ABOUT MY EVIL SPIRIT...
...I MEAN, MY "STAND"?
I DON'T GET IT.

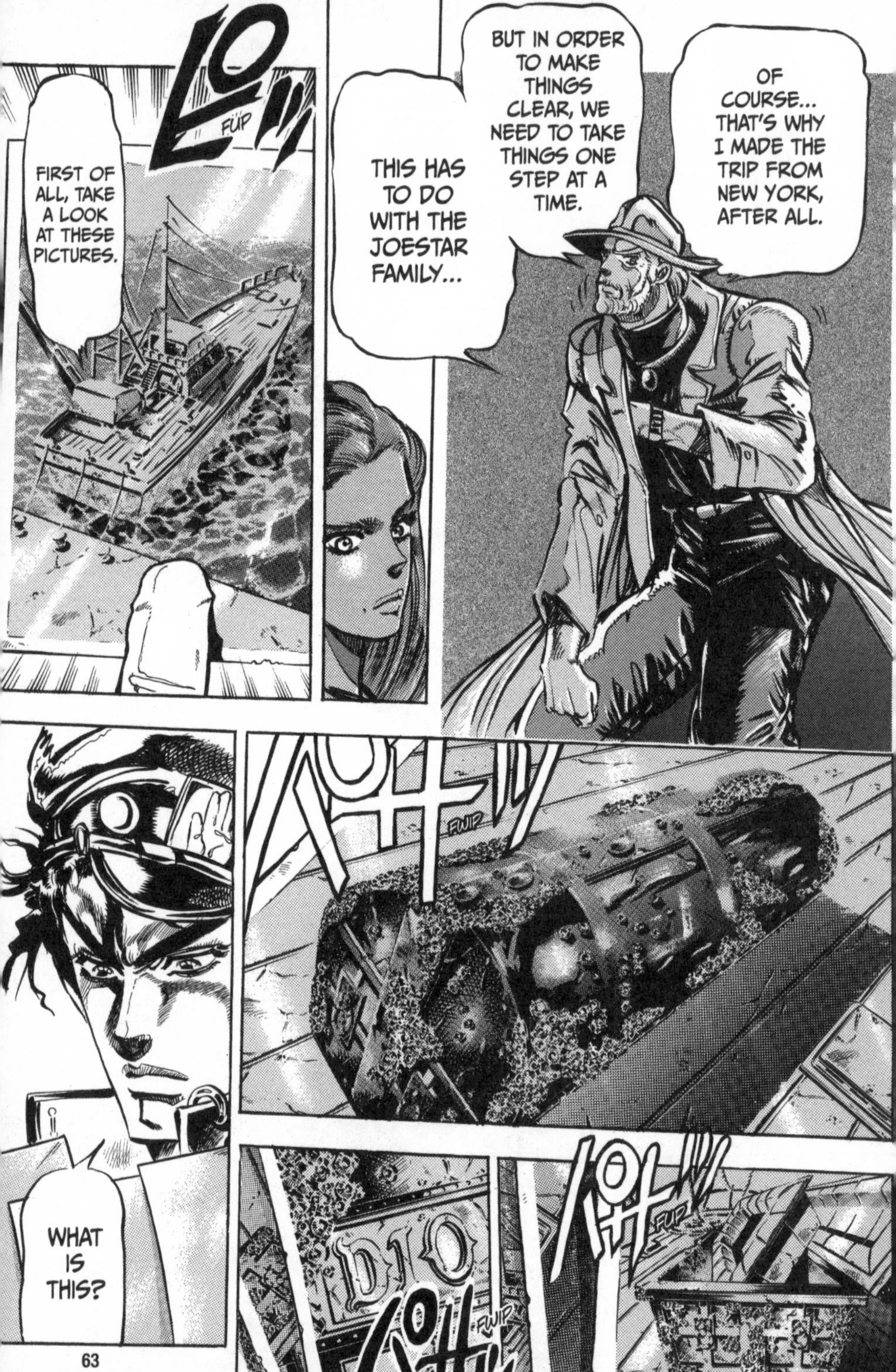
THIS HAS TO DO WITH THE JOESTAR FAMILY...
OF COURSE... THAT'S WHY I MADE THE TRIP FROM NEW YORK, AFTER ALL.
BUT IN ORDER TO MAKE THINGS CLEAR, WE NEED TO TAKE THINGS ONE STEP AT A TIME.
FÜP
FIRST OF ALL, TAKE A LOOK AT THESE PICTURES.
FWIP
FÜP
FWIP
WHAT IS THIS?

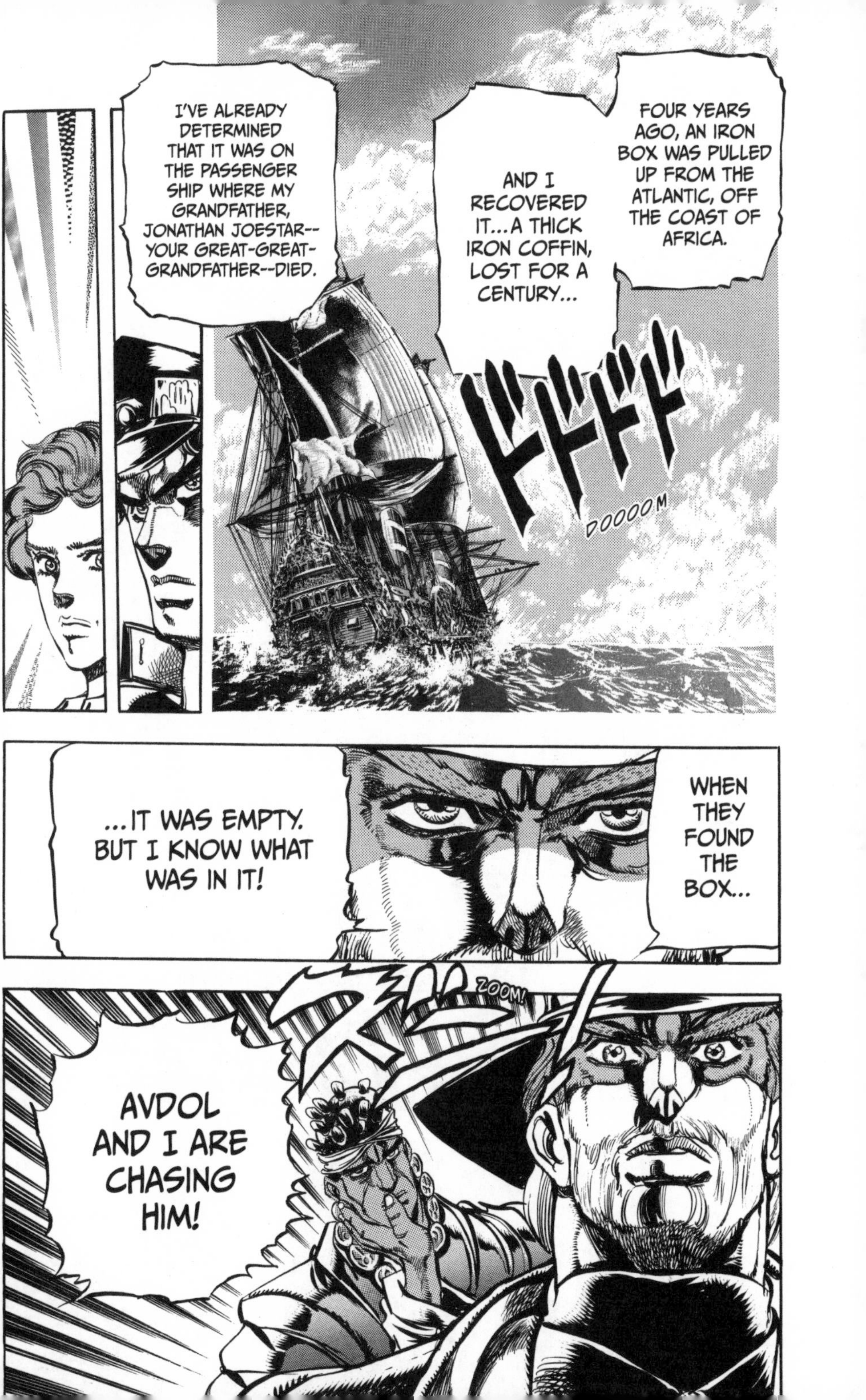
FOUR YEARS AGO, AN IRON BOX WAS PULLED UP FROM THE ATLANTIC, OFF THE COAST OF AFRICA.
AND I RECOVERED IT...A THICK IRON COFFIN, LOST FOR A CENTURY...
I'VE ALREADY DETERMINED THAT IT WAS ON THE PASSENGER SHIP WHERE MY GRANDFATHER, JONATHAN JOESTAR--YOUR GREAT-GREAT-GRANDFATHER--DIED.
ドドドド
DOOOOM
WHEN THEY FOUND THE BOX...
...IT WAS EMPTY. BUT I KNOW WHAT WAS IN IT!
ZOOM!
AVDOL AND I ARE CHASING HIM!

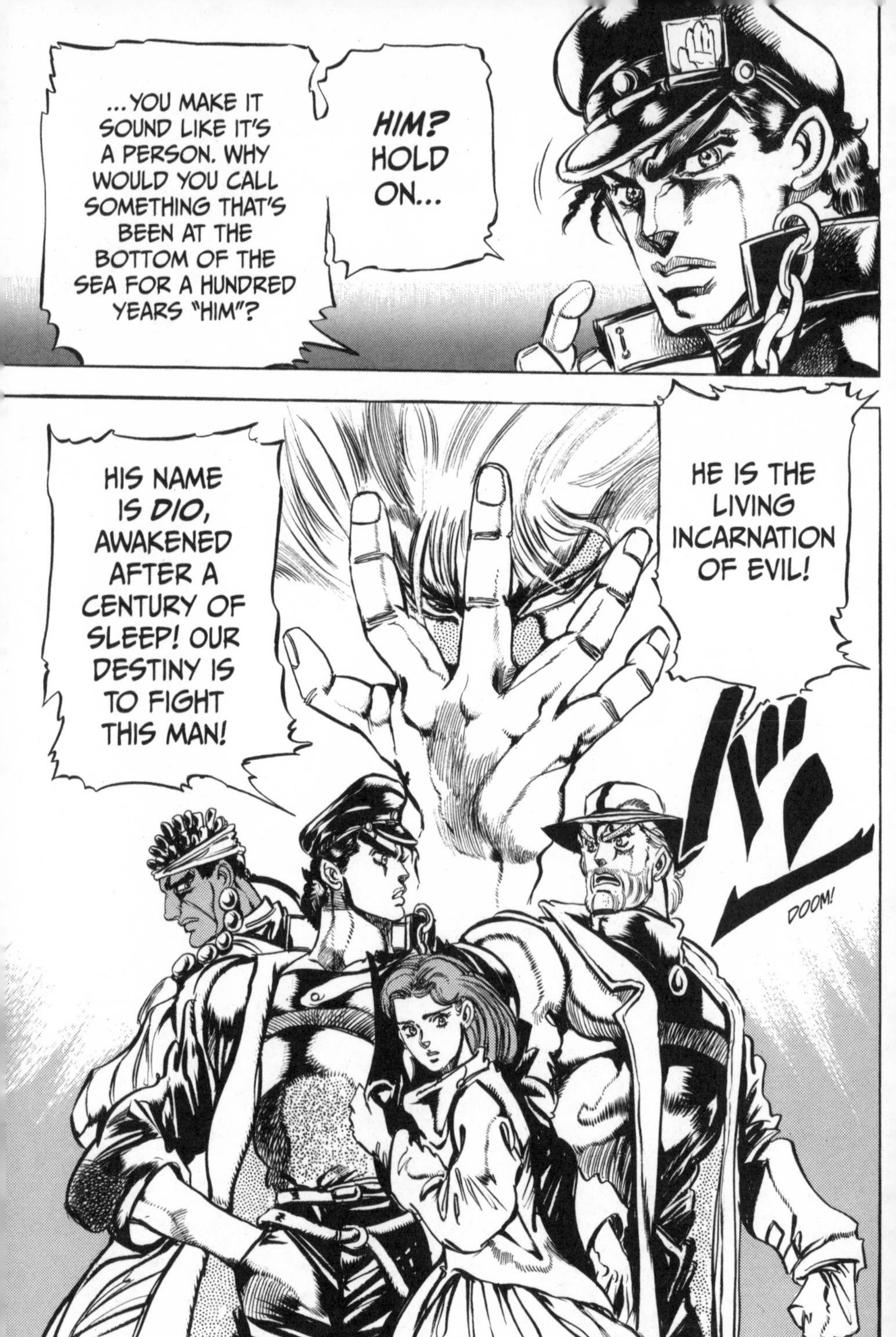
HIM? HOLD ON...
...YOU MAKE IT SOUND LIKE IT'S A PERSON. WHY WOULD YOU CALL SOMETHING THAT'S BEEN AT THE BOTTOM OF THE SEA FOR A HUNDRED YEARS "HIM"?
HE IS THE LIVING INCARNATION OF EVIL!
HIS NAME IS *DIO*, AWAKENED AFTER A CENTURY OF SLEEP! OUR DESTINY IS TO FIGHT THIS MAN!
DOOM!

JOESTAR FAMILY TREE

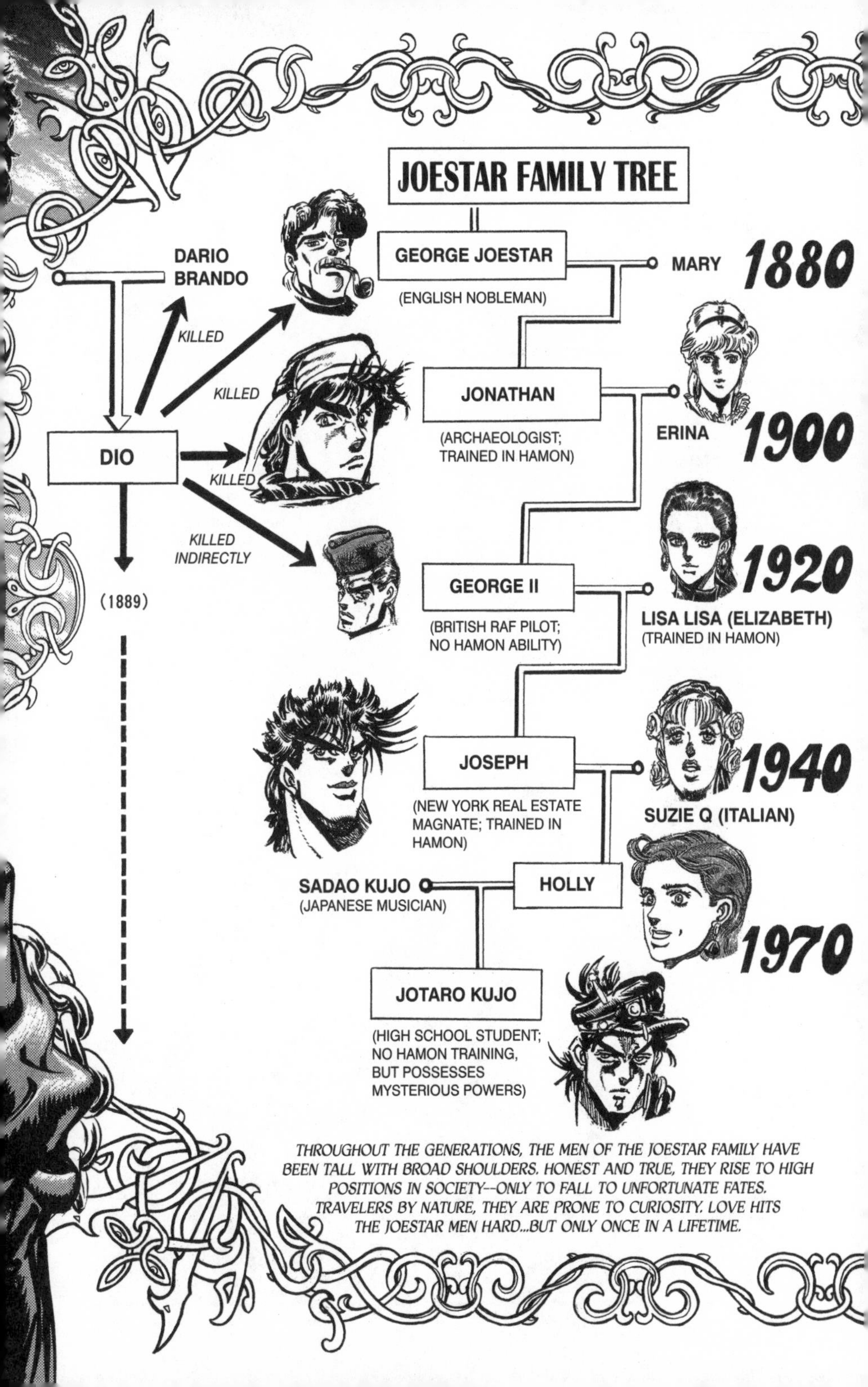

GEORGE JOESTAR
(ENGLISH NOBLEMAN)
MARY
1880
DARIO BRANDO
KILLED
KILLED
DIO
KILLED
KILLED INDIRECTLY
(1889)
JONATHAN
(ARCHAEOLOGIST; TRAINED IN HAMON)
ERINA
1900
GEORGE II
(BRITISH RAF PILOT; NO HAMON ABILITY)
LISA LISA (ELIZABETH)
(TRAINED IN HAMON)
1920
JOSEPH
(NEW YORK REAL ESTATE MAGNATE; TRAINED IN HAMON)
SUZIE Q (ITALIAN)
1940
SADAO KUJO
(JAPANESE MUSICIAN)
HOLLY
1970
JOTARO KUJO
(HIGH SCHOOL STUDENT; NO HAMON TRAINING, BUT POSSESSES MYSTERIOUS POWERS)

THROUGHOUT THE GENERATIONS, THE MEN OF THE JOESTAR FAMILY HAVE BEEN TALL WITH BROAD SHOULDERS. HONEST AND TRUE, THEY RISE TO HIGH POSITIONS IN SOCIETY--ONLY TO FALL TO UNFORTUNATE FATES. TRAVELERS BY NATURE, THEY ARE PRONE TO CURIOSITY. LOVE HITS THE JOESTAR MEN HARD...BUT ONLY ONCE IN A LIFETIME.

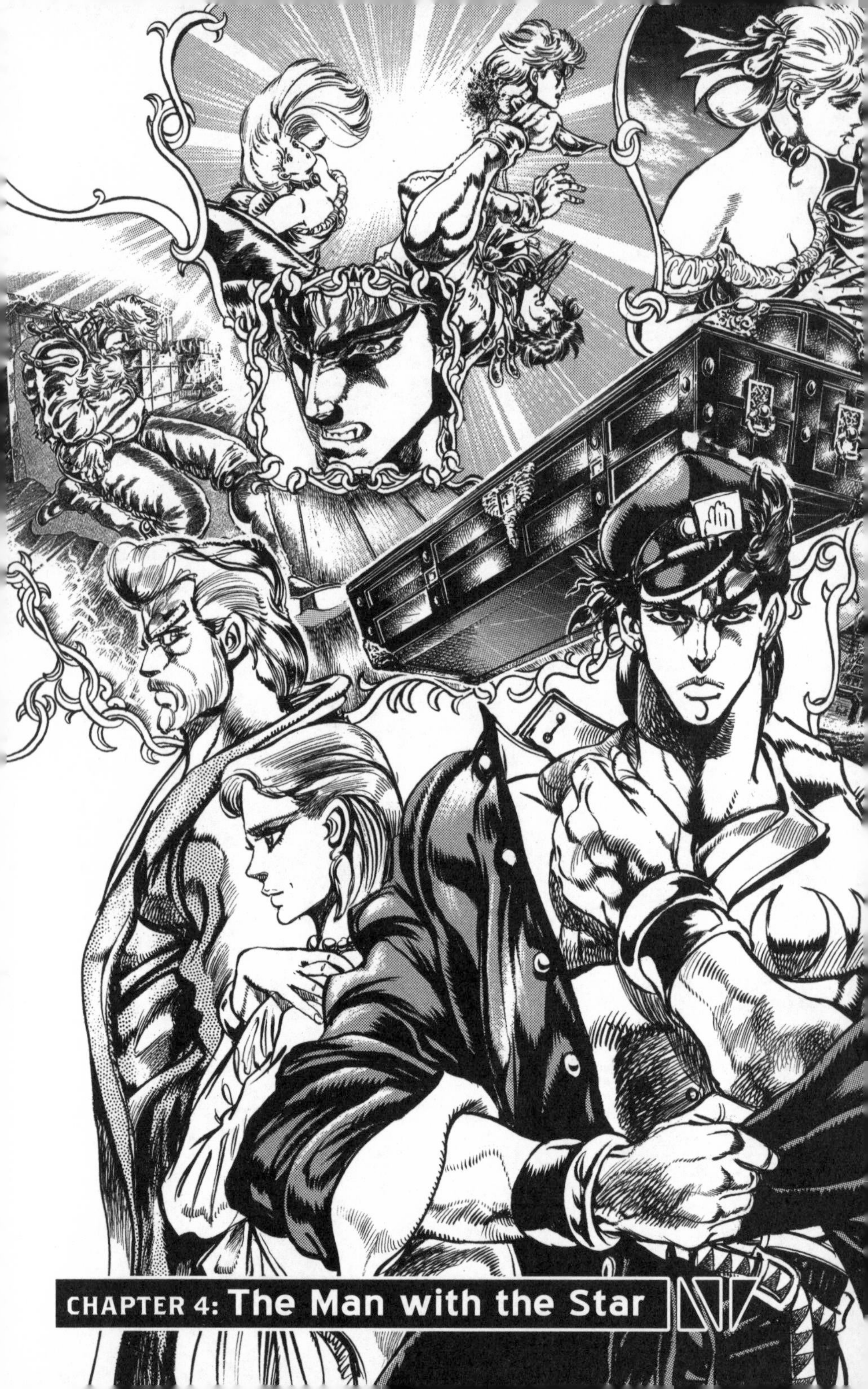

CHAPTER 4: The Man with the Star

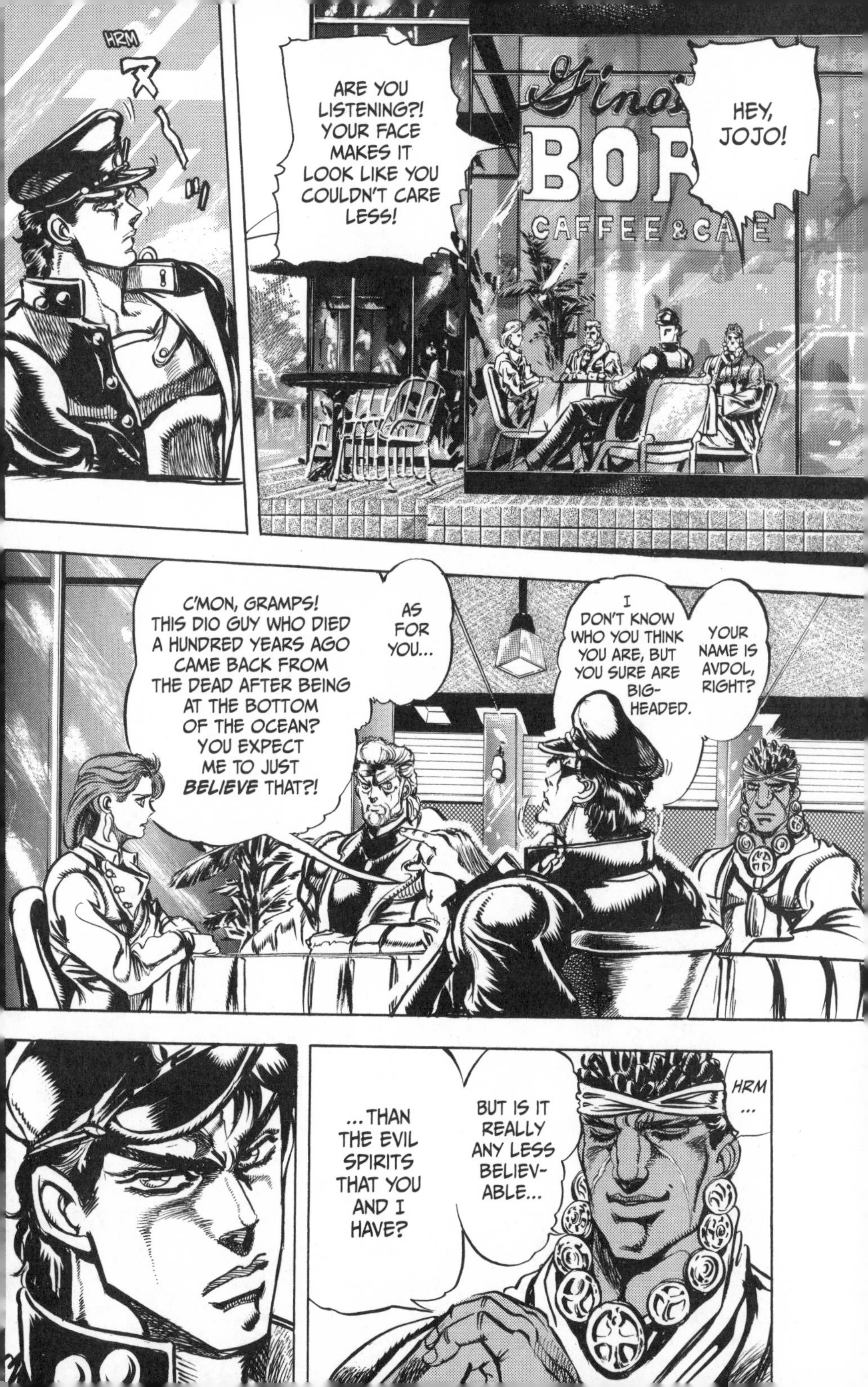
HEY, JOJO!
ARE YOU LISTENING?! YOUR FACE MAKES IT LOOK LIKE YOU COULDN'T CARE LESS!
HRM
YOUR NAME IS AVDOL, RIGHT?
I DON'T KNOW WHO YOU THINK YOU ARE, BUT YOU SURE ARE BIG-HEADED.
AS FOR YOU...
C'MON, GRAMPS! THIS DIO GUY WHO DIED A HUNDRED YEARS AGO CAME BACK FROM THE DEAD AFTER BEING AT THE BOTTOM OF THE OCEAN? YOU EXPECT ME TO JUST *BELIEVE* THAT?!
HRM...
BUT IS IT REALLY ANY LESS BELIEV-ABLE...
...THAN THE EVIL SPIRITS THAT YOU AND I HAVE?

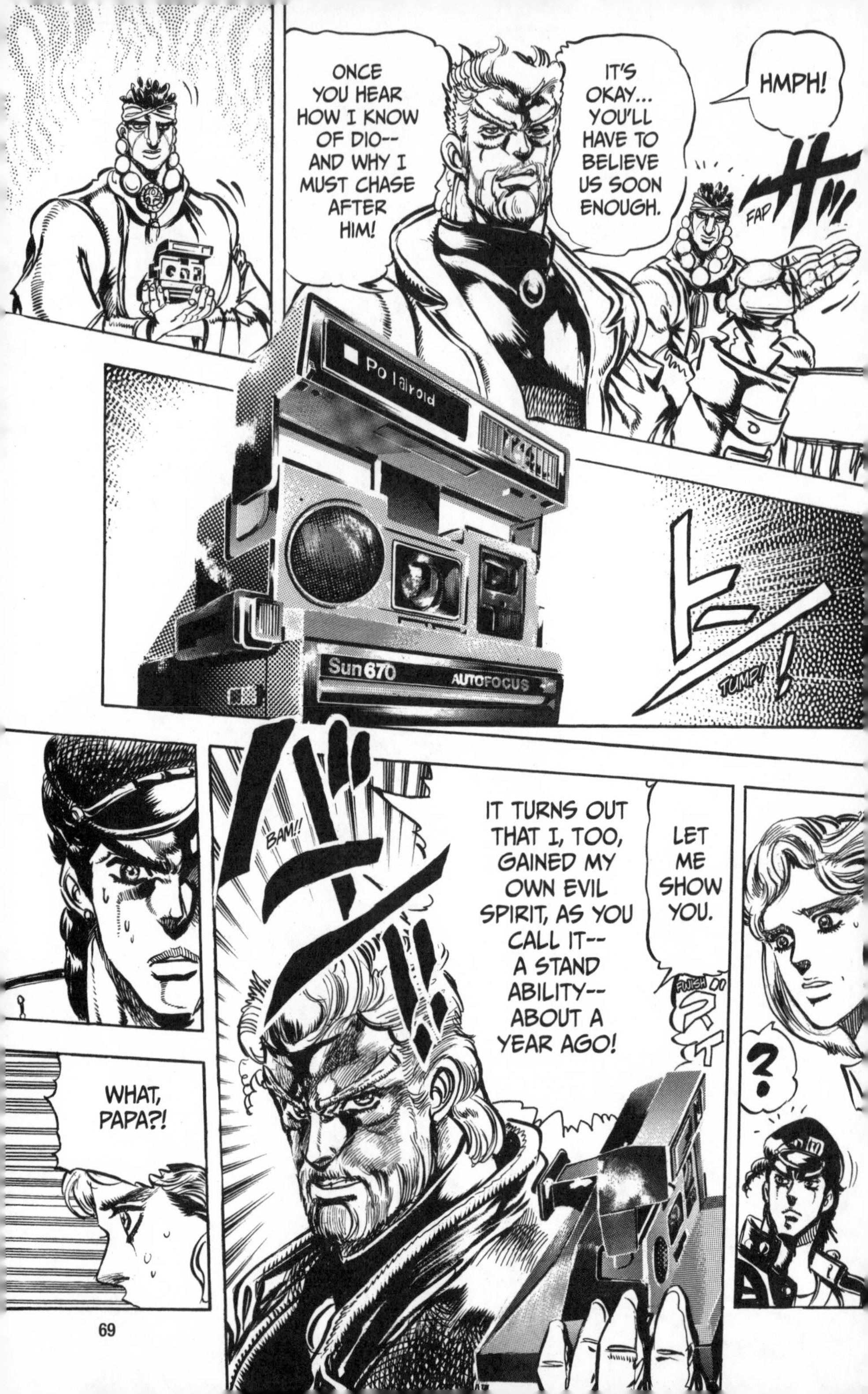
HMPH!
FAP
IT'S OKAY... YOU'LL HAVE TO BELIEVE US SOON ENOUGH.
ONCE YOU HEAR HOW I KNOW OF DIO-- AND WHY I MUST CHASE AFTER HIM!
Polaroid
Sun 670
AUTOFOCUS
TUMP!
?
LET ME SHOW YOU.
FWISH
IT TURNS OUT THAT I, TOO, GAINED MY OWN EVIL SPIRIT, AS YOU CALL IT-- A STAND ABILITY-- ABOUT A YEAR AGO!
BAM!!
WHAT, PAPA?!

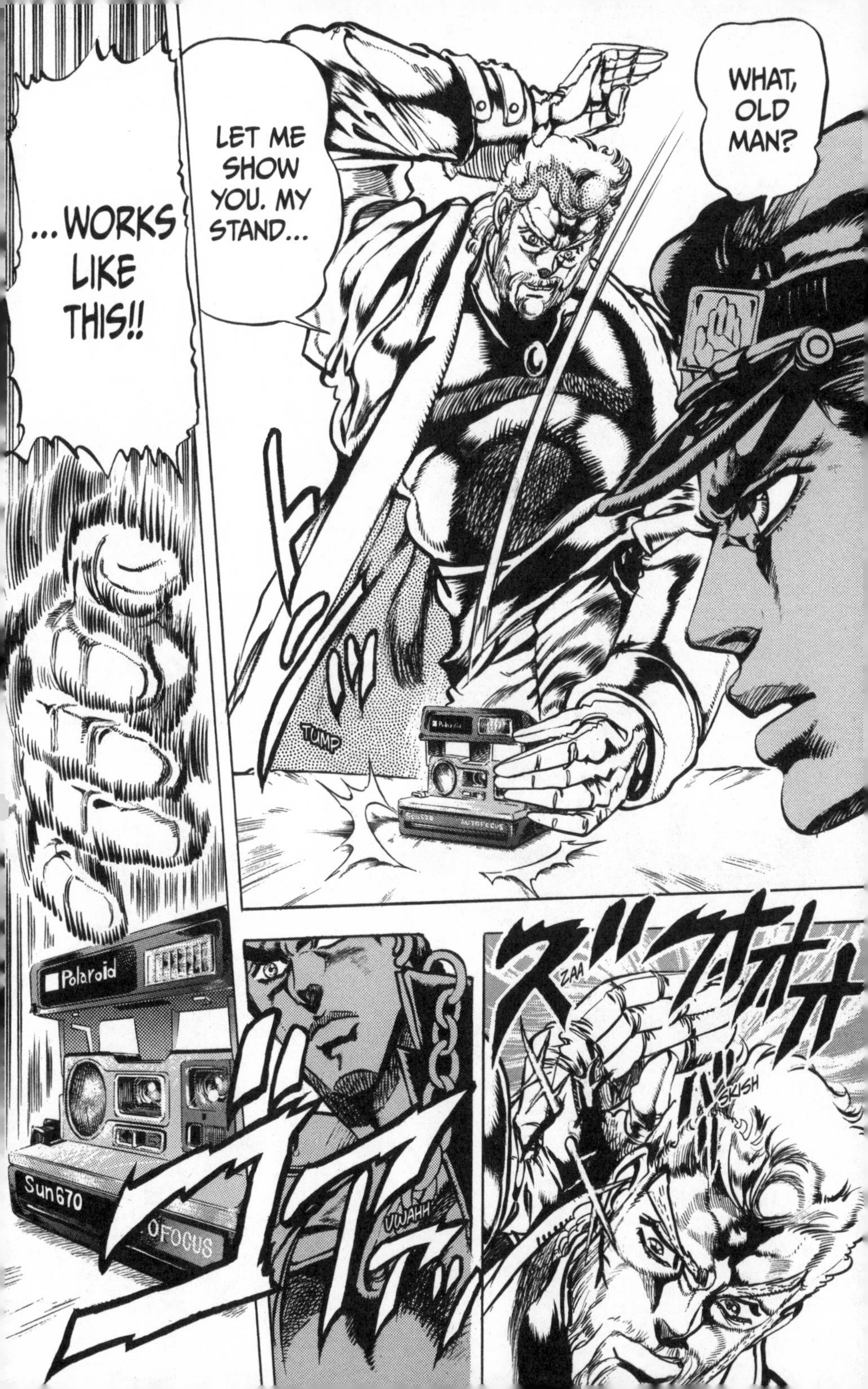
WHAT, OLD MAN?
LET ME SHOW YOU. MY STAND...
TUMP
...WORKS LIKE THIS!!
ZAA
SKISH
UWAHH
Polaroid
Sun670
OFOCUS

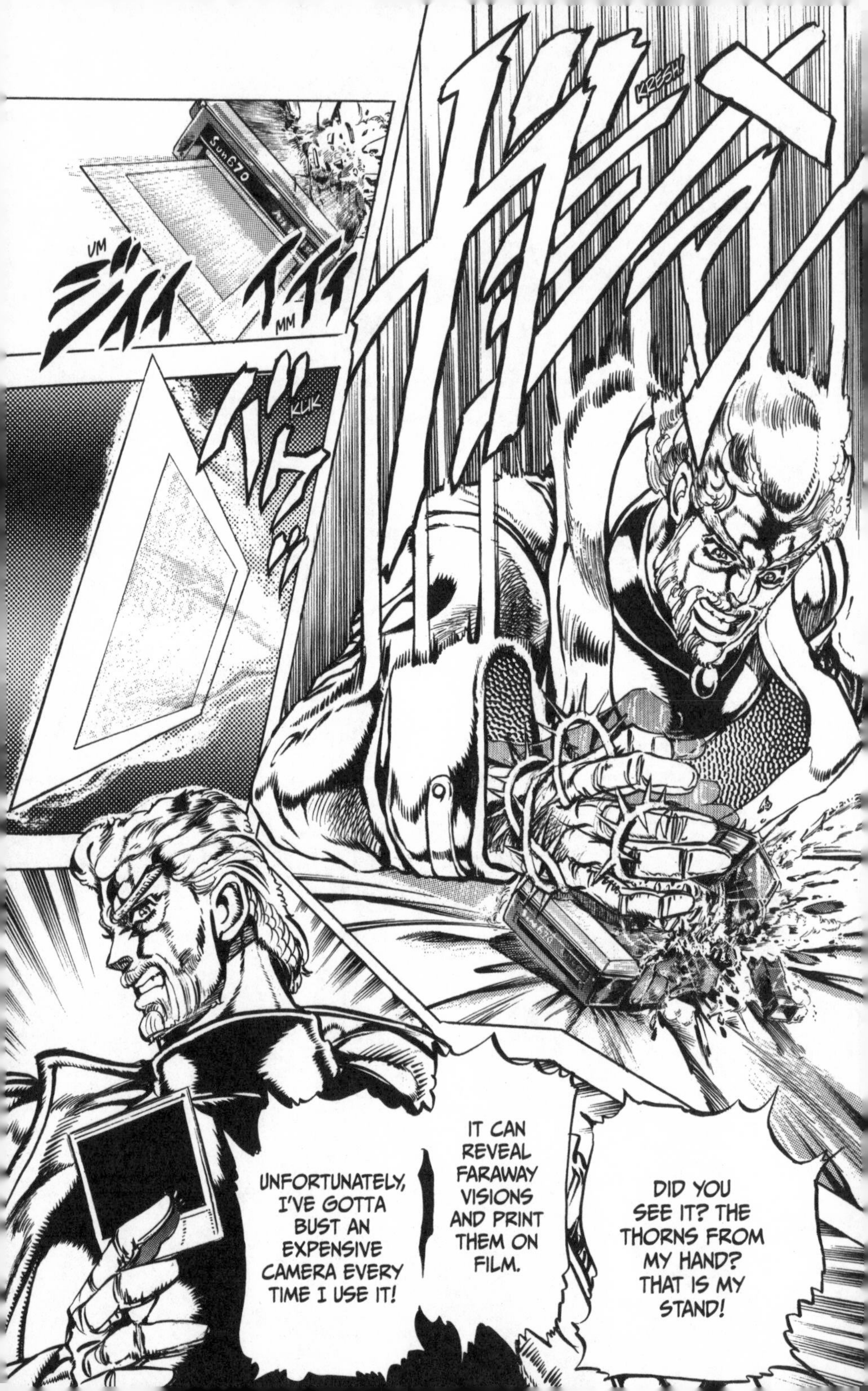
KRESH!
UM
MM
KUK
DID YOU SEE IT? THE THORNS FROM MY HAND? THAT IS MY STAND!
IT CAN REVEAL FARAWAY VISIONS AND PRINT THEM ON FILM.
UNFORTUNATELY, I'VE GOTTA BUST AN EXPENSIVE CAMERA EVERY TIME I USE IT!

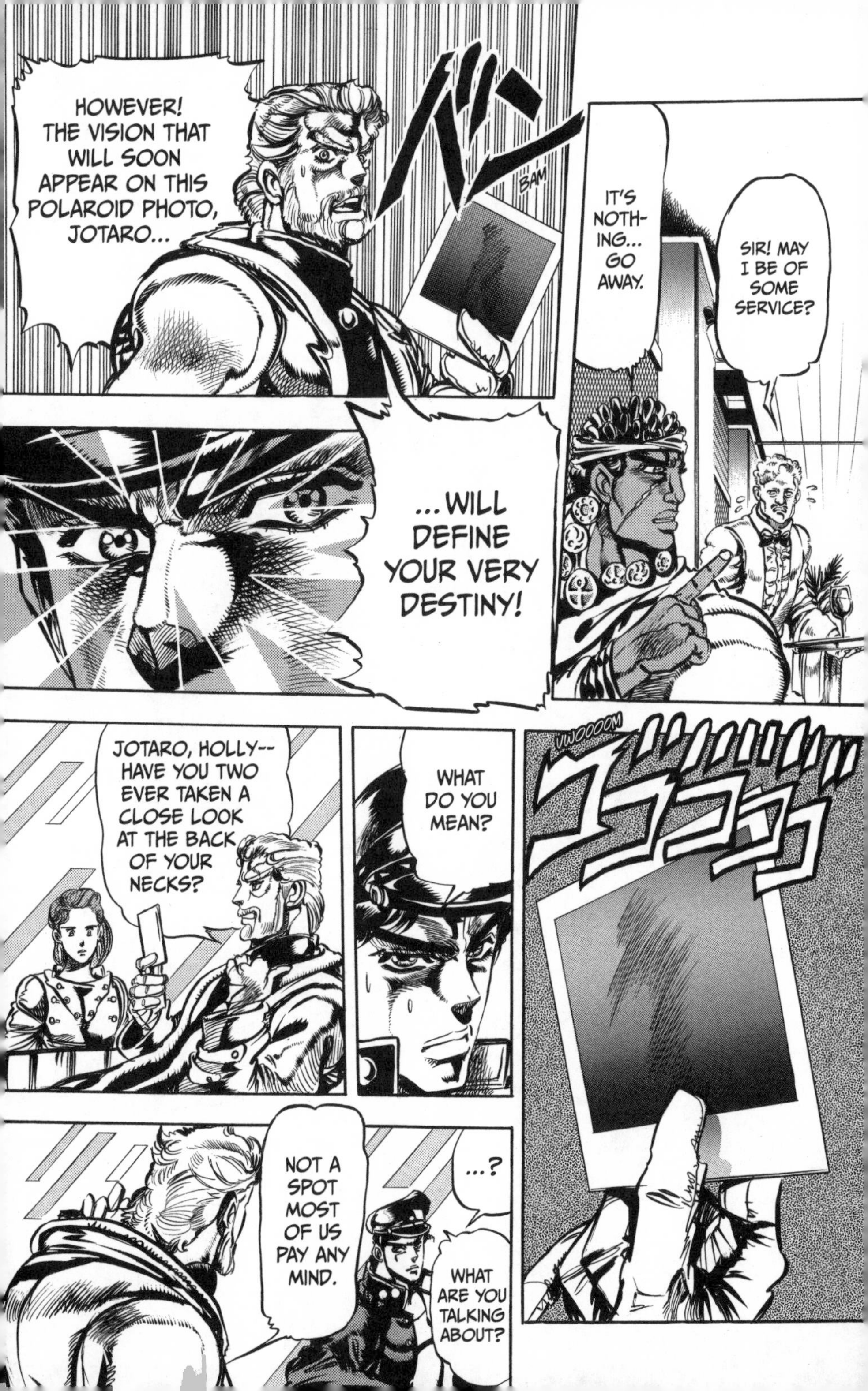
SIR! MAY I BE OF SOME SERVICE?
IT'S NOTHING... GO AWAY.
HOWEVER! THE VISION THAT WILL SOON APPEAR ON THIS POLAROID PHOTO, JOTARO...
BAM
...WILL DEFINE YOUR VERY DESTINY!
UWOOOOM
WHAT DO YOU MEAN?
JOTARO, HOLLY-- HAVE YOU TWO EVER TAKEN A CLOSE LOOK AT THE BACK OF YOUR NECKS?
...?
NOT A SPOT MOST OF US PAY ANY MIND.
WHAT ARE YOU TALKING ABOUT?

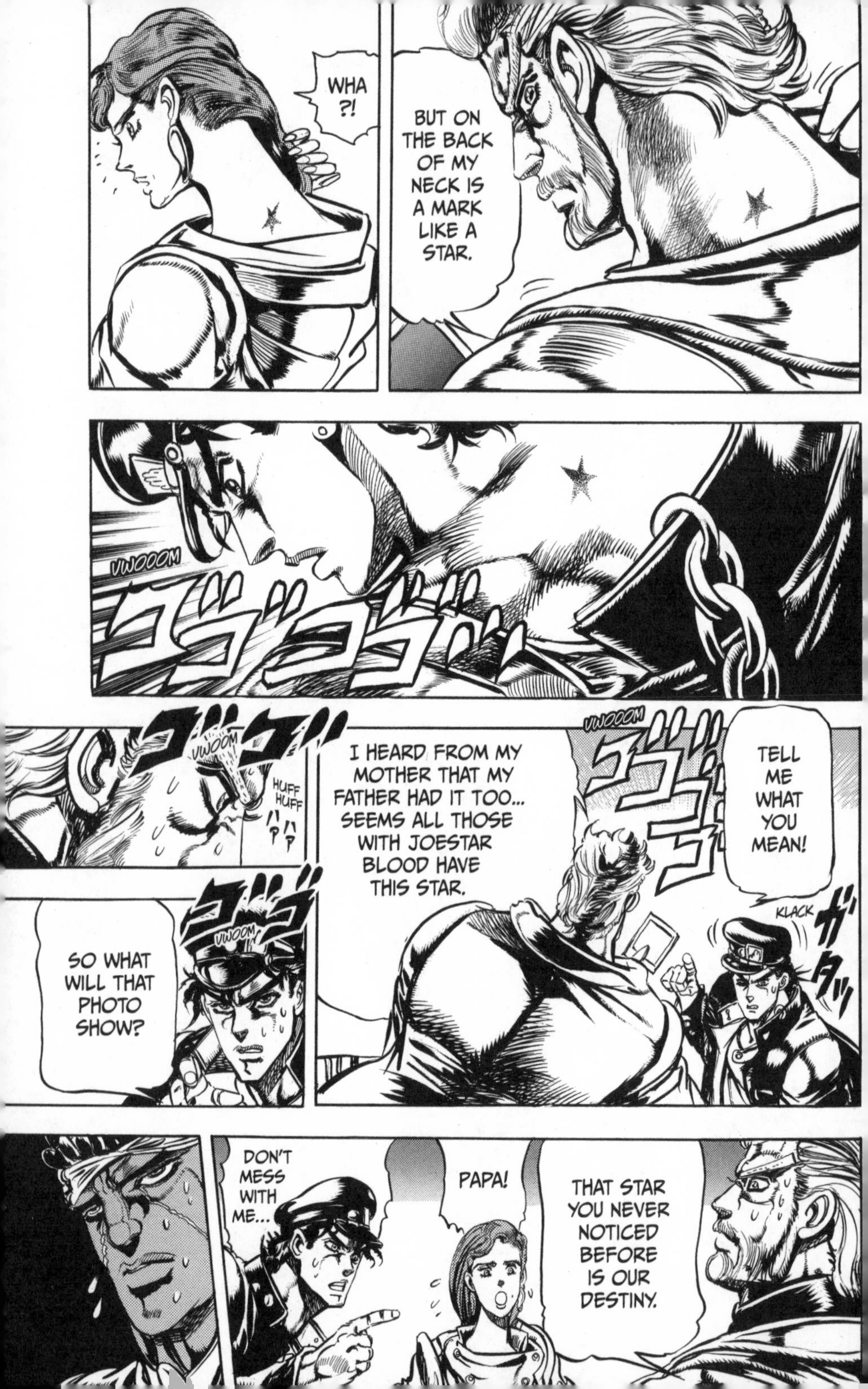
BUT ON THE BACK OF MY NECK IS A MARK LIKE A STAR.
WHA ?!
VWOOOM
VWOOOM
TELL ME WHAT YOU MEAN!
KLACK
I HEARD FROM MY MOTHER THAT MY FATHER HAD IT TOO... SEEMS ALL THOSE WITH JOESTAR BLOOD HAVE THIS STAR.
VWOOOM
HUFF HUFF
VWOOOM
SO WHAT WILL THAT PHOTO SHOW?
THAT STAR YOU NEVER NOTICED BEFORE IS OUR DESTINY.
PAPA!
DON'T MESS WITH ME...

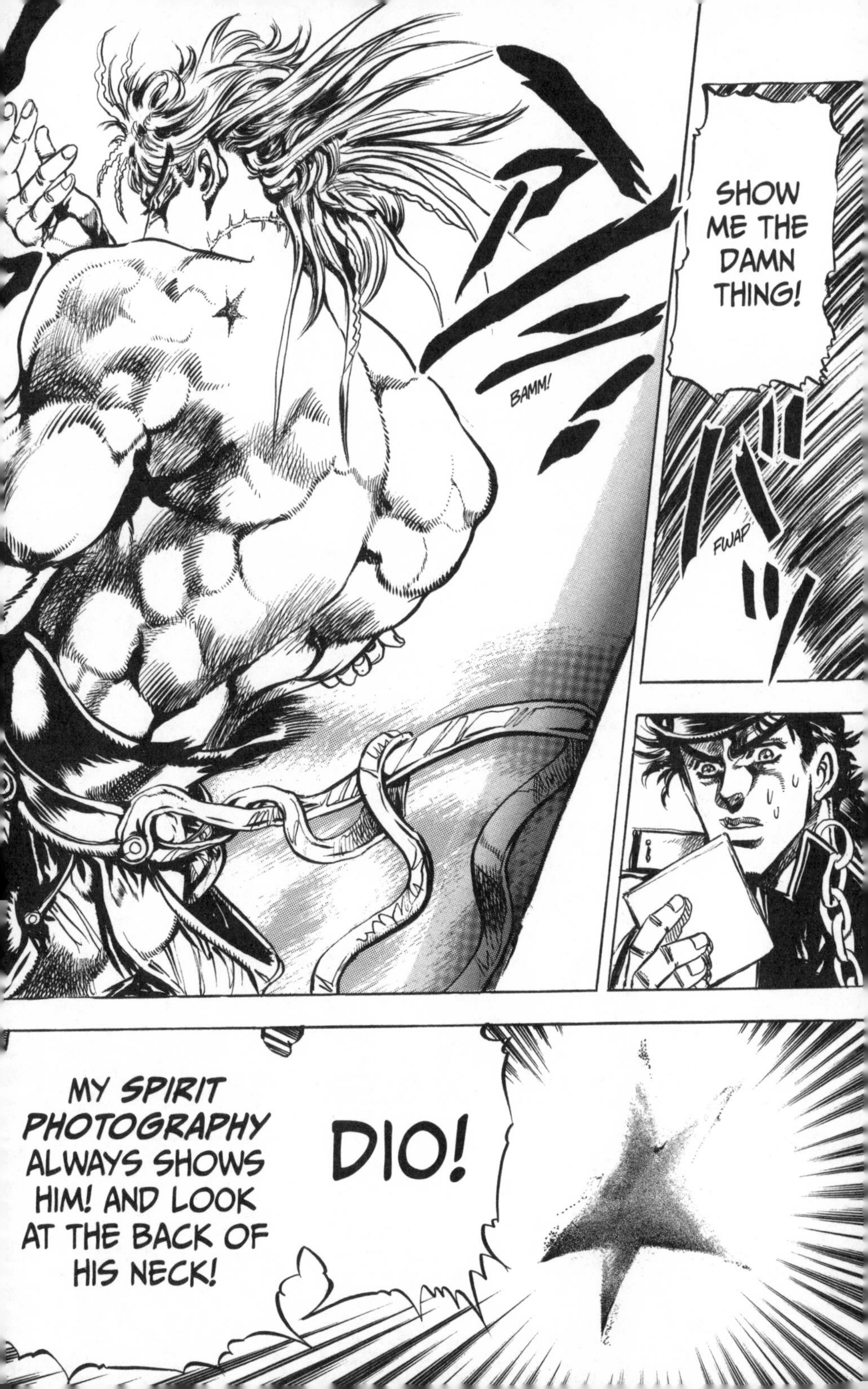
SHOW ME THE DAMN THING!
FWAP
BAMM!
DIO!
MY SPIRIT PHOTOGRAPHY ALWAYS SHOWS HIM! AND LOOK AT THE BACK OF HIS NECK!

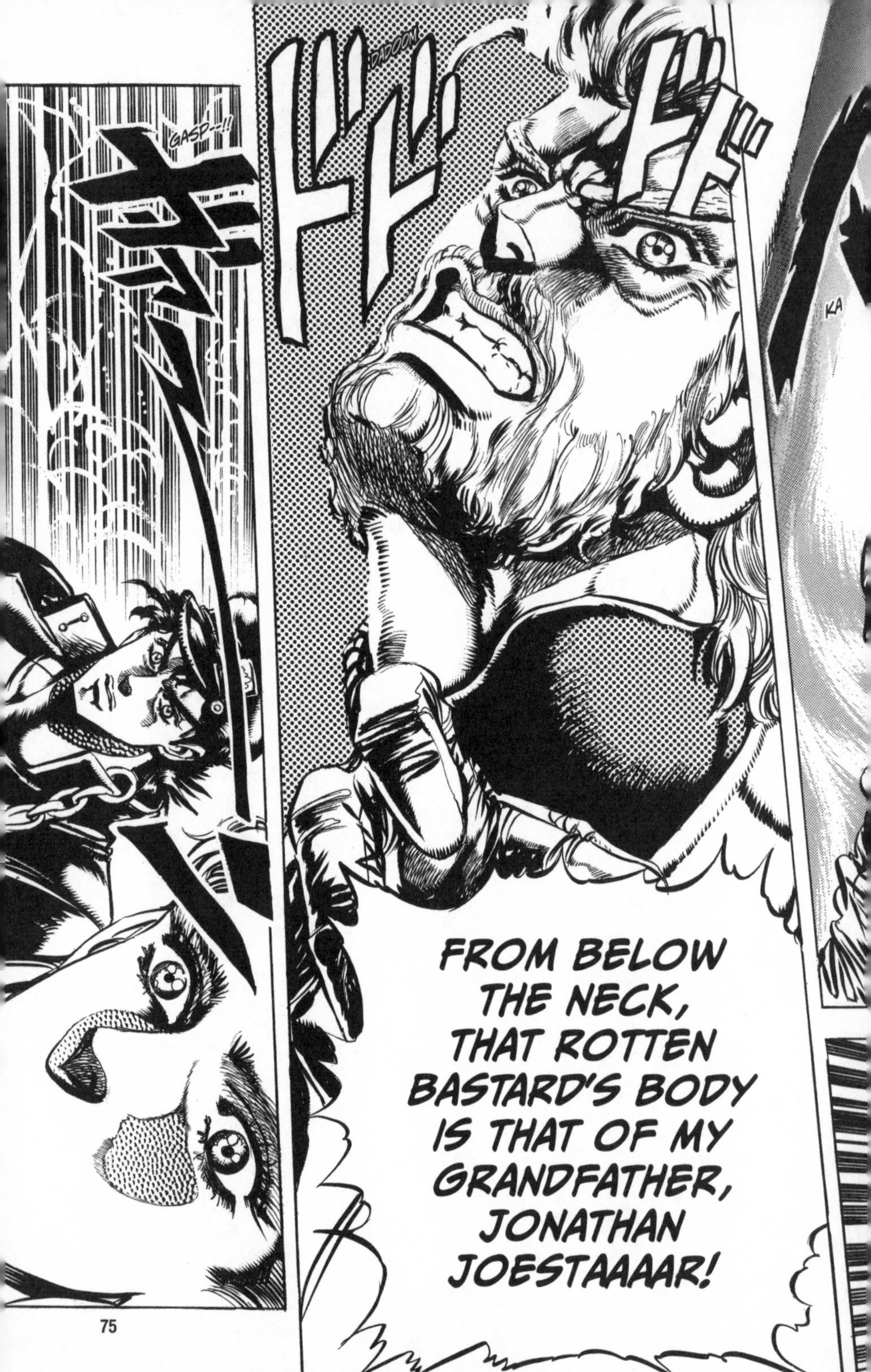
KA
DADOOM
FROM BELOW THE NECK, THAT ROTTEN BASTARD'S BODY IS THAT OF MY GRANDFATHER, JONATHAN JOESTAAAAR!
GASP--!!

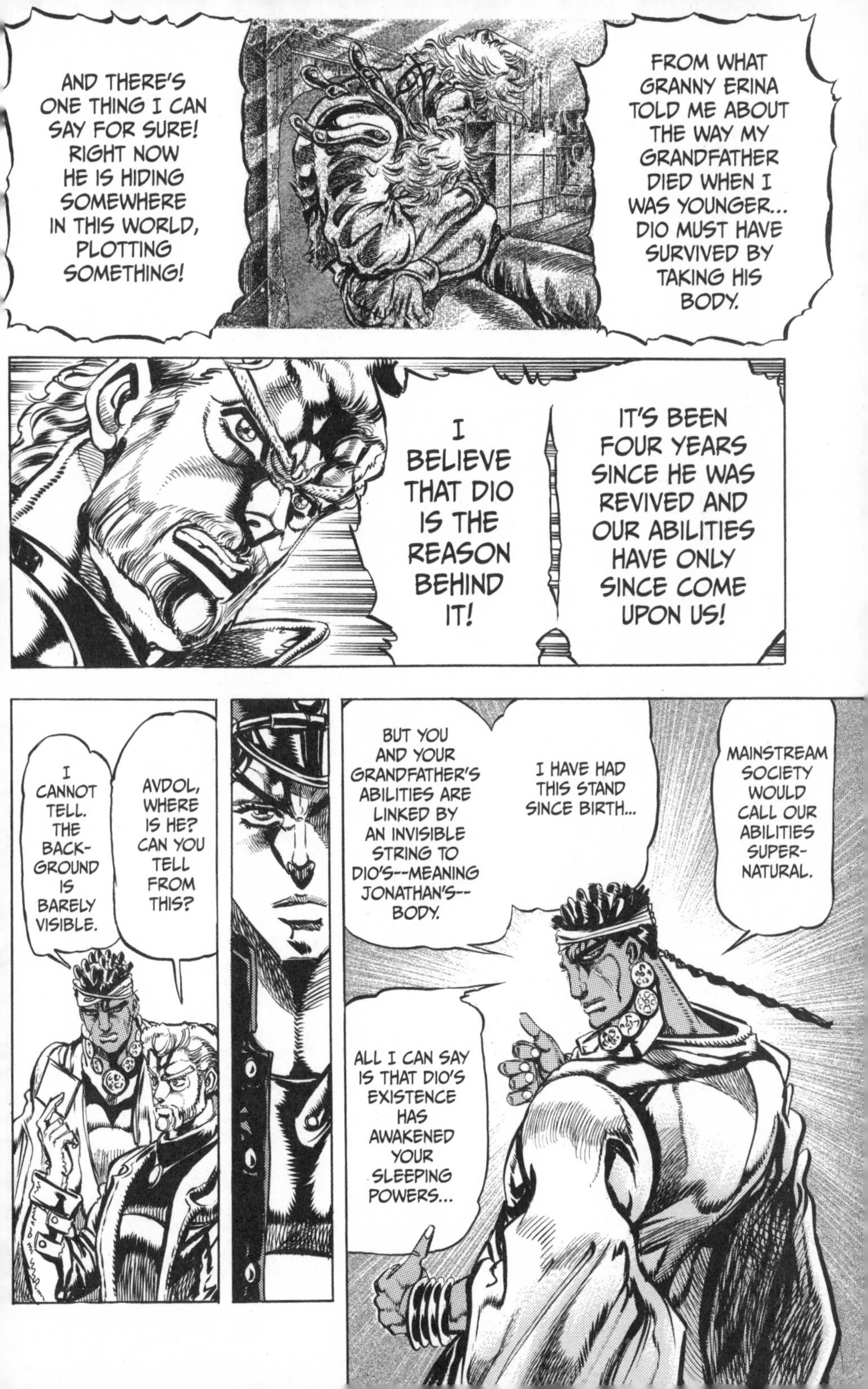
FROM WHAT GRANNY ERINA TOLD ME ABOUT THE WAY MY GRANDFATHER DIED WHEN I WAS YOUNGER... DIO MUST HAVE SURVIVED BY TAKING HIS BODY.
AND THERE'S ONE THING I CAN SAY FOR SURE! RIGHT NOW HE IS HIDING SOMEWHERE IN THIS WORLD, PLOTTING SOMETHING!
IT'S BEEN FOUR YEARS SINCE HE WAS REVIVED AND OUR ABILITIES HAVE ONLY SINCE COME UPON US!
I BELIEVE THAT DIO IS THE REASON BEHIND IT!
MAINSTREAM SOCIETY WOULD CALL OUR ABILITIES SUPER-NATURAL.
I HAVE HAD THIS STAND SINCE BIRTH...
BUT YOU AND YOUR GRANDFATHER'S ABILITIES ARE LINKED BY AN INVISIBLE STRING TO DIO'S--MEANING JONATHAN'S--BODY.
ALL I CAN SAY IS THAT DIO'S EXISTENCE HAS AWAKENED YOUR SLEEPING POWERS...
AVDOL, WHERE IS HE? CAN YOU TELL FROM THIS?
I CANNOT TELL. THE BACK-GROUND IS BARELY VISIBLE.

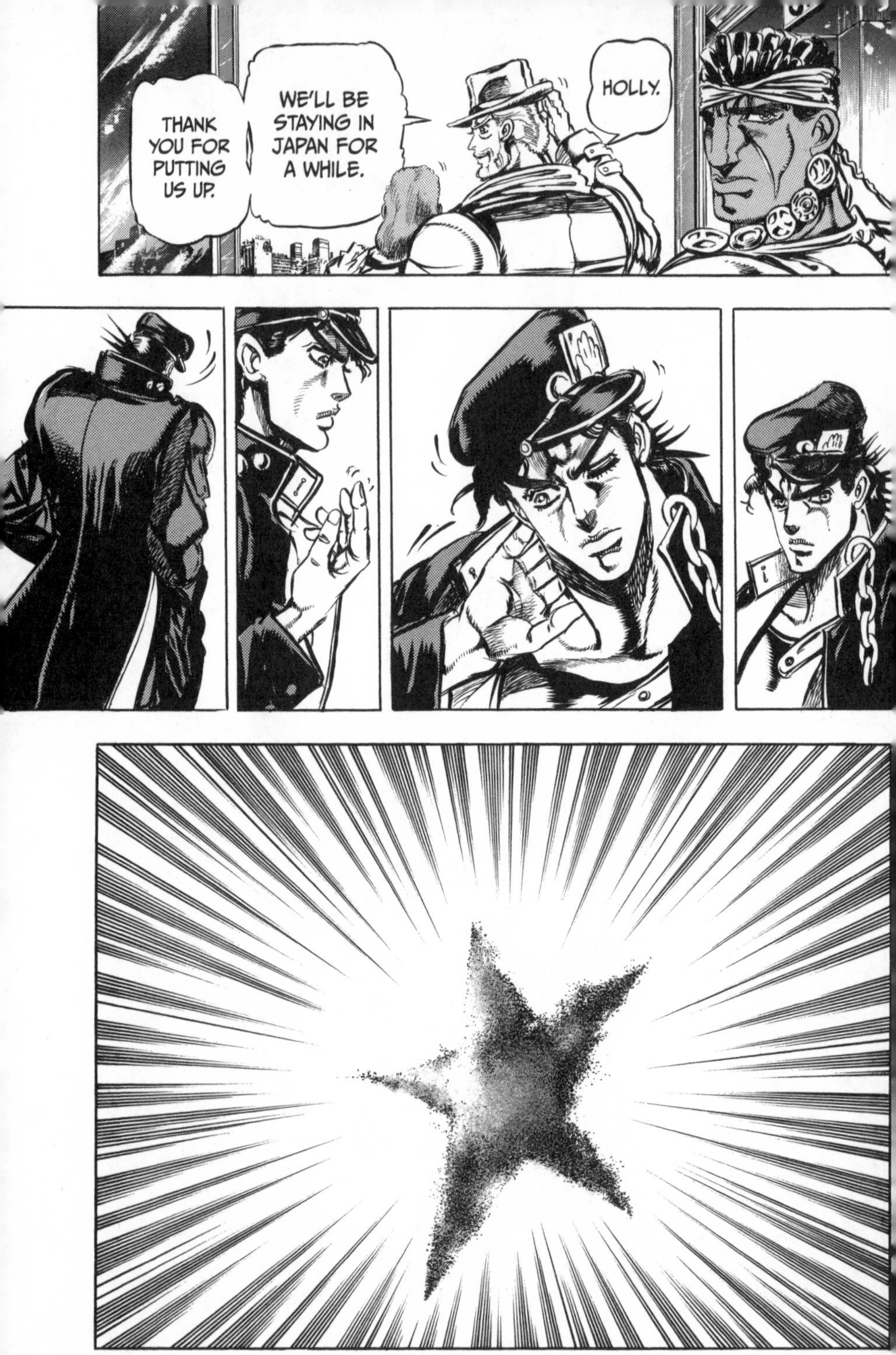
HOLLY.
WE'LL BE STAYING IN JAPAN FOR A WHILE.
THANK YOU FOR PUTTING US UP.

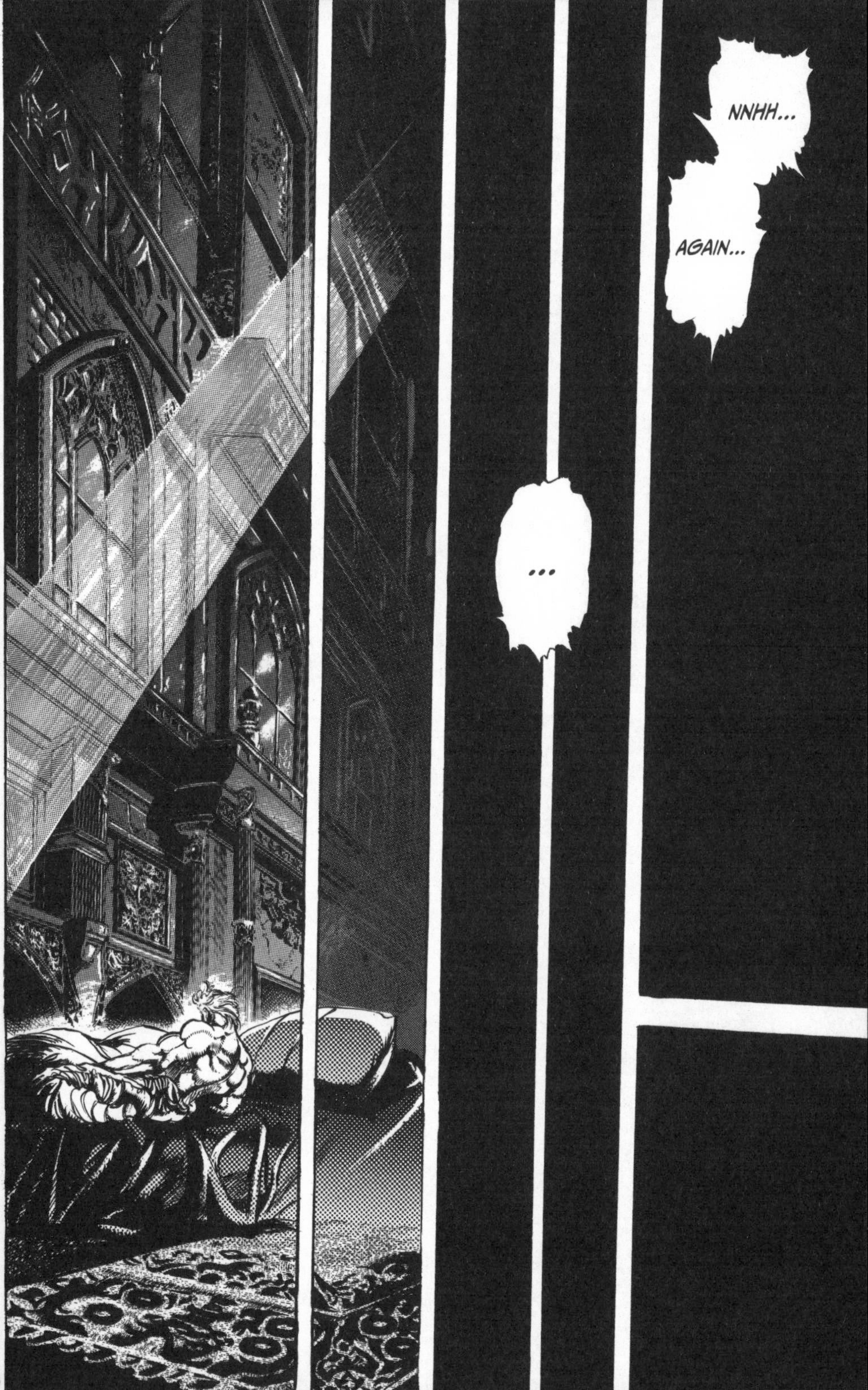
NNHH...
AGAIN...
...

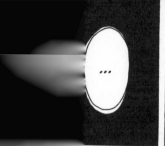

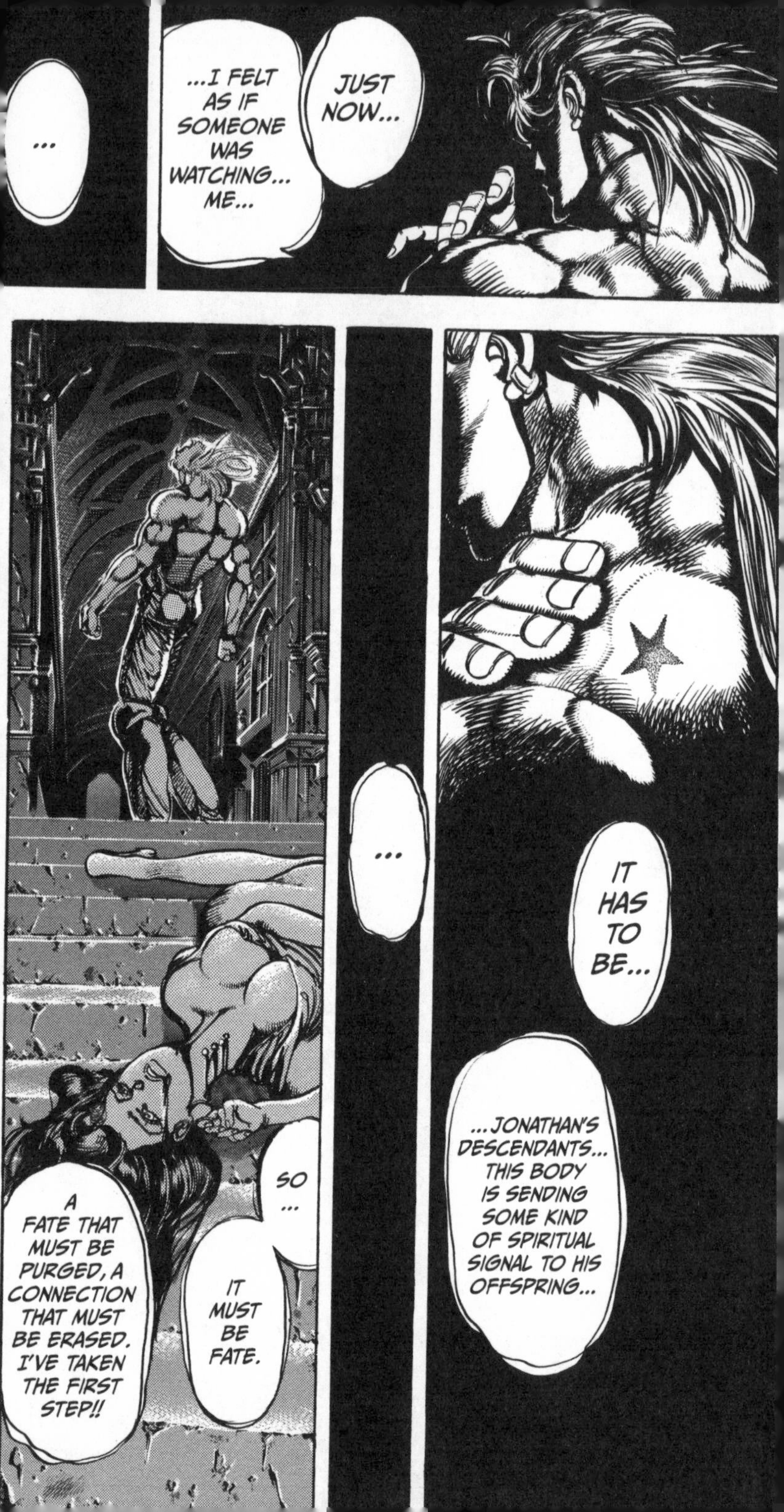
JUST NOW...
...I FELT AS IF SOMEONE WAS WATCHING... ME...
...
IT HAS TO BE...
...JONATHAN'S DESCENDANTS... THIS BODY IS SENDING SOME KIND OF SPIRITUAL SIGNAL TO HIS OFFSPRING...
...
SO ...
IT MUST BE FATE.
A FATE THAT MUST BE PURGED, A CONNECTION THAT MUST BE ERASED. I'VE TAKEN THE FIRST STEP!!

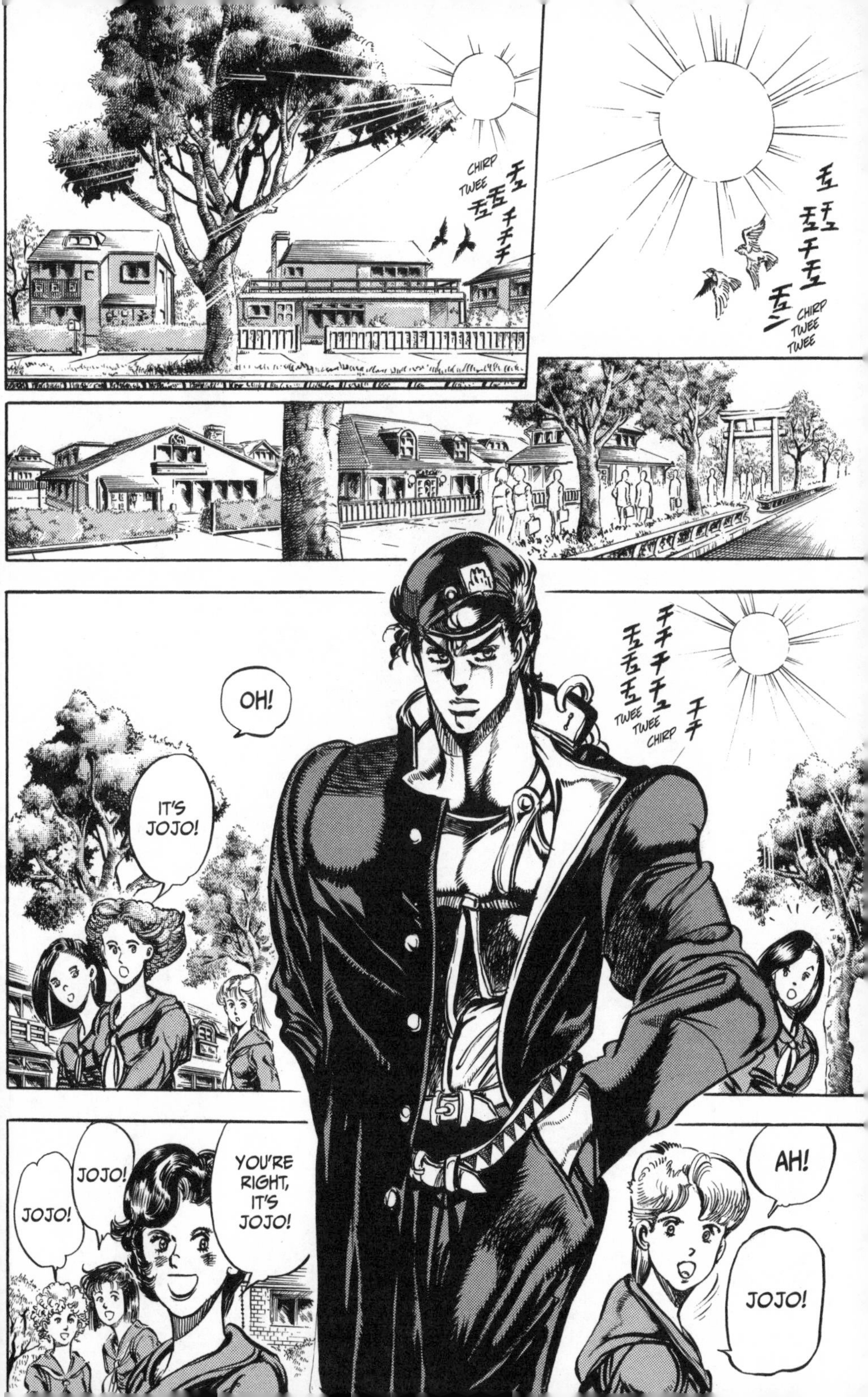
CHIRP TWEE TWEE
CHIRP TWEE
TWEE TWEE CHIRP
OH!
IT'S JOJO!
AH!
JOJO!
YOU'RE RIGHT, IT'S JOJO!
JOJO!
JOJO!

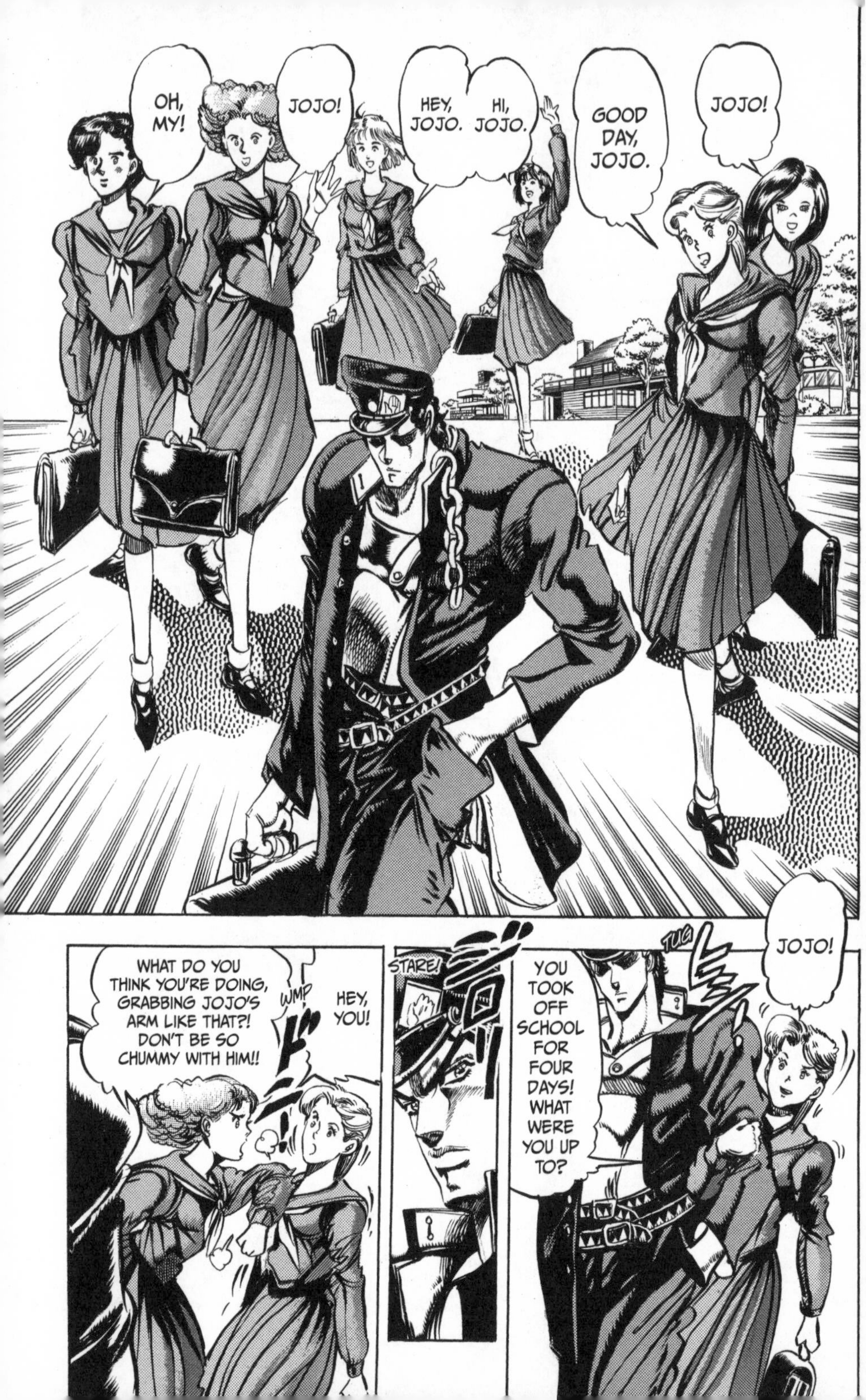
JOJO!
GOOD DAY, JOJO.
HI, JOJO.
HEY, JOJO.
JOJO!
OH, MY!
JOJO!
TUG
YOU TOOK OFF SCHOOL FOR FOUR DAYS! WHAT WERE YOU UP TO?
STARE!
HEY, YOU!
WMP
WHAT DO YOU THINK YOU'RE DOING, GRABBING JOJO'S ARM LIKE THAT?! DON'T BE SO CHUMMY WITH HIM!!

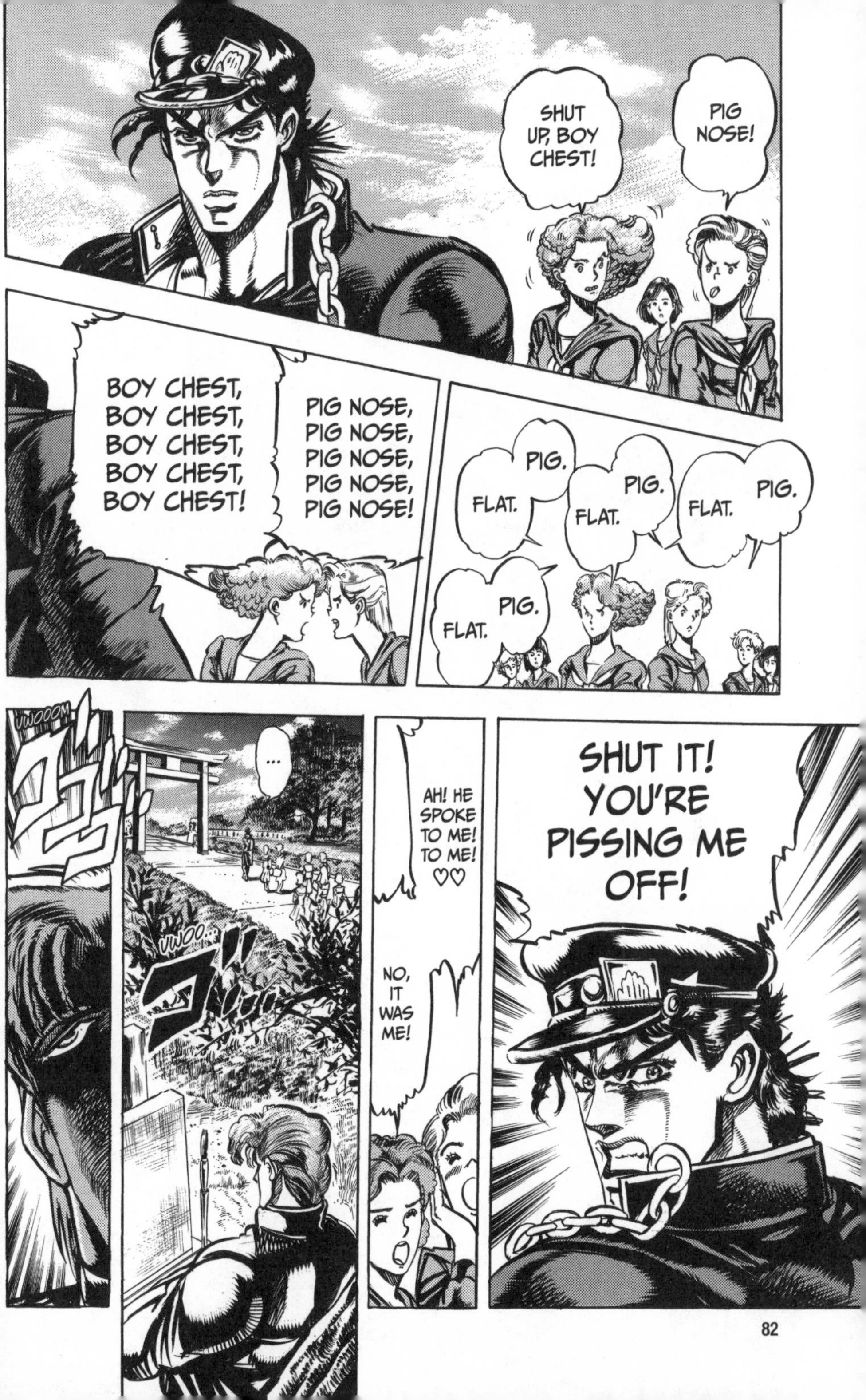
PIG NOSE!
SHUT UP, BOY CHEST!
FLAT. PIG.
FLAT. PIG.
FLAT. PIG.
FLAT. PIG.
PIG NOSE, PIG NOSE, PIG NOSE, PIG NOSE, PIG NOSE!
BOY CHEST, BOY CHEST, BOY CHEST, BOY CHEST, BOY CHEST!
SHUT IT! YOU'RE PISSING ME OFF!
AH! HE SPOKE TO ME! TO ME! ♡♡
NO, IT WAS ME!
...
UWOO...
UWOOOM

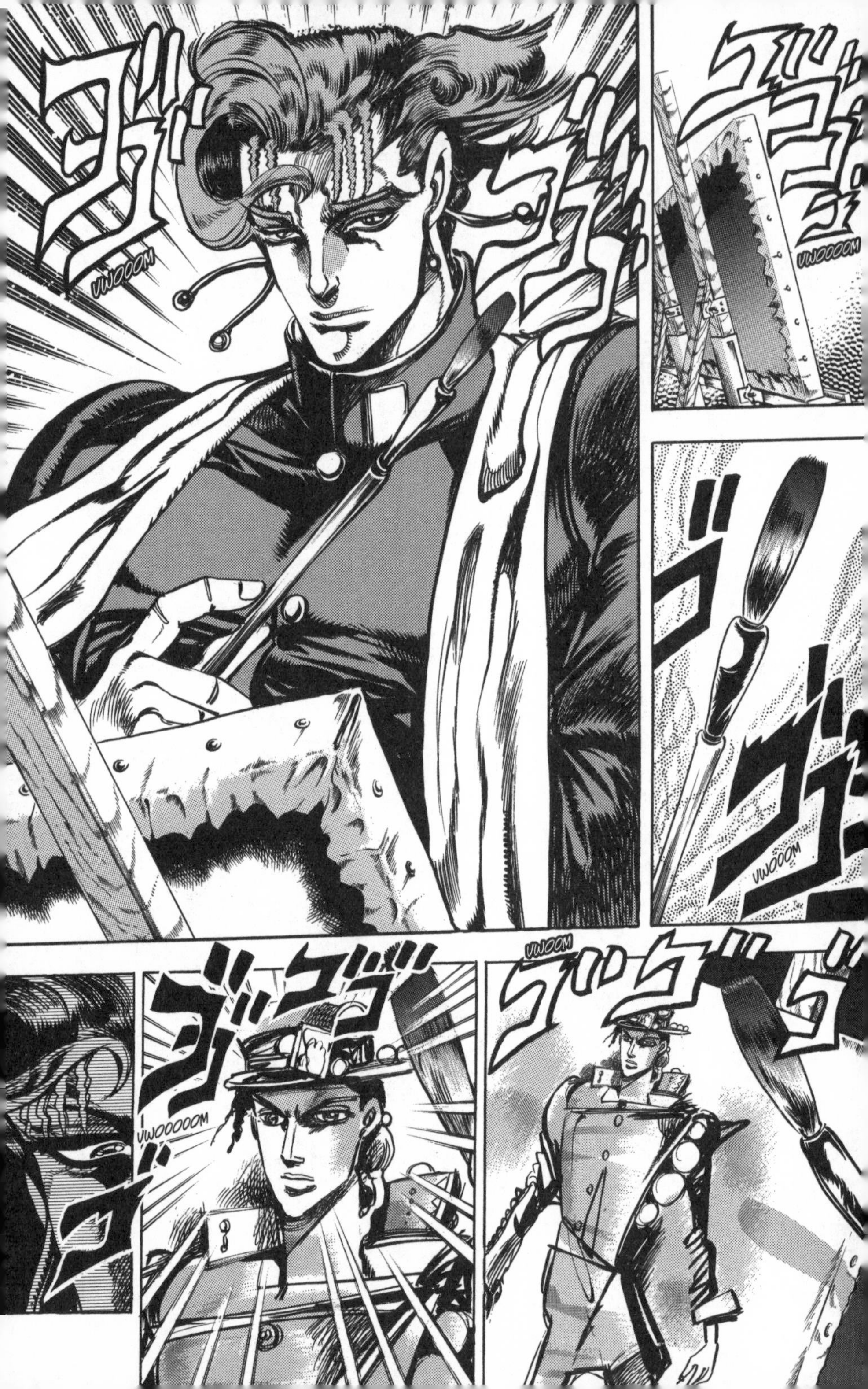
VWOOOOM
VWOOOM
VWOOOM
VWOOM
VWOOOOOM

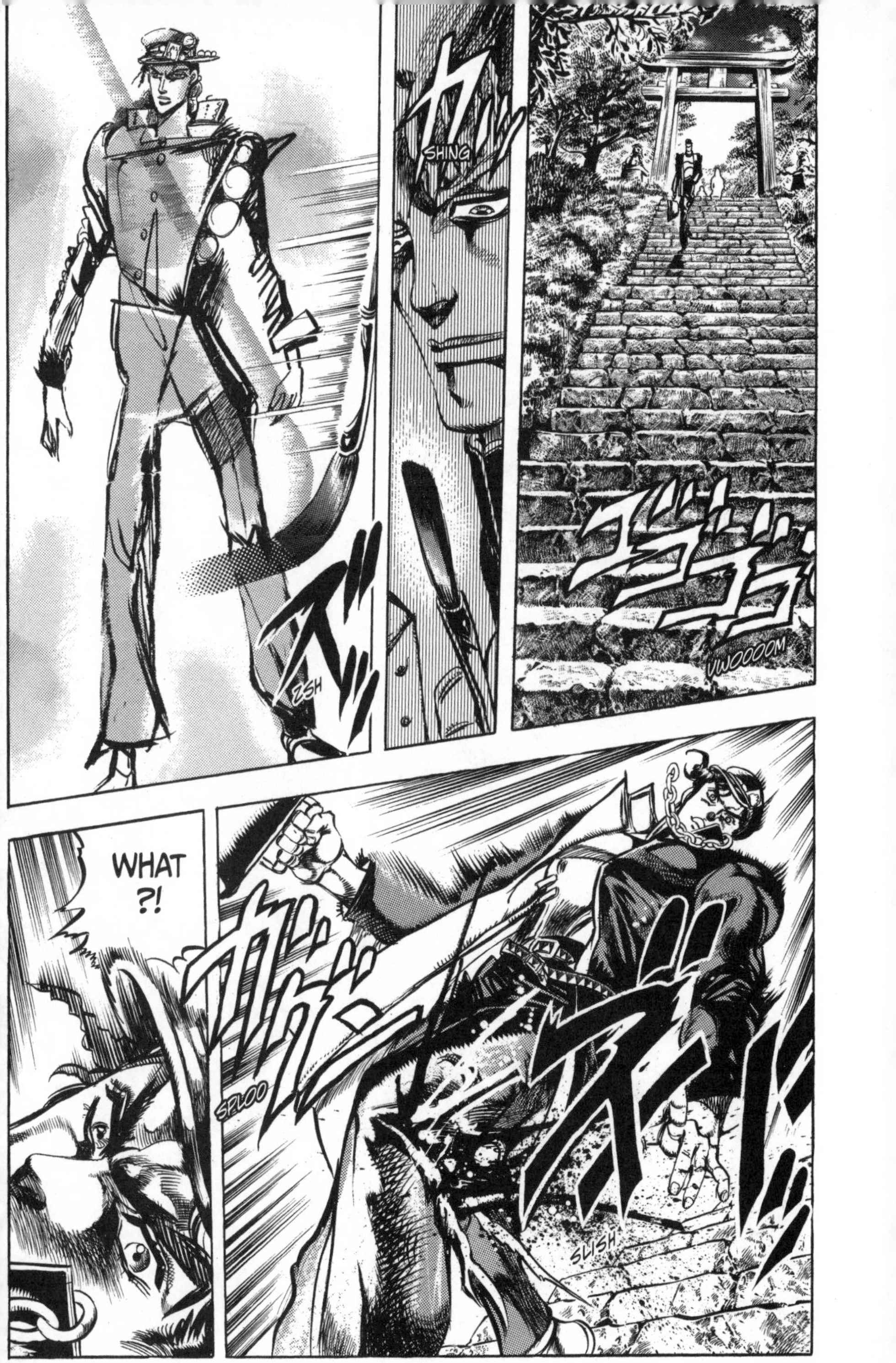
VWOOOOM
SHING
ZSH
SPLOO
SLISH
WHAT ?!

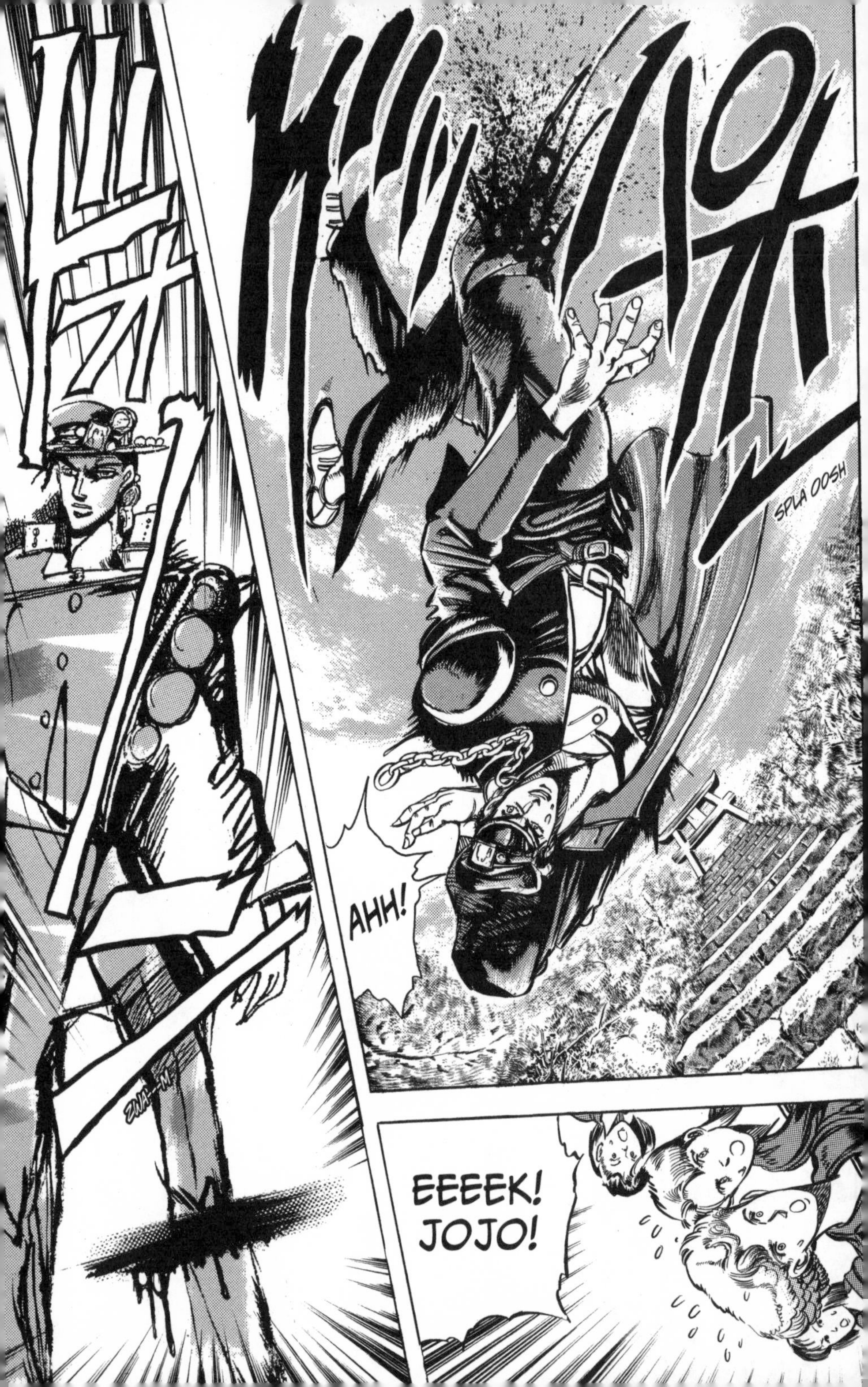
SPLA OOSH
AHH!
EEEEK! JOJO!
ZWA—M

LUCKYLAND
THE HERMIT 9

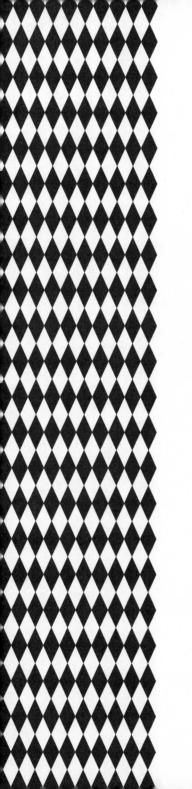

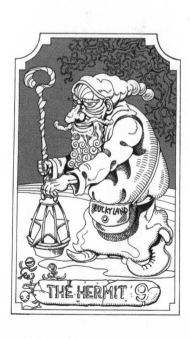

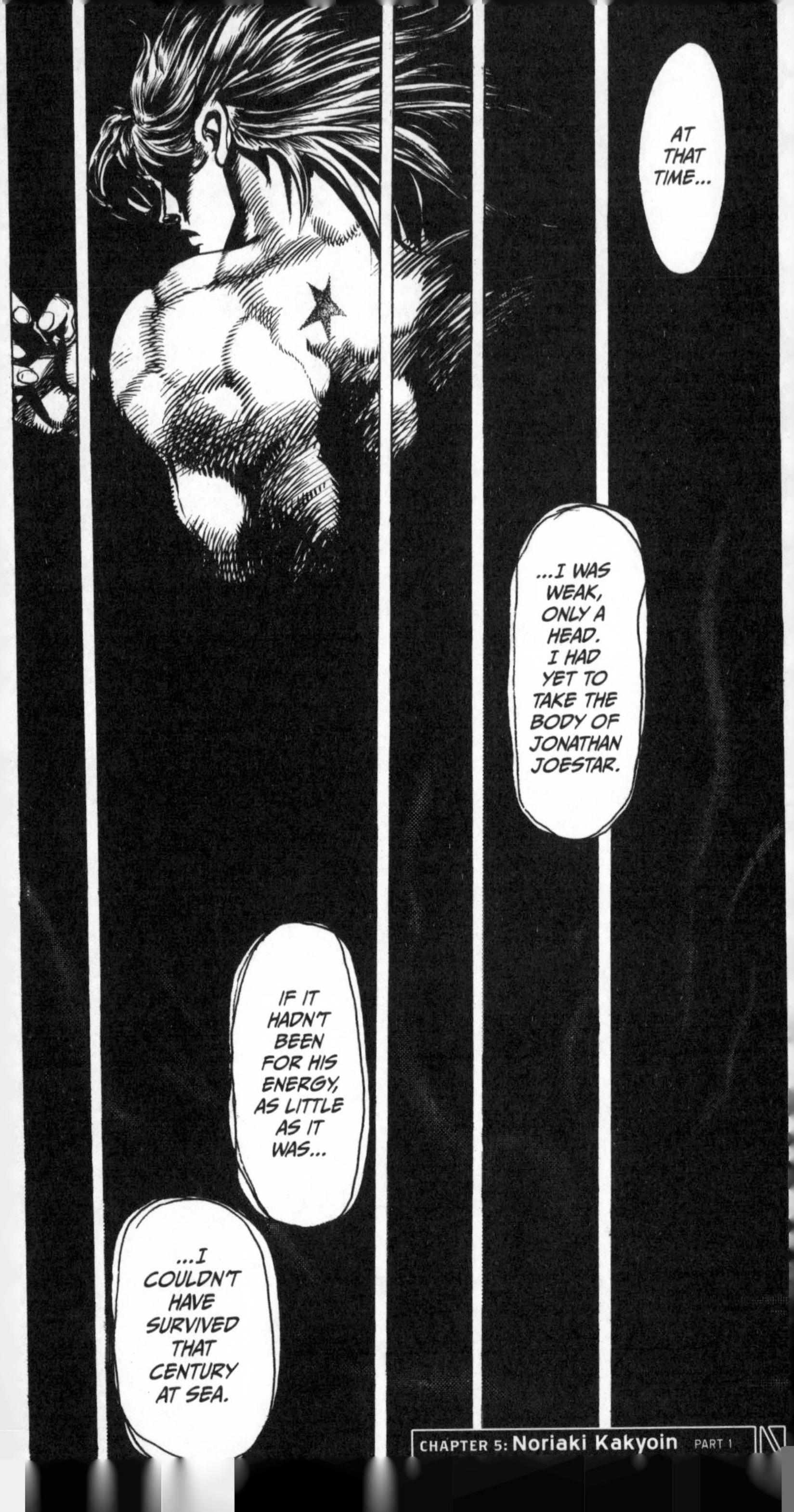
AT THAT TIME...
...I WAS WEAK, ONLY A HEAD. I HAD YET TO TAKE THE BODY OF JONATHAN JOESTAR.
IF IT HADN'T BEEN FOR HIS ENERGY, AS LITTLE AS IT WAS...
...I COULDN'T HAVE SURVIVED THAT CENTURY AT SEA.

CHAPTER 5: Noriaki Kakyoin PART 1

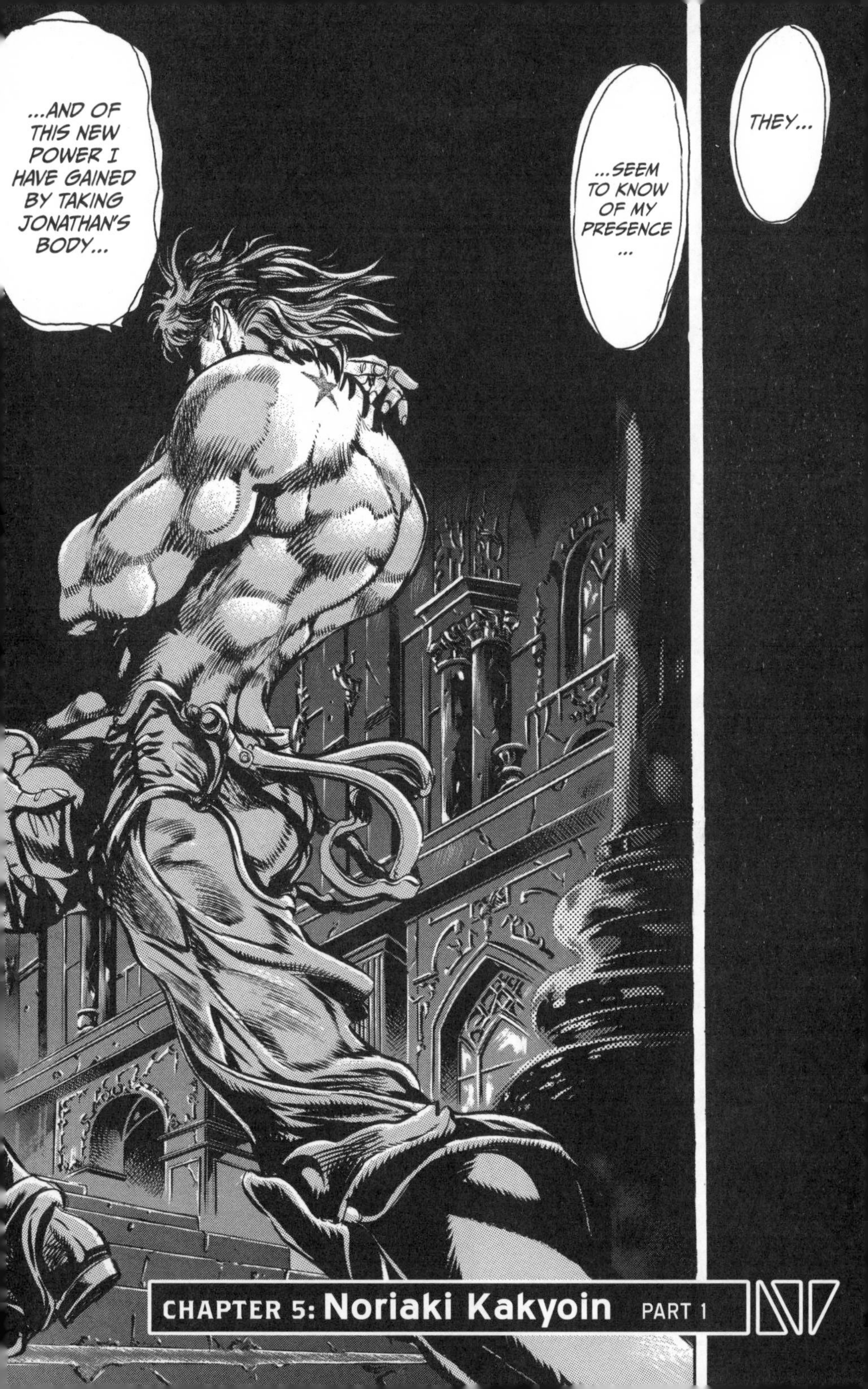
THEY...
...SEEM TO KNOW OF MY PRESENCE ...
...AND OF THIS NEW POWER I HAVE GAINED BY TAKING JONATHAN'S BODY...
CHAPTER 5: Noriaki Kakyoin PART 1

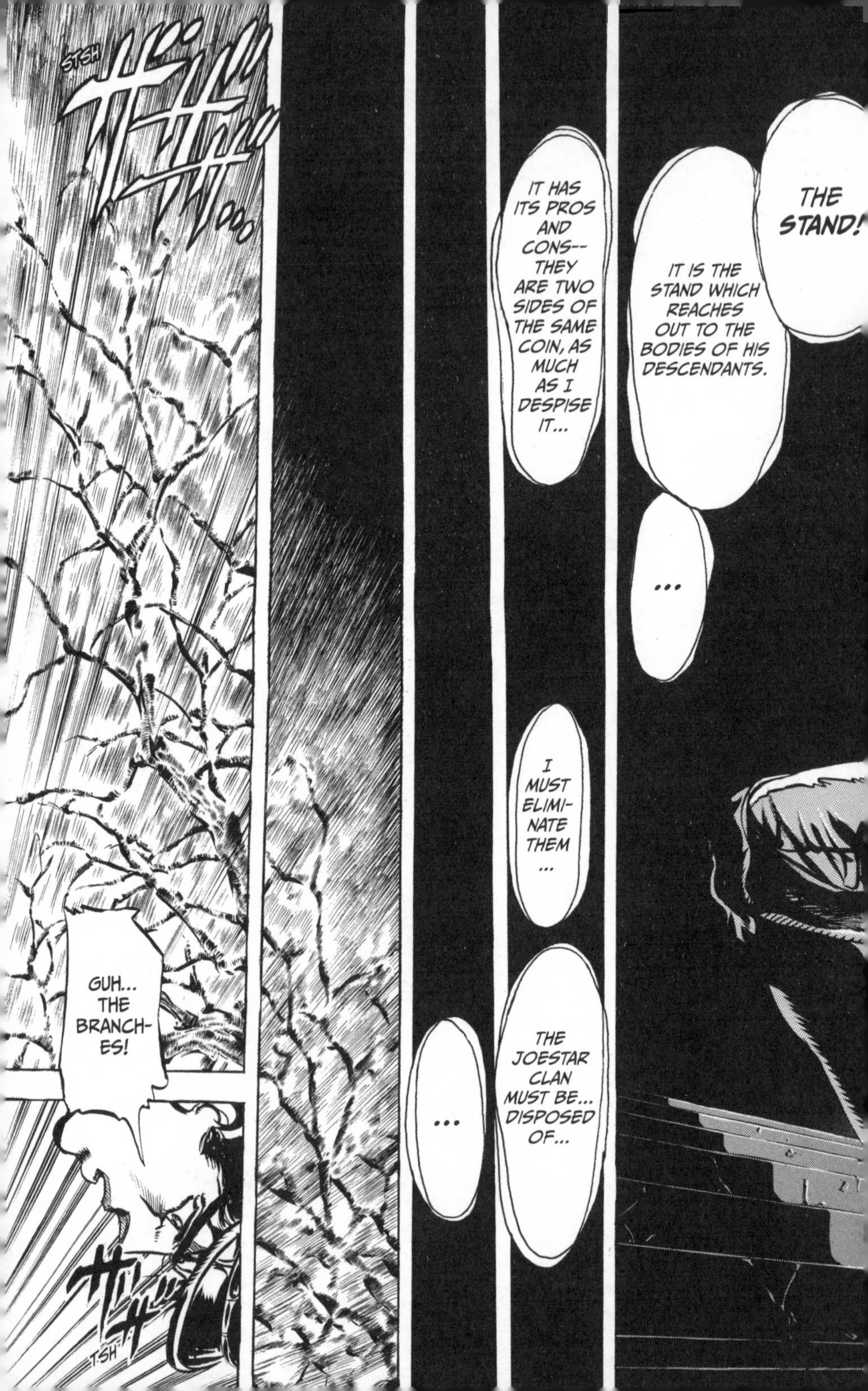
THE STAND!
IT IS THE STAND WHICH REACHES OUT TO THE BODIES OF HIS DESCENDANTS.
...
IT HAS ITS PROS AND CONS-- THEY ARE TWO SIDES OF THE SAME COIN, AS MUCH AS I DESPISE IT...
I MUST ELIMINATE THEM...
THE JOESTAR CLAN MUST BE... DISPOSED OF...
...
STSH
GUH... THE BRANCHES!
TSH

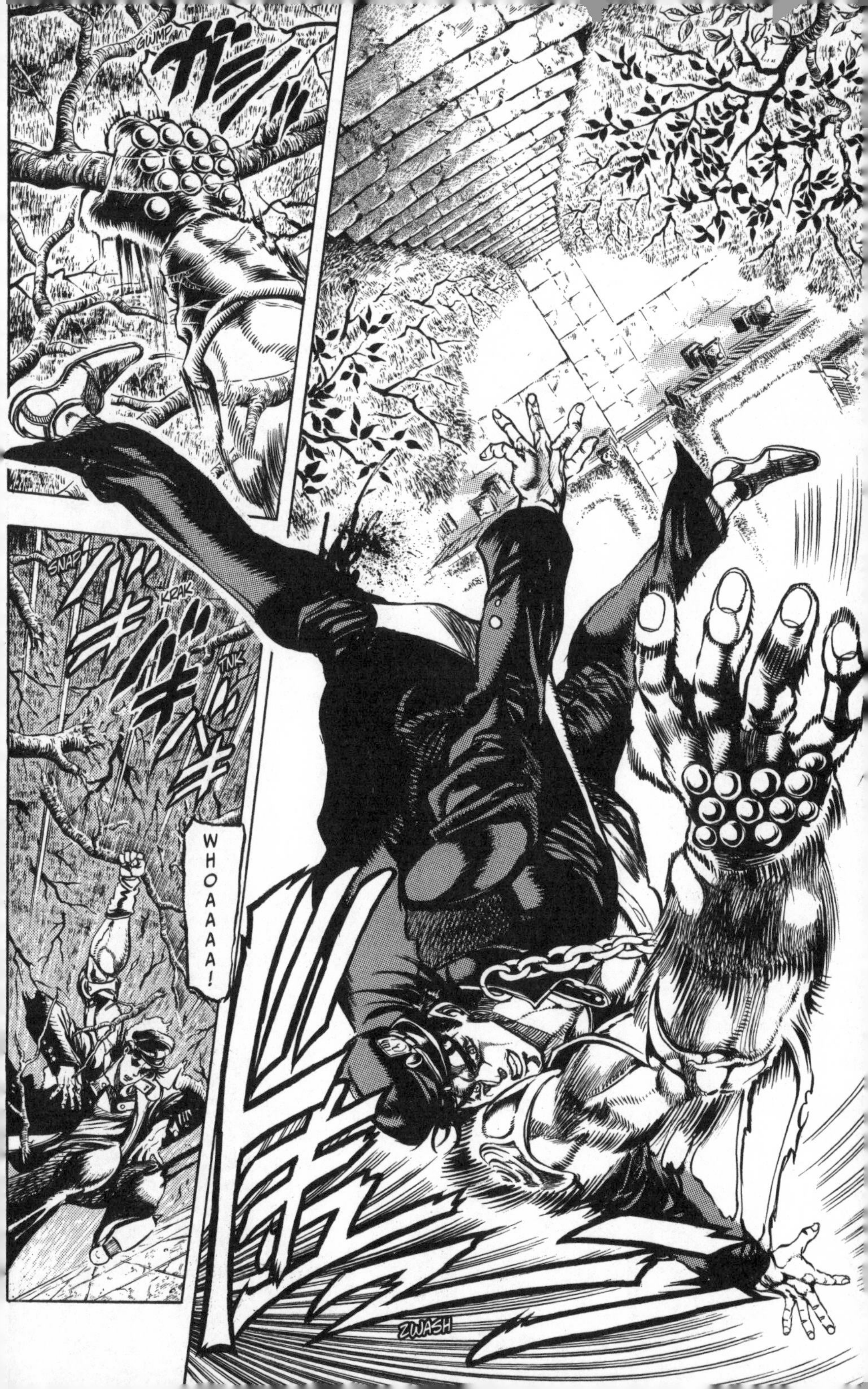
ZWASH
GWUMP
SNAP
KRAK
TNK
WHOAAAAA!

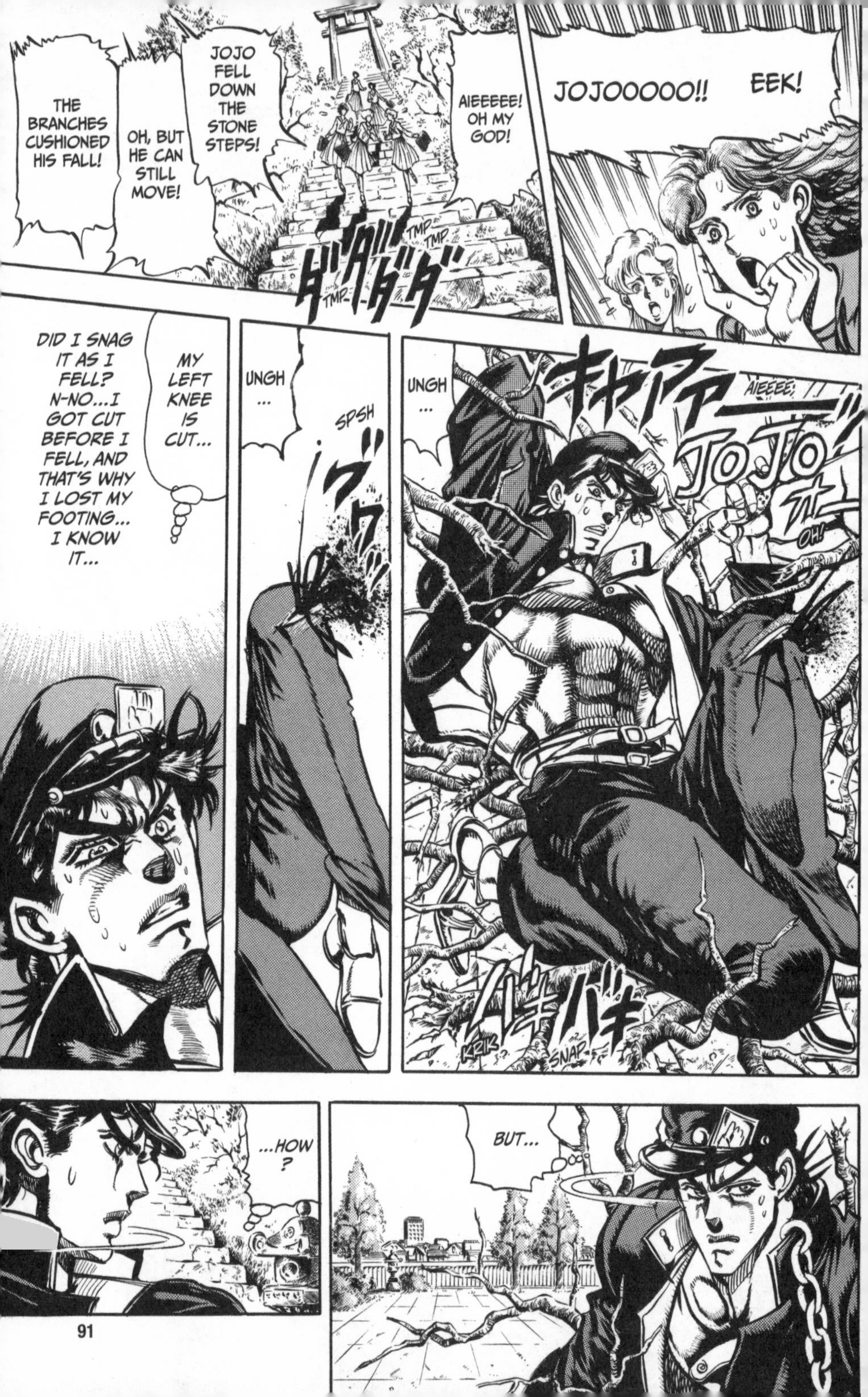
JOJOOOOO!!
EEK!
AIEEEEE! OH MY GOD!
JOJO FELL DOWN THE STONE STEPS!
OH, BUT HE CAN STILL MOVE!
THE BRANCHES CUSHIONED HIS FALL!
TMP TMP
TMP
AIEEEE!
JOJO!
OH!
UNGH...
SNAP
UNGH...
SPSH
MY LEFT KNEE IS CUT...
DID I SNAG IT AS I FELL? N-NO...I GOT CUT BEFORE I FELL, AND THAT'S WHY I LOST MY FOOTING... I KNOW IT...
BUT...
...HOW?

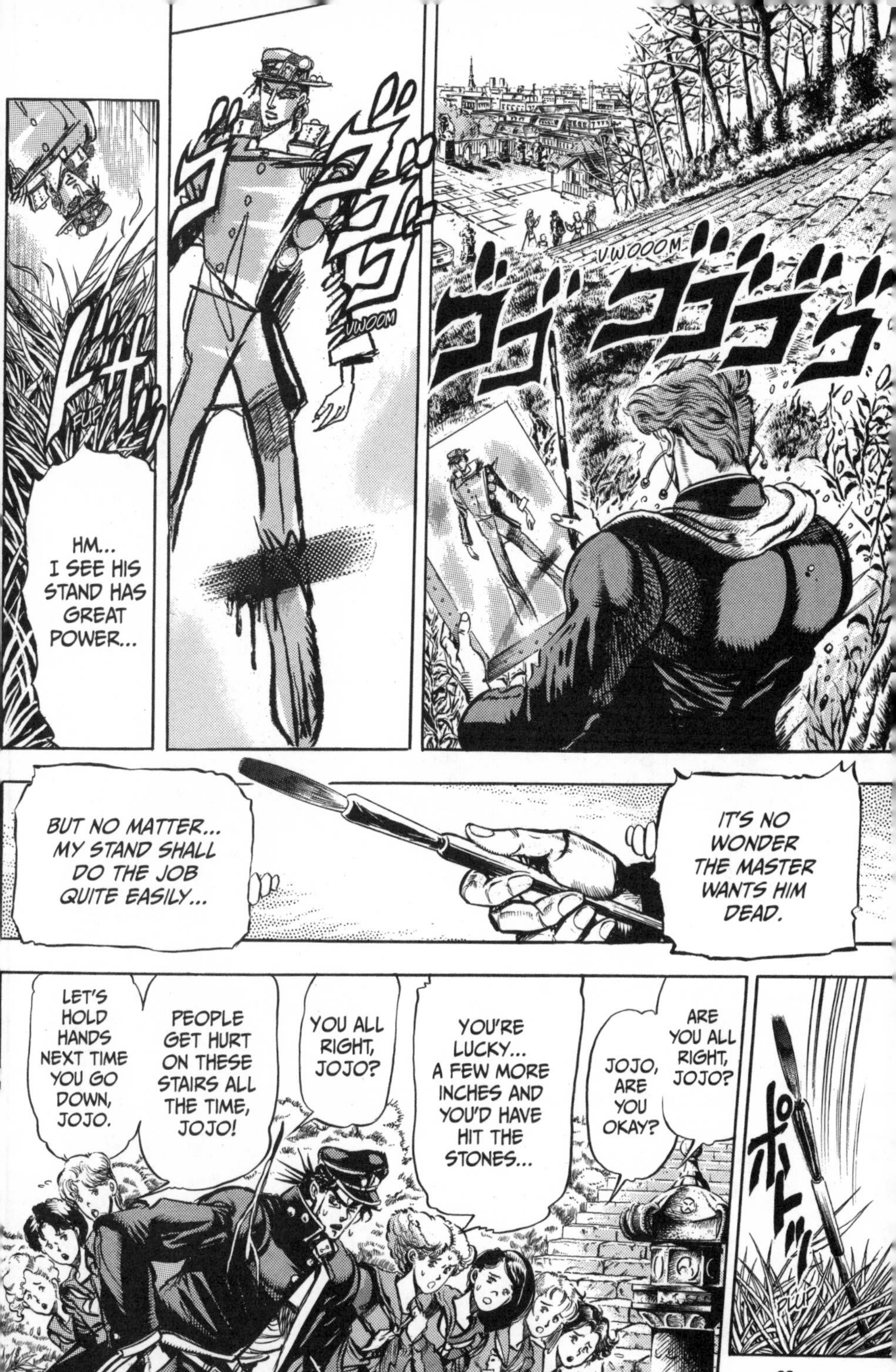

VWOOOM
VWOOM
FUP
HM... I SEE HIS STAND HAS GREAT POWER...
IT'S NO WONDER THE MASTER WANTS HIM DEAD.
BUT NO MATTER... MY STAND SHALL DO THE JOB QUITE EASILY...
PLUP
ARE YOU ALL RIGHT, JOJO?
JOJO, ARE YOU OKAY?
YOU'RE LUCKY... A FEW MORE INCHES AND YOU'D HAVE HIT THE STONES...
YOU ALL RIGHT, JOJO?
PEOPLE GET HURT ON THESE STAIRS ALL THE TIME, JOJO!
LET'S HOLD HANDS NEXT TIME YOU GO DOWN, JOJO.

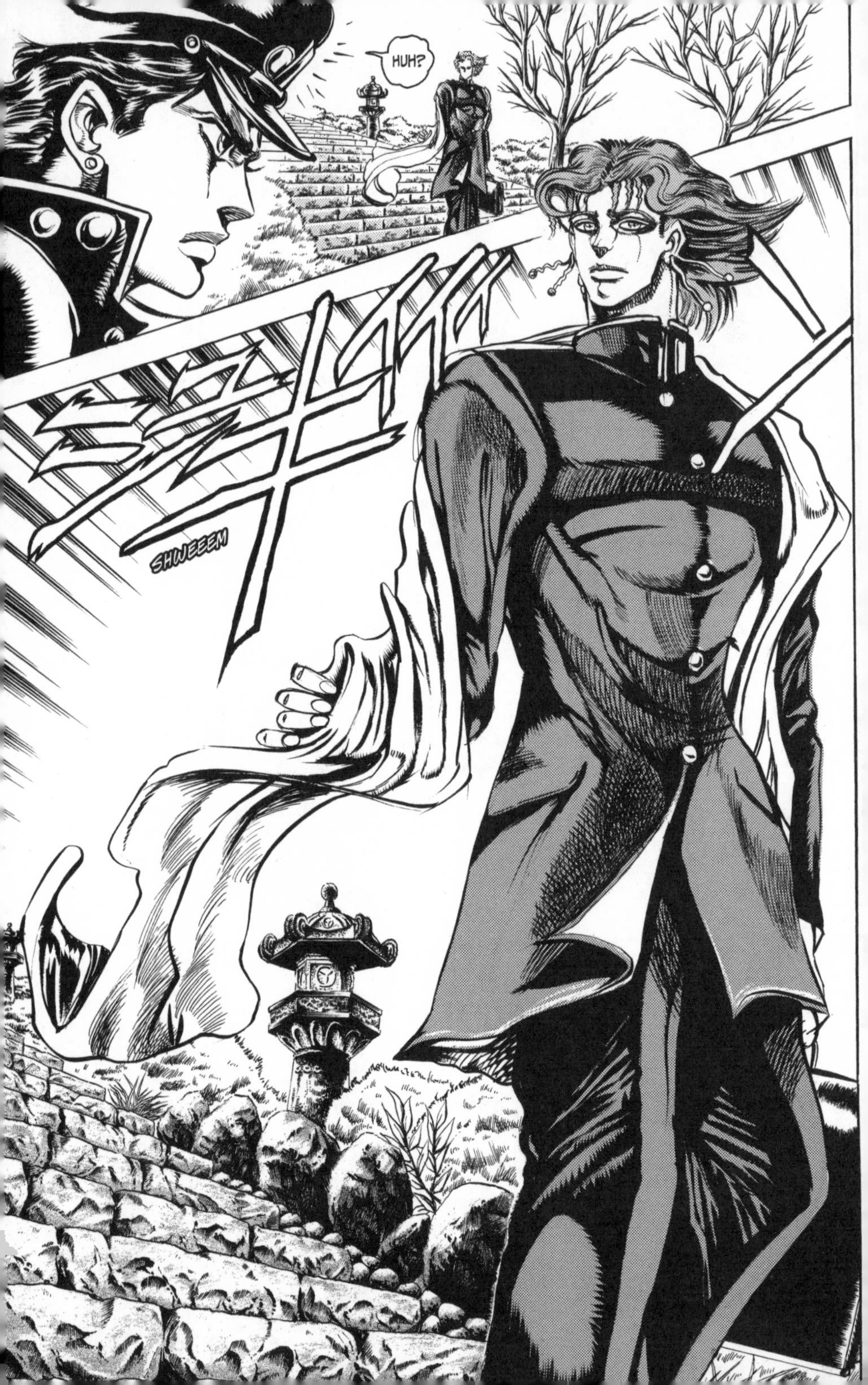
HUH?
SHWEEEM

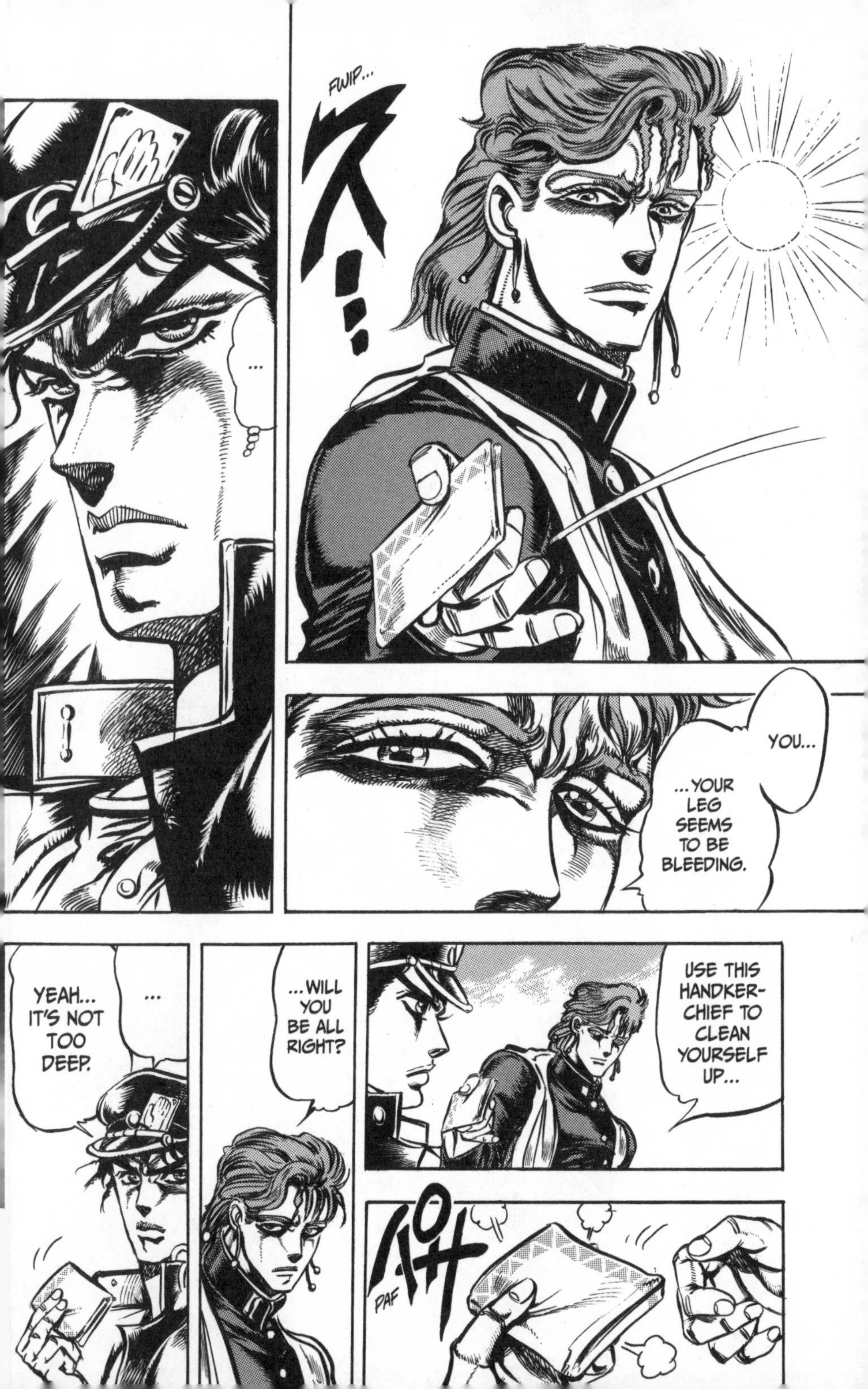
FWIP...
YOU...
...YOUR LEG SEEMS TO BE BLEEDING.
...
USE THIS HANDKER-CHIEF TO CLEAN YOURSELF UP...
PAF
...WILL YOU BE ALL RIGHT?
...
YEAH... IT'S NOT TOO DEEP.

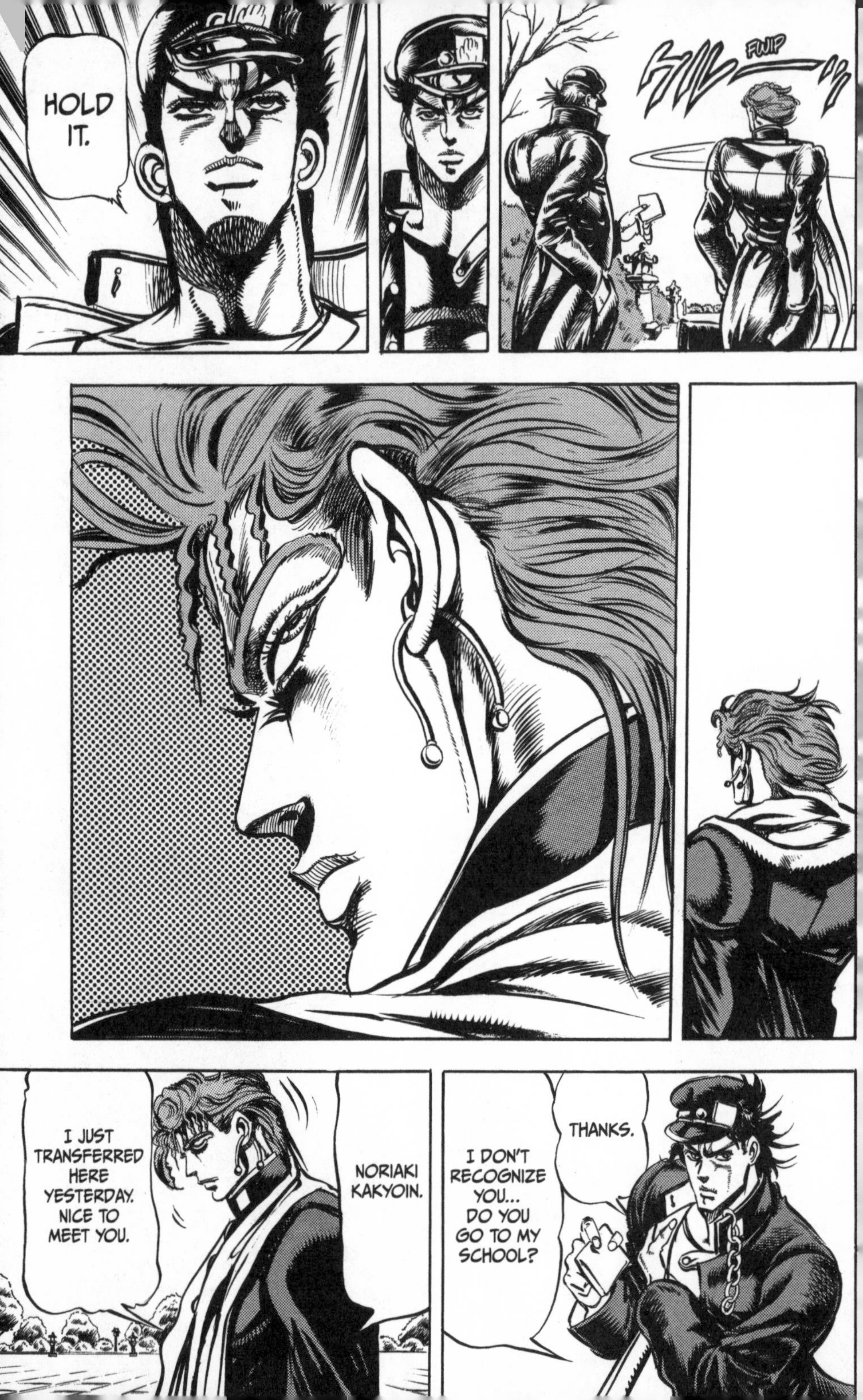
FWIP
HOLD IT.
THANKS.
I DON'T RECOGNIZE YOU... DO YOU GO TO MY SCHOOL?
NORIAKI KAKYOIN.
I JUST TRANSFERRED HERE YESTERDAY. NICE TO MEET YOU.

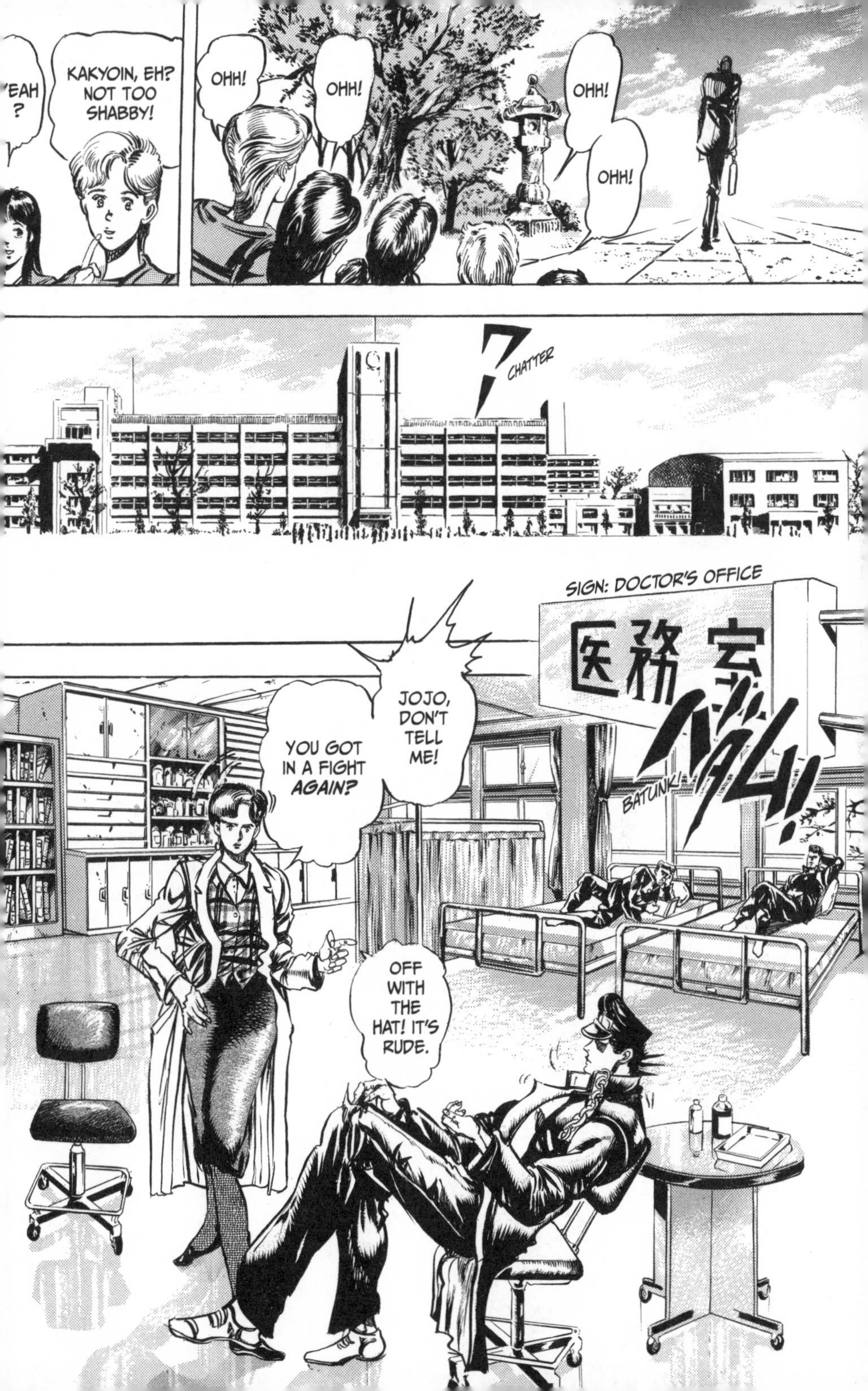
OHH!
OHH!
OHH!
OHH!
KAKYOIN, EH? NOT TOO SHABBY!
'EAH ?
CHATTER
SIGN: DOCTOR'S OFFICE
医務室
BATUNK!
JOJO, DON'T TELL ME!
YOU GOT IN A FIGHT AGAIN?
OFF WITH THE HAT! IT'S RUDE.

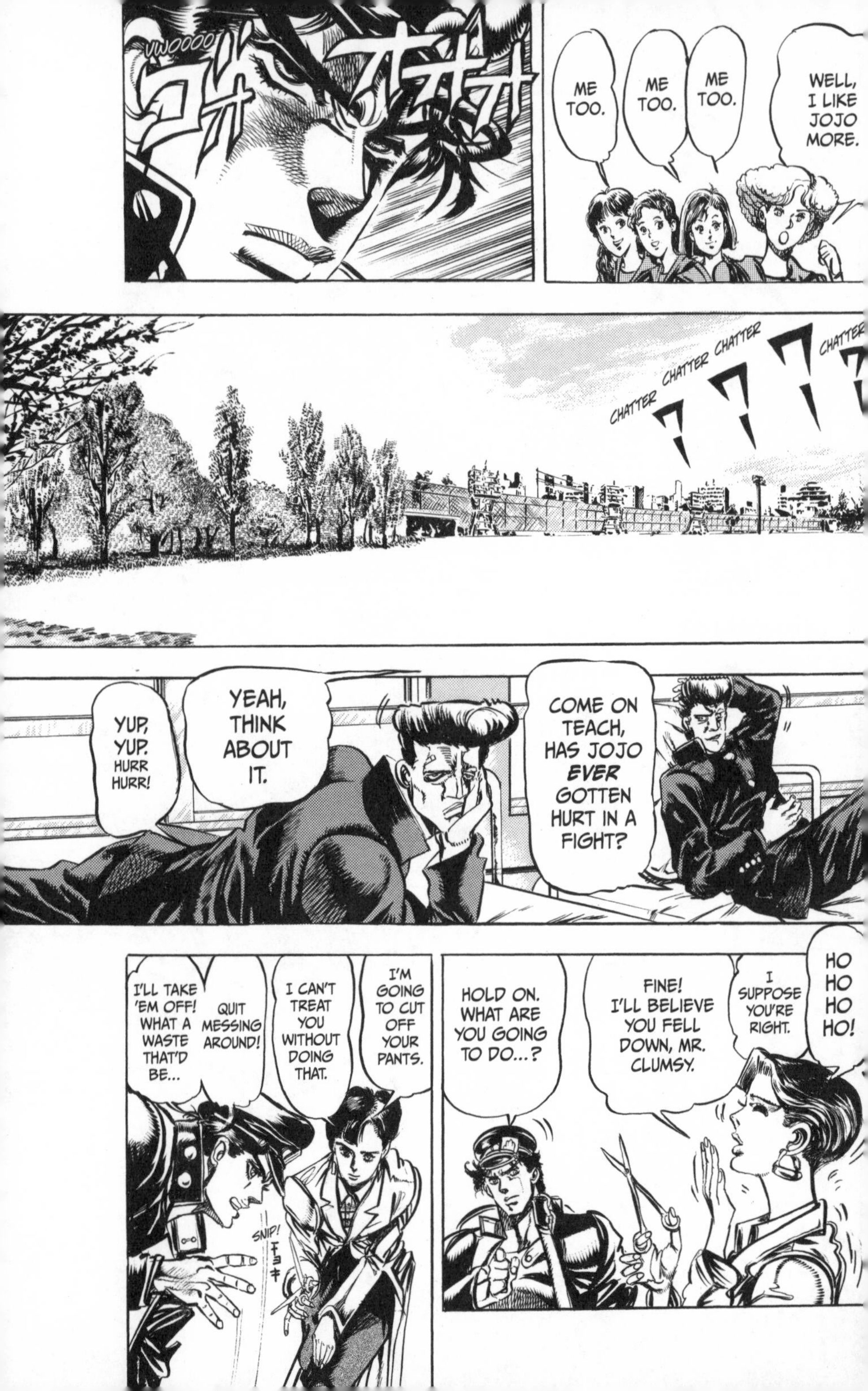
WELL, I LIKE JOJO MORE.
ME TOO.
ME TOO.
ME TOO.
VWOOOO
CHATTER CHATTER CHATTER CHATTER
COME ON TEACH, HAS JOJO **EVER** GOTTEN HURT IN A FIGHT?
YEAH, THINK ABOUT IT.
YUP, YUP. HURR HURR!
HO HO HO HO!
I SUPPOSE YOU'RE RIGHT.
FINE! I'LL BELIEVE YOU FELL DOWN, MR. CLUMSY.
HOLD ON. WHAT ARE YOU GOING TO DO...?
I'M GOING TO CUT OFF YOUR PANTS.
I CAN'T TREAT YOU WITHOUT DOING THAT.
QUIT MESSING AROUND!
I'LL TAKE 'EM OFF! WHAT A WASTE THAT'D BE...
SNIP!

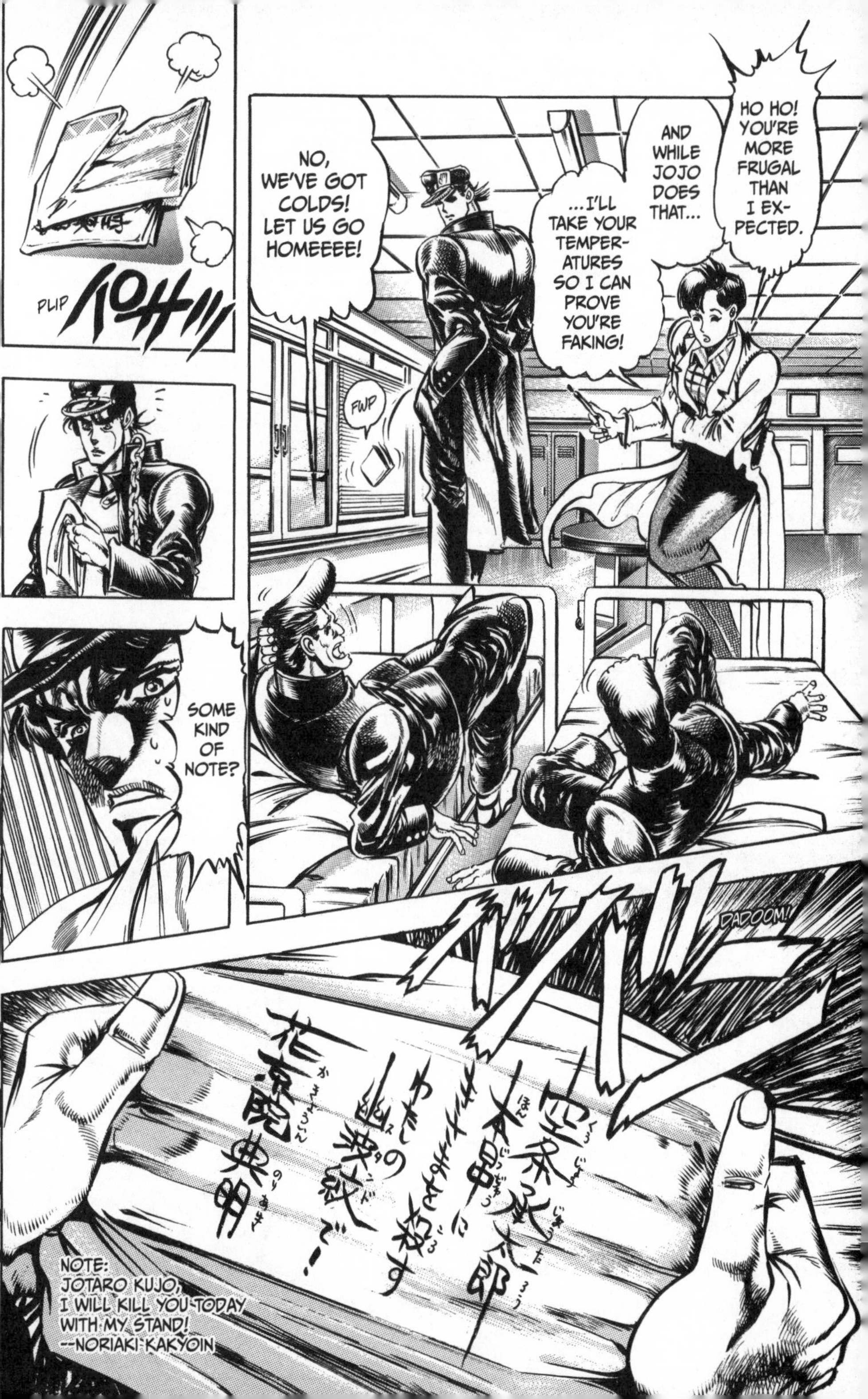
HO HO! YOU'RE MORE FRUGAL THAN I EXPECTED.
AND WHILE JOJO DOES THAT...
...I'LL TAKE YOUR TEMPERATURES SO I CAN PROVE YOU'RE FAKING!
NO, WE'VE GOT COLDS! LET US GO HOMEEEE!
FWP
PLIP
SOME KIND OF NOTE?
DADOOM!
空条承太郎
本日オマエを殺す
わたしの幽波紋で！
花京院典明
NOTE:
JOTARO KUJO,
I WILL KILL YOU TODAY
WITH MY STAND!
--NORIAKI KAKYOIN

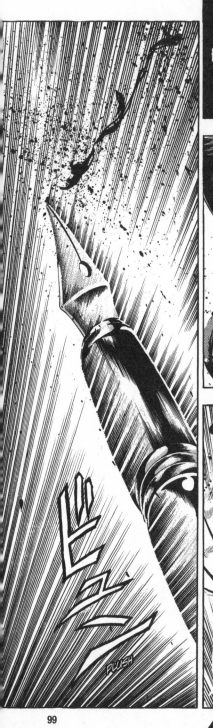

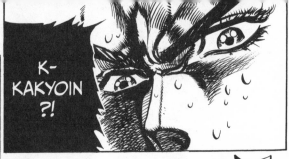

K-
KAKYOIN
?!
DUH...
DOCTOR! WHAT ARE YOU DOING?!
SKSH
AIEEEE!
TSH
!!?
PLUSH
PLASH
PLUSH

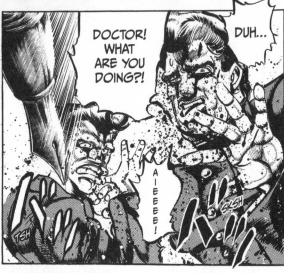

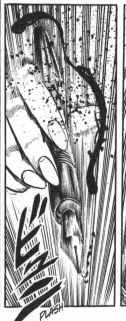

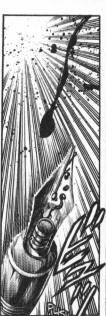

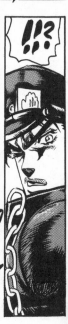

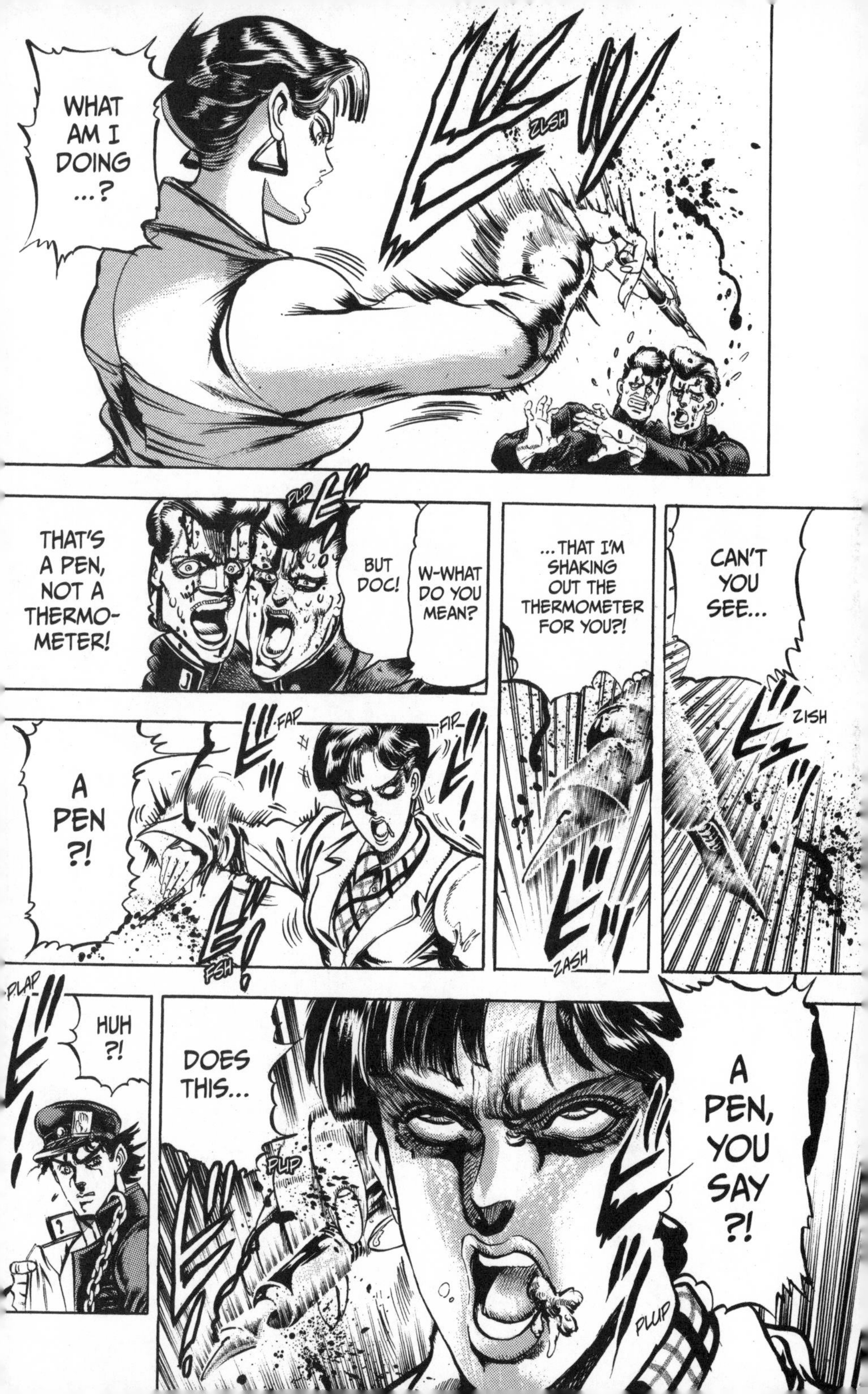
WHAT AM I DOING ...?
ZLISH
CAN'T YOU SEE...
ZISH
...THAT I'M SHAKING OUT THE THERMOMETER FOR YOU?!
ZASH
W-WHAT DO YOU MEAN?
BUT DOC!
PLIP
THAT'S A PEN, NOT A THERMO-METER!
FIP
FAP
A PEN ?!
PSH
A PEN, YOU SAY ?!
DOES THIS...
PLIP
PLUP
HUH ?!
P.LAP

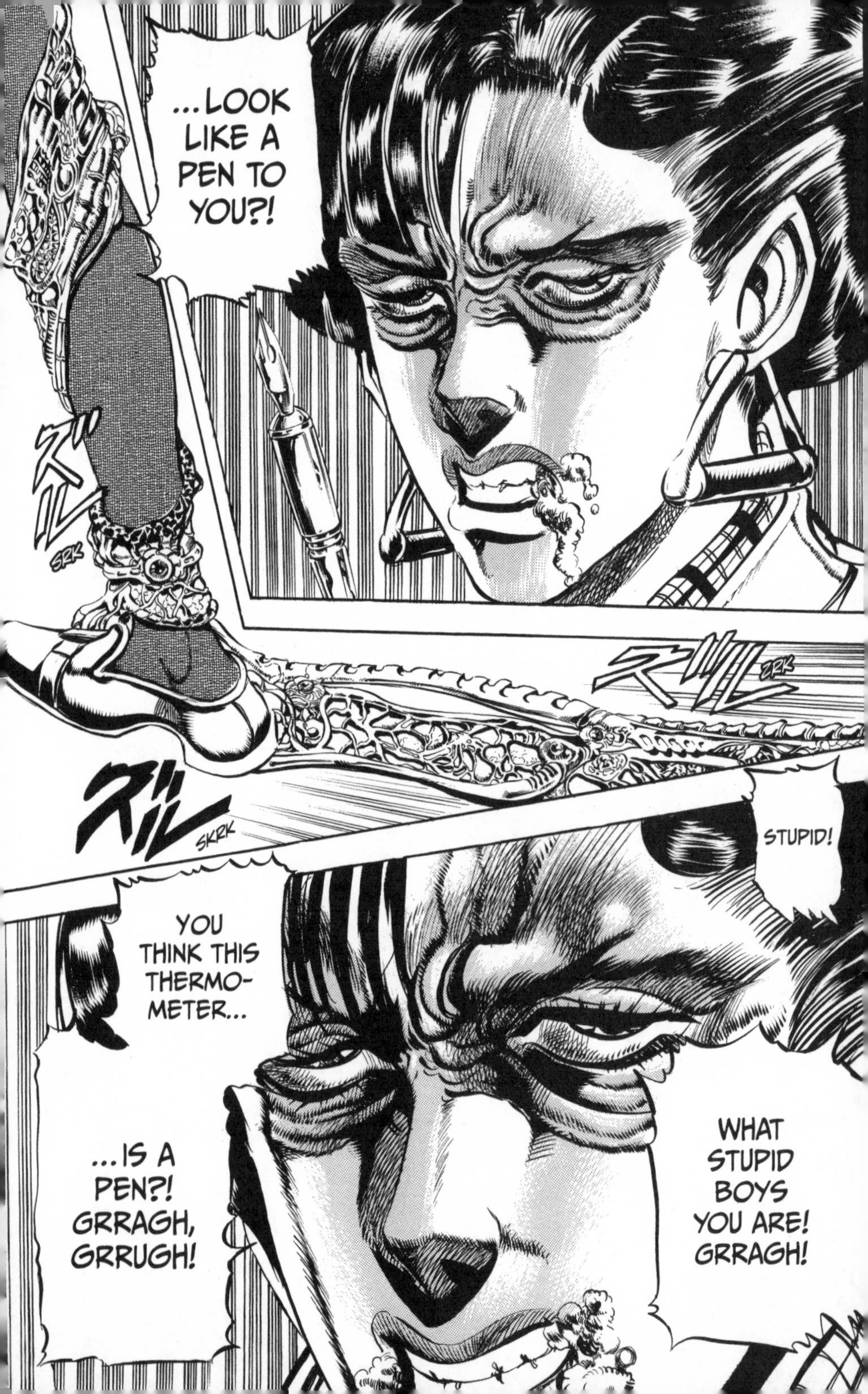
...LOOK LIKE A PEN TO YOU?!
SRK
SRK
SKRK
STUPID!
WHAT STUPID BOYS YOU ARE! GRRAGH!
YOU THINK THIS THERMO-METER...
...IS A PEN?! GRRAGH, GRRUGH!

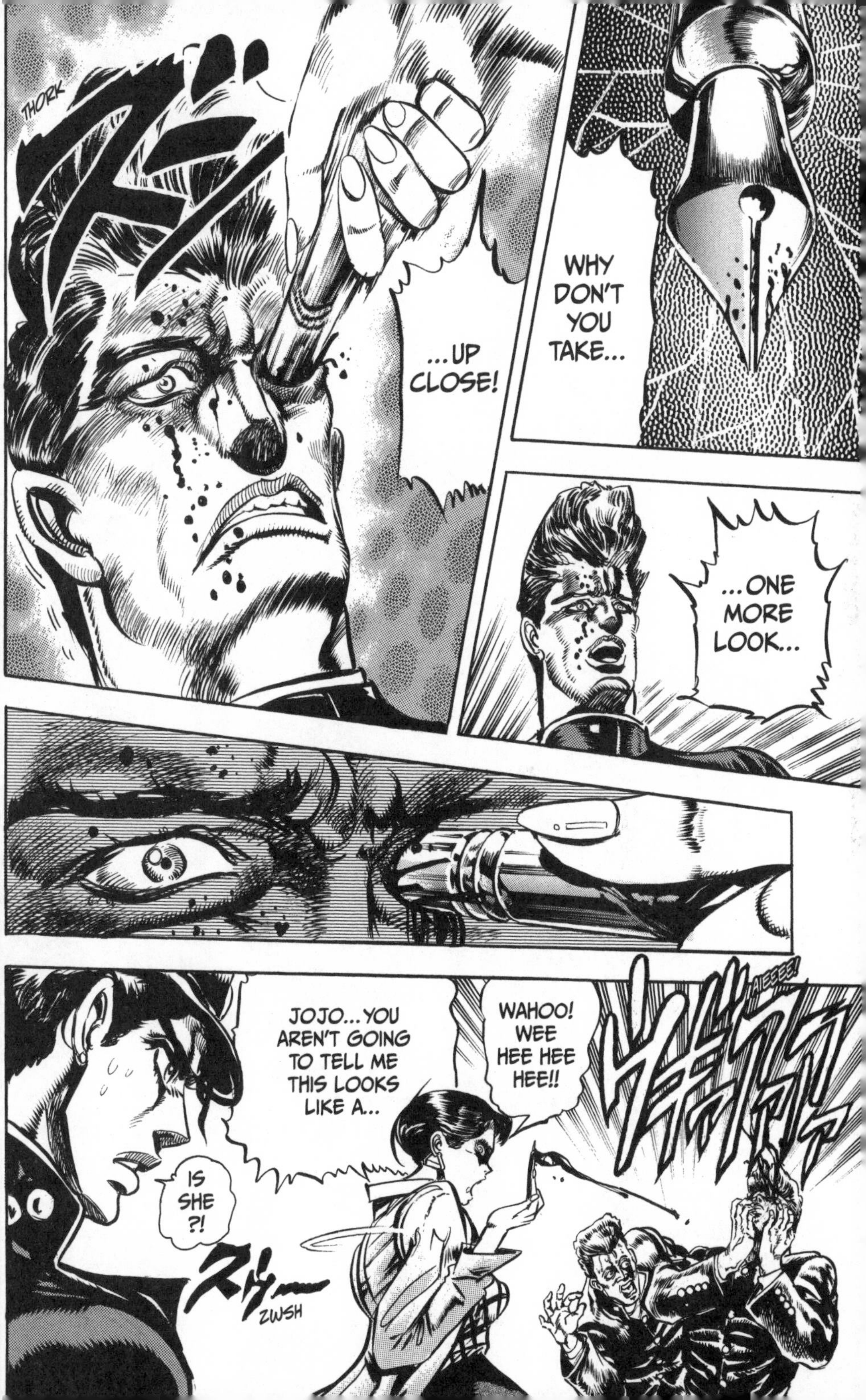
WHY DON'T YOU TAKE...
...ONE MORE LOOK...
...UP CLOSE!
THORK
AIEEEE!
WAHOO! WEE HEE HEE HEE!!
JOJO... YOU AREN'T GOING TO TELL ME THIS LOOKS LIKE A...
IS SHE ?!
ZWSH

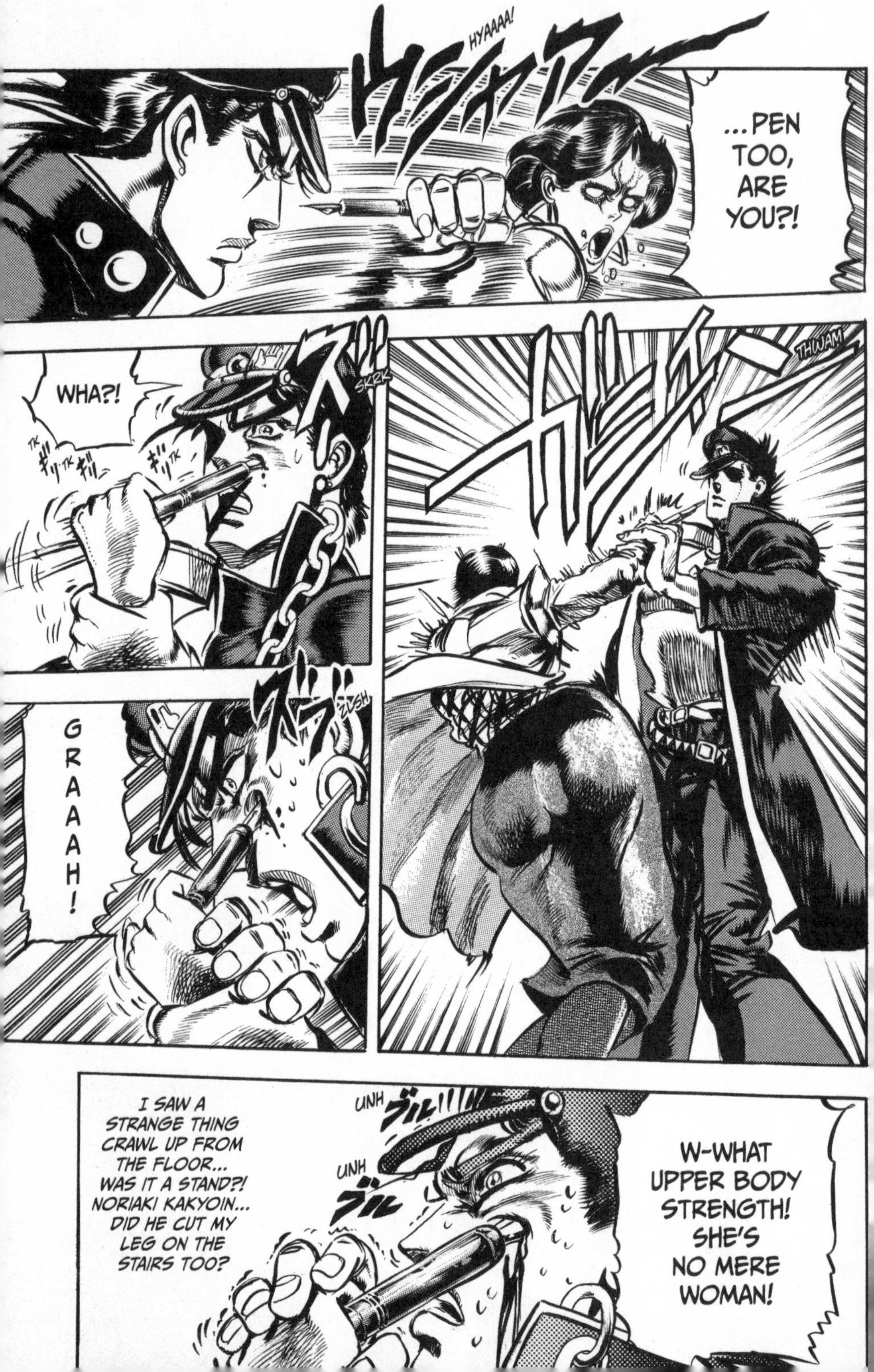
HYAAAA!
...PEN TOO, ARE YOU?!
THWAM
SKRK
WHA?!
TK TK TK
ZUSH
GRAAAAH!
W-WHAT UPPER BODY STRENGTH! SHE'S NO MERE WOMAN!
UNH
UNH
I SAW A STRANGE THING CRAWL UP FROM THE FLOOR... WAS IT A STAND?! NORIAKI KAKYOIN... DID HE CUT MY LEG ON THE STAIRS TOO?

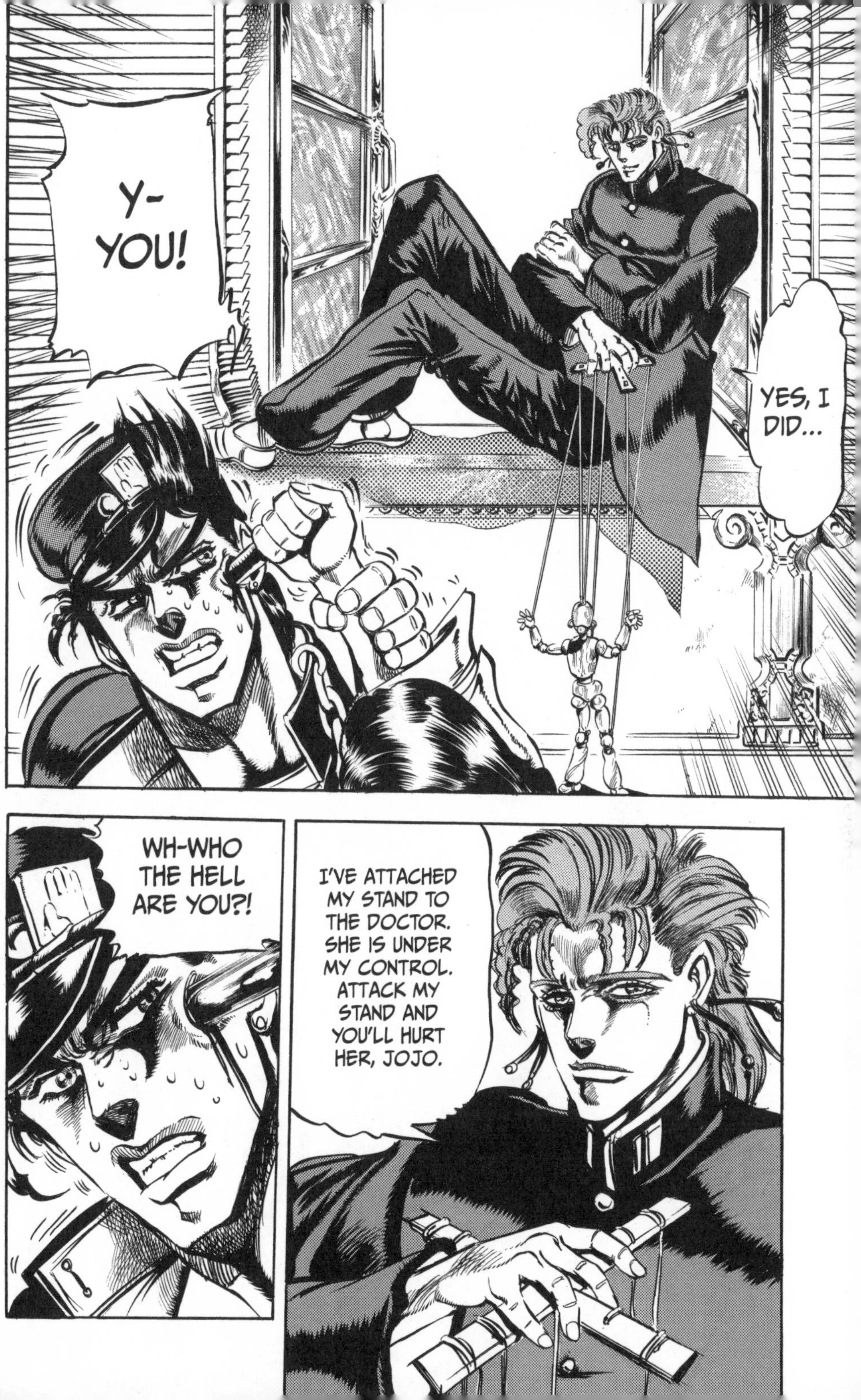
YES, I DID...
Y- YOU!
I'VE ATTACHED MY STAND TO THE DOCTOR. SHE IS UNDER MY CONTROL. ATTACK MY STAND AND YOU'LL HURT HER, JOJO.
WH-WHO THE HELL ARE YOU?!

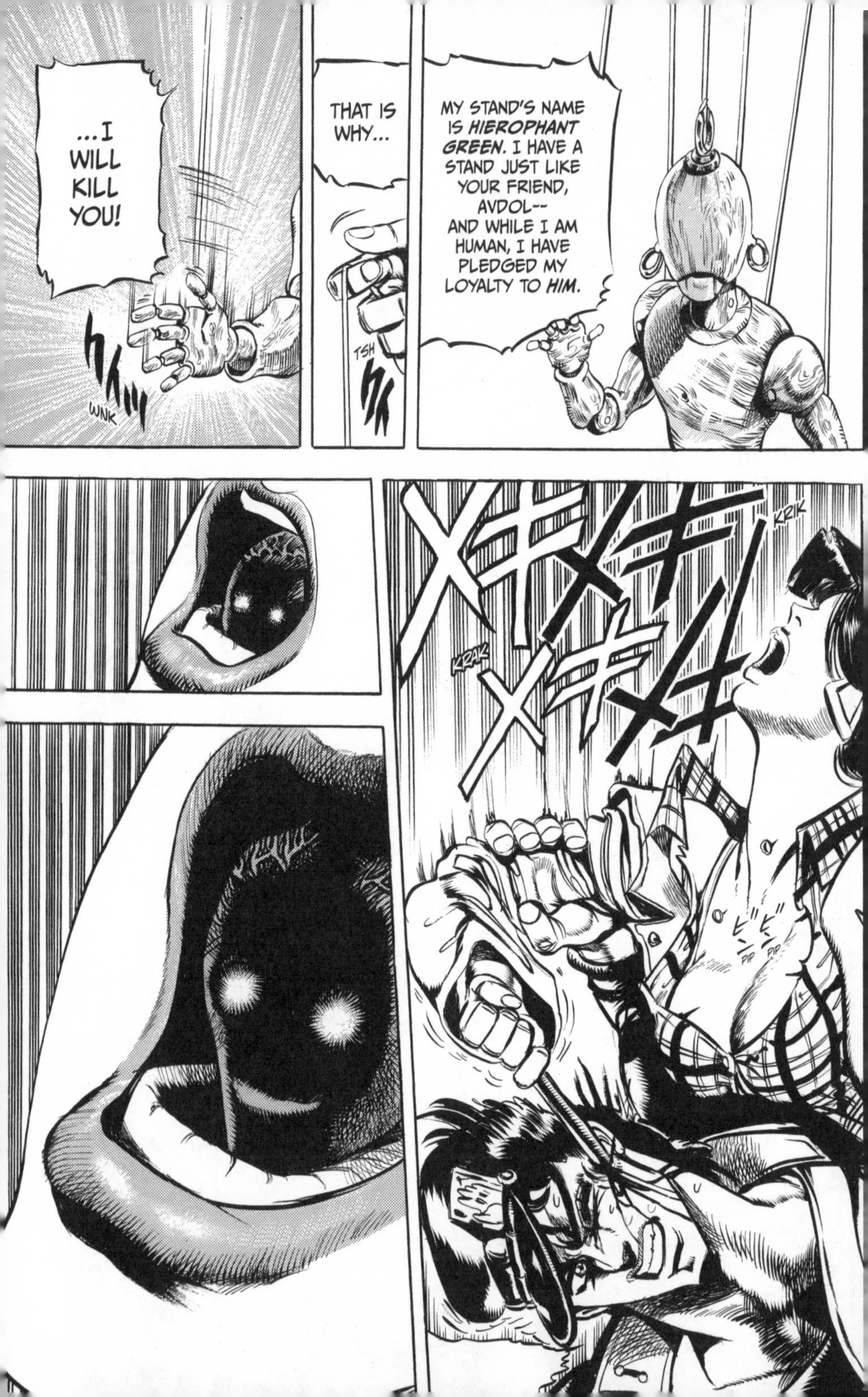
MY STAND'S NAME IS *HIEROPHANT GREEN*. I HAVE A STAND JUST LIKE YOUR FRIEND, AVDOL-- AND WHILE I AM HUMAN, I HAVE PLEDGED MY LOYALTY TO *HIM*.
THAT IS WHY...
TSH
...I WILL KILL YOU!
WNK
KRIK
KRAK
PIP PIP

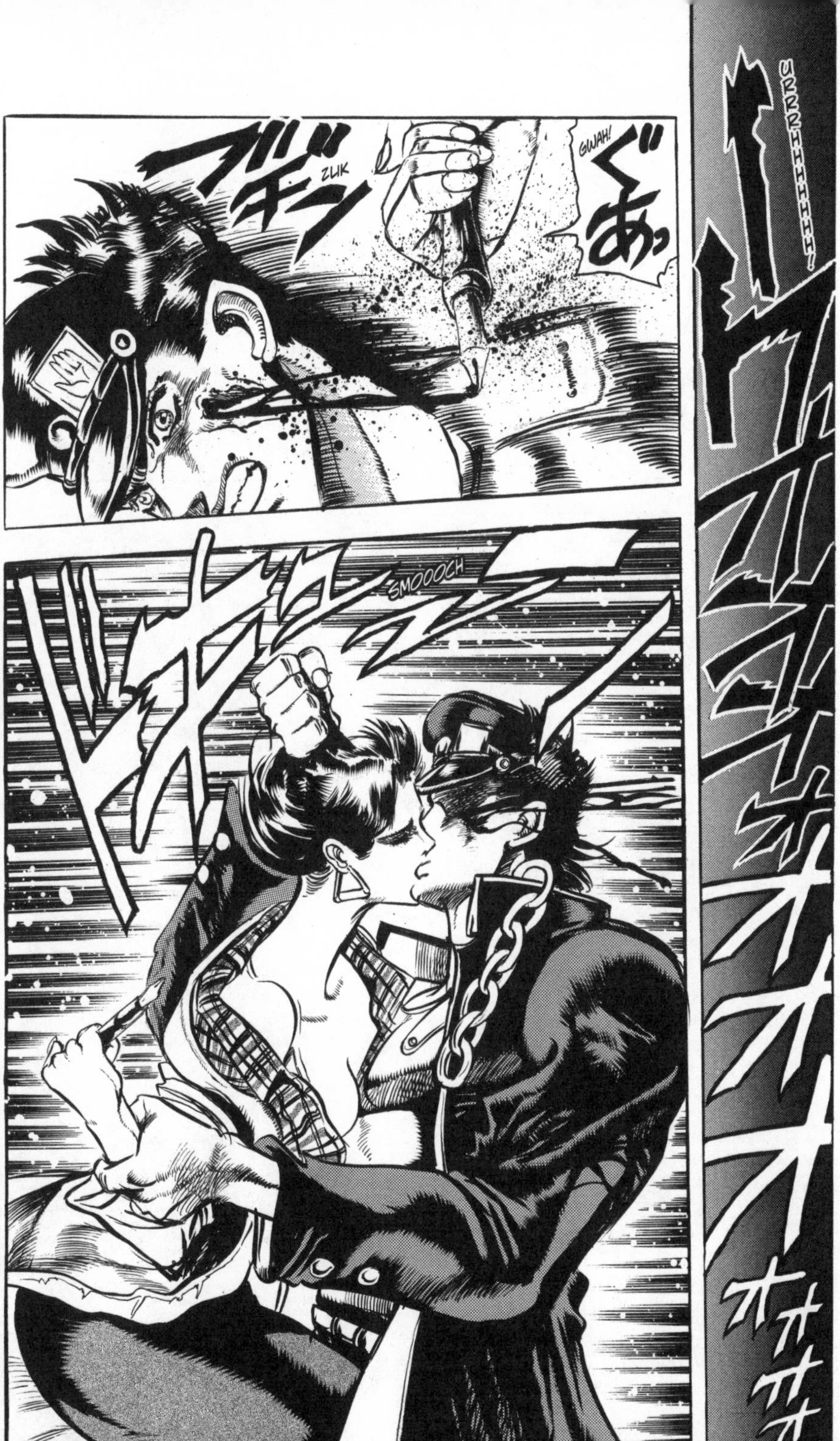
URRRHHHHHHHH!
GWAH!
ぐあっ
ZLIK
SMOOOCH

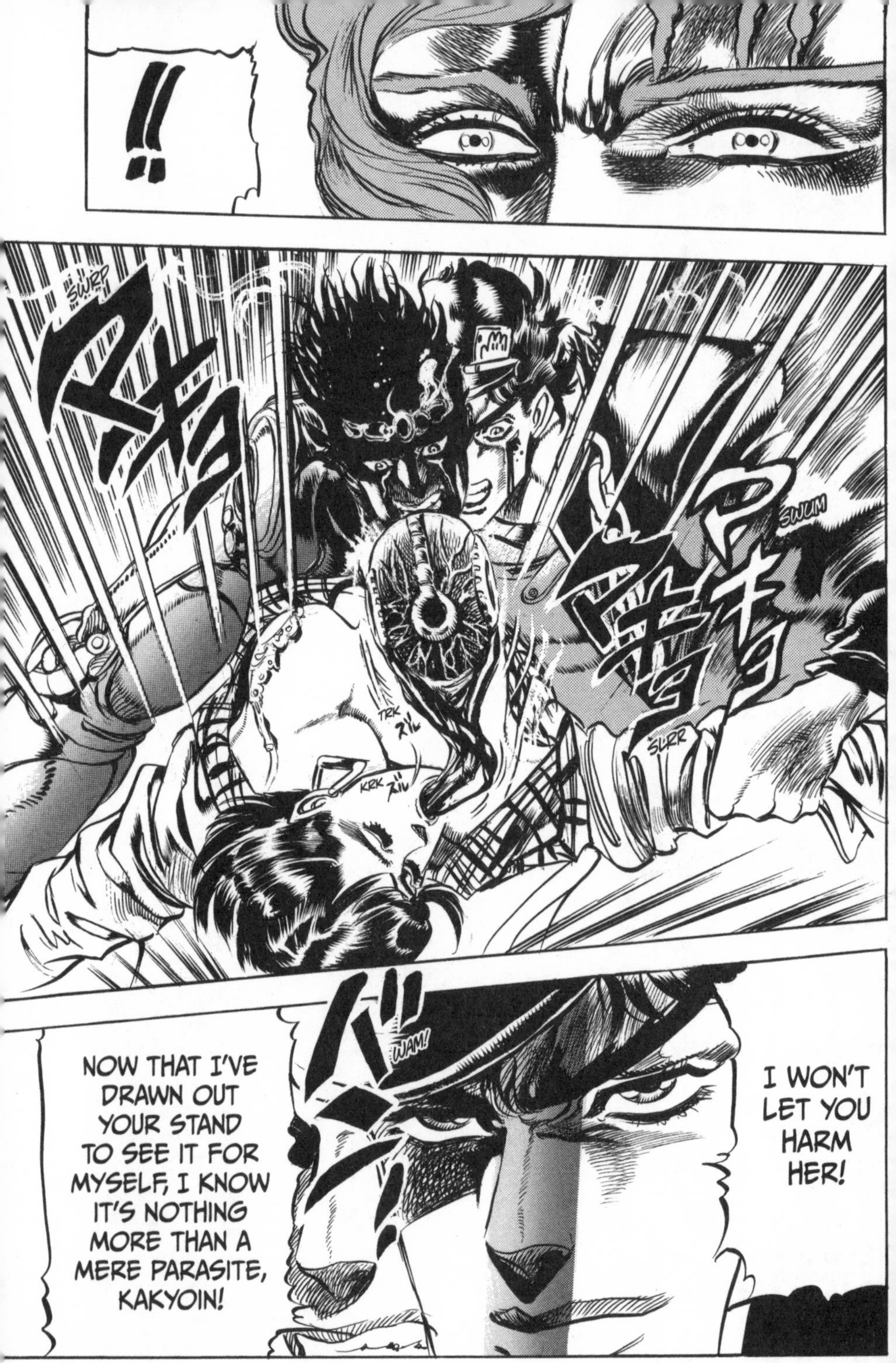
!!
SWRP
SWUM
TRK
KRK
SLRR
I WON'T LET YOU HARM HER!
WAM!
NOW THAT I'VE DRAWN OUT YOUR STAND TO SEE IT FOR MYSELF, I KNOW IT'S NOTHING MORE THAN A MERE PARASITE, KAKYOIN!

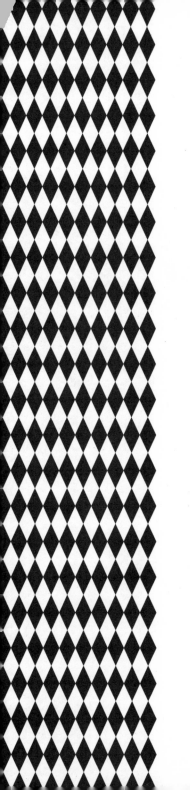

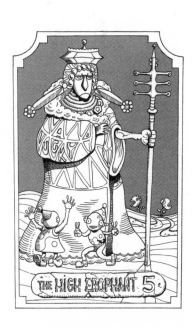

THE HIGH EROPHANT 5

CHAPTER 5: Noriaki Kakyoin PART 2

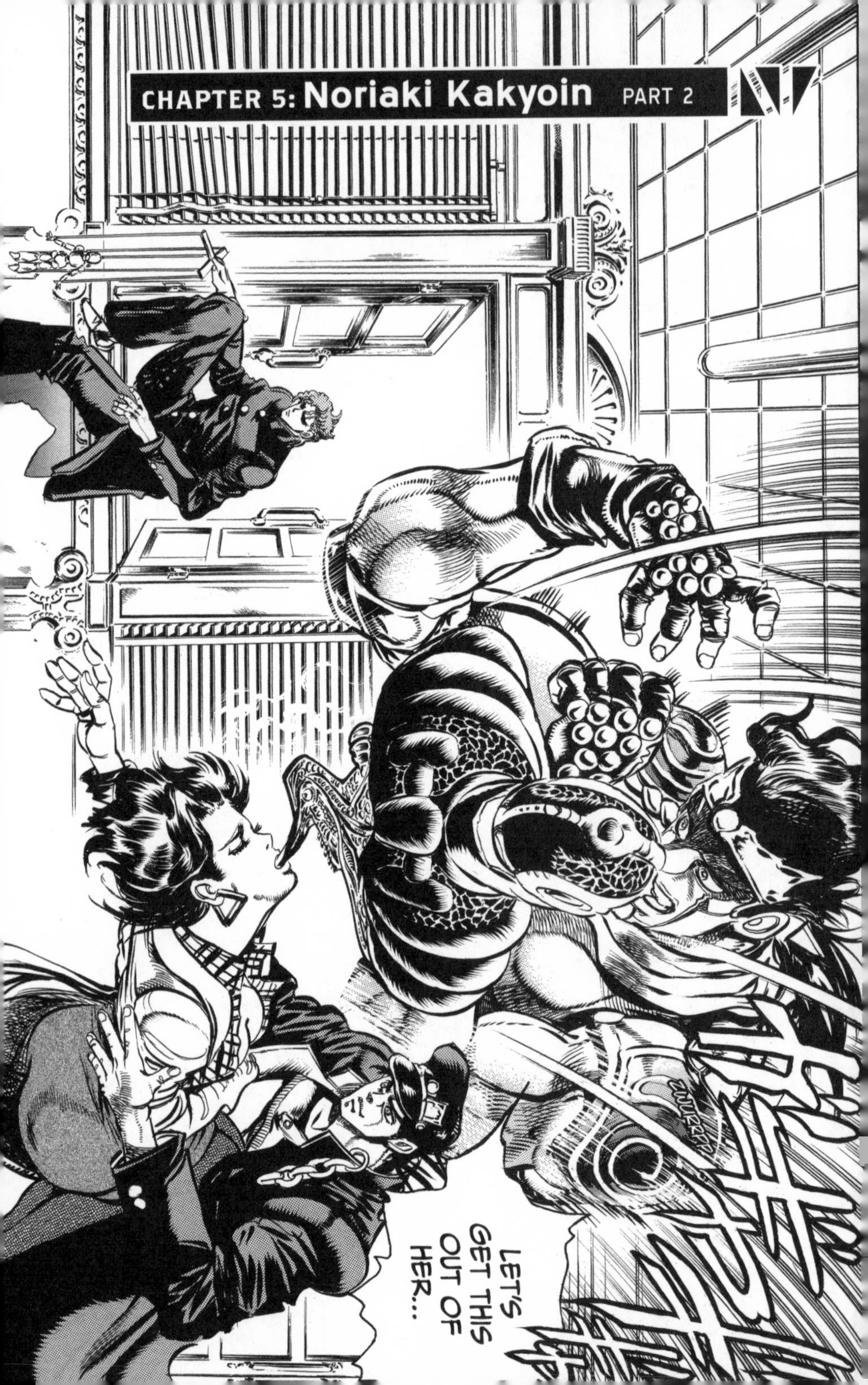
LET'S GET THIS OUT OF HER...

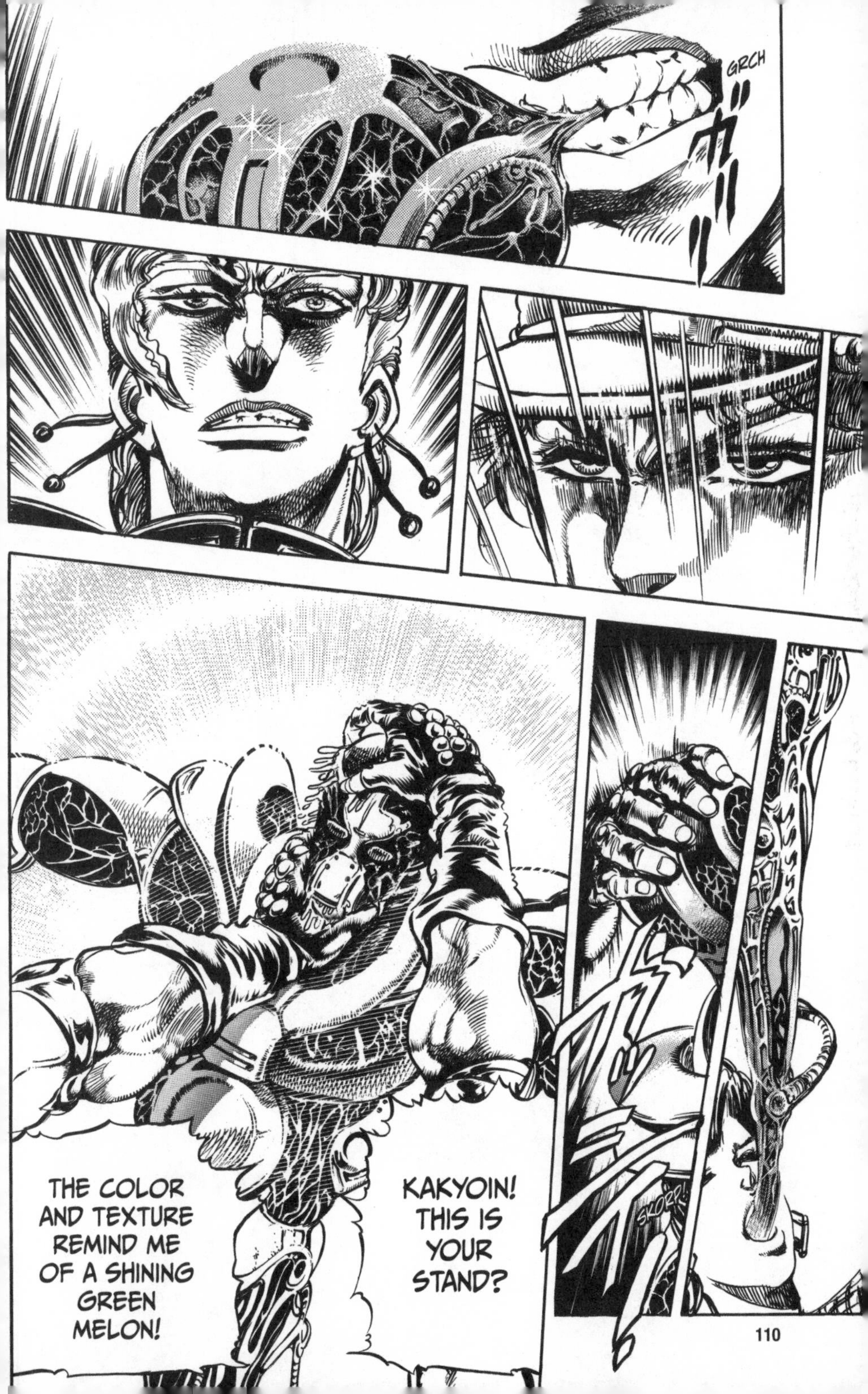
GRCH
SKORR
KAKYOIN! THIS IS YOUR STAND?
THE COLOR AND TEXTURE REMIND ME OF A SHINING GREEN MELON!

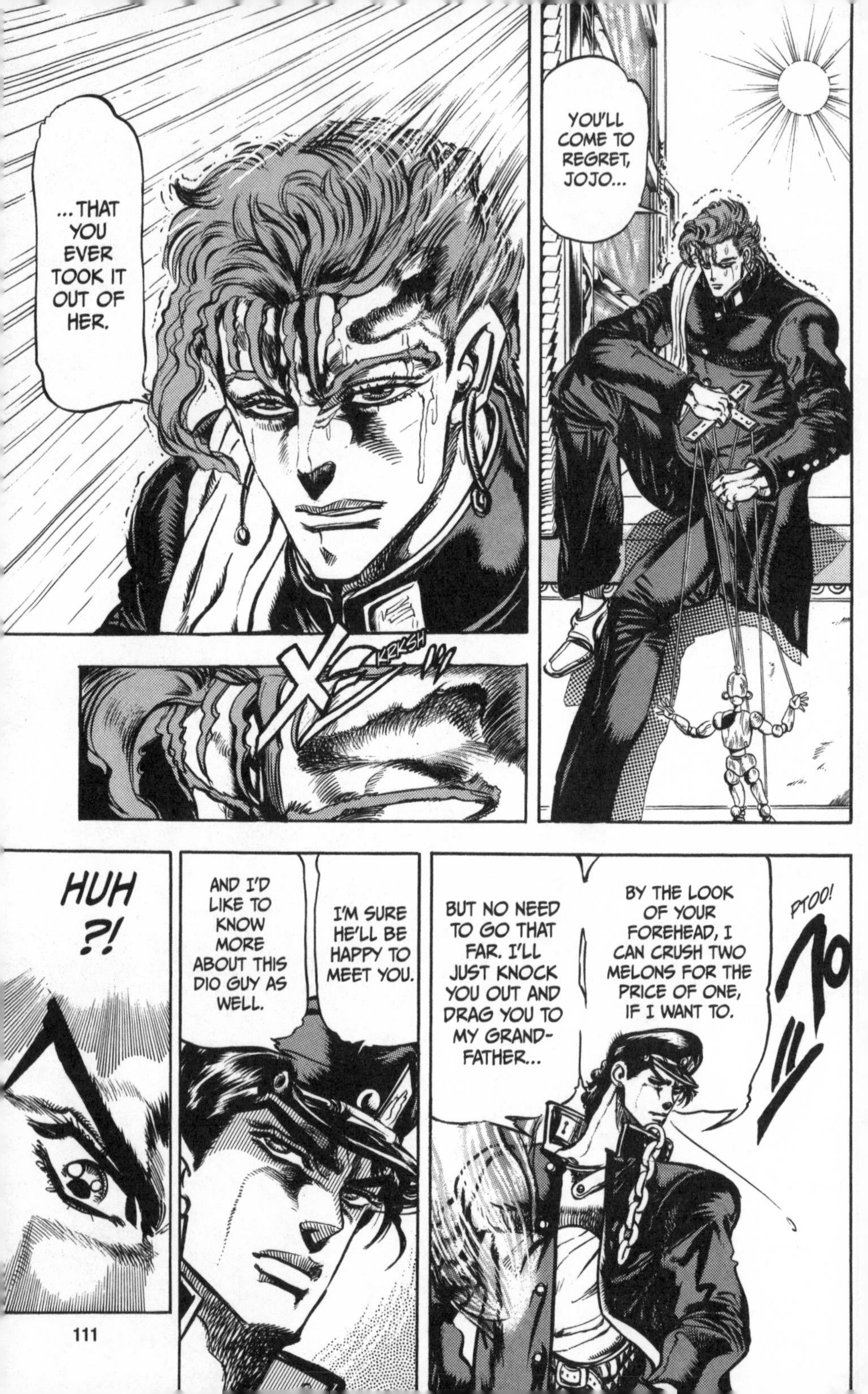
YOU'LL COME TO REGRET, JOJO...
...THAT YOU EVER TOOK IT OUT OF HER.
KRKSH
PTOO!
BY THE LOOK OF YOUR FOREHEAD, I CAN CRUSH TWO MELONS FOR THE PRICE OF ONE, IF I WANT TO.
BUT NO NEED TO GO THAT FAR. I'LL JUST KNOCK YOU OUT AND DRAG YOU TO MY GRAND-FATHER...
I'M SURE HE'LL BE HAPPY TO MEET YOU.
AND I'D LIKE TO KNOW MORE ABOUT THIS DIO GUY AS WELL.
HUH ?!

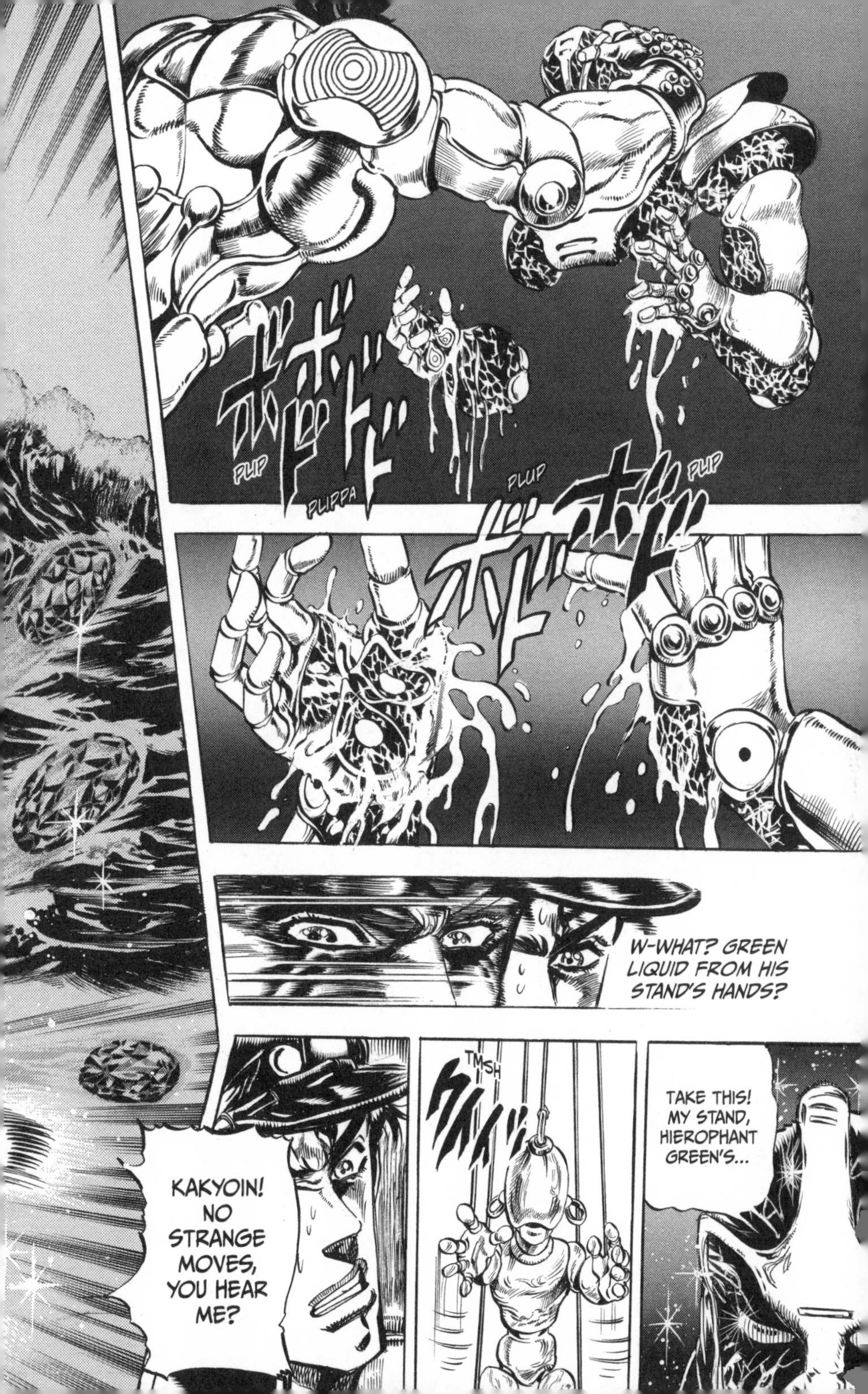
PLUP
PLUP
PLUPPA
PLUP
W-WHAT? GREEN LIQUID FROM HIS STAND'S HANDS?
TAKE THIS! MY STAND, HIEROPHANT GREEN'S...
TMSH
KAKYOIN! NO STRANGE MOVES, YOU HEAR ME?

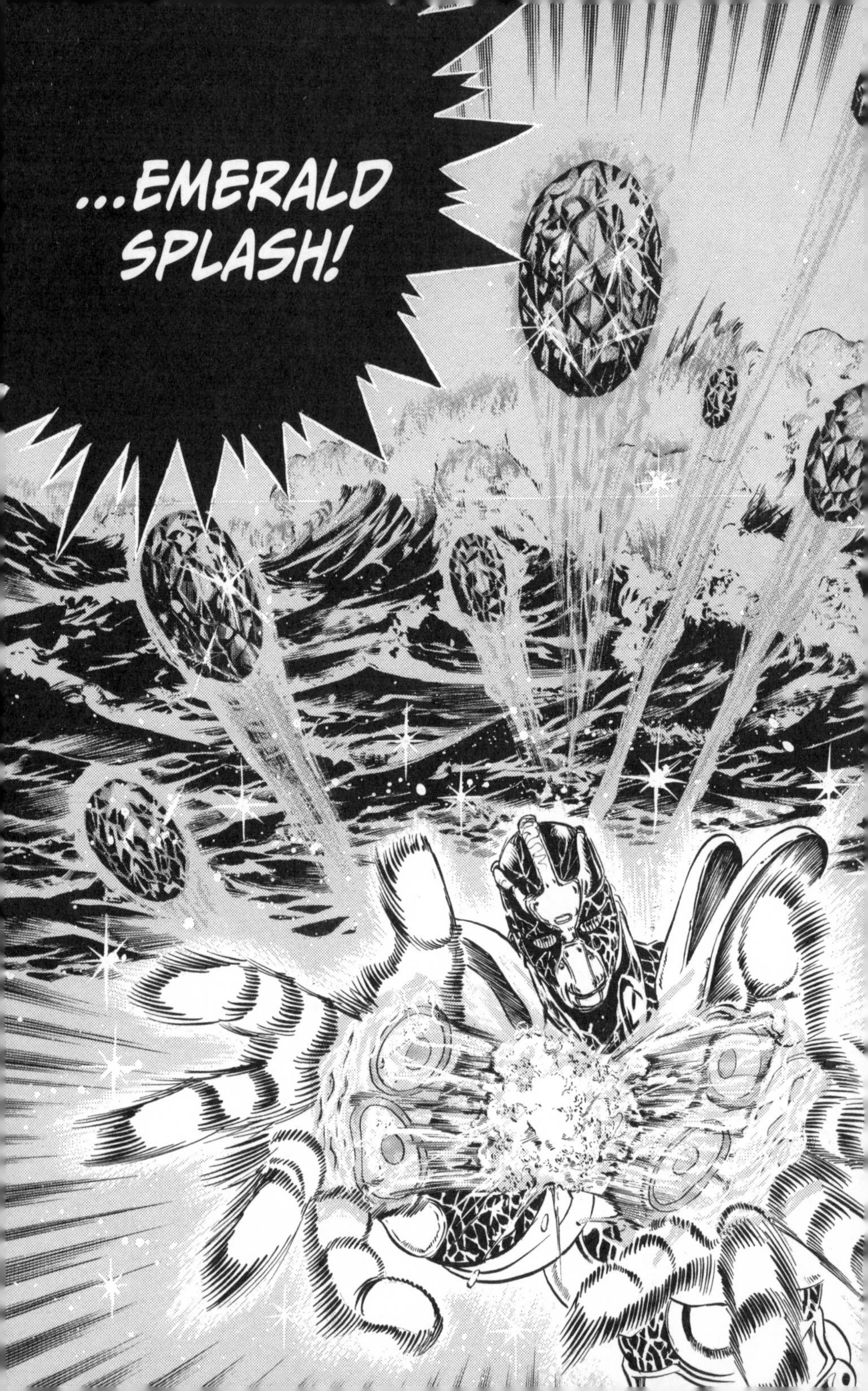
...EMERALD SPLASH!

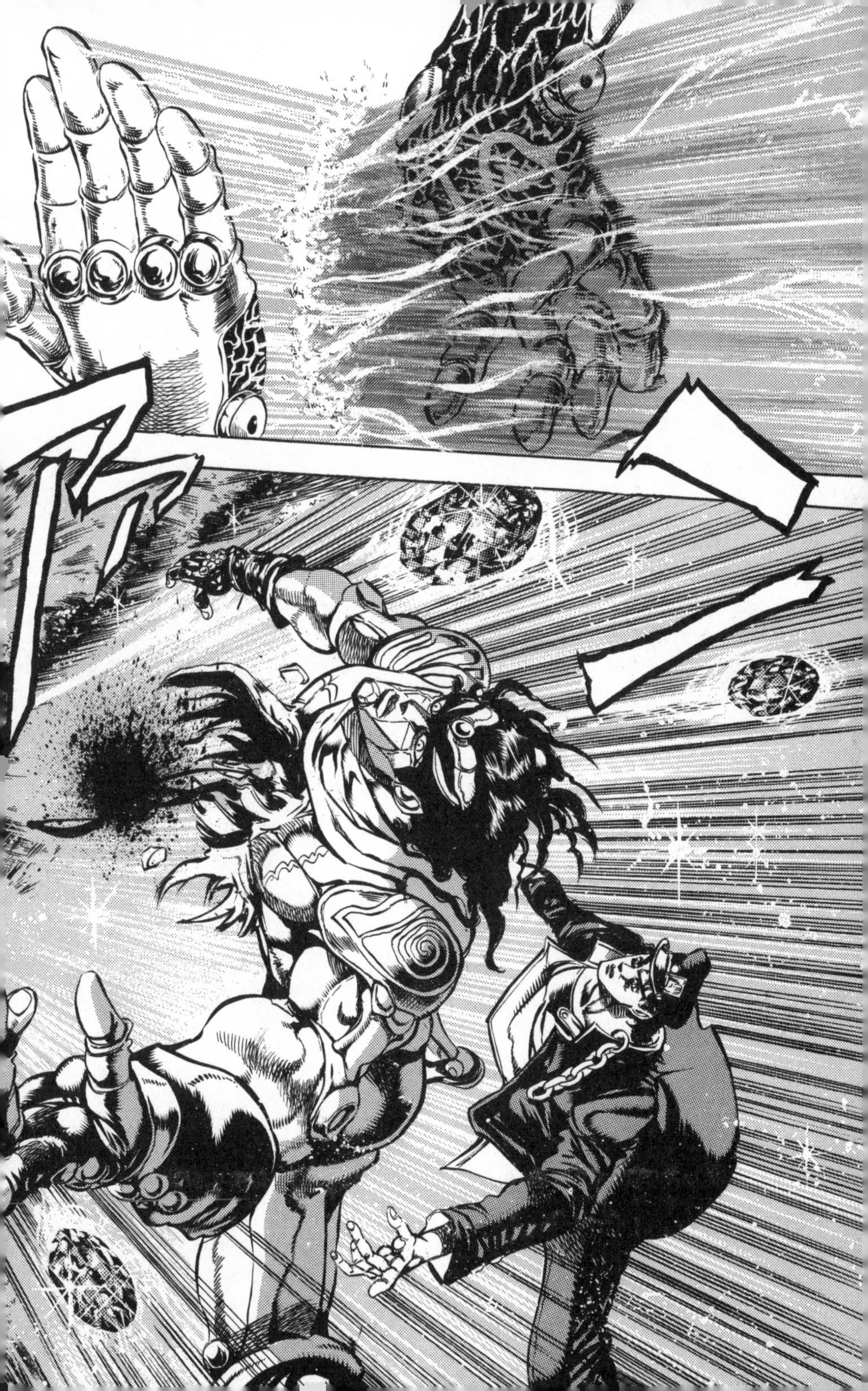

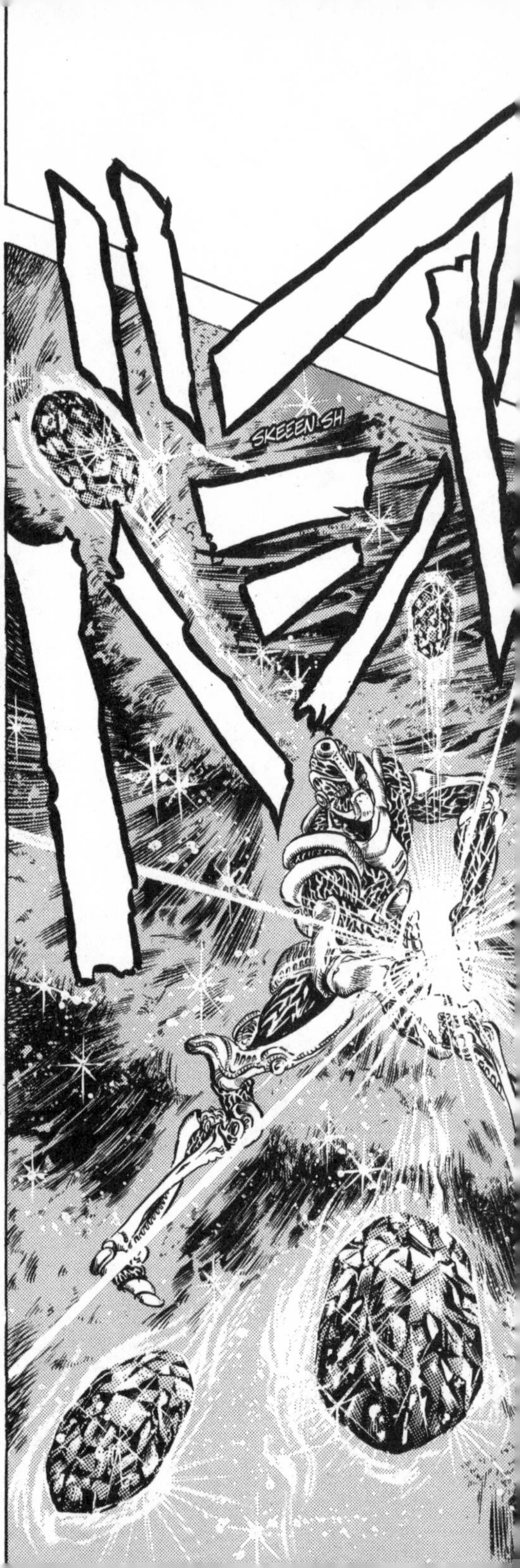
SKEEEN SH
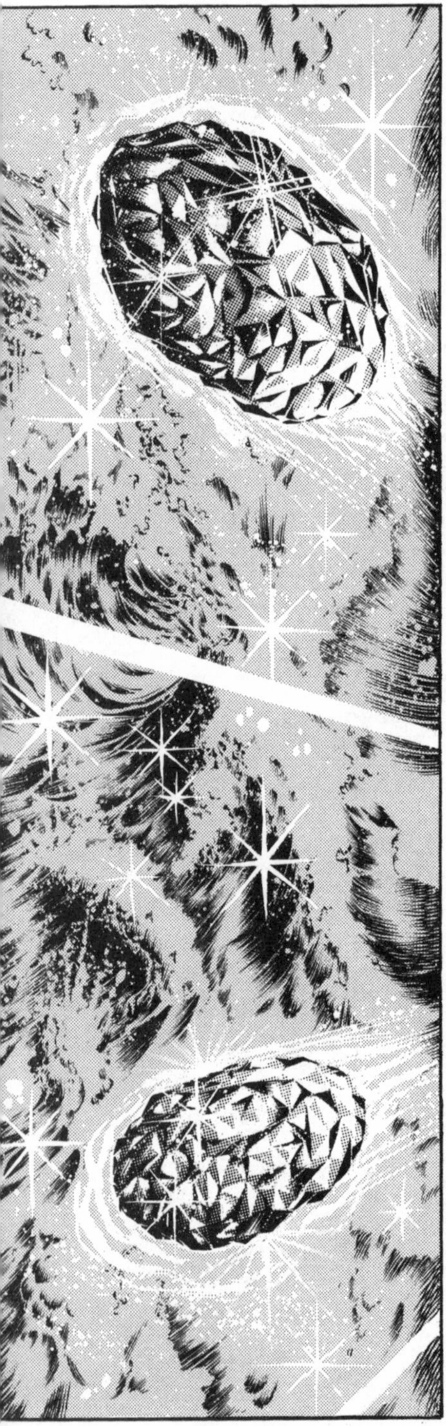

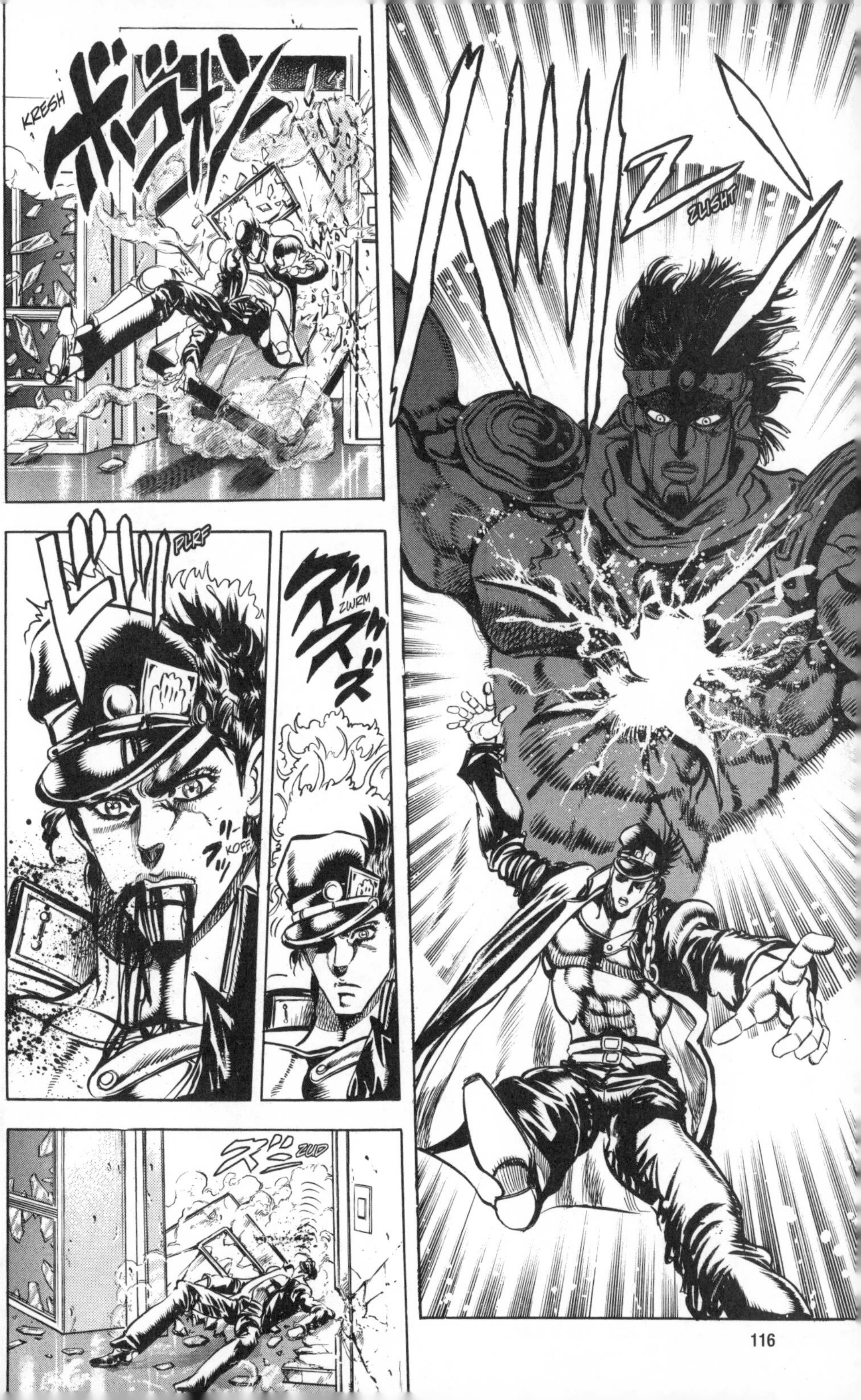
ZLISHT
KRESH
ZWRM
PLRF
KOFF
ZUD

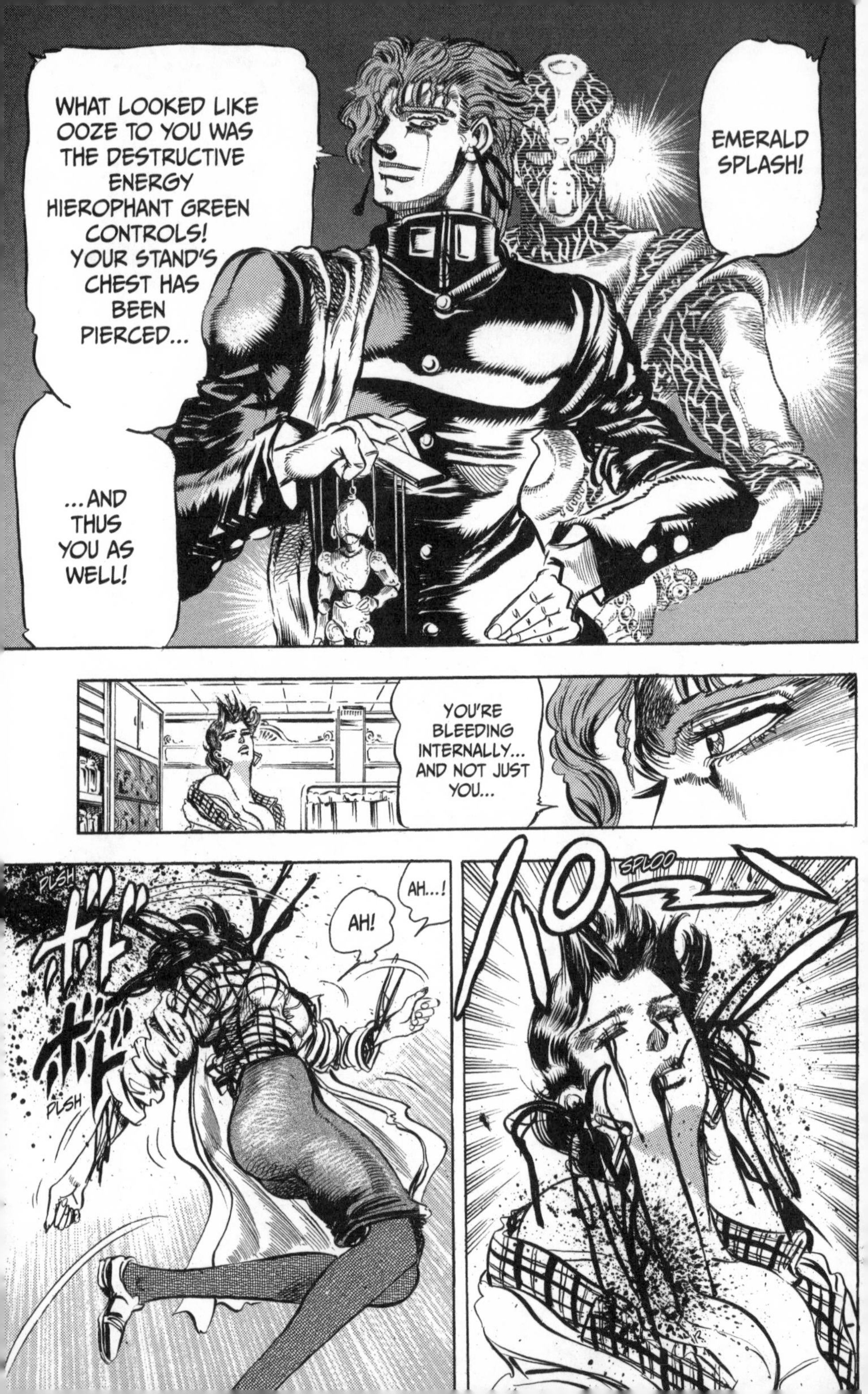

EMERALD SPLASH!
WHAT LOOKED LIKE OOZE TO YOU WAS THE DESTRUCTIVE ENERGY HIEROPHANT GREEN CONTROLS! YOUR STAND'S CHEST HAS BEEN PIERCED...
...AND THUS YOU AS WELL!
YOU'RE BLEEDING INTERNALLY... AND NOT JUST YOU...
SPLOO
AH...!
AH!
PLSH
PLSH

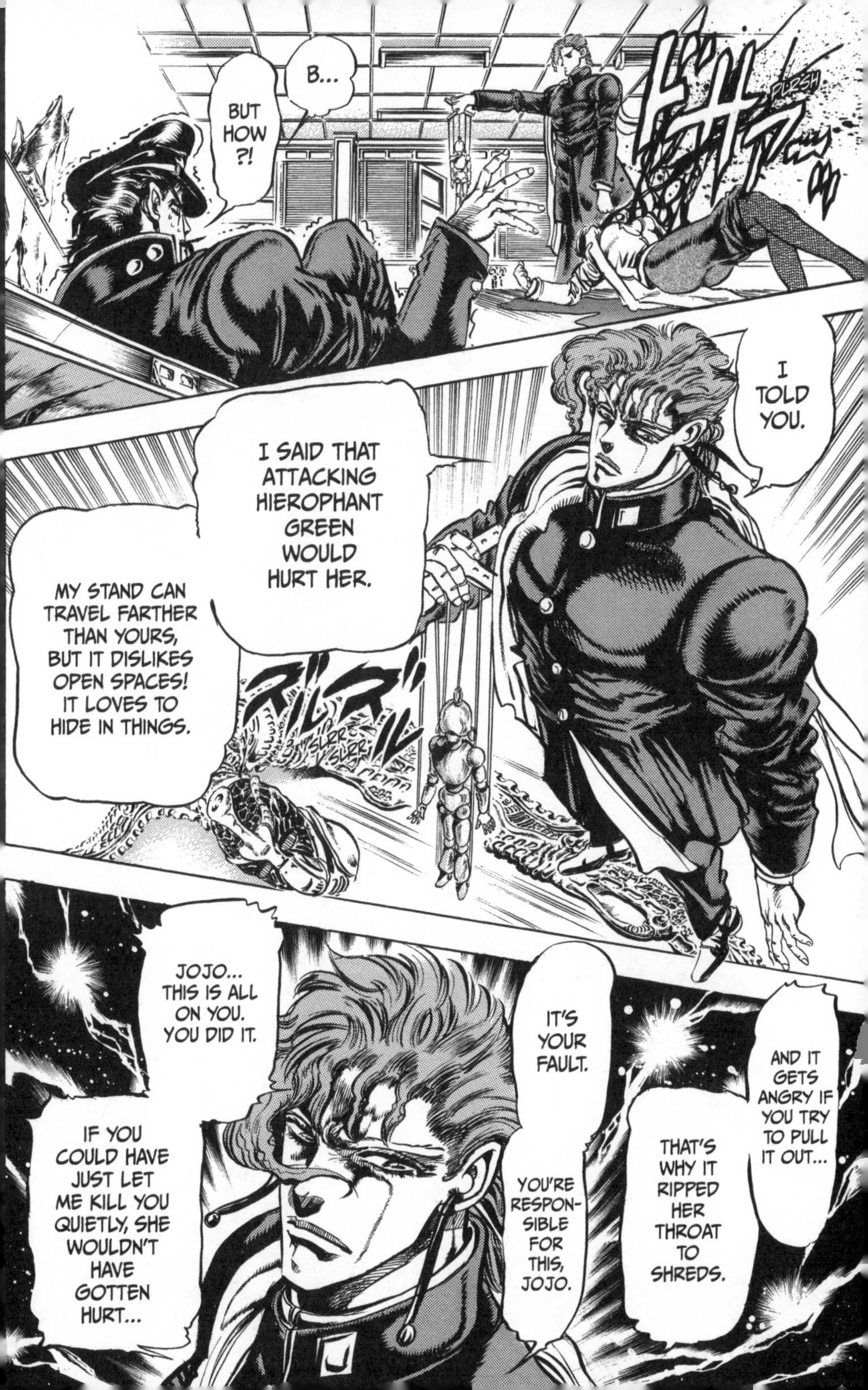
PLRSH
B...
BUT HOW ?!
I TOLD YOU.
I SAID THAT ATTACKING HIEROPHANT GREEN WOULD HURT HER.
MY STAND CAN TRAVEL FARTHER THAN YOURS, BUT IT DISLIKES OPEN SPACES! IT LOVES TO HIDE IN THINGS.
SLRR SLRR
AND IT GETS ANGRY IF YOU TRY TO PULL IT OUT...
THAT'S WHY IT RIPPED HER THROAT TO SHREDS.
IT'S YOUR FAULT.
YOU'RE RESPONSIBLE FOR THIS, JOJO.
JOJO... THIS IS ALL ON YOU. YOU DID IT.
IF YOU COULD HAVE JUST LET ME KILL YOU QUIETLY, SHE WOULDN'T HAVE GOTTEN HURT...

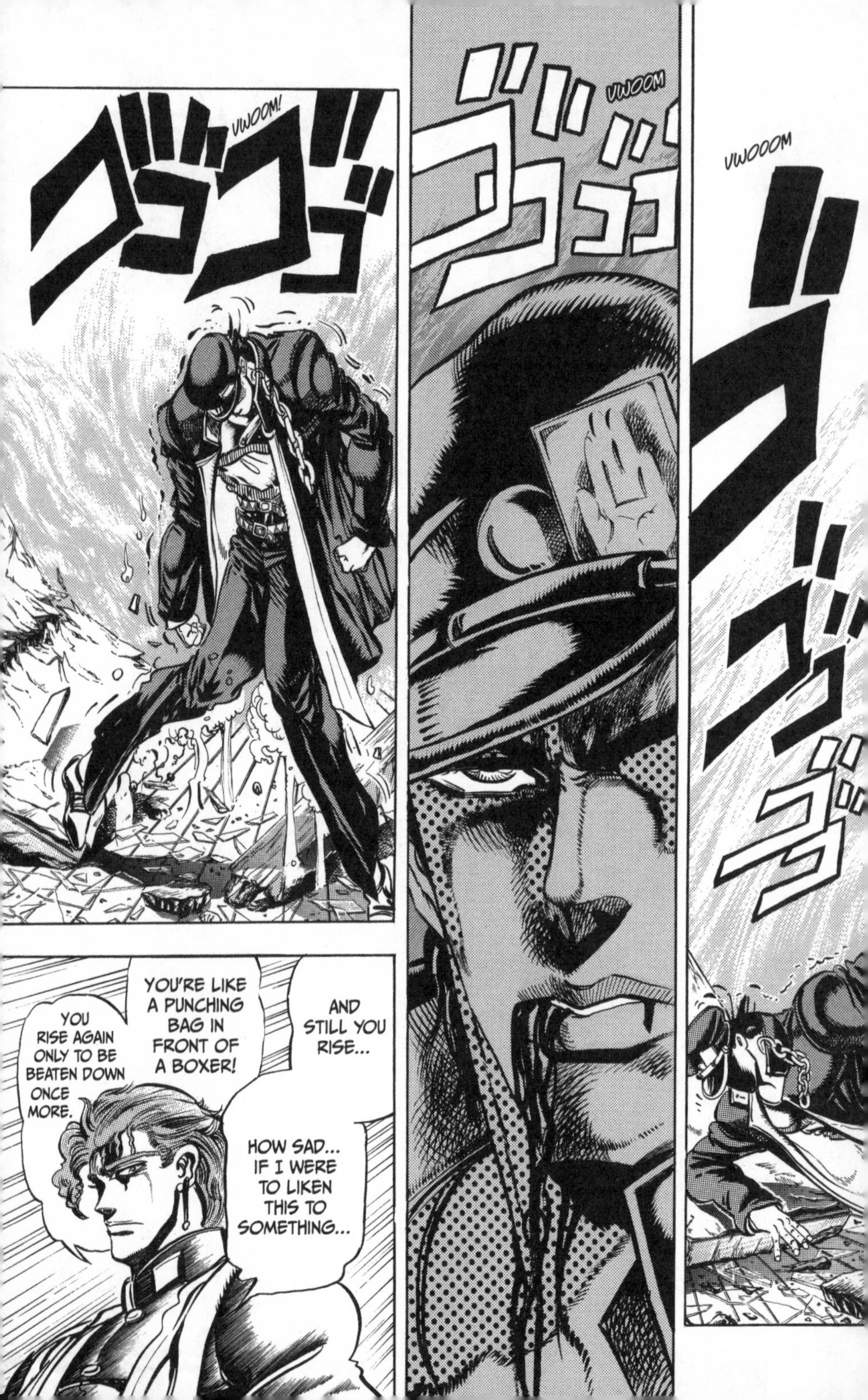
VWOOOM
VWOOM
VWOOM!
AND STILL YOU RISE...
HOW SAD... IF I WERE TO LIKEN THIS TO SOMETHING...
YOU'RE LIKE A PUNCHING BAG IN FRONT OF A BOXER!
YOU RISE AGAIN ONLY TO BE BEATEN DOWN ONCE MORE.

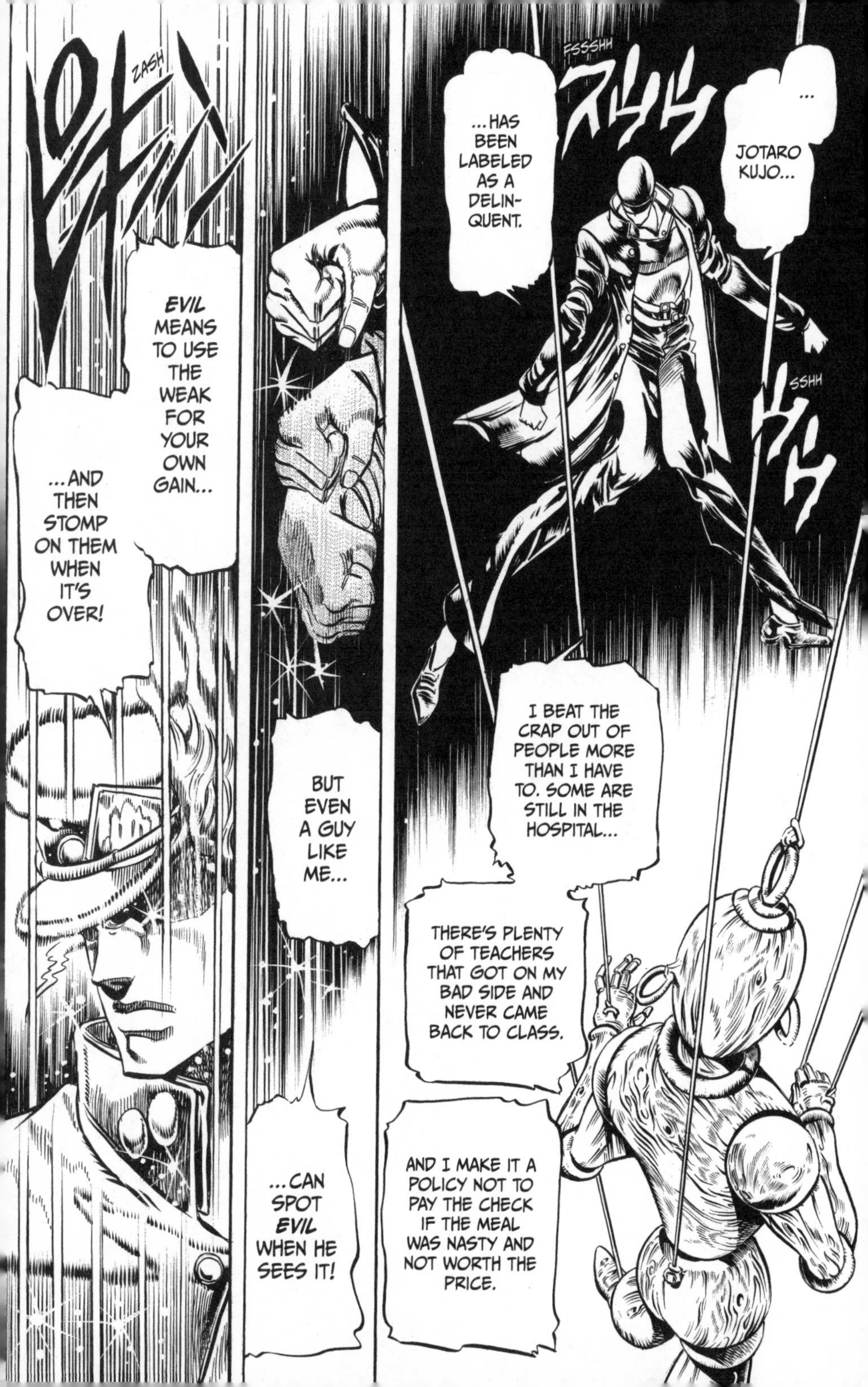
...
JOTARO KUJO...
SSHH
FSSSHH
...HAS BEEN LABELED AS A DELINQUENT.
I BEAT THE CRAP OUT OF PEOPLE MORE THAN I HAVE TO. SOME ARE STILL IN THE HOSPITAL...
THERE'S PLENTY OF TEACHERS THAT GOT ON MY BAD SIDE AND NEVER CAME BACK TO CLASS.
AND I MAKE IT A POLICY NOT TO PAY THE CHECK IF THE MEAL WAS NASTY AND NOT WORTH THE PRICE.
BUT EVEN A GUY LIKE ME...
...CAN SPOT *EVIL* WHEN HE SEES IT!
ZASH
EVIL MEANS TO USE THE WEAK FOR YOUR OWN GAIN...
...AND THEN STOMP ON THEM WHEN IT'S OVER!

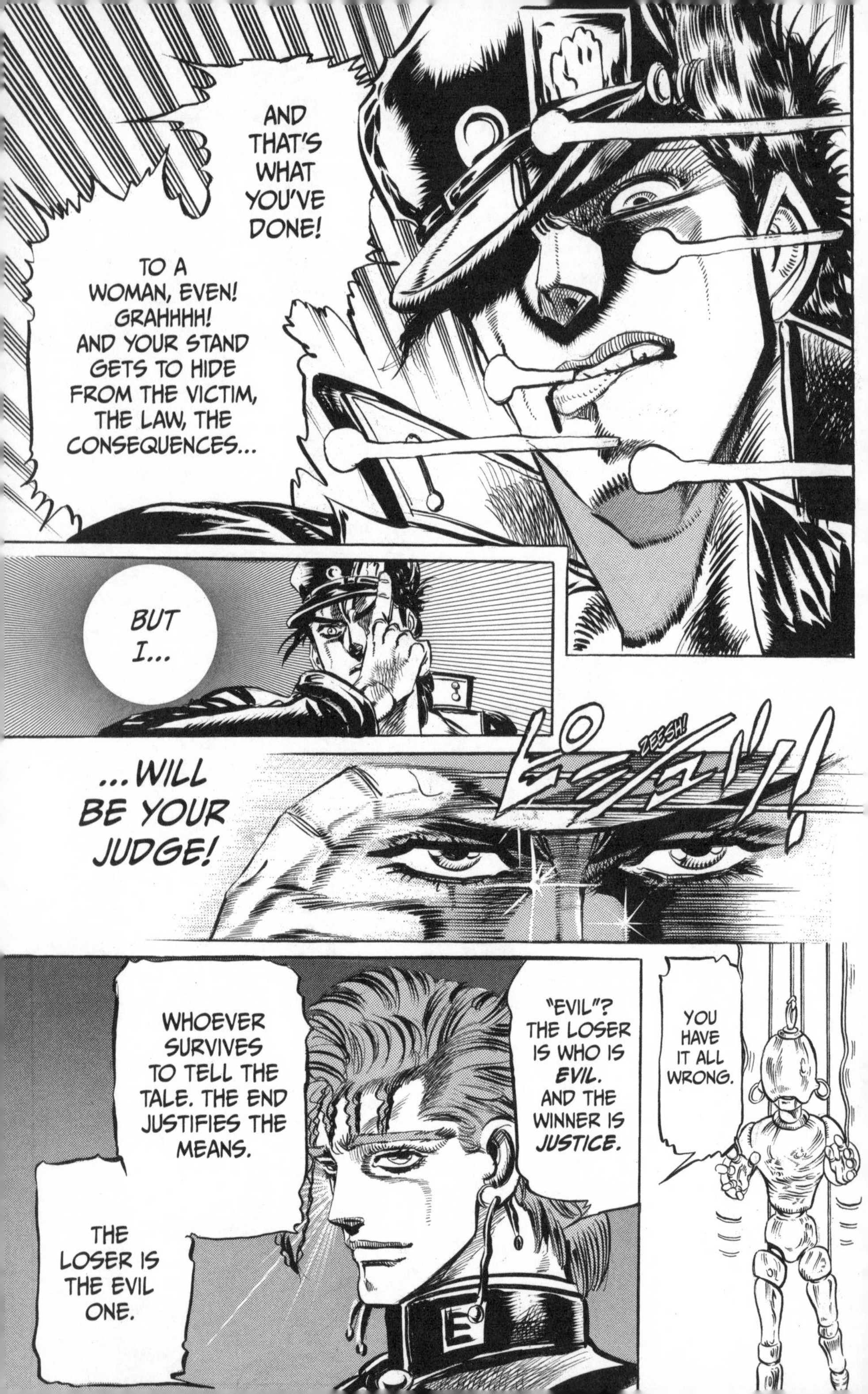
AND THAT'S WHAT YOU'VE DONE!
TO A WOMAN, EVEN! GRAHHHH! AND YOUR STAND GETS TO HIDE FROM THE VICTIM, THE LAW, THE CONSEQUENCES...
BUT I...
ZEESH!
...WILL BE YOUR JUDGE!
YOU HAVE IT ALL WRONG.
"EVIL"? THE LOSER IS WHO IS *EVIL*. AND THE WINNER IS *JUSTICE*.
WHOEVER SURVIVES TO TELL THE TALE. THE END JUSTIFIES THE MEANS.
THE LOSER IS THE EVIL ONE.

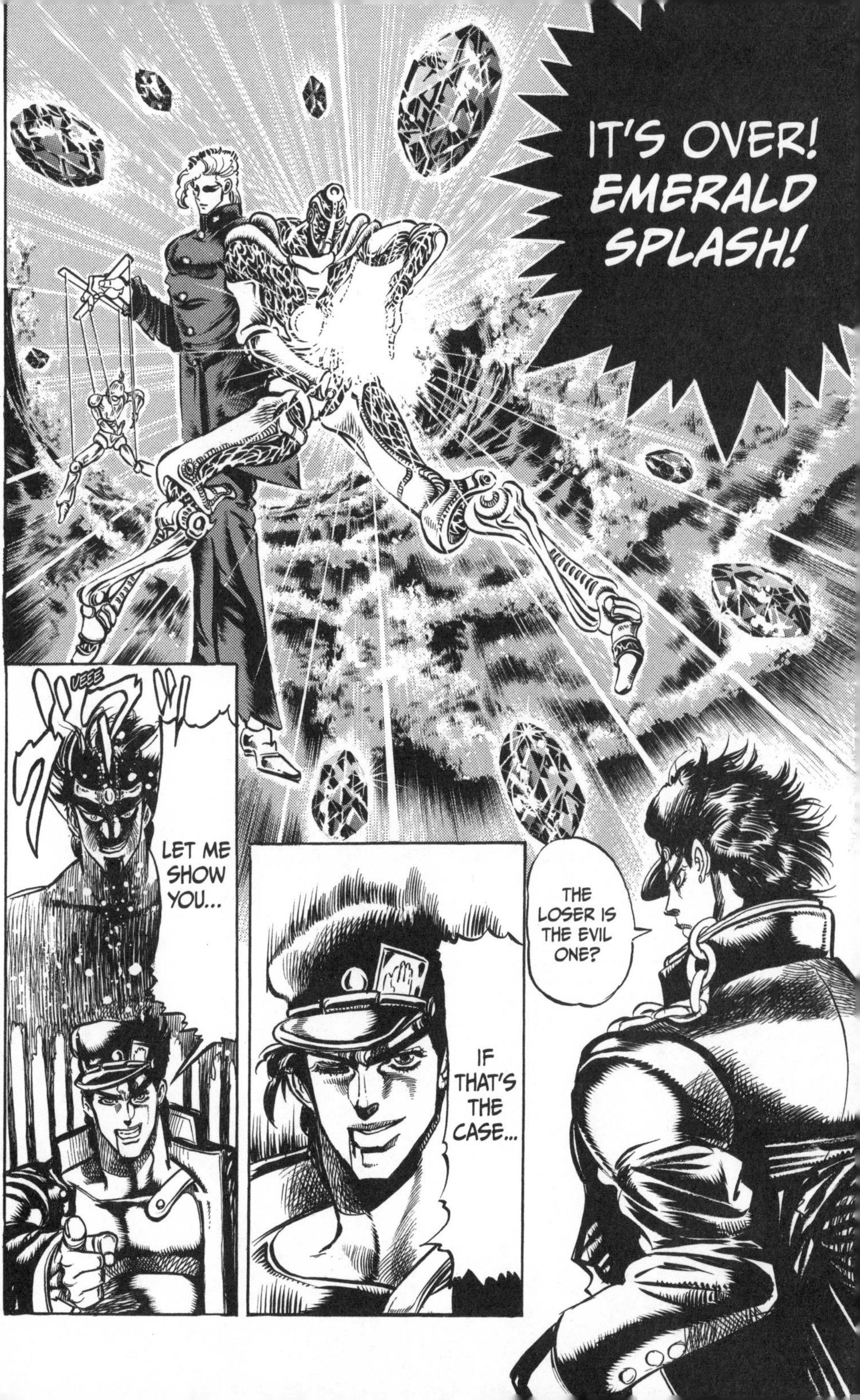
IT'S OVER! EMERALD SPLASH!
THE LOSER IS THE EVIL ONE?
IF THAT'S THE CASE...
VEEE
LET ME SHOW YOU...

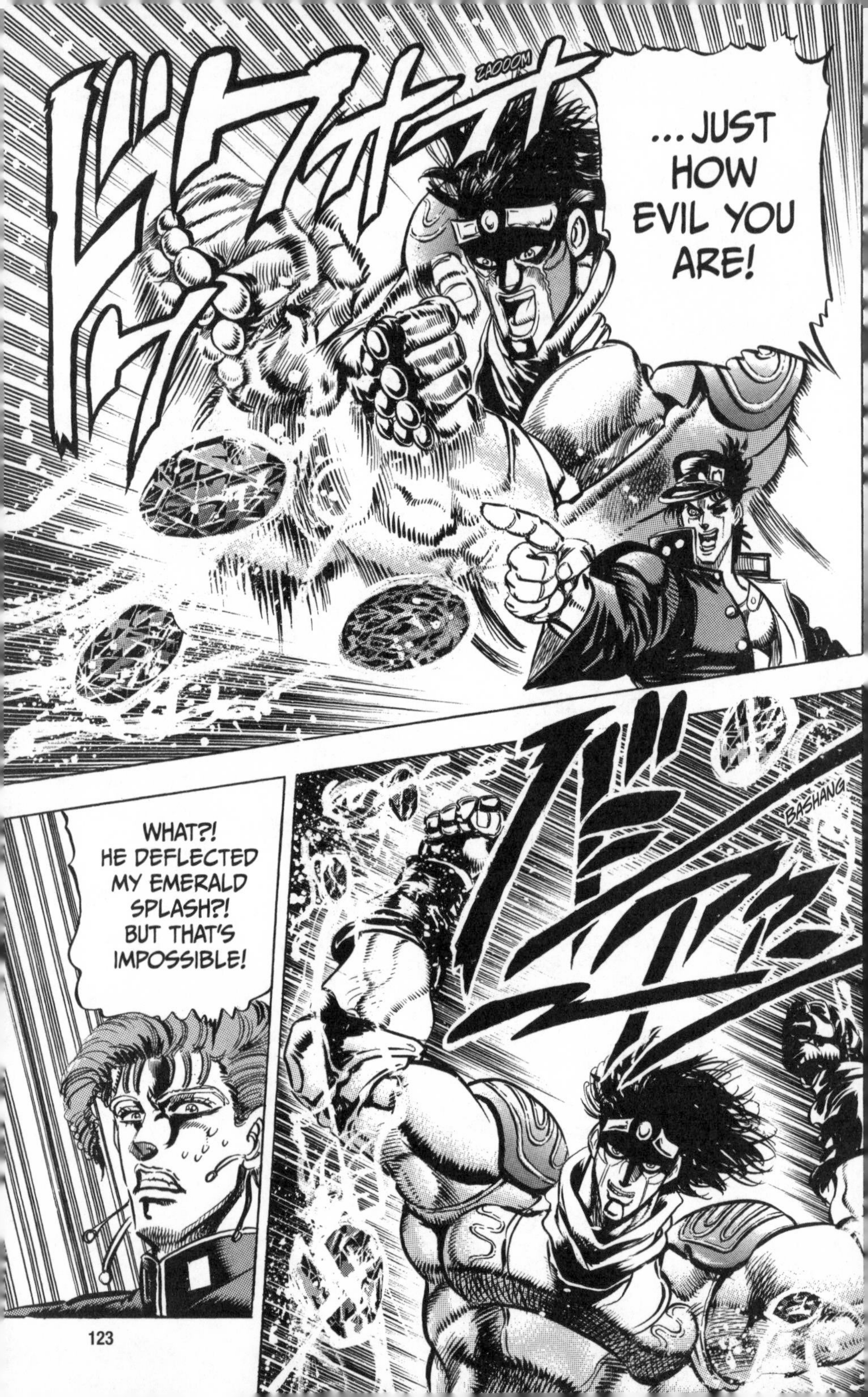
ZAOOOM
...JUST HOW EVIL YOU ARE!
BASHANG
WHAT?! HE DEFLECTED MY EMERALD SPLASH?! BUT THAT'S IMPOSSIBLE!

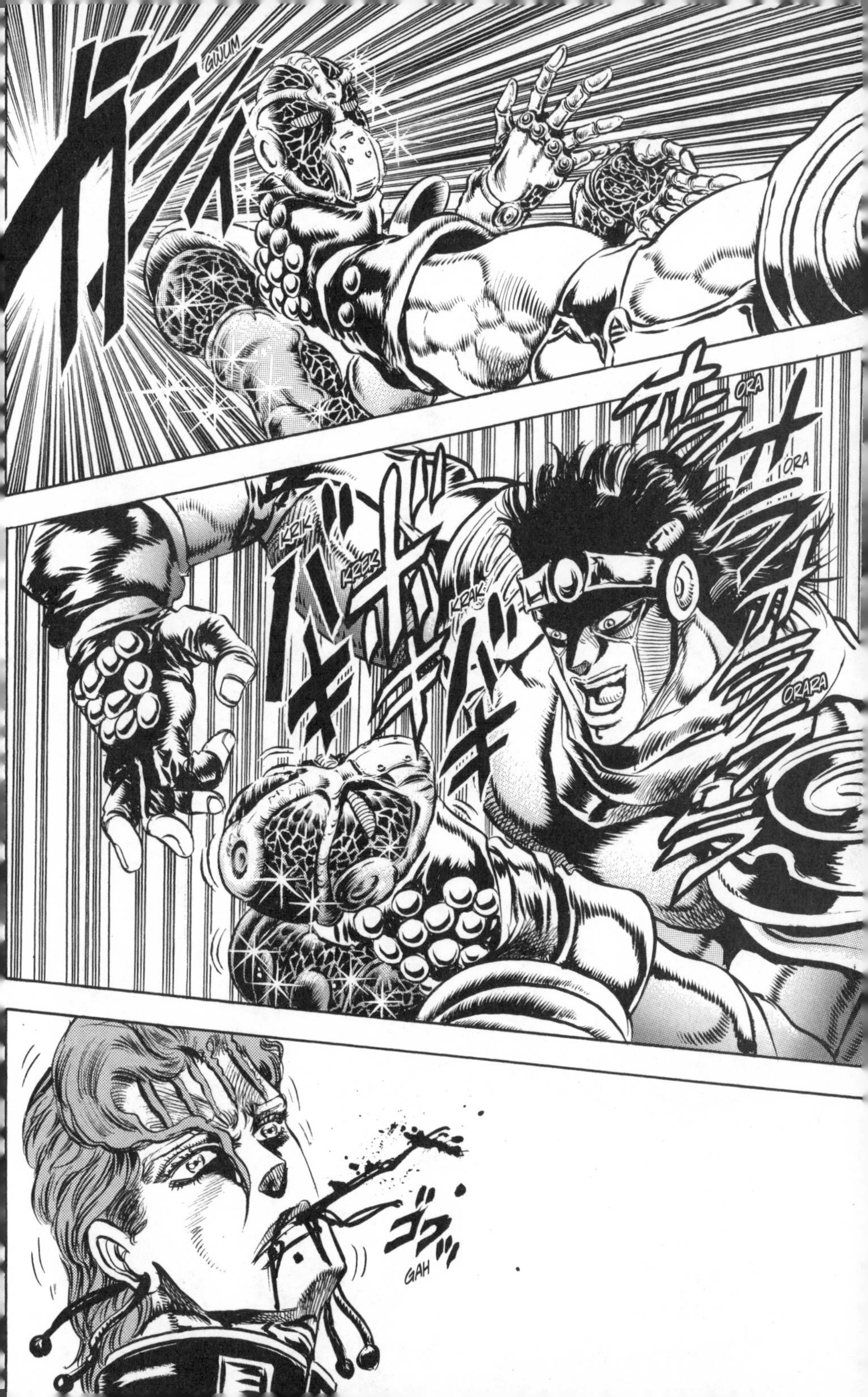
GWUM
ORA
ORA
ORARA
KRIK
KREK
KRAK
GAH

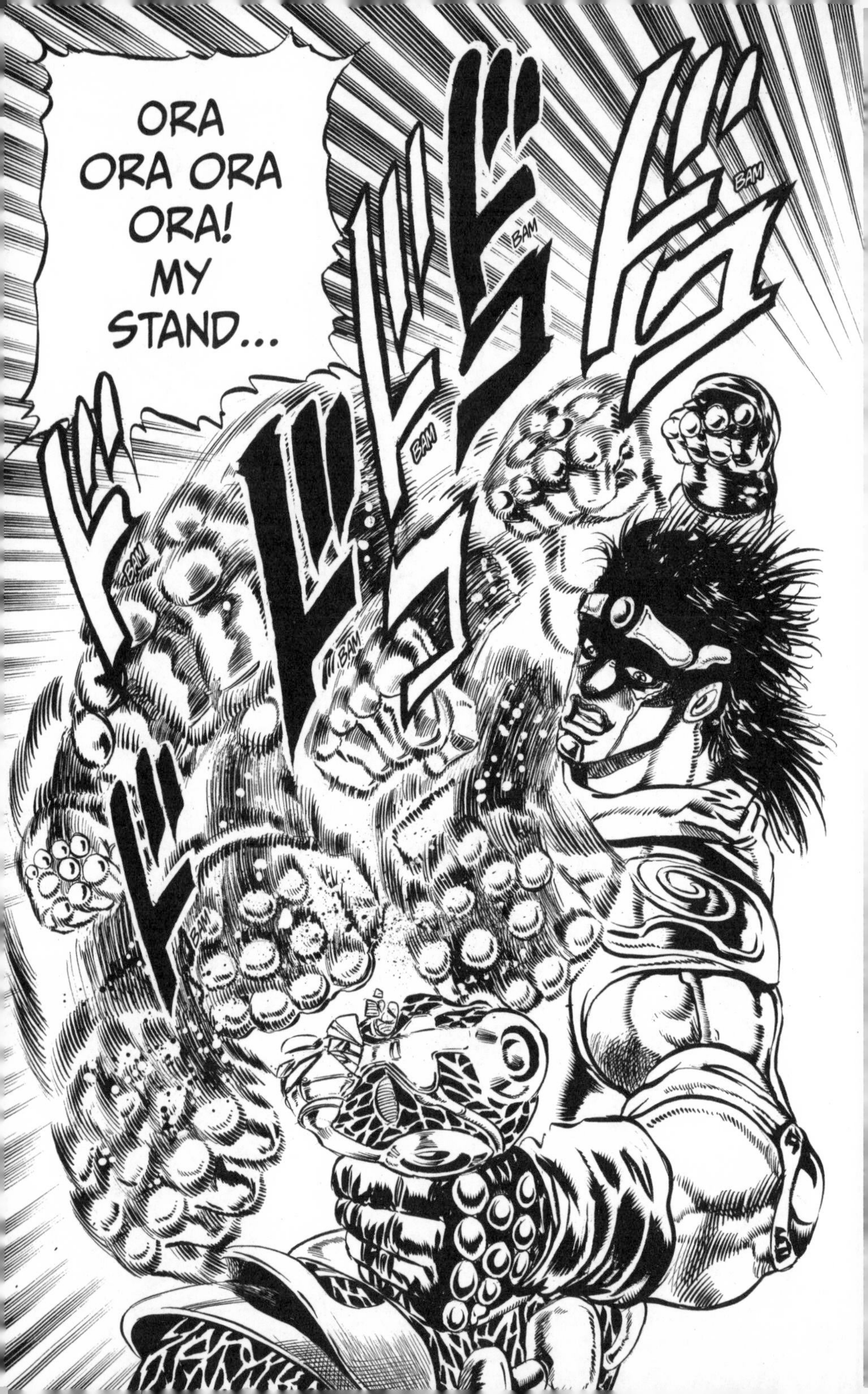
ORA ORA ORA ORA ORA! MY STAND...
BAM
BAM
BAM
BAM
BAM
BAM

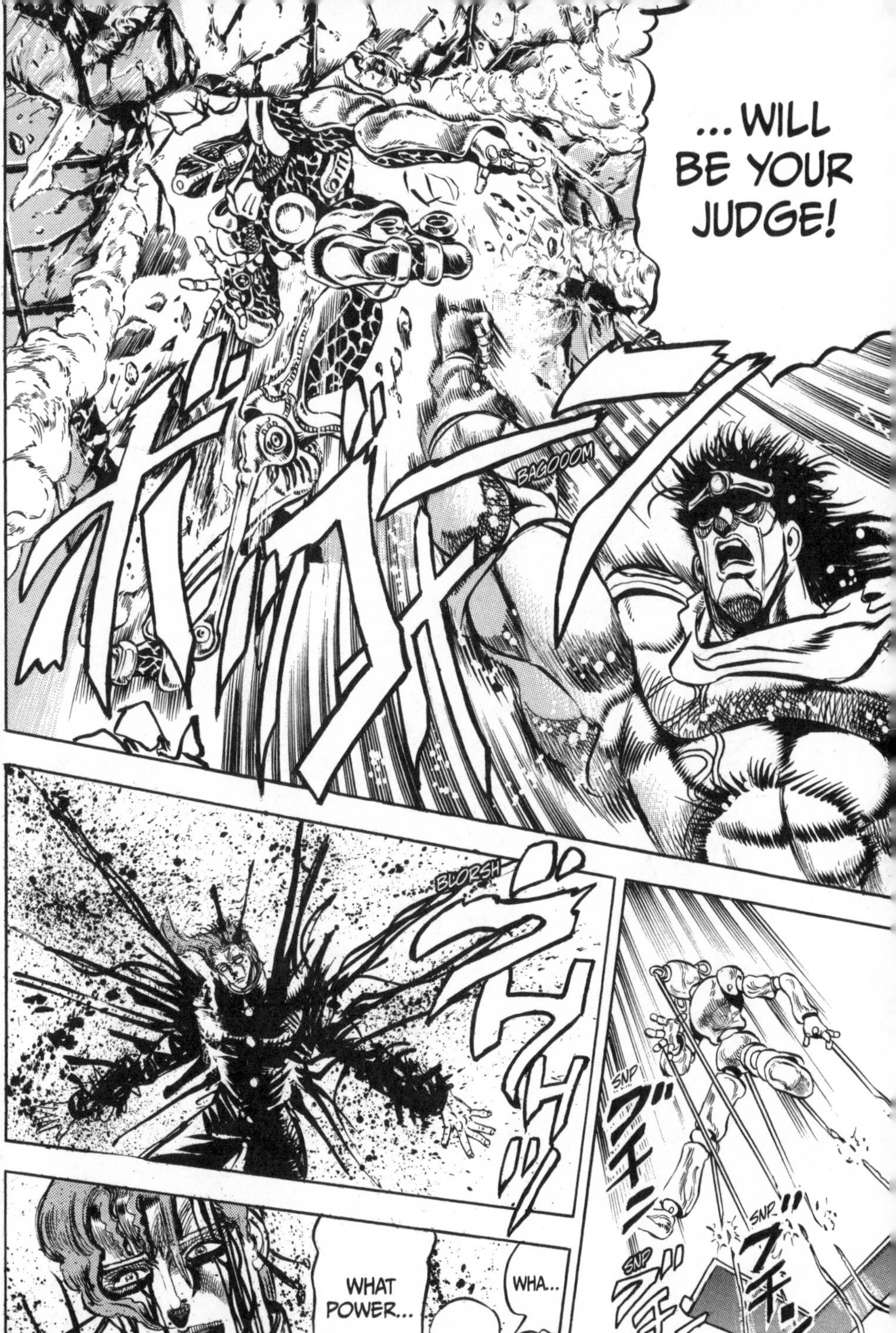

...WILL BE YOUR JUDGE!
BAGOOOM
SNP
SNP
SNP
BLORSH
WHA...
...
WHAT POWER...

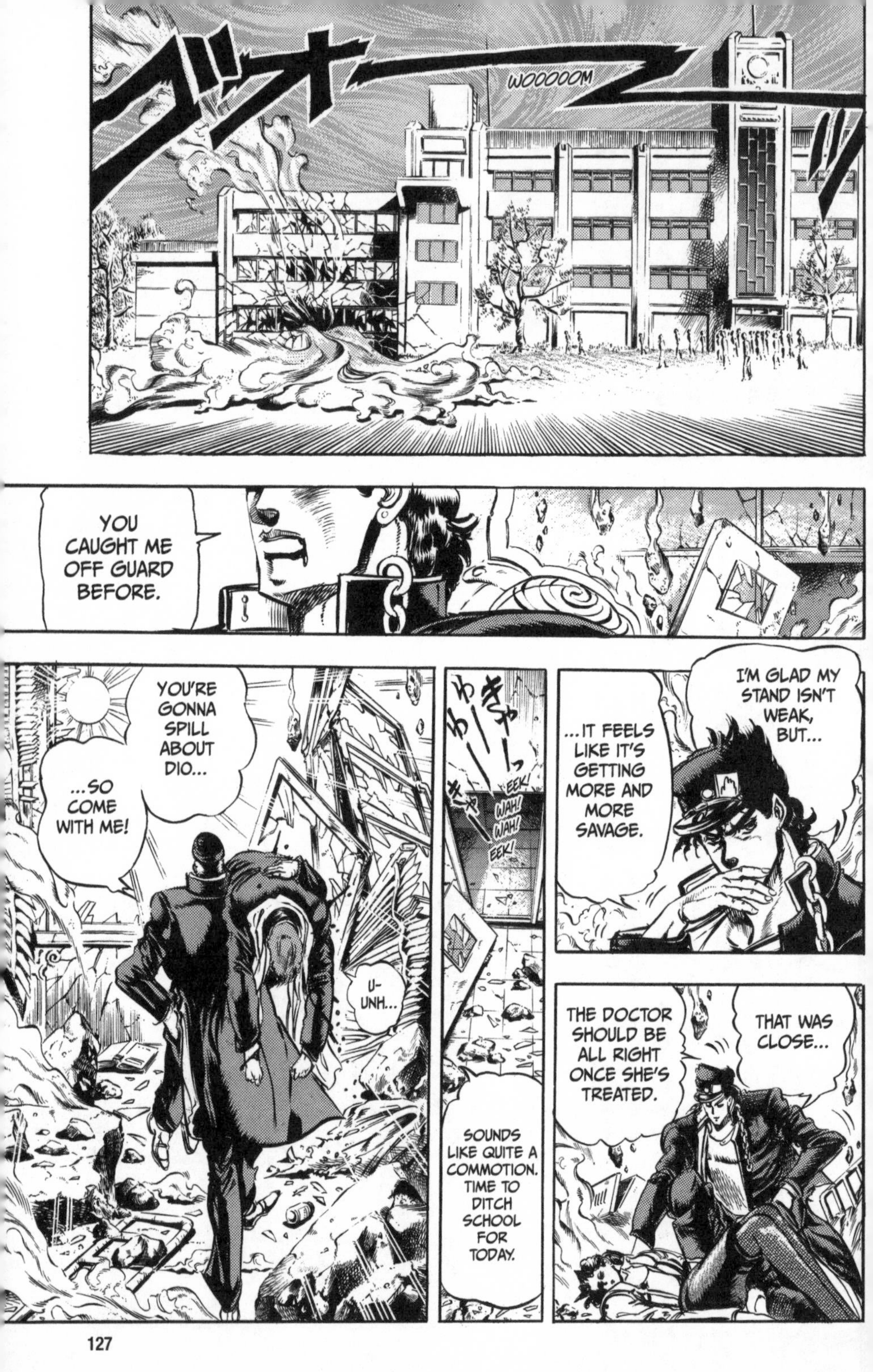
WOOOOOM
YOU CAUGHT ME OFF GUARD BEFORE.
I'M GLAD MY STAND ISN'T WEAK, BUT...
...IT FEELS LIKE IT'S GETTING MORE AND MORE SAVAGE.
THAT WAS CLOSE...
THE DOCTOR SHOULD BE ALL RIGHT ONCE SHE'S TREATED.
EEK!
WAH!
WAH!
EEK!
U-UNH...
SOUNDS LIKE QUITE A COMMOTION. TIME TO DITCH SCHOOL FOR TODAY.
YOU'RE GONNA SPILL ABOUT DIO...
...SO COME WITH ME!

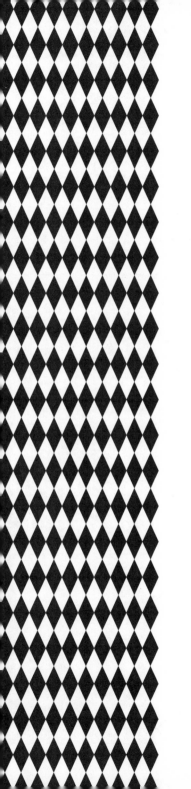

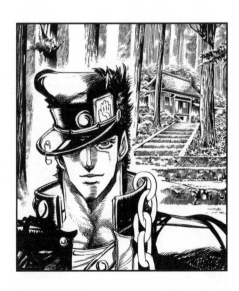

CHAPTER 7: Noriaki Kakyoin PART 3

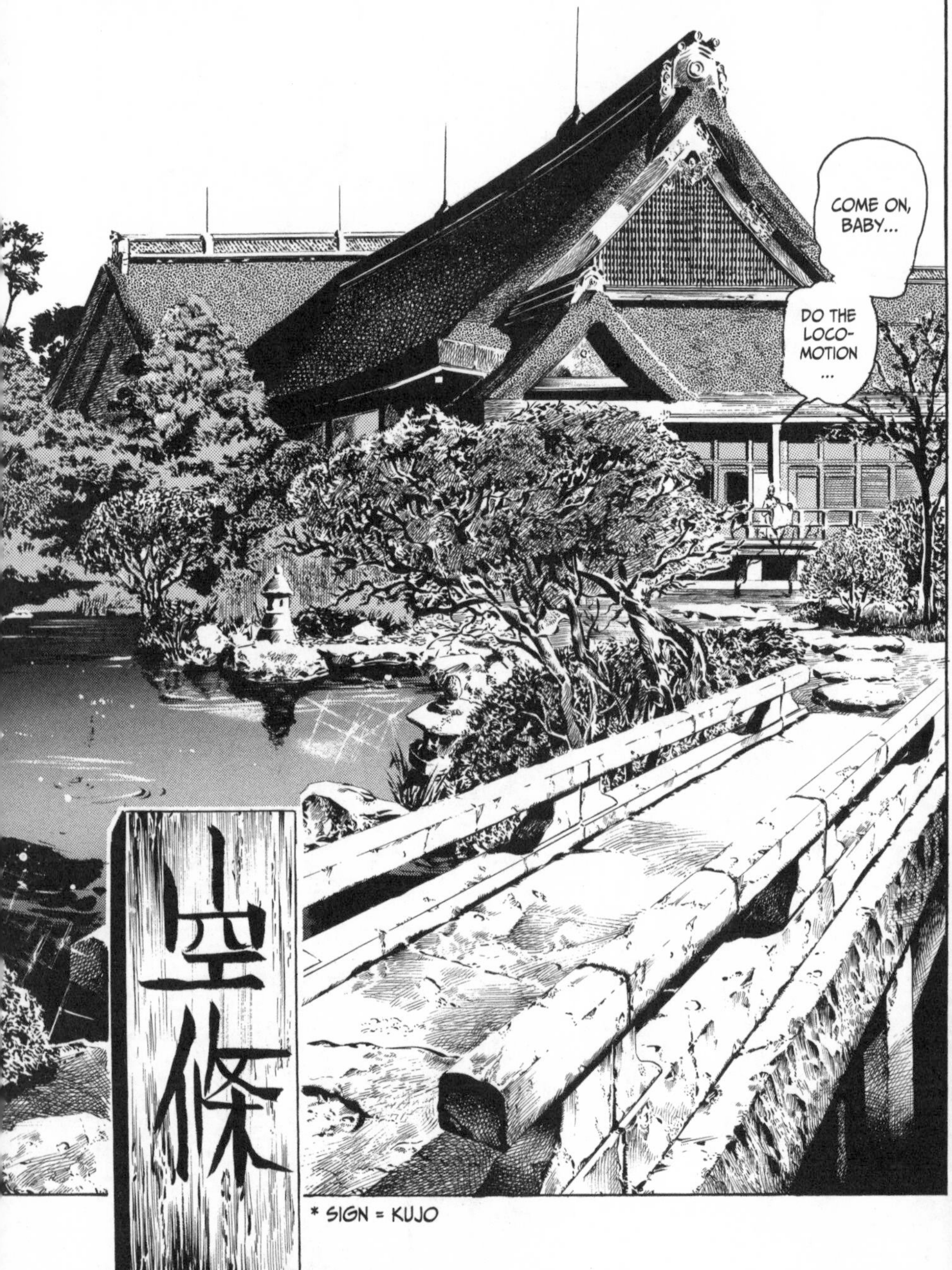
COME ON, BABY...
DO THE LOCO-MOTION ...
空條

* SIGN = KUJO

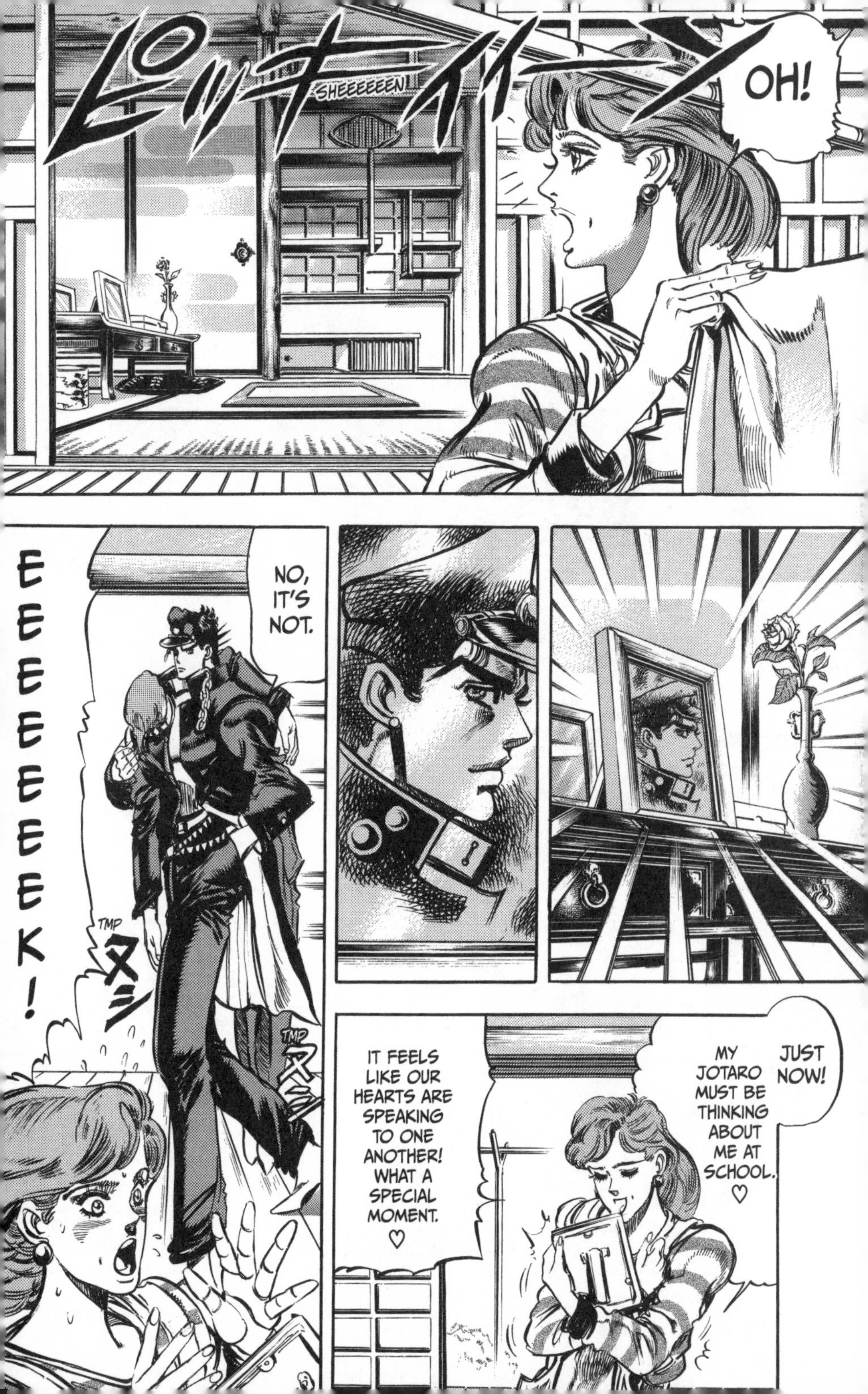
SHEEEEEEEN
OH!
JUST NOW!
MY JOTARO MUST BE THINKING ABOUT ME AT SCHOOL. ♡
IT FEELS LIKE OUR HEARTS ARE SPEAKING TO ONE ANOTHER! WHAT A SPECIAL MOMENT. ♡
NO, IT'S NOT.
EEEEEEEEK!
TMP
TMP

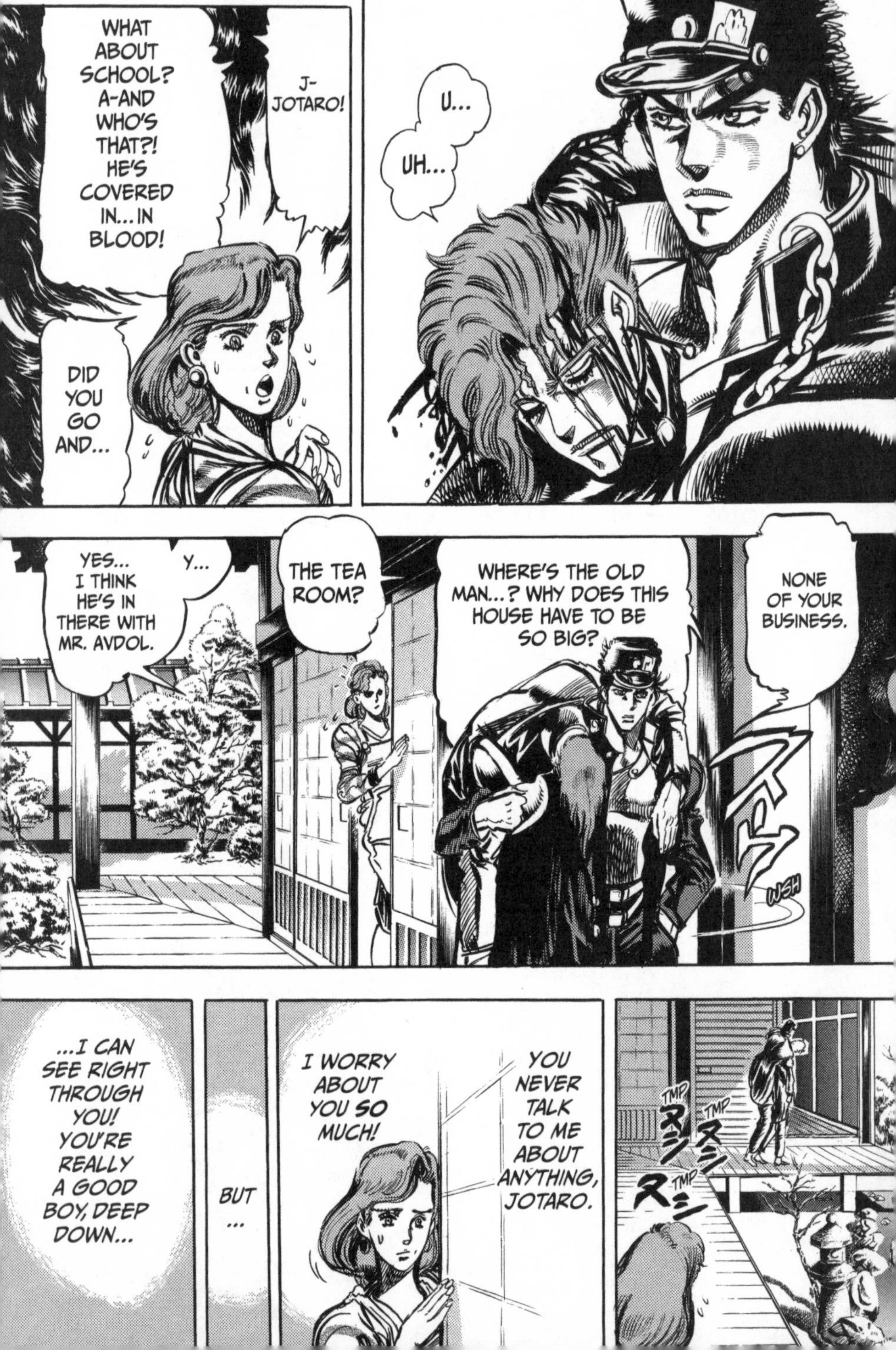
U...
UH...
J- JOTARO!
WHAT ABOUT SCHOOL? A-AND WHO'S THAT?! HE'S COVERED IN...IN BLOOD!
DID YOU GO AND...
NONE OF YOUR BUSINESS.
WHERE'S THE OLD MAN...? WHY DOES THIS HOUSE HAVE TO BE SO BIG?
THE TEA ROOM?
Y...
YES... I THINK HE'S IN THERE WITH MR. AVDOL.
WSH
TMP
TMP
TMP
YOU NEVER TALK TO ME ABOUT ANYTHING, JOTARO.
I WORRY ABOUT YOU SO MUCH!
BUT ...
...I CAN SEE RIGHT THROUGH YOU! YOU'RE REALLY A GOOD BOY, DEEP DOWN...

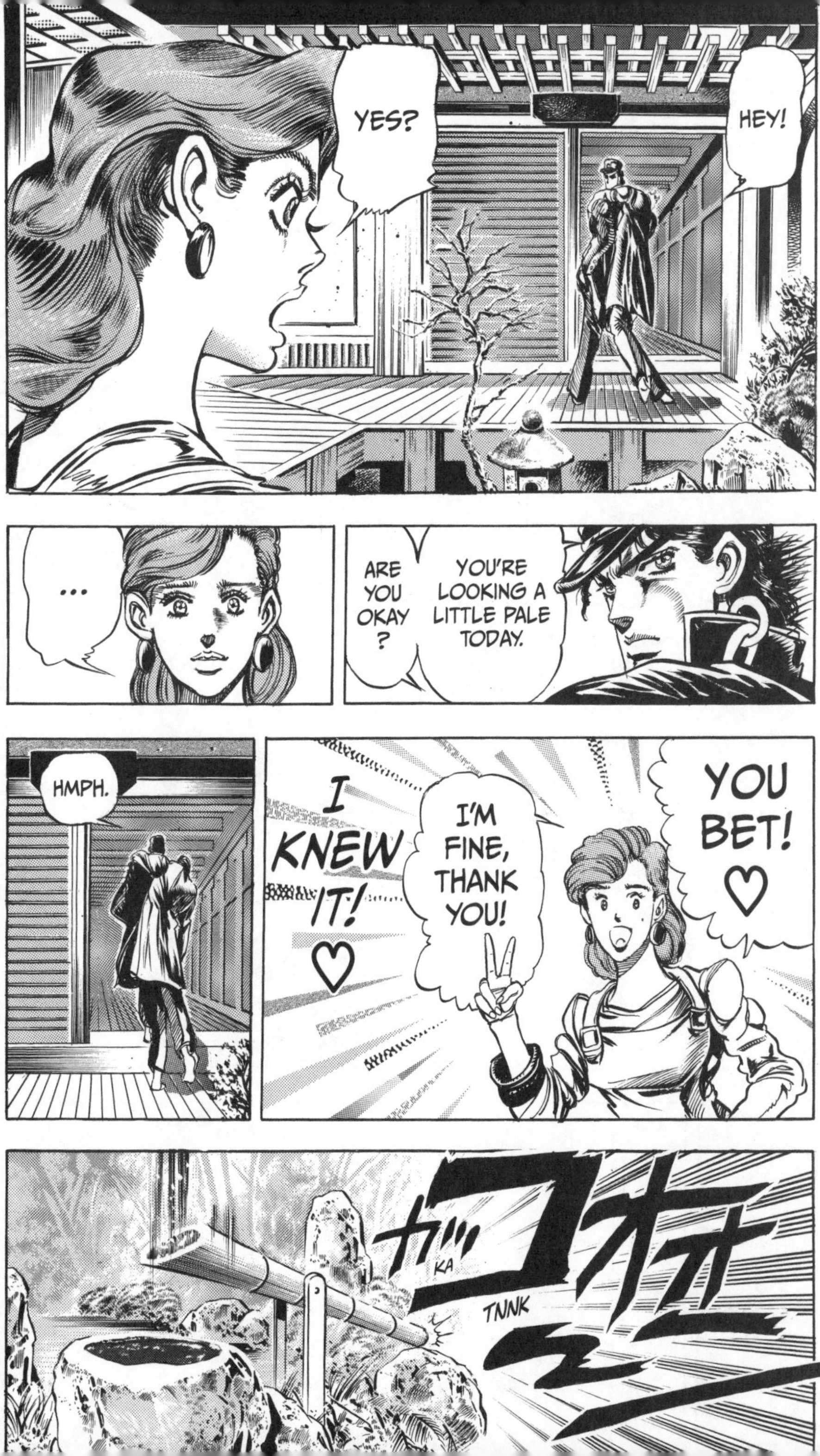
HEY!
YES?
YOU'RE LOOKING A LITTLE PALE TODAY.
ARE YOU OKAY?
...
YOU BET! ♥
I'M FINE, THANK YOU!
I KNEW IT! ♥
HMPH.
KA
TNNK

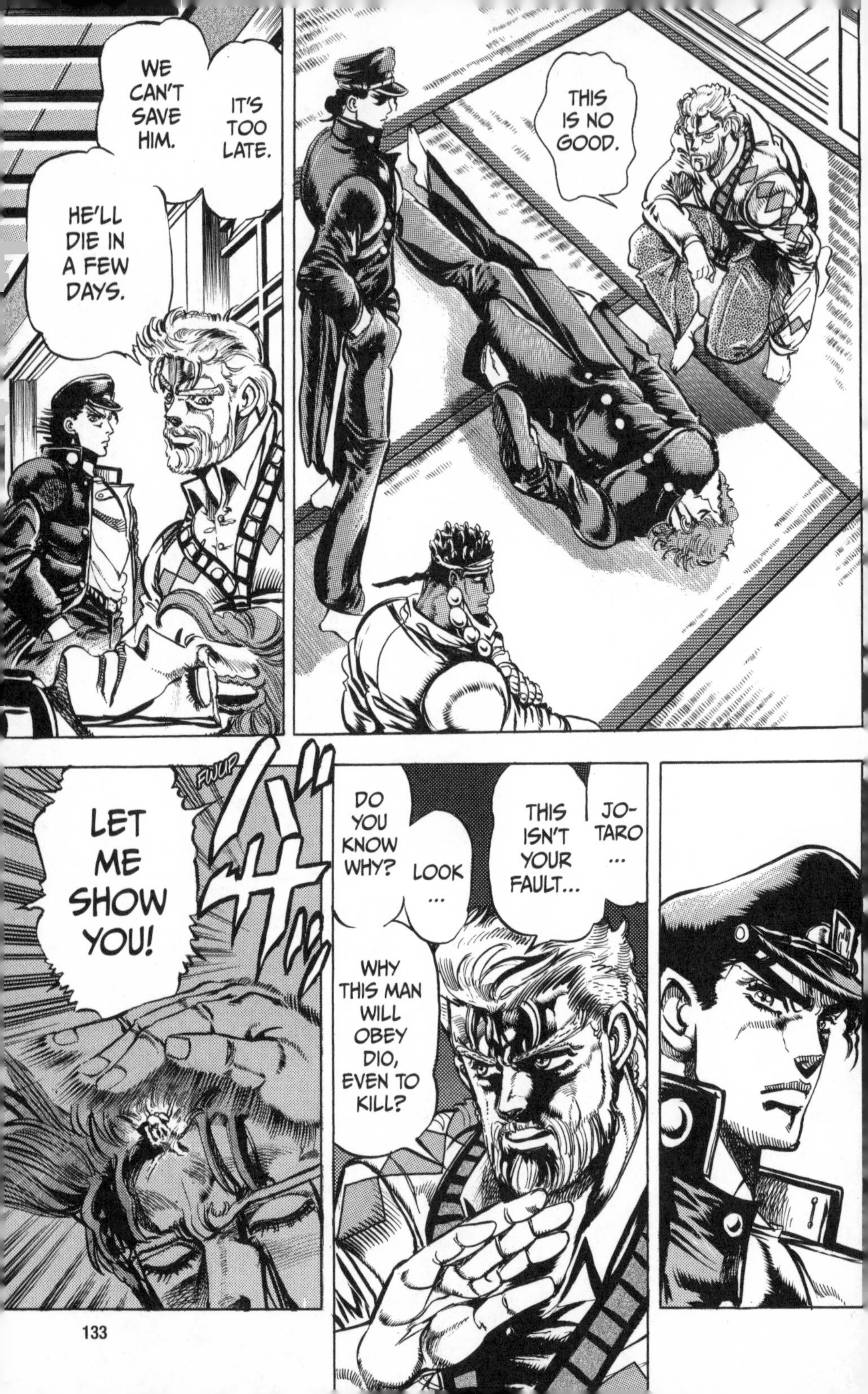
THIS IS NO GOOD.
WE CAN'T SAVE HIM.
IT'S TOO LATE.
HE'LL DIE IN A FEW DAYS.
JO-TARO ...
THIS ISN'T YOUR FAULT...
LOOK ...
DO YOU KNOW WHY?
WHY THIS MAN WILL OBEY DIO, EVEN TO KILL?
FWUP
LET ME SHOW YOU!

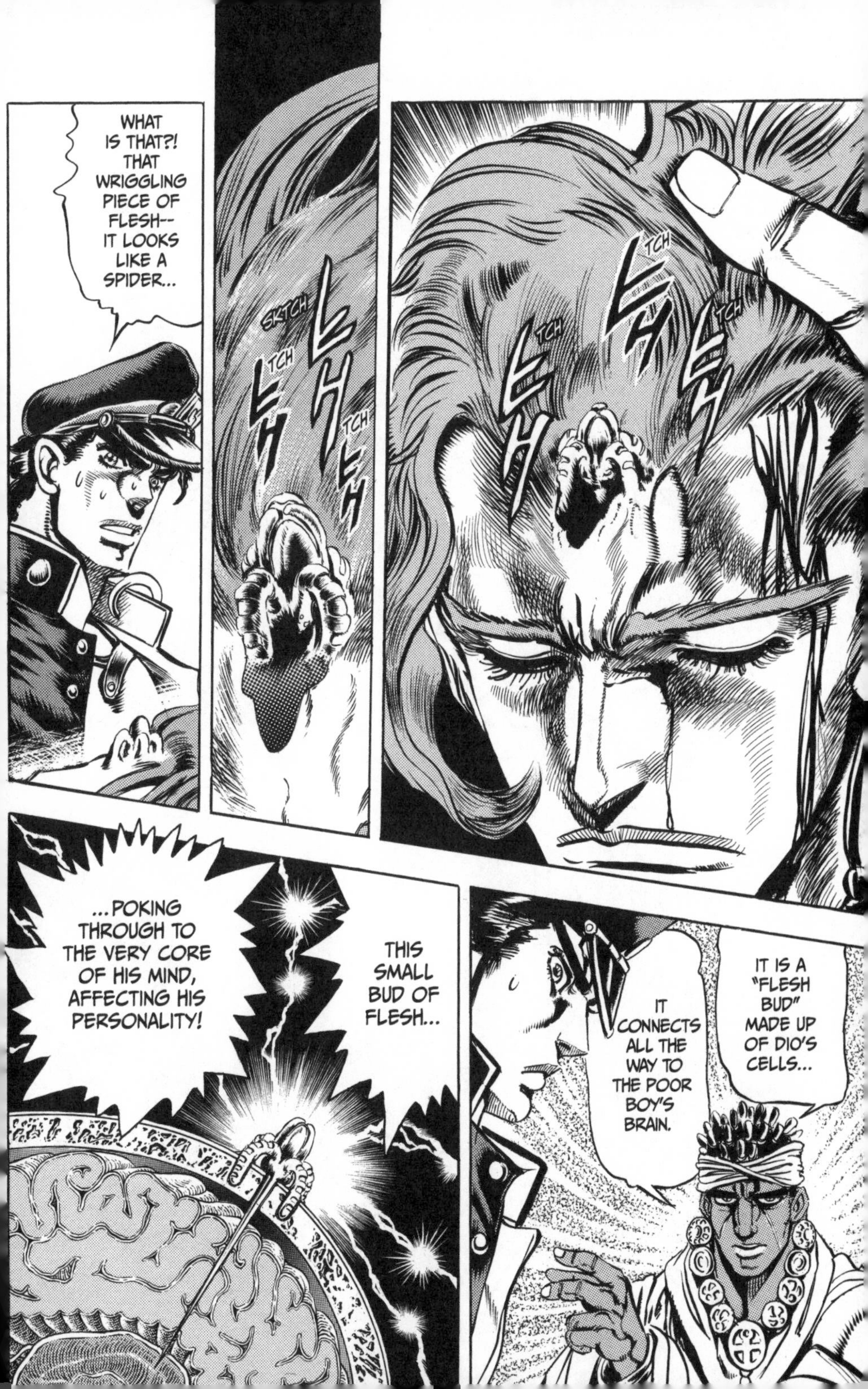
TCH
TCH
TCH
SKTCH
TCH
TCH
WHAT IS THAT?! THAT WRIGGLING PIECE OF FLESH-- IT LOOKS LIKE A SPIDER...
IT IS A "FLESH BUD" MADE UP OF DIO'S CELLS...
IT CONNECTS ALL THE WAY TO THE POOR BOY'S BRAIN.
THIS SMALL BUD OF FLESH...
...POKING THROUGH TO THE VERY CORE OF HIS MIND, AFFECTING HIS PERSONALITY!

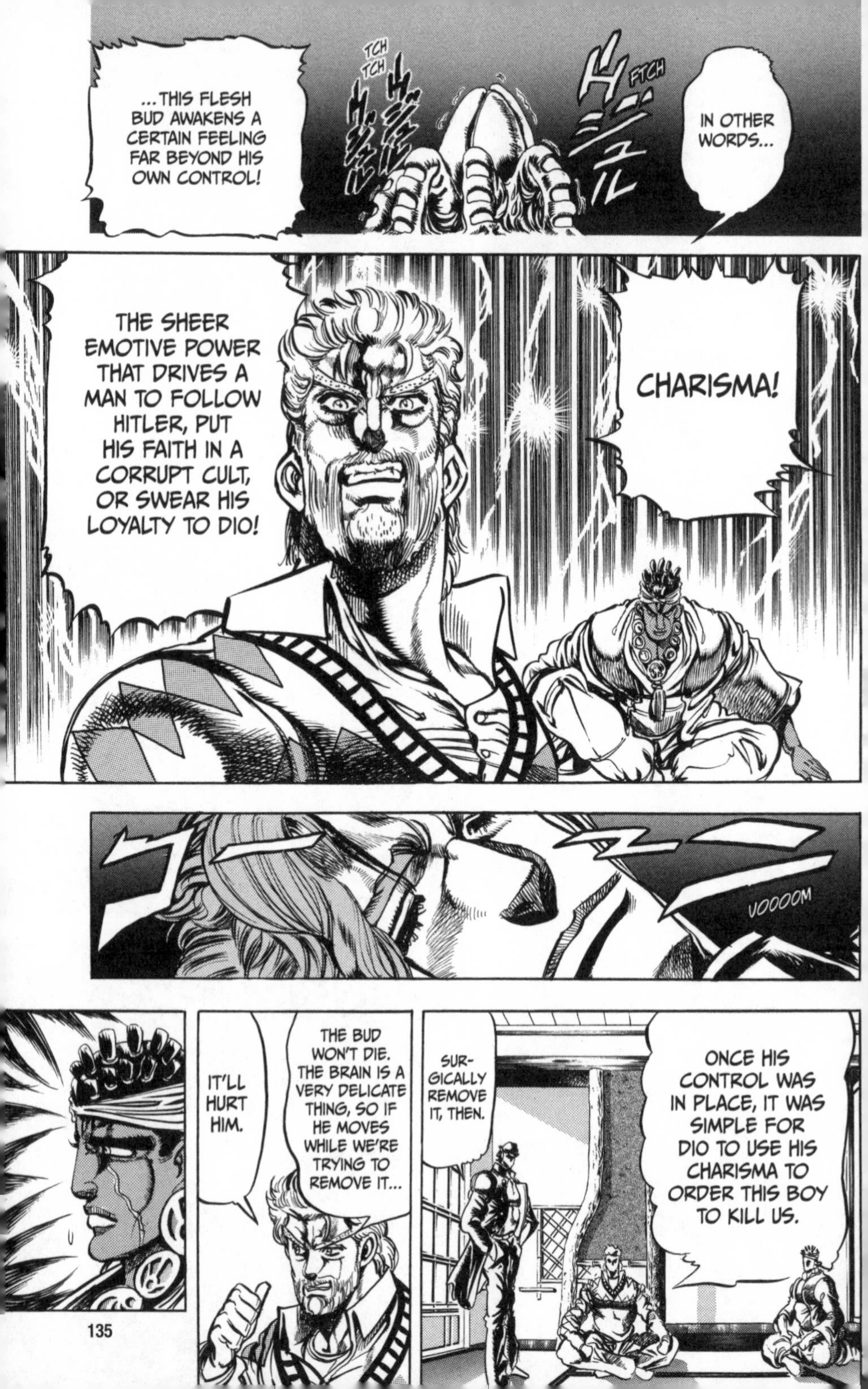
FTCH
IN OTHER WORDS...
TCH TCH
...THIS FLESH BUD AWAKENS A CERTAIN FEELING FAR BEYOND HIS OWN CONTROL!
CHARISMA!
THE SHEER EMOTIVE POWER THAT DRIVES A MAN TO FOLLOW HITLER, PUT HIS FAITH IN A CORRUPT CULT, OR SWEAR HIS LOYALTY TO DIO!
VOOOOM
ONCE HIS CONTROL WAS IN PLACE, IT WAS SIMPLE FOR DIO TO USE HIS CHARISMA TO ORDER THIS BOY TO KILL US.
SUR-GICALLY REMOVE IT, THEN.
THE BUD WON'T DIE. THE BRAIN IS A VERY DELICATE THING, SO IF HE MOVES WHILE WE'RE TRYING TO REMOVE IT...
IT'LL HURT HIM.

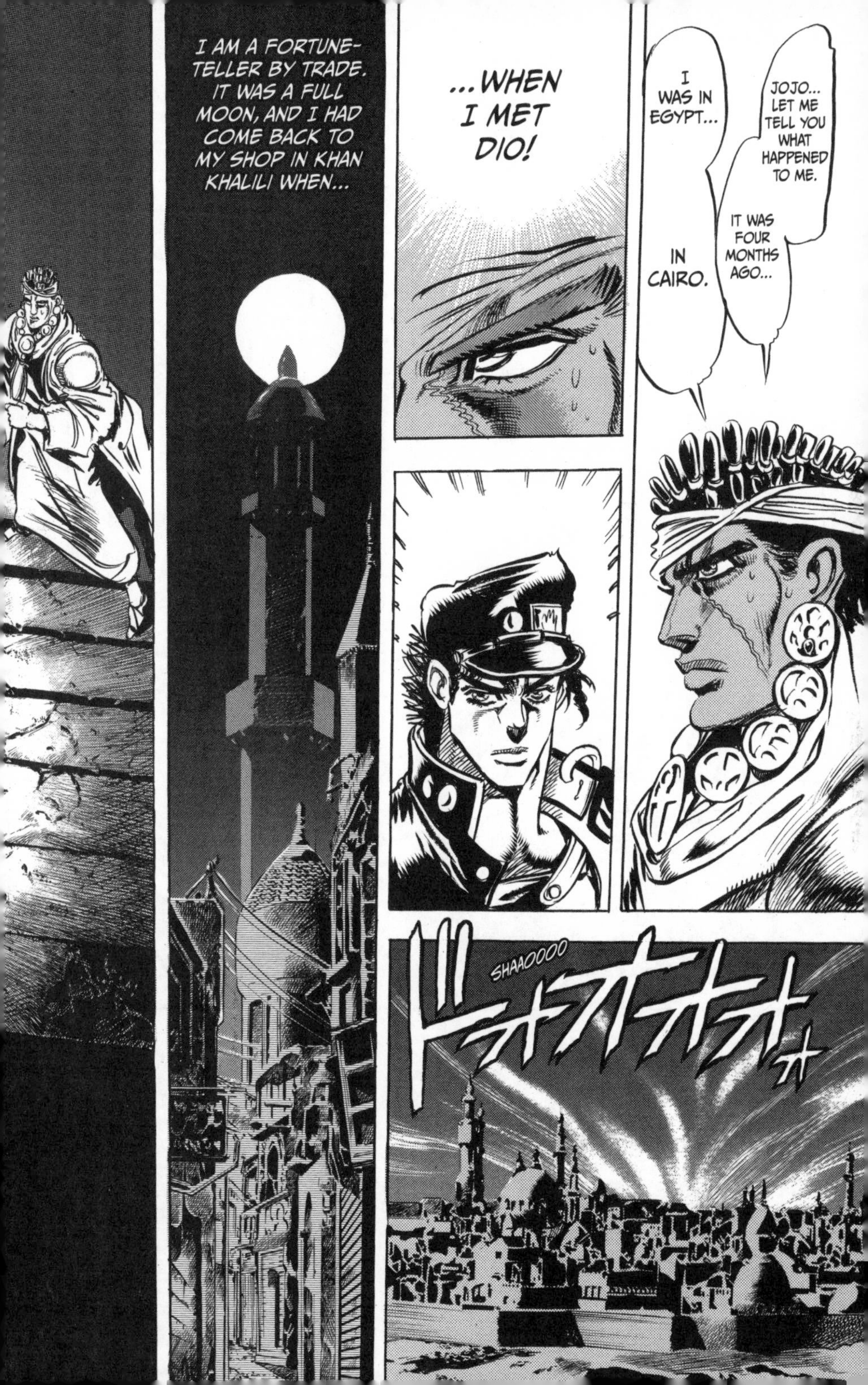
JOJO... LET ME TELL YOU WHAT HAPPENED TO ME.
IT WAS FOUR MONTHS AGO...
I WAS IN EGYPT...
IN CAIRO.
...WHEN I MET DIO!
SHAAOOOO
I AM A FORTUNE-TELLER BY TRADE. IT WAS A FULL MOON, AND I HAD COME BACK TO MY SHOP IN KHAN KHALILI WHEN...

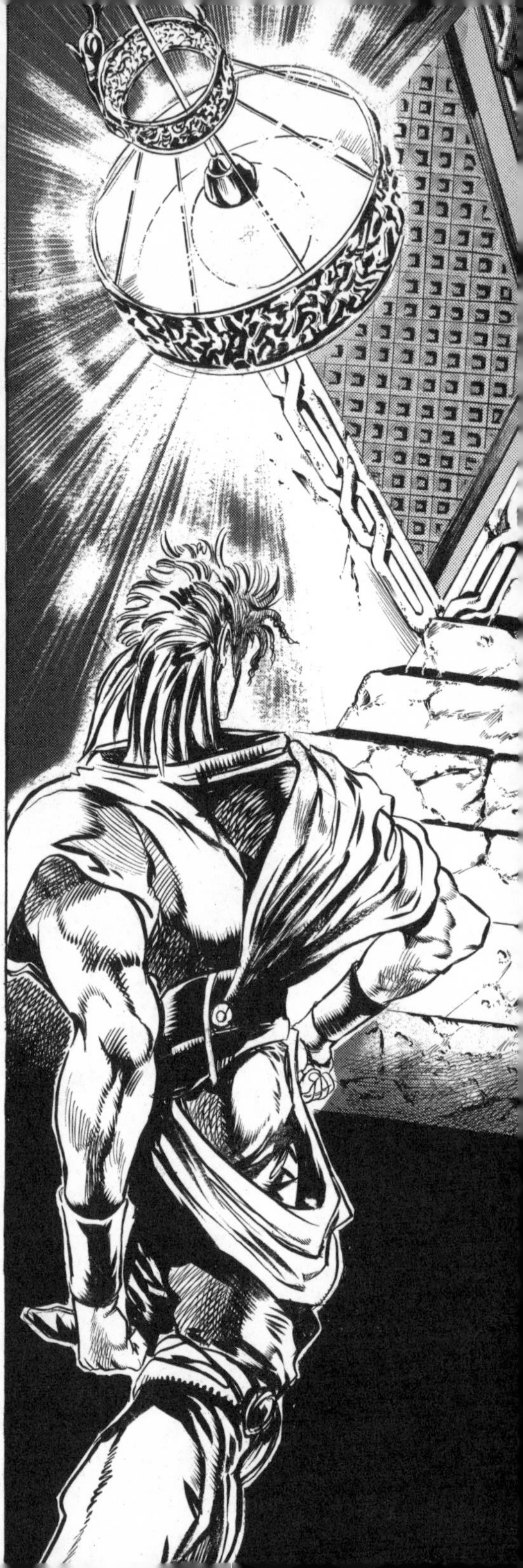

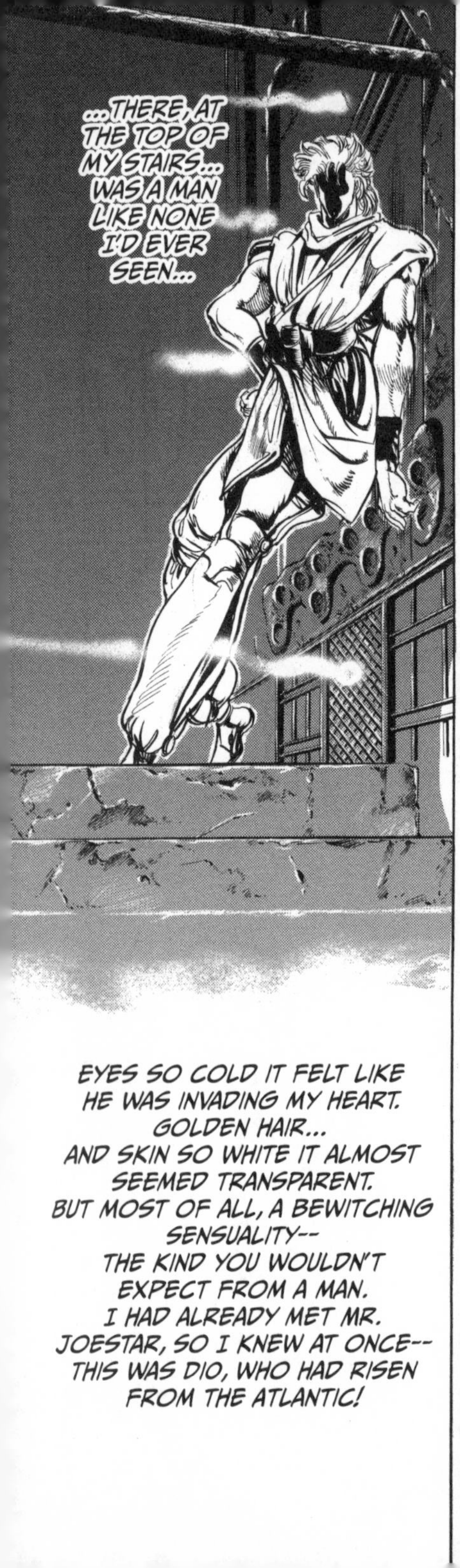
...THERE, AT THE TOP OF MY STAIRS... WAS A MAN LIKE NONE I'D EVER SEEN...
EYES SO COLD IT FELT LIKE HE WAS INVADING MY HEART. GOLDEN HAIR... AND SKIN SO WHITE IT ALMOST SEEMED TRANSPARENT. BUT MOST OF ALL, A BEWITCHING SENSUALITY-- THE KIND YOU WOULDN'T EXPECT FROM A MAN. I HAD ALREADY MET MR. JOESTAR, SO I KNEW AT ONCE-- THIS WAS DIO, WHO HAD RISEN FROM THE ATLANTIC!

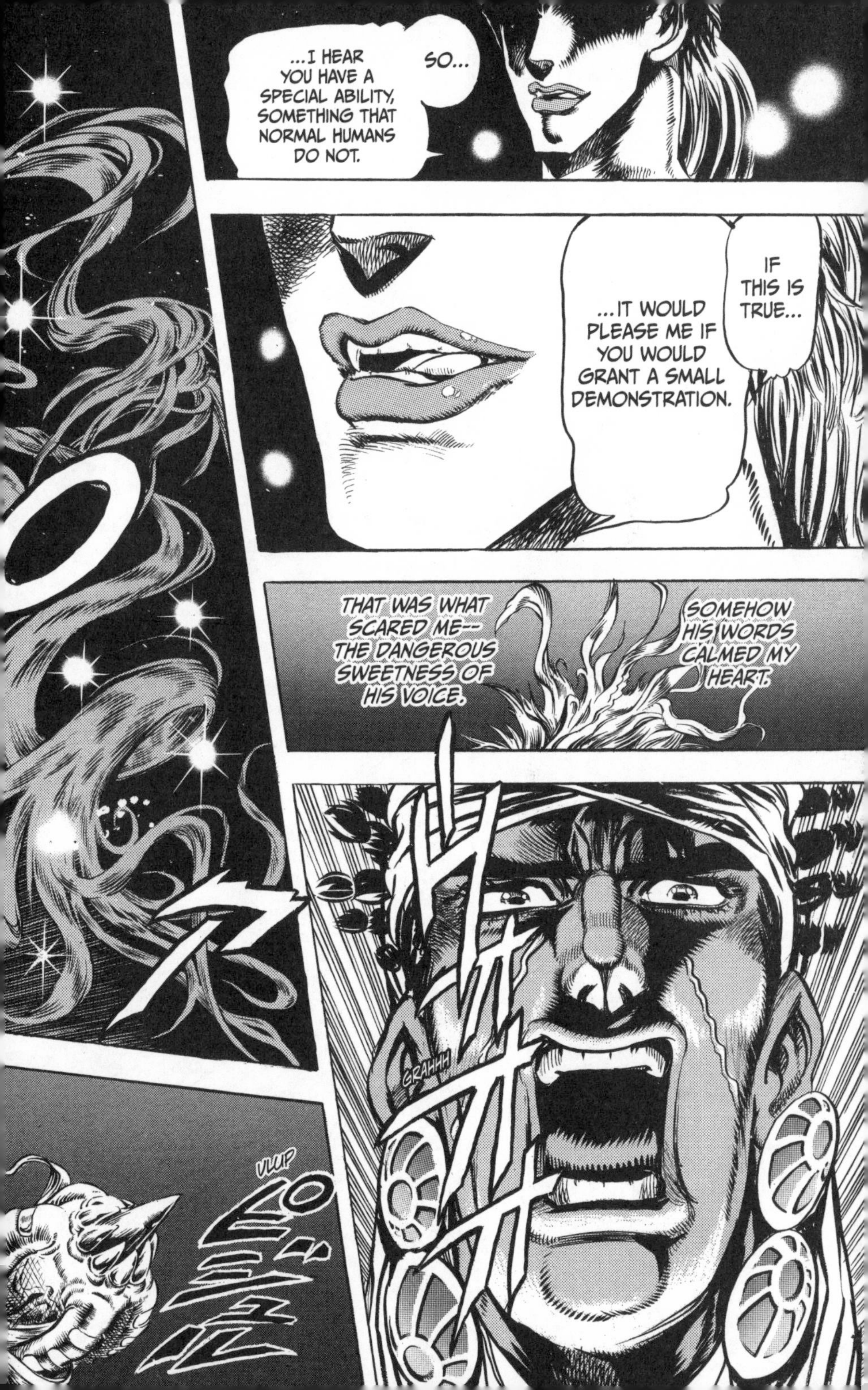
SO...
...I HEAR YOU HAVE A SPECIAL ABILITY, SOMETHING THAT NORMAL HUMANS DO NOT.
IF THIS IS TRUE...
...IT WOULD PLEASE ME IF YOU WOULD GRANT A SMALL DEMONSTRATION.
SOMEHOW HIS WORDS CALMED MY HEART.
THAT WAS WHAT SCARED ME-- THE DANGEROUS SWEETNESS OF HIS VOICE.
GRAHHH
ULUP

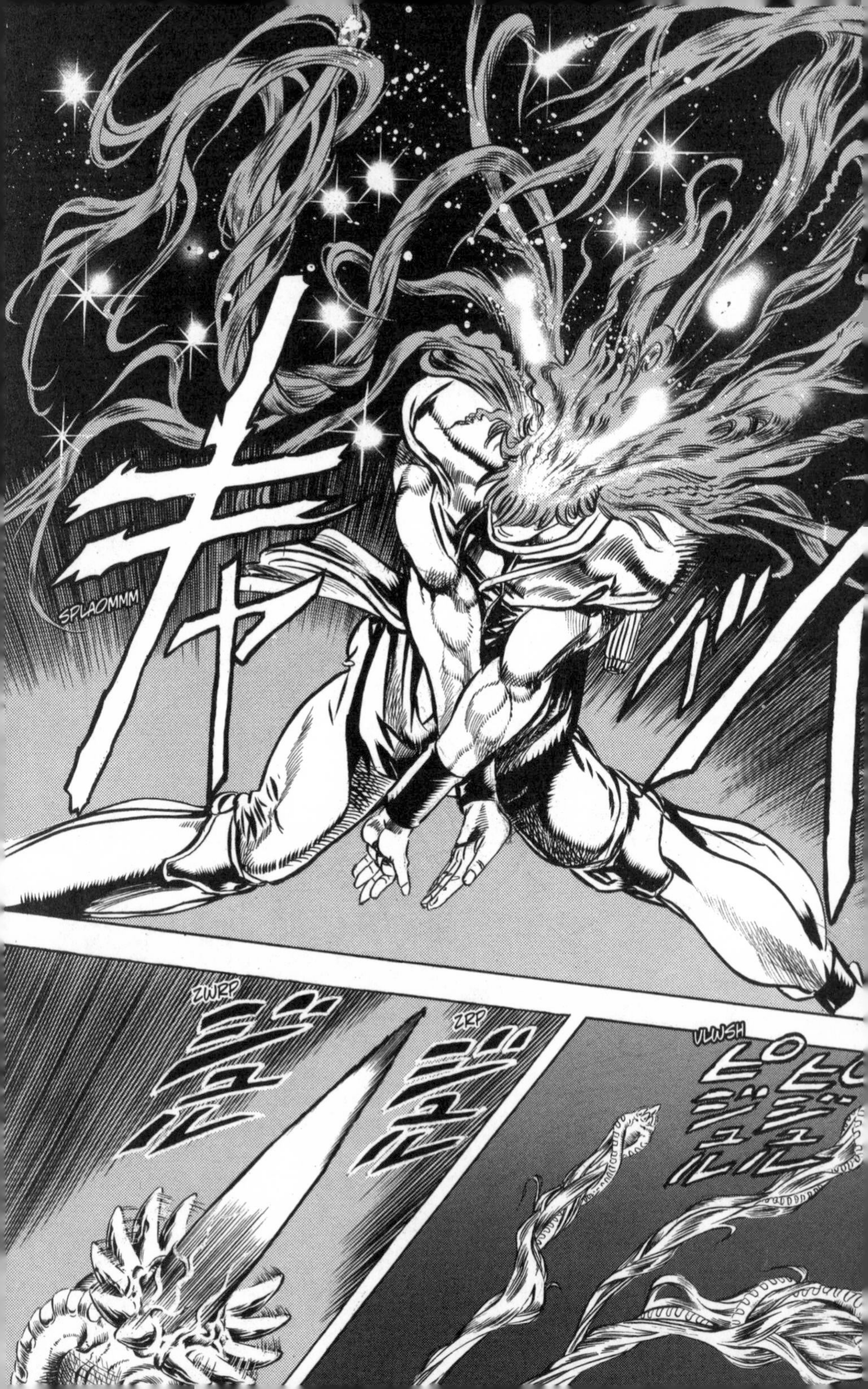
キャ
SPLAOMMM
ZWRP
ZRP
VLWSH
ピュ
ピュ

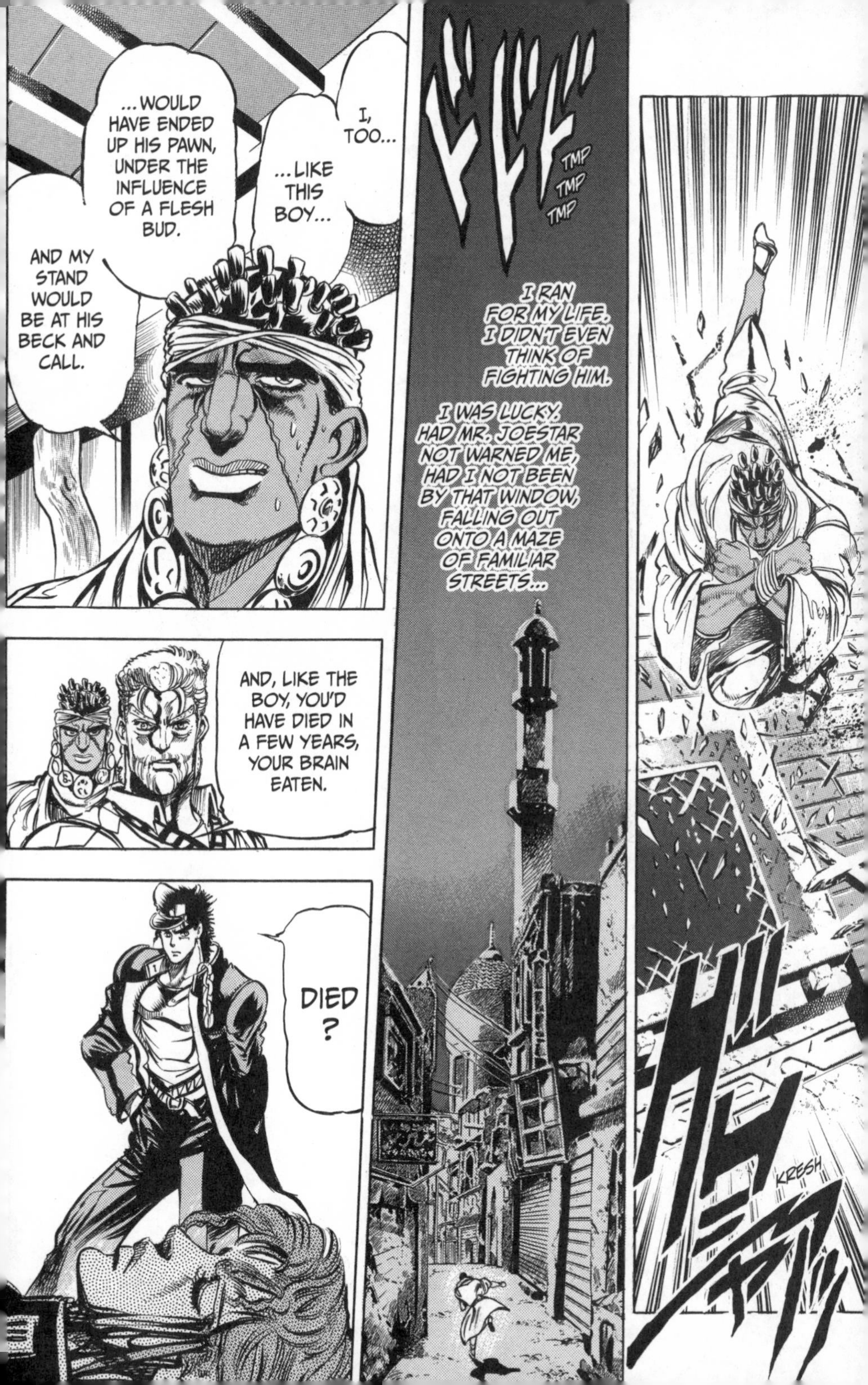
KRESH
TMP TMP TMP
I RAN FOR MY LIFE. I DIDN'T EVEN THINK OF FIGHTING HIM.
I WAS LUCKY. HAD MR. JOESTAR NOT WARNED ME, HAD I NOT BEEN BY THAT WINDOW, FALLING OUT ONTO A MAZE OF FAMILIAR STREETS...
I, TOO...
...LIKE THIS BOY...
...WOULD HAVE ENDED UP HIS PAWN, UNDER THE INFLUENCE OF A FLESH BUD.
AND MY STAND WOULD BE AT HIS BECK AND CALL.
AND, LIKE THE BOY, YOU'D HAVE DIED IN A FEW YEARS, YOUR BRAIN EATEN.
DIED?

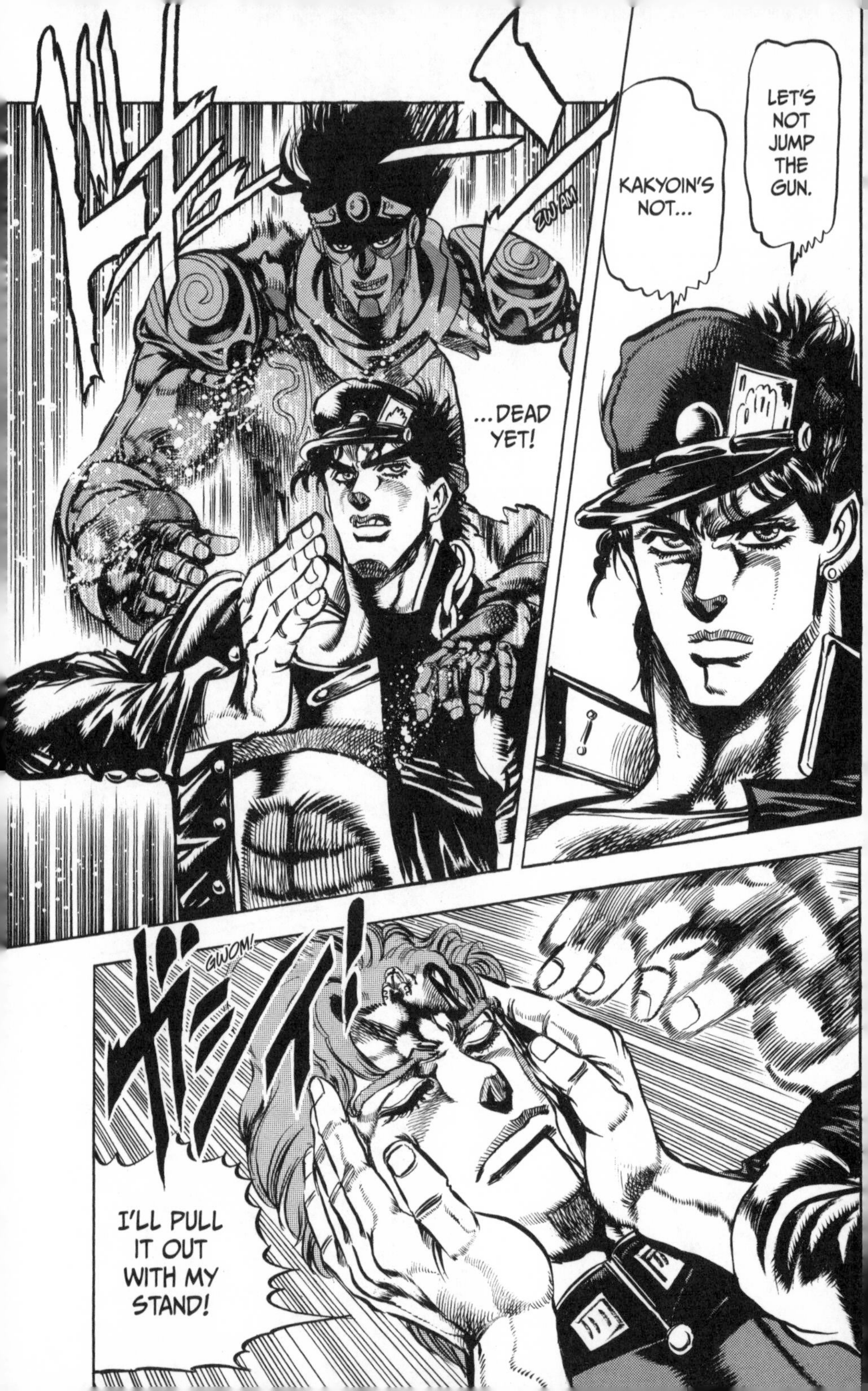
LET'S NOT JUMP THE GUN.
KAKYOIN'S NOT...
ZWAM
...DEAD YET!
GWOM!
I'LL PULL IT OUT WITH MY STAND!

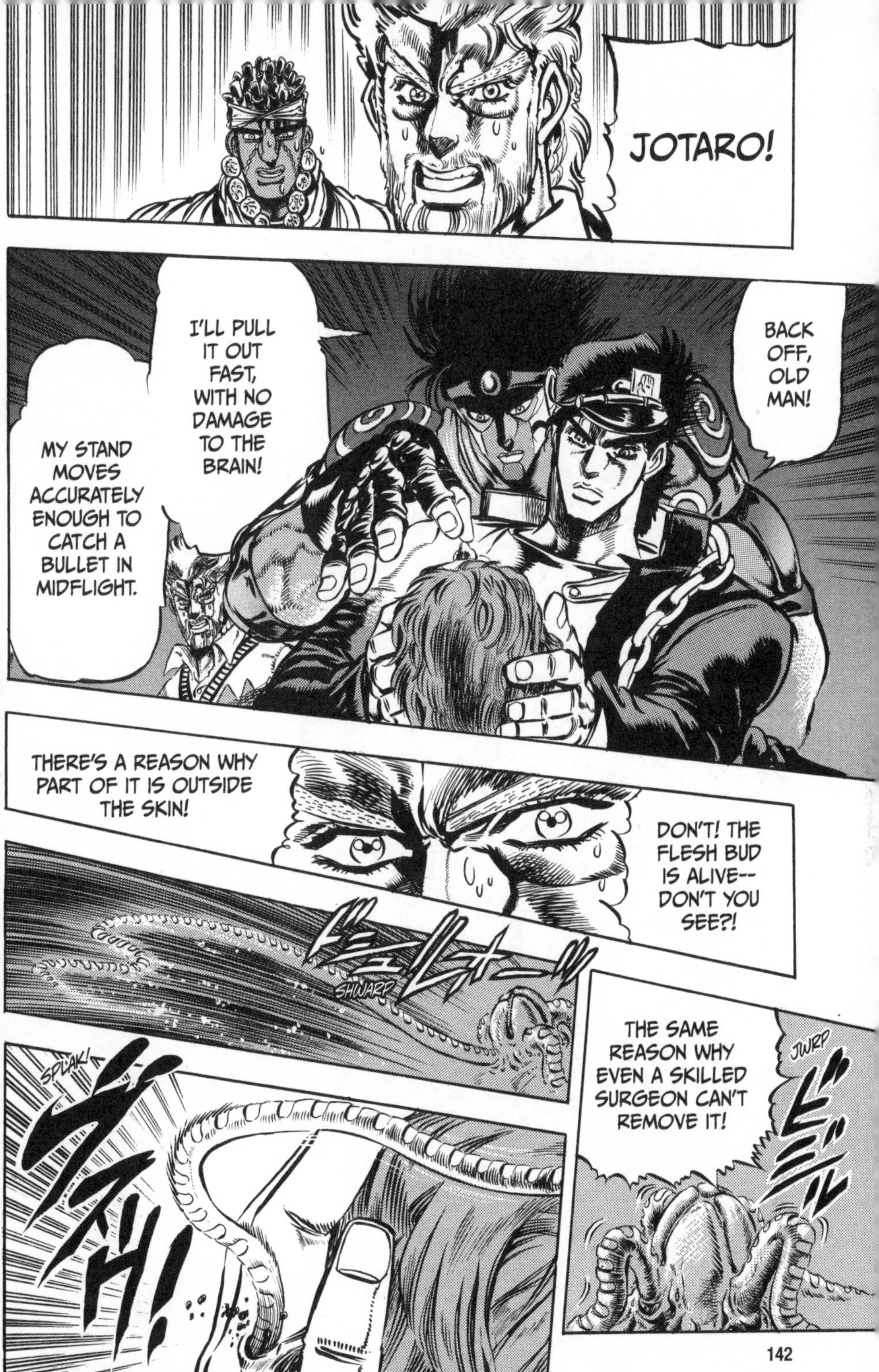
JOTARO!
BACK OFF, OLD MAN!
I'LL PULL IT OUT FAST, WITH NO DAMAGE TO THE BRAIN!
MY STAND MOVES ACCURATELY ENOUGH TO CATCH A BULLET IN MIDFLIGHT.
DON'T! THE FLESH BUD IS ALIVE-- DON'T YOU SEE?!
THERE'S A REASON WHY PART OF IT IS OUTSIDE THE SKIN!
SHWARP
JWRP
THE SAME REASON WHY EVEN A SKILLED SURGEON CAN'T REMOVE IT!
SPLAK!

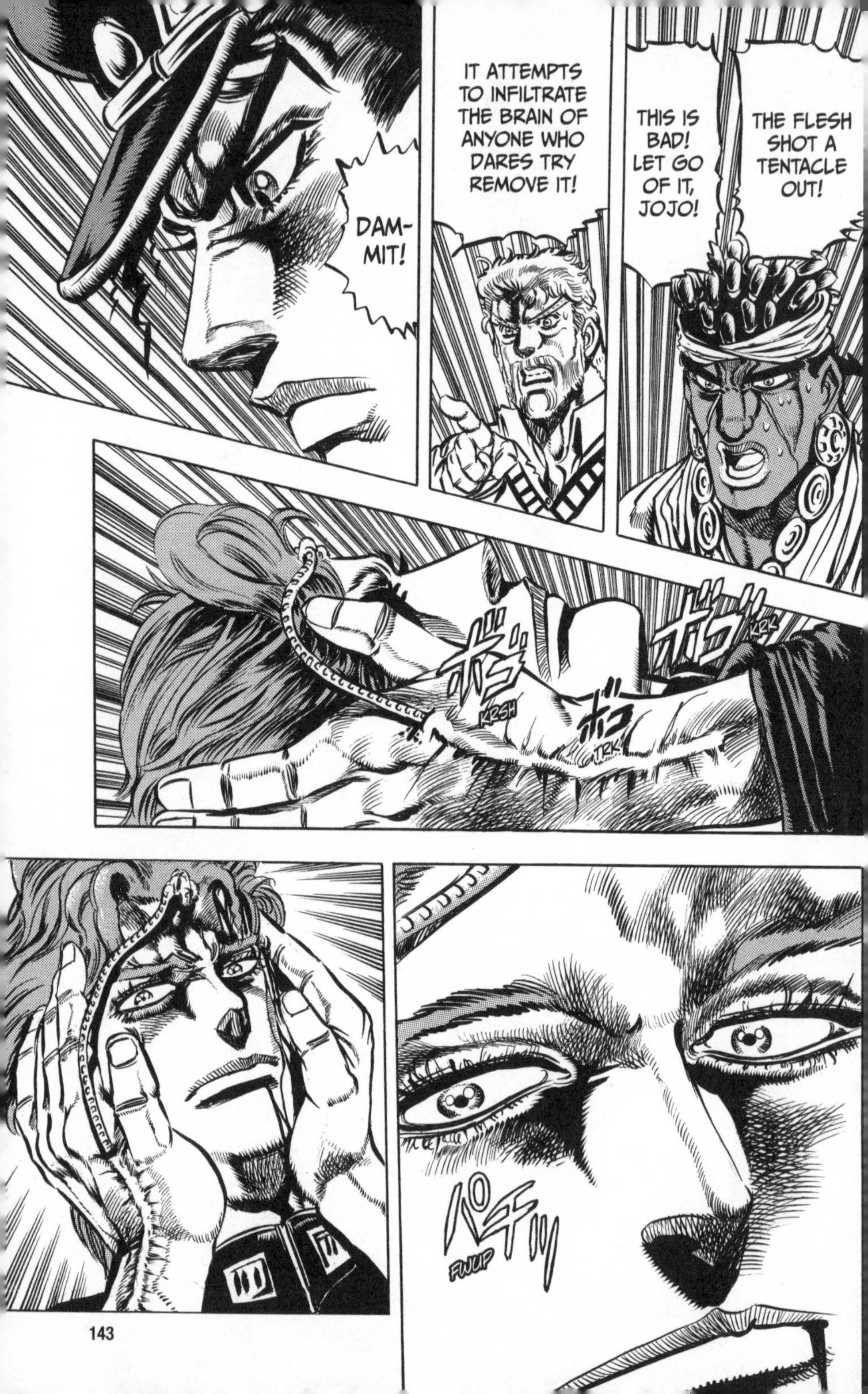
THE FLESH SHOT A TENTACLE OUT!
THIS IS BAD! LET GO OF IT, JOJO!
IT ATTEMPTS TO INFILTRATE THE BRAIN OF ANYONE WHO DARES TRY REMOVE IT!
DAM-MIT!
KRK
KRSH
TRK
FWUP

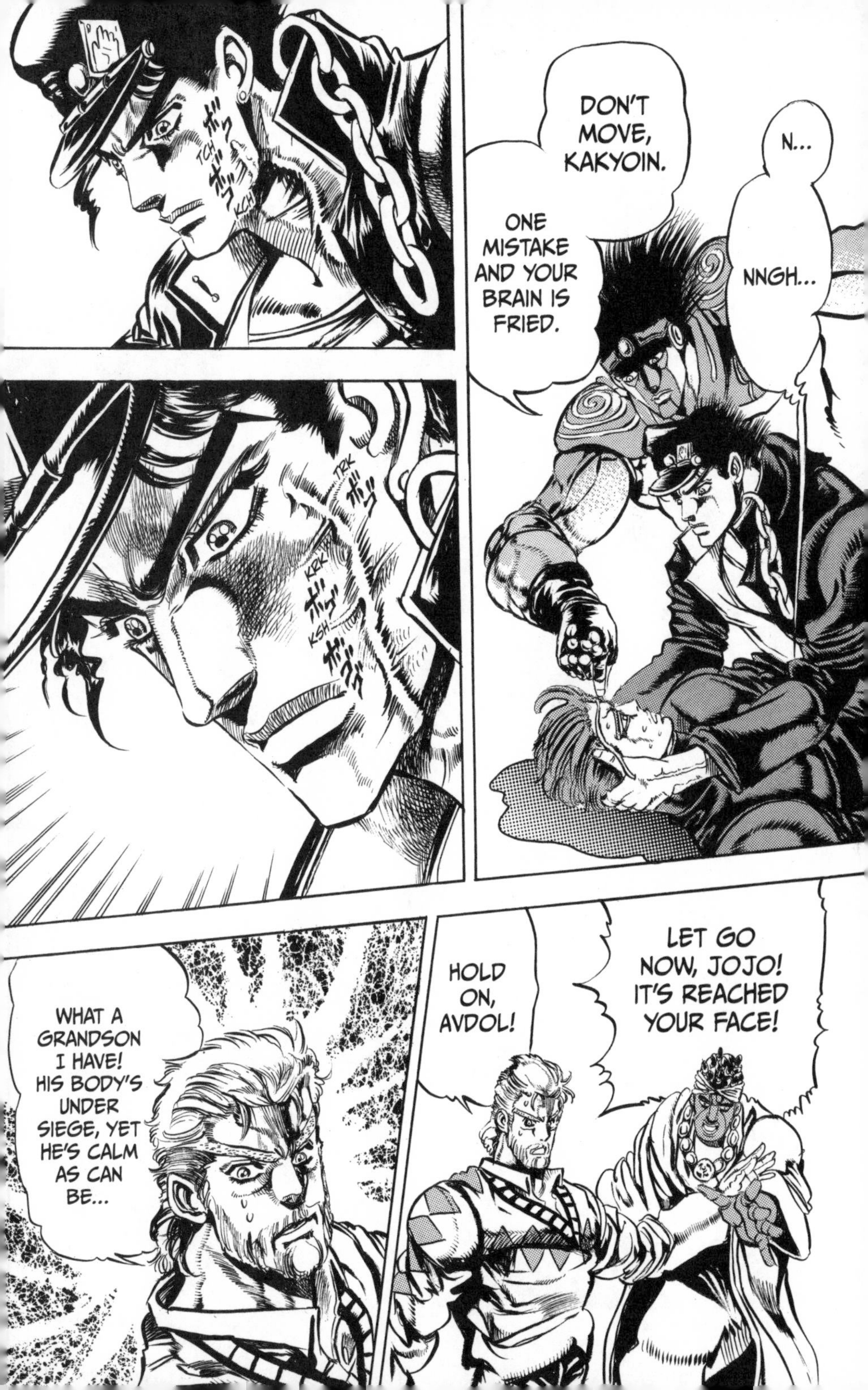
DON'T MOVE, KAKYOIN.
N...
NNGH...
ONE MISTAKE AND YOUR BRAIN IS FRIED.
TCH
KCH
TRK
KRK
KSH
LET GO NOW, JOJO! IT'S REACHED YOUR FACE!
HOLD ON, AVDOL!
WHAT A GRANDSON I HAVE! HIS BODY'S UNDER SIEGE, YET HE'S CALM AS CAN BE...

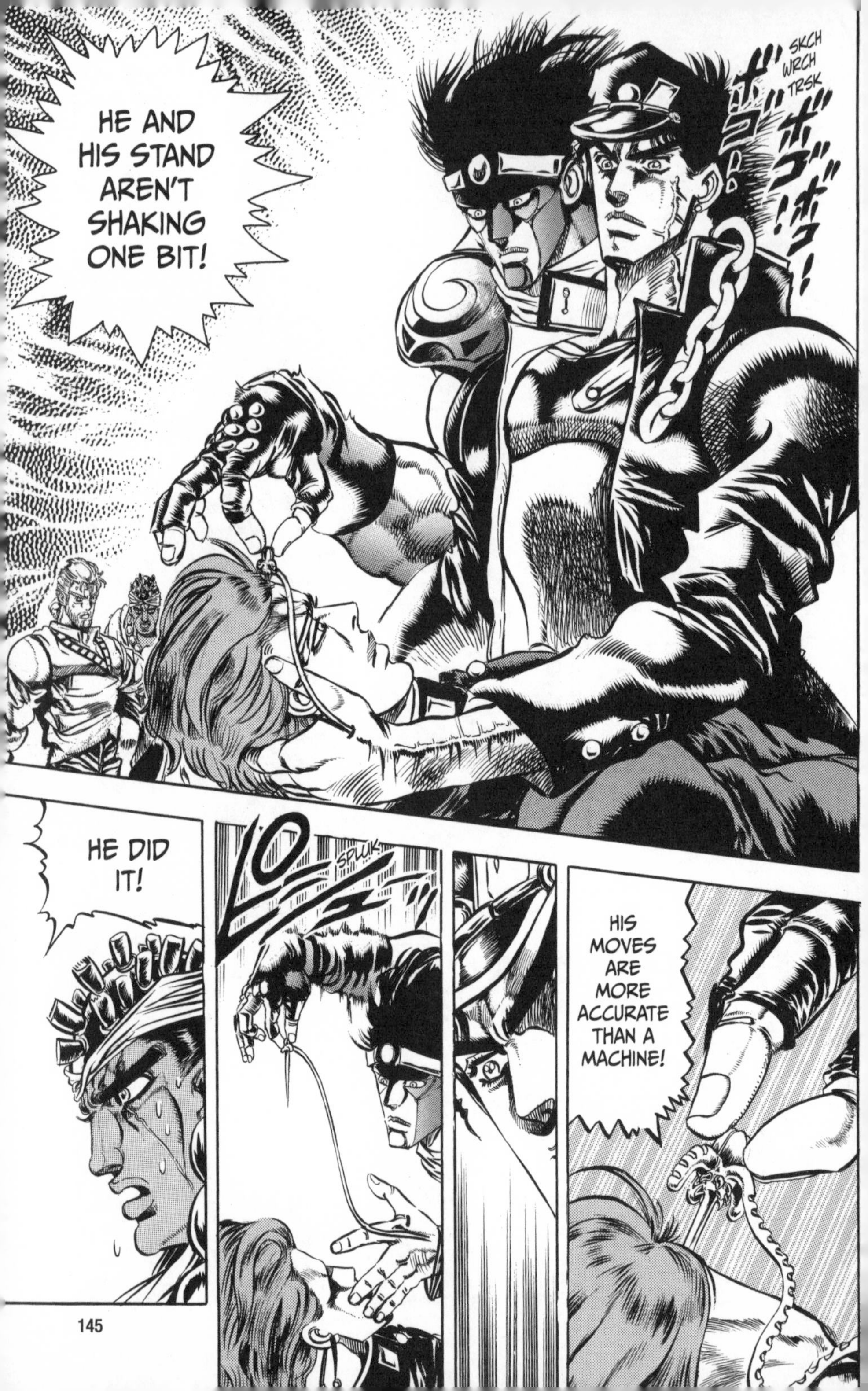
SKCH
WRCH
TRSK
HE AND HIS STAND AREN'T SHAKING ONE BIT!
HIS MOVES ARE MORE ACCURATE THAN A MACHINE!
SPLUK
HE DID IT!

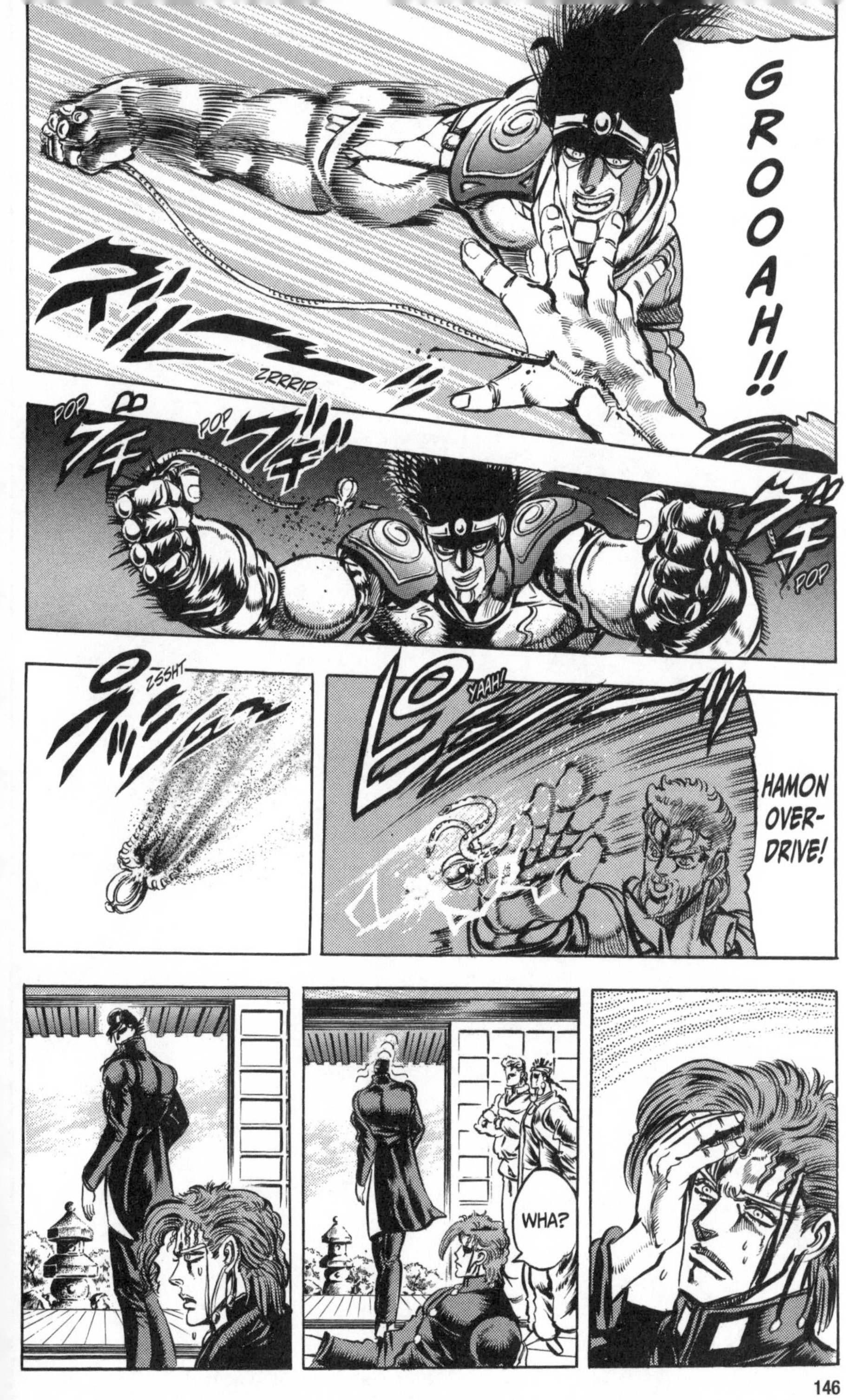
GROOOAH!!
ZRRRIP
POP
POP
POP
YAAH!
HAMON OVER-DRIVE!
ZSSHT
WHA?

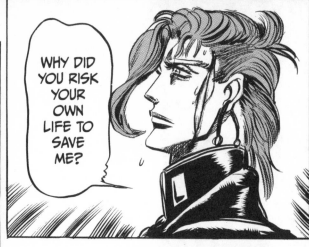

WHY DID YOU RISK YOUR OWN LIFE TO SAVE ME?

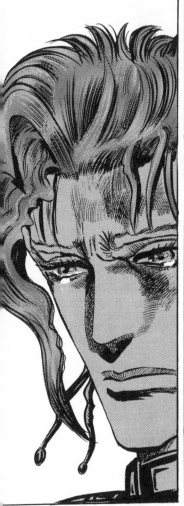

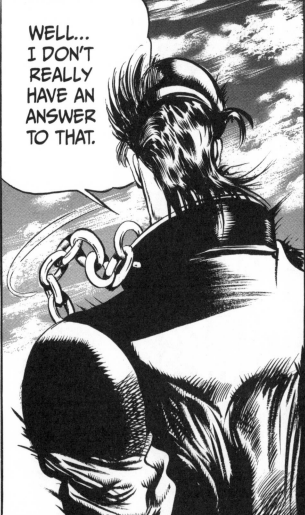

WELL... I DON'T REALLY HAVE AN ANSWER TO THAT.

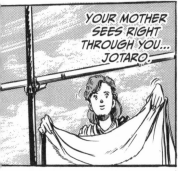

YOUR MOTHER SEES RIGHT THROUGH YOU... JOTARO.

147

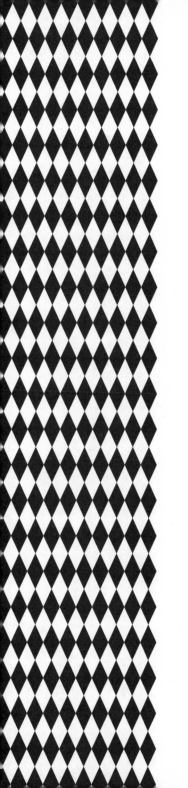
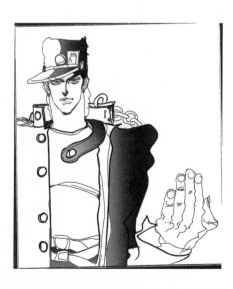

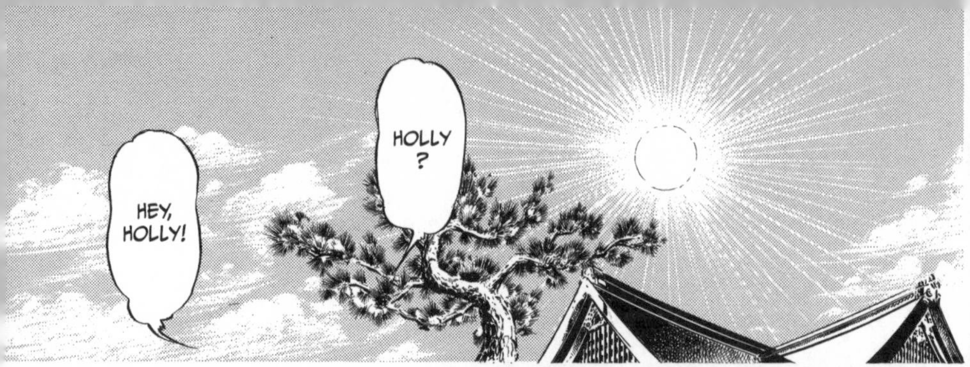
HOLLY ?
HEY, HOLLY!

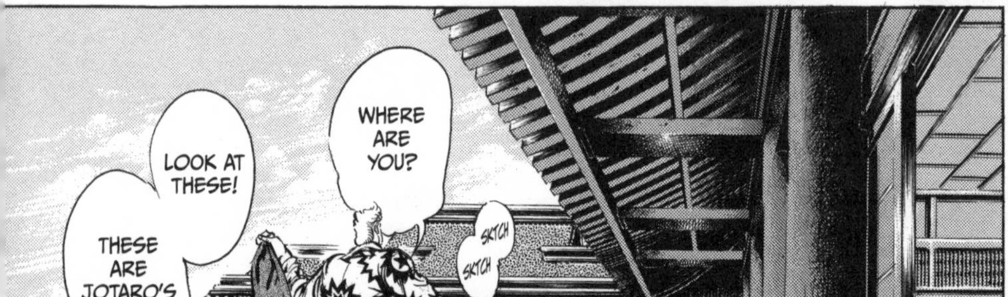
WHERE ARE YOU?
SKTCH SKTCH
LOOK AT THESE!
THESE ARE JOTARO'S PANTS!
SHF

CHAPTER 8: The Power Called a "Stand"

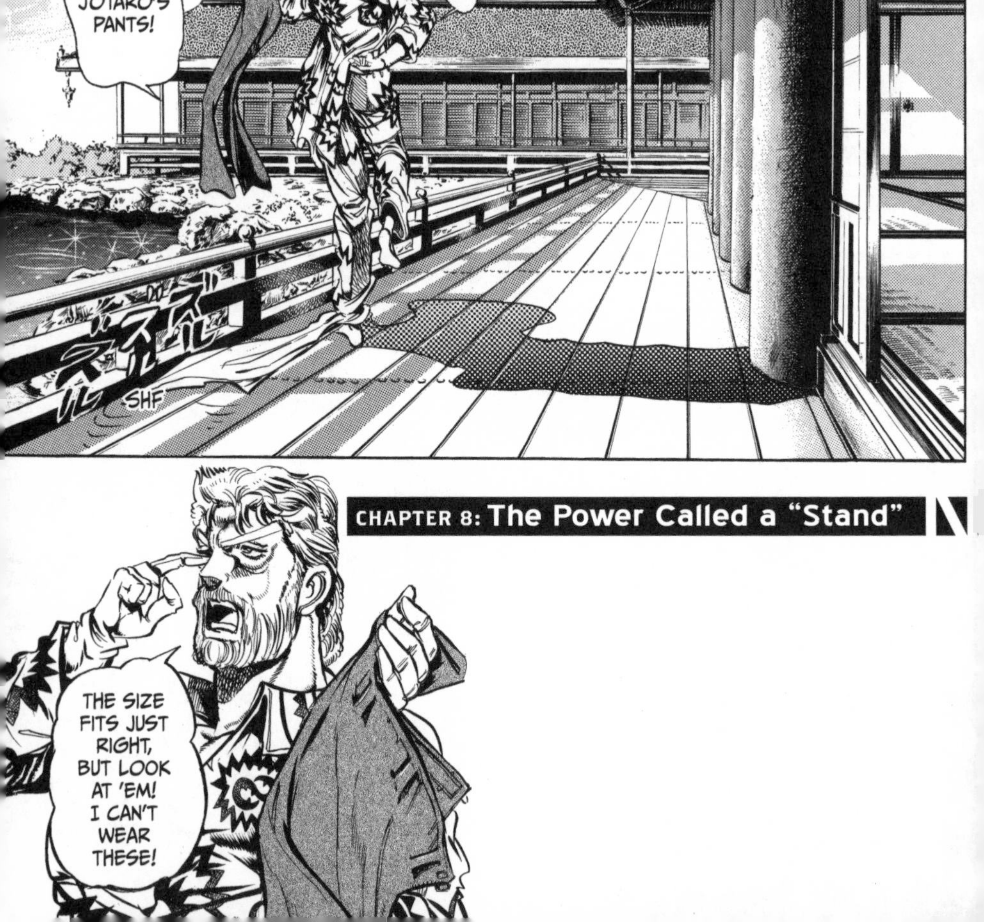
THE SIZE FITS JUST RIGHT, BUT LOOK AT 'EM! I CAN'T WEAR THESE!

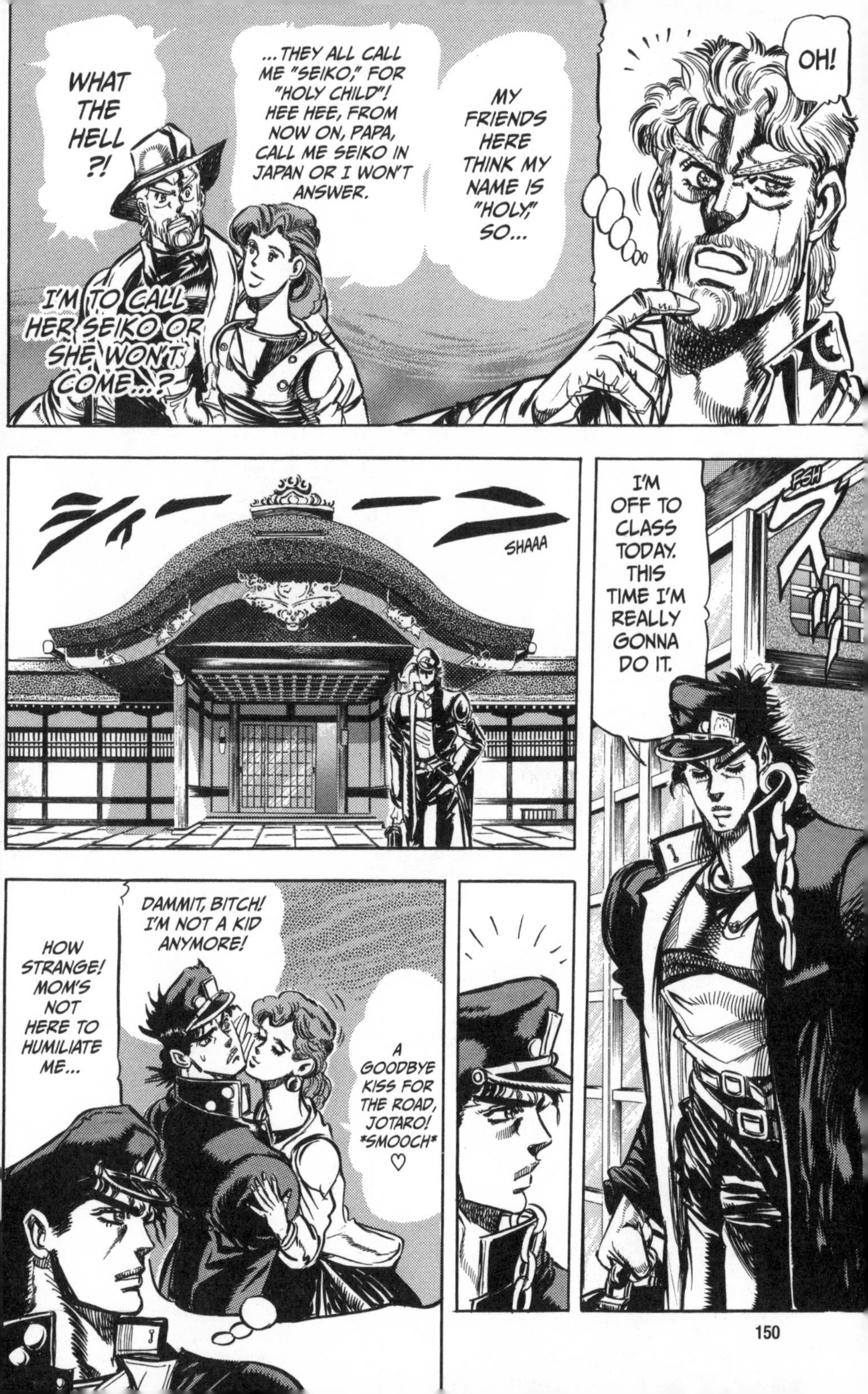
OH!
MY FRIENDS HERE THINK MY NAME IS "HOLY," SO...
...THEY ALL CALL ME "SEIKO," FOR "HOLY CHILD"! HEE HEE, FROM NOW ON, PAPA, CALL ME SEIKO IN JAPAN OR I WON'T ANSWER.
WHAT THE HELL ?!
I'M TO CALL HER SEIKO OR SHE WON'T COME...?
FSH
I'M OFF TO CLASS TODAY. THIS TIME I'M REALLY GONNA DO IT.
シィーーー
SHAAA
A GOODBYE KISS FOR THE ROAD, JOTARO! *SMOOCH* ♡
DAMMIT, BITCH! I'M NOT A KID ANYMORE!
HOW STRANGE! MOM'S NOT HERE TO HUMILIATE ME...

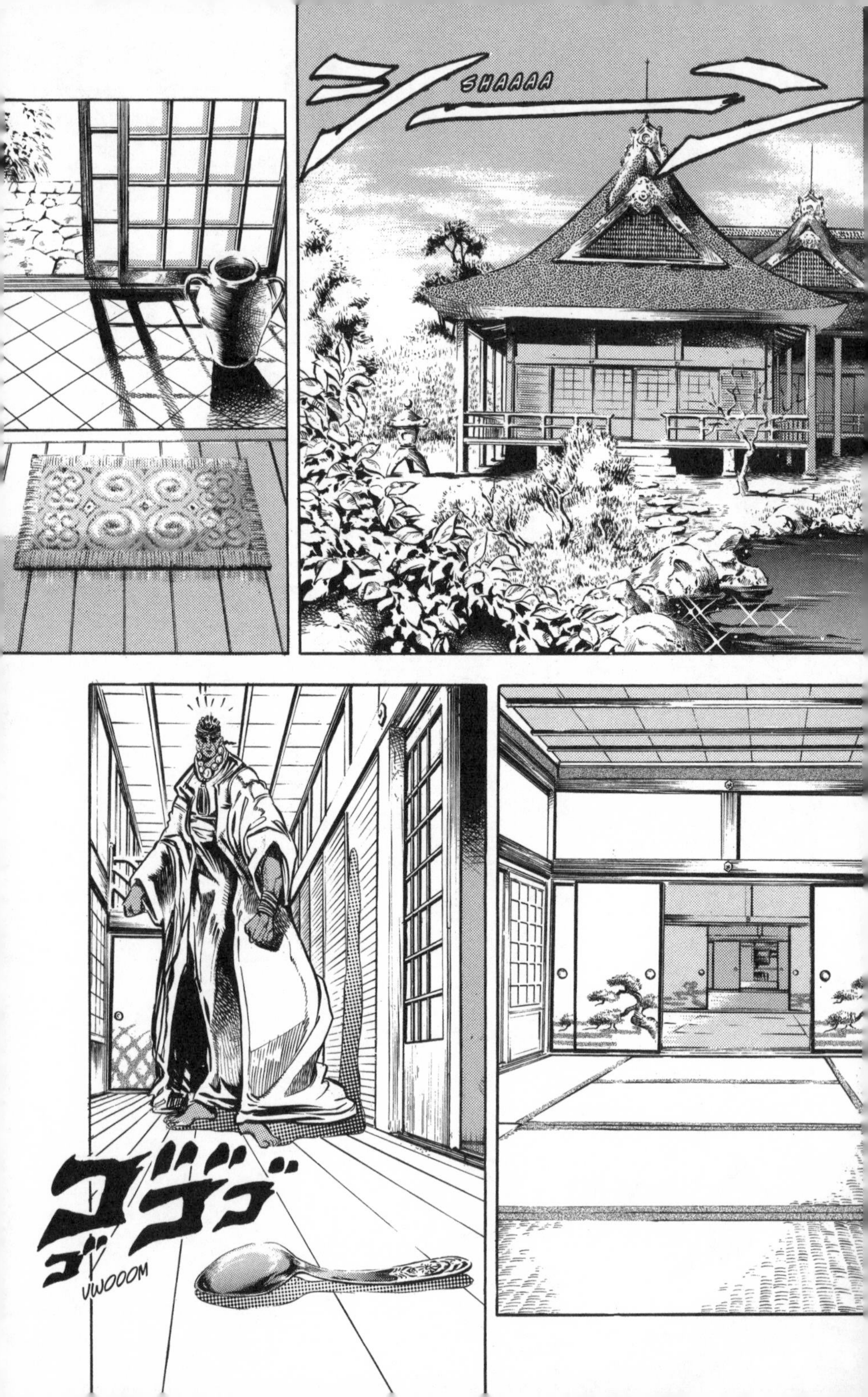
SHAAAA
ゴゴゴゴ
VWOOOM

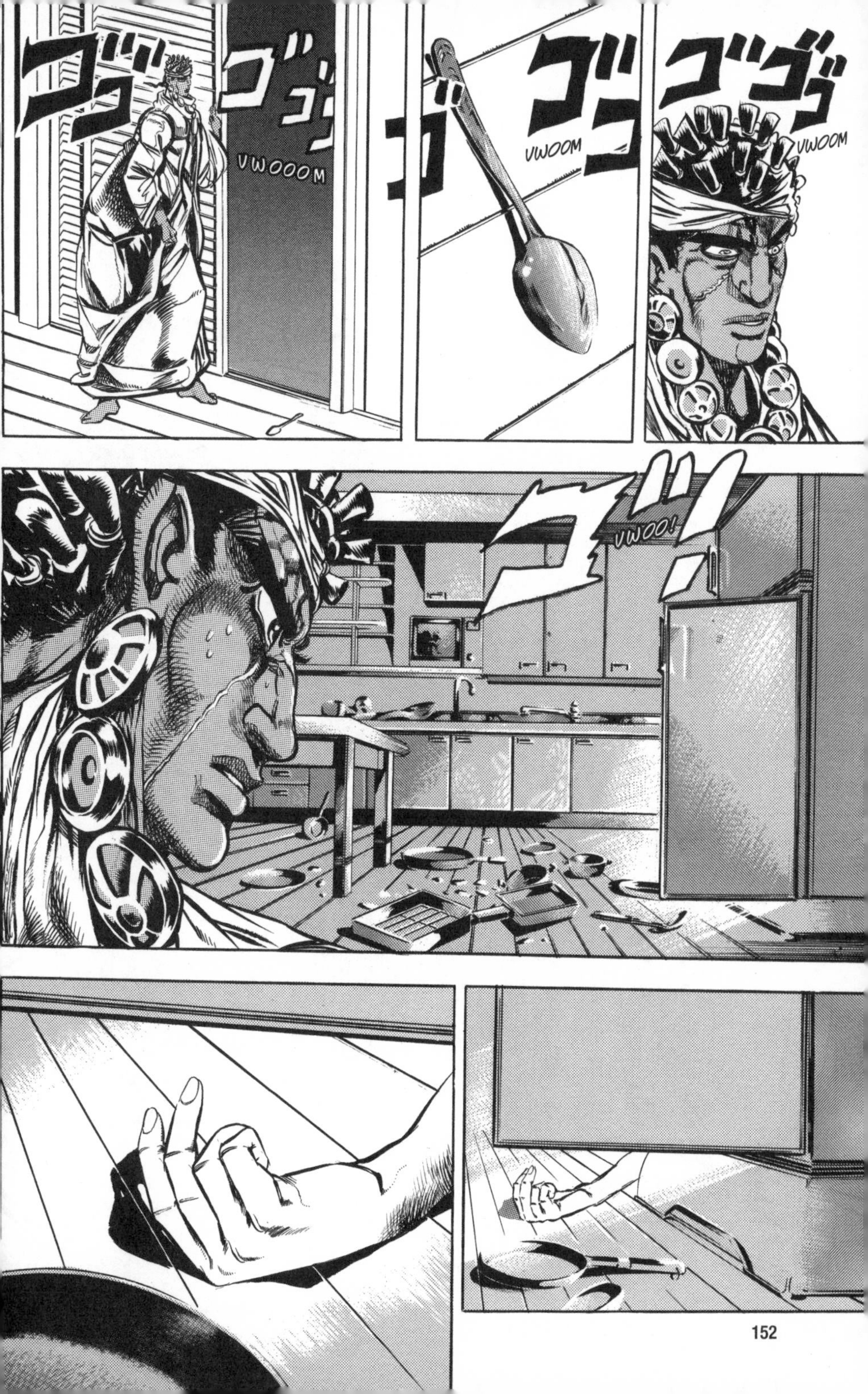
VWOOM
VWOOM
VWOOOM
VWOO!

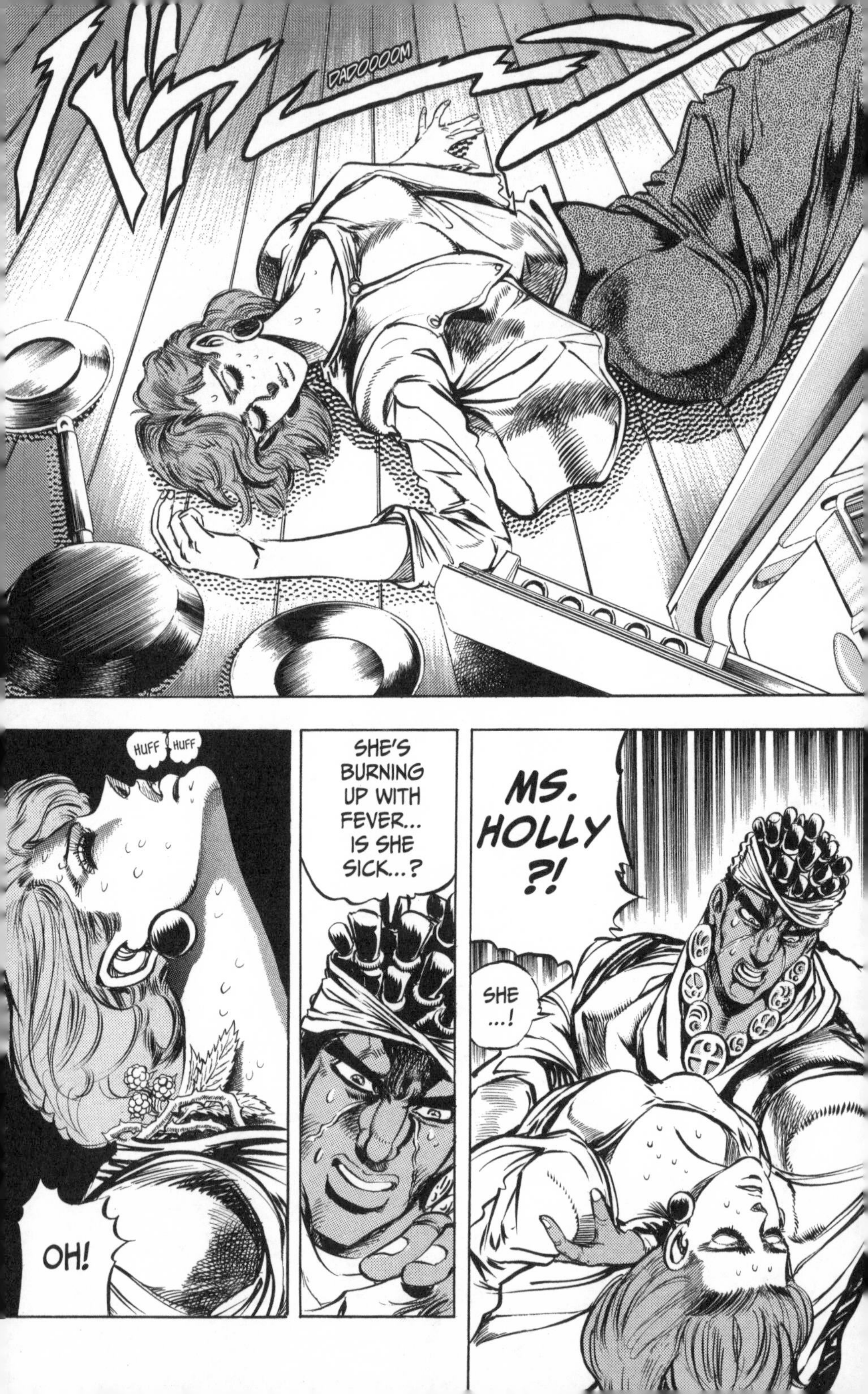
DADOOOOM
MS. HOLLY ?!
SHE ...!
SHE'S BURNING UP WITH FEVER... IS SHE SICK...?
HUFF HUFF
OH!

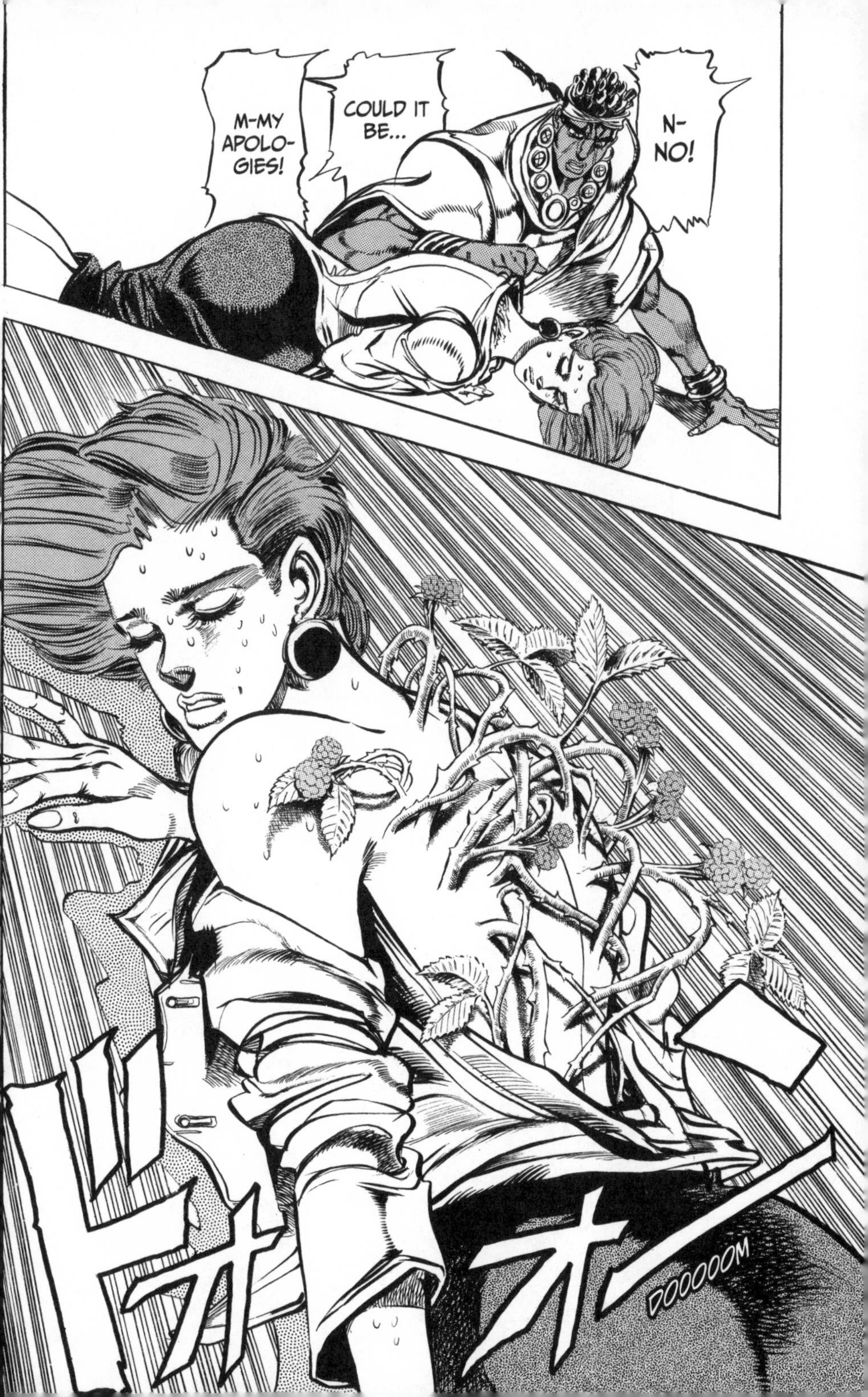
N-
NO!
COULD IT BE...
M-MY APOLOGIES!
ドォオオー
DOOOOOM

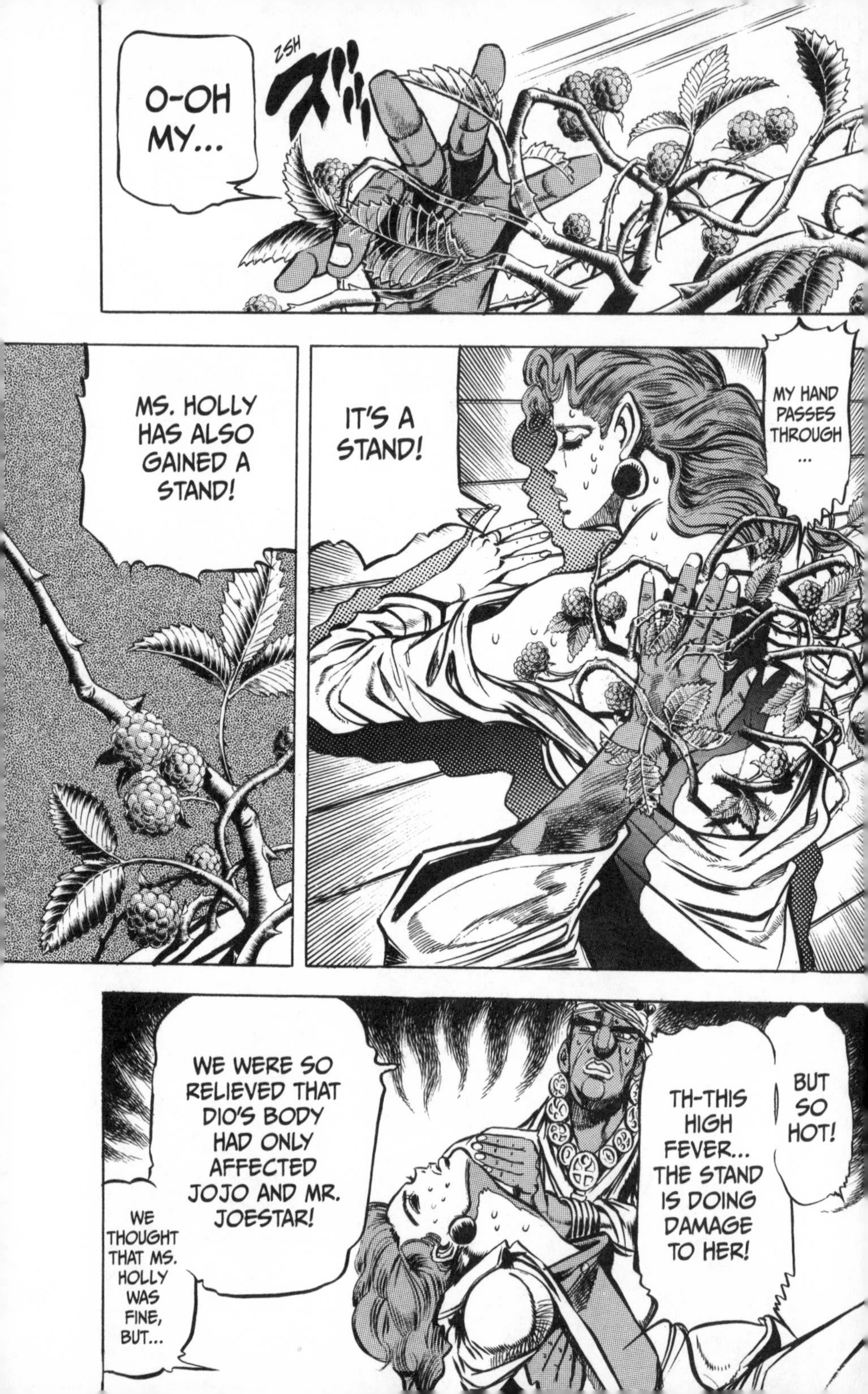
ZSH
O-OH MY...
MY HAND PASSES THROUGH ...
IT'S A STAND!
MS. HOLLY HAS ALSO GAINED A STAND!
BUT SO HOT!
TH-THIS HIGH FEVER... THE STAND IS DOING DAMAGE TO HER!
WE WERE SO RELIEVED THAT DIO'S BODY HAD ONLY AFFECTED JOJO AND MR. JOESTAR!
WE THOUGHT THAT MS. HOLLY WAS FINE, BUT...

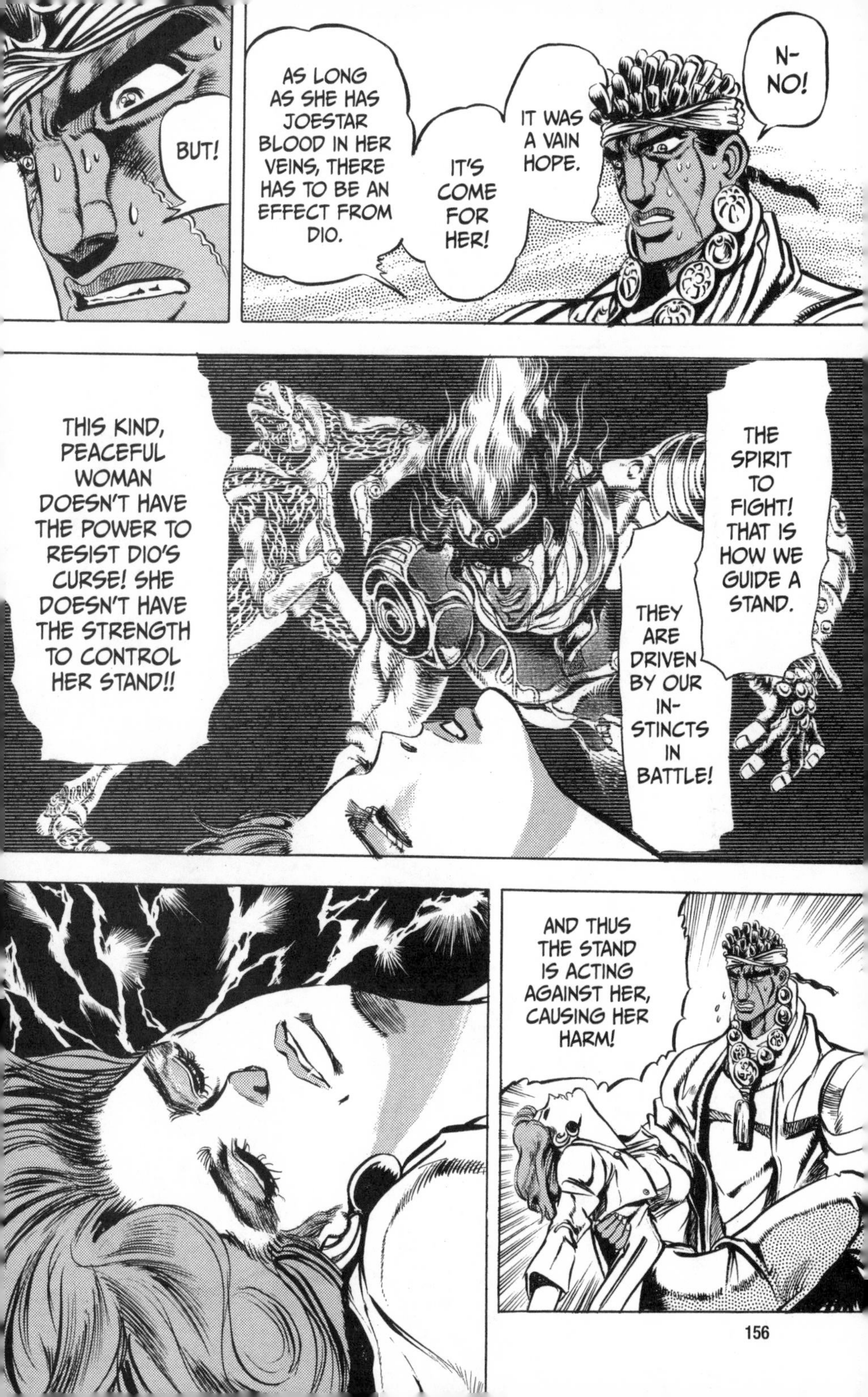
N-NO!
IT WAS A VAIN HOPE.
IT'S COME FOR HER!
AS LONG AS SHE HAS JOESTAR BLOOD IN HER VEINS, THERE HAS TO BE AN EFFECT FROM DIO.
BUT!
THE SPIRIT TO FIGHT! THAT IS HOW WE GUIDE A STAND.
THEY ARE DRIVEN BY OUR IN-STINCTS IN BATTLE!
THIS KIND, PEACEFUL WOMAN DOESN'T HAVE THE POWER TO RESIST DIO'S CURSE! SHE DOESN'T HAVE THE STRENGTH TO CONTROL HER STAND!!
AND THUS THE STAND IS ACTING AGAINST HER, CAUSING HER HARM!

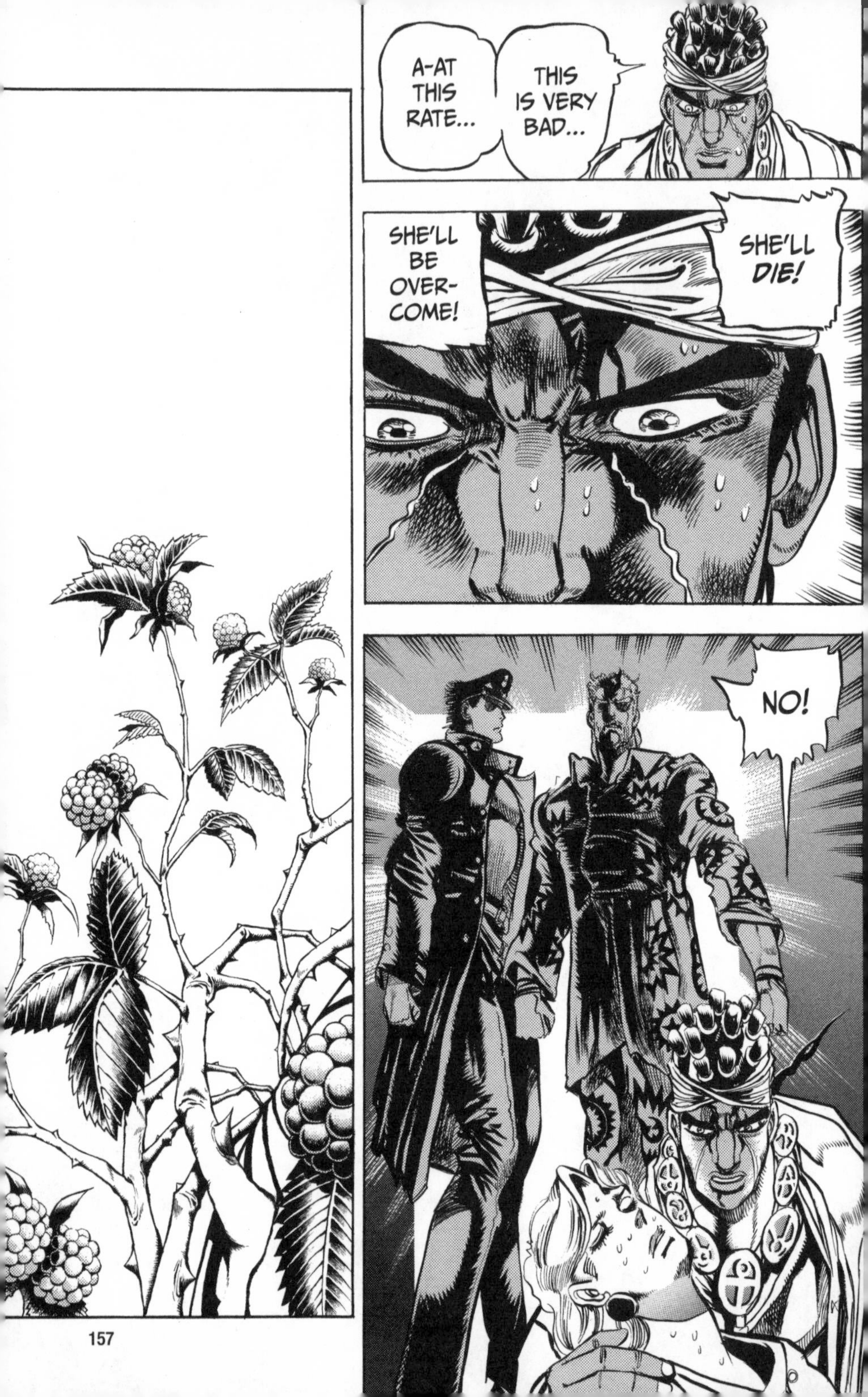
THIS IS VERY BAD...
A-AT THIS RATE...
SHE'LL *DIE!*
SHE'LL BE OVER-COME!
NO!

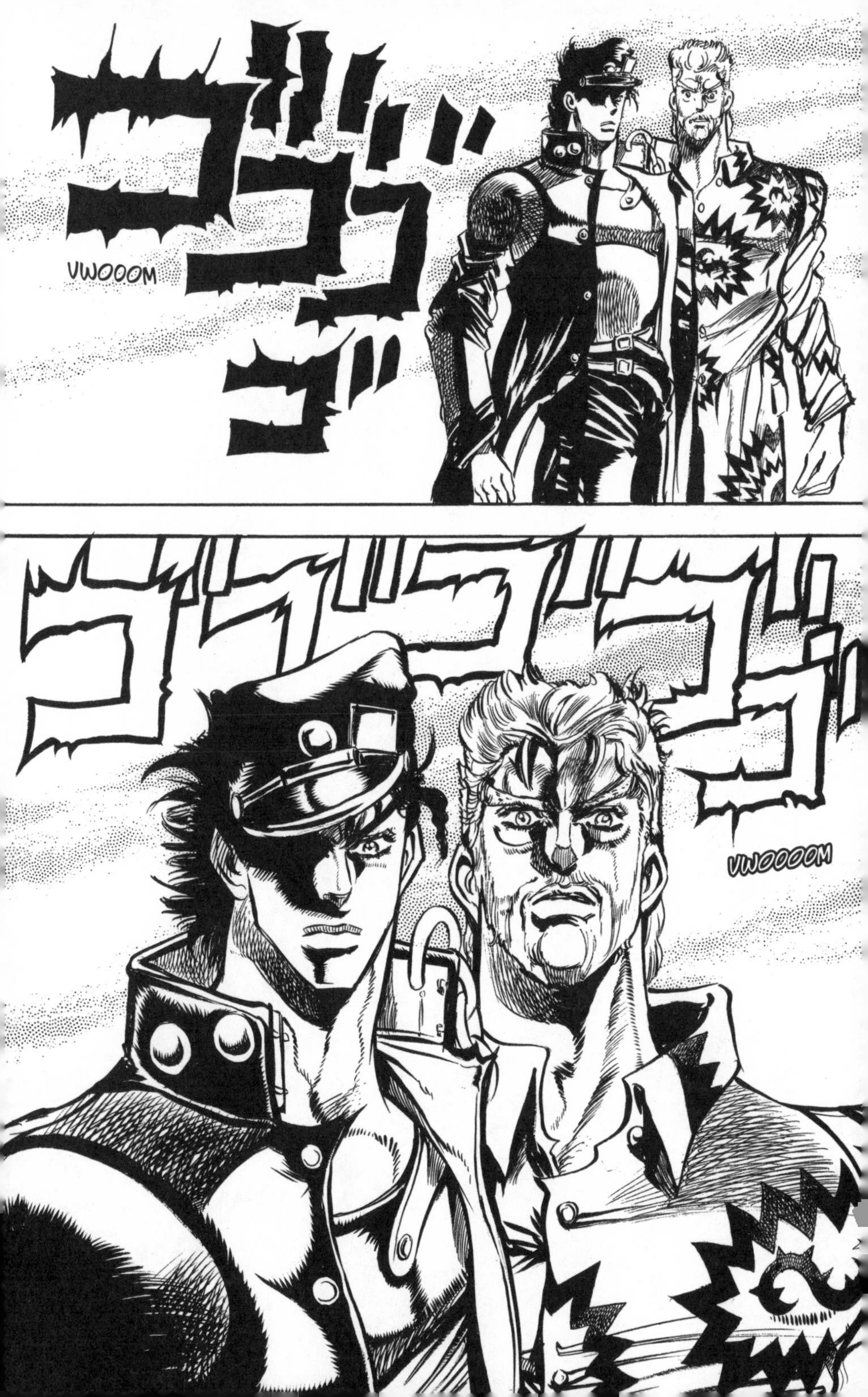
ゴゴゴゴ
VWOOOM
ゴゴゴゴゴ
VWOOOOM

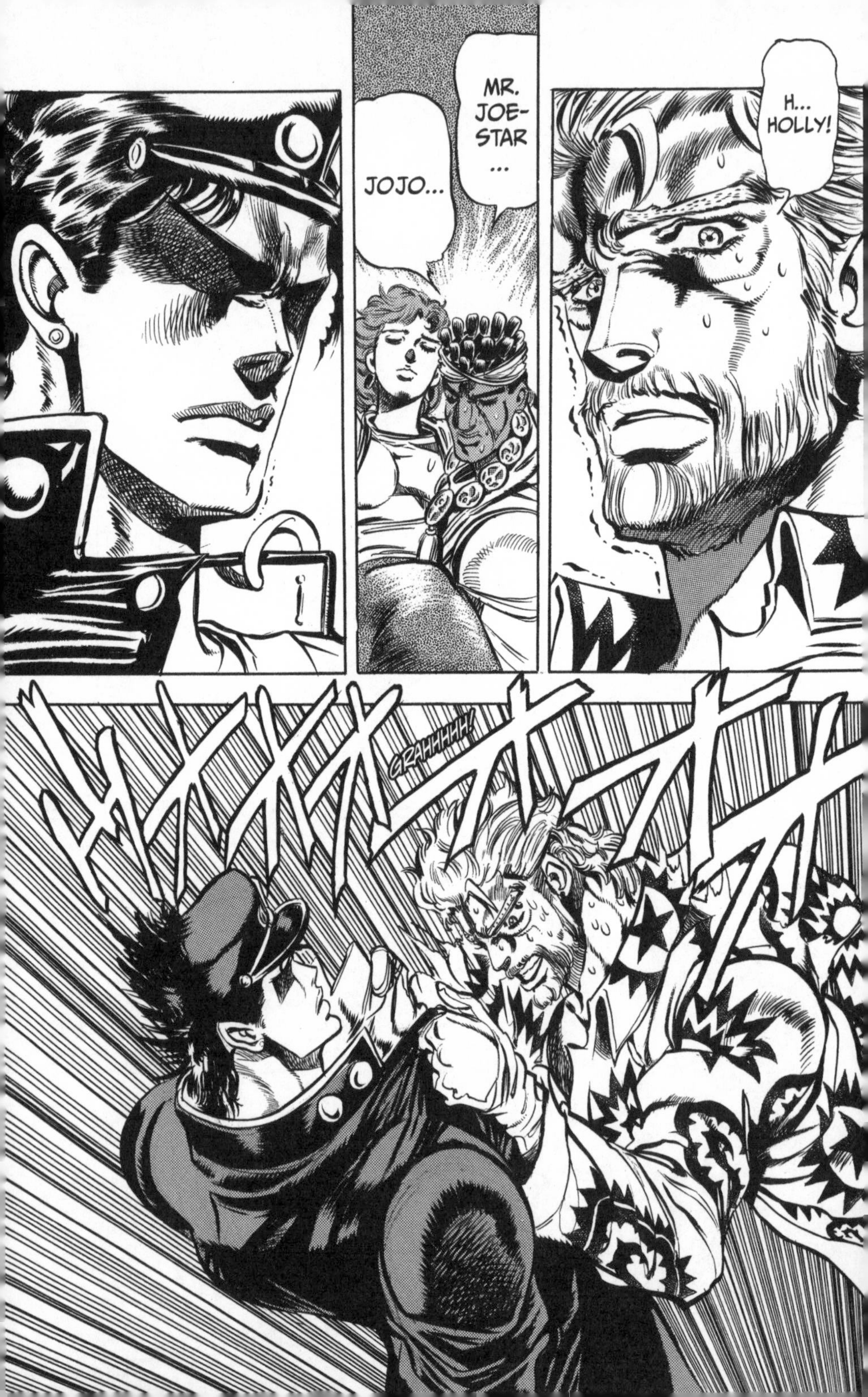
H... HOLLY!
MR. JOE-STAR...
JOJO...
GRAHHHHH!

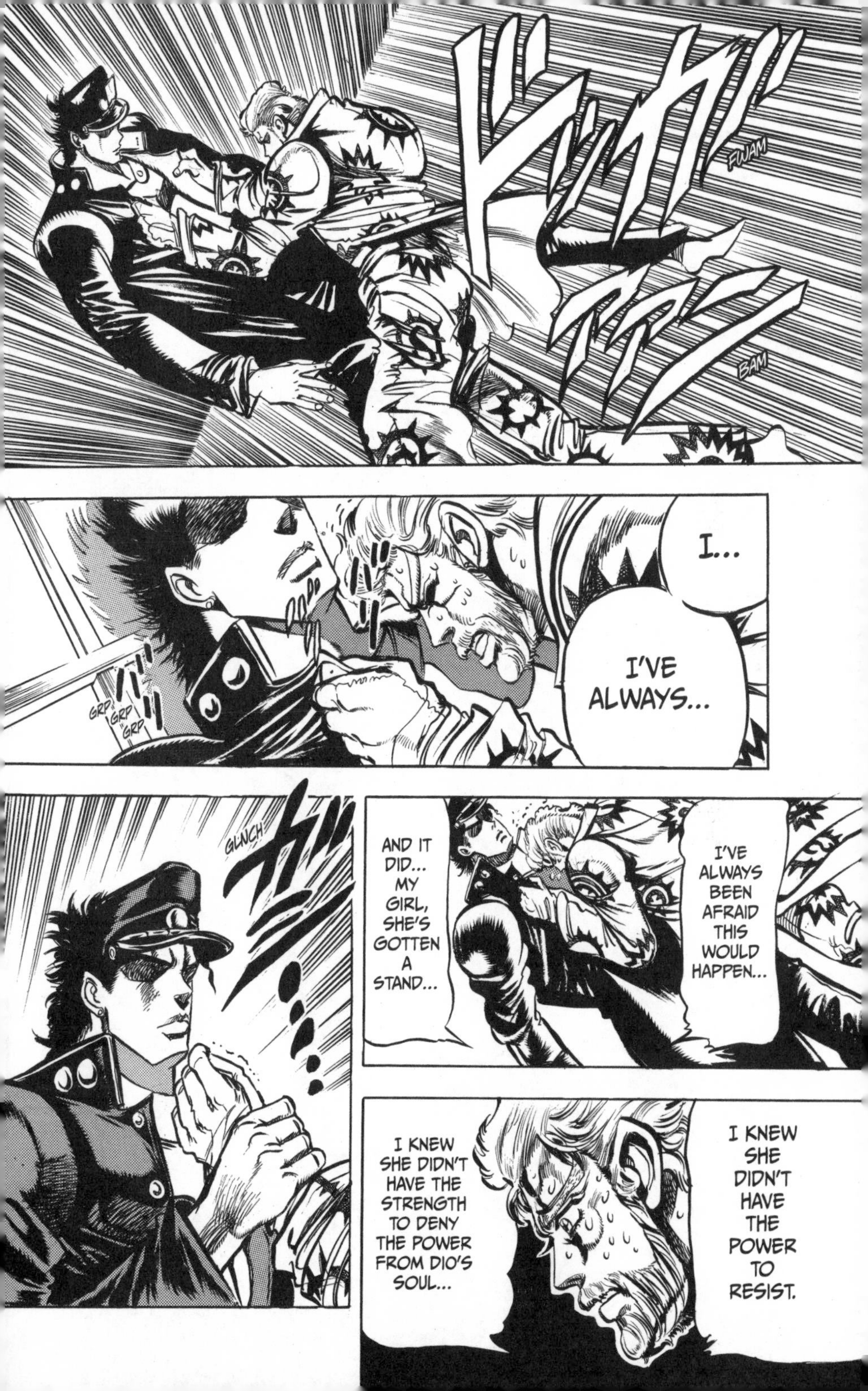
FWAM
BAM
I...
I'VE ALWAYS...
GRP GRP GRP
I'VE ALWAYS BEEN AFRAID THIS WOULD HAPPEN...
AND IT DID... MY GIRL, SHE'S GOTTEN A STAND...
I KNEW SHE DIDN'T HAVE THE POWER TO RESIST.
I KNEW SHE DIDN'T HAVE THE STRENGTH TO DENY THE POWER FROM DIO'S SOUL...
GLNCH

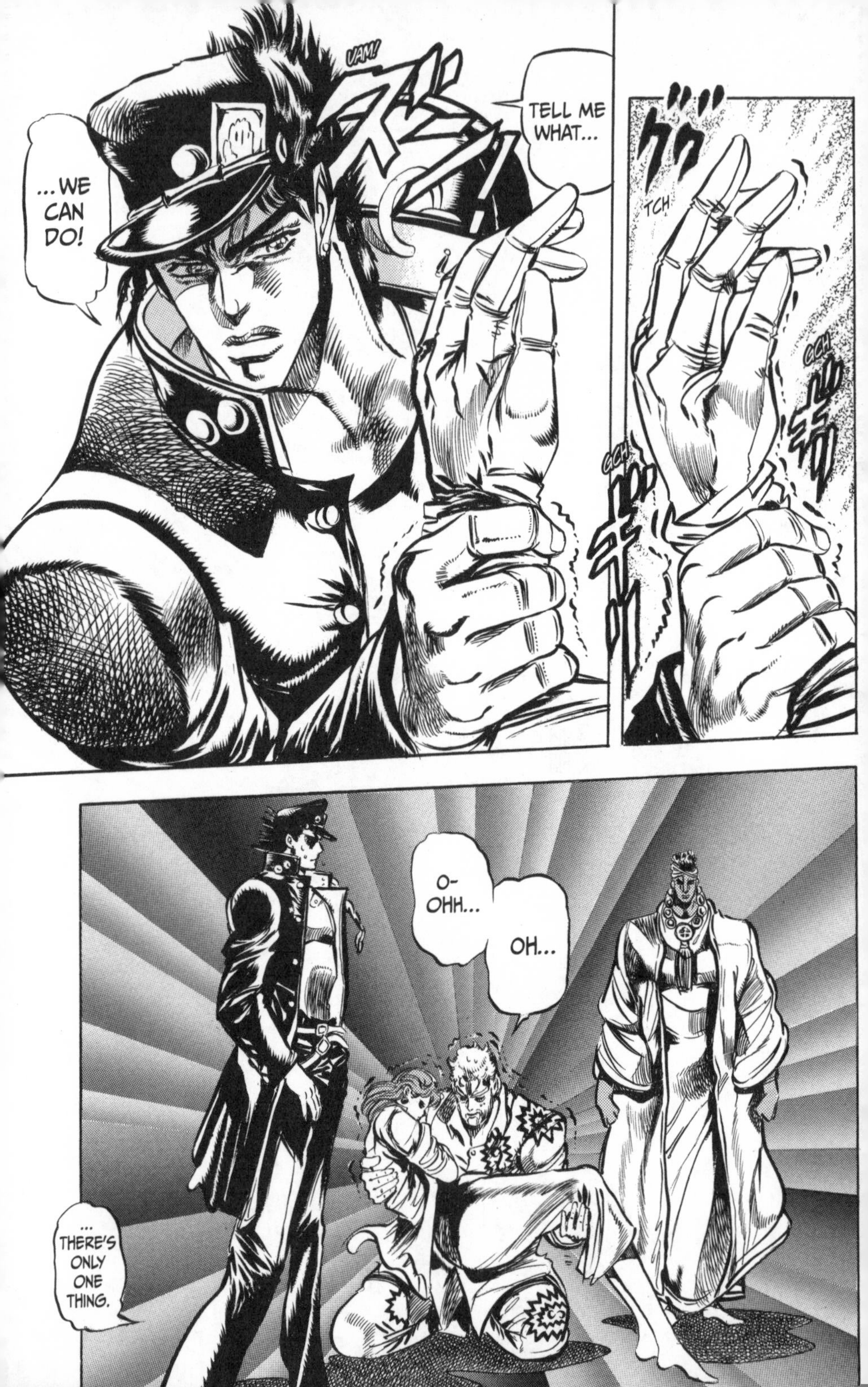
TCH
CCH
CCH
UAM!
TELL ME WHAT...
...WE CAN DO!
O-OHH...
OH...
...THERE'S ONLY ONE THING.

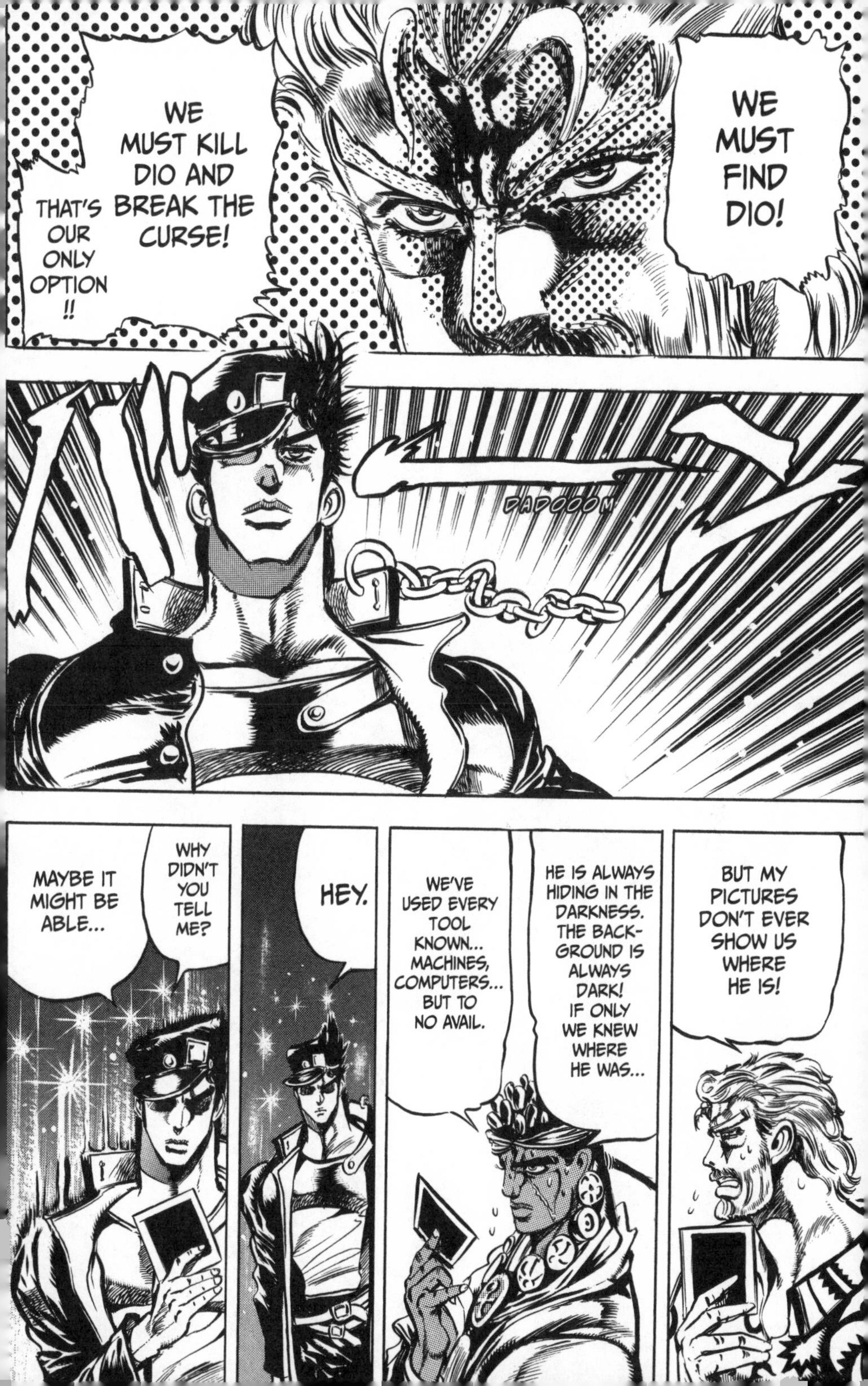
WE MUST FIND DIO!
WE MUST KILL DIO AND BREAK THE CURSE!
THAT'S OUR ONLY OPTION !!
DADOOOOM
BUT MY PICTURES DON'T EVER SHOW US WHERE HE IS!
HE IS ALWAYS HIDING IN THE DARKNESS. THE BACKGROUND IS ALWAYS DARK! IF ONLY WE KNEW WHERE HE WAS...
WE'VE USED EVERY TOOL KNOWN... MACHINES, COMPUTERS... BUT TO NO AVAIL.
HEY.
WHY DIDN'T YOU TELL ME?
MAYBE IT MIGHT BE ABLE...

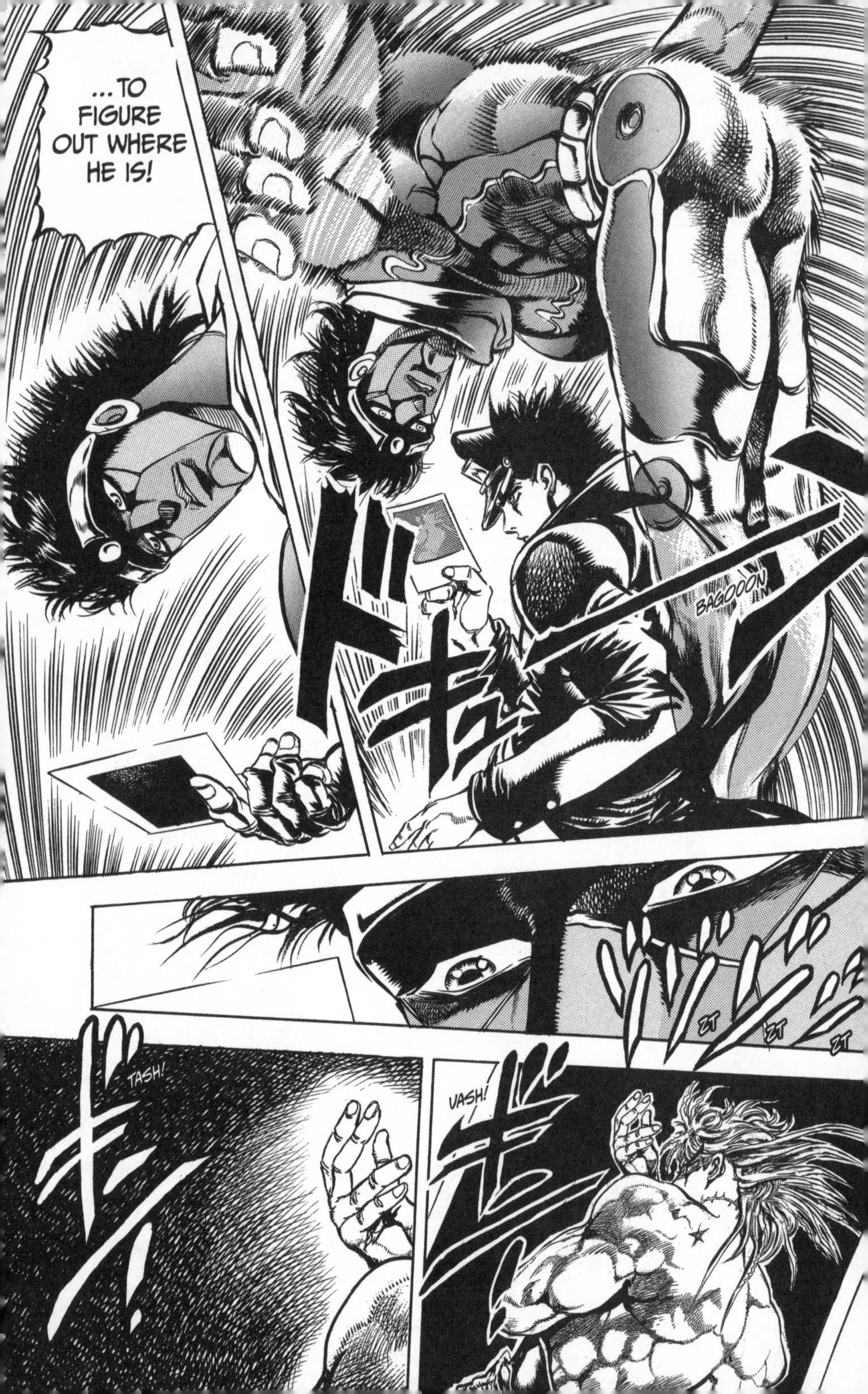
...TO FIGURE OUT WHERE HE IS!
BAGOOON
ZT
ZT
ZT
VASH!
TASH!

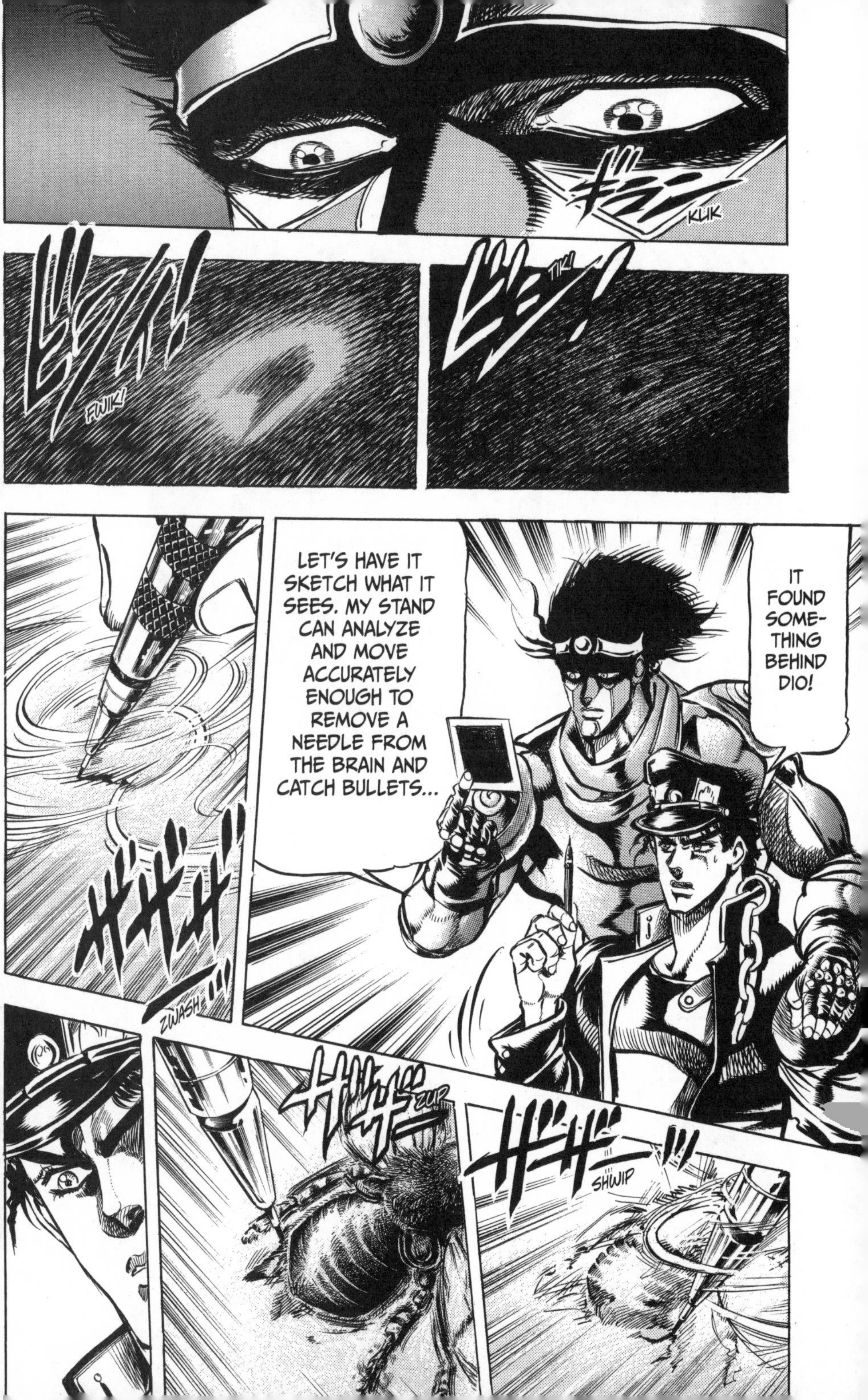
KLIK
TIK!
FWIK!
IT FOUND SOME-THING BEHIND DIO!
LET'S HAVE IT SKETCH WHAT IT SEES. MY STAND CAN ANALYZE AND MOVE ACCURATELY ENOUGH TO REMOVE A NEEDLE FROM THE BRAIN AND CATCH BULLETS...
ZWASH
SHWIP
ZUP

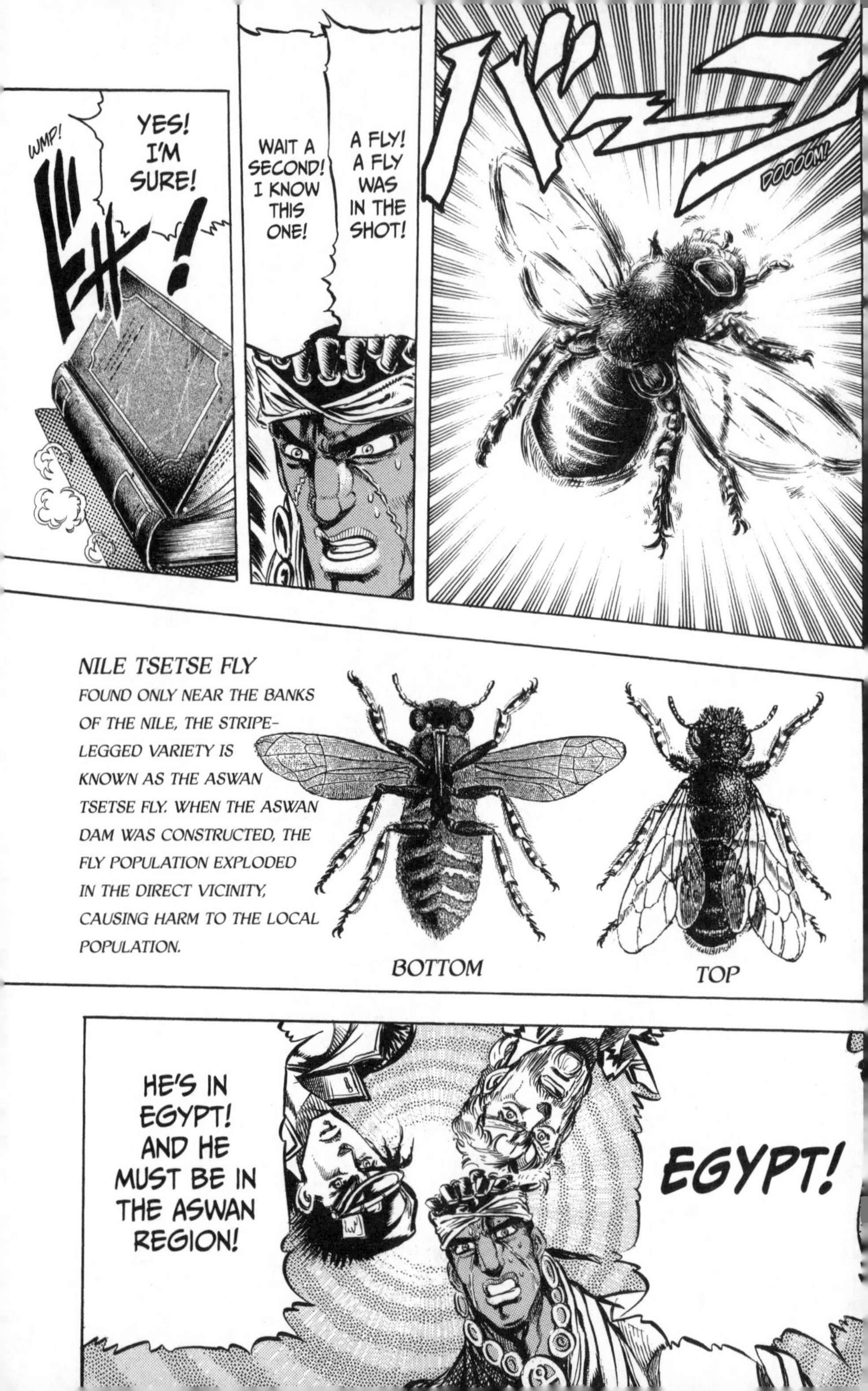
DOOOOM!
A FLY! A FLY WAS IN THE SHOT!
WAIT A SECOND! I KNOW THIS ONE!
YES! I'M SURE!
WMP!
NILE TSETSE FLY
FOUND ONLY NEAR THE BANKS OF THE NILE, THE STRIPE-LEGGED VARIETY IS KNOWN AS THE ASWAN TSETSE FLY. WHEN THE ASWAN DAM WAS CONSTRUCTED, THE FLY POPULATION EXPLODED IN THE DIRECT VICINITY, CAUSING HARM TO THE LOCAL POPULATION.
TOP
BOTTOM
EGYPT!
HE'S IN EGYPT! AND HE MUST BE IN THE ASWAN REGION!

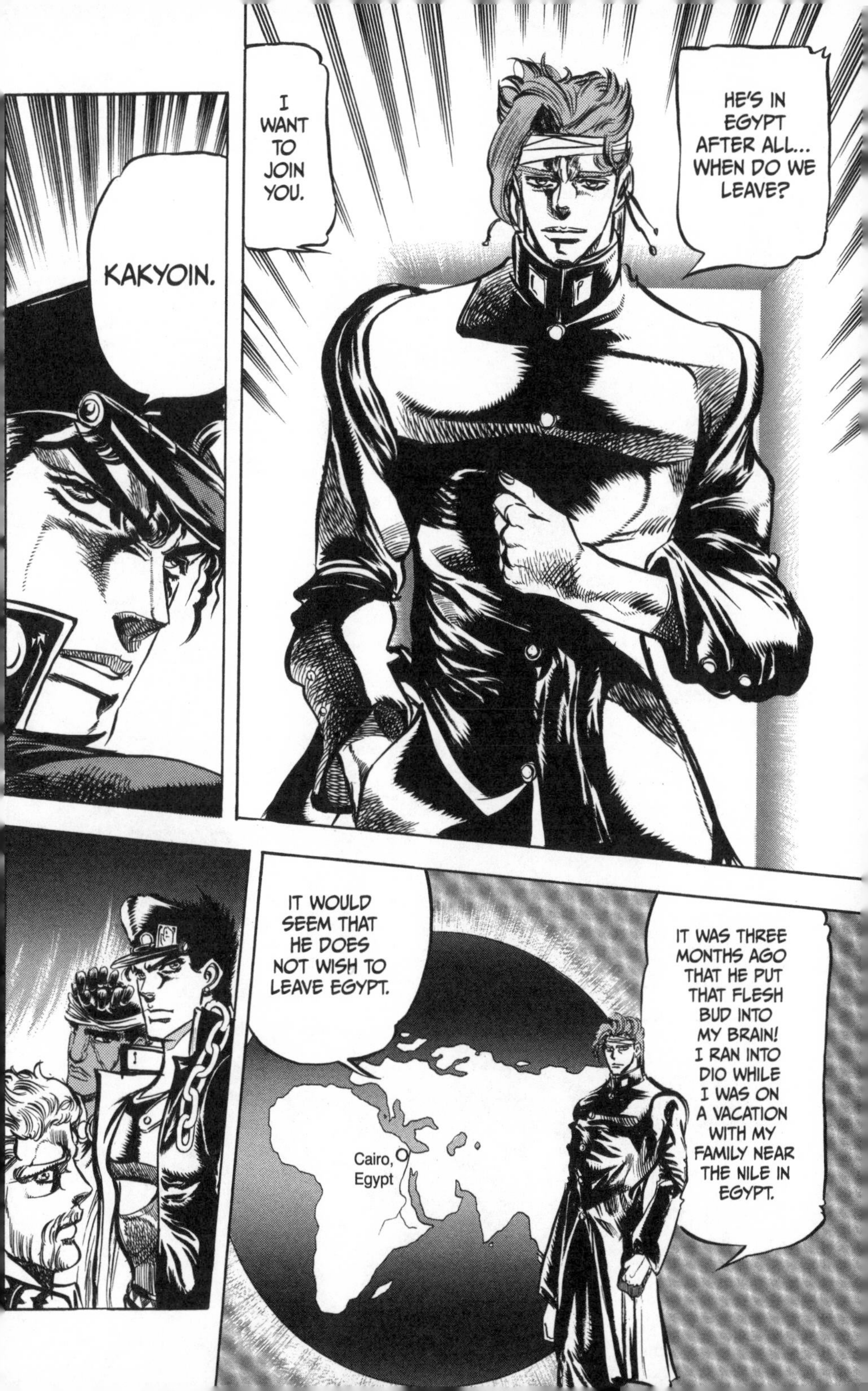
HE'S IN EGYPT AFTER ALL... WHEN DO WE LEAVE?
I WANT TO JOIN YOU.
KAKYOIN.
IT WAS THREE MONTHS AGO THAT HE PUT THAT FLESH BUD INTO MY BRAIN! I RAN INTO DIO WHILE I WAS ON A VACATION WITH MY FAMILY NEAR THE NILE IN EGYPT.
IT WOULD SEEM THAT HE DOES NOT WISH TO LEAVE EGYPT.
Cairo, Egypt

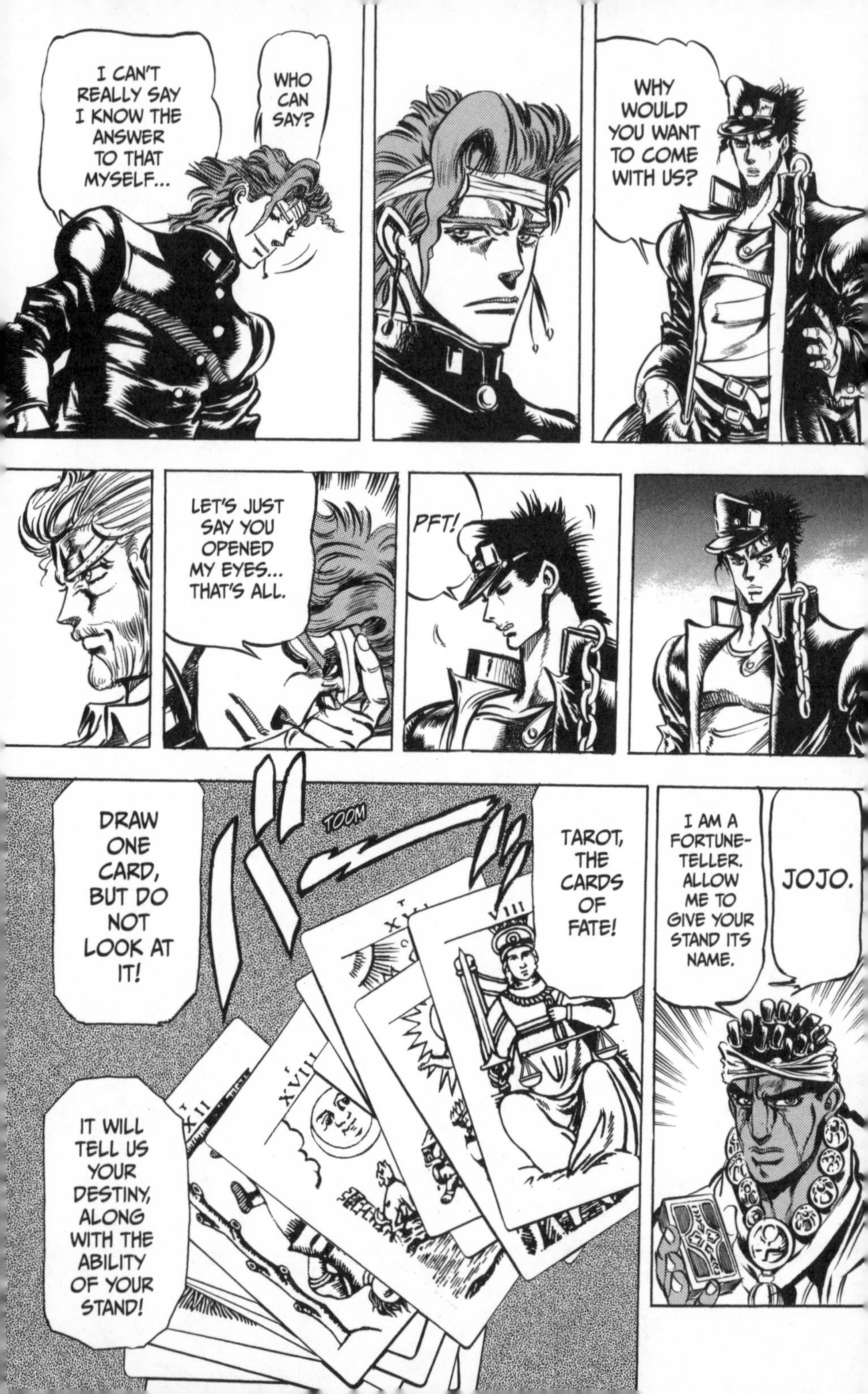
WHY WOULD YOU WANT TO COME WITH US?
WHO CAN SAY?
I CAN'T REALLY SAY I KNOW THE ANSWER TO THAT MYSELF...
PFT!
LET'S JUST SAY YOU OPENED MY EYES... THAT'S ALL.
JOJO.
I AM A FORTUNE-TELLER. ALLOW ME TO GIVE YOUR STAND ITS NAME.
TAROT, THE CARDS OF FATE!
TOOM
DRAW ONE CARD, BUT DO NOT LOOK AT IT!
IT WILL TELL US YOUR DESTINY, ALONG WITH THE ABILITY OF YOUR STAND!

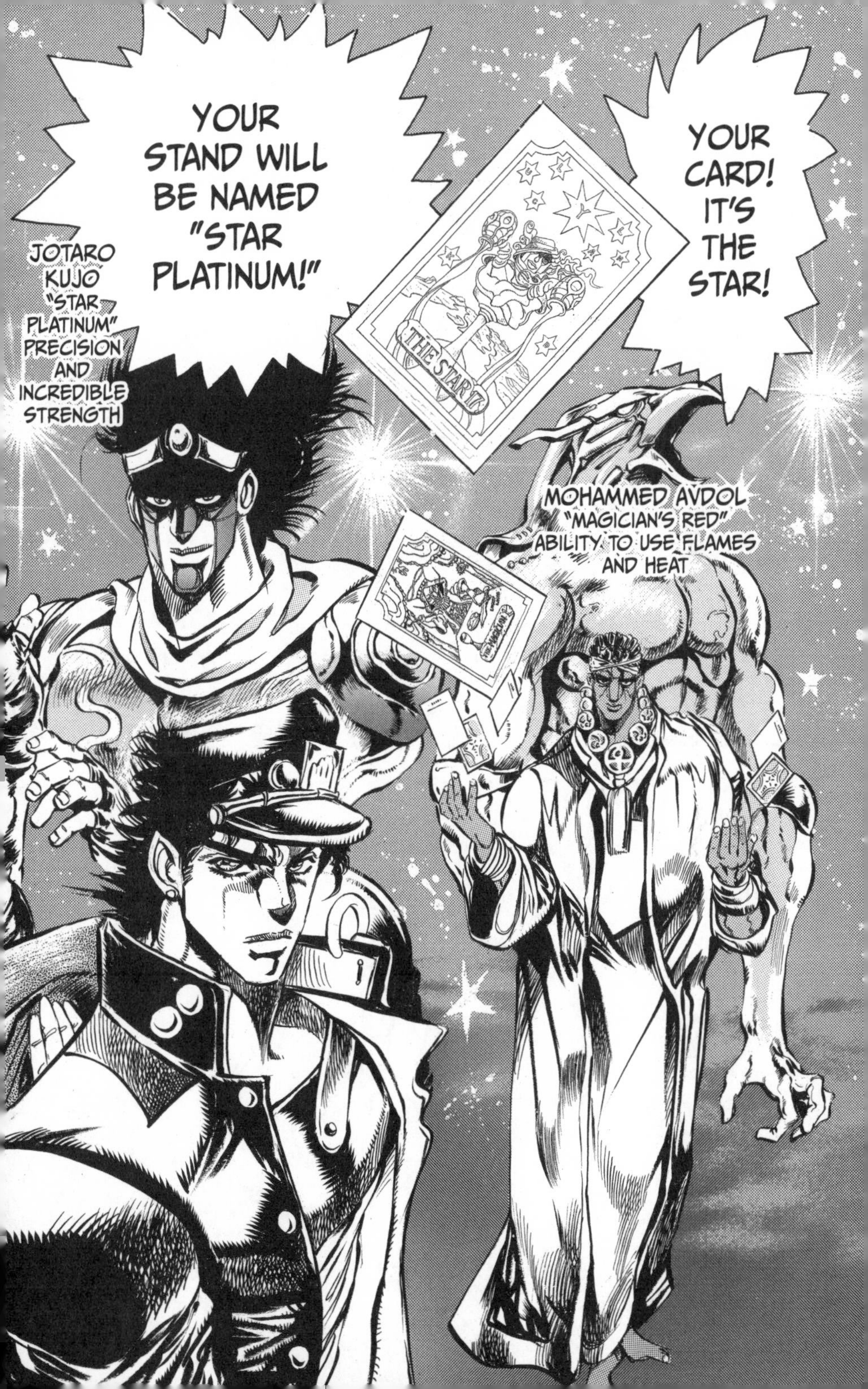
YOUR CARD! IT'S THE STAR!
YOUR STAND WILL BE NAMED "STAR PLATINUM!"
THE STAR 17
JOTARO KUJO "STAR PLATINUM" PRECISION AND INCREDIBLE STRENGTH
MOHAMMED AVDOL "MAGICIAN'S RED" ABILITY TO USE FLAMES AND HEAT

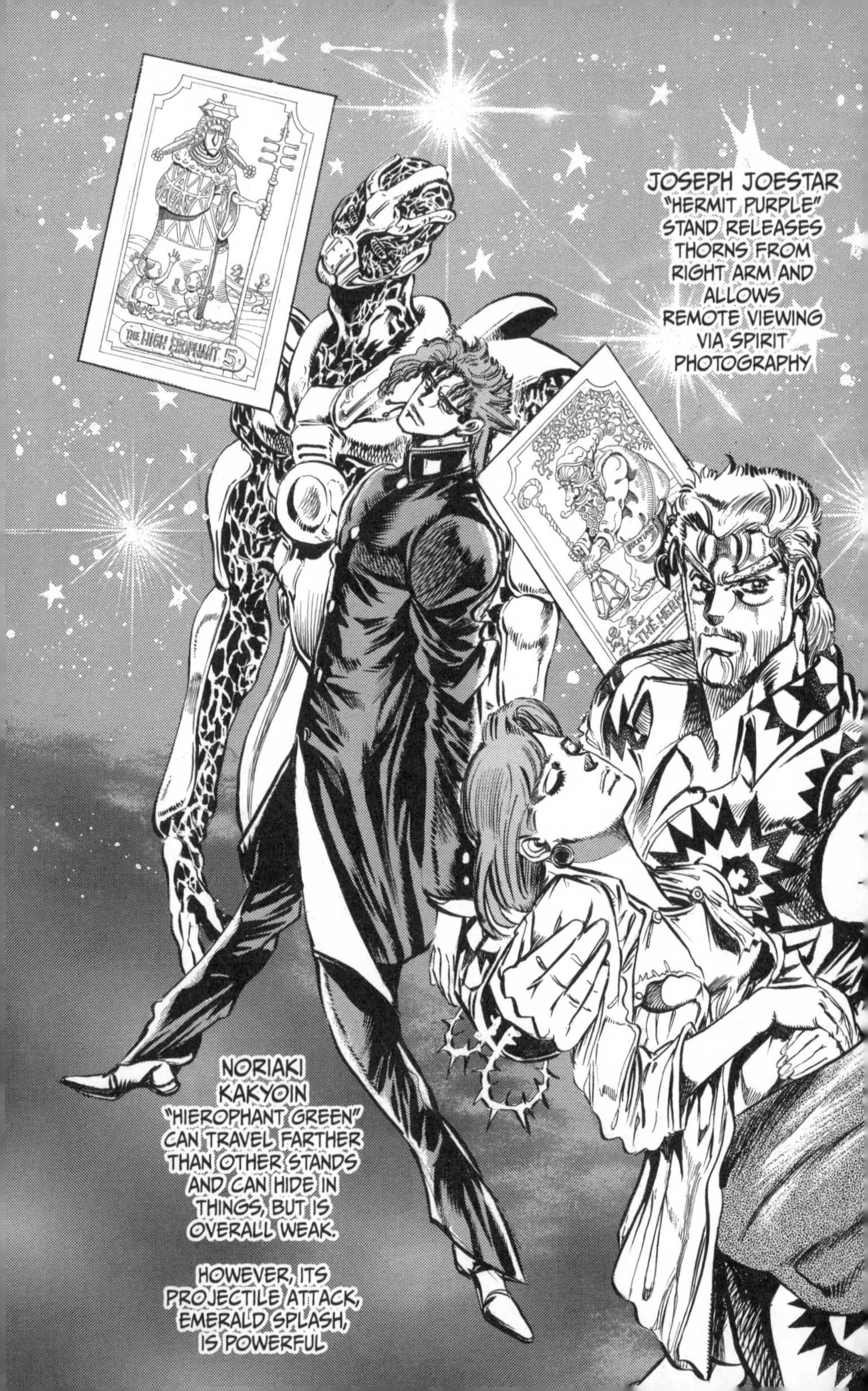
THE HIGH EROPHANT 5
JOSEPH JOESTAR "HERMIT PURPLE" STAND RELEASES THORNS FROM RIGHT ARM AND ALLOWS REMOTE VIEWING VIA SPIRIT PHOTOGRAPHY
NORIAKI KAKYOIN "HIEROPHANT GREEN" CAN TRAVEL FARTHER THAN OTHER STANDS AND CAN HIDE IN THINGS, BUT IS OVERALL WEAK.
HOWEVER, ITS PROJECTILE ATTACK, EMERALD SPLASH, IS POWERFUL

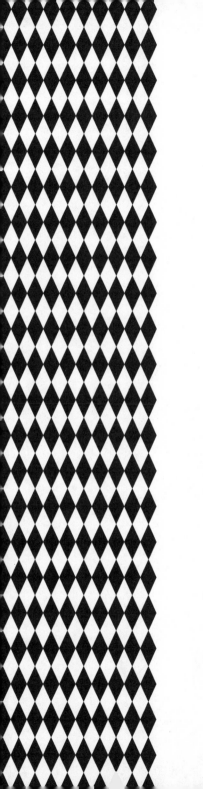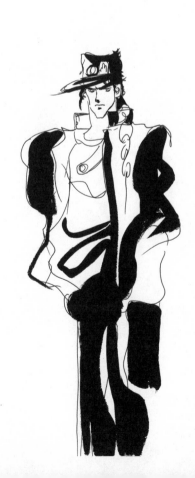

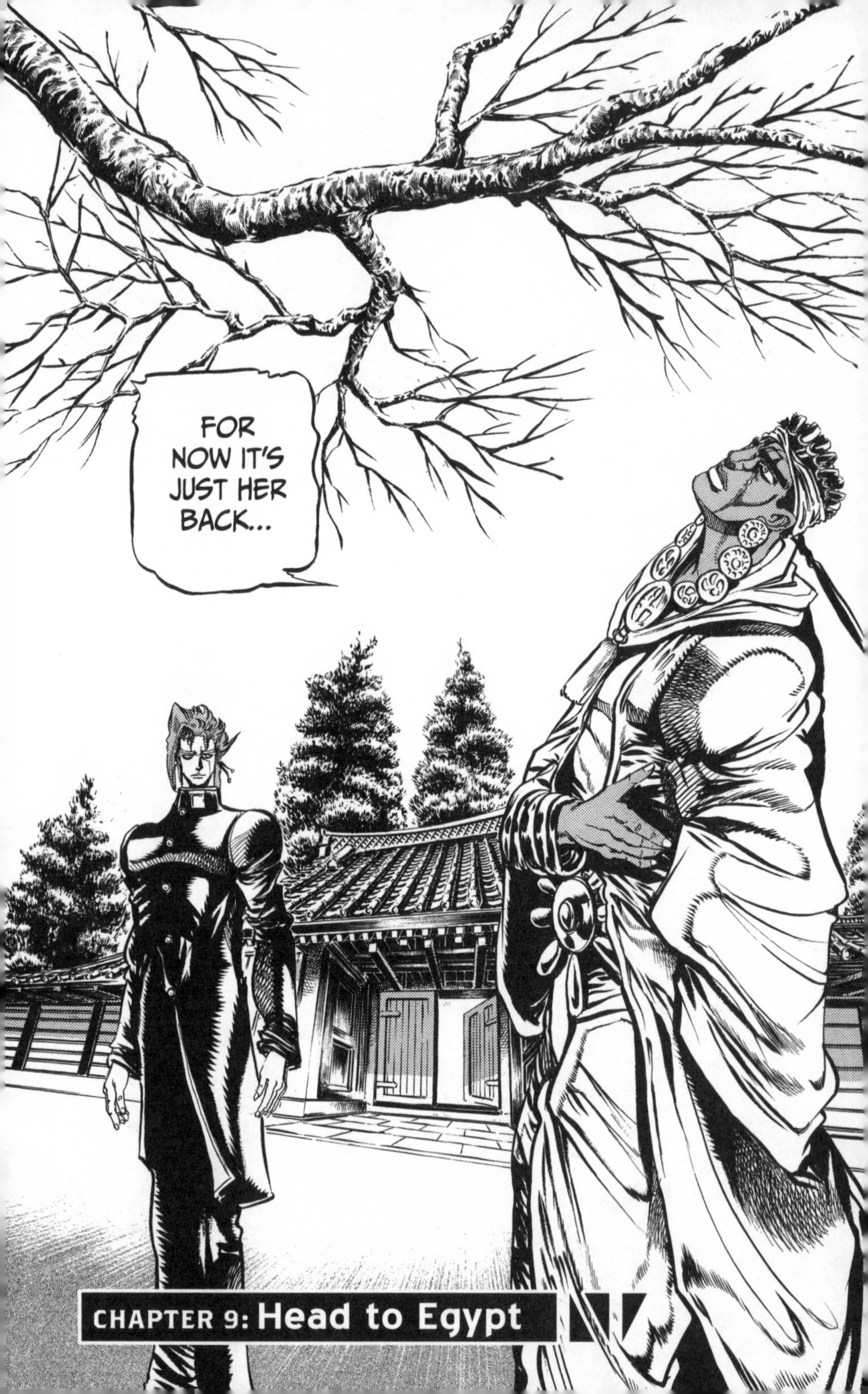
FOR NOW IT'S JUST HER BACK...
CHAPTER 9: Head to Egypt

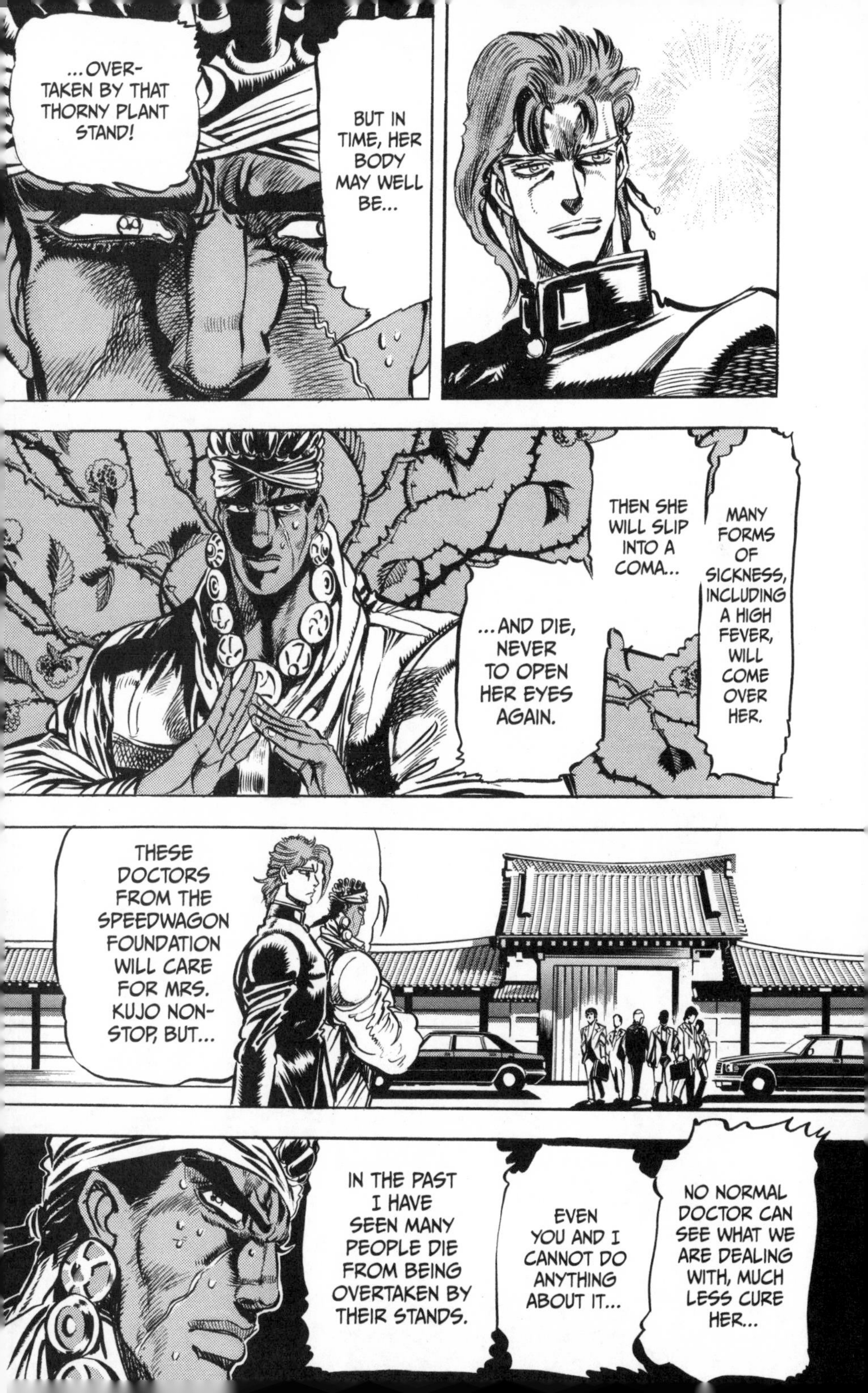
BUT IN TIME, HER BODY MAY WELL BE...
...OVER-TAKEN BY THAT THORNY PLANT STAND!
MANY FORMS OF SICKNESS, INCLUDING A HIGH FEVER, WILL COME OVER HER.
THEN SHE WILL SLIP INTO A COMA...
...AND DIE, NEVER TO OPEN HER EYES AGAIN.
THESE DOCTORS FROM THE SPEEDWAGON FOUNDATION WILL CARE FOR MRS. KUJO NON-STOP, BUT...
NO NORMAL DOCTOR CAN SEE WHAT WE ARE DEALING WITH, MUCH LESS CURE HER...
EVEN YOU AND I CANNOT DO ANYTHING ABOUT IT...
IN THE PAST I HAVE SEEN MANY PEOPLE DIE FROM BEING OVERTAKEN BY THEIR STANDS.

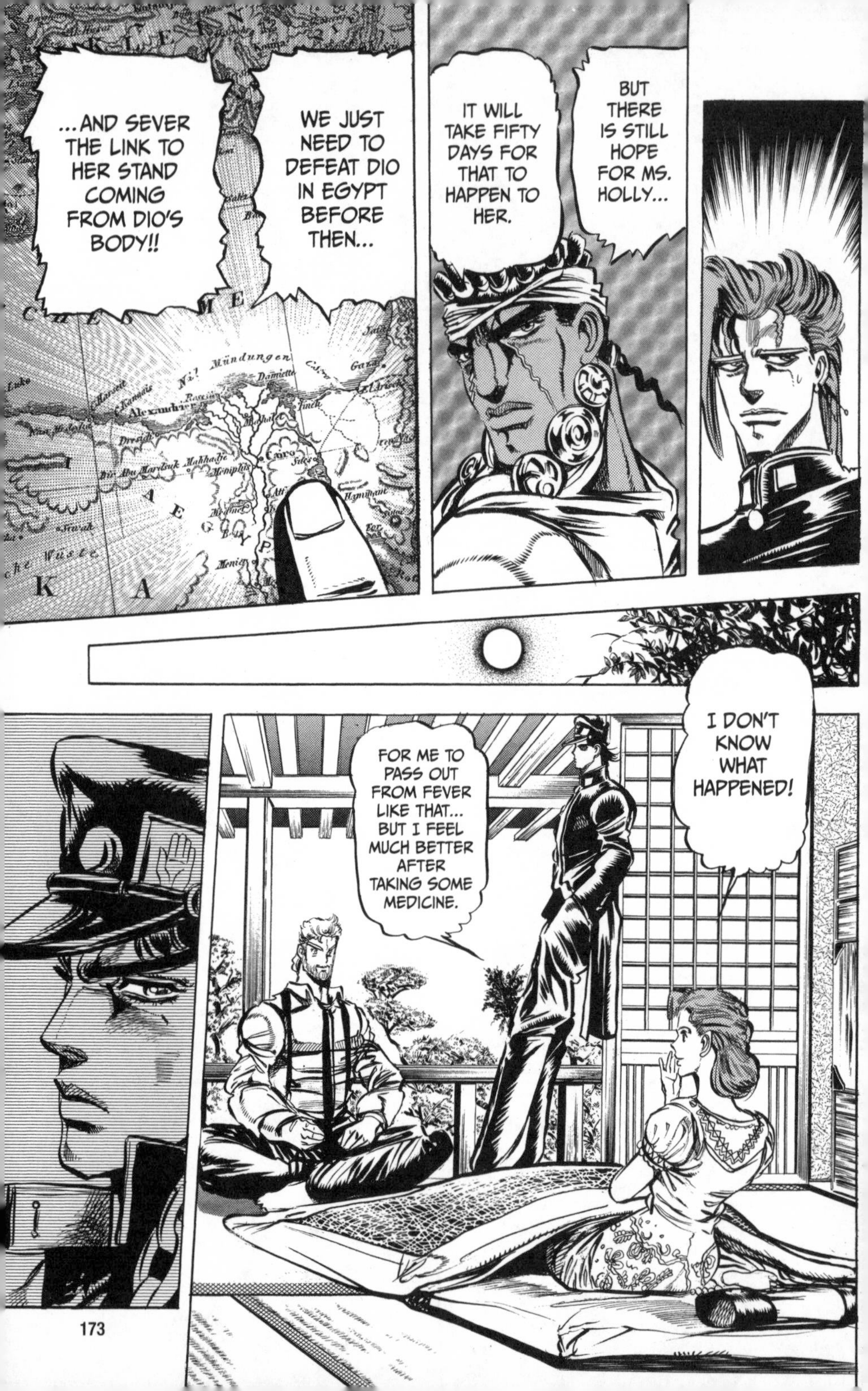
BUT THERE IS STILL HOPE FOR MS. HOLLY...
IT WILL TAKE FIFTY DAYS FOR THAT TO HAPPEN TO HER.
WE JUST NEED TO DEFEAT DIO IN EGYPT BEFORE THEN...
...AND SEVER THE LINK TO HER STAND COMING FROM DIO'S BODY!!
I DON'T KNOW WHAT HAPPENED!
FOR ME TO PASS OUT FROM FEVER LIKE THAT... BUT I FEEL MUCH BETTER AFTER TAKING SOME MEDICINE.

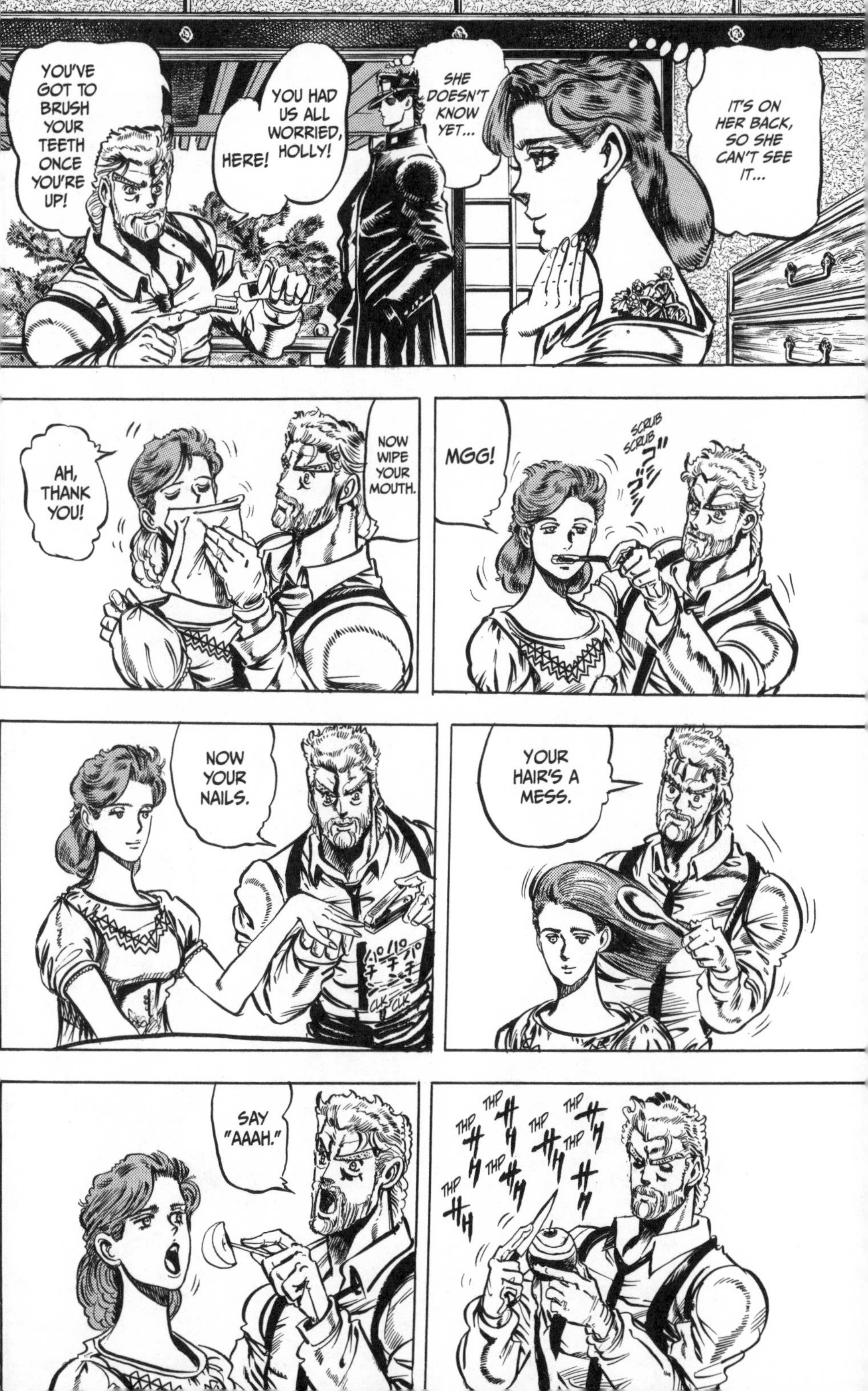
IT'S ON HER BACK, SO SHE CAN'T SEE IT...
SHE DOESN'T KNOW YET...
YOU HAD US ALL WORRIED, HOLLY!
HERE!
YOU'VE GOT TO BRUSH YOUR TEETH ONCE YOU'RE UP!
SCRUB SCRUB
MGG!
NOW WIPE YOUR MOUTH.
AH, THANK YOU!
YOUR HAIR'S A MESS.
NOW YOUR NAILS.
CLK CLK
THP THP THP THP THP THP THP
SAY "AAAH."

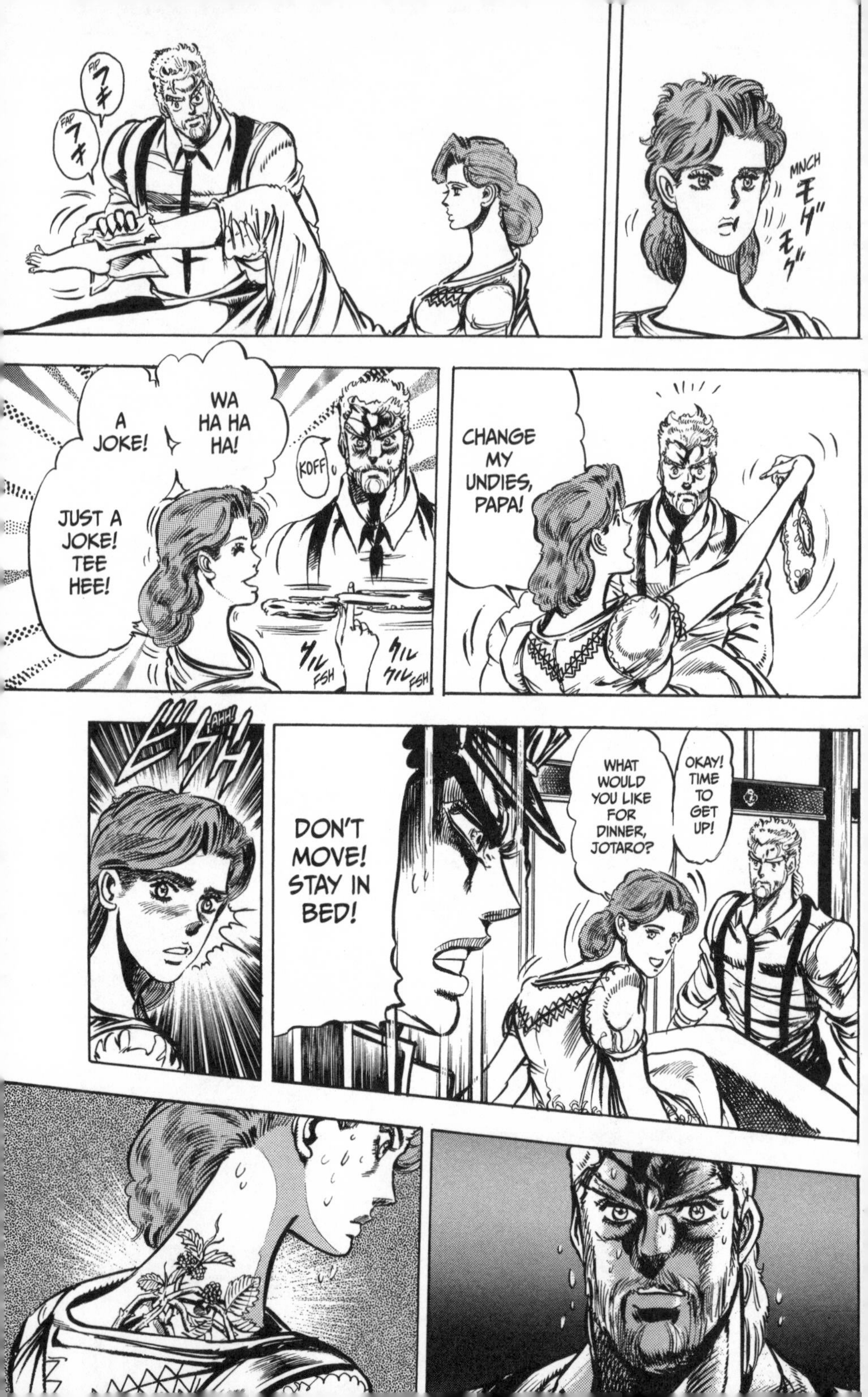
MNCH
FIP
FAP
CHANGE MY UNDIES, PAPA!
KOFF
WA HA HA HA!
A JOKE!
JUST A JOKE! TEE HEE!
FSH
FSH
OKAY! TIME TO GET UP!
WHAT WOULD YOU LIKE FOR DINNER, JOTARO?
DON'T MOVE! STAY IN BED!
AHH!

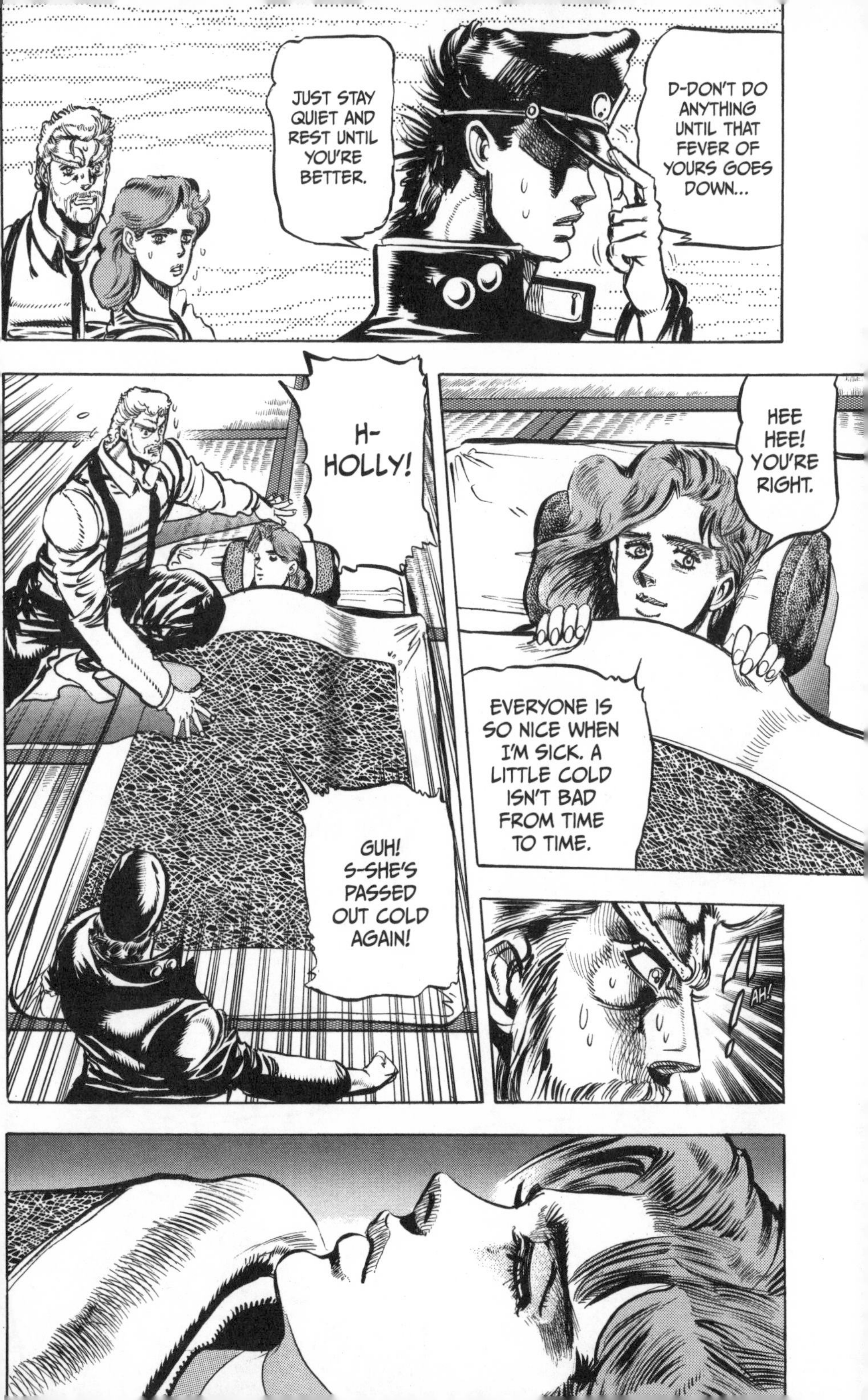
D-DON'T DO ANYTHING UNTIL THAT FEVER OF YOURS GOES DOWN...
JUST STAY QUIET AND REST UNTIL YOU'RE BETTER.
HEE HEE! YOU'RE RIGHT.
EVERYONE IS SO NICE WHEN I'M SICK. A LITTLE COLD ISN'T BAD FROM TIME TO TIME.
AH!
H- HOLLY!
GUH! S-SHE'S PASSED OUT COLD AGAIN!

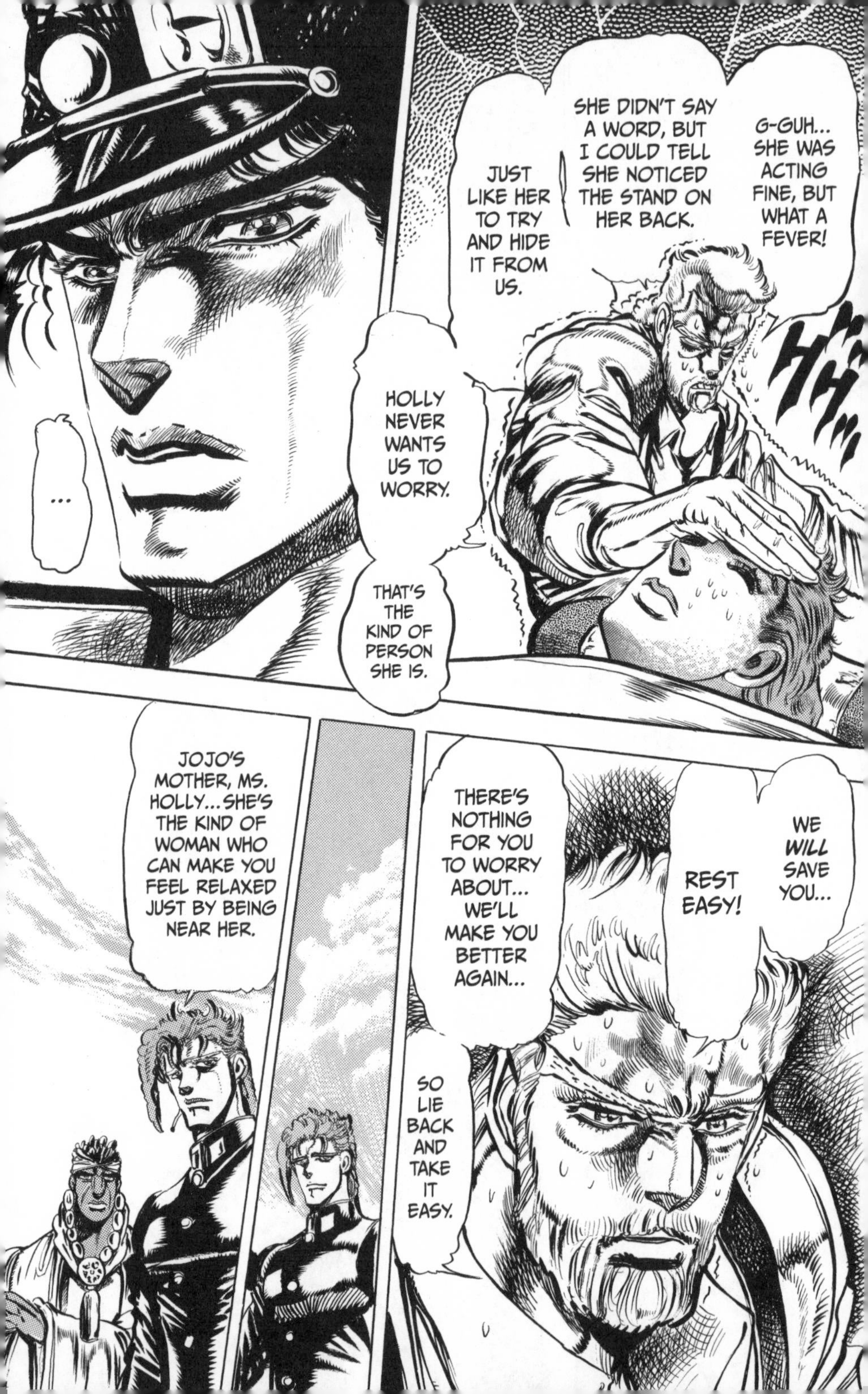
G-GUH... SHE WAS ACTING FINE, BUT WHAT A FEVER!
SHE DIDN'T SAY A WORD, BUT I COULD TELL SHE NOTICED THE STAND ON HER BACK.
JUST LIKE HER TO TRY AND HIDE IT FROM US.
HOLLY NEVER WANTS US TO WORRY.
THAT'S THE KIND OF PERSON SHE IS.
...
WE *WILL* SAVE YOU...
REST EASY!
THERE'S NOTHING FOR YOU TO WORRY ABOUT... WE'LL MAKE YOU BETTER AGAIN...
SO LIE BACK AND TAKE IT EASY.
JOJO'S MOTHER, MS. HOLLY...SHE'S THE KIND OF WOMAN WHO CAN MAKE YOU FEEL RELAXED JUST BY BEING NEAR HER.

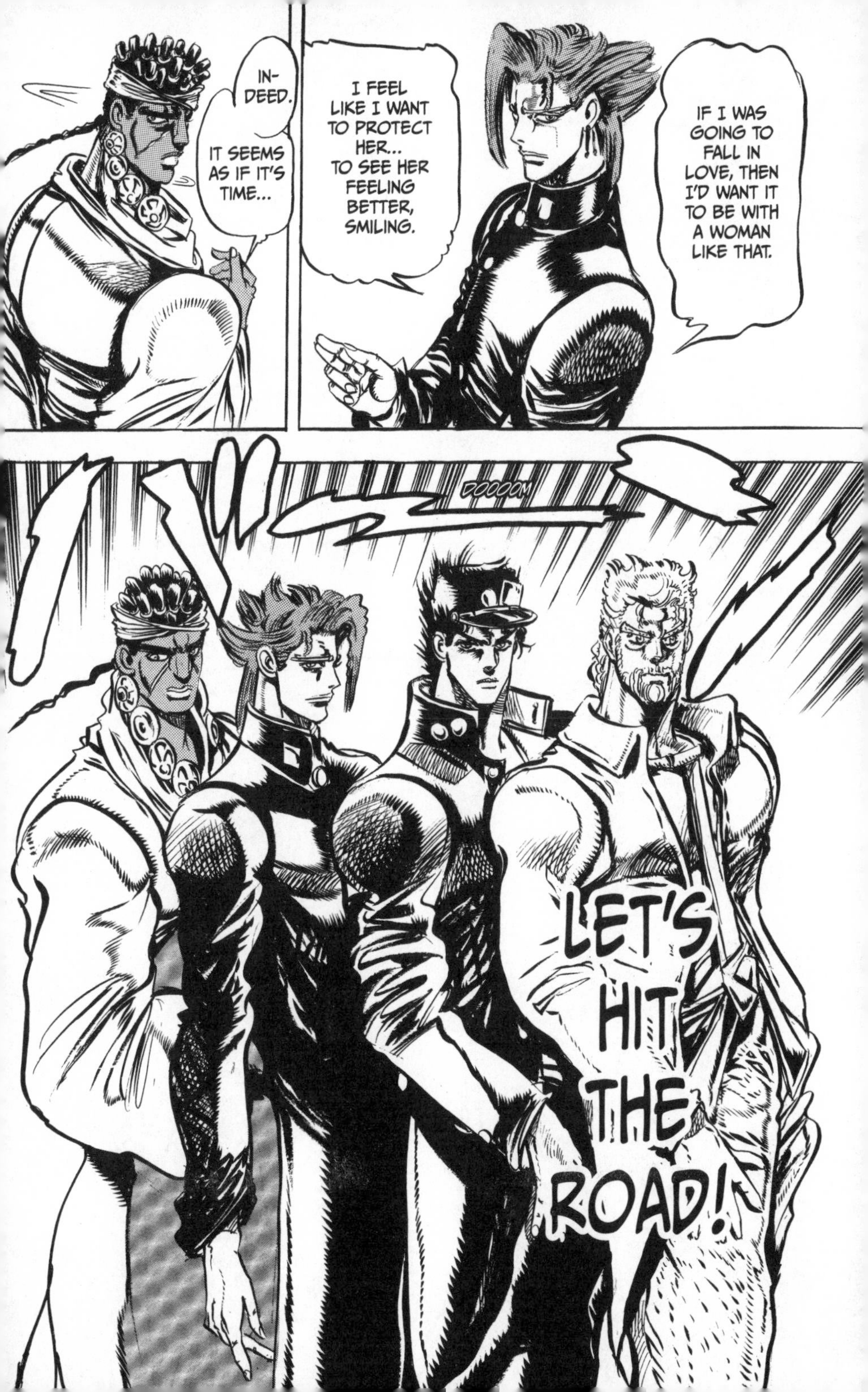
I FEEL LIKE I WANT TO PROTECT HER... TO SEE HER FEELING BETTER, SMILING.
IF I WAS GOING TO FALL IN LOVE, THEN I'D WANT IT TO BE WITH A WOMAN LIKE THAT.
IN-DEED.
IT SEEMS AS IF IT'S TIME...
DOOOOM
LET'S HIT THE ROAD!

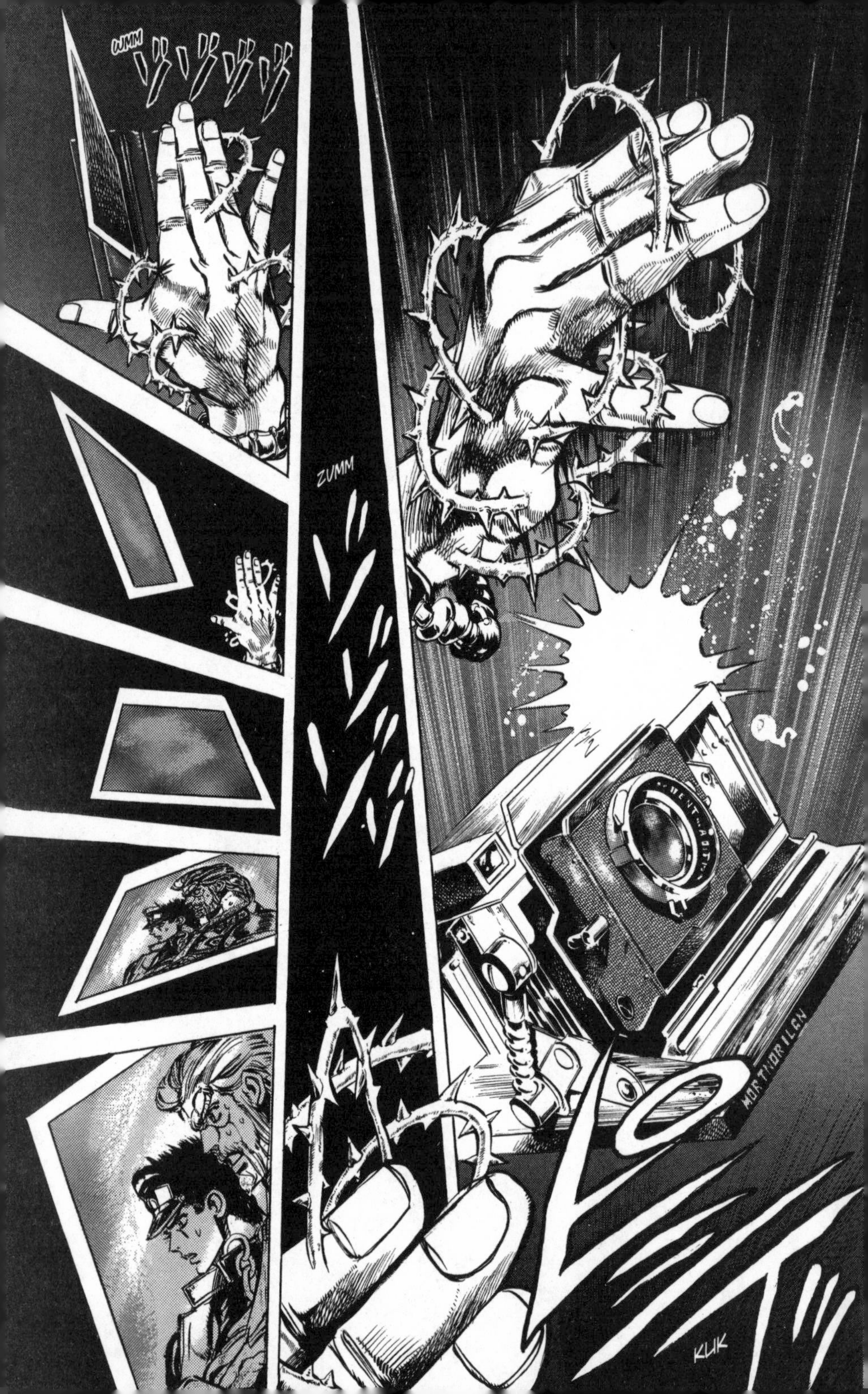
KLIK
ZUMM
WMM ジジジジ

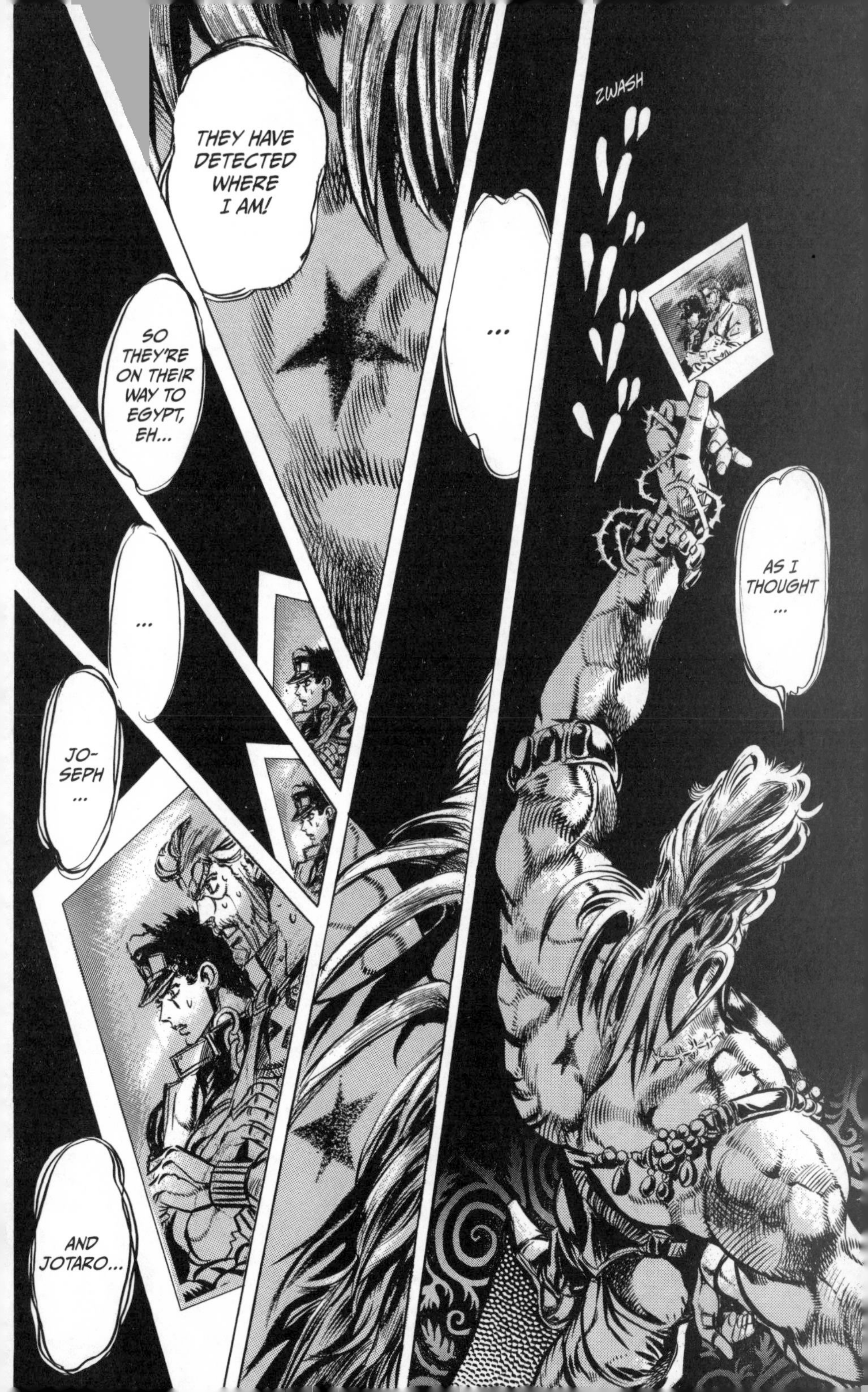
ZWASH
AS I THOUGHT ...
...
THEY HAVE DETECTED WHERE I AM!
SO THEY'RE ON THEIR WAY TO EGYPT, EH...
...
JO-SEPH ...
AND JOTARO...

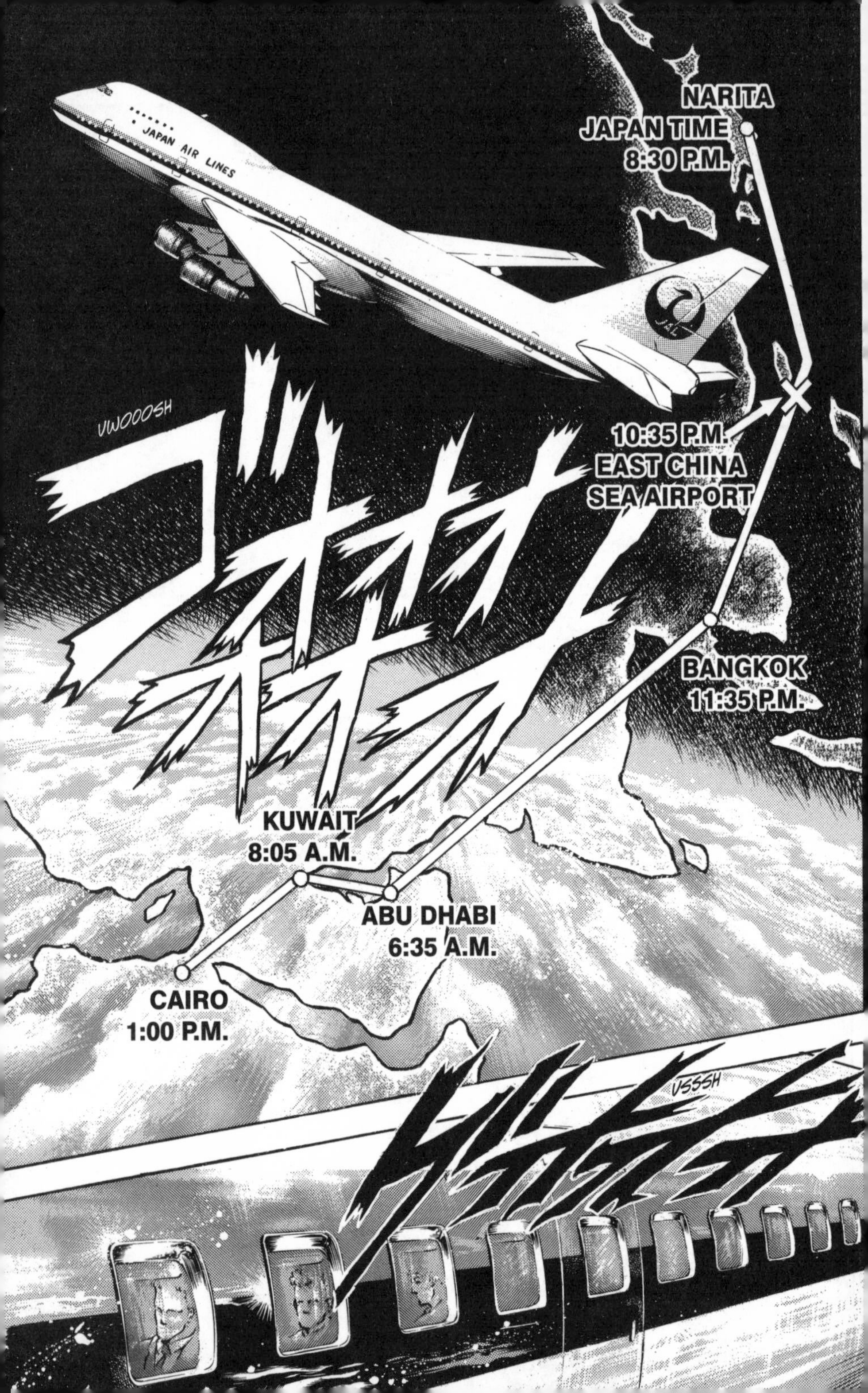
NARITA
JAPAN TIME
8:30 P.M.
10:35 P.M.
EAST CHINA
SEA AIRPORT
BANGKOK
11:35 P.M.
ABU DHABI
6:35 A.M.
KUWAIT
8:05 A.M.
CAIRO
1:00 P.M.
JAPAN AIR LINES
VWOOOSH
VSSSH

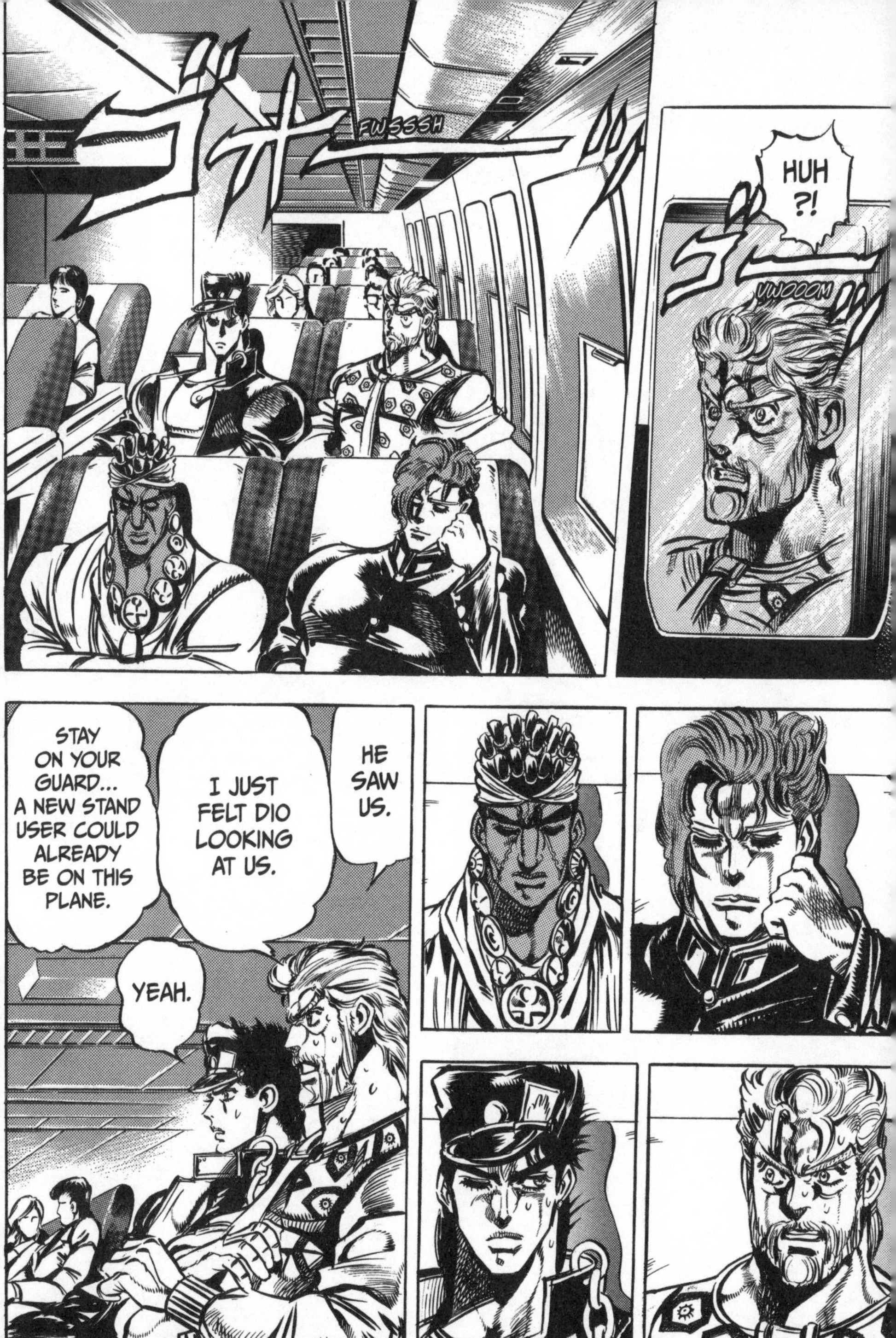
HUH ?!
VWOOOM
FWSSSH
HE SAW US.
I JUST FELT DIO LOOKING AT US.
STAY ON YOUR GUARD... A NEW STAND USER COULD ALREADY BE ON THIS PLANE.
YEAH.

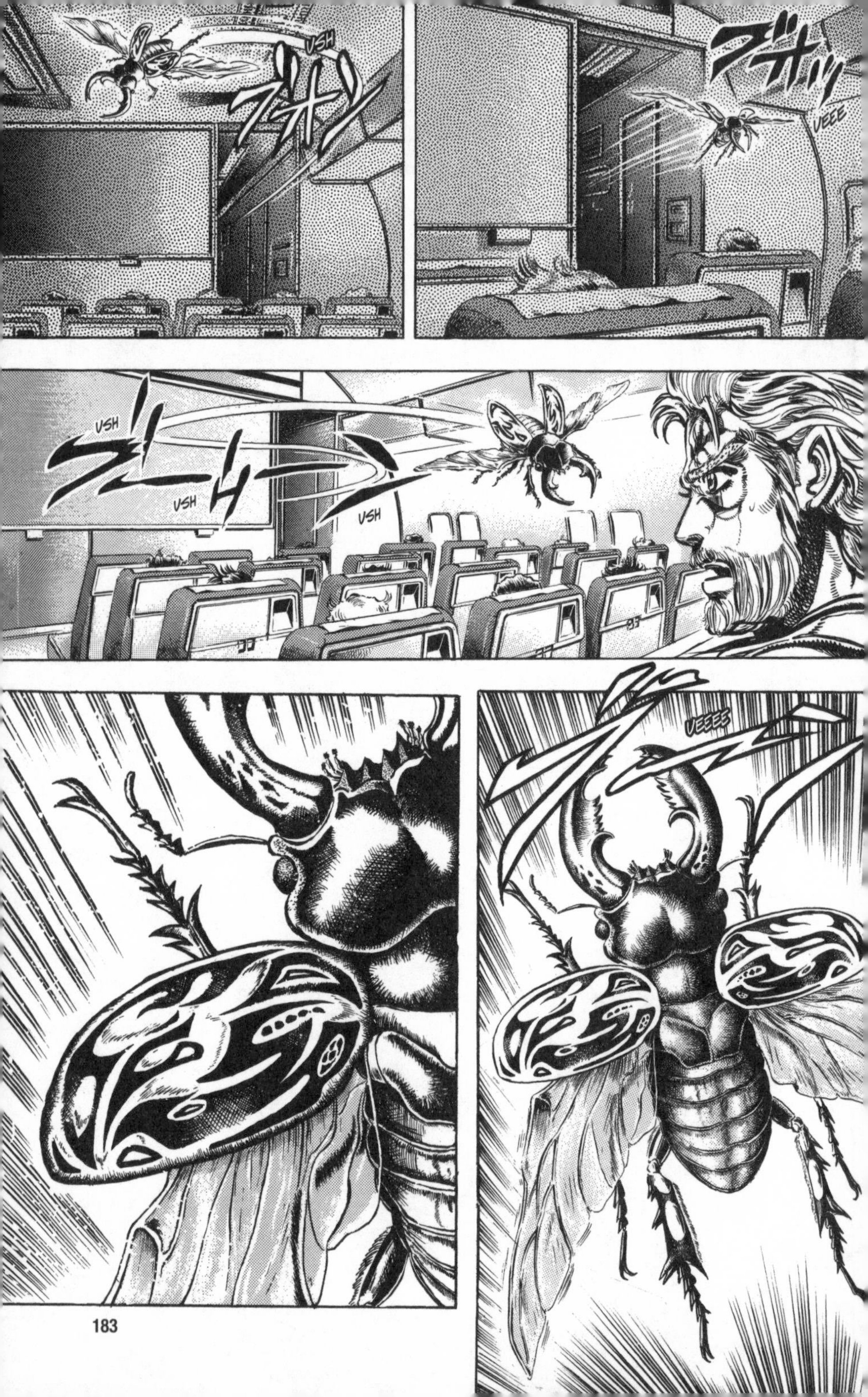
VEEE
VSH
VSH
VSH
VSH
VEEEE

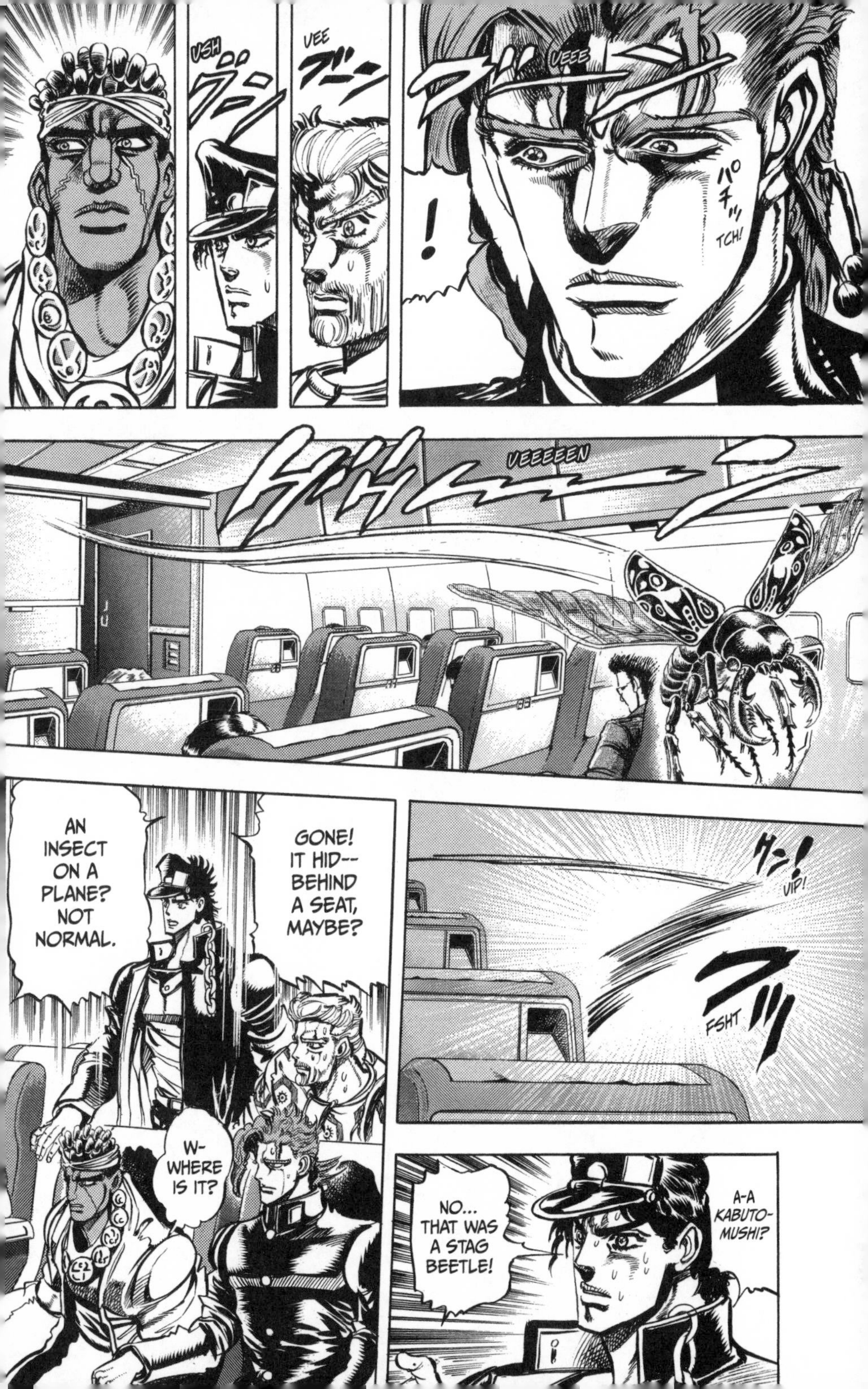
VEEE
TCH!
!
VEE
USH
VEEEEEN
VIP!
FSHT
A-A KABUTO-MUSHI?
NO... THAT WAS A STAG BEETLE!
GONE! IT HID-- BEHIND A SEAT, MAYBE?
AN INSECT ON A PLANE? NOT NORMAL.
W-WHERE IS IT?

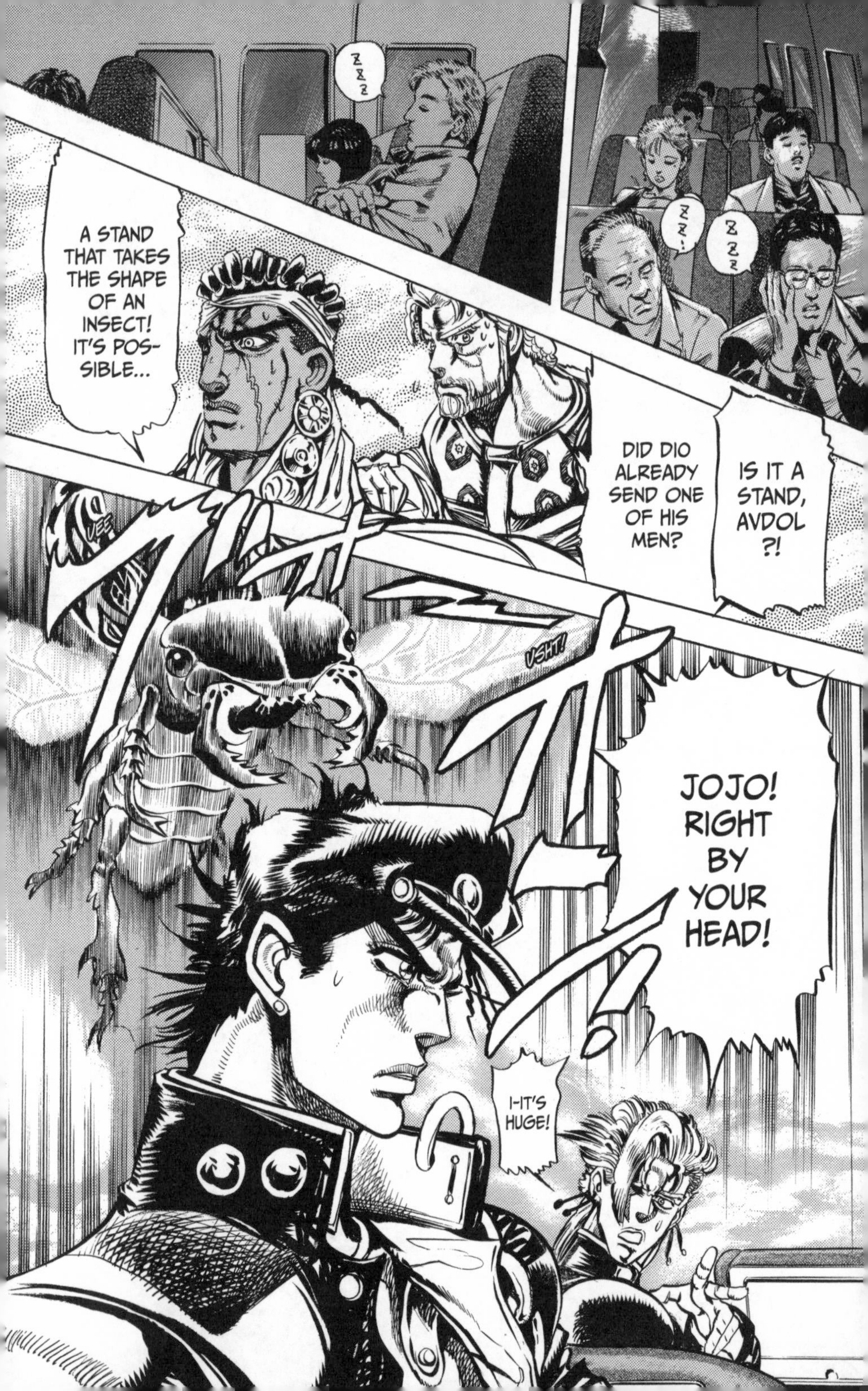
ZZZ
ZZ...
ZZZ
IS IT A STAND, AVDOL?!
DID DIO ALREADY SEND ONE OF HIS MEN?
A STAND THAT TAKES THE SHAPE OF AN INSECT! IT'S POS-SIBLE...
VEE
VSHT!
JOJO! RIGHT BY YOUR HEAD!
I-IT'S HUGE!

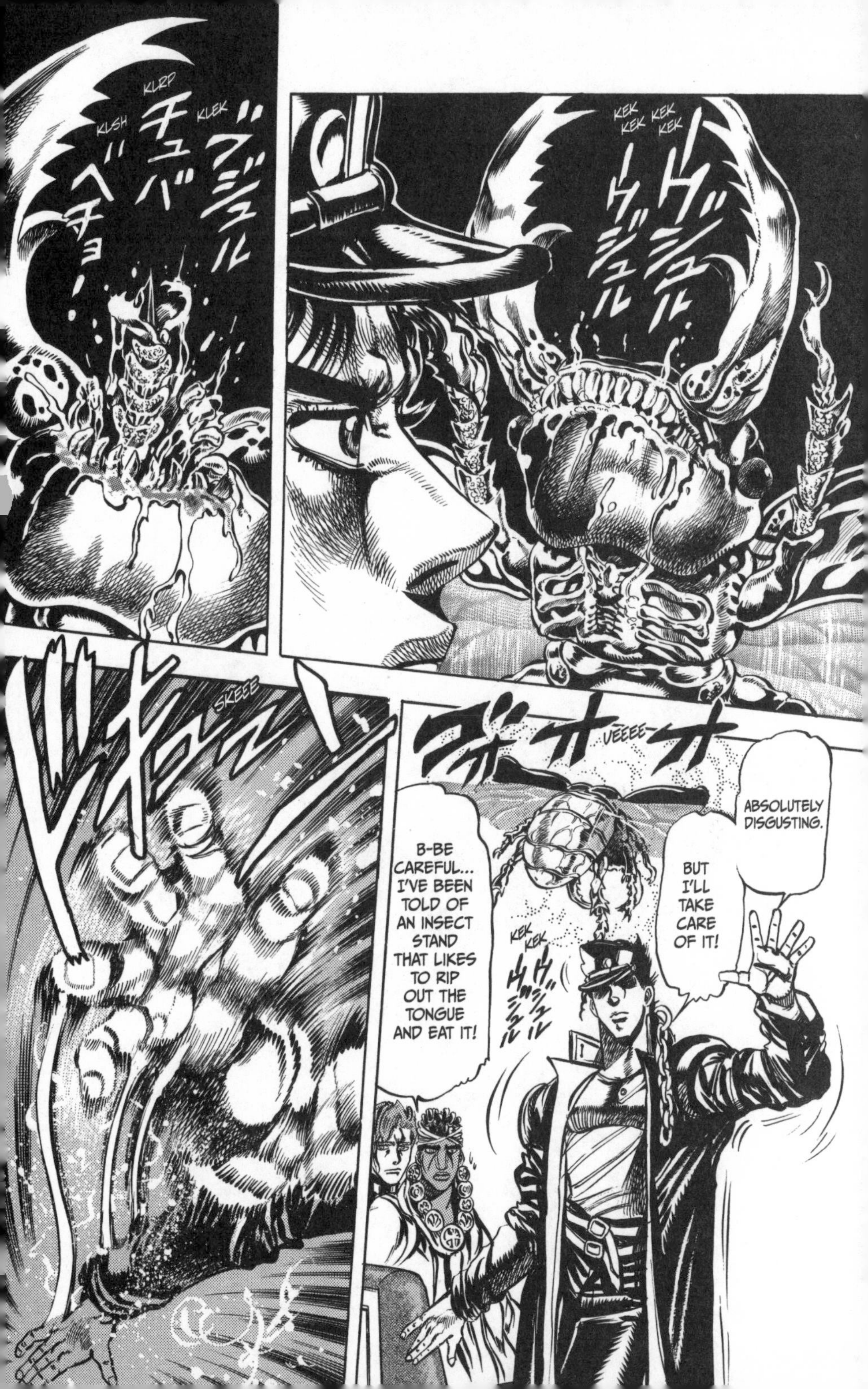

KEK KEK KEK KEK
KLRP
KLEK
KLSH
ブジュル
チュバ
ベチョ!
VEEEE
ABSOLUTELY DISGUSTING.
BUT I'LL TAKE CARE OF IT!
B-BE CAREFUL... I'VE BEEN TOLD OF AN INSECT STAND THAT LIKES TO RIP OUT THE TONGUE AND EAT IT!
KEK KEK
SKEEE

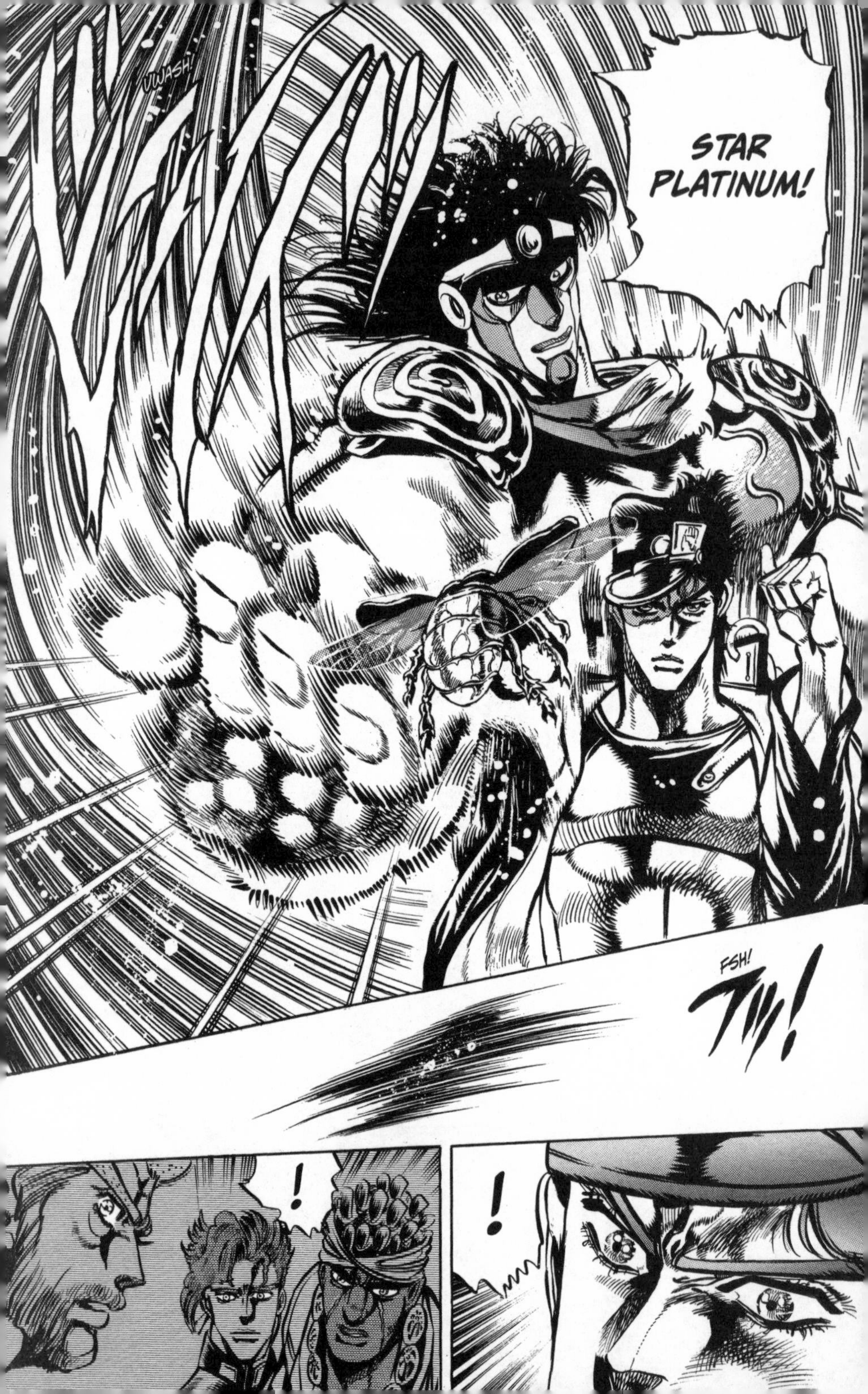

STAR PLATINUM!
UWASH!
FSH!
!
!

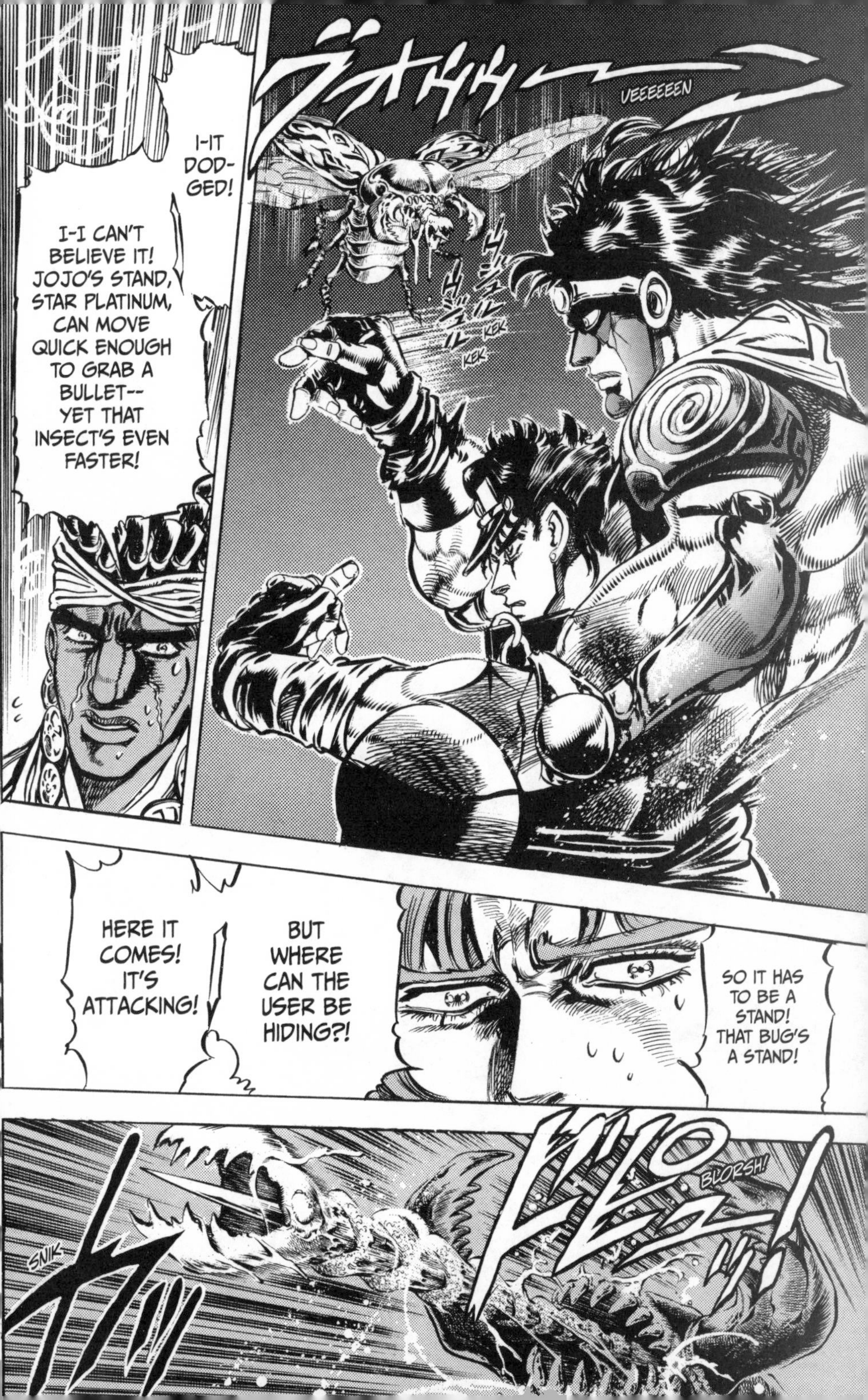
VEEEEEEN
KEK
KEK
I-IT DODGED!
I-I CAN'T BELIEVE IT! JOJO'S STAND, STAR PLATINUM, CAN MOVE QUICK ENOUGH TO GRAB A BULLET-- YET THAT INSECT'S EVEN FASTER!
SO IT HAS TO BE A STAND! THAT BUG'S A STAND!
BUT WHERE CAN THE USER BE HIDING?!
HERE IT COMES! IT'S ATTACKING!
BLORSH!
SNIK

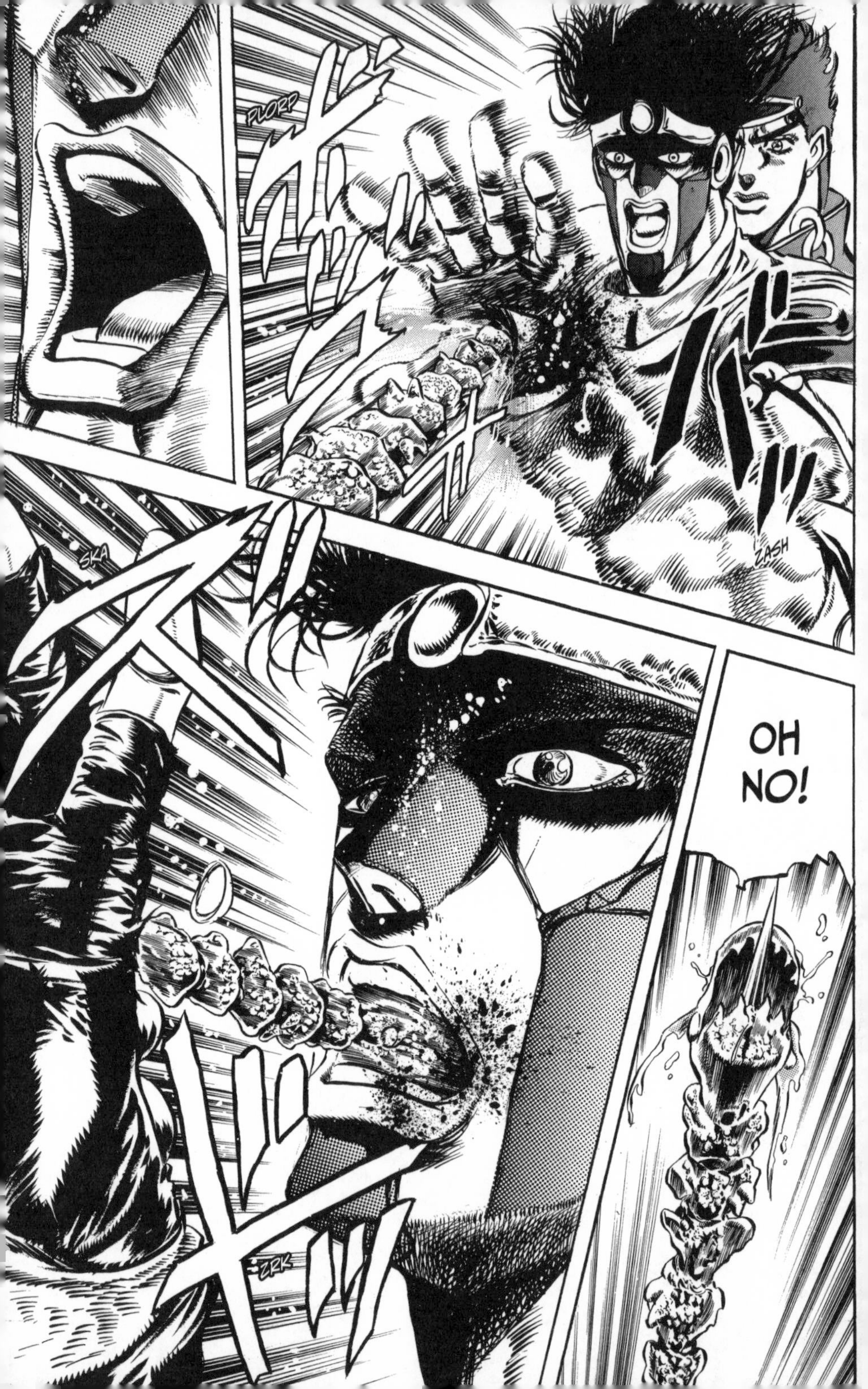
PLORP
ZASH
SKA
OH NO!
ZRK

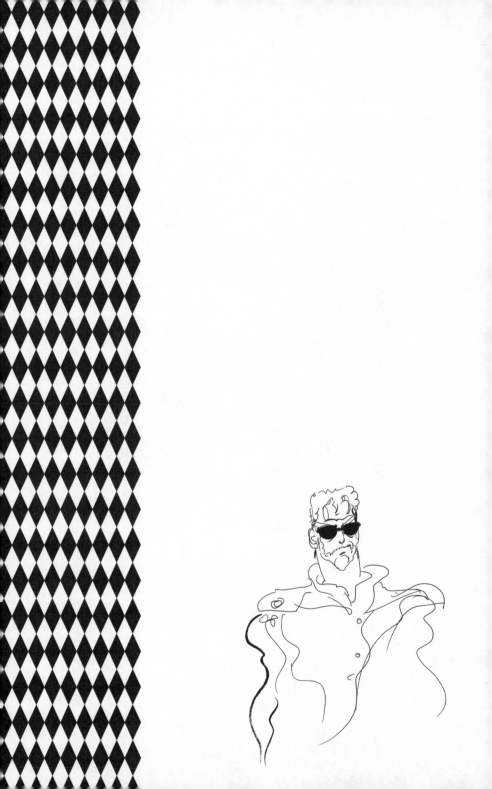

CHAPTER 10: Tower of Gray

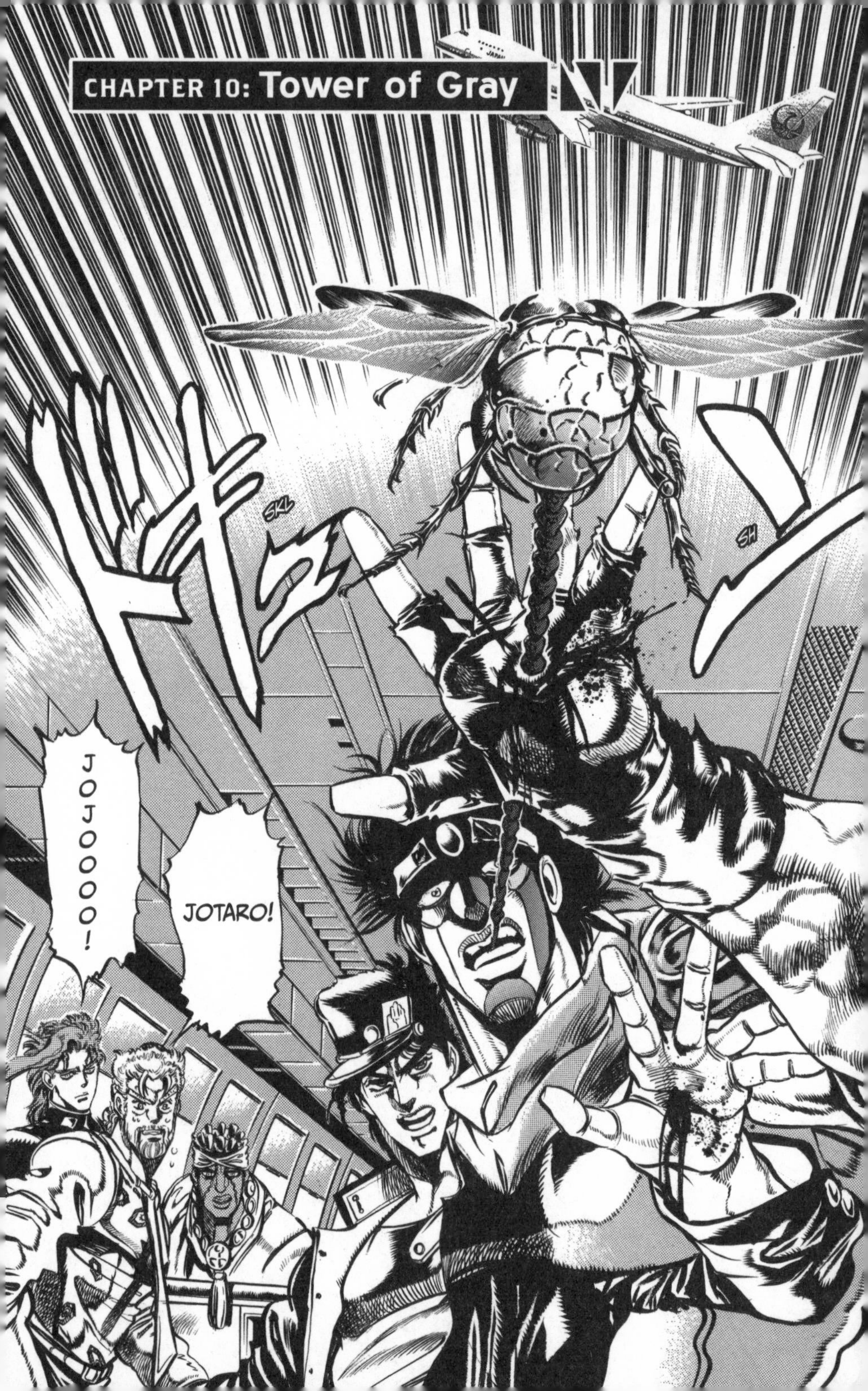
SH
SKL
JOTARO!
JOJOOOOO!

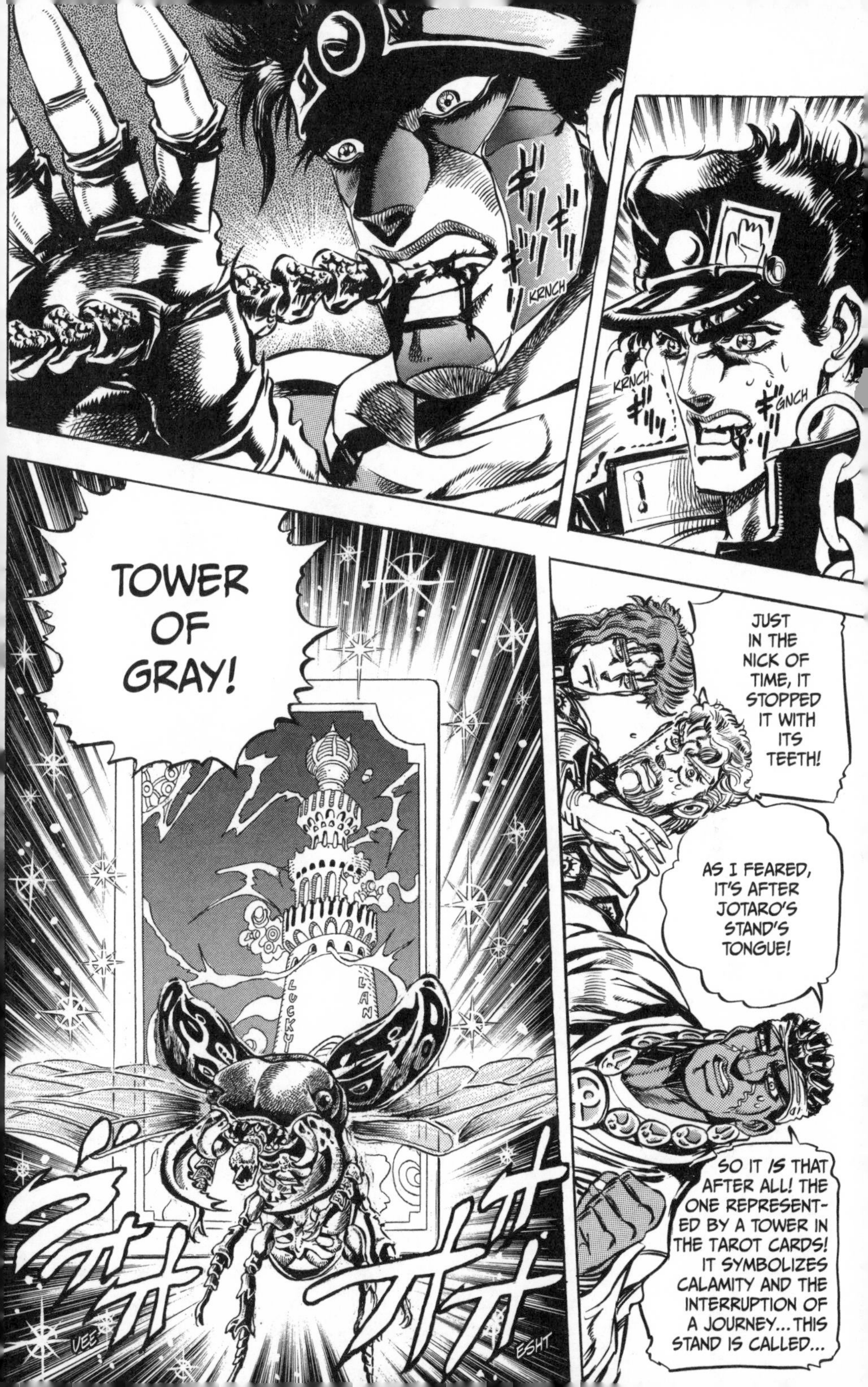
KRNCH
GNCH
KRNCH
JUST IN THE NICK OF TIME, IT STOPPED IT WITH ITS TEETH!
AS I FEARED, IT'S AFTER JOTARO'S STAND'S TONGUE!
SO IT *IS* THAT AFTER ALL! THE ONE REPRESENTED BY A TOWER IN THE TAROT CARDS! IT SYMBOLIZES CALAMITY AND THE INTERRUPTION OF A JOURNEY... THIS STAND IS CALLED...
TOWER OF GRAY!
UEE
ESHT

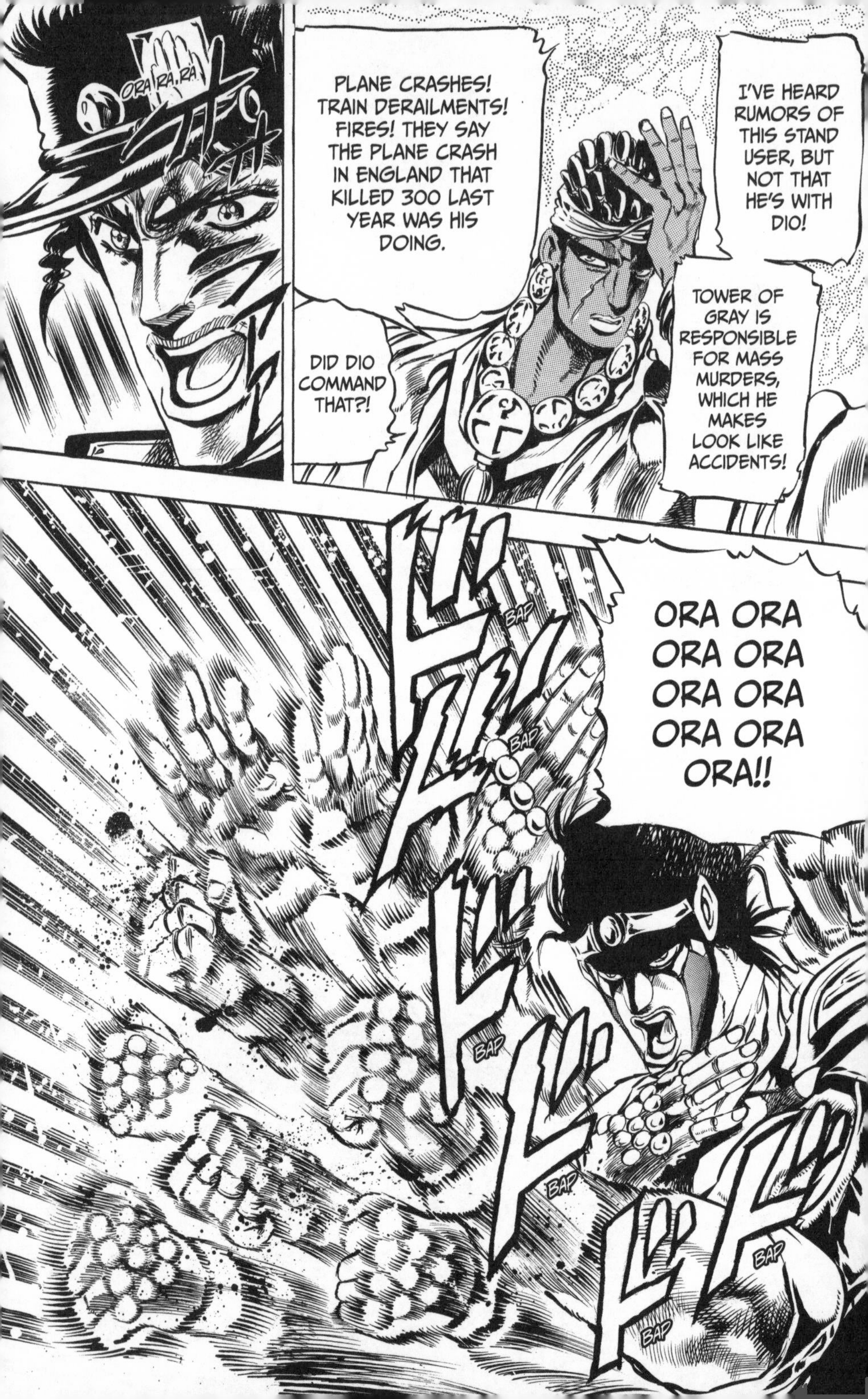
I'VE HEARD RUMORS OF THIS STAND USER, BUT NOT THAT HE'S WITH DIO!
TOWER OF GRAY IS RESPONSIBLE FOR MASS MURDERS, WHICH HE MAKES LOOK LIKE ACCIDENTS!
PLANE CRASHES! TRAIN DERAILMENTS! FIRES! THEY SAY THE PLANE CRASH IN ENGLAND THAT KILLED 300 LAST YEAR WAS HIS DOING.
DID DIO COMMAND THAT?!
ORA RA RA
ORA ORA ORA ORA ORA ORA ORA ORA ORA!!
BAP
BAP
BAP
BAP
BAP
BAP

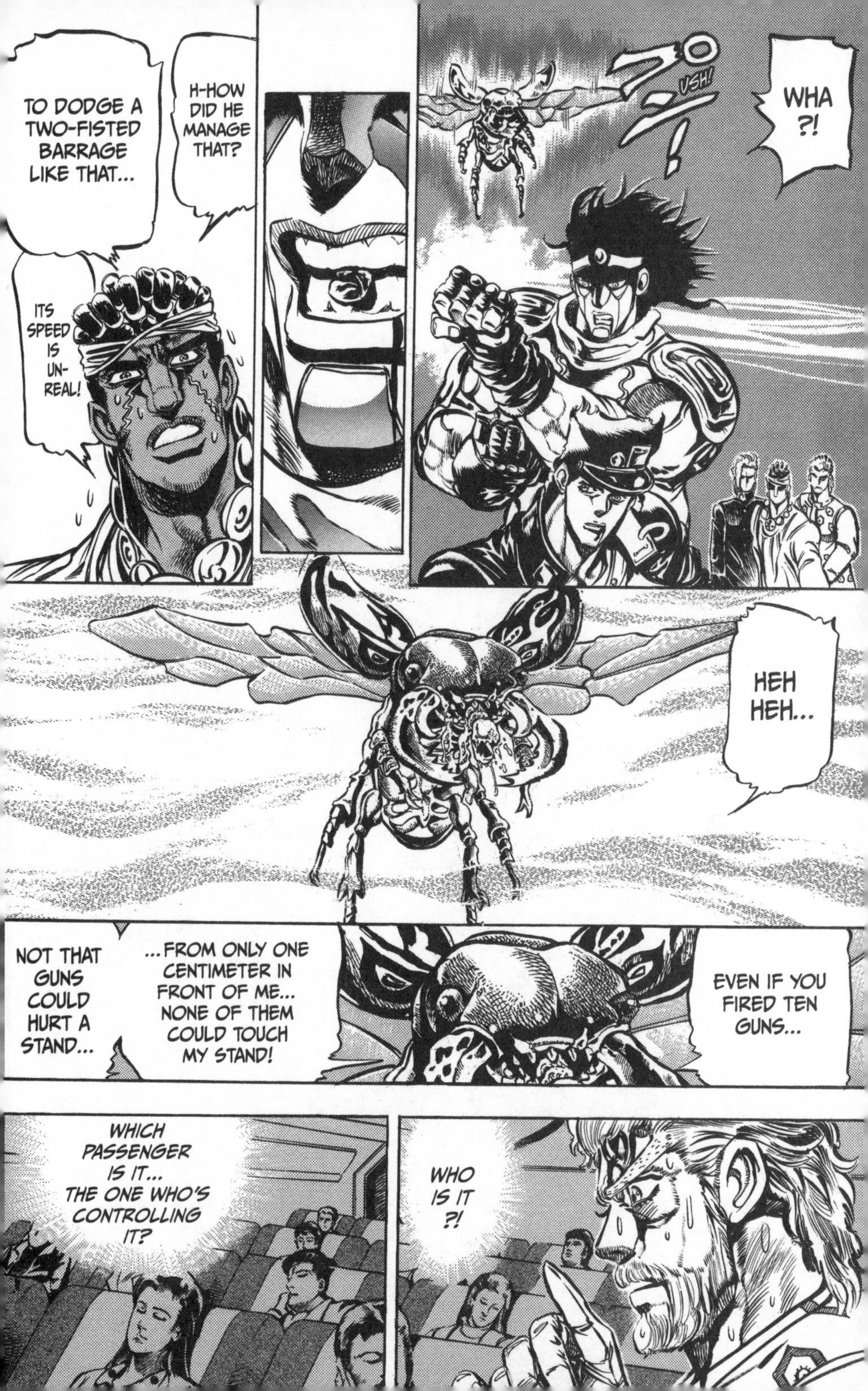
WHA ?!
VSH!
H-HOW DID HE MANAGE THAT?
TO DODGE A TWO-FISTED BARRAGE LIKE THAT...
ITS SPEED IS UN-REAL!
HEH HEH...
EVEN IF YOU FIRED TEN GUNS...
...FROM ONLY ONE CENTIMETER IN FRONT OF ME... NONE OF THEM COULD TOUCH MY STAND!
NOT THAT GUNS COULD HURT A STAND...
WHO IS IT ?!
WHICH PASSENGER IS IT... THE ONE WHO'S CONTROLLING IT?

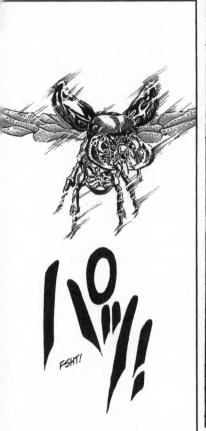

FSHT!

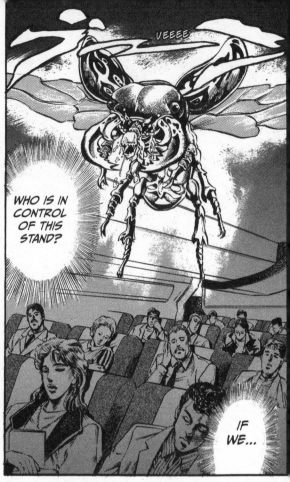

VEEEE

WHO IS IN CONTROL OF THIS STAND?

IF WE...

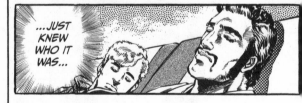

...JUST KNEW WHO IT WAS...

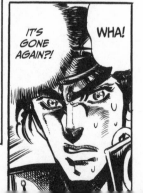

IT'S GONE AGAIN?!

WHA!

VSH

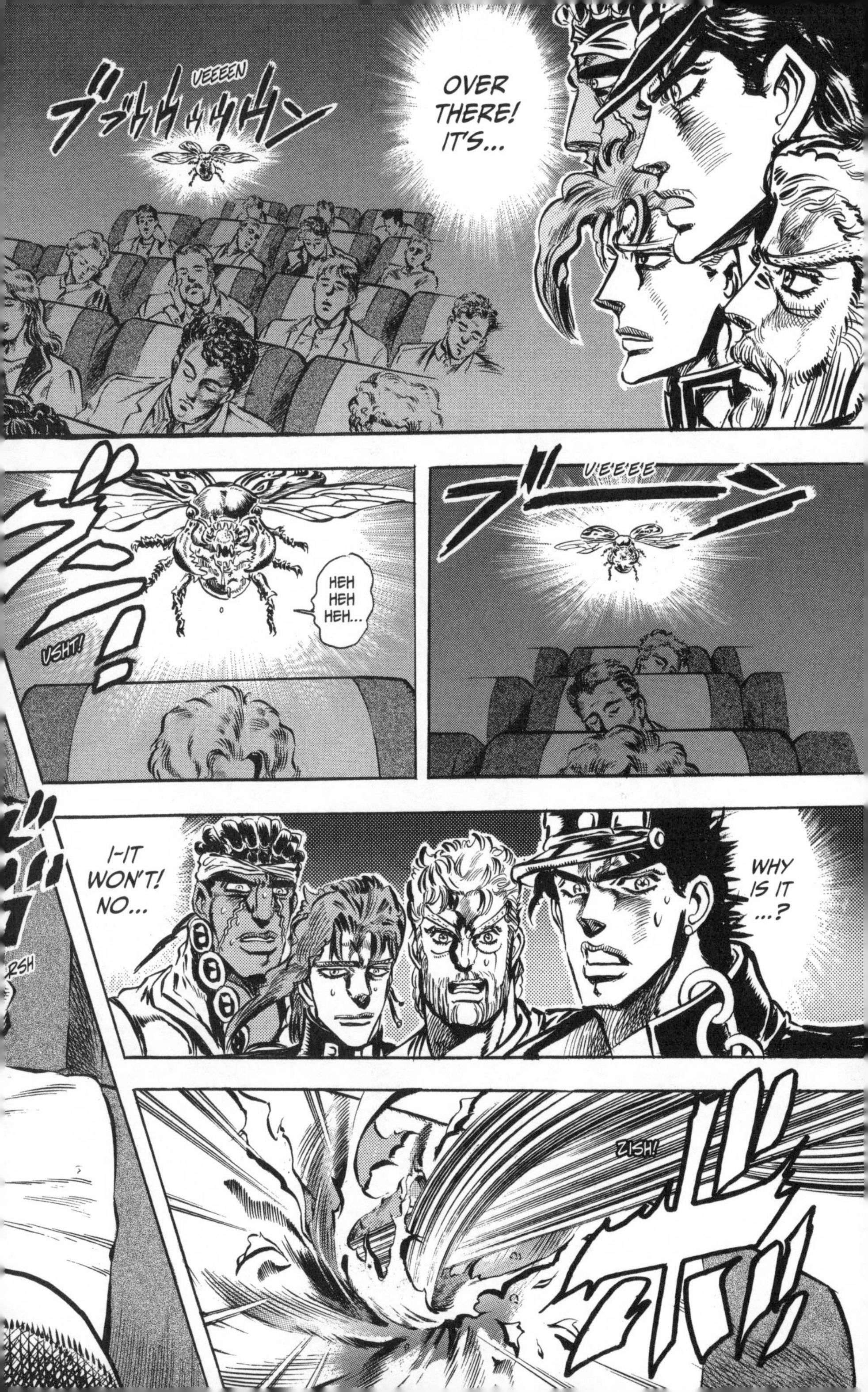
OVER THERE! IT'S...
VEEEEN
VEEEE
HEH HEH HEH...
VSHT!
WHY IS IT ...?
I-IT WON'T! NO...
ZISH!

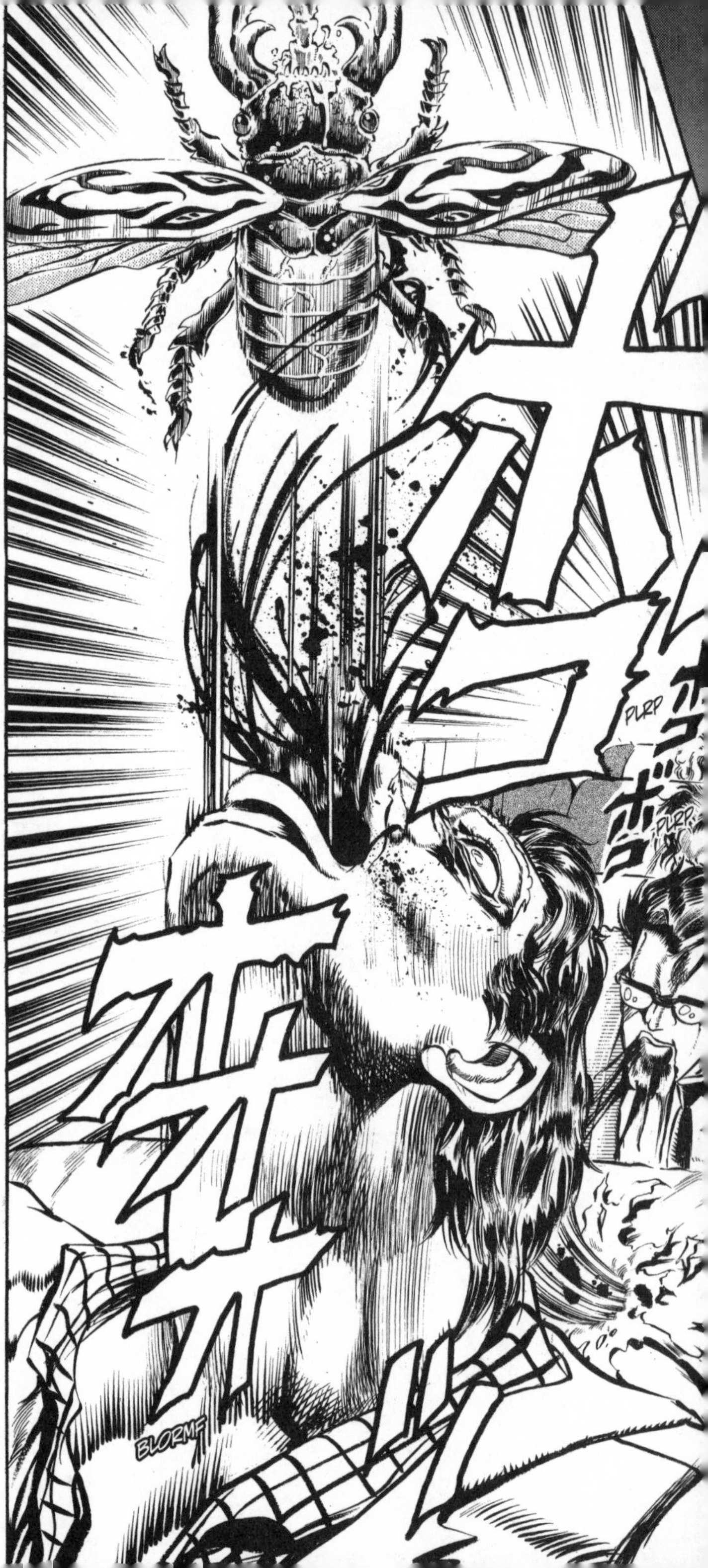
PLRP
PLRP
BLORMF

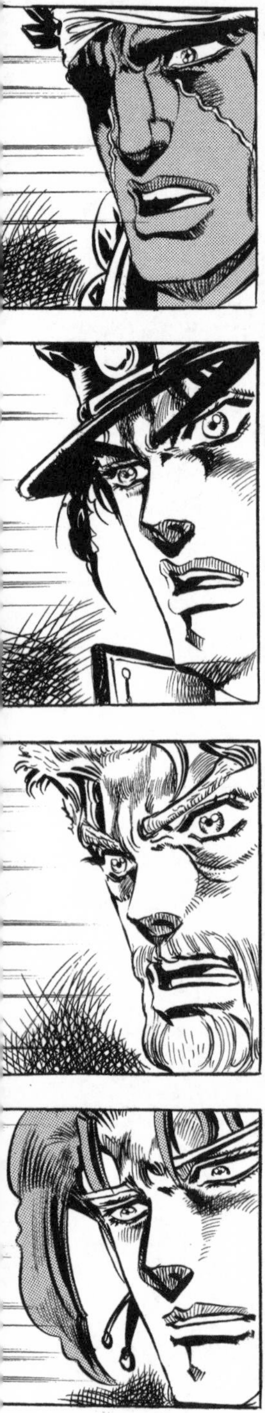

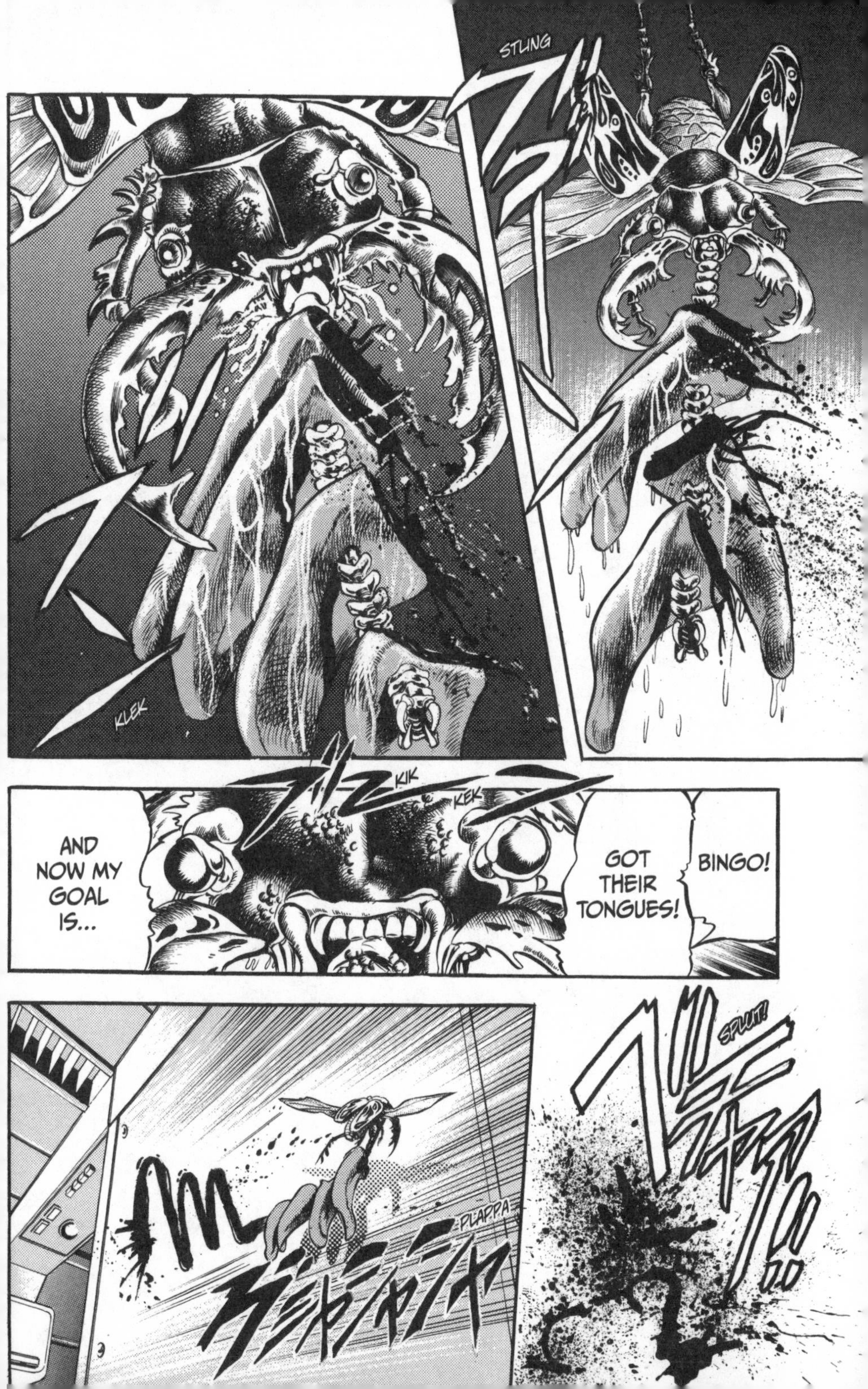
STLING
KLEK
KIK
KEK
BINGO!
GOT THEIR TONGUES!
AND NOW MY GOAL IS...
SPLUT!
PLAPPA

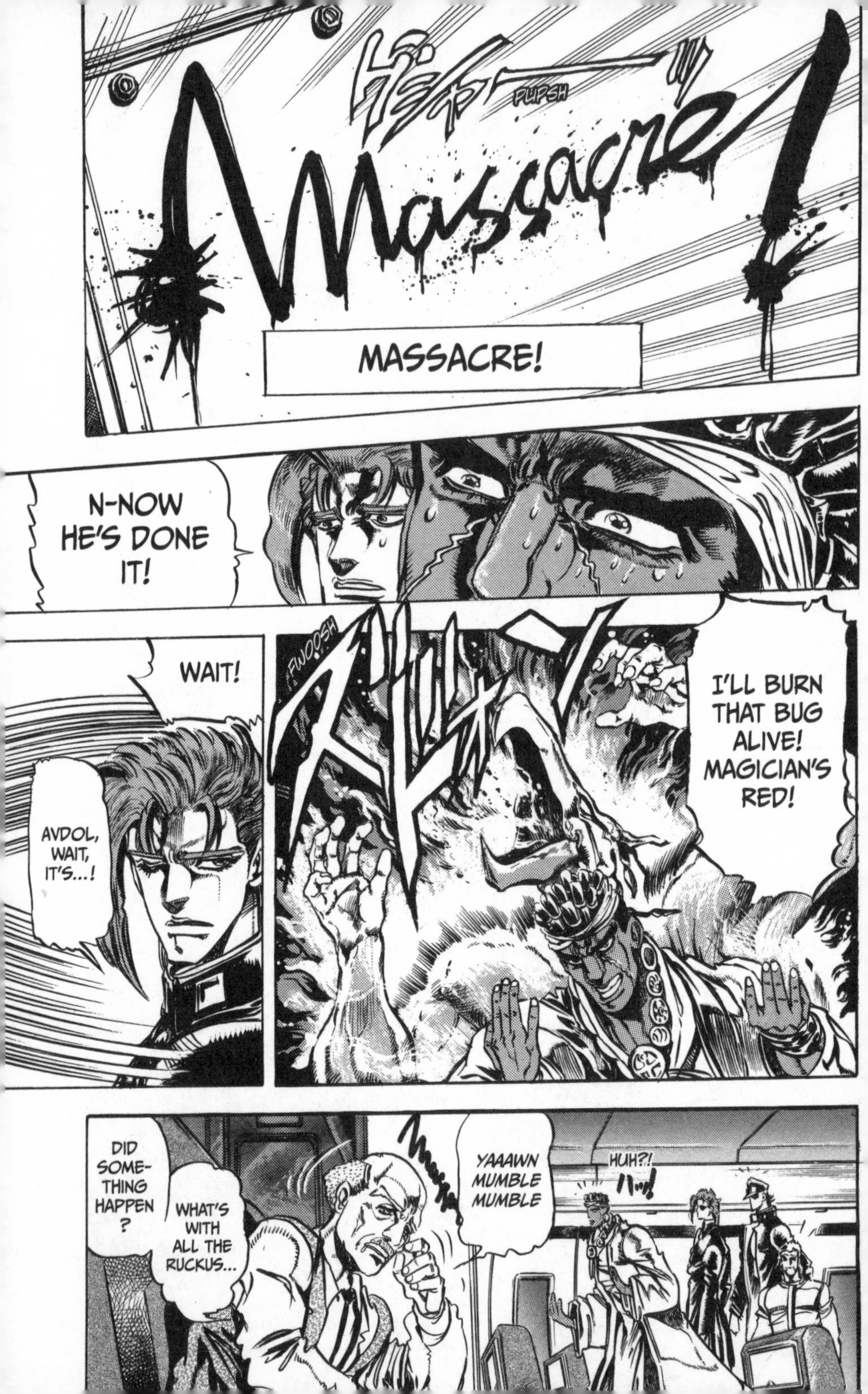
PUPSH
Massacre!
MASSACRE!
N-NOW HE'S DONE IT!
FWOOSH
I'LL BURN THAT BUG ALIVE! MAGICIAN'S RED!
WAIT!
AVDOL, WAIT, IT'S...!
HUH?!
YAAAWN MUMBLE MUMBLE
WHAT'S WITH ALL THE RUCKUS...
DID SOME-THING HAPPEN?

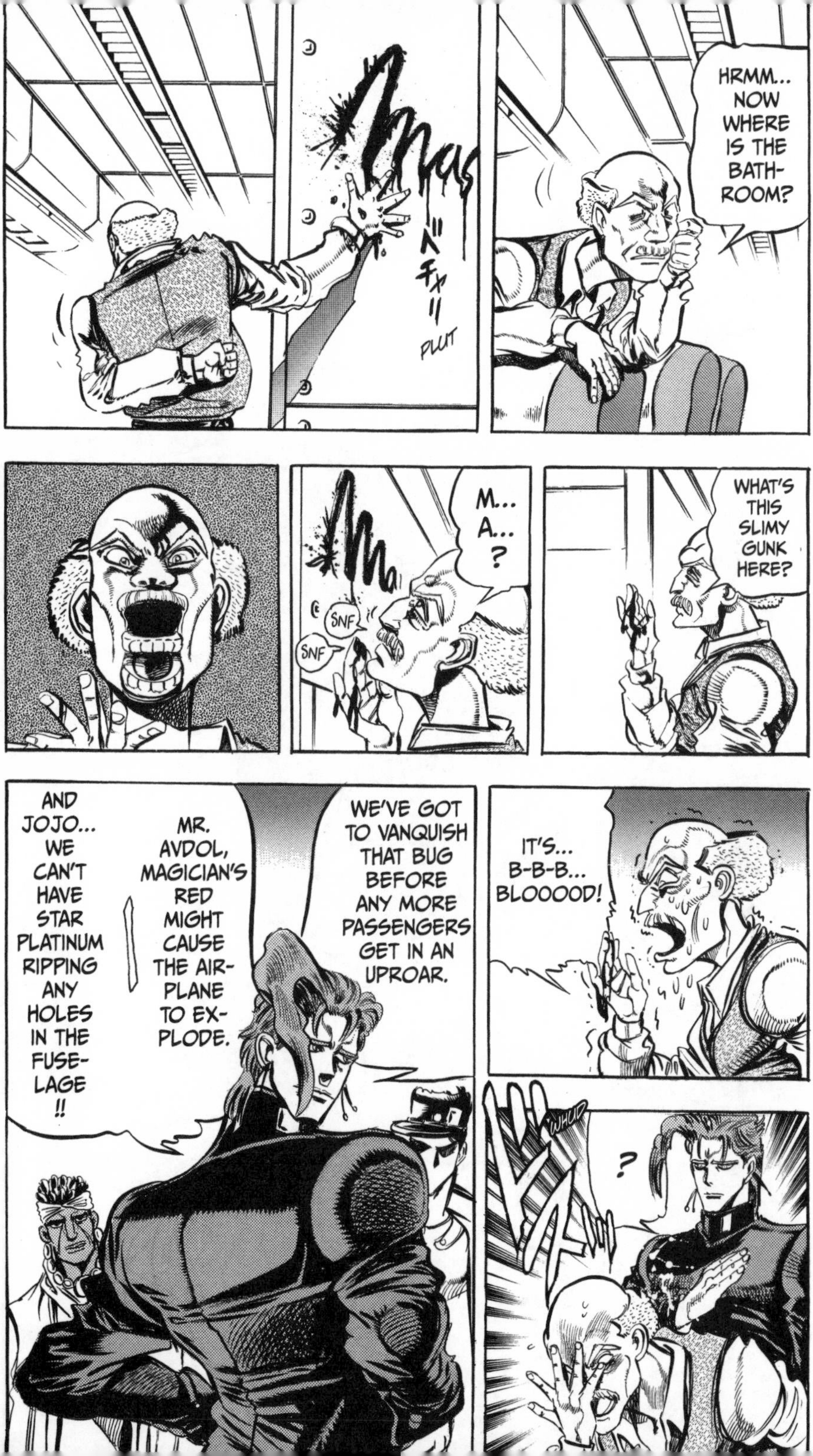
HRMM... NOW WHERE IS THE BATH-ROOM?
ベチャリ
PLUT
WHAT'S THIS SLIMY GUNK HERE?
M... A... ?
SNF
SNF
IT'S... B-B-B... BLOOOOD!
WHUD
?
WE'VE GOT TO VANQUISH THAT BUG BEFORE ANY MORE PASSENGERS GET IN AN UPROAR.
MR. AVDOL, MAGICIAN'S RED MIGHT CAUSE THE AIR-PLANE TO EX-PLODE.
AND JOJO... WE CAN'T HAVE STAR PLATINUM RIPPING ANY HOLES IN THE FUSE-LAGE !!

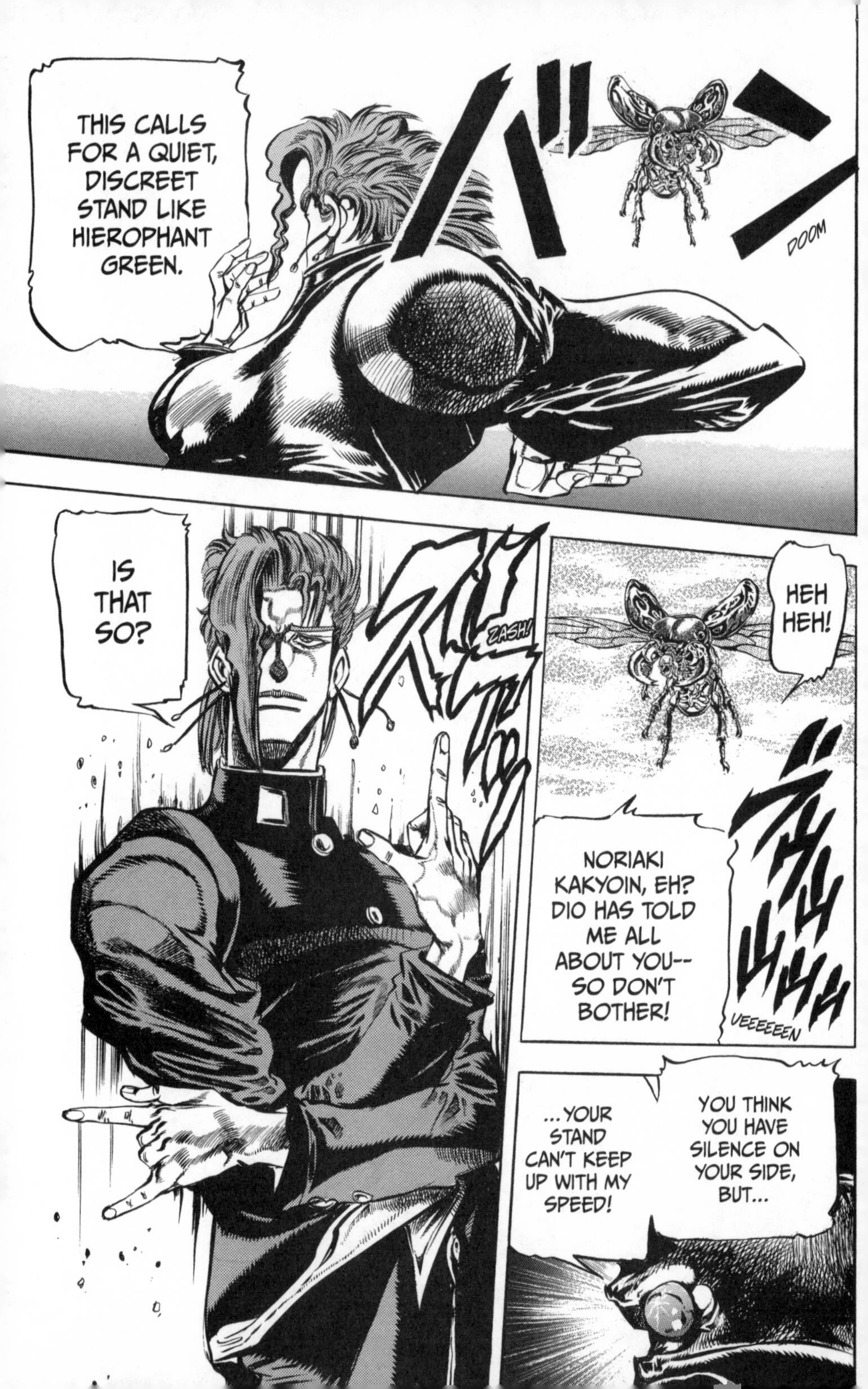
THIS CALLS FOR A QUIET, DISCREET STAND LIKE HIEROPHANT GREEN.
DOOM
HEH HEH!
NORIAKI KAKYOIN, EH? DIO HAS TOLD ME ALL ABOUT YOU-- SO DON'T BOTHER!
VEEEEEEN
YOU THINK YOU HAVE SILENCE ON YOUR SIDE, BUT...
...YOUR STAND CAN'T KEEP UP WITH MY SPEED!
IS THAT SO?
ZASH!

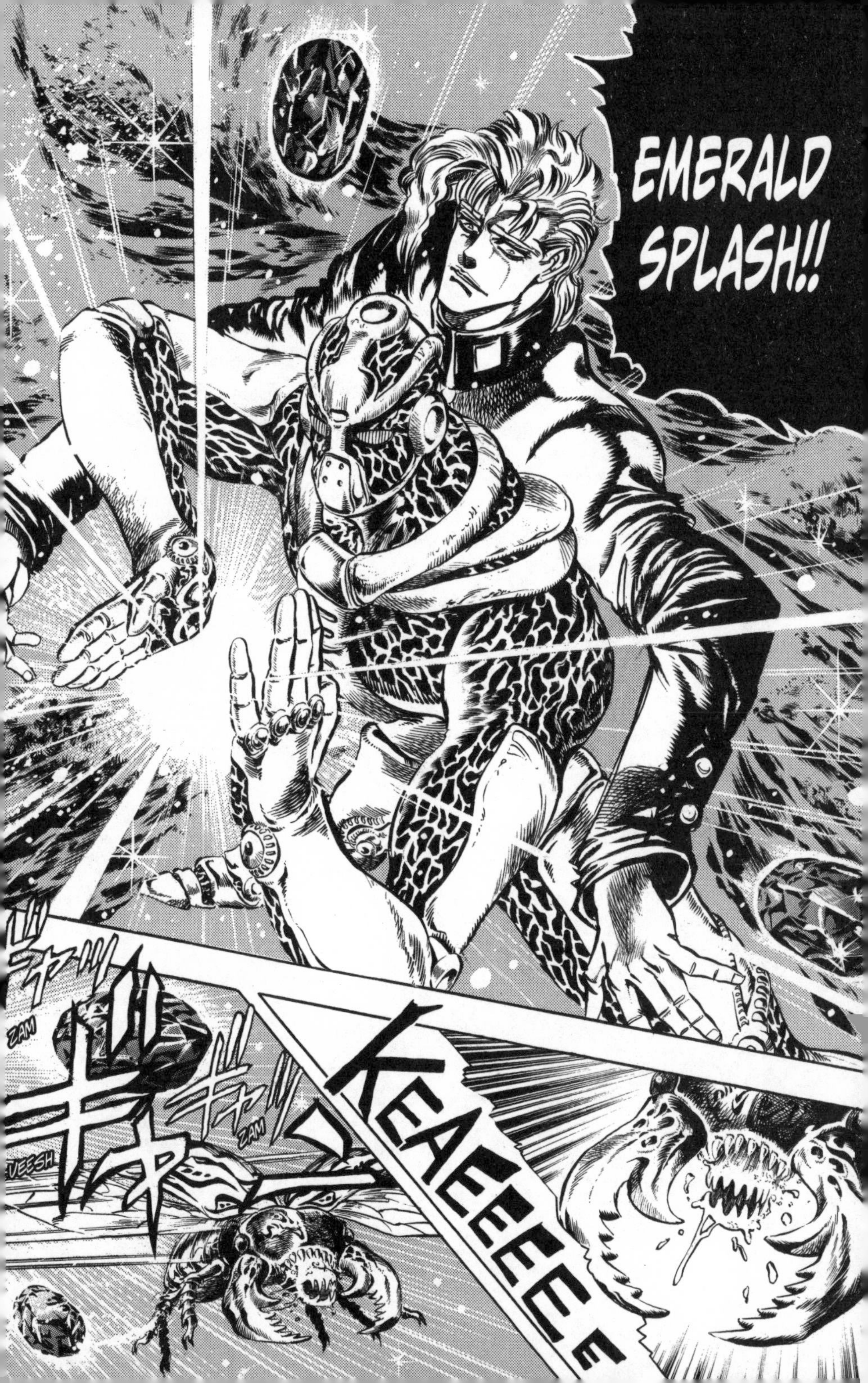
EMERALD SPLASH!!
KEAEEEEEE E
ZAM
ZAM
VEESH

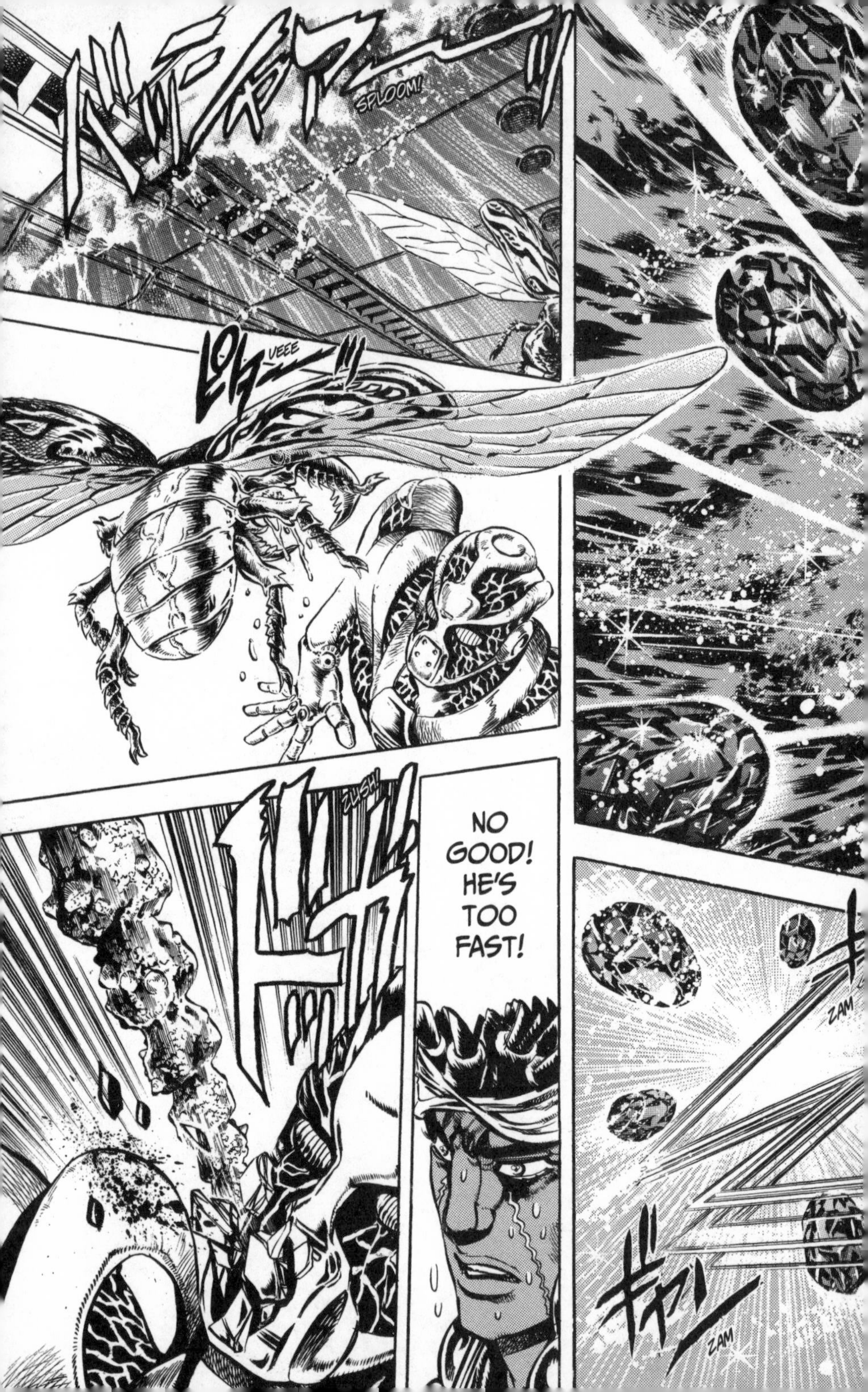
SPLOOM!
VEEE
ZAM
ZAM
NO GOOD! HE'S TOO FAST!
ZUSH!

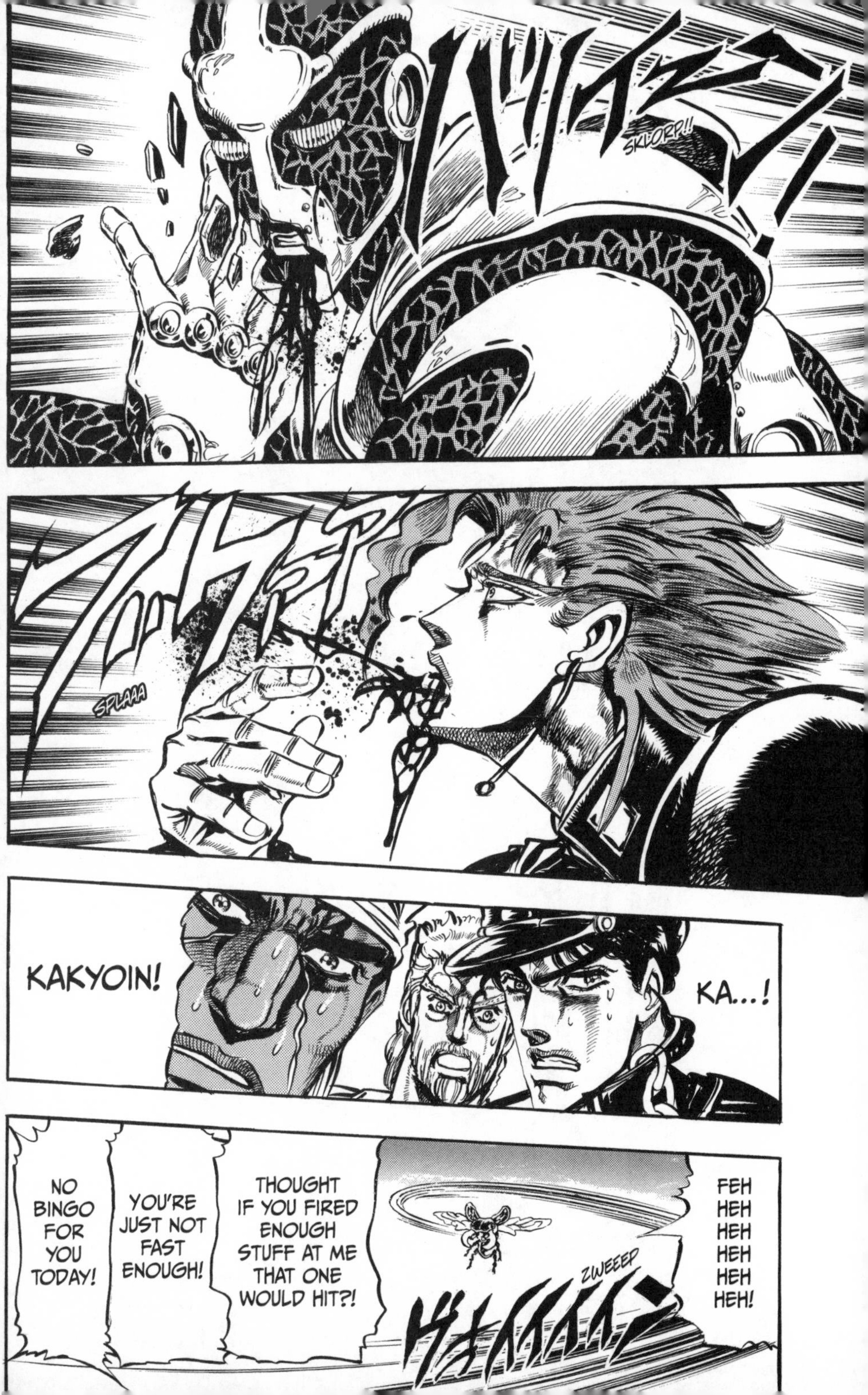
SKLORP!!
SPLAAA
KA...!
KAKYOIN!
FEH HEH HEH HEH HEH HEH!
ZWEEEP
THOUGHT IF YOU FIRED ENOUGH STUFF AT ME THAT ONE WOULD HIT?!
YOU'RE JUST NOT FAST ENOUGH!
NO BINGO FOR YOU TODAY!

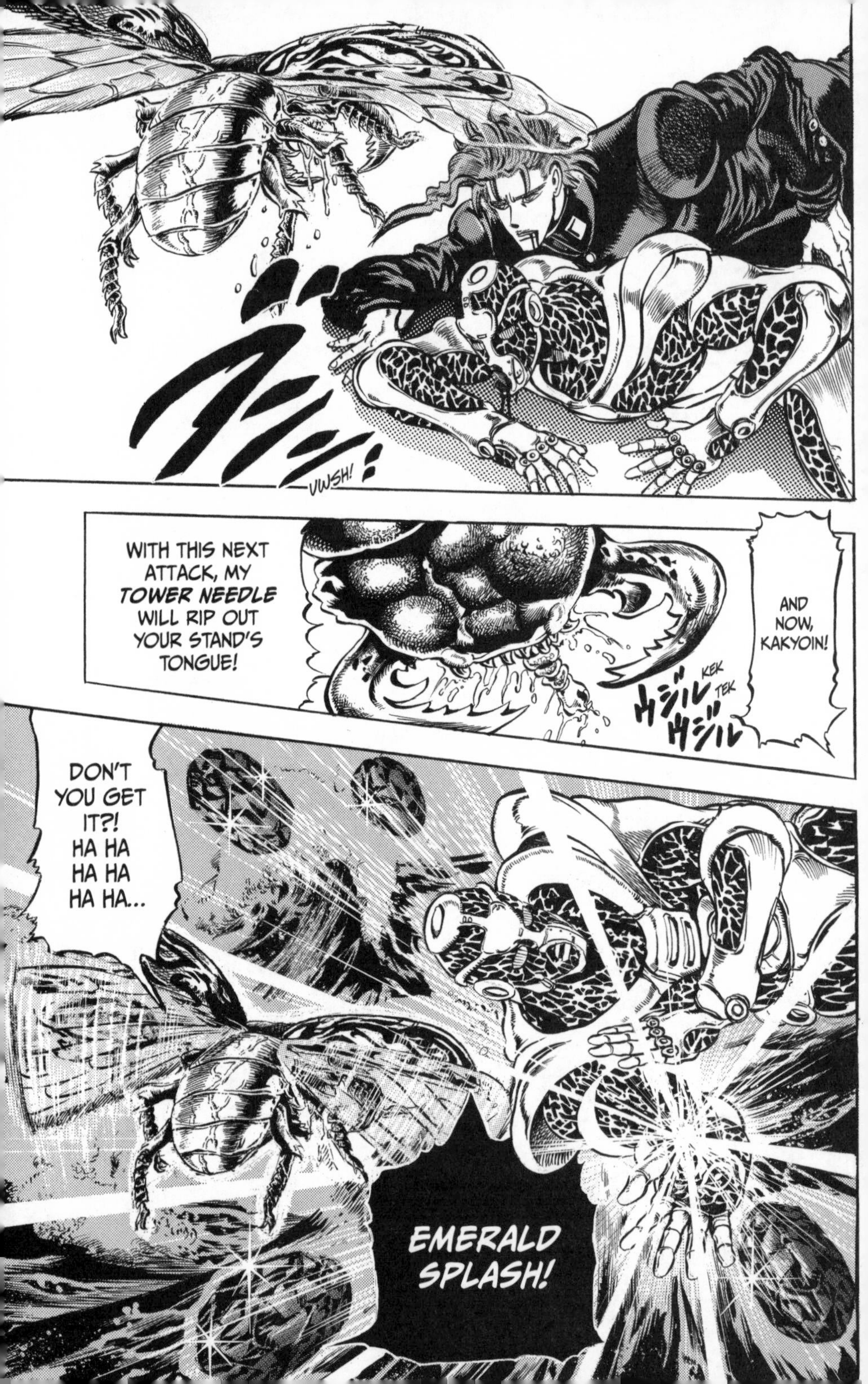
VWSH!
AND NOW, KAKYOIN!
KEK
TEK
WITH THIS NEXT ATTACK, MY *TOWER NEEDLE* WILL RIP OUT YOUR STAND'S TONGUE!
DON'T YOU GET IT?! HA HA HA HA HA HA...
EMERALD SPLASH!

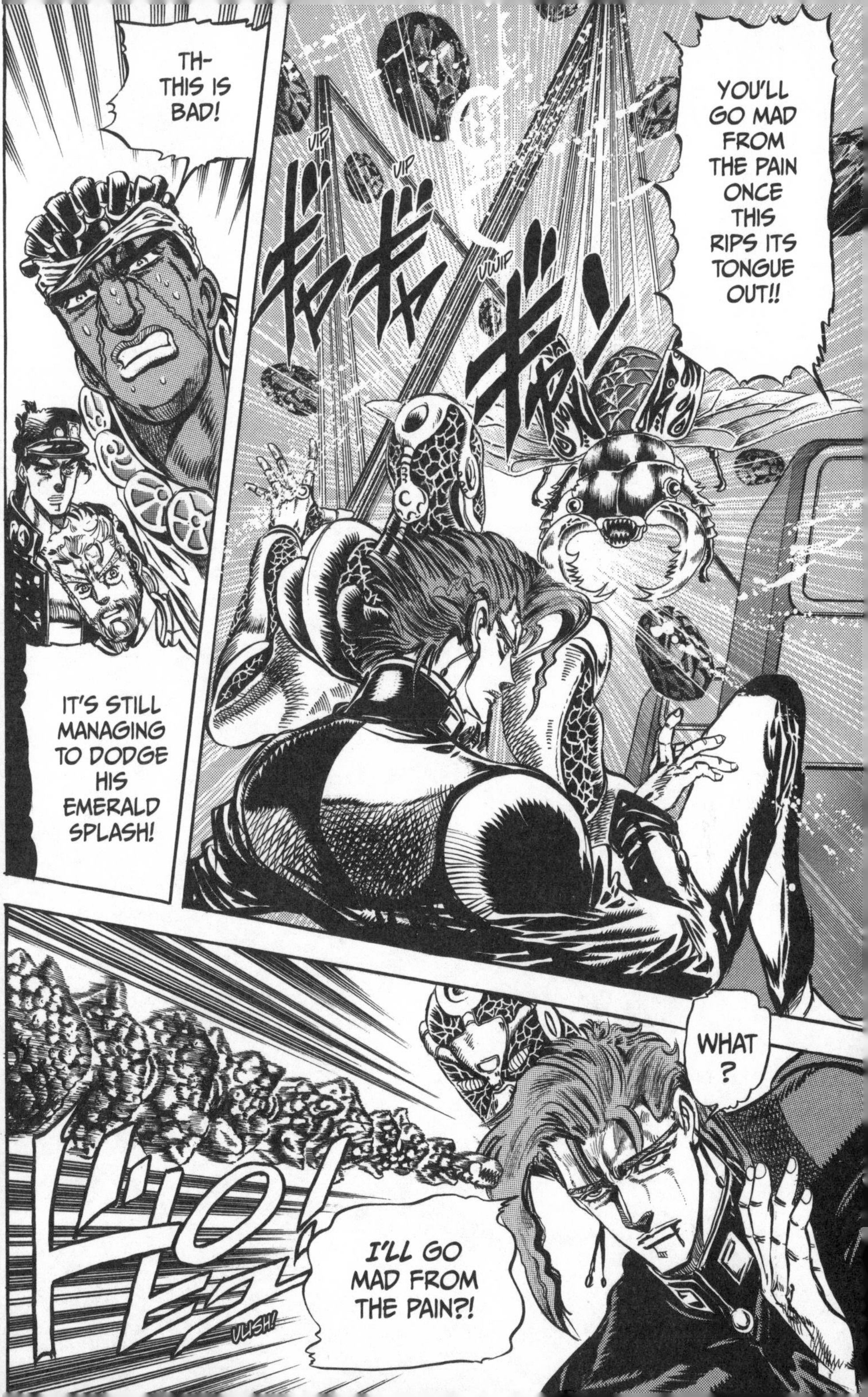
YOU'LL GO MAD FROM THE PAIN ONCE THIS RIPS ITS TONGUE OUT!!
UIP
UIP
UWIP
TH-THIS IS BAD!
IT'S STILL MANAGING TO DODGE HIS EMERALD SPLASH!
WHAT?
I'LL GO MAD FROM THE PAIN?!
VLISH!

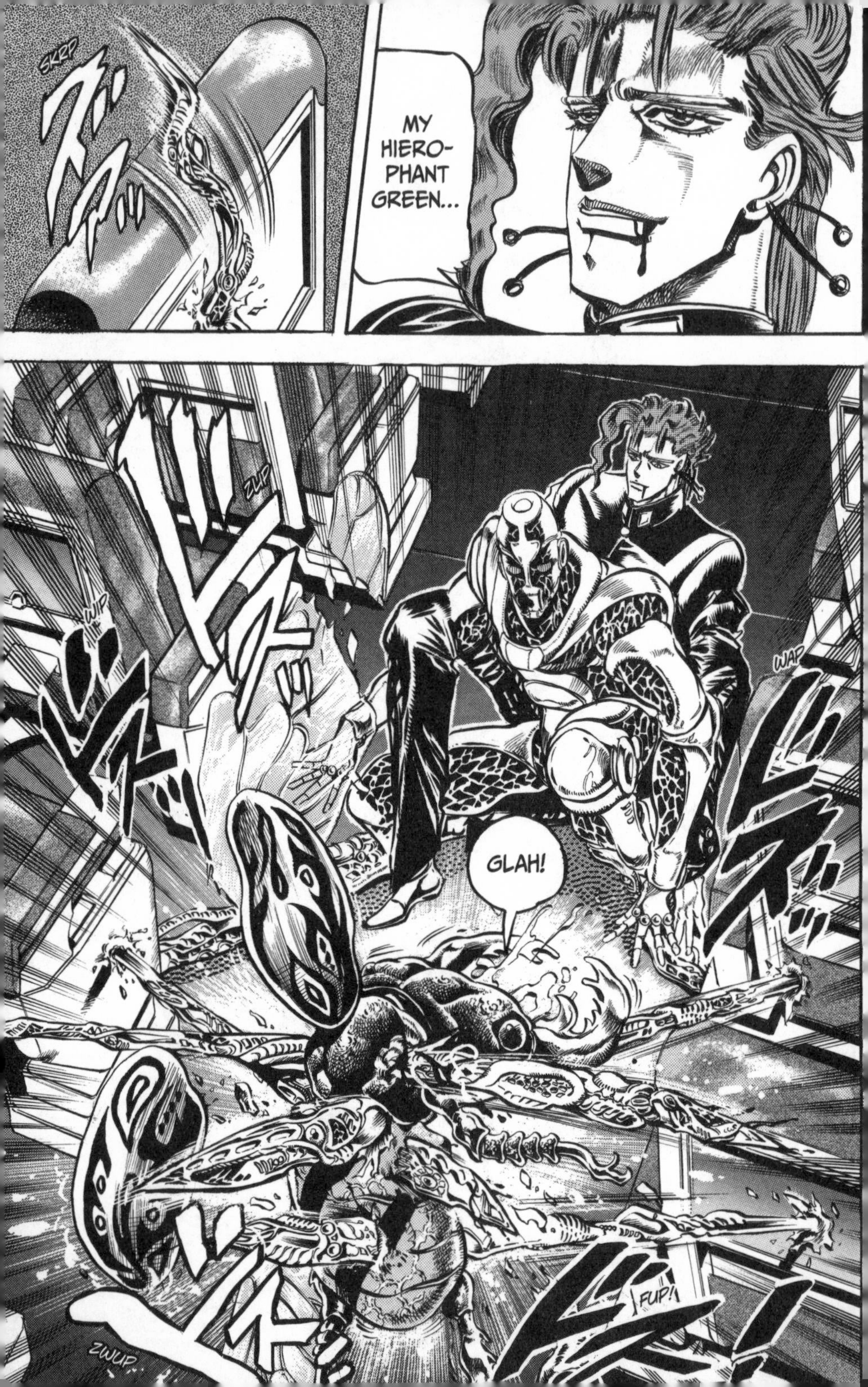
MY HIERO-PHANT GREEN...
SKRP
WAP
ZUP
WIP
GLAH!
FUP!
ZWUP

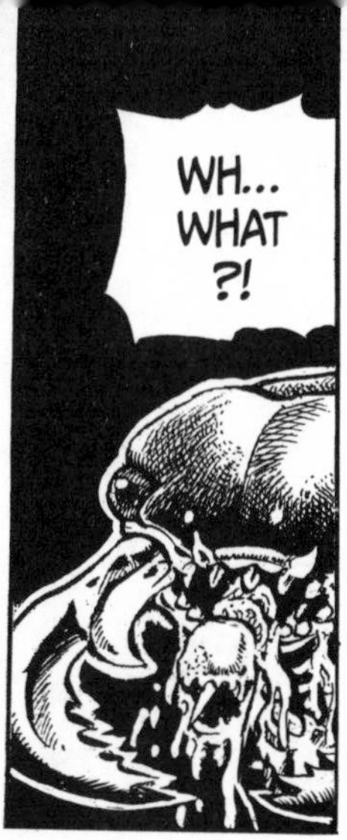
WH... WHAT ?!
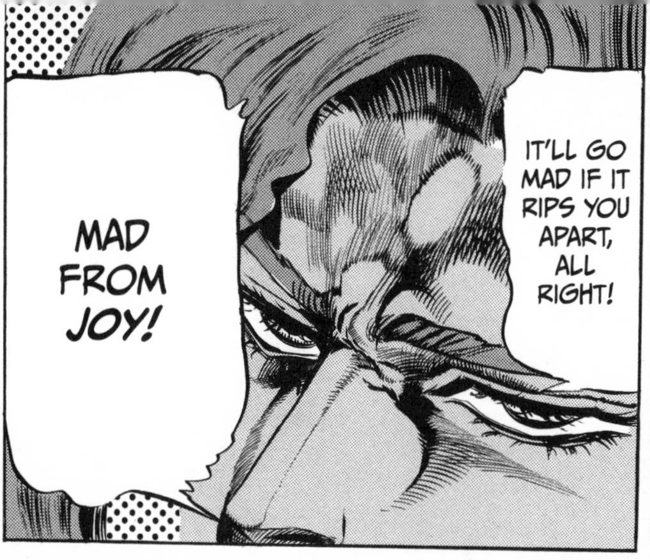
IT'LL GO MAD IF IT RIPS YOU APART, ALL RIGHT!
MAD FROM JOY!
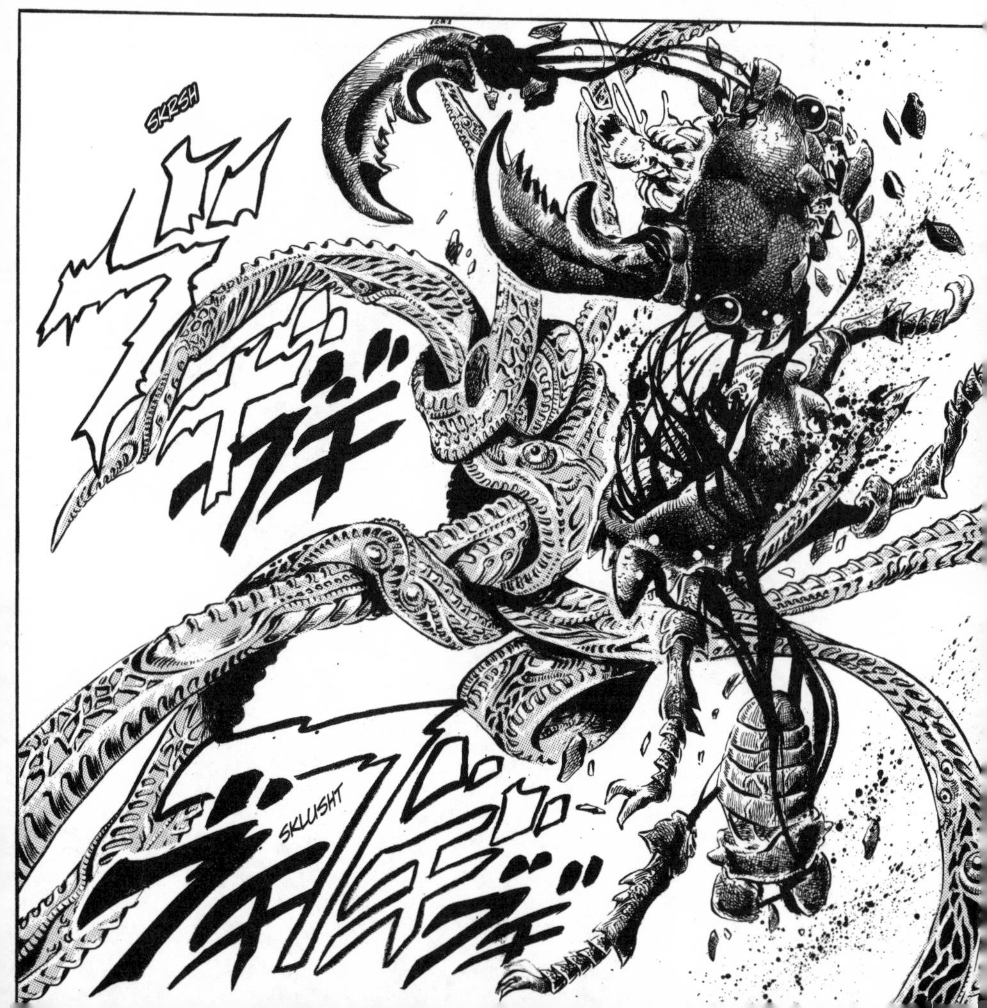
SKRSH
SKLUSHT

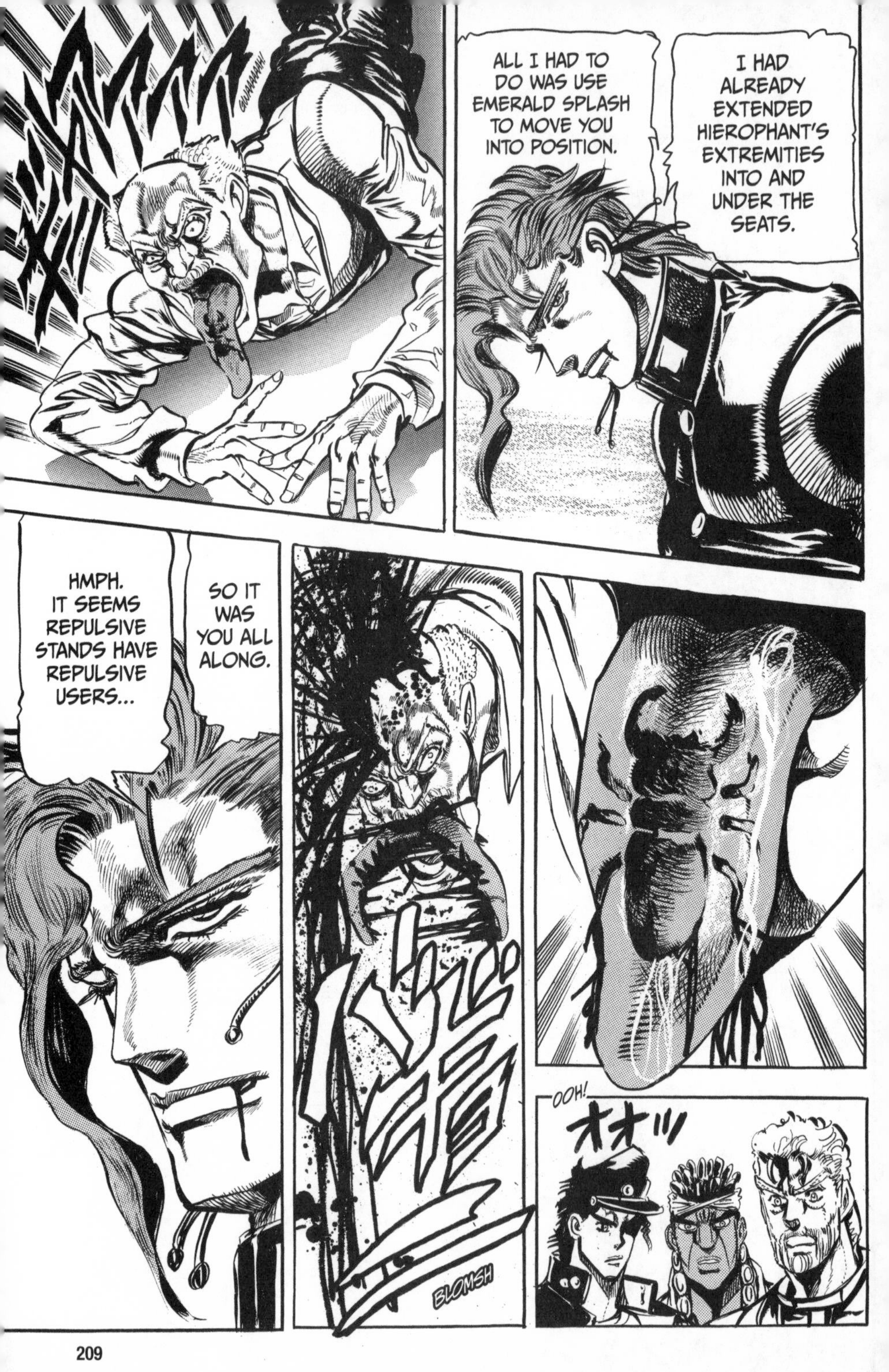
I HAD ALREADY EXTENDED HIEROPHANT'S EXTREMITIES INTO AND UNDER THE SEATS.
ALL I HAD TO DO WAS USE EMERALD SPLASH TO MOVE YOU INTO POSITION.
GUAAAAAH!
OOH!
オオッ
BLOMSH
SO IT WAS YOU ALL ALONG.
HMPH. IT SEEMS REPULSIVE STANDS HAVE REPULSIVE USERS...

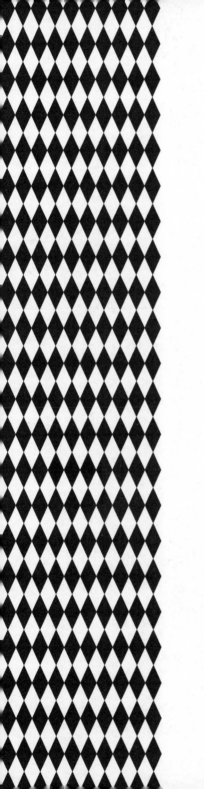

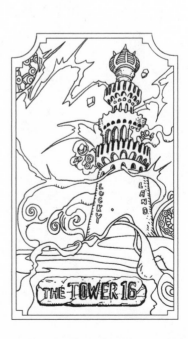

THE TOWER 16

LUCKY LAND

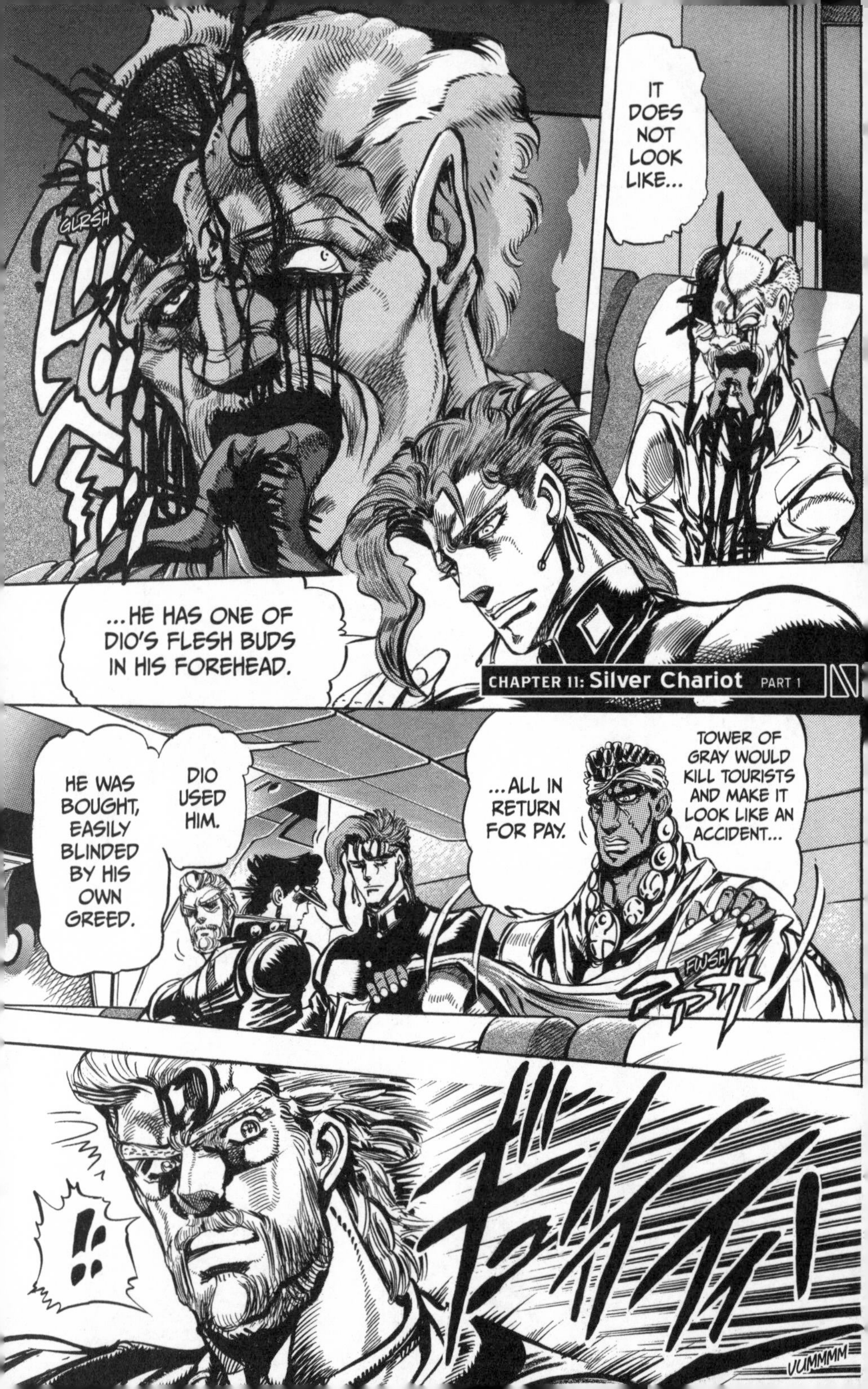
IT DOES NOT LOOK LIKE...
GLRSH
...HE HAS ONE OF DIO'S FLESH BUDS IN HIS FOREHEAD.
CHAPTER 11: Silver Chariot PART 1
TOWER OF GRAY WOULD KILL TOURISTS AND MAKE IT LOOK LIKE AN ACCIDENT...
...ALL IN RETURN FOR PAY.
FWSH
DIO USED HIM.
HE WAS BOUGHT, EASILY BLINDED BY HIS OWN GREED.
VUMMMM
!!

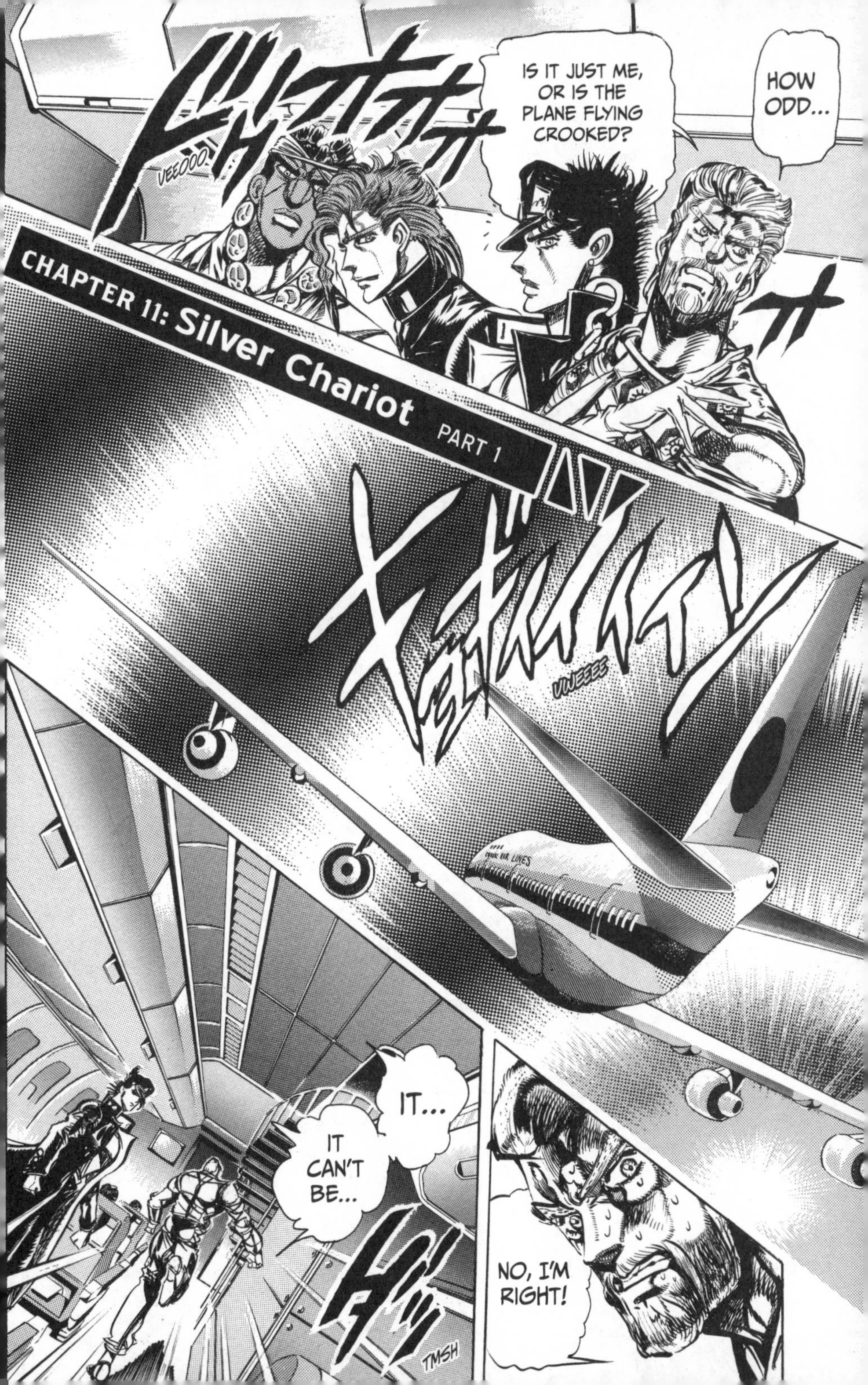
HOW ODD...
IS IT JUST ME, OR IS THE PLANE FLYING CROOKED?
VEEOOO
CHAPTER 11: Silver Chariot PART 1
UWEEEE
NO, I'M RIGHT!
IT...
IT CAN'T BE...
TMSH

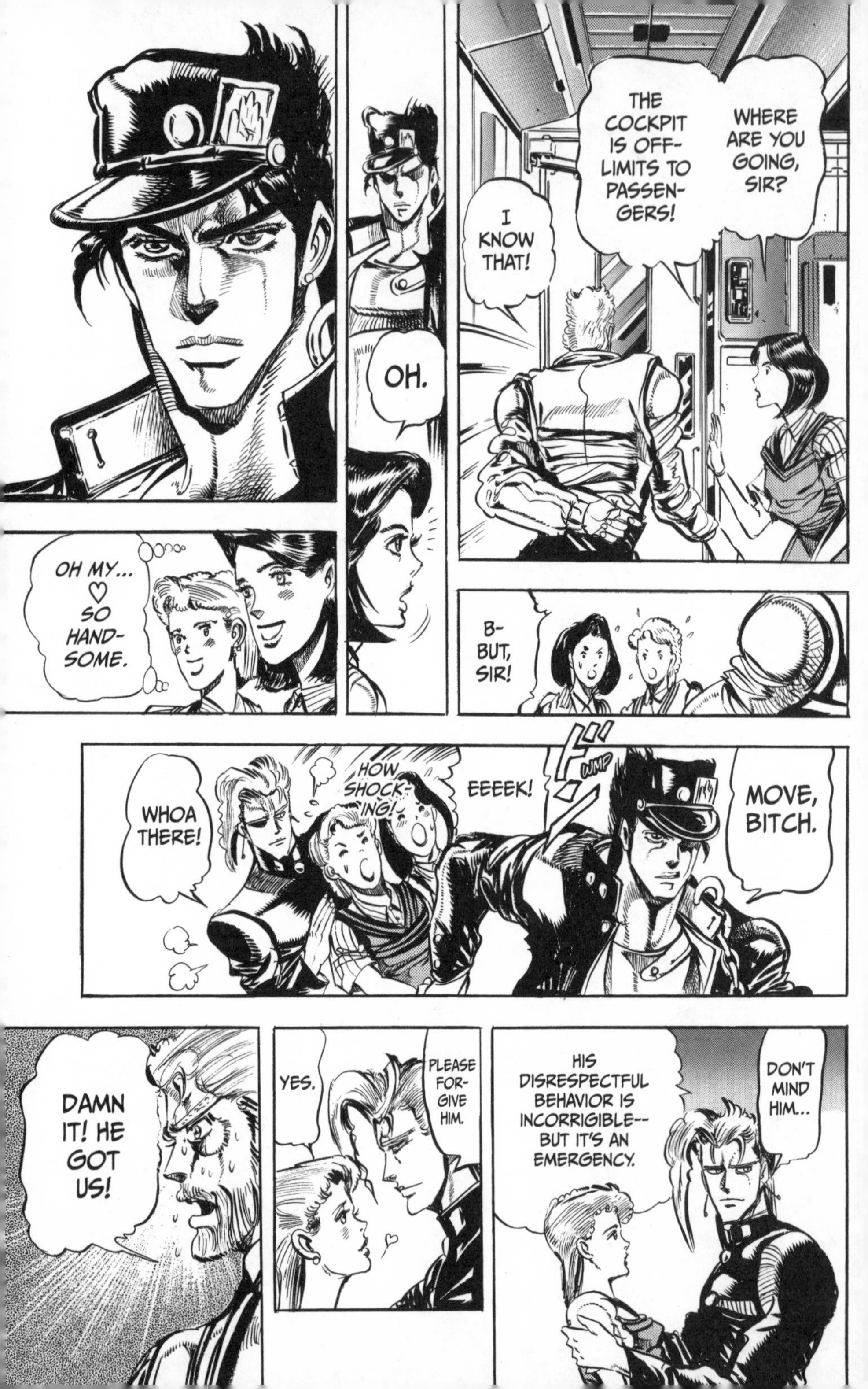
WHERE ARE YOU GOING, SIR?
THE COCKPIT IS OFF-LIMITS TO PASSENGERS!
I KNOW THAT!
B-BUT, SIR!
OH.
OH MY... ♡ SO HANDSOME.
MOVE, BITCH.
WUMP
EEEEK!
HOW SHOCKING!
WHOA THERE!
DON'T MIND HIM...
HIS DISRESPECTFUL BEHAVIOR IS INCORRIGIBLE-- BUT IT'S AN EMERGENCY.
PLEASE FOR-GIVE HIM.
YES.
DAMN IT! HE GOT US!

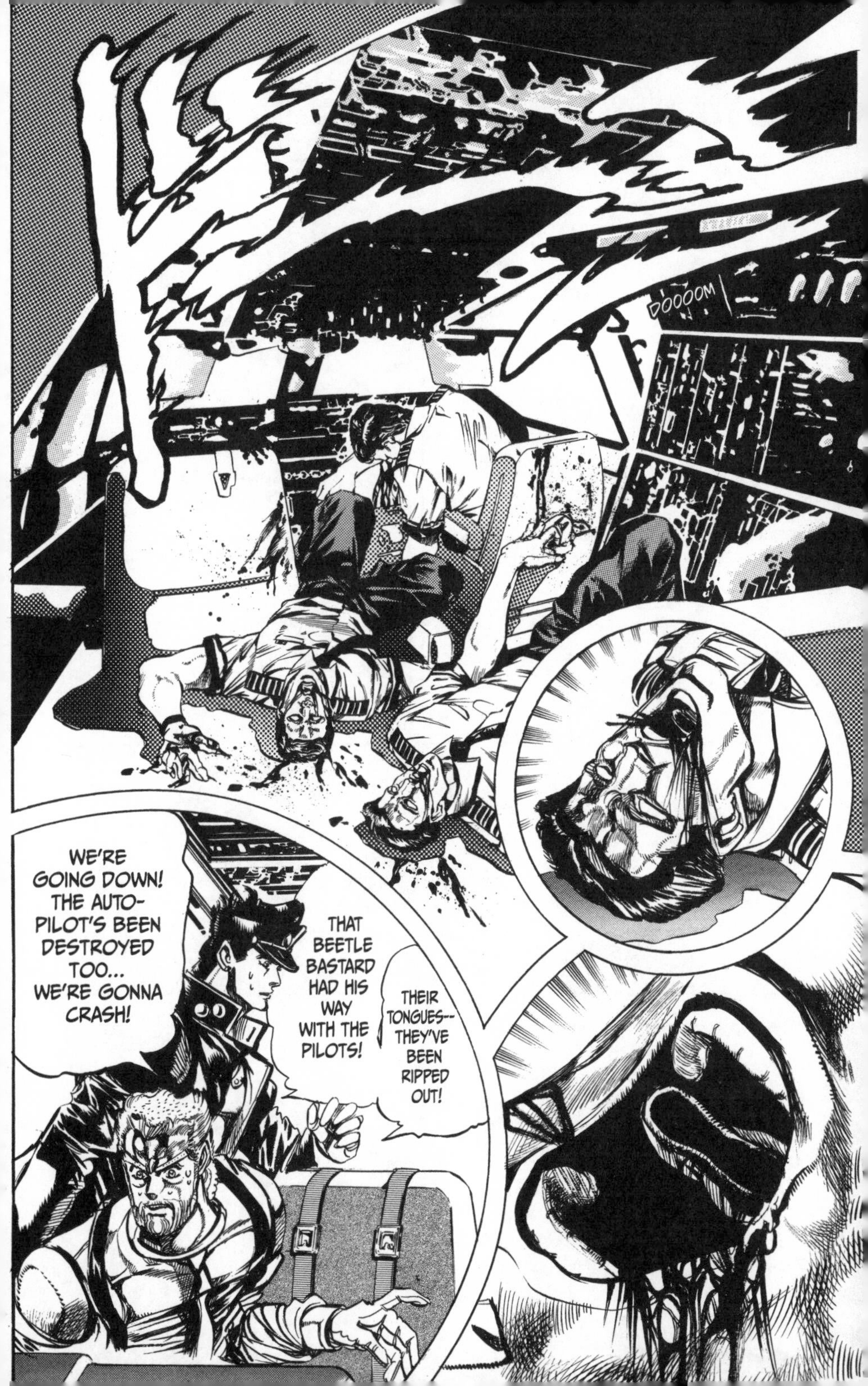
DOOOOM
THEIR TONGUES-- THEY'VE BEEN RIPPED OUT!
THAT BEETLE BASTARD HAD HIS WAY WITH THE PILOTS!
WE'RE GOING DOWN! THE AUTO-PILOT'S BEEN DESTROYED TOO... WE'RE GONNA CRASH!

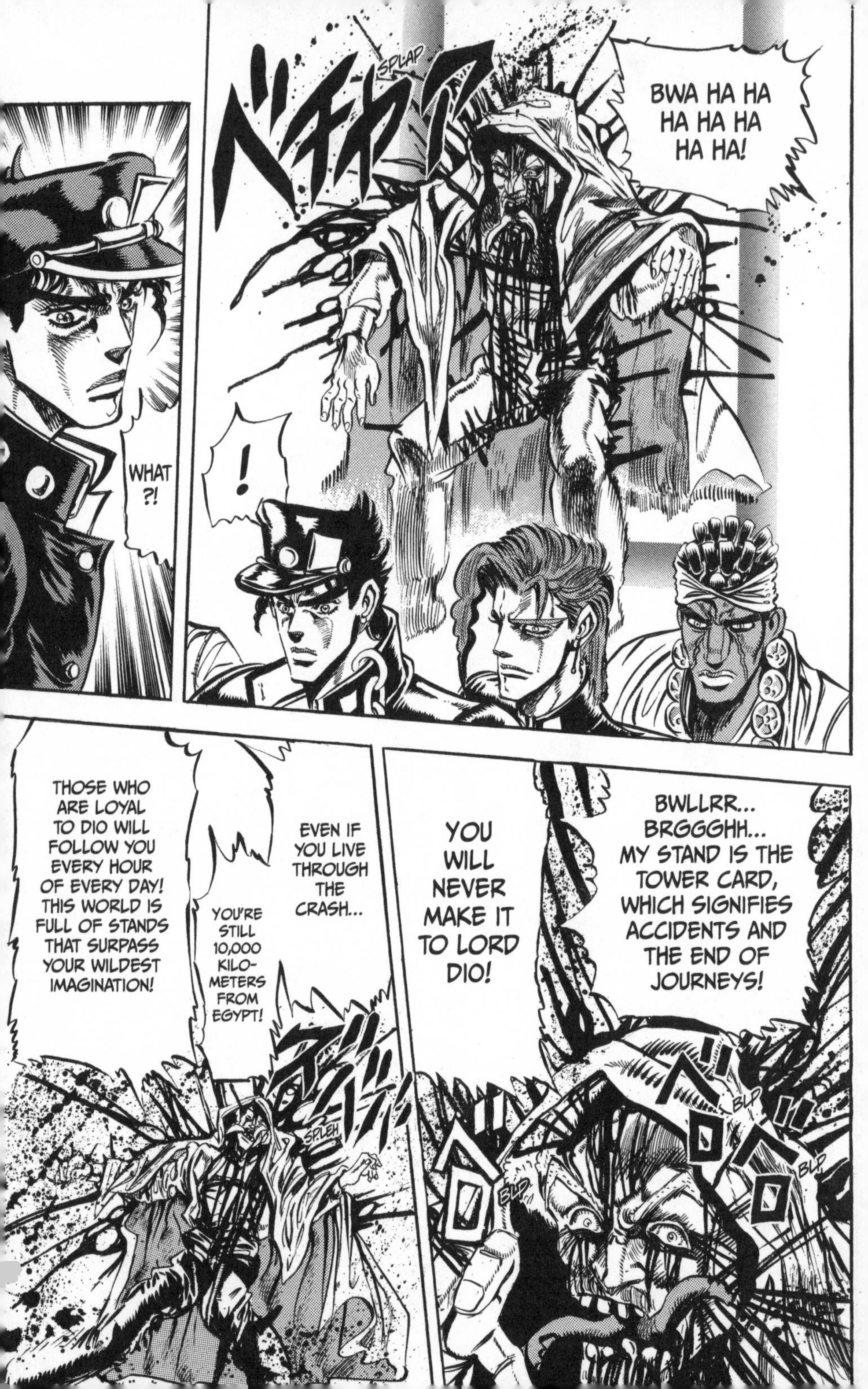
SPLAP
BWA HA HA HA HA HA HA HA!
!
WHAT ?!
BWLLRR... BRGGGHH... MY STAND IS THE TOWER CARD, WHICH SIGNIFIES ACCIDENTS AND THE END OF JOURNEYS!
YOU WILL NEVER MAKE IT TO LORD DIO!
BLP
BLP
BLP
EVEN IF YOU LIVE THROUGH THE CRASH...
YOU'RE STILL 10,000 KILO-METERS FROM EGYPT!
THOSE WHO ARE LOYAL TO DIO WILL FOLLOW YOU EVERY HOUR OF EVERY DAY! THIS WORLD IS FULL OF STANDS THAT SURPASS YOUR WILDEST IMAGINATION!
SPLEH

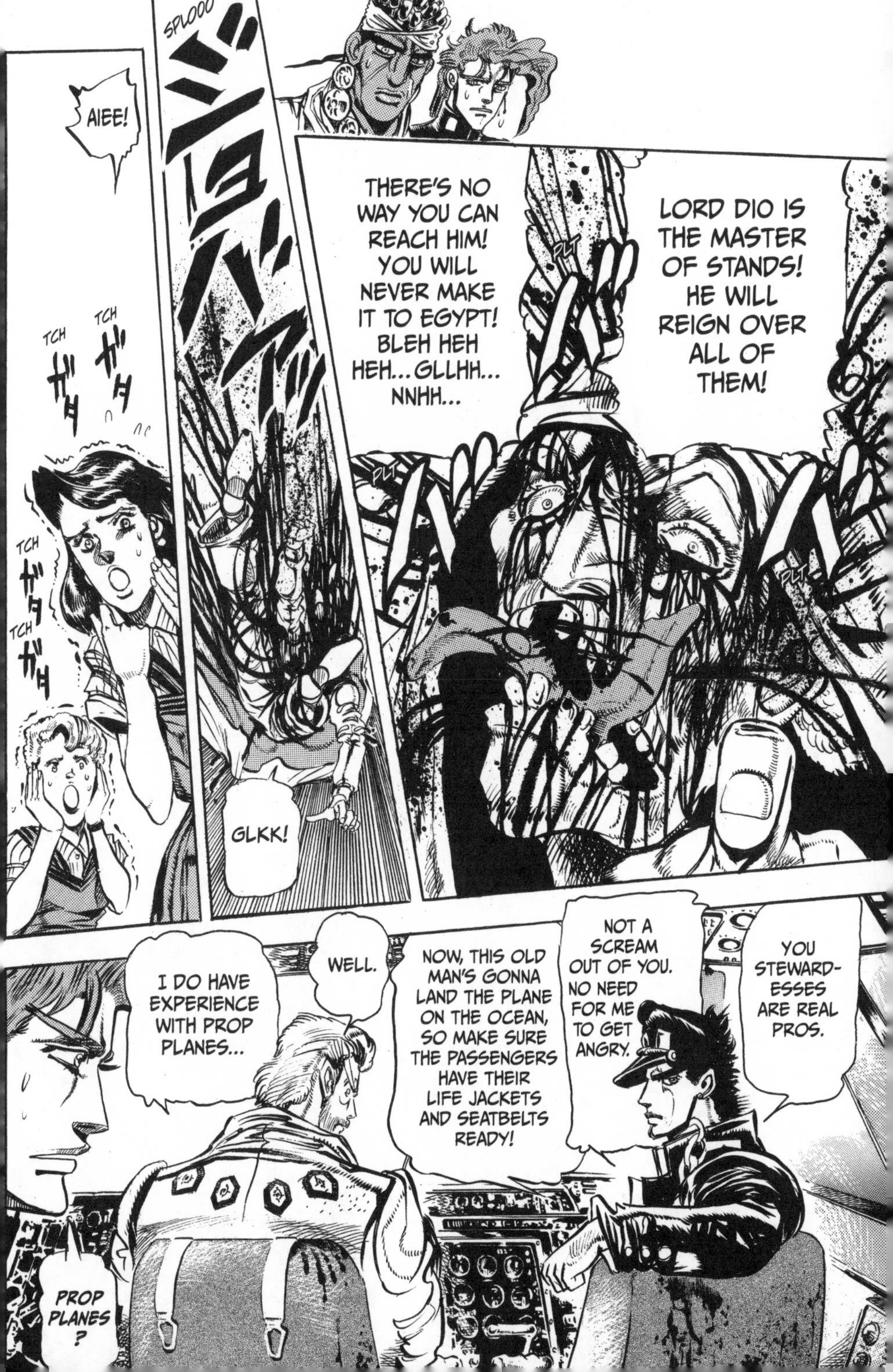

LORD DIO IS THE MASTER OF STANDS! HE WILL REIGN OVER ALL OF THEM!
THERE'S NO WAY YOU CAN REACH HIM! YOU WILL NEVER MAKE IT TO EGYPT! BLEH HEH HEH... GLLHH... NNHH...
PLT
PLT
PLT
SPLOOO
GLKK!
AIEE!
TCH
TCH
TCH
TCH
YOU STEWARD-ESSES ARE REAL PROS.
NOT A SCREAM OUT OF YOU. NO NEED FOR ME TO GET ANGRY.
NOW, THIS OLD MAN'S GONNA LAND THE PLANE ON THE OCEAN, SO MAKE SURE THE PASSENGERS HAVE THEIR LIFE JACKETS AND SEATBELTS READY!
WELL.
I DO HAVE EXPERIENCE WITH PROP PLANES...
PROP PLANES?

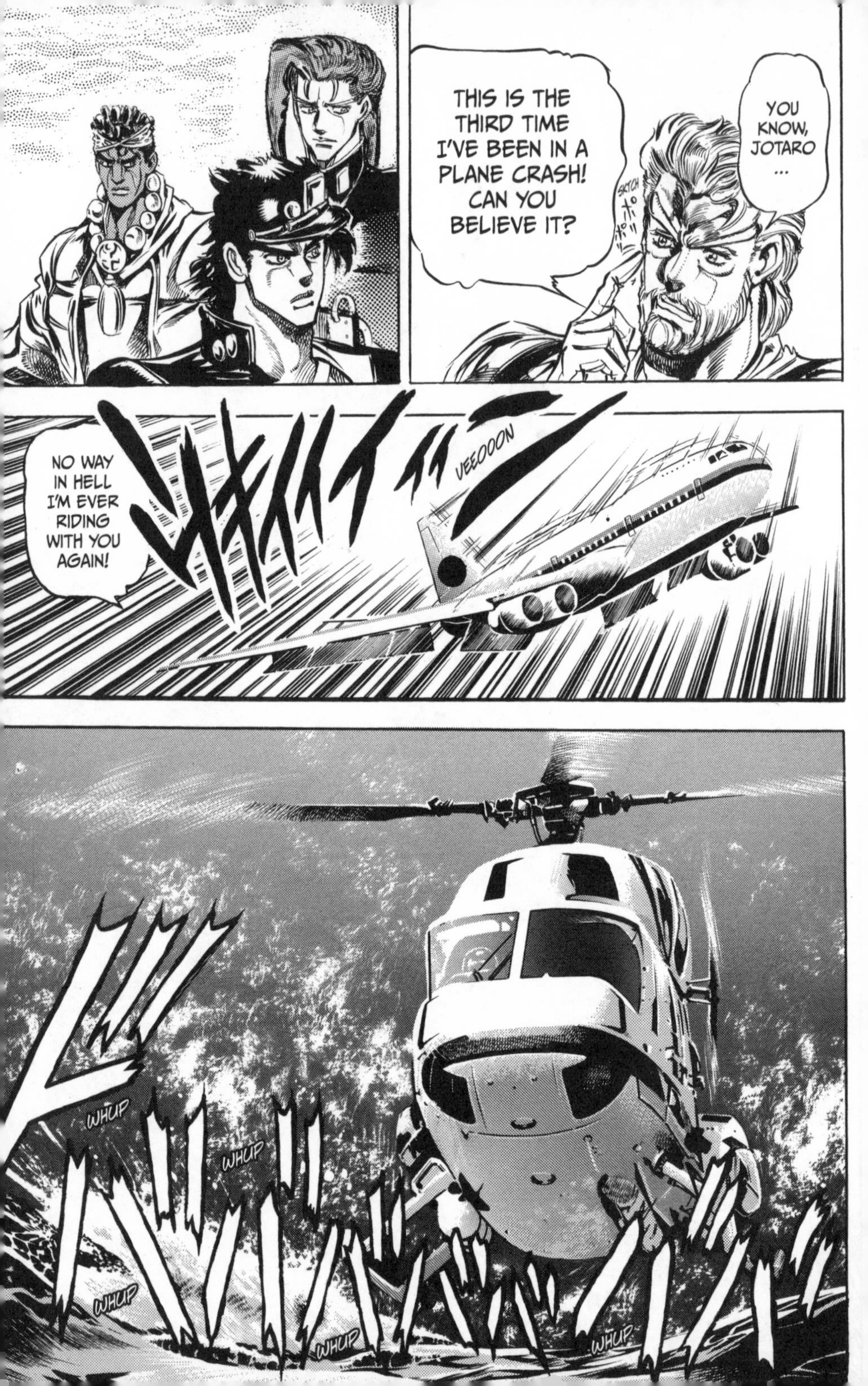
YOU KNOW, JOTARO ...
SKTCH
THIS IS THE THIRD TIME I'VE BEEN IN A PLANE CRASH! CAN YOU BELIEVE IT?
VEEOOON
NO WAY IN HELL I'M EVER RIDING WITH YOU AGAIN!
WHUP
WHUP
WHUP
WHUP
WHUP

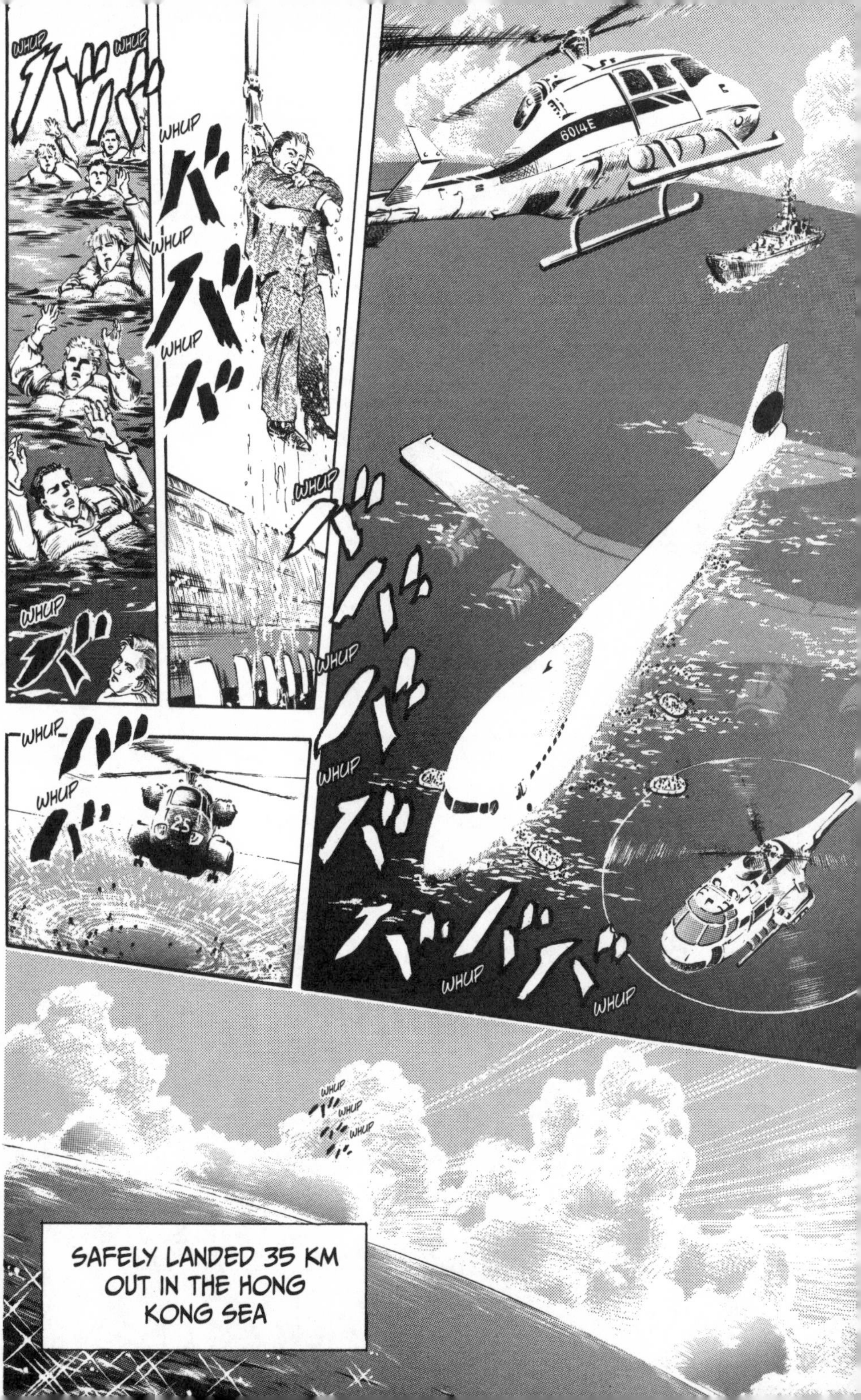
WHUP
WHUP
WHUP
WHUP
WHUP
WHUP
WHUP
WHUP
WHUP
WHUP
WHUP
WHUP
WHUP
WHUP
WHUP
WHUP
WHUP
SAFELY LANDED 35 KM OUT IN THE HONG KONG SEA

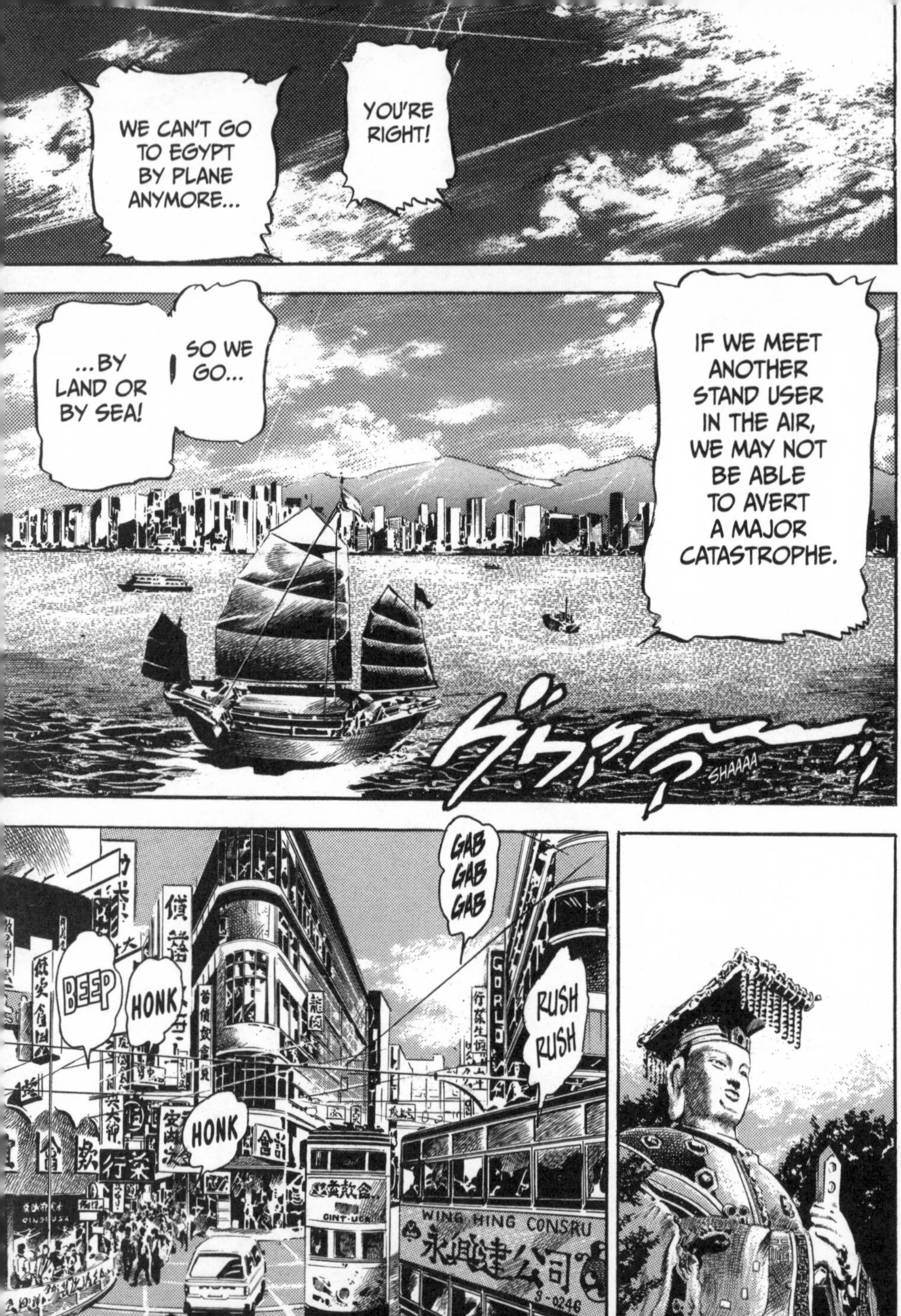
YOU'RE RIGHT!
WE CAN'T GO TO EGYPT BY PLANE ANYMORE...
IF WE MEET ANOTHER STAND USER IN THE AIR, WE MAY NOT BE ABLE TO AVERT A MAJOR CATASTROPHE.
SO WE GO...
...BY LAND OR BY SEA!
SHAAAA
GAB GAB GAB
RUSH RUSH
HONK
BEEP
HONK
WING HING CONSRU
3-0246
VRMMM

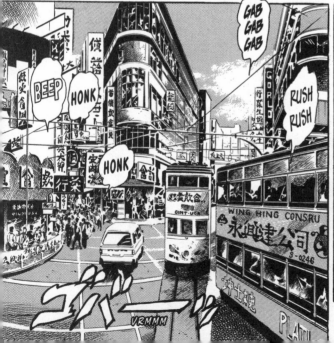

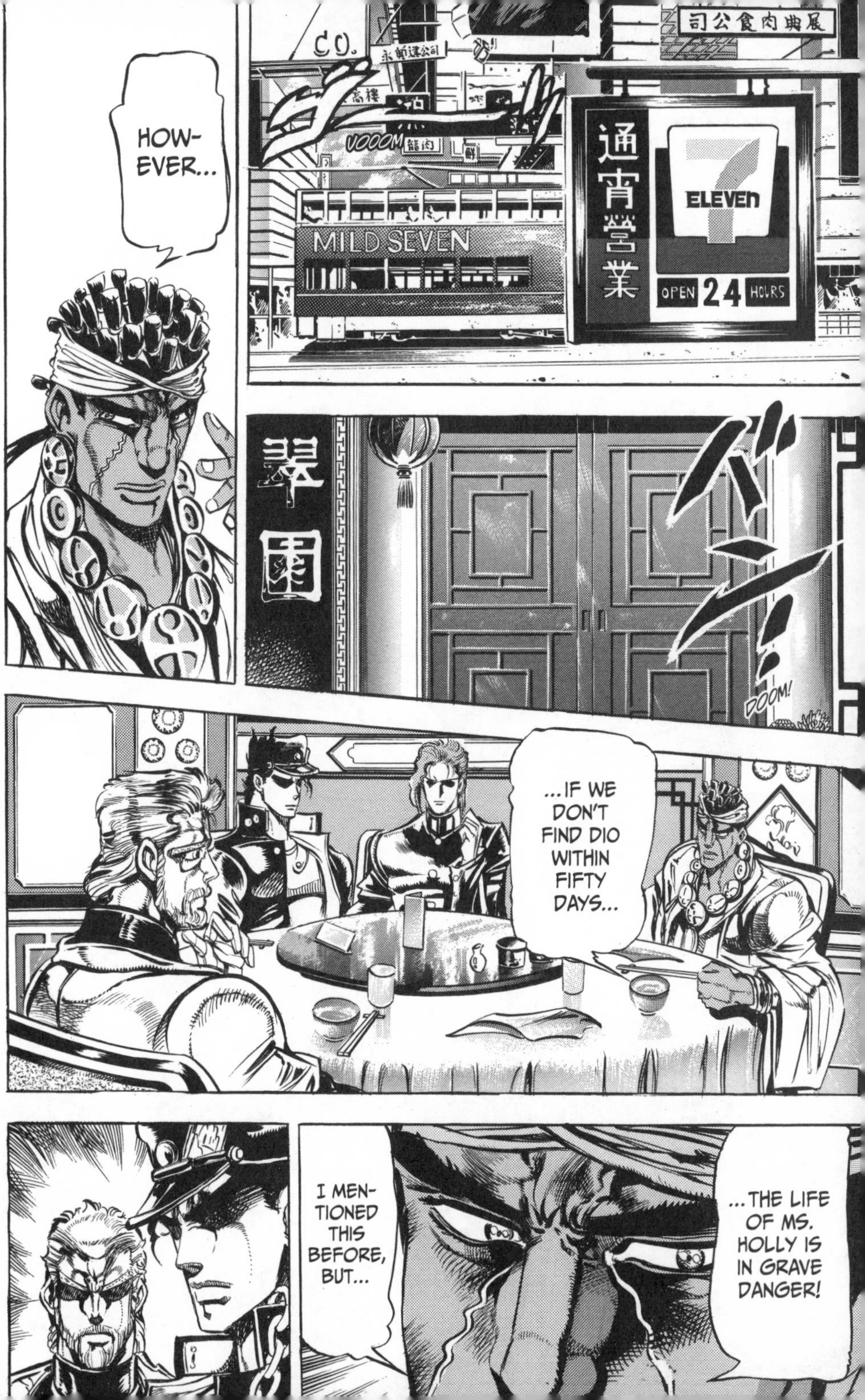

VOOOM
MILD SEVEN
通宵營業
ELEVEn
OPEN 24 HOURS
DOOM!
翠園
HOW-EVER...
...IF WE DON'T FIND DIO WITHIN FIFTY DAYS...
I MEN-TIONED THIS BEFORE, BUT...
...THE LIFE OF MS. HOLLY IS IN GRAVE DANGER!

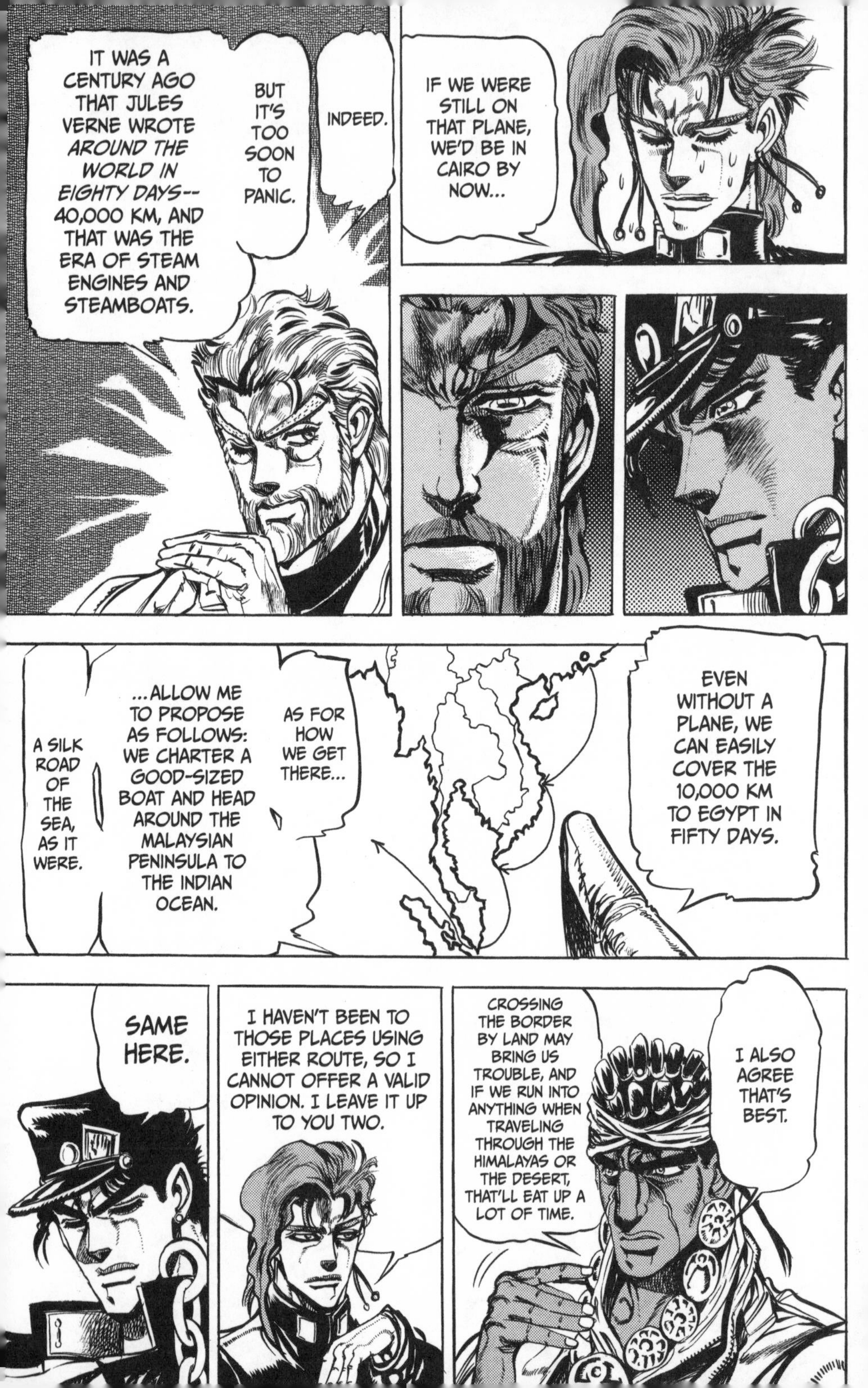
IF WE WERE STILL ON THAT PLANE, WE'D BE IN CAIRO BY NOW...
INDEED.
BUT IT'S TOO SOON TO PANIC.
IT WAS A CENTURY AGO THAT JULES VERNE WROTE *AROUND THE WORLD IN EIGHTY DAYS*--40,000 KM, AND THAT WAS THE ERA OF STEAM ENGINES AND STEAMBOATS.
EVEN WITHOUT A PLANE, WE CAN EASILY COVER THE 10,000 KM TO EGYPT IN FIFTY DAYS.
AS FOR HOW WE GET THERE...
...ALLOW ME TO PROPOSE AS FOLLOWS: WE CHARTER A GOOD-SIZED BOAT AND HEAD AROUND THE MALAYSIAN PENINSULA TO THE INDIAN OCEAN.
A SILK ROAD OF THE SEA, AS IT WERE.
I ALSO AGREE THAT'S BEST.
CROSSING THE BORDER BY LAND MAY BRING US TROUBLE, AND IF WE RUN INTO ANYTHING WHEN TRAVELING THROUGH THE HIMALAYAS OR THE DESERT, THAT'LL EAT UP A LOT OF TIME.
I HAVEN'T BEEN TO THOSE PLACES USING EITHER ROUTE, SO I CANNOT OFFER A VALID OPINION. I LEAVE IT UP TO YOU TWO.
SAME HERE.

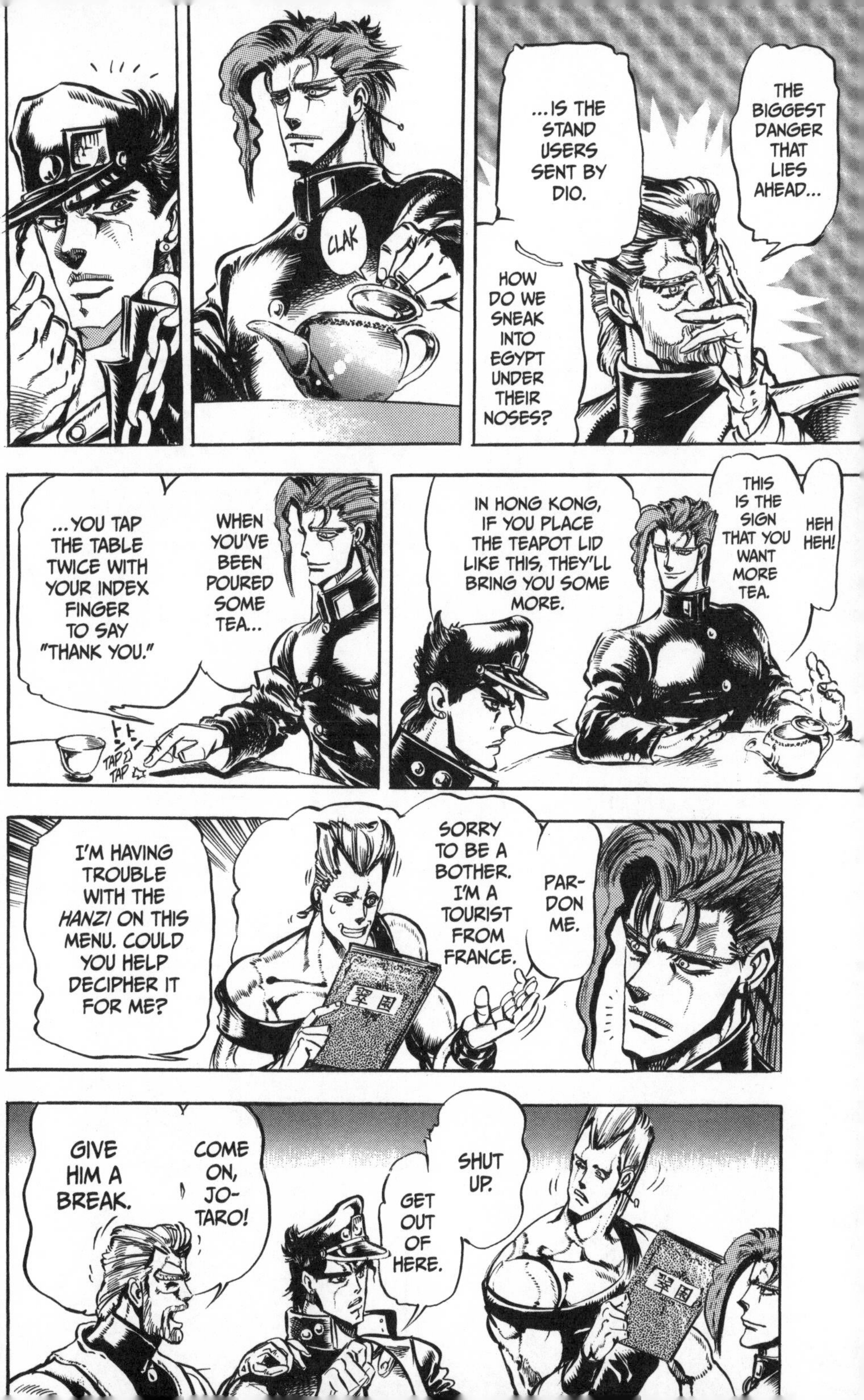
THE BIGGEST DANGER THAT LIES AHEAD...
...IS THE STAND USERS SENT BY DIO.
HOW DO WE SNEAK INTO EGYPT UNDER THEIR NOSES?
CLAK
HEH HEH!
THIS IS THE SIGN THAT YOU WANT MORE TEA.
IN HONG KONG, IF YOU PLACE THE TEAPOT LID LIKE THIS, THEY'LL BRING YOU SOME MORE.
WHEN YOU'VE BEEN POURED SOME TEA...
...YOU TAP THE TABLE TWICE WITH YOUR INDEX FINGER TO SAY "THANK YOU."
TAP TAP
PAR-DON ME.
SORRY TO BE A BOTHER. I'M A TOURIST FROM FRANCE.
I'M HAVING TROUBLE WITH THE *HANZI* ON THIS MENU. COULD YOU HELP DECIPHER IT FOR ME?
SHUT UP.
GET OUT OF HERE.
COME ON, JO-TARO!
GIVE HIM A BREAK.

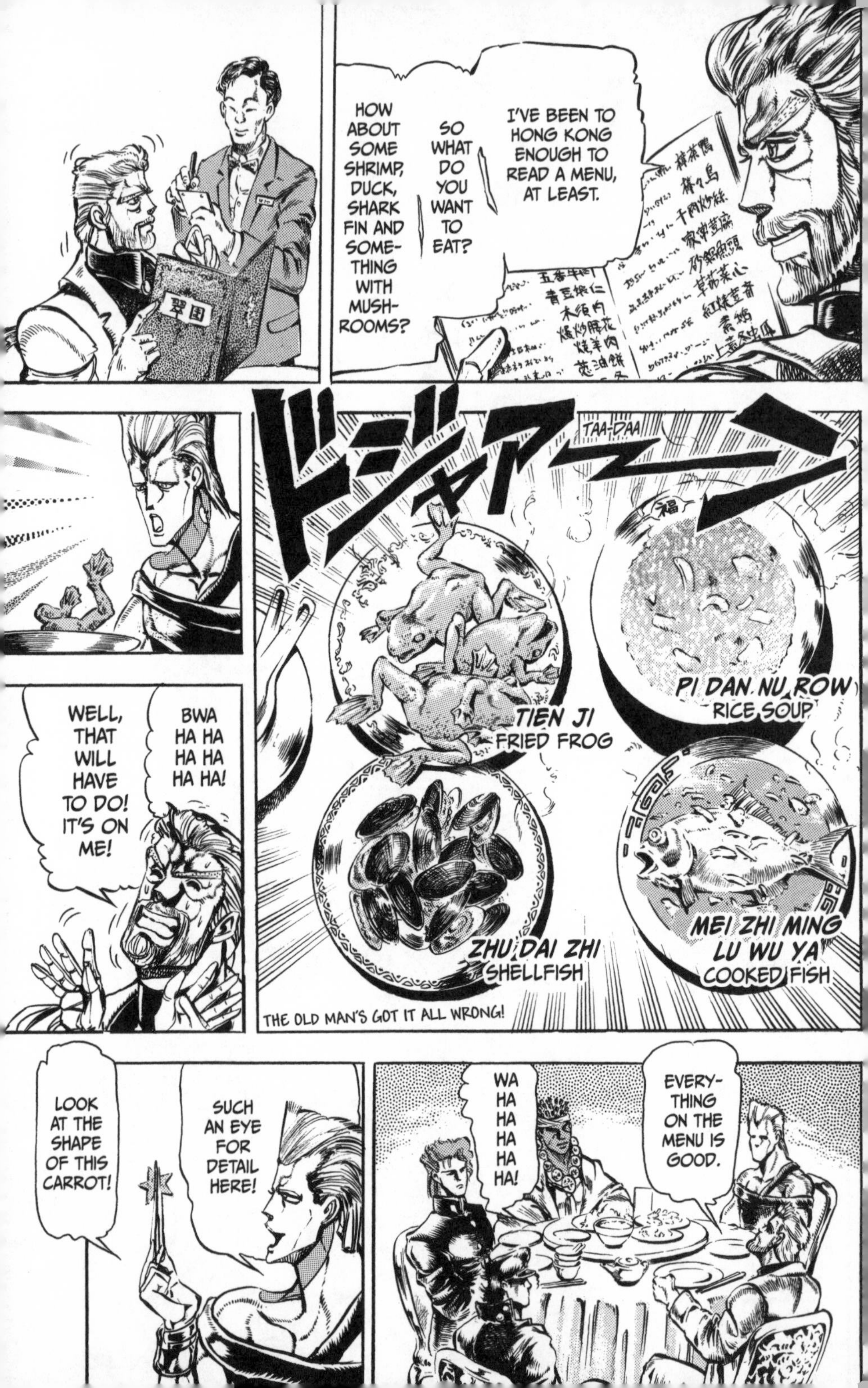
I'VE BEEN TO HONG KONG ENOUGH TO READ A MENU, AT LEAST.
SO WHAT DO YOU WANT TO EAT?
HOW ABOUT SOME SHRIMP, DUCK, SHARK FIN AND SOMETHING WITH MUSHROOMS?
ドジャアーン
TAA-DAA
PI DAN NU ROW
RICE SOUP
TIEN JI
FRIED FROG
MEI ZHI MING LU WU YA
COOKED FISH
ZHU DAI ZHI
SHELLFISH
THE OLD MAN'S GOT IT ALL WRONG!
BWA HA HA HA HA HA HA!
WELL, THAT WILL HAVE TO DO! IT'S ON ME!
EVERYTHING ON THE MENU IS GOOD.
WA HA HA HA HA HA HA!
SUCH AN EYE FOR DETAIL HERE!
LOOK AT THE SHAPE OF THIS CARROT!

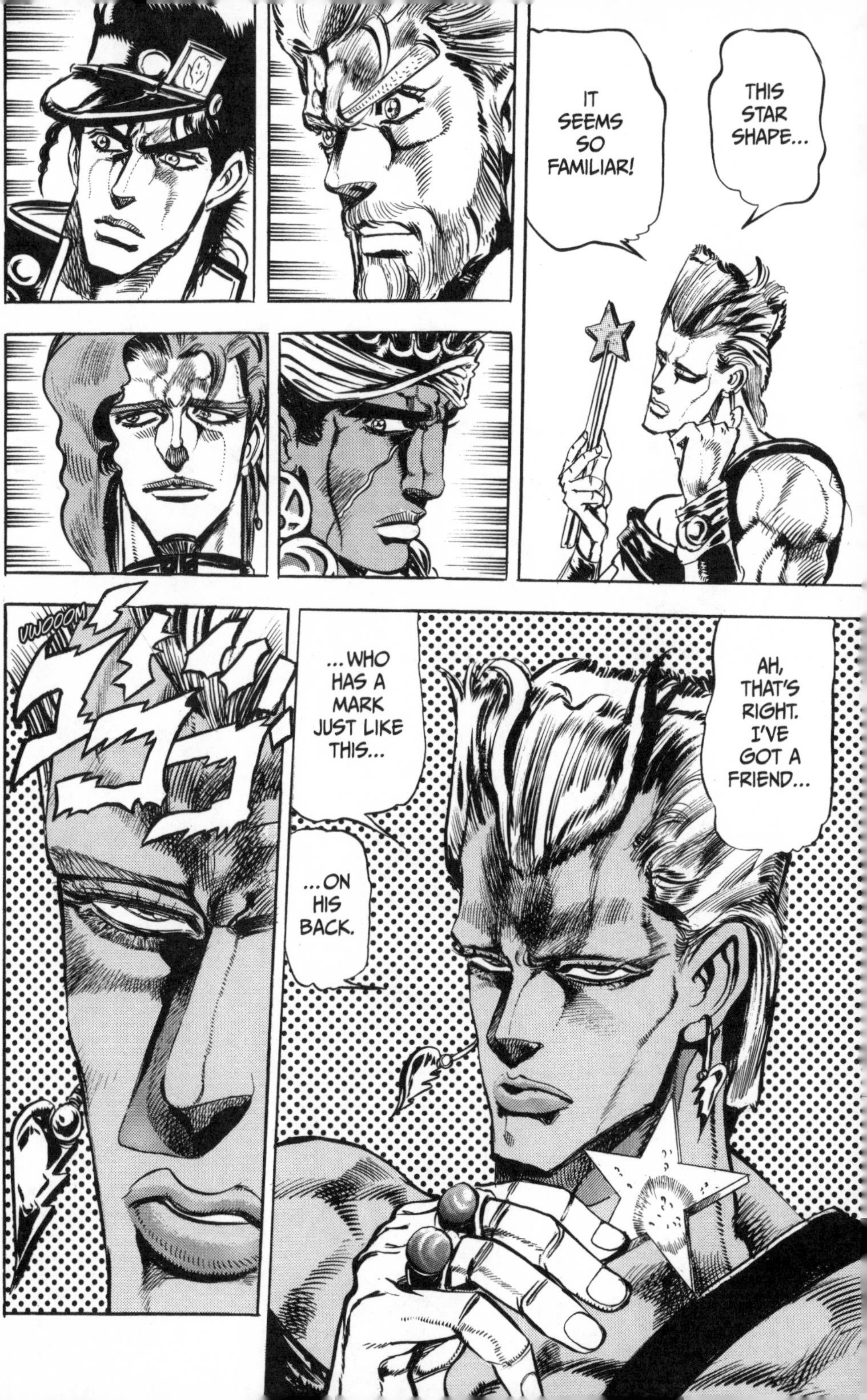
THIS STAR SHAPE...
IT SEEMS SO FAMILIAR!
AH, THAT'S RIGHT. I'VE GOT A FRIEND...
...WHO HAS A MARK JUST LIKE THIS...
...ON HIS BACK.
UWOOOM

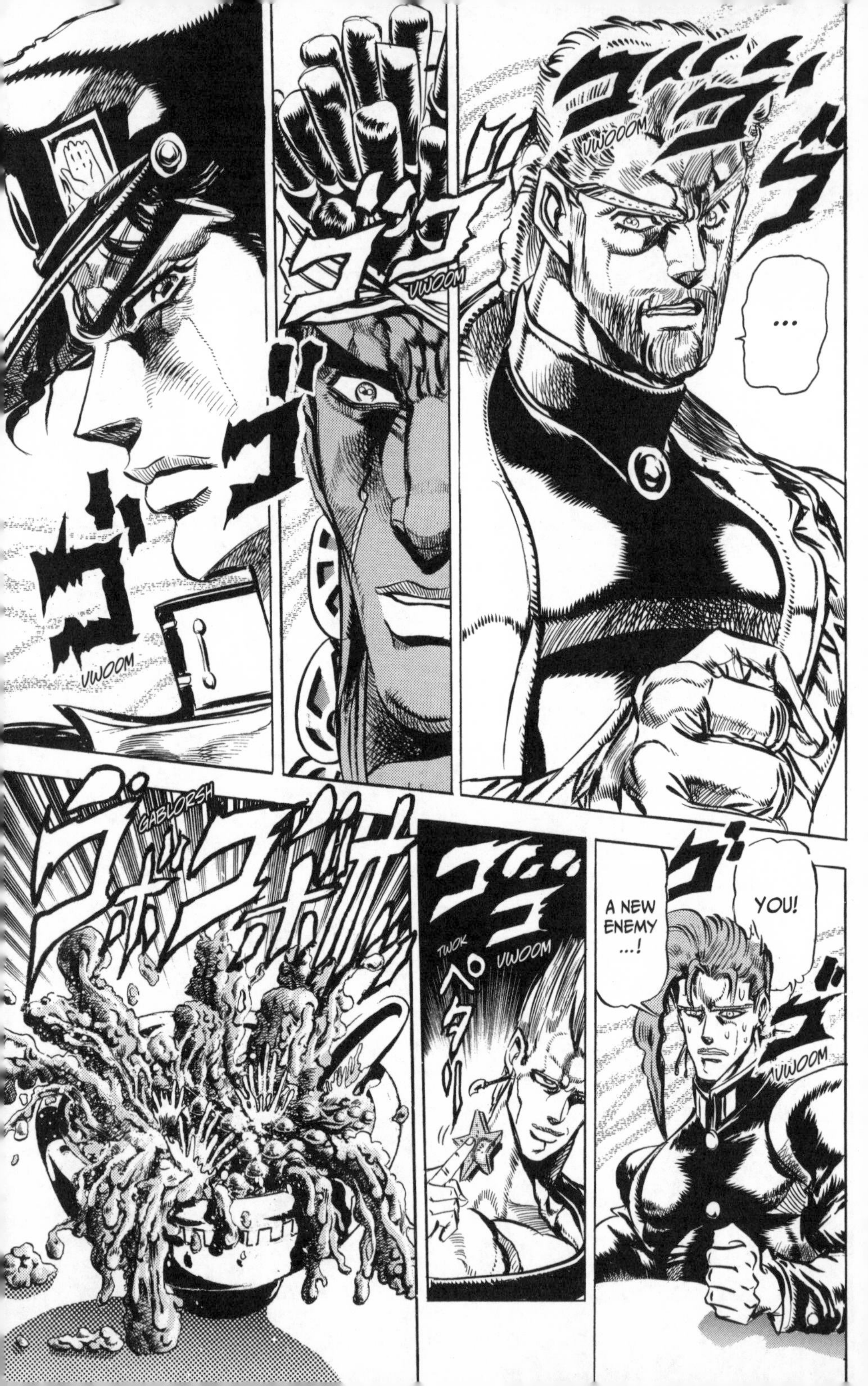
VWOOOM
...
VWOOM
VWOOM
YOU!
A NEW ENEMY ...!
VWOOM
TWOK
VWOOM
GABLORSH

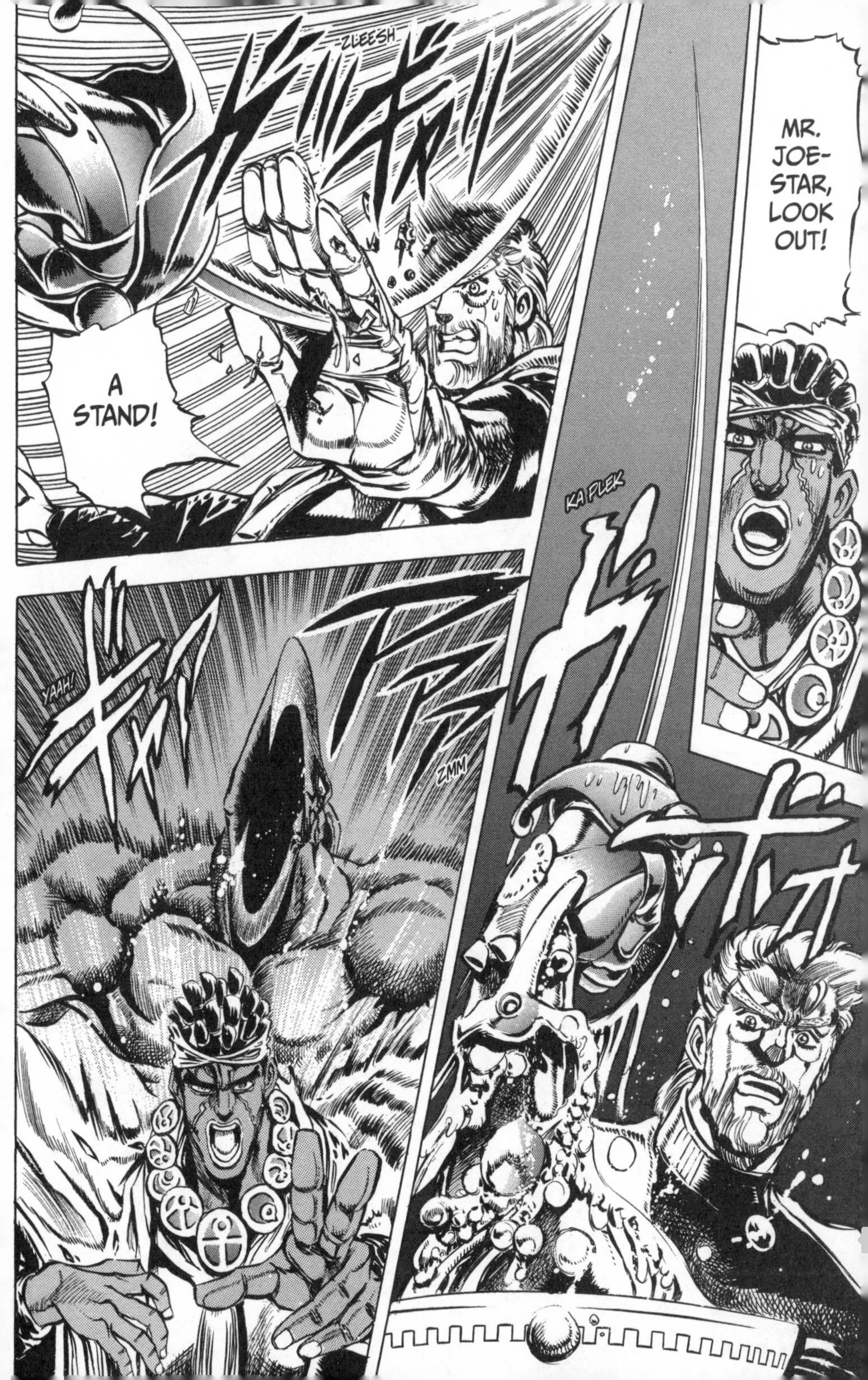
MR. JOE-STAR, LOOK OUT!
ZLEESH
A STAND!
KA-PLEK
YAAH!
ZMM

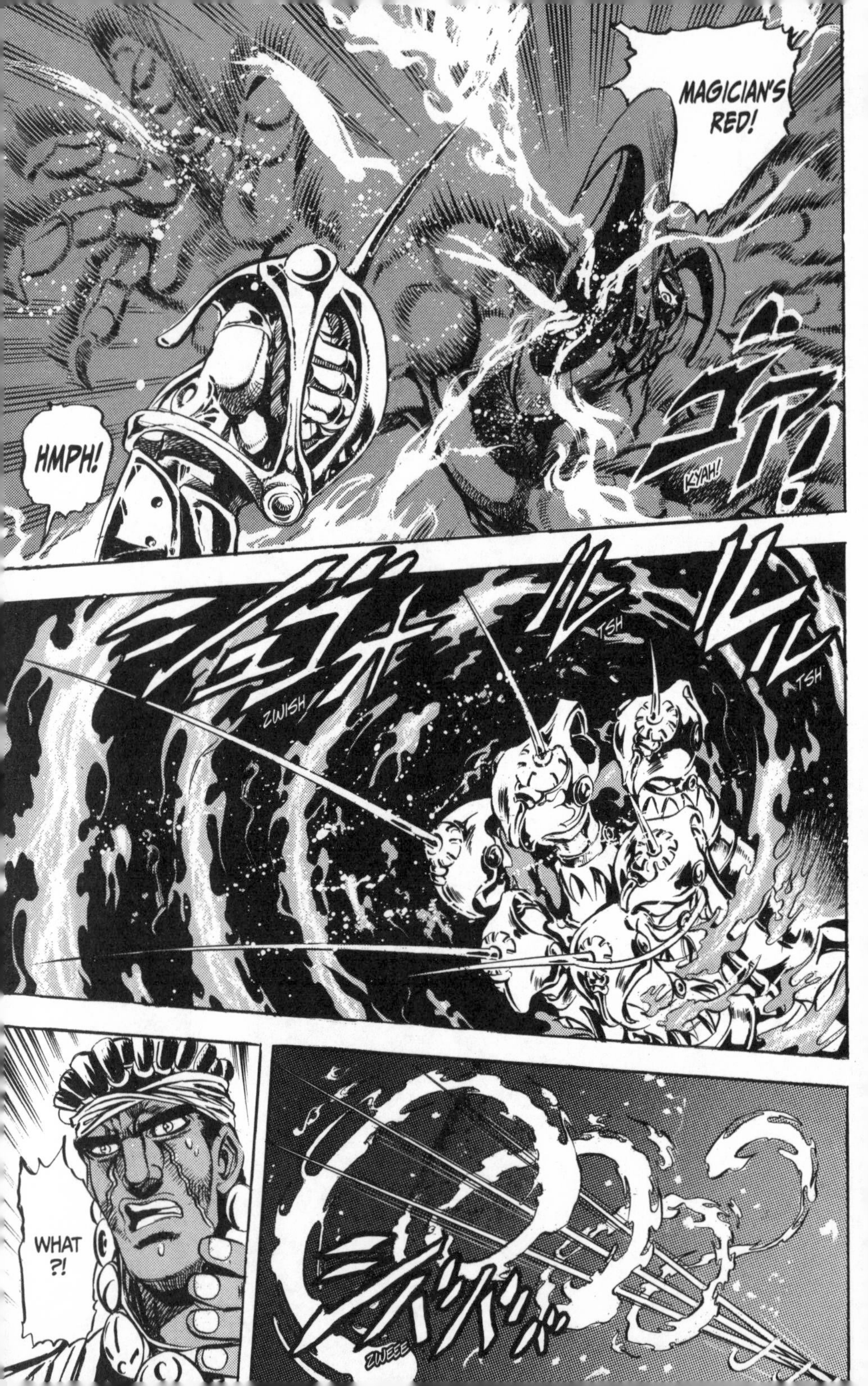
MAGICIAN'S RED!
KYAH!
HMPH!
TSH
TSH
ZWISH
ZWEEE
WHAT ?!

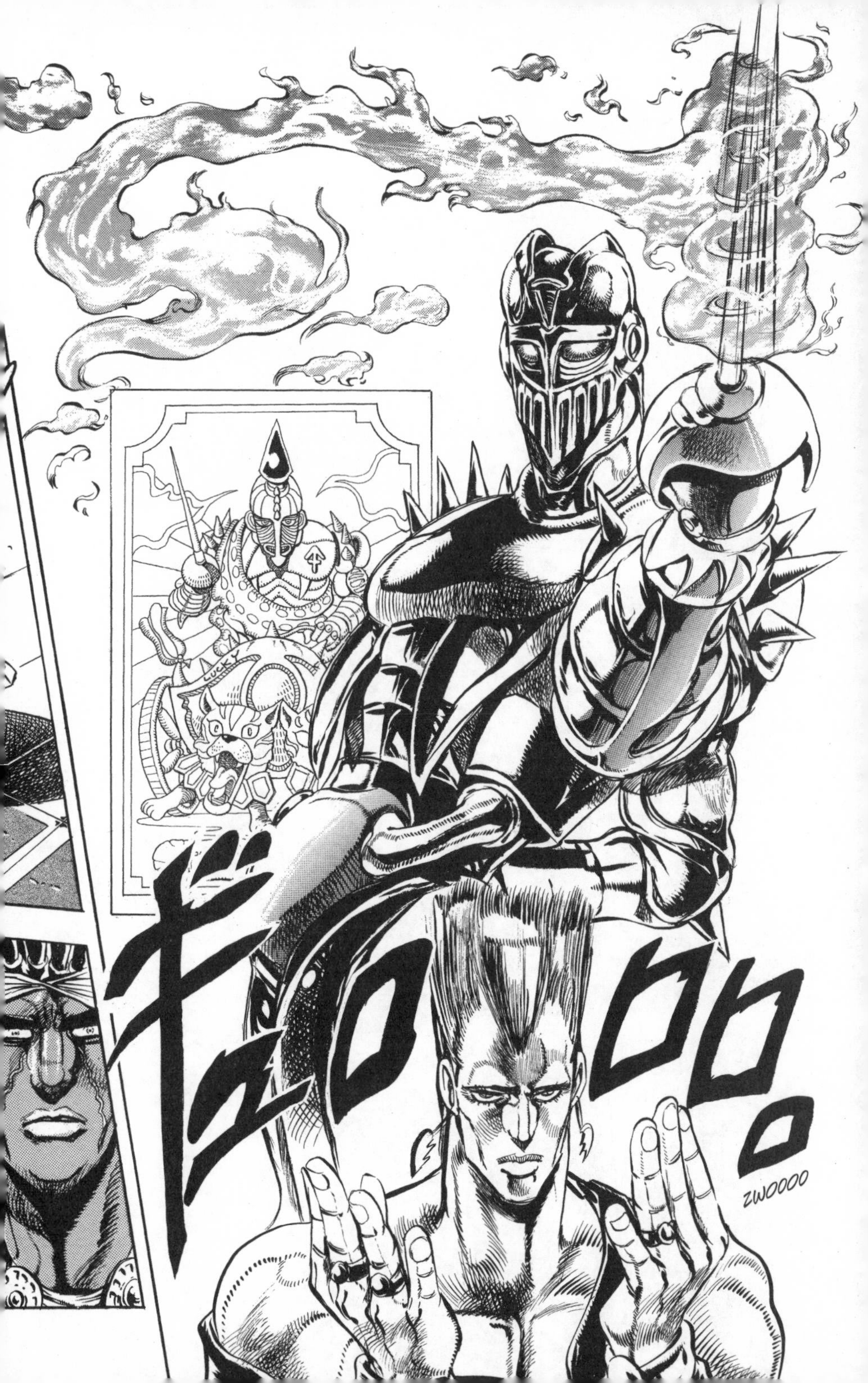
LUCKY
ZWOOOO

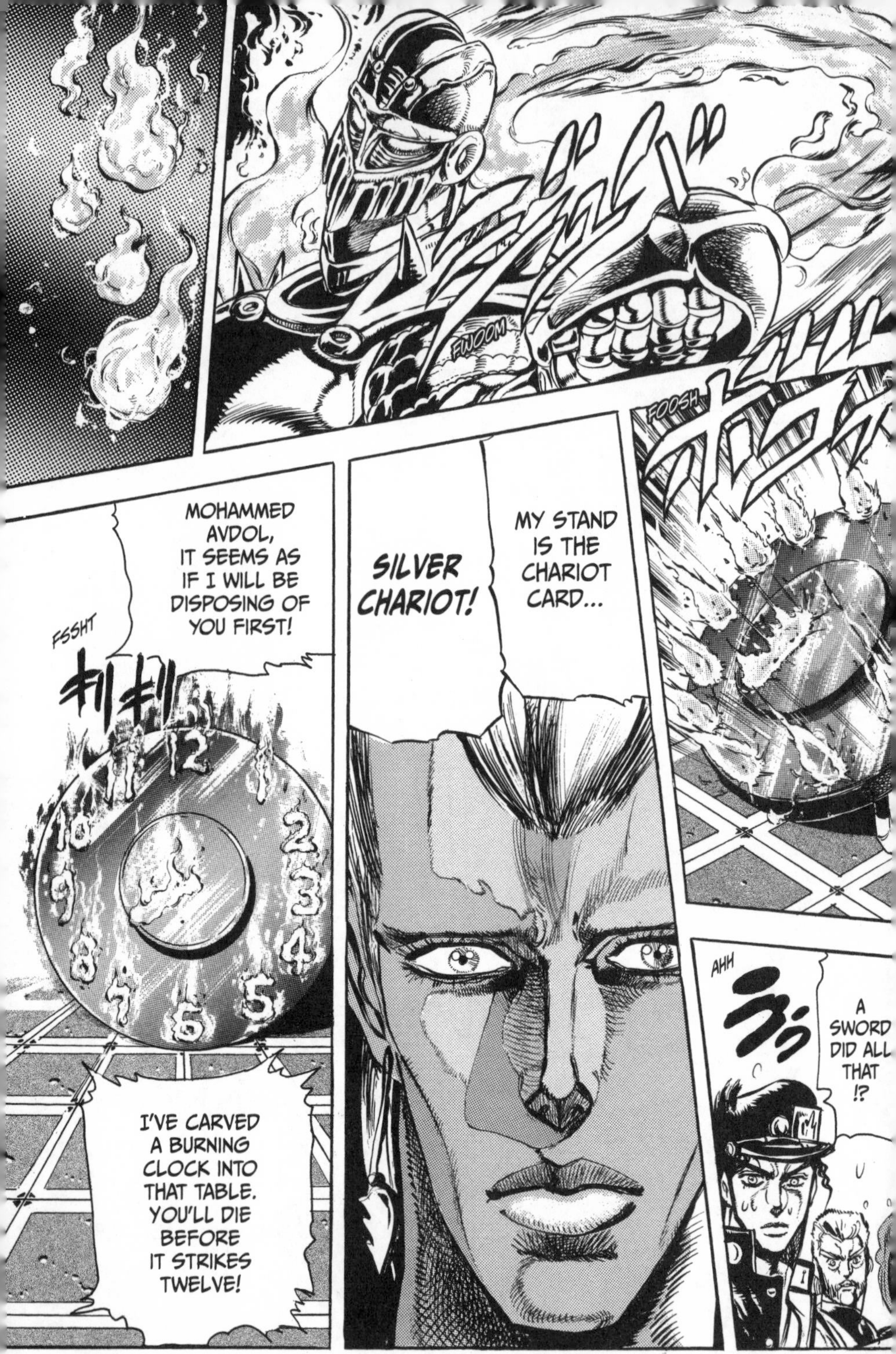
FWOOM
FOOSH
AHH
A SWORD DID ALL THAT!?
MY STAND IS THE CHARIOT CARD...
SILVER CHARIOT!
MOHAMMED AVDOL, IT SEEMS AS IF I WILL BE DISPOSING OF YOU FIRST!
FSSHT
I'VE CARVED A BURNING CLOCK INTO THAT TABLE. YOU'LL DIE BEFORE IT STRIKES TWELVE!

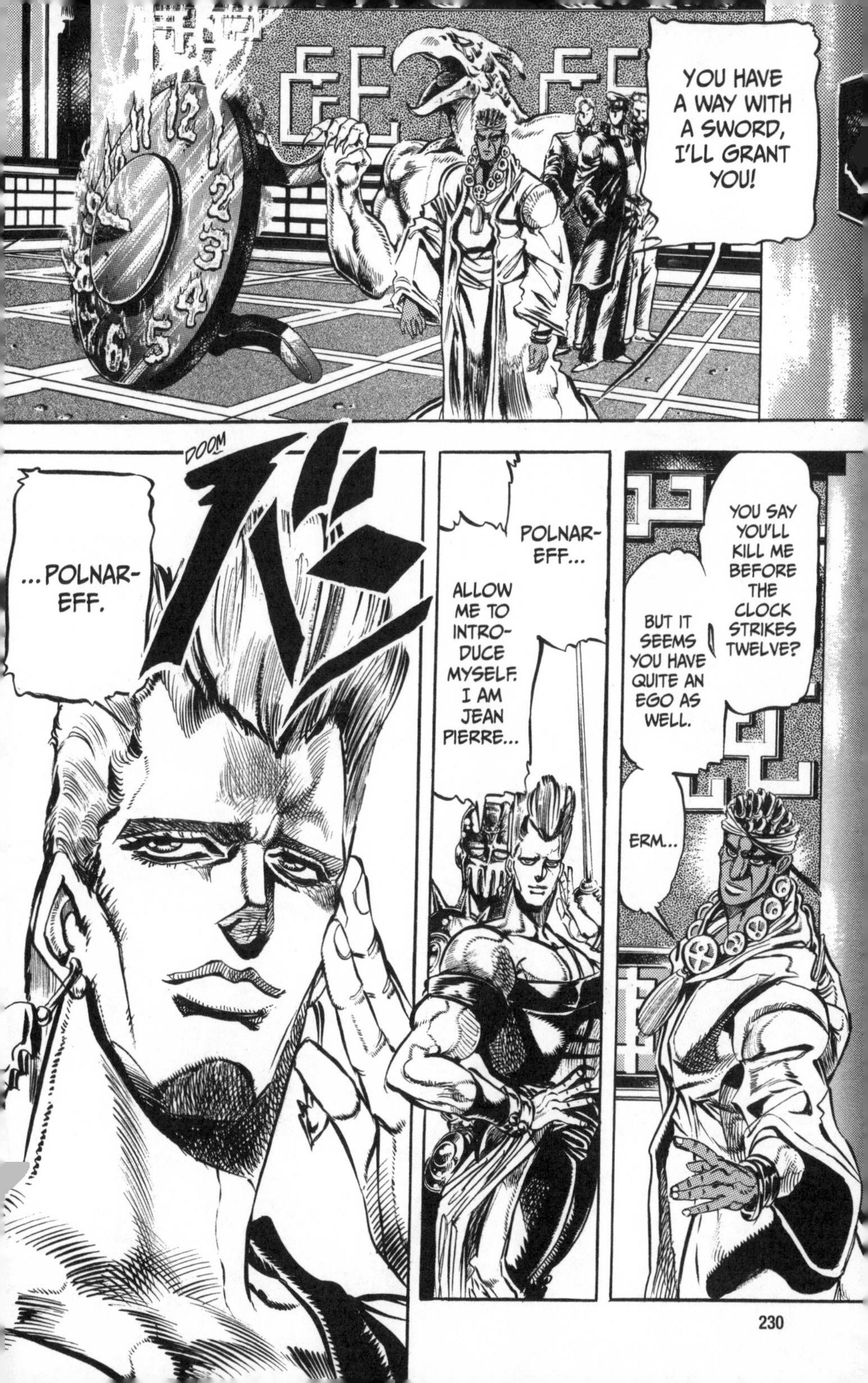
YOU HAVE A WAY WITH A SWORD, I'LL GRANT YOU!
YOU SAY YOU'LL KILL ME BEFORE THE CLOCK STRIKES TWELVE?
BUT IT SEEMS YOU HAVE QUITE AN EGO AS WELL.
ERM...
POLNAREFF...
ALLOW ME TO INTRODUCE MYSELF. I AM JEAN PIERRE...
DOOM
...POLNAREFF.

CHAPTER 12: Silver Chariot PART 2

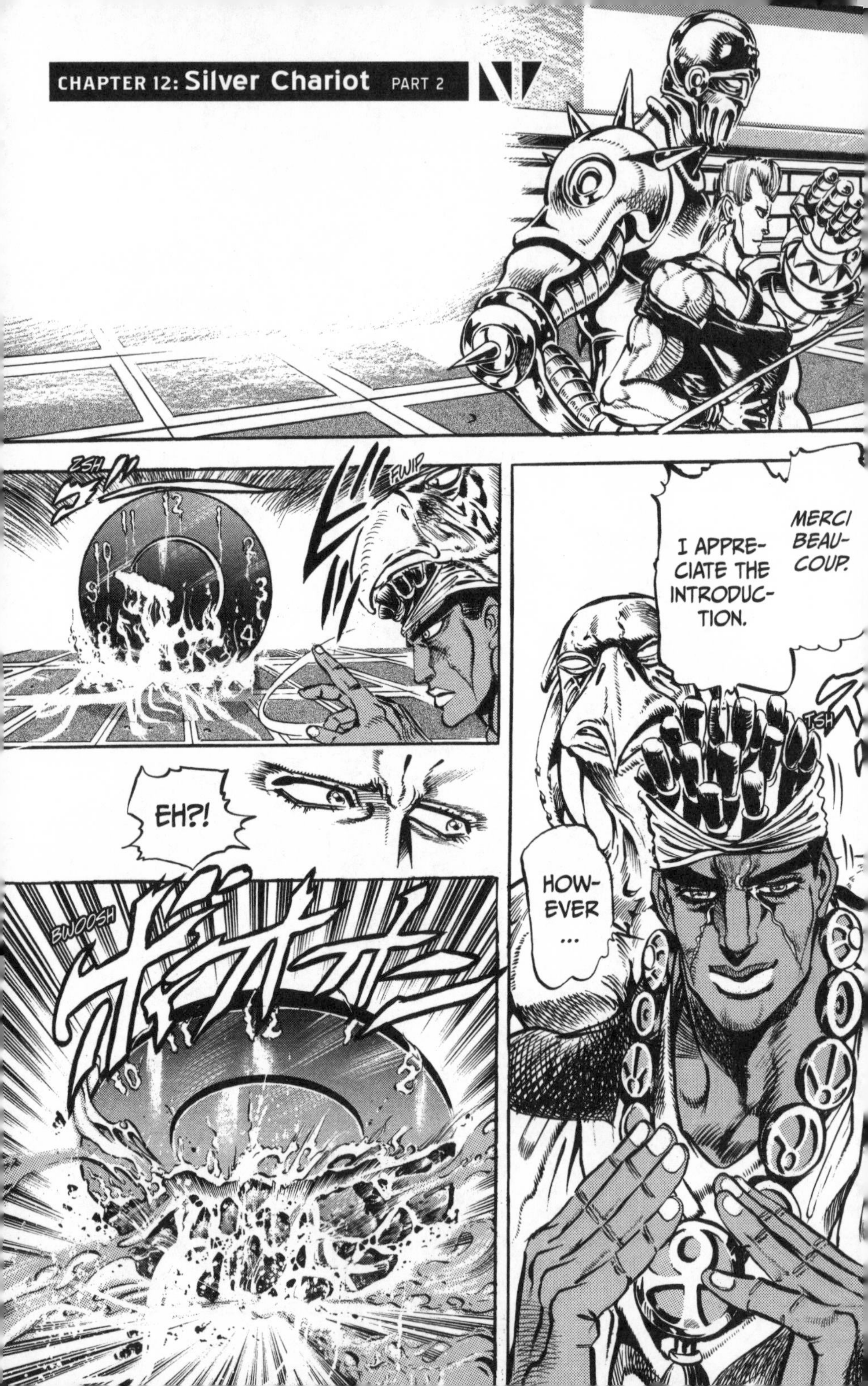
MERCI BEAU-COUP.
I APPRE-CIATE THE INTRODUC-TION.
TSH
HOW-EVER ...
FWIP
ZSH
EH?!
BWOOSH

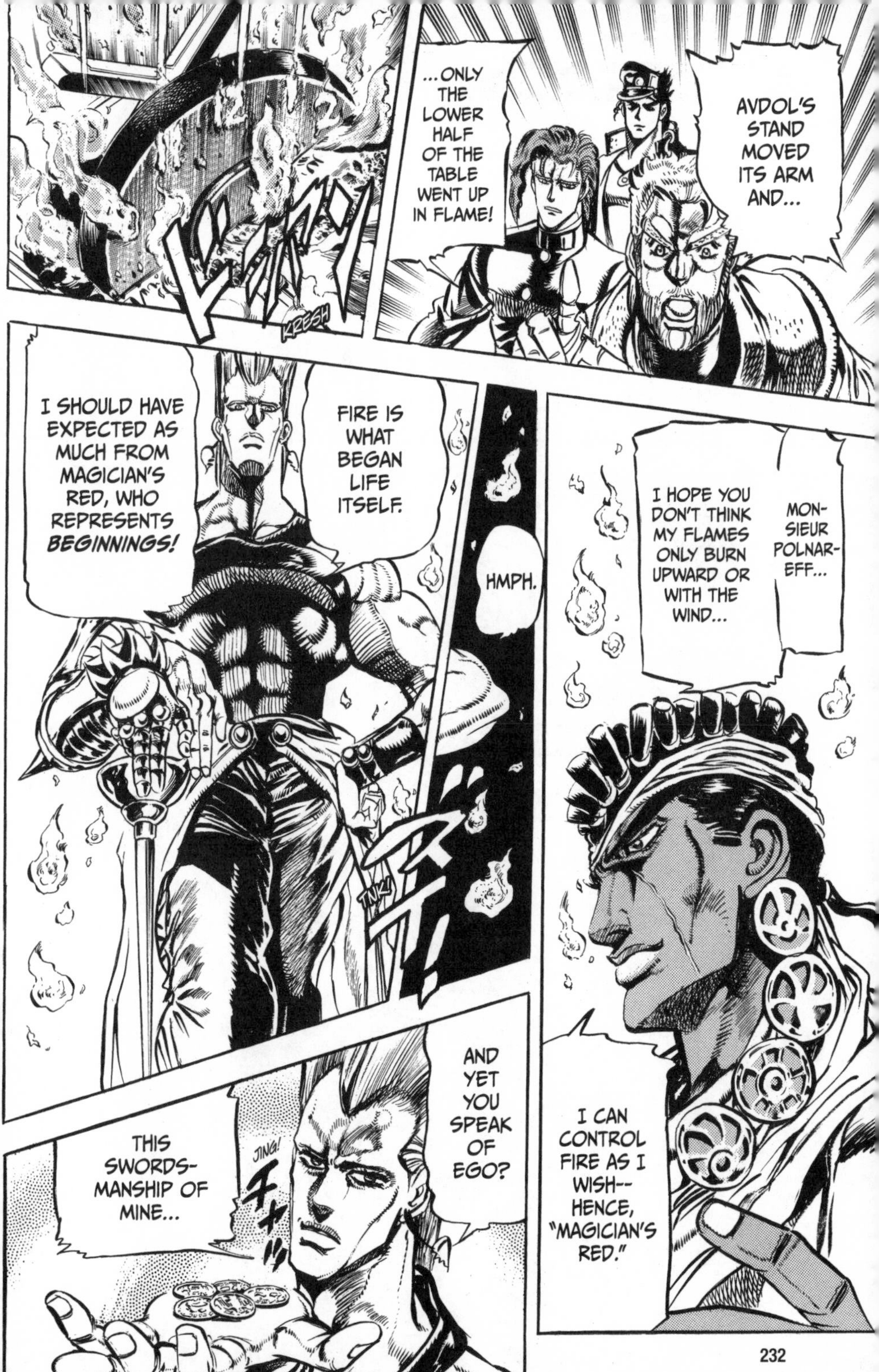
AVDOL'S STAND MOVED ITS ARM AND...
...ONLY THE LOWER HALF OF THE TABLE WENT UP IN FLAME!
KRESH
MON-SIEUR POLNAR-EFF...
I HOPE YOU DON'T THINK MY FLAMES ONLY BURN UPWARD OR WITH THE WIND...
I CAN CONTROL FIRE AS I WISH-- HENCE, "MAGICIAN'S RED."
HMPH.
FIRE IS WHAT BEGAN LIFE ITSELF.
I SHOULD HAVE EXPECTED AS MUCH FROM MAGICIAN'S RED, WHO REPRESENTS *BEGINNINGS!*
TINK!
AND YET YOU SPEAK OF EGO?
JING!
THIS SWORDS-MANSHIP OF MINE...

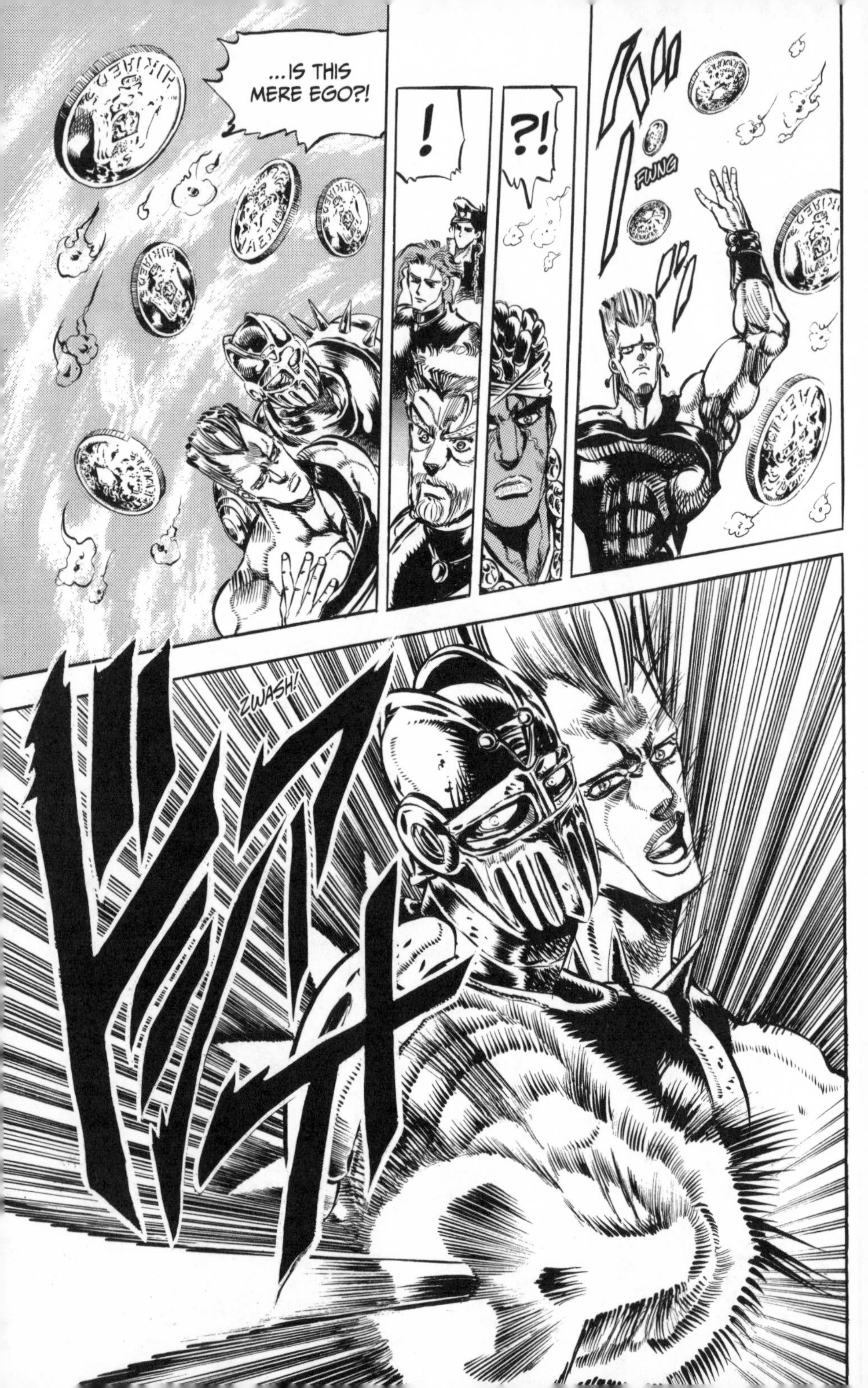
FUNG
?!
!
...IS THIS
MERE EGO?!
ZWASH!

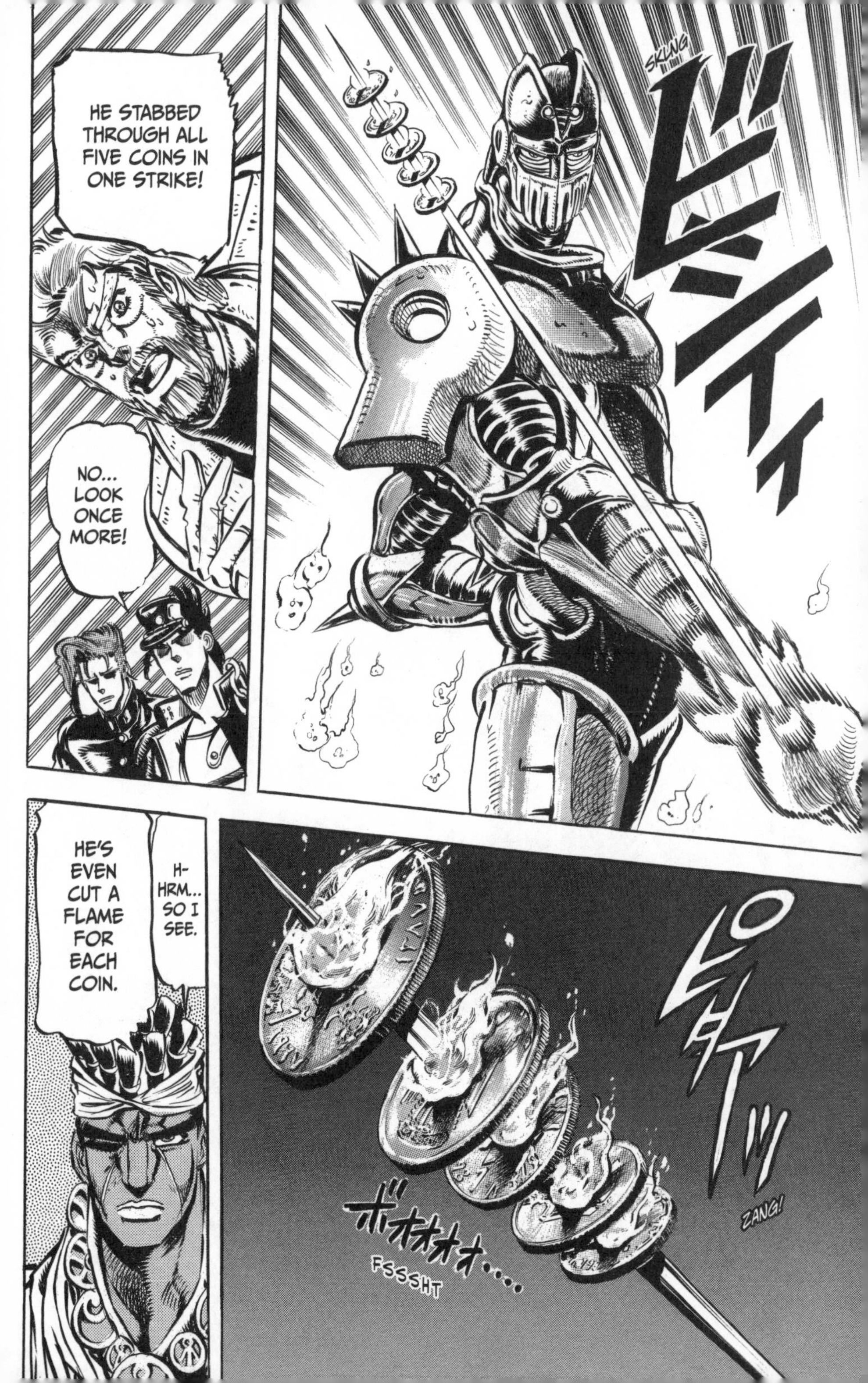
SKLNG
HE STABBED THROUGH ALL FIVE COINS IN ONE STRIKE!
NO... LOOK ONCE MORE!
ZANG!
FSSSHT
H-HRM... SO I SEE.
HE'S EVEN CUT A FLAME FOR EACH COIN.

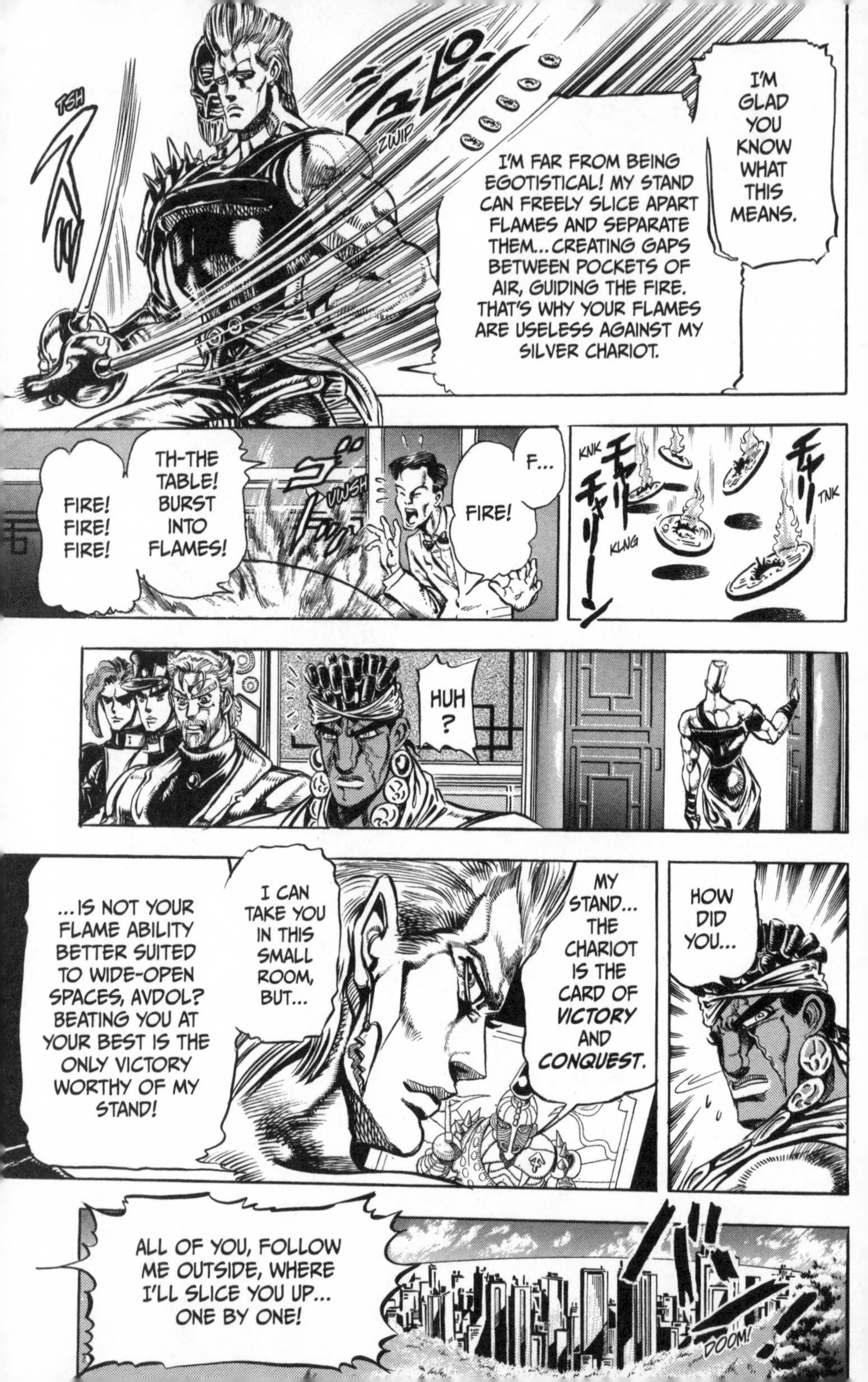
I'M GLAD YOU KNOW WHAT THIS MEANS.
I'M FAR FROM BEING EGOTISTICAL! MY STAND CAN FREELY SLICE APART FLAMES AND SEPARATE THEM...CREATING GAPS BETWEEN POCKETS OF AIR, GUIDING THE FIRE. THAT'S WHY YOUR FLAMES ARE USELESS AGAINST MY SILVER CHARIOT.
ZWIP
TSH
TNK
KNK
KLNG
F...
FIRE!
TH-THE TABLE! BURST INTO FLAMES!
FIRE! FIRE! FIRE!
VWSH
HUH?
HOW DID YOU...
MY STAND... THE CHARIOT IS THE CARD OF VICTORY AND CONQUEST.
I CAN TAKE YOU IN THIS SMALL ROOM, BUT...
...IS NOT YOUR FLAME ABILITY BETTER SUITED TO WIDE-OPEN SPACES, AVDOL? BEATING YOU AT YOUR BEST IS THE ONLY VICTORY WORTHY OF MY STAND!
ALL OF YOU, FOLLOW ME OUTSIDE, WHERE I'LL SLICE YOU UP... ONE BY ONE!
DOOM!

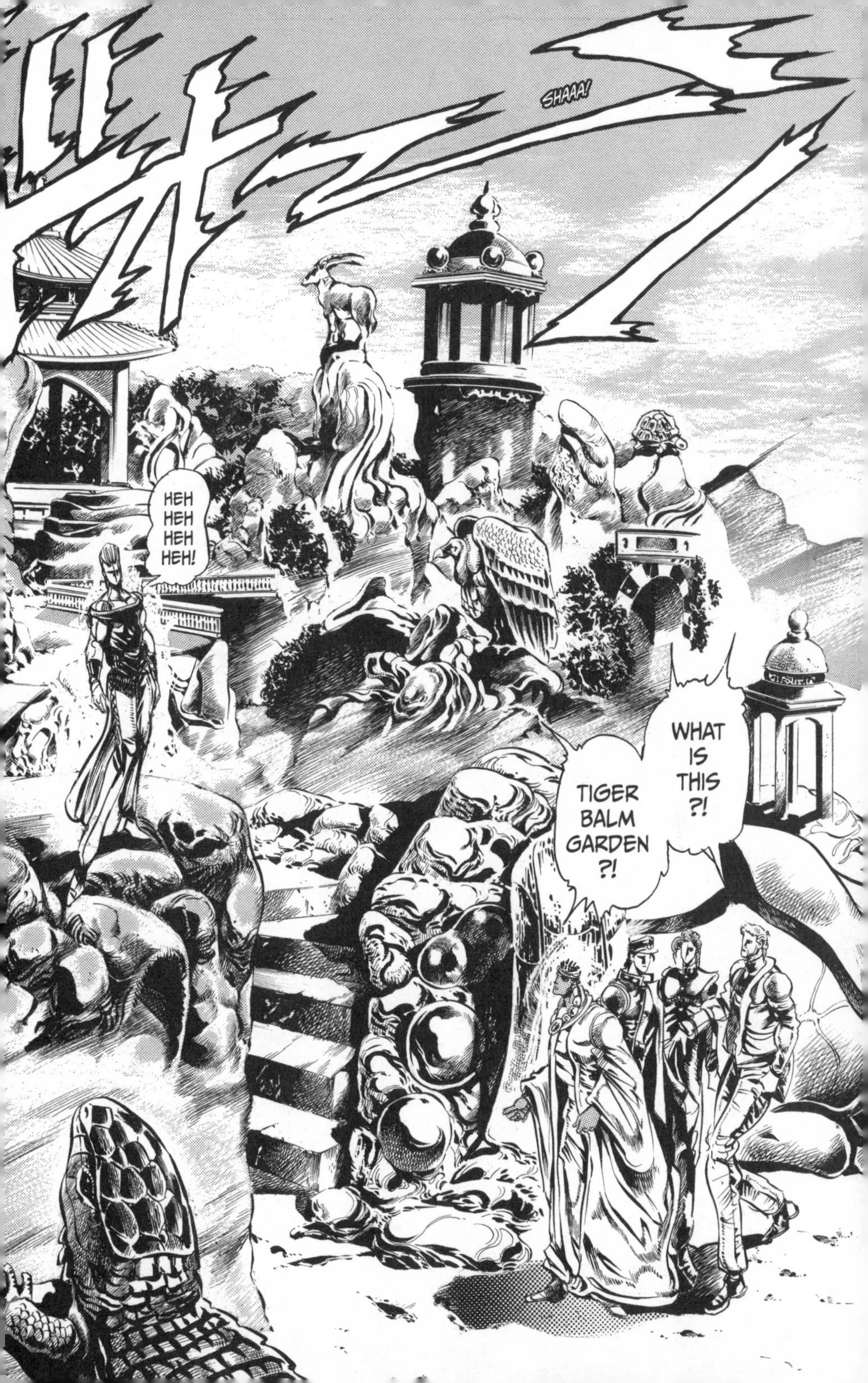
SHAAA!
HEH HEH HEH HEH!
WHAT IS THIS ?!
TIGER BALM GARDEN ?!

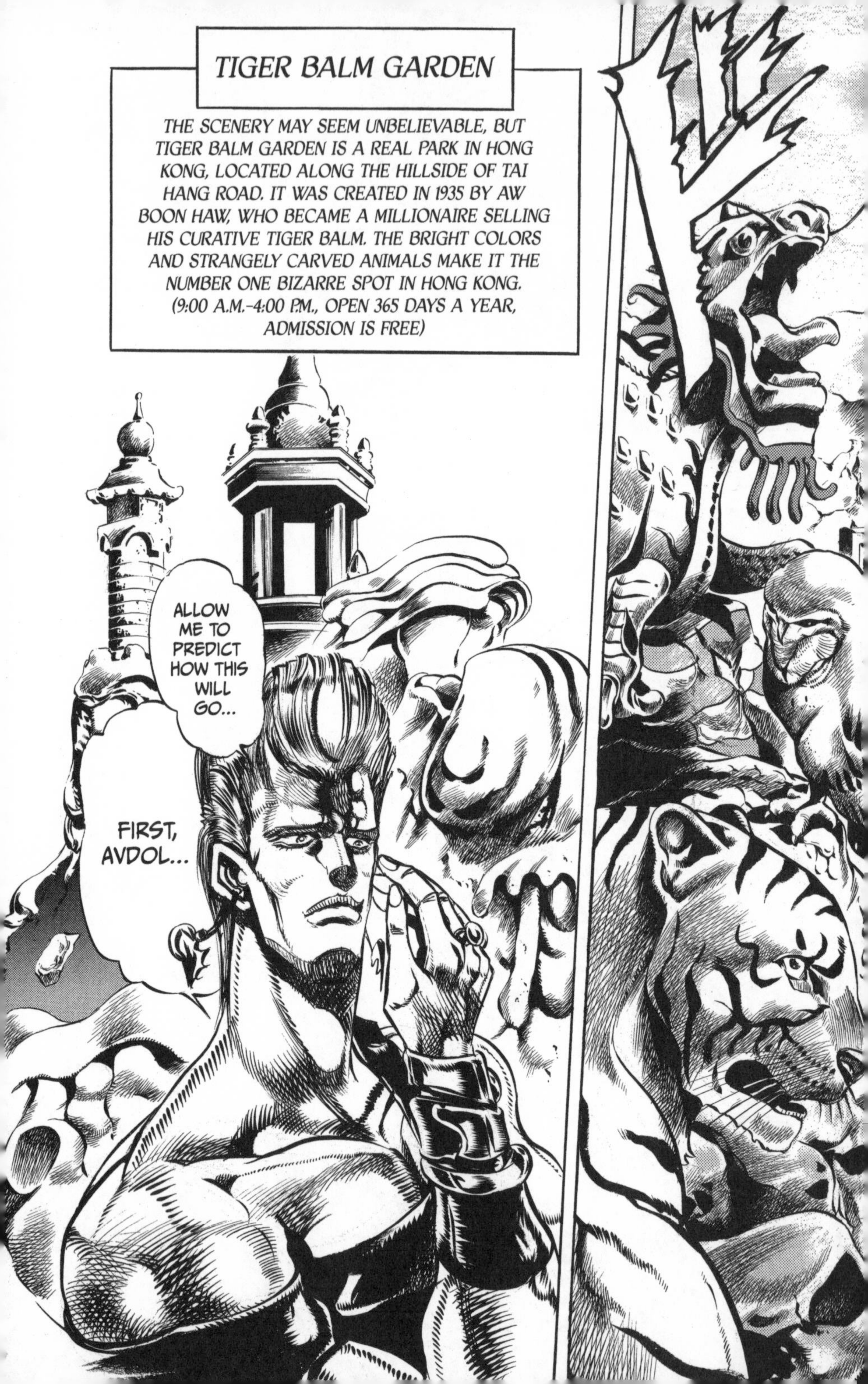
TIGER BALM GARDEN
THE SCENERY MAY SEEM UNBELIEVABLE, BUT TIGER BALM GARDEN IS A REAL PARK IN HONG KONG, LOCATED ALONG THE HILLSIDE OF TAI HANG ROAD. IT WAS CREATED IN 1935 BY AW BOON HAW, WHO BECAME A MILLIONAIRE SELLING HIS CURATIVE TIGER BALM. THE BRIGHT COLORS AND STRANGELY CARVED ANIMALS MAKE IT THE NUMBER ONE BIZARRE SPOT IN HONG KONG. (9:00 A.M.-4:00 P.M., OPEN 365 DAYS A YEAR, ADMISSION IS FREE)
ALLOW ME TO PREDICT HOW THIS WILL GO...
FIRST, AVDOL...

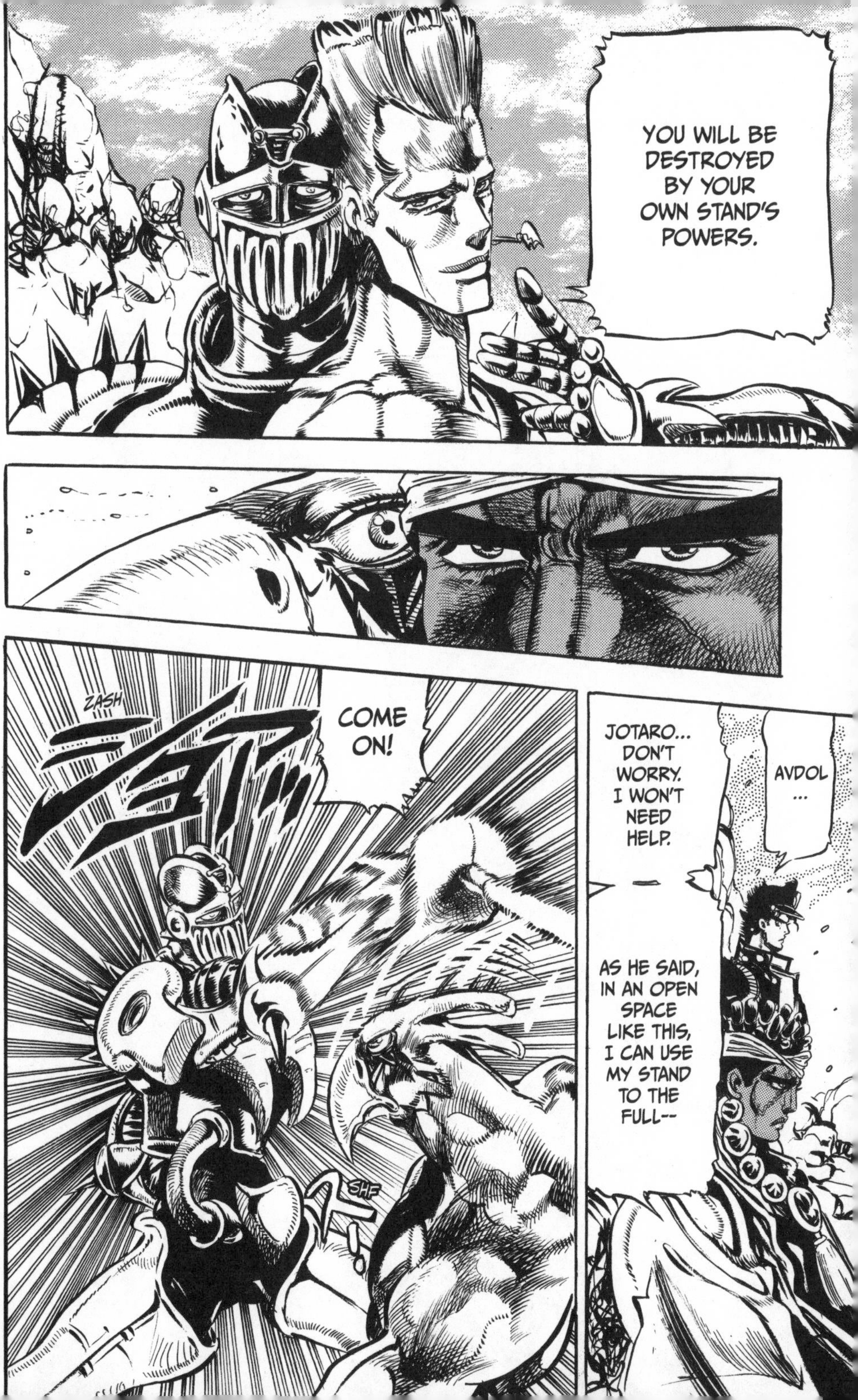
YOU WILL BE DESTROYED BY YOUR OWN STAND'S POWERS.
AVDOL ...
JOTARO... DON'T WORRY. I WON'T NEED HELP.
AS HE SAID, IN AN OPEN SPACE LIKE THIS, I CAN USE MY STAND TO THE FULL--
ZASH
COME ON!
SHF

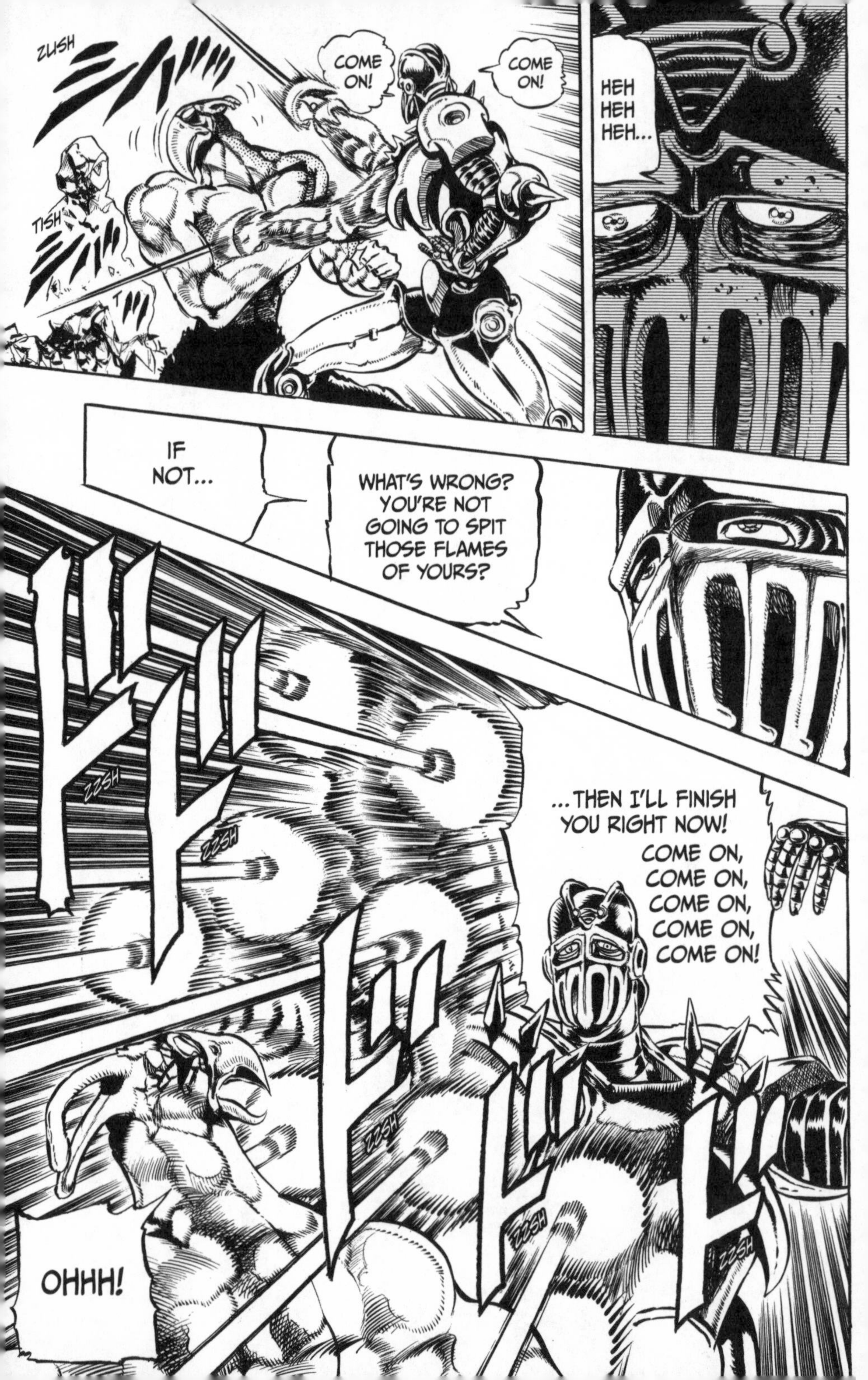
HEH HEH HEH...
COME ON!
COME ON!
ZUSH
TISH
WHAT'S WRONG? YOU'RE NOT GOING TO SPIT THOSE FLAMES OF YOURS?
IF NOT...
...THEN I'LL FINISH YOU RIGHT NOW!
COME ON, COME ON, COME ON, COME ON, COME ON!
ZZSH
ZZSH
ZZSH
ZZSH
ZZSH
OHHH!

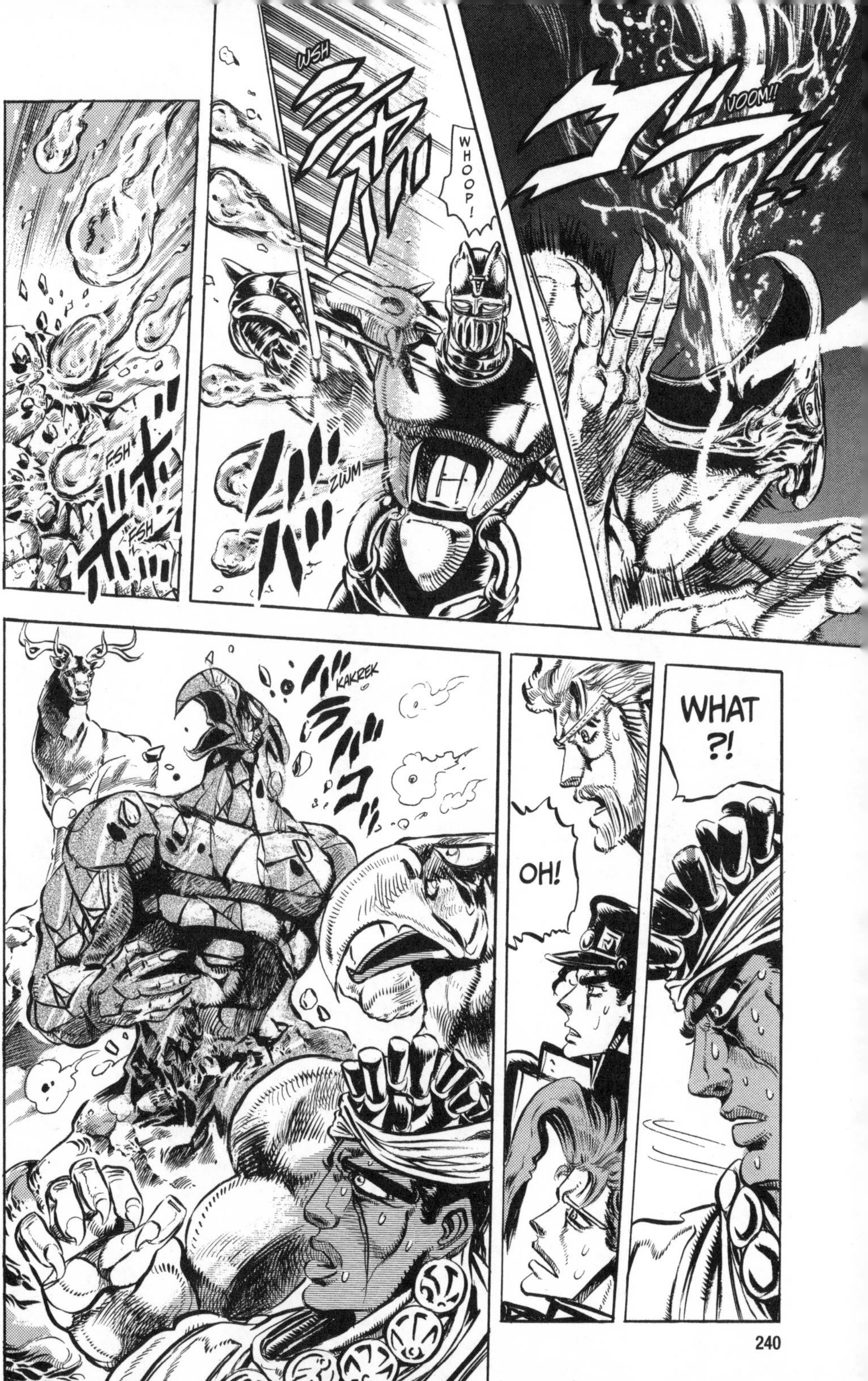
VOOM!!
WSH
WHOOP!
ZWUM
FSH
FSH
WHAT ?!
OH!
KAKREK

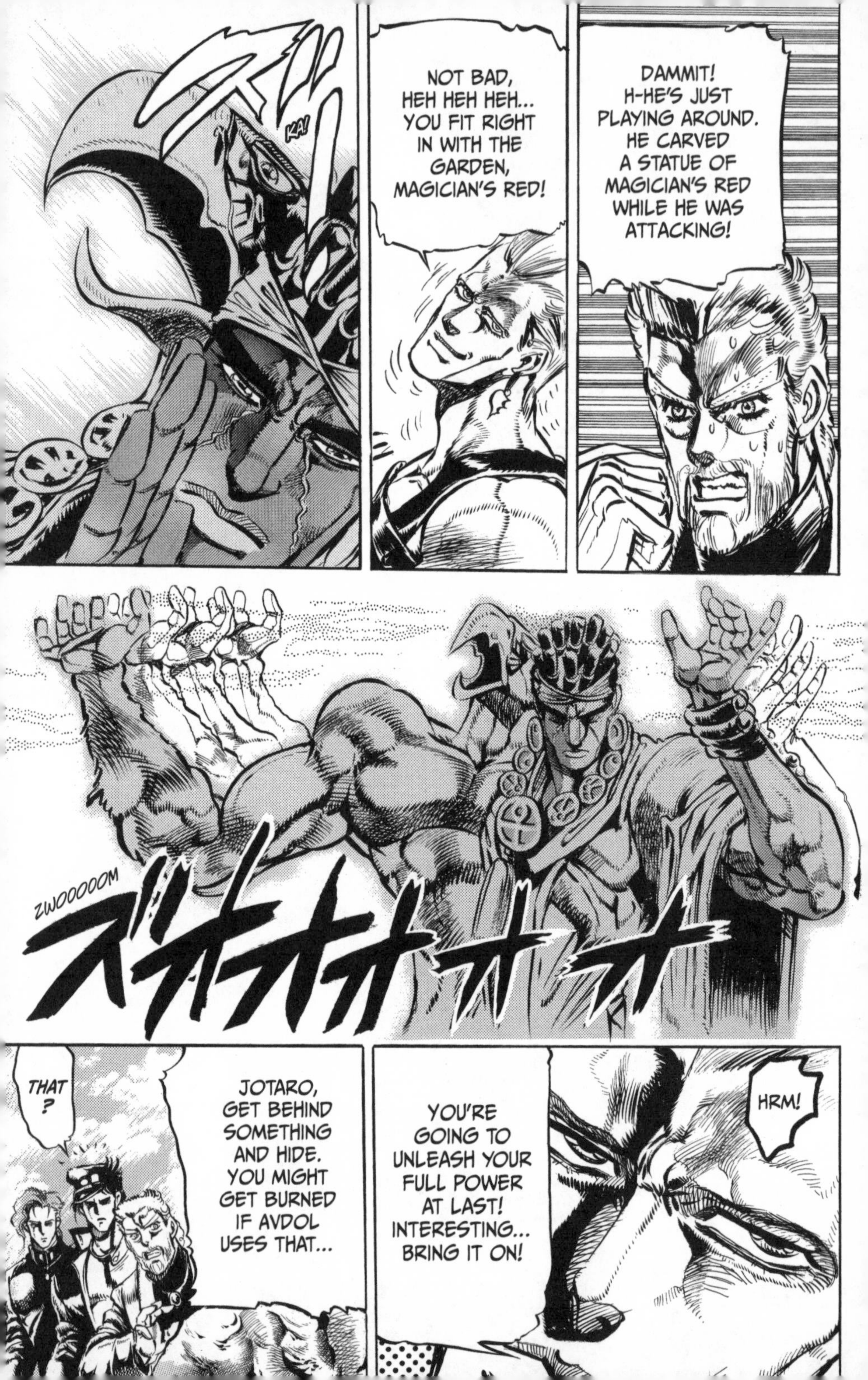
DAMMIT! H-HE'S JUST PLAYING AROUND. HE CARVED A STATUE OF MAGICIAN'S RED WHILE HE WAS ATTACKING!
NOT BAD, HEH HEH HEH... YOU FIT RIGHT IN WITH THE GARDEN, MAGICIAN'S RED!
KA!
ZWOOOOOOM
HRM!
YOU'RE GOING TO UNLEASH YOUR FULL POWER AT LAST! INTERESTING... BRING IT ON!
JOTARO, GET BEHIND SOMETHING AND HIDE. YOU MIGHT GET BURNED IF AVDOL USES THAT...
THAT ?

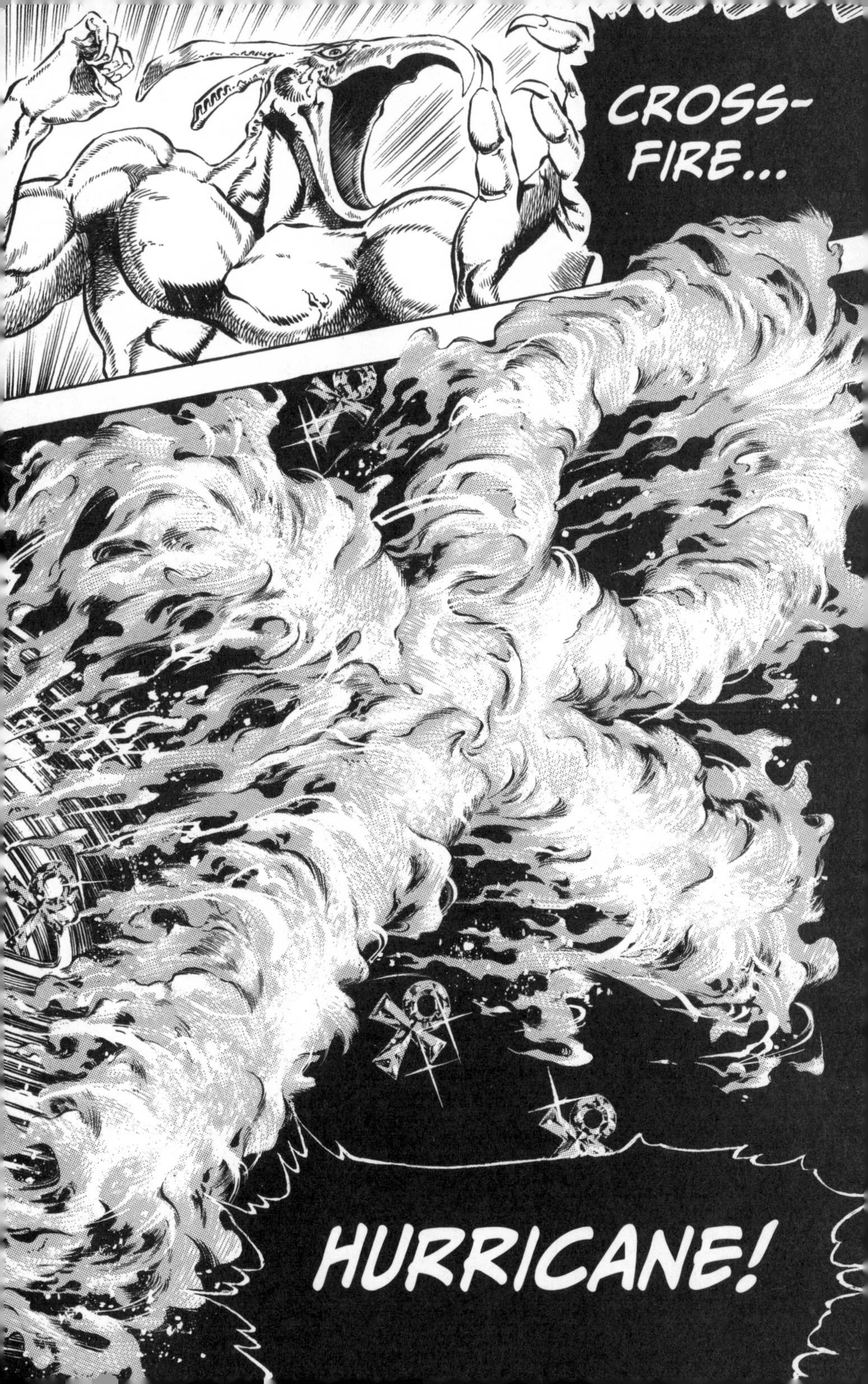
CROSS-
FIRE...
HURRICANE!

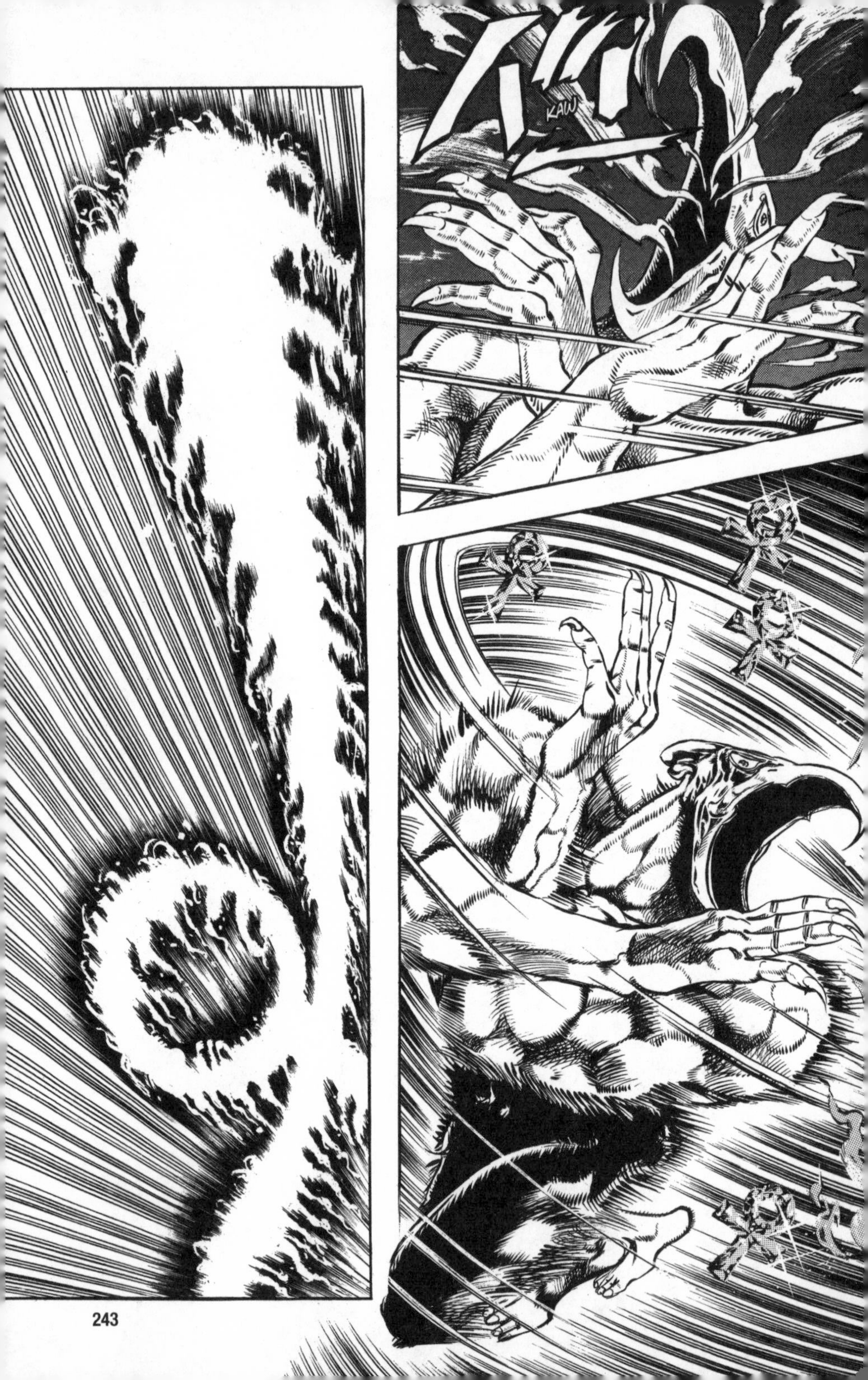
KAW

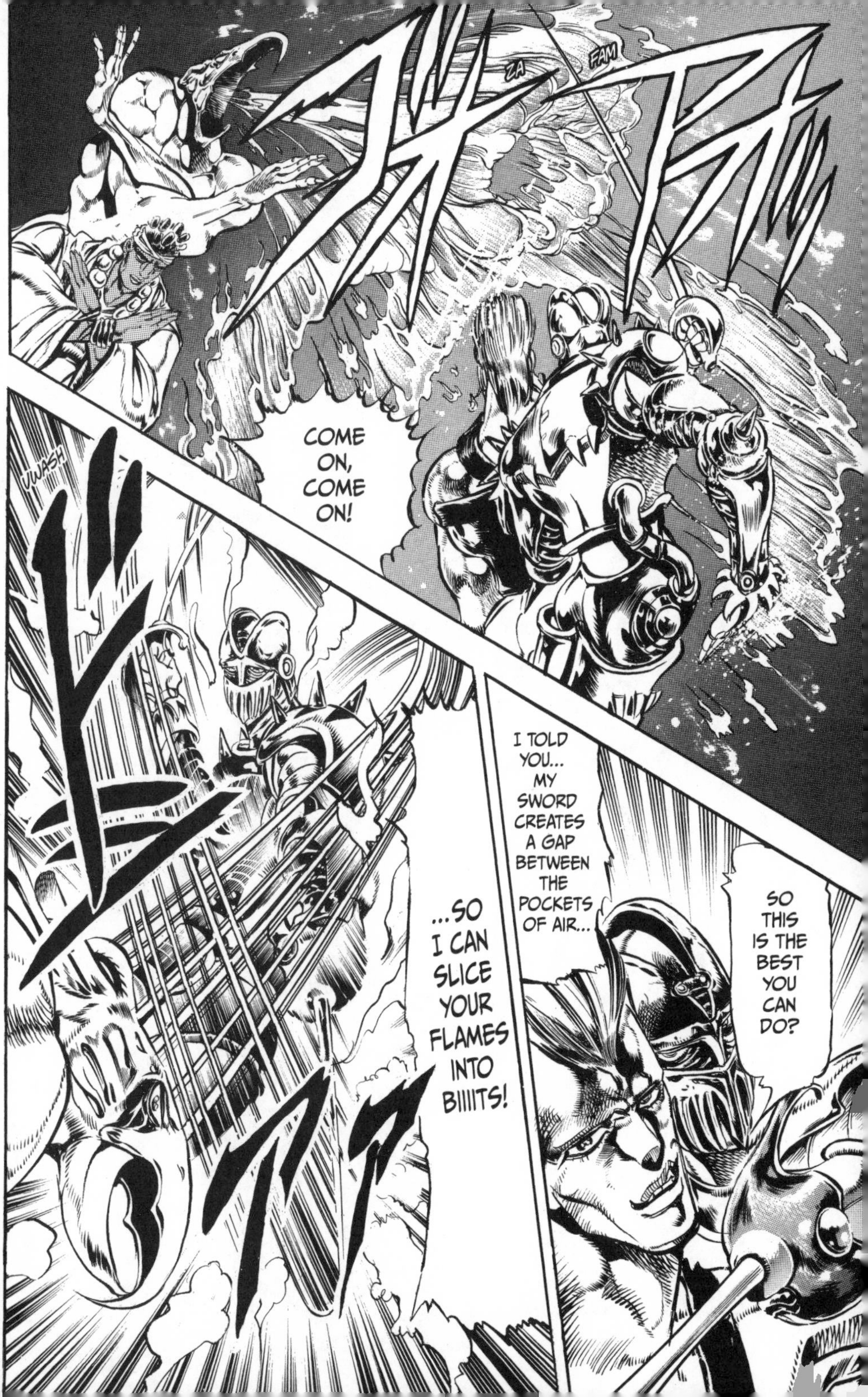
ZA
FAM
COME ON, COME ON!
SO THIS IS THE BEST YOU CAN DO?
I TOLD YOU... MY SWORD CREATES A GAP BETWEEN THE POCKETS OF AIR...
...SO I CAN SLICE YOUR FLAMES INTO BIIIITS!
VWASH

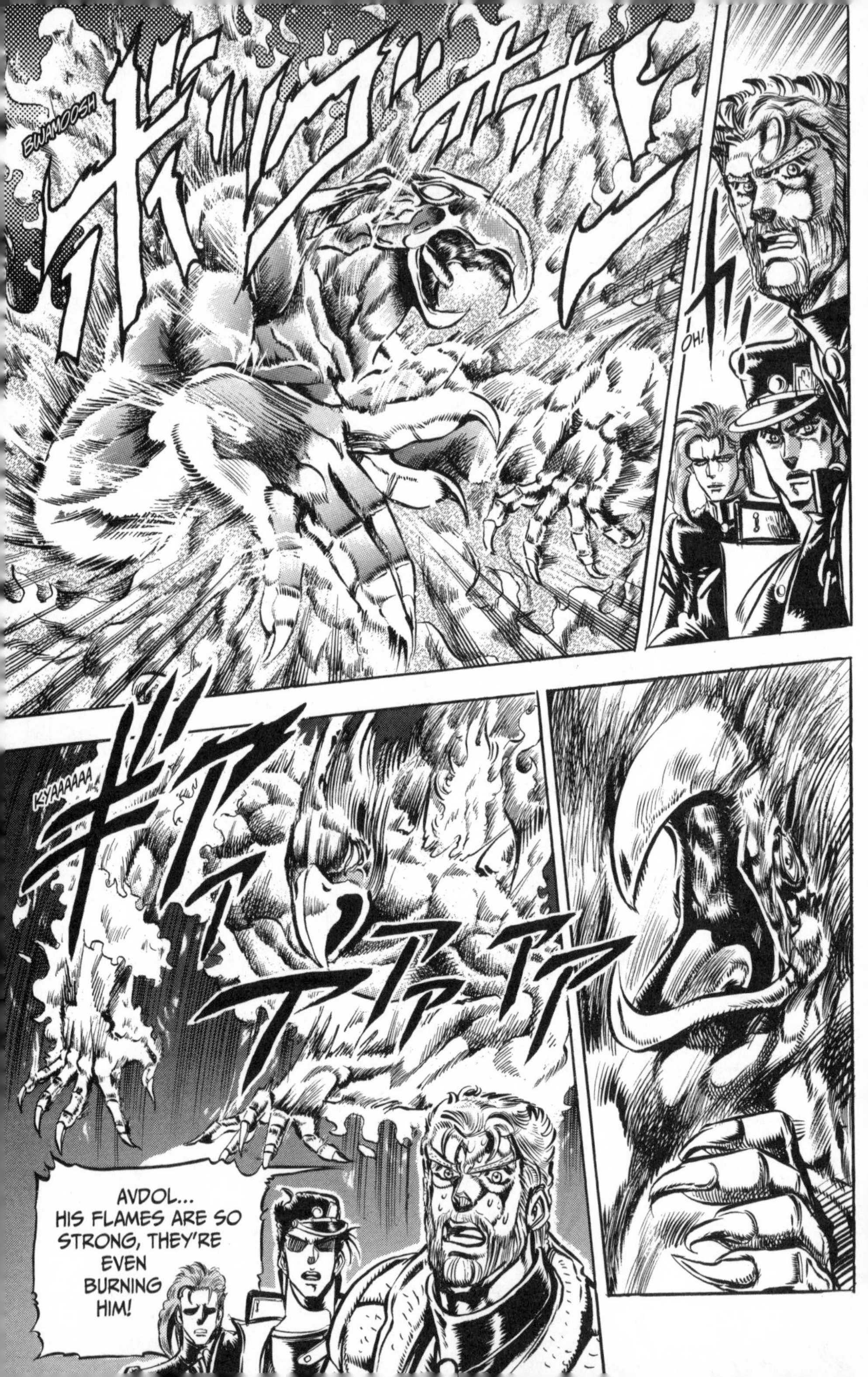
OH!
BWAMOOSH
KYAAAAAA
AVDOL... HIS FLAMES ARE SO STRONG, THEY'RE EVEN BURNING HIM!

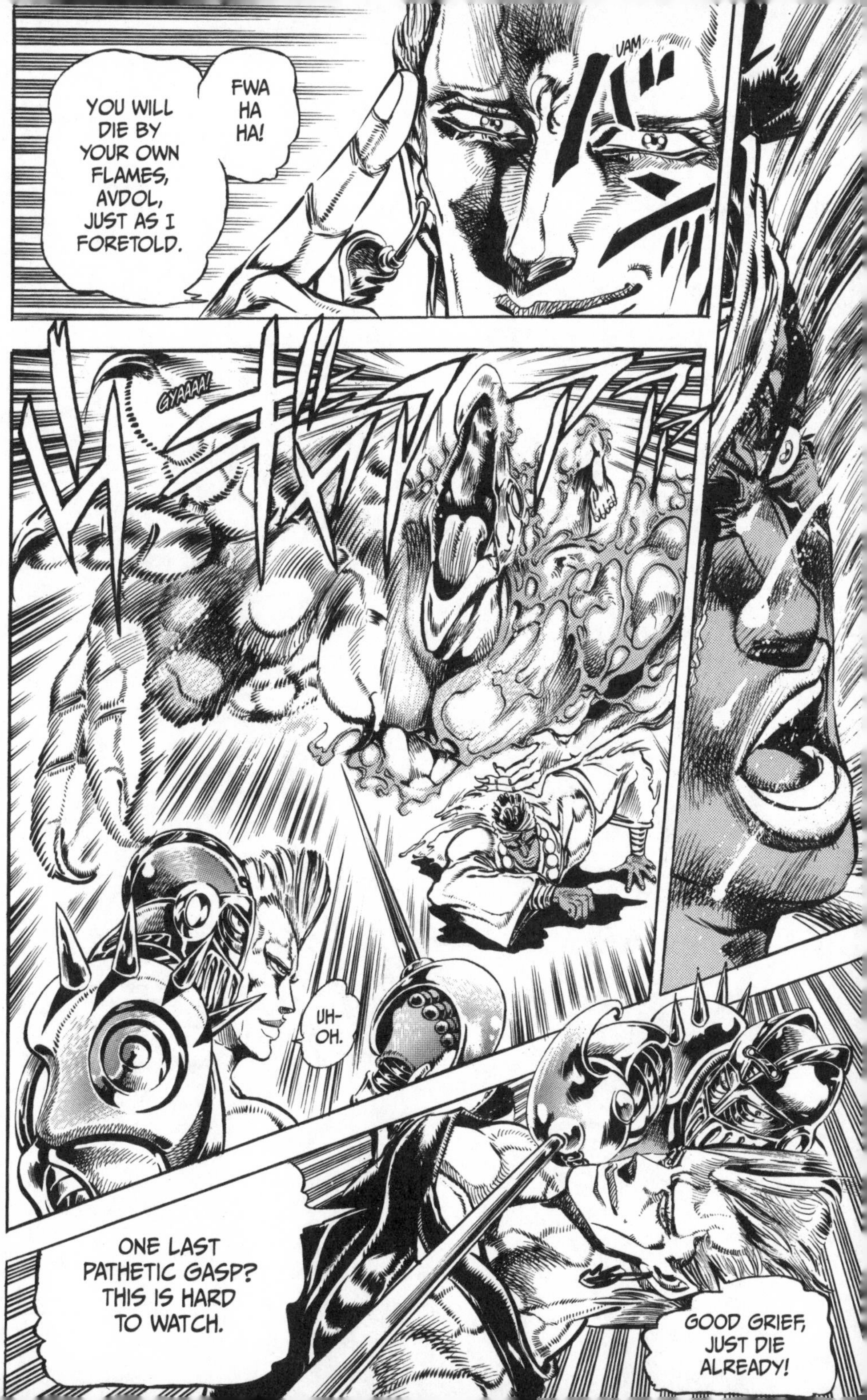
VAM
FWA HA HA!
YOU WILL DIE BY YOUR OWN FLAMES, AVDOL, JUST AS I FORETOLD.
GYAAAA!
UH-OH.
GOOD GRIEF, JUST DIE ALREADY!
ONE LAST PATHETIC GASP? THIS IS HARD TO WATCH.

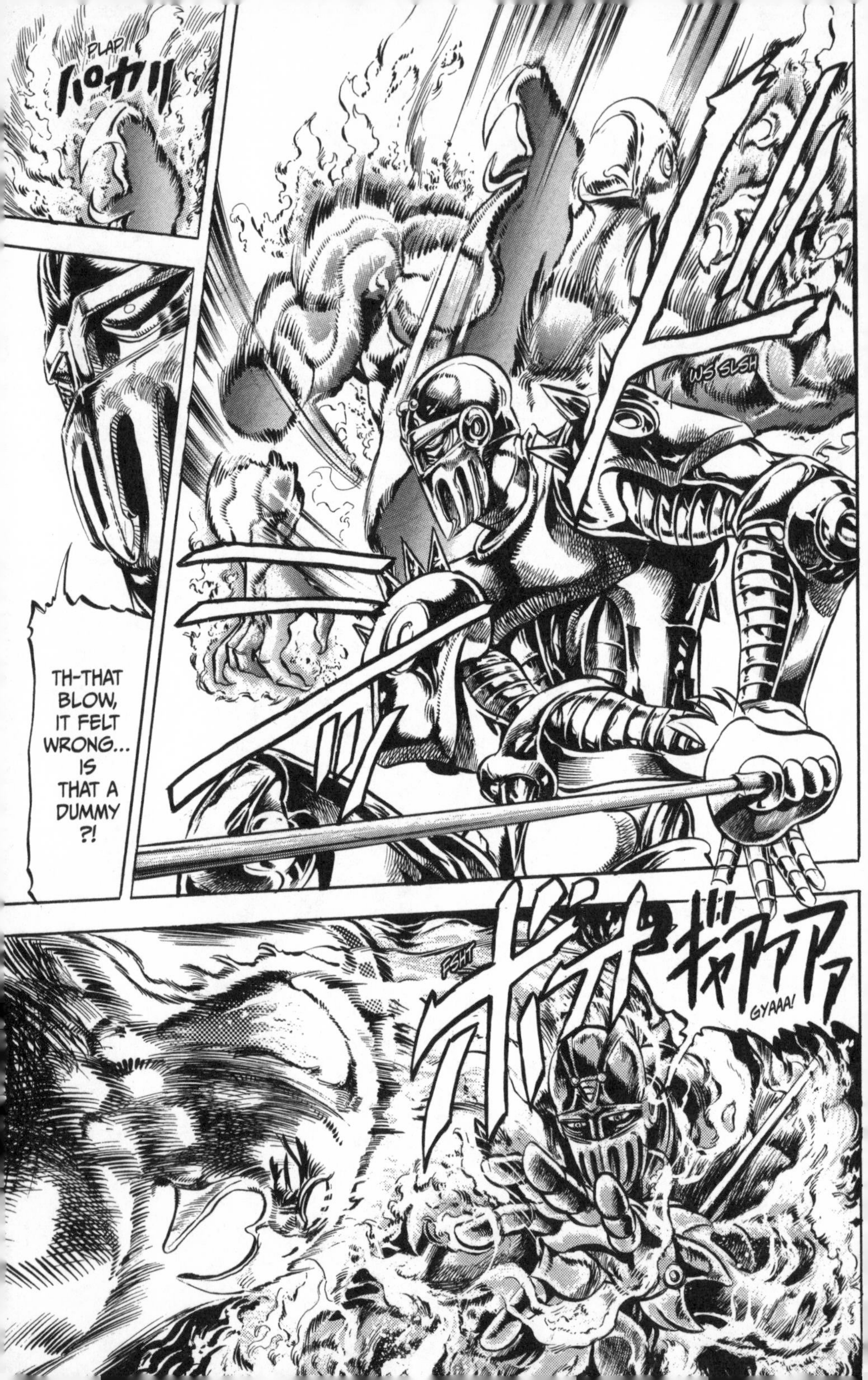
WS SLSH
PLAP
TH-THAT BLOW, IT FELT WRONG... IS THAT A DUMMY ?!
FSHT
GYAAA!

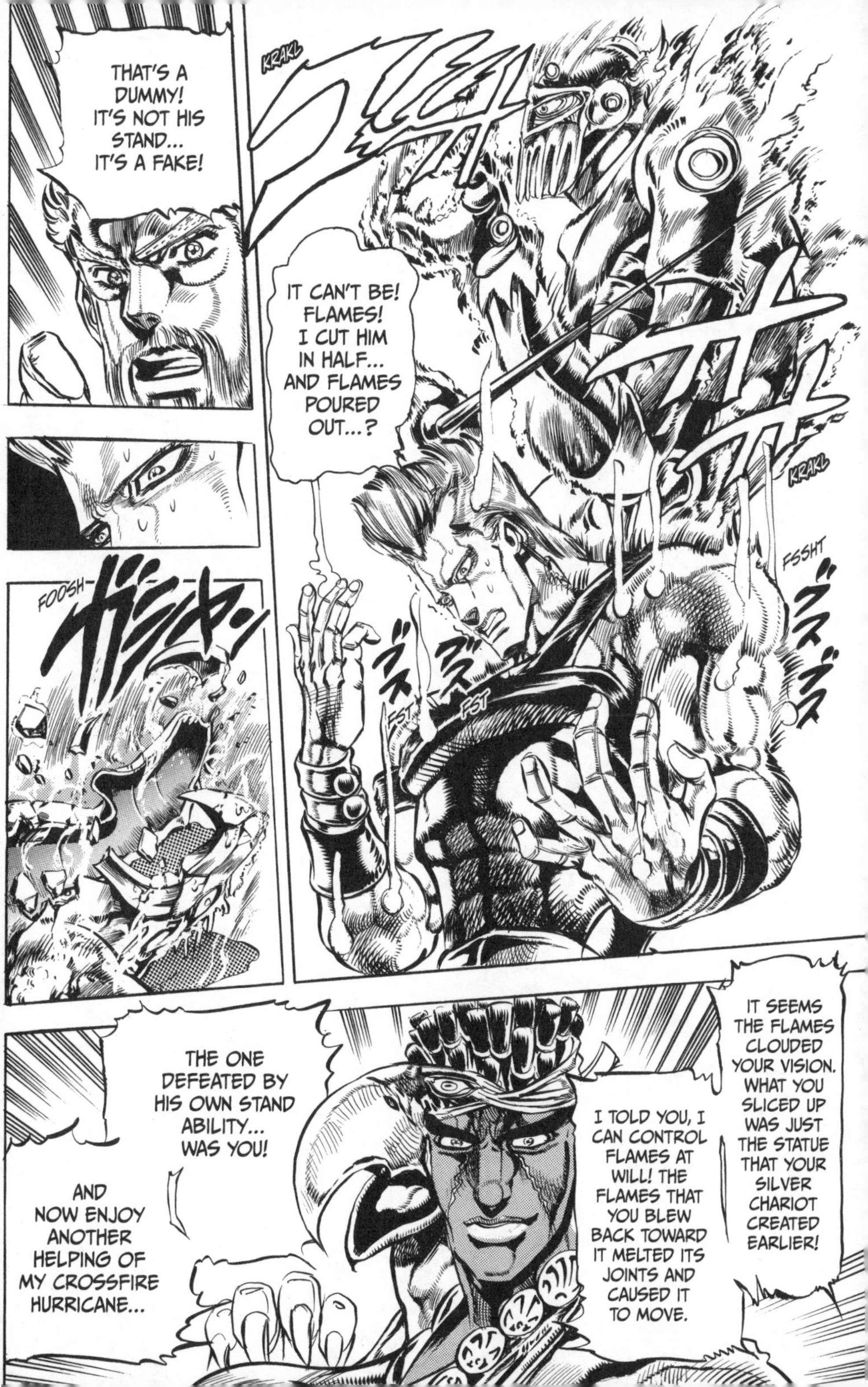
KRAKL
IT CAN'T BE! FLAMES! I CUT HIM IN HALF... AND FLAMES POURED OUT...?
KRAKL
FSSHT
FST
FST
THAT'S A DUMMY! IT'S NOT HIS STAND... IT'S A FAKE!
FOOSH
IT SEEMS THE FLAMES CLOUDED YOUR VISION. WHAT YOU SLICED UP WAS JUST THE STATUE THAT YOUR SILVER CHARIOT CREATED EARLIER!
I TOLD YOU, I CAN CONTROL FLAMES AT WILL! THE FLAMES THAT YOU BLEW BACK TOWARD IT MELTED ITS JOINTS AND CAUSED IT TO MOVE.
THE ONE DEFEATED BY HIS OWN STAND ABILITY... WAS YOU!
AND NOW ENJOY ANOTHER HELPING OF MY CROSSFIRE HURRICANE...

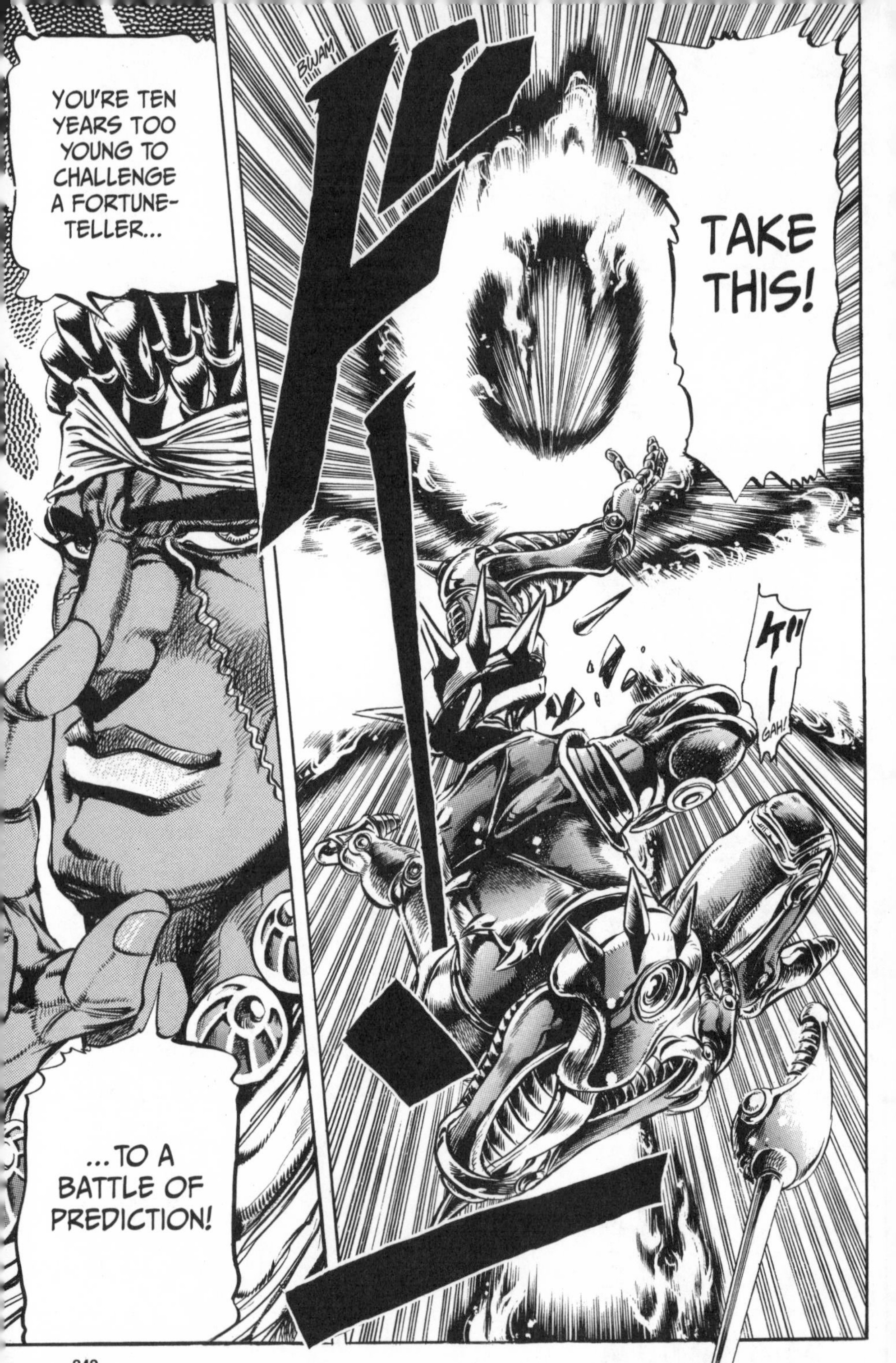
BWAM
TAKE THIS!
GAH!
YOU'RE TEN YEARS TOO YOUNG TO CHALLENGE A FORTUNE-TELLER...
...TO A BATTLE OF PREDICTION!

LUCKY
THE CHARIOT 7

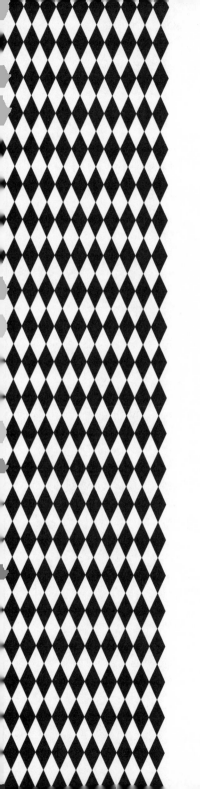

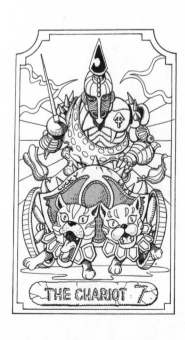

CHAPTER 13: Silver Chariot PART 3

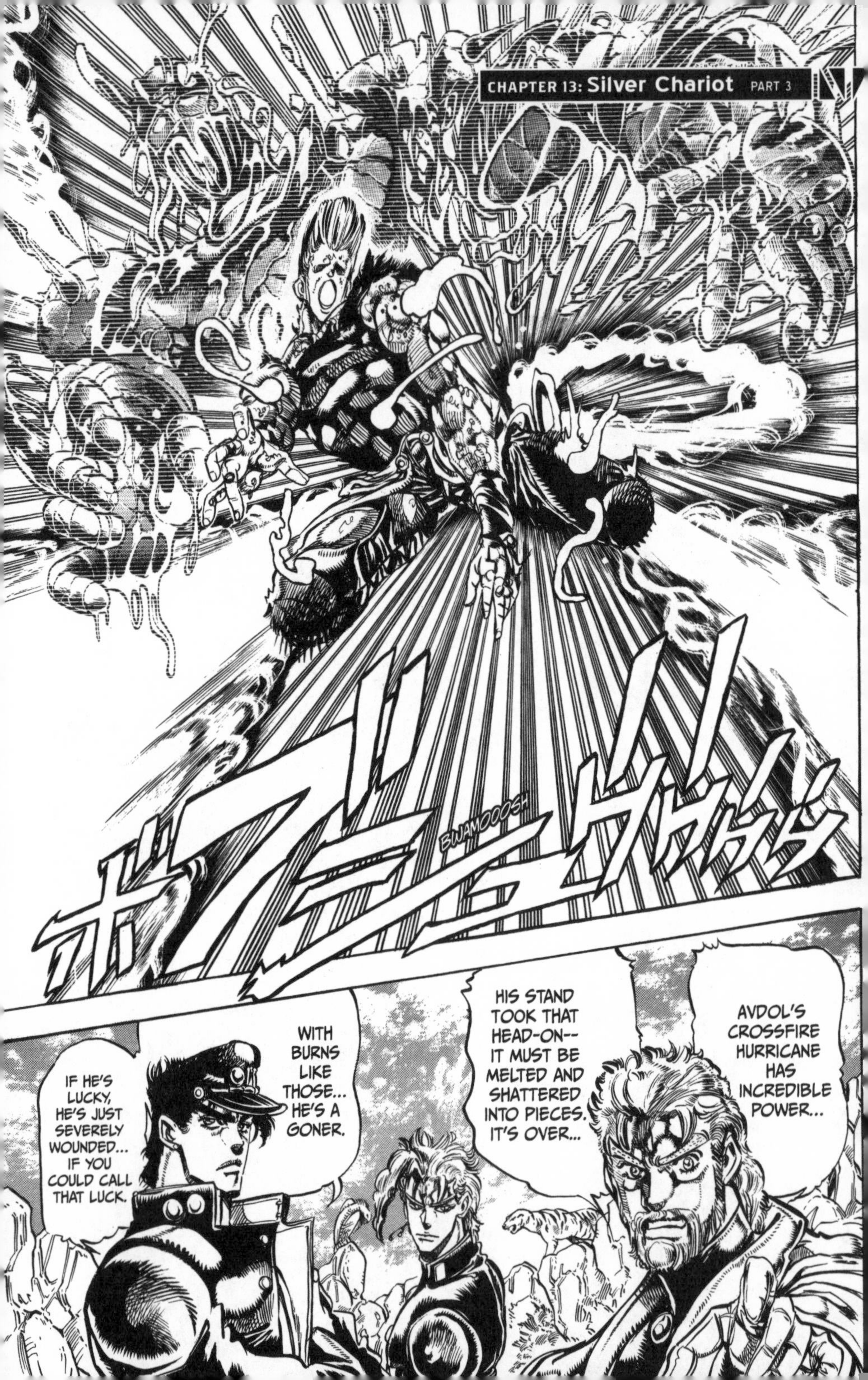
BWAMOOOSH
AVDOL'S CROSSFIRE HURRICANE HAS INCREDIBLE POWER...
HIS STAND TOOK THAT HEAD-ON-- IT MUST BE MELTED AND SHATTERED INTO PIECES. IT'S OVER...
WITH BURNS LIKE THOSE... HE'S A GONER.
IF HE'S LUCKY, HE'S JUST SEVERELY WOUNDED... IF YOU COULD CALL THAT LUCK.

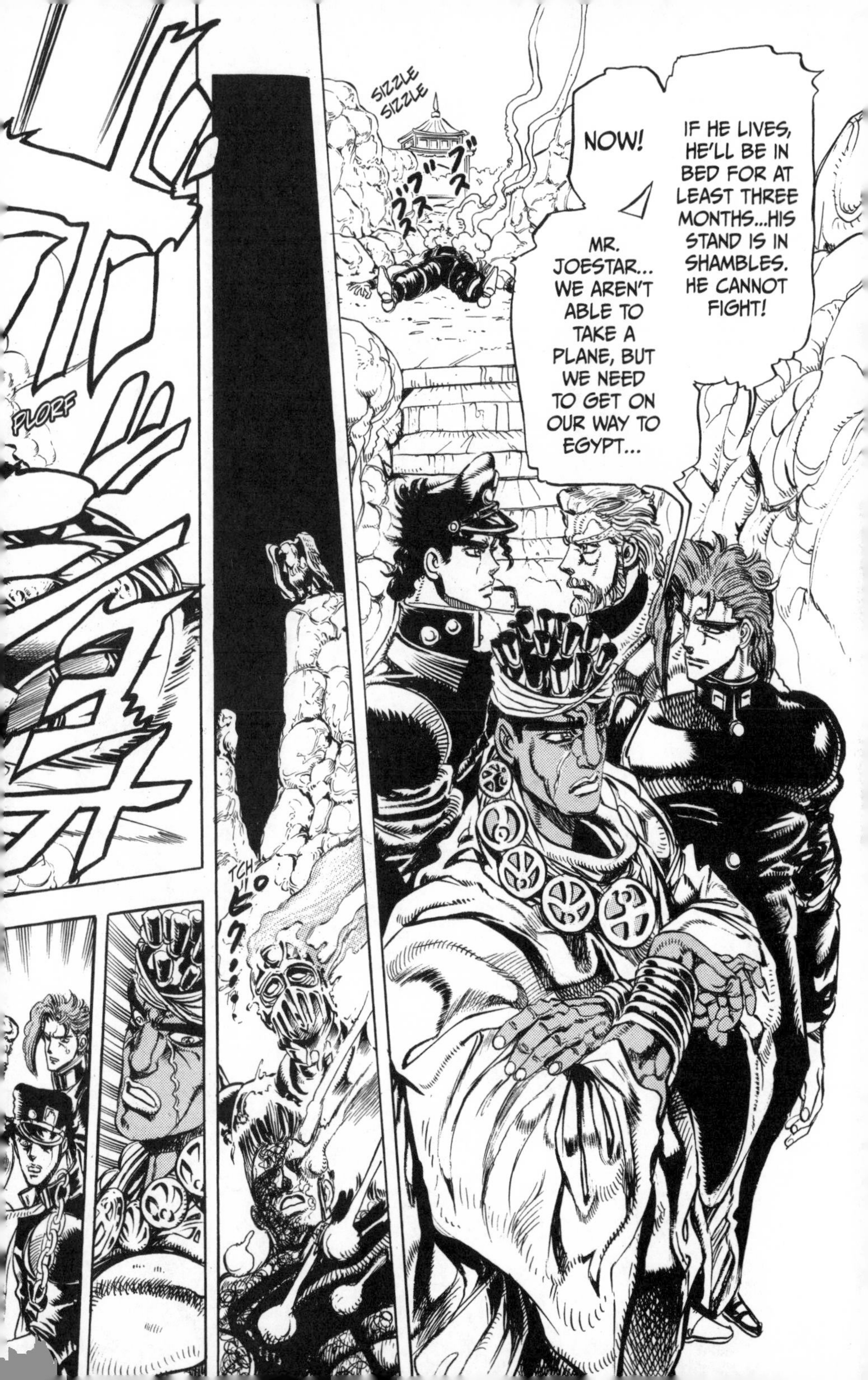
IF HE LIVES, HE'LL BE IN BED FOR AT LEAST THREE MONTHS...HIS STAND IS IN SHAMBLES. HE CANNOT FIGHT!
NOW!
MR. JOESTAR... WE AREN'T ABLE TO TAKE A PLANE, BUT WE NEED TO GET ON OUR WAY TO EGYPT...
SIZZLE SIZZLE
TCH
PLORF

CHAPTER 13: Silver Chariot PART 3

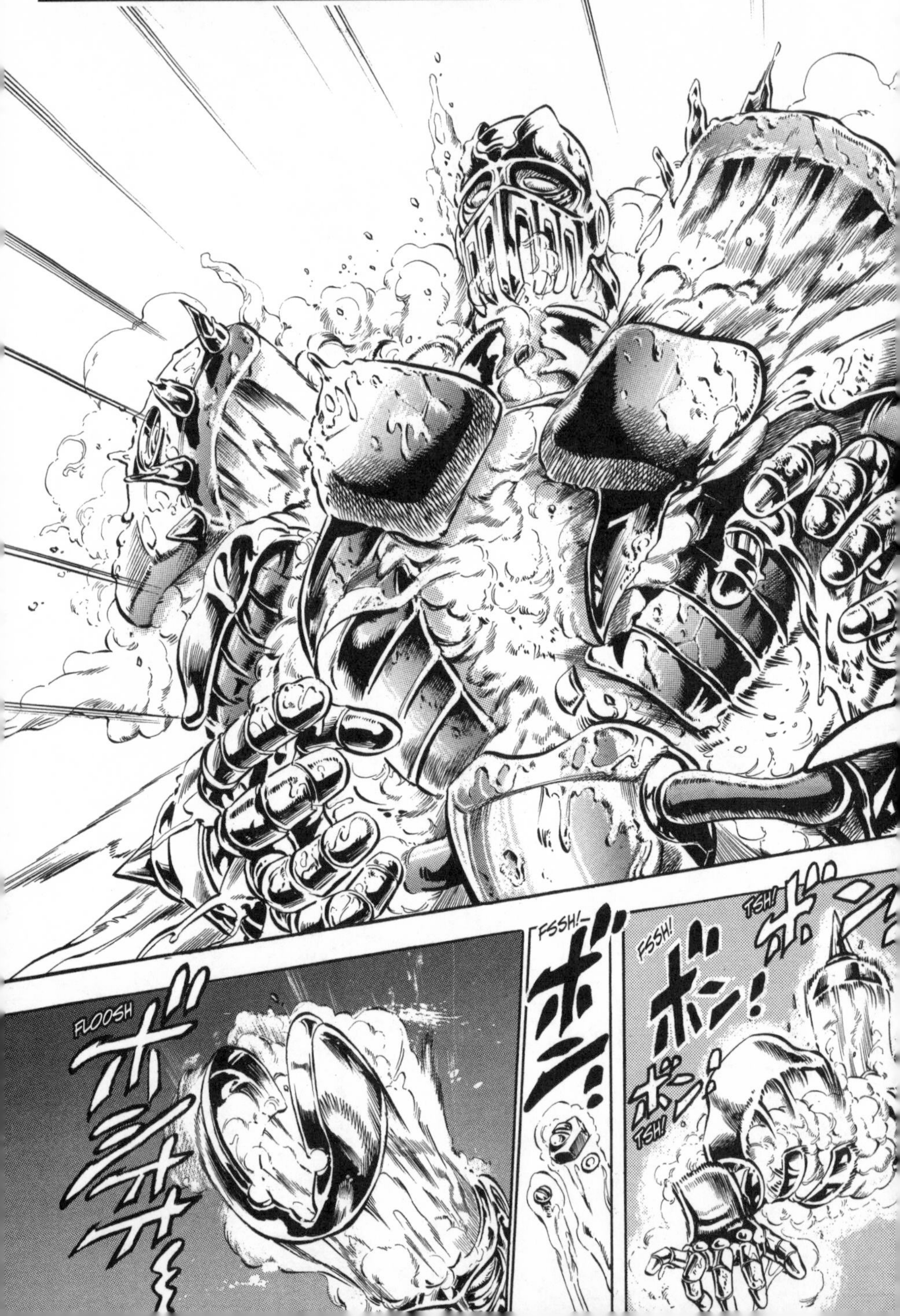
TSH!
FSSH!
TSH!
FSSH!
FLOOSH

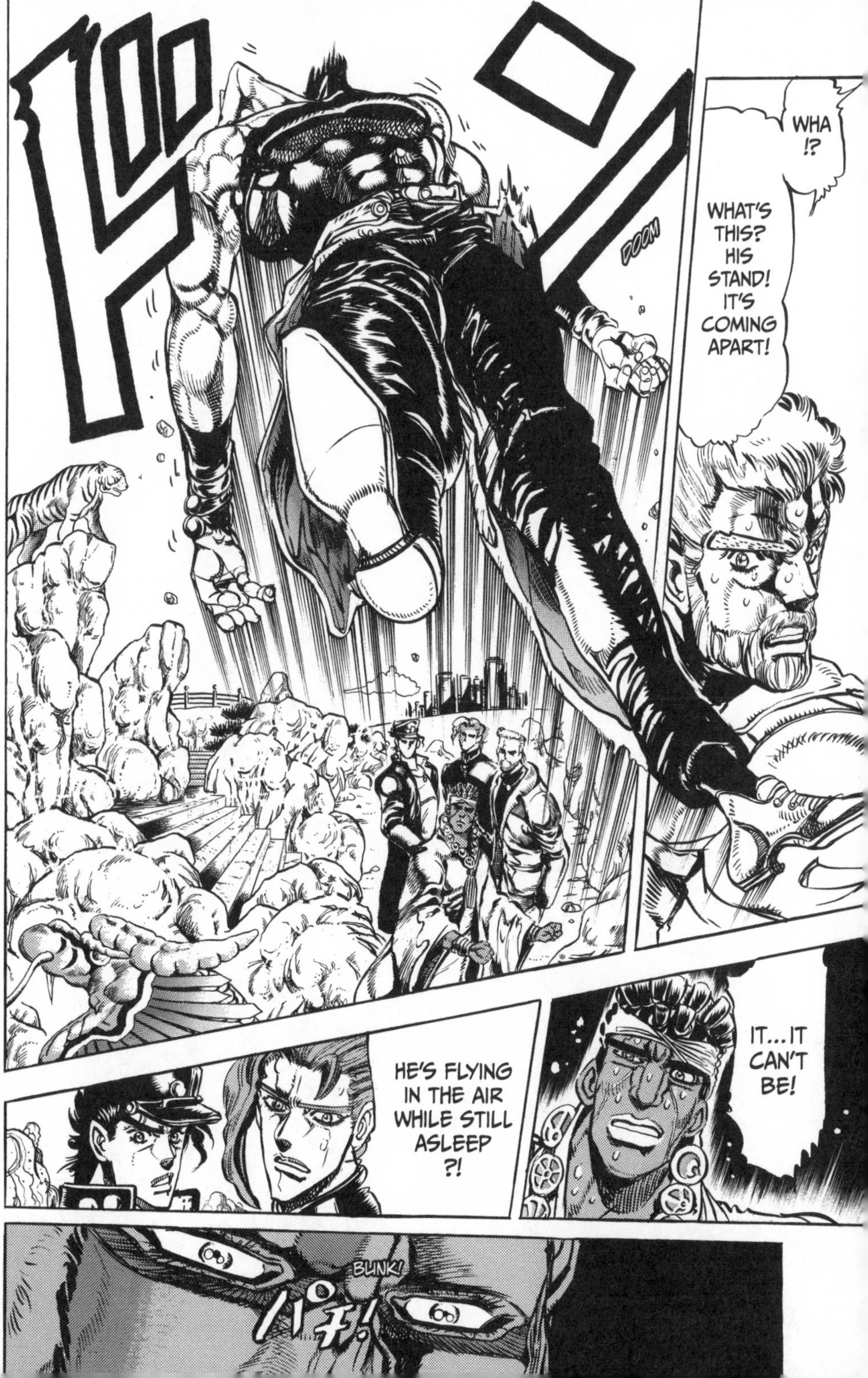
WHA !?
WHAT'S THIS? HIS STAND! IT'S COMING APART!
DOOM
IT...IT CAN'T BE!
HE'S FLYING IN THE AIR WHILE STILL ASLEEP ?!
BLINK!
パチ!

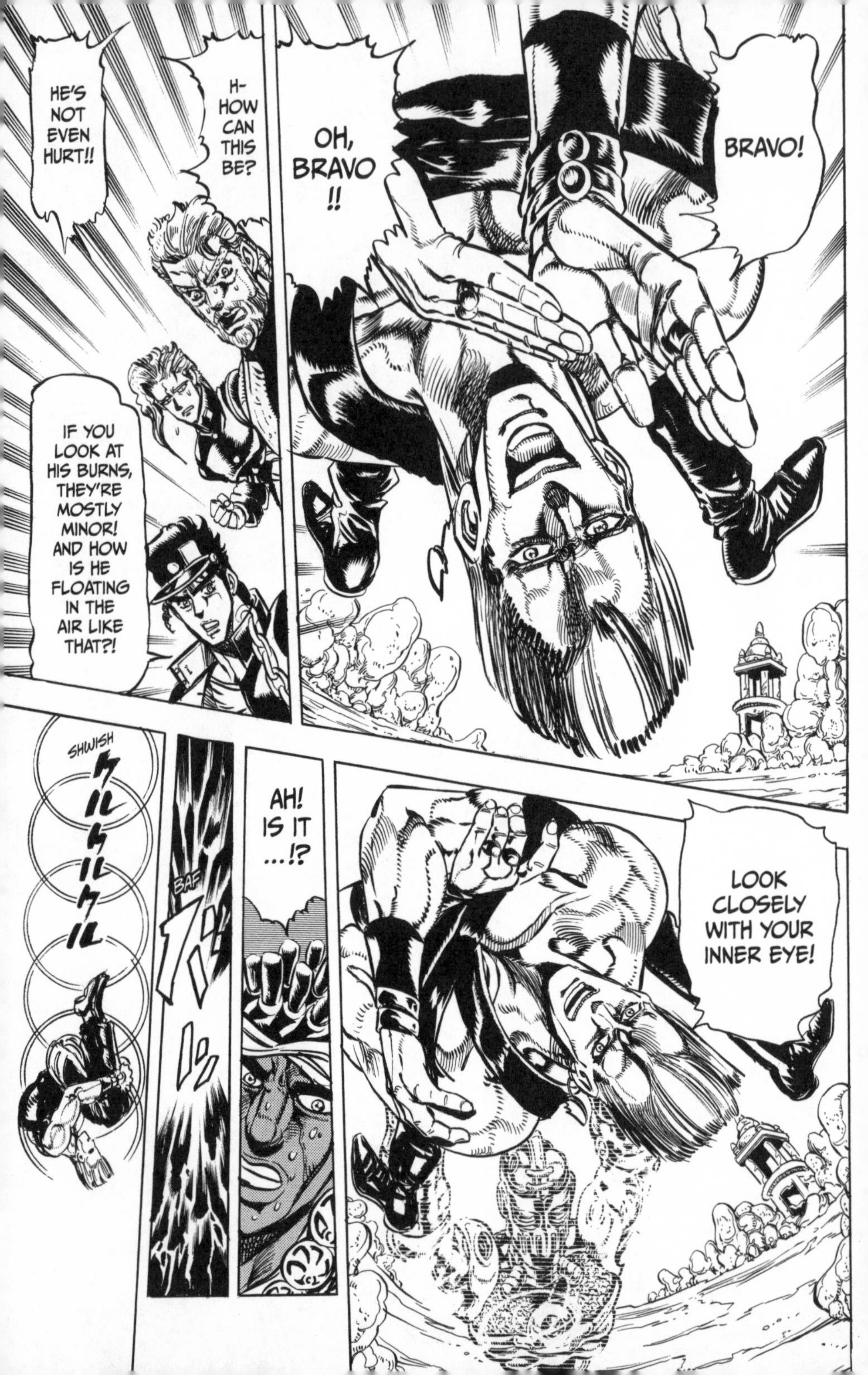
BRAVO!
OH, BRAVO!!
H-HOW CAN THIS BE?
HE'S NOT EVEN HURT!!
IF YOU LOOK AT HIS BURNS, THEY'RE MOSTLY MINOR! AND HOW IS HE FLOATING IN THE AIR LIKE THAT?!
LOOK CLOSELY WITH YOUR INNER EYE!
AH! IS IT ...!?
BAF
SHWISH

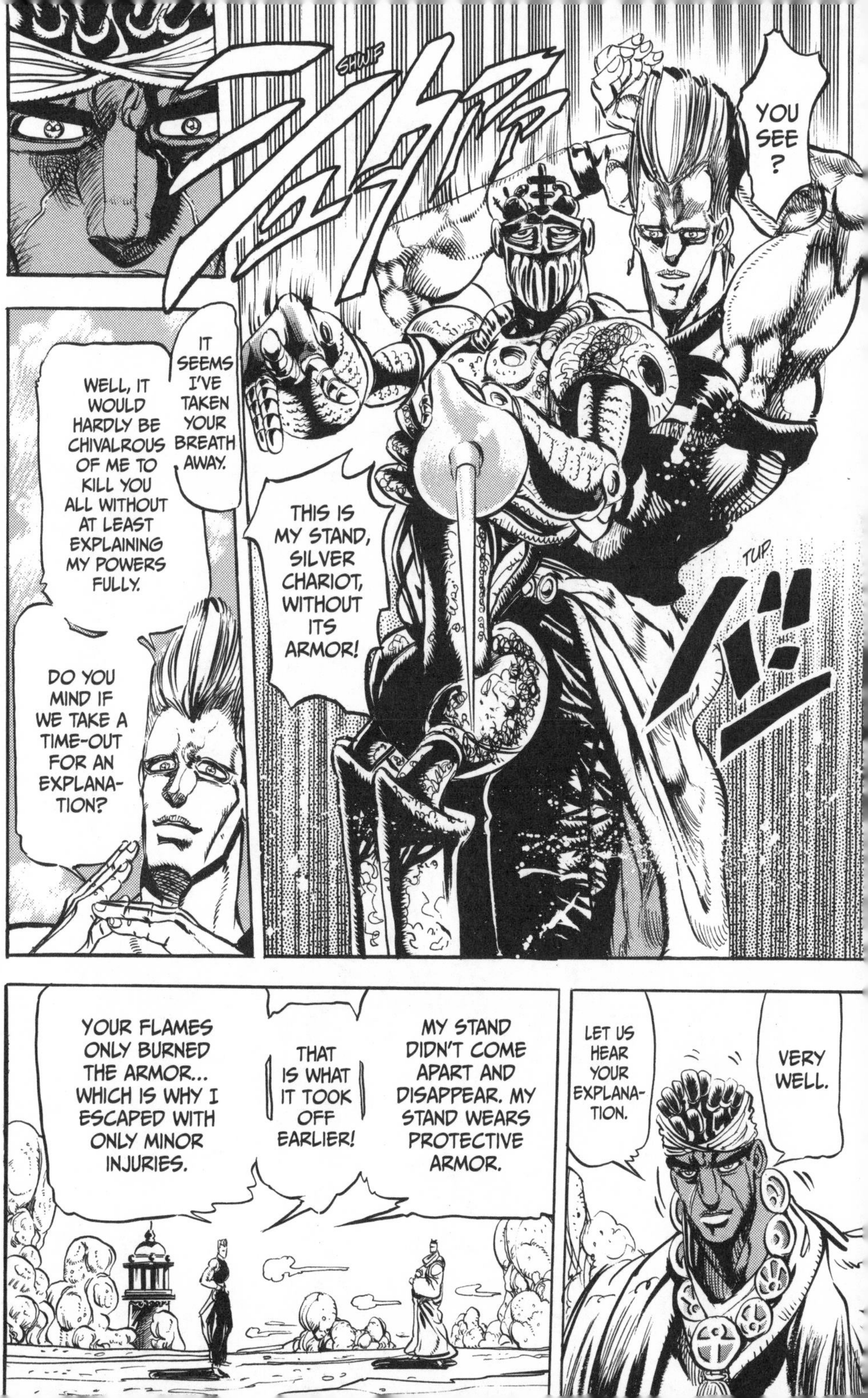
YOU SEE?
SHWIF
THIS IS MY STAND, SILVER CHARIOT, WITHOUT ITS ARMOR!
TUP
IT SEEMS I'VE TAKEN YOUR BREATH AWAY.
WELL, IT WOULD HARDLY BE CHIVALROUS OF ME TO KILL YOU ALL WITHOUT AT LEAST EXPLAINING MY POWERS FULLY.
DO YOU MIND IF WE TAKE A TIME-OUT FOR AN EXPLANATION?
VERY WELL.
LET US HEAR YOUR EXPLANATION.
MY STAND DIDN'T COME APART AND DISAPPEAR. MY STAND WEARS PROTECTIVE ARMOR.
THAT IS WHAT IT TOOK OFF EARLIER!
YOUR FLAMES ONLY BURNED THE ARMOR... WHICH IS WHY I ESCAPED WITH ONLY MINOR INJURIES.

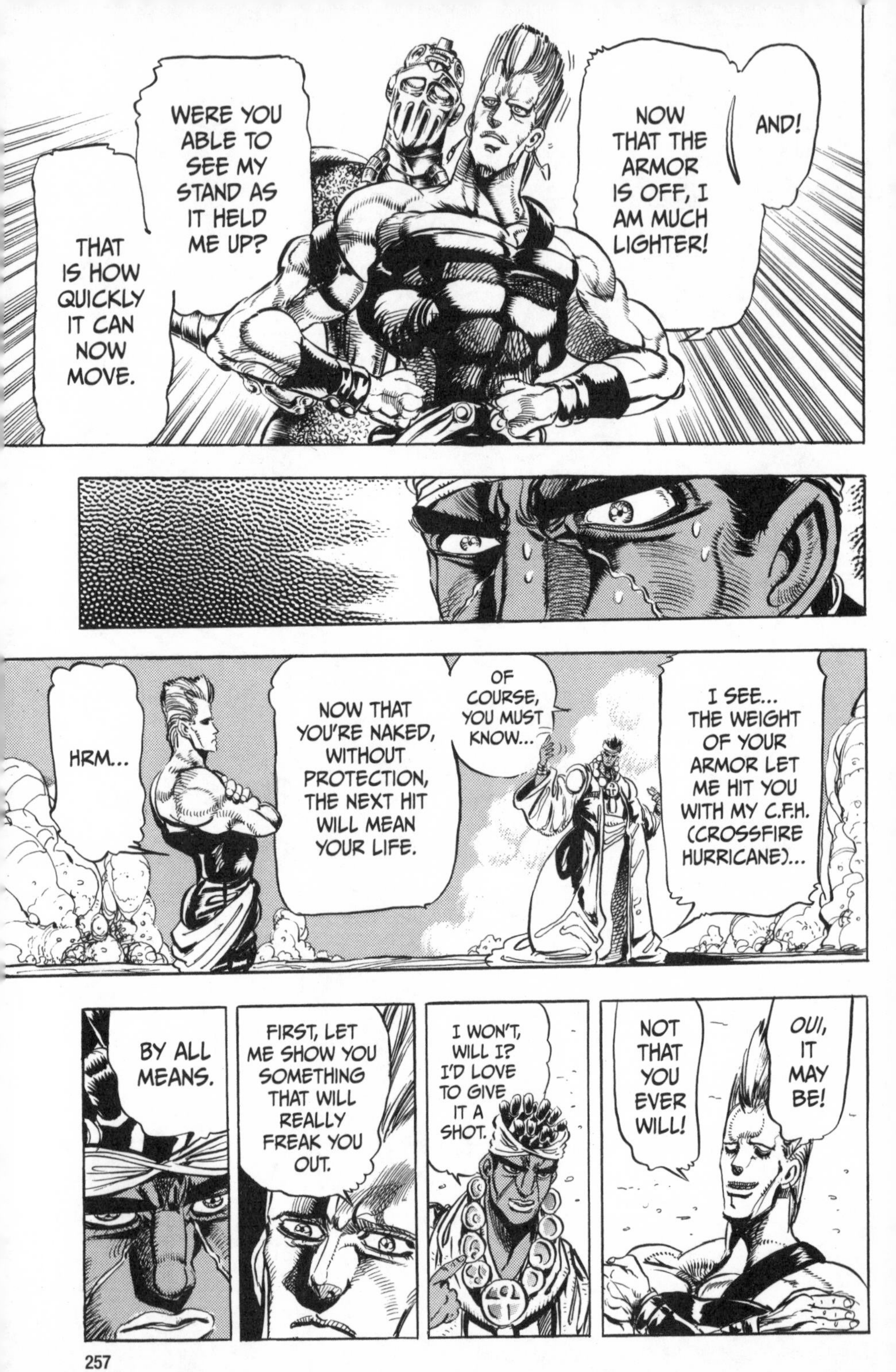
AND!
NOW THAT THE ARMOR IS OFF, I AM MUCH LIGHTER!
WERE YOU ABLE TO SEE MY STAND AS IT HELD ME UP?
THAT IS HOW QUICKLY IT CAN NOW MOVE.
I SEE... THE WEIGHT OF YOUR ARMOR LET ME HIT YOU WITH MY C.F.H. (CROSSFIRE HURRICANE)...
OF COURSE, YOU MUST KNOW...
NOW THAT YOU'RE NAKED, WITHOUT PROTECTION, THE NEXT HIT WILL MEAN YOUR LIFE.
HRM...
OUI, IT MAY BE!
NOT THAT YOU EVER WILL!
I WON'T, WILL I? I'D LOVE TO GIVE IT A SHOT.
FIRST, LET ME SHOW YOU SOMETHING THAT WILL REALLY FREAK YOU OUT.
BY ALL MEANS.

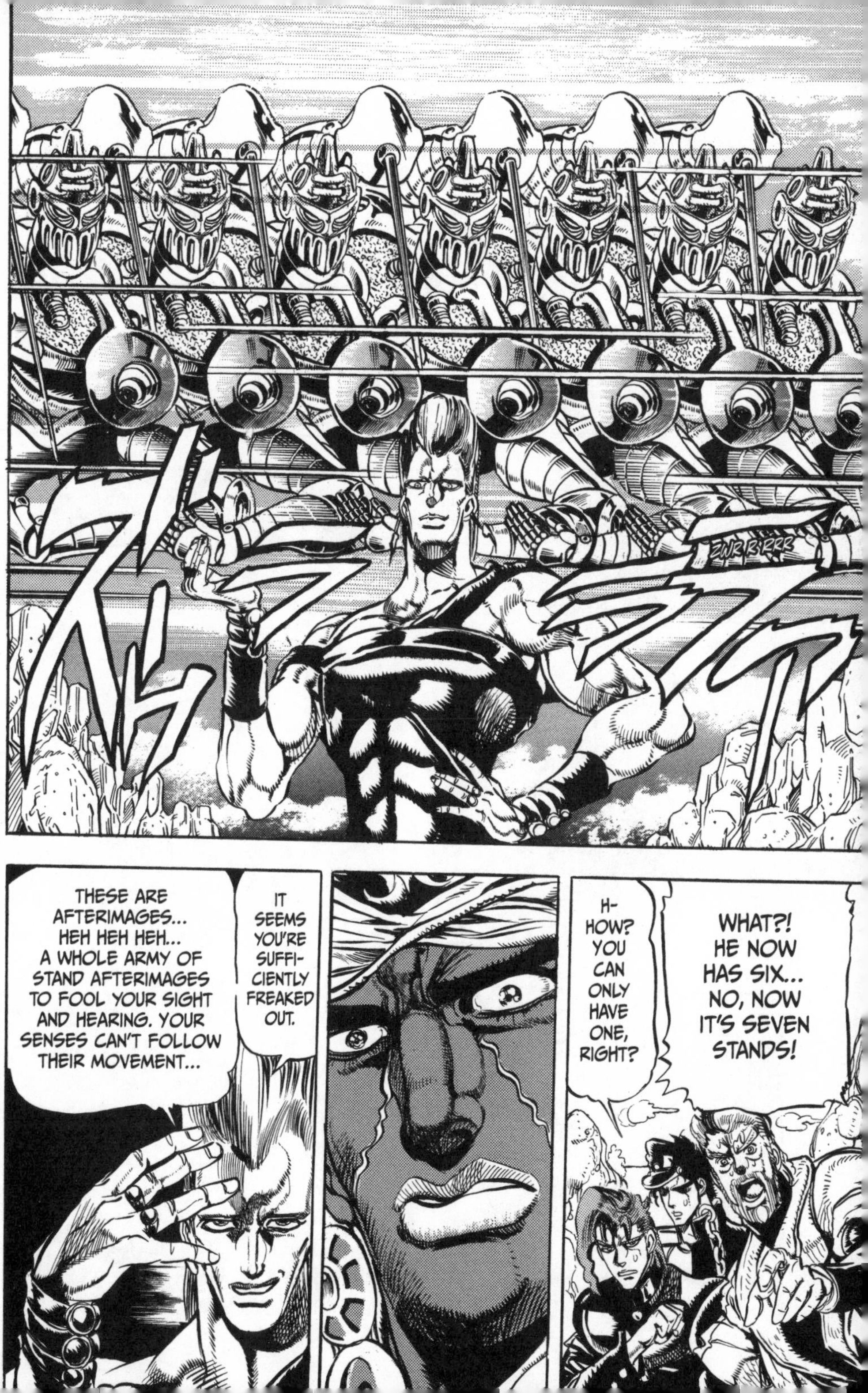
ZWR R RRR
WHAT?! HE NOW HAS SIX... NO, NOW IT'S SEVEN STANDS!
H-HOW? YOU CAN ONLY HAVE ONE, RIGHT?
IT SEEMS YOU'RE SUFFICIENTLY FREAKED OUT.
THESE ARE AFTERIMAGES... HEH HEH HEH... A WHOLE ARMY OF STAND AFTERIMAGES TO FOOL YOUR SIGHT AND HEARING. YOUR SENSES CAN'T FOLLOW THEIR MOVEMENT...

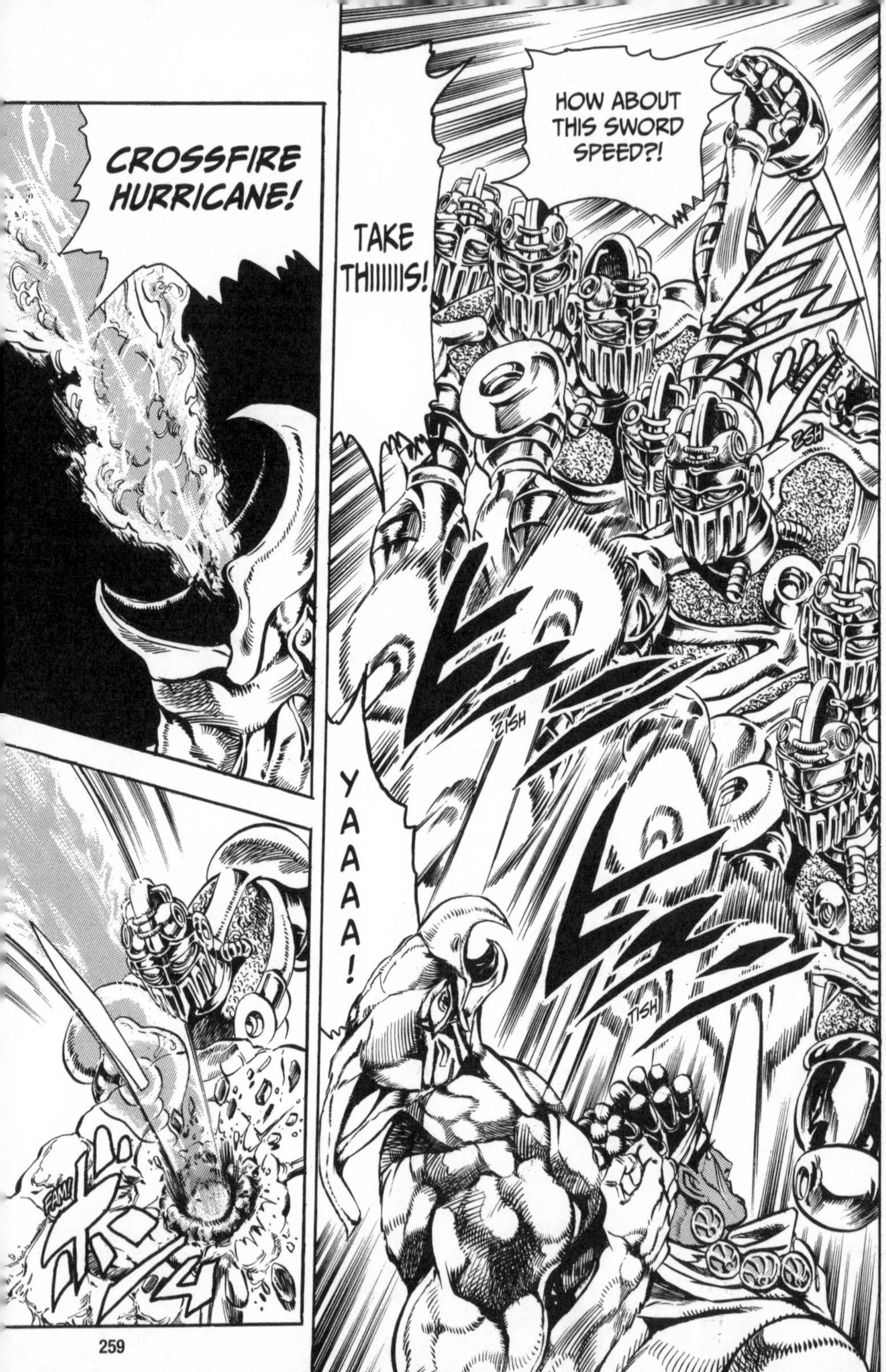

HOW ABOUT THIS SWORD SPEED?!
TAKE THIIIIIIS!
ZISH
ZISH
YAAAAAA!
TISH
CROSSFIRE HURRICANE!
FAM!

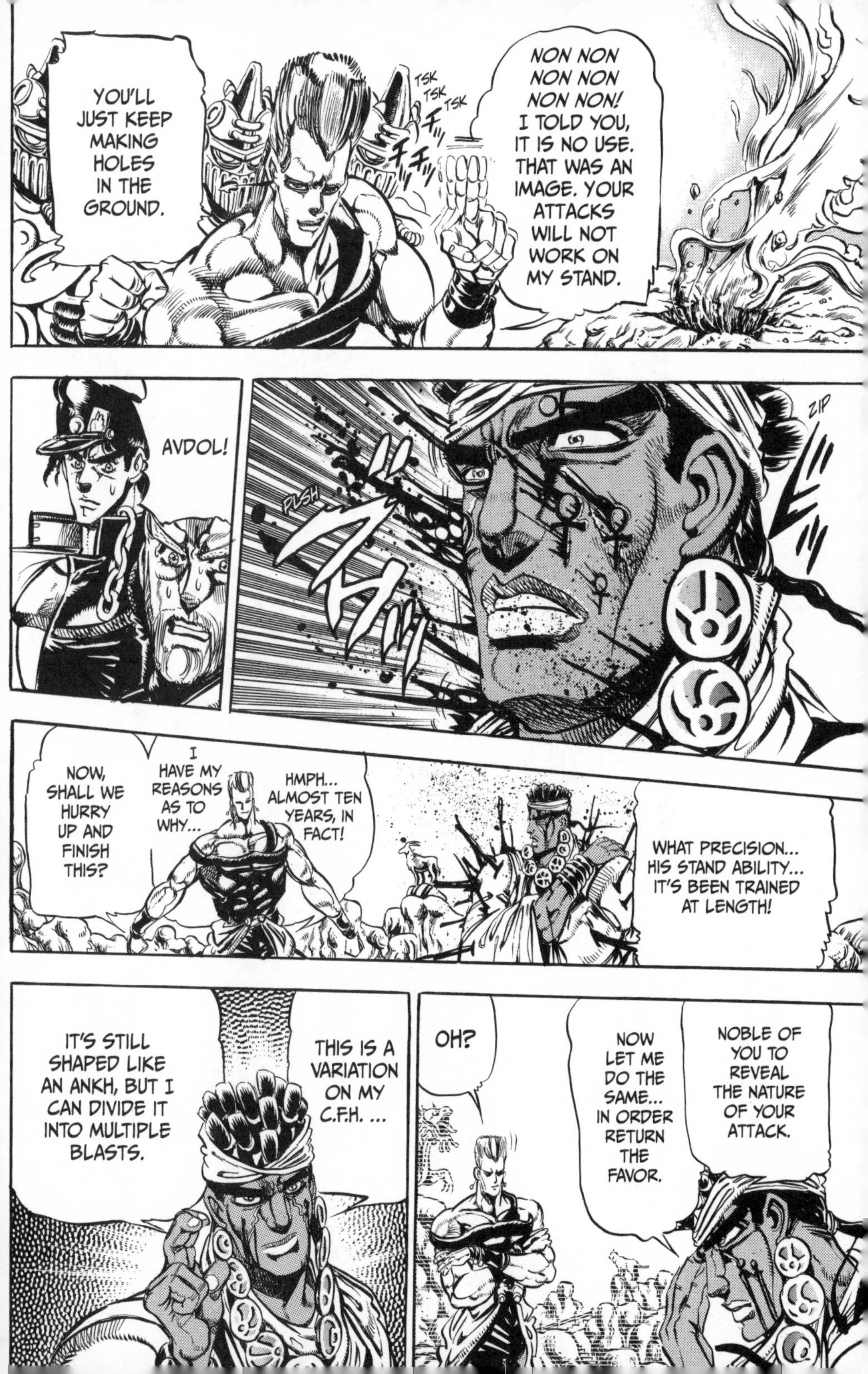
NON NON NON NON NON NON! I TOLD YOU, IT IS NO USE. THAT WAS AN IMAGE. YOUR ATTACKS WILL NOT WORK ON MY STAND.
TSK TSK TSK
YOU'LL JUST KEEP MAKING HOLES IN THE GROUND.
ZIP
PLSH
AVDOL!
WHAT PRECISION... HIS STAND ABILITY... IT'S BEEN TRAINED AT LENGTH!
HMPH... ALMOST TEN YEARS, IN FACT!
I HAVE MY REASONS AS TO WHY...
NOW, SHALL WE HURRY UP AND FINISH THIS?
NOBLE OF YOU TO REVEAL THE NATURE OF YOUR ATTACK.
NOW LET ME DO THE SAME... IN ORDER RETURN THE FAVOR.
OH?
THIS IS A VARIATION ON MY C.F.H. ...
IT'S STILL SHAPED LIKE AN ANKH, BUT I CAN DIVIDE IT INTO MULTIPLE BLASTS.

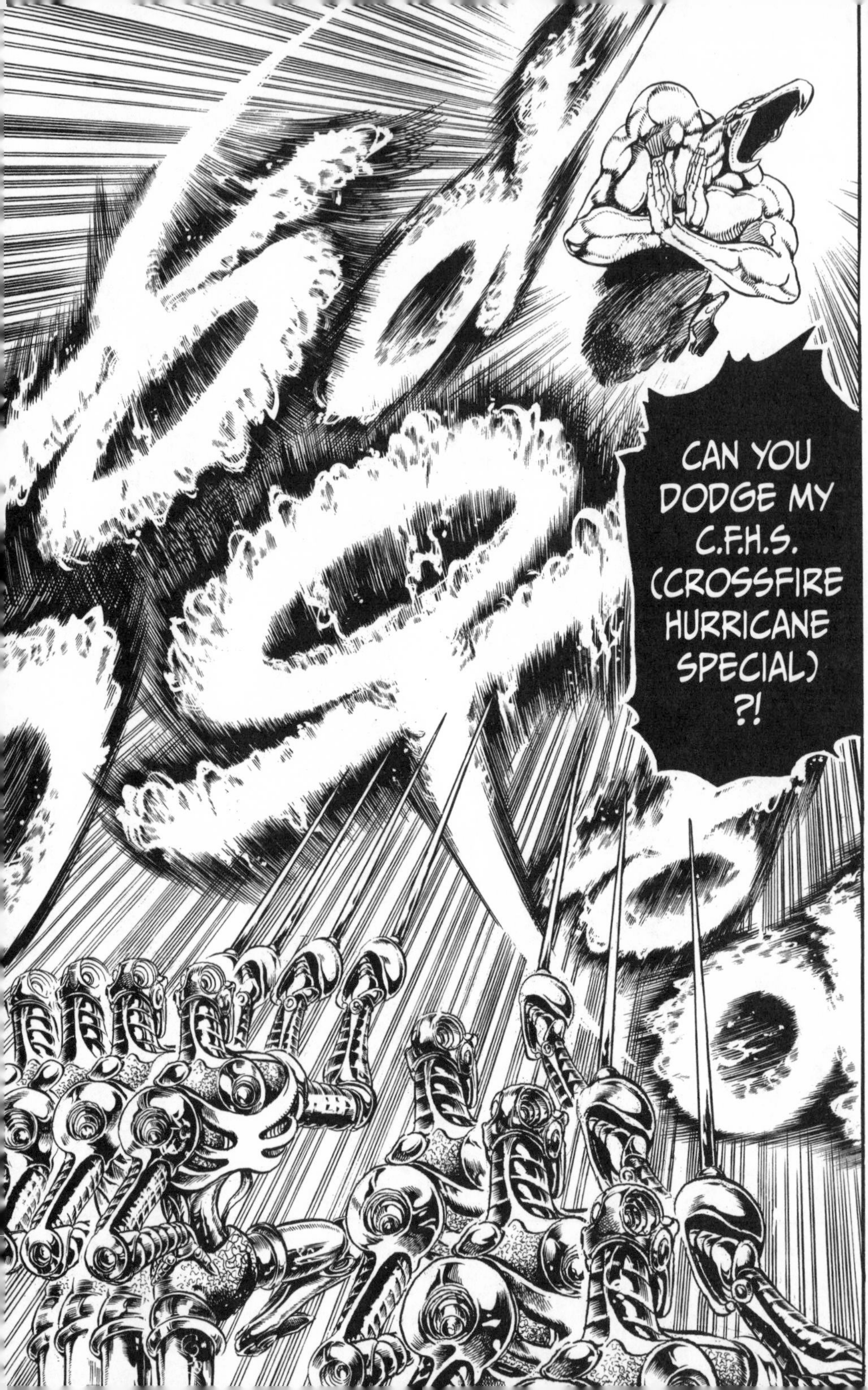
CAN YOU DODGE MY C.F.H.S. (CROSSFIRE HURRICANE SPECIAL) ?!

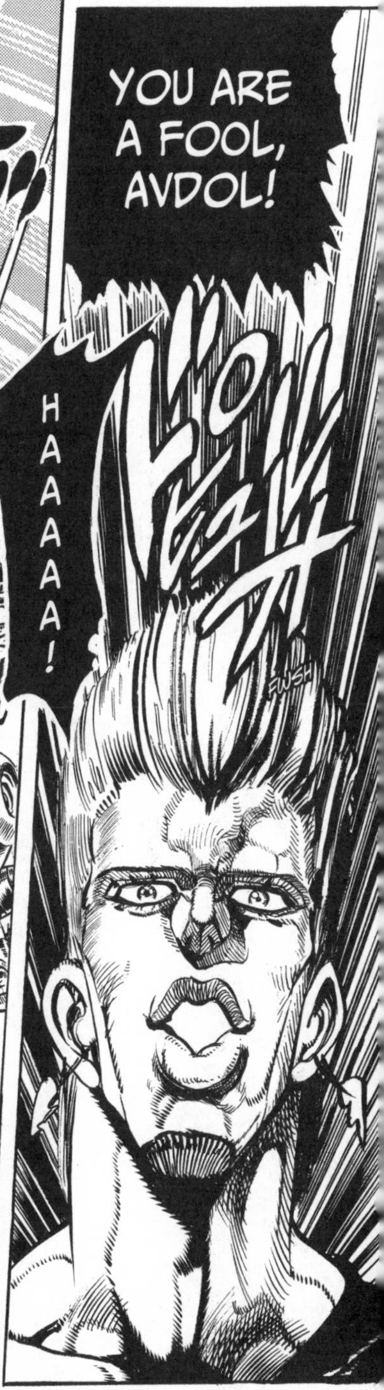
YOU ARE A FOOL, AVDOL!
HAAAAAA!
FWSH

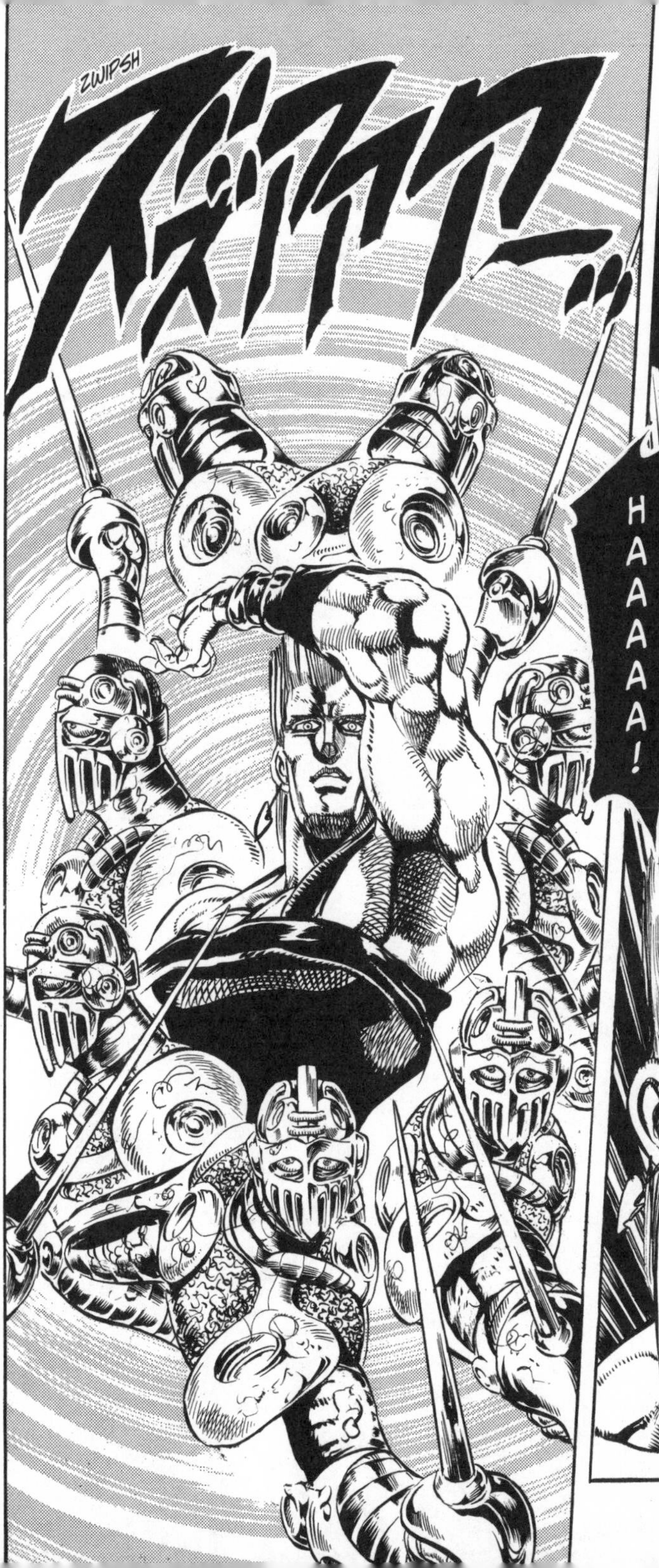
ZWIPSH

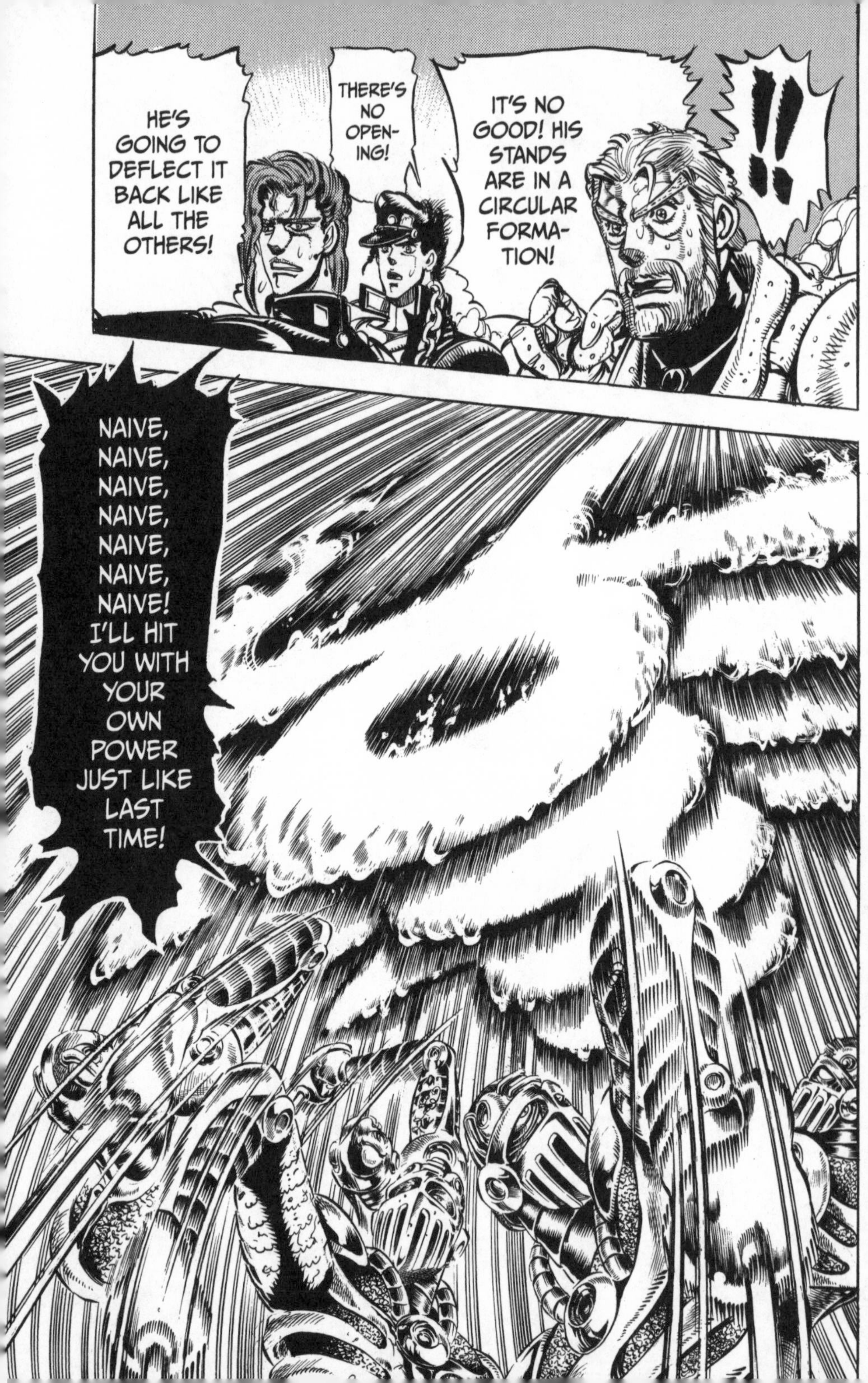
!!
IT'S NO GOOD! HIS STANDS ARE IN A CIRCULAR FORMATION!
THERE'S NO OPENING!
HE'S GOING TO DEFLECT IT BACK LIKE ALL THE OTHERS!
NAIVE, NAIVE, NAIVE, NAIVE, NAIVE, NAIVE, NAIVE! I'LL HIT YOU WITH YOUR OWN POWER JUST LIKE LAST TIME!

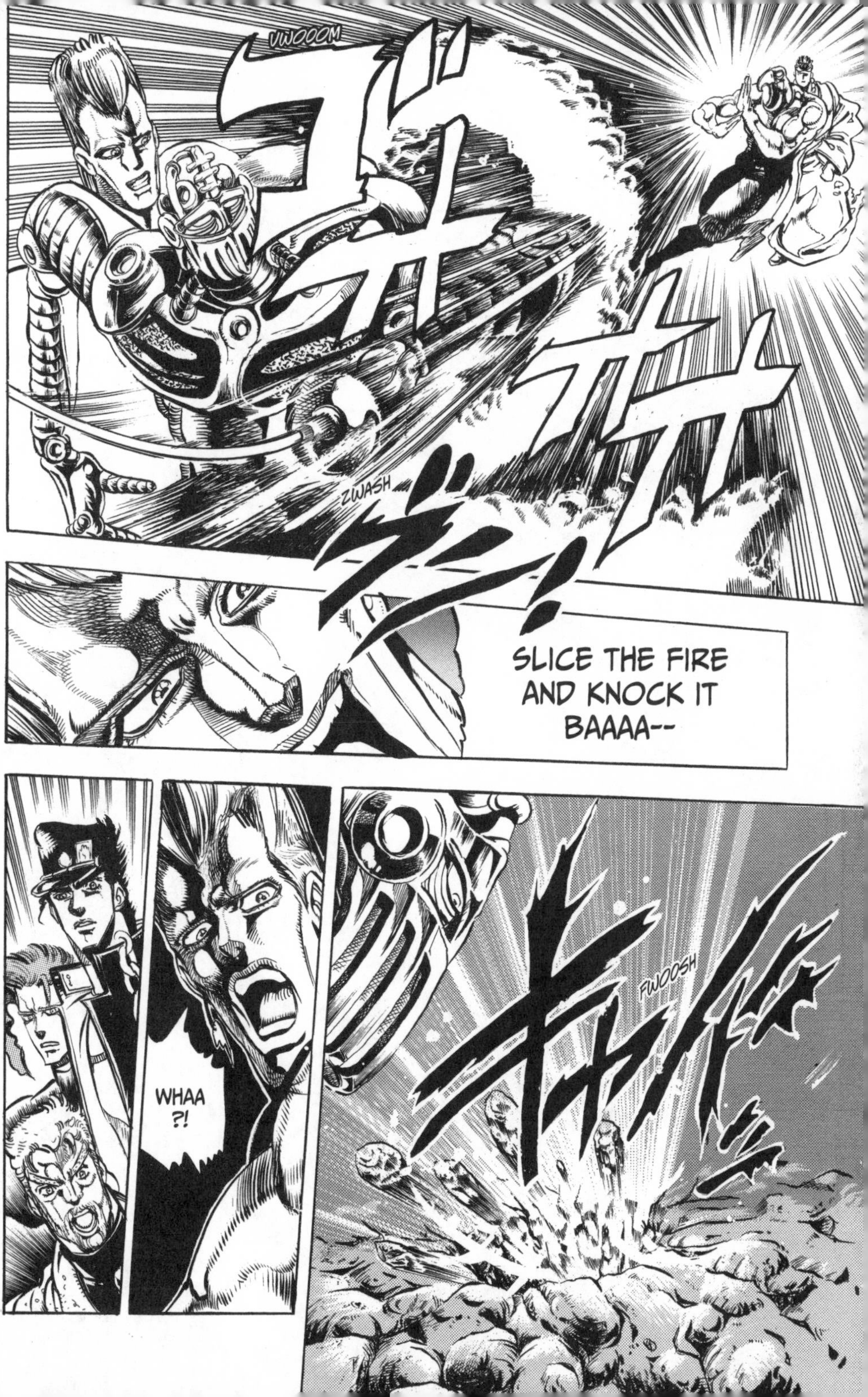
VWOOOM
ZWASH
SLICE THE FIRE AND KNOCK IT BAAAA--
FWOOSH
WHAA ?!

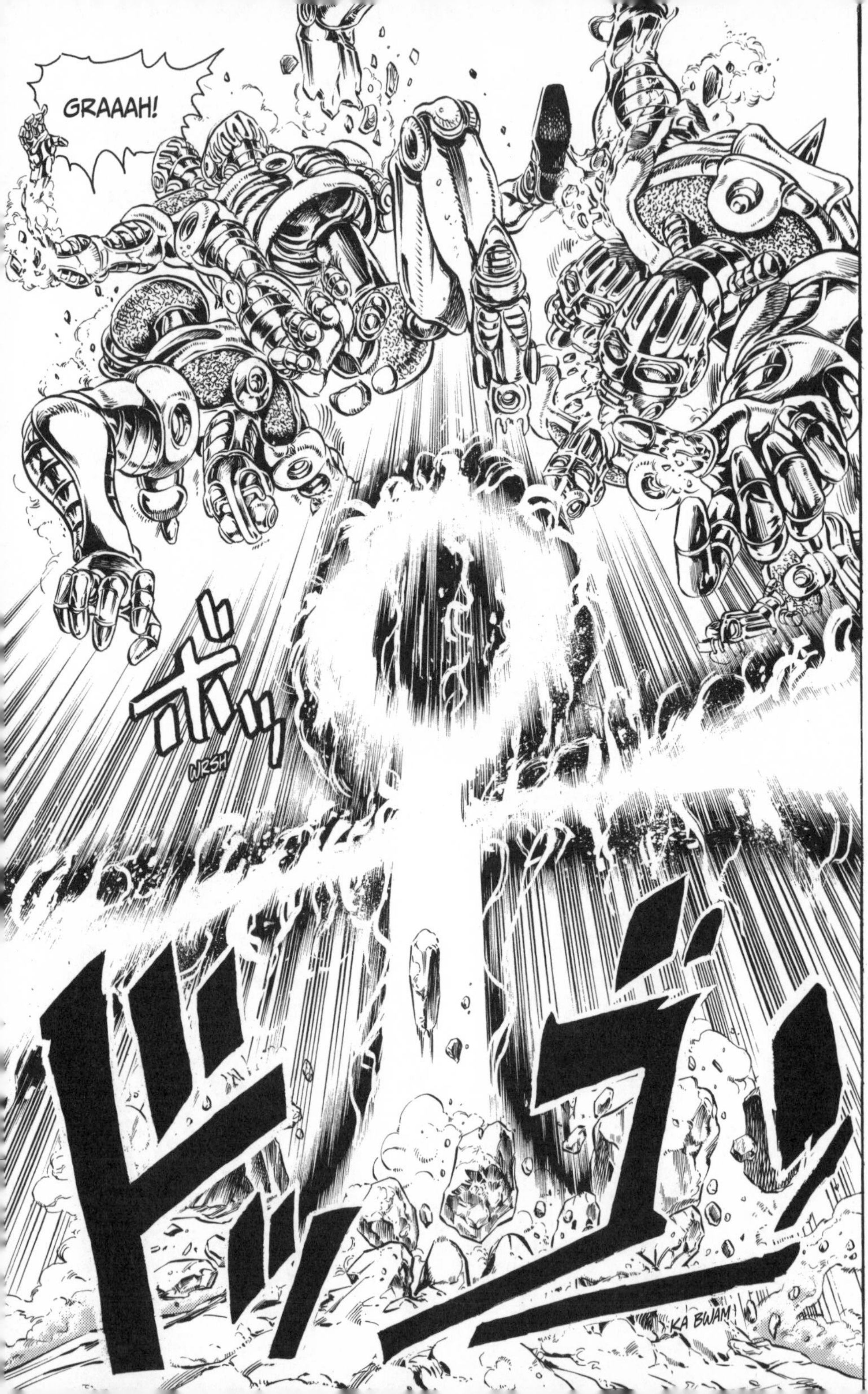
GRAAAH!
WRSH
KA BWAM!

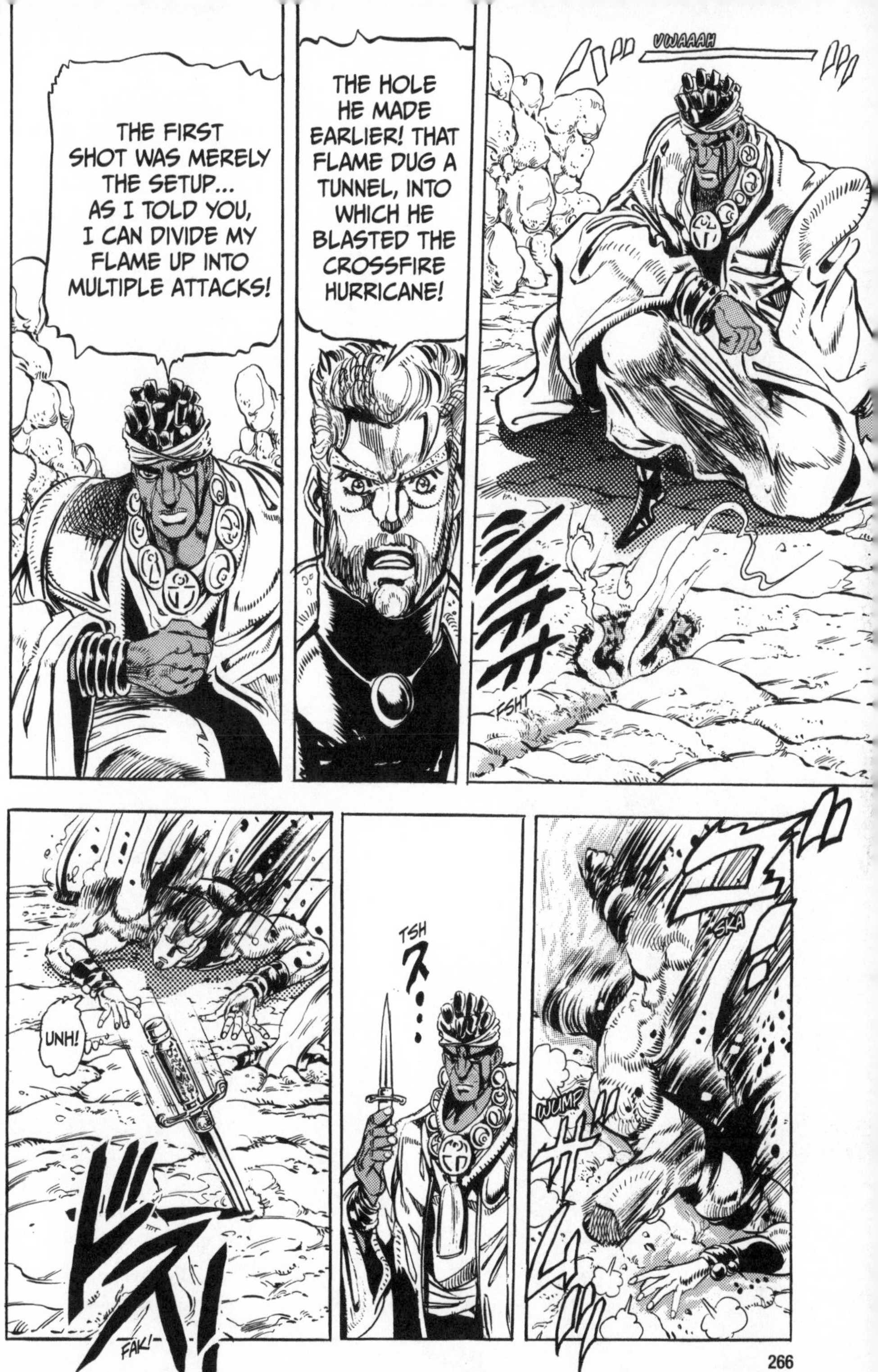
UWAAAH
FSHT
THE HOLE HE MADE EARLIER! THAT FLAME DUG A TUNNEL, INTO WHICH HE BLASTED THE CROSSFIRE HURRICANE!
THE FIRST SHOT WAS MERELY THE SETUP... AS I TOLD YOU, I CAN DIVIDE MY FLAME UP INTO MULTIPLE ATTACKS!
SKA
WUMP
TSH
UNH!
FAK!

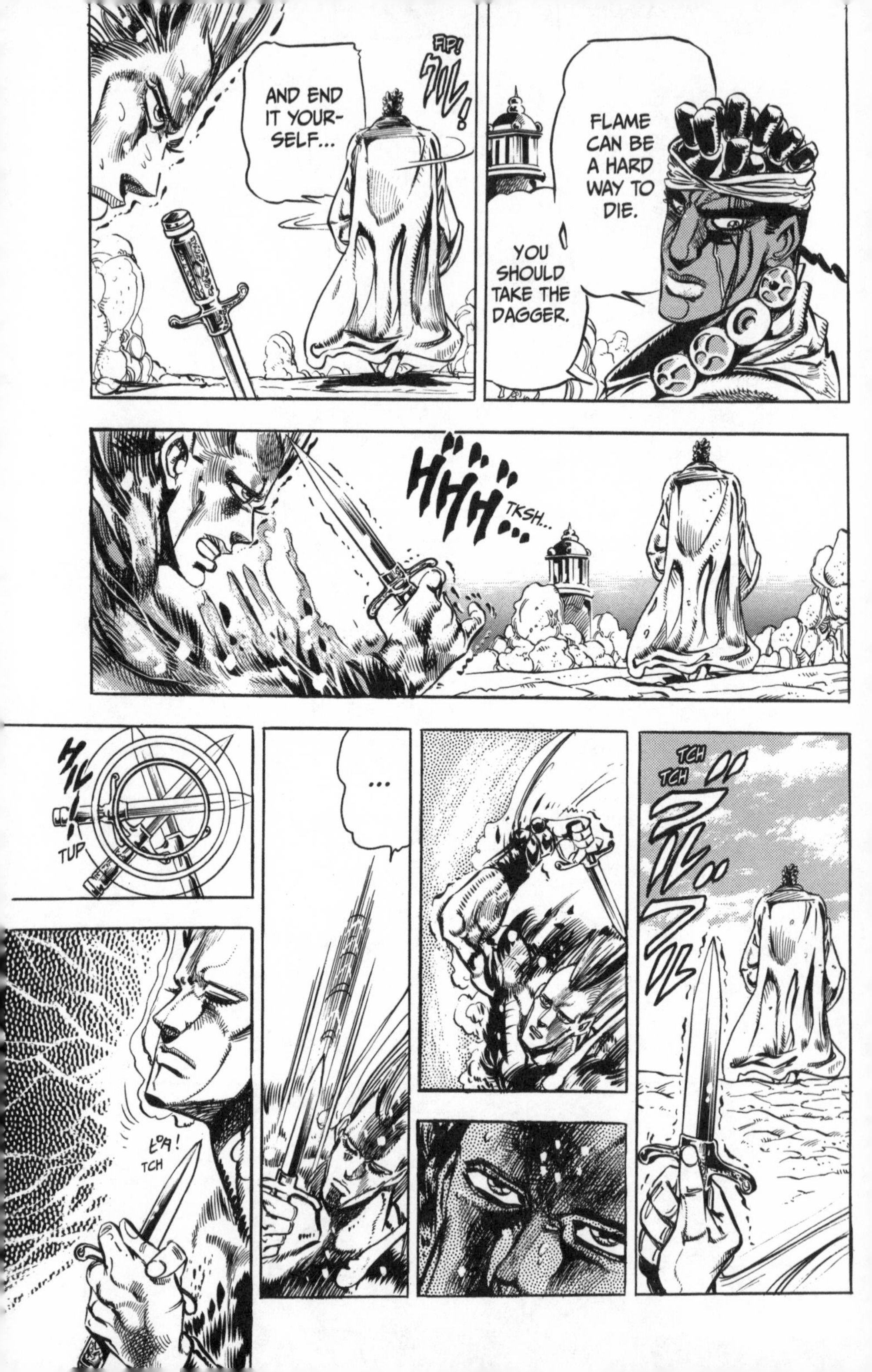
FLAME CAN BE A HARD WAY TO DIE.
YOU SHOULD TAKE THE DAGGER.
FLP!
AND END IT YOURSELF...
TKSH...
TCH TCH
...
TUP
TCH

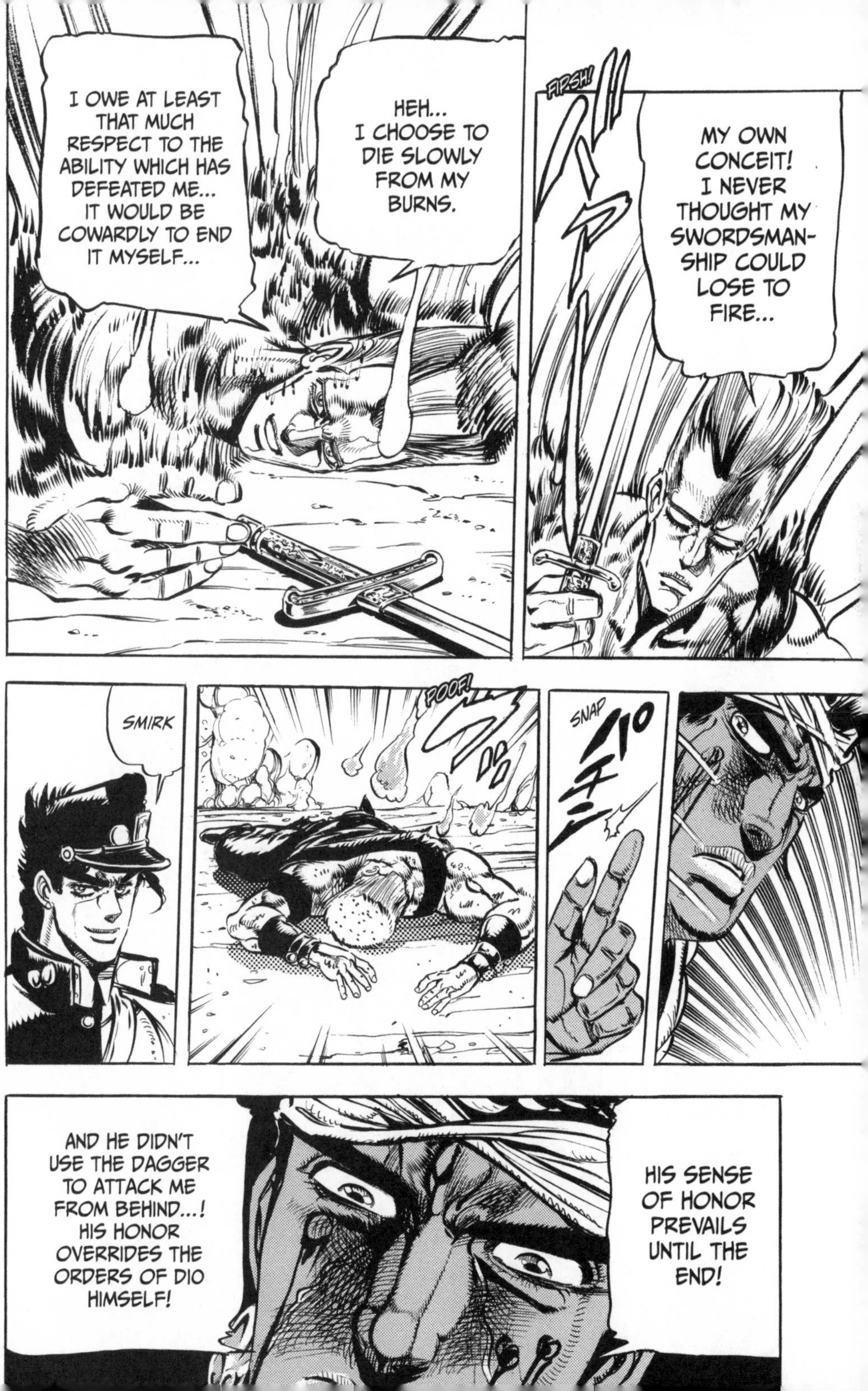

FIRSH!
MY OWN CONCEIT! I NEVER THOUGHT MY SWORDSMAN-SHIP COULD LOSE TO FIRE...
HEH... I CHOOSE TO DIE SLOWLY FROM MY BURNS.
I OWE AT LEAST THAT MUCH RESPECT TO THE ABILITY WHICH HAS DEFEATED ME... IT WOULD BE COWARDLY TO END IT MYSELF...
SNAP
POOF!
SMIRK
HIS SENSE OF HONOR PREVAILS UNTIL THE END!
AND HE DIDN'T USE THE DAGGER TO ATTACK ME FROM BEHIND...! HIS HONOR OVERRIDES THE ORDERS OF DIO HIMSELF!

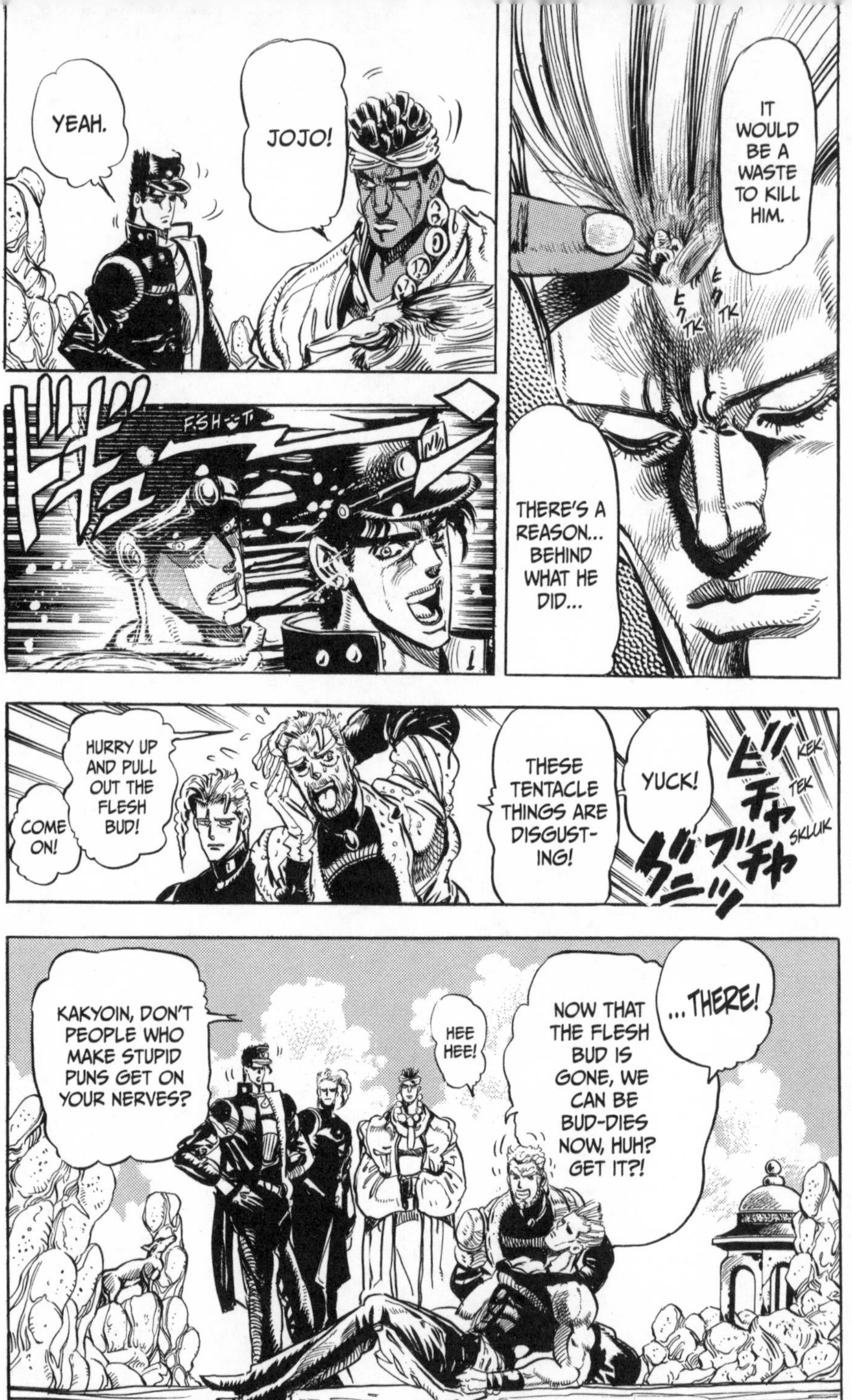
IT WOULD BE A WASTE TO KILL HIM.
TK TK
THERE'S A REASON... BEHIND WHAT HE DID...
JOJO!
YEAH.
F-SH-T
KEK
TEK
SKLUK
YUCK!
THESE TENTACLE THINGS ARE DISGUST-ING!
HURRY UP AND PULL OUT THE FLESH BUD!
COME ON!
...THERE!
NOW THAT THE FLESH BUD IS GONE, WE CAN BE BUD-DIES NOW, HUH? GET IT?!
HEE HEE!
KAKYOIN, DON'T PEOPLE WHO MAKE STUPID PUNS GET ON YOUR NERVES?

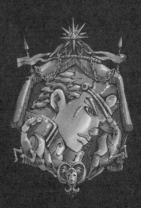

JoJo's
BIZARRE ADVENTURE

(01)

END

To Be Continued

JoJo's BIZARRE ADVENTURE

01

Jo

荒木飛呂彦が
語る
キャラクター一
誕生秘話

Hirohiko Araki talks about character creation!

JoJo's BIZARRE ADVENTURE
PART 3
STARDUST CRUSADERS

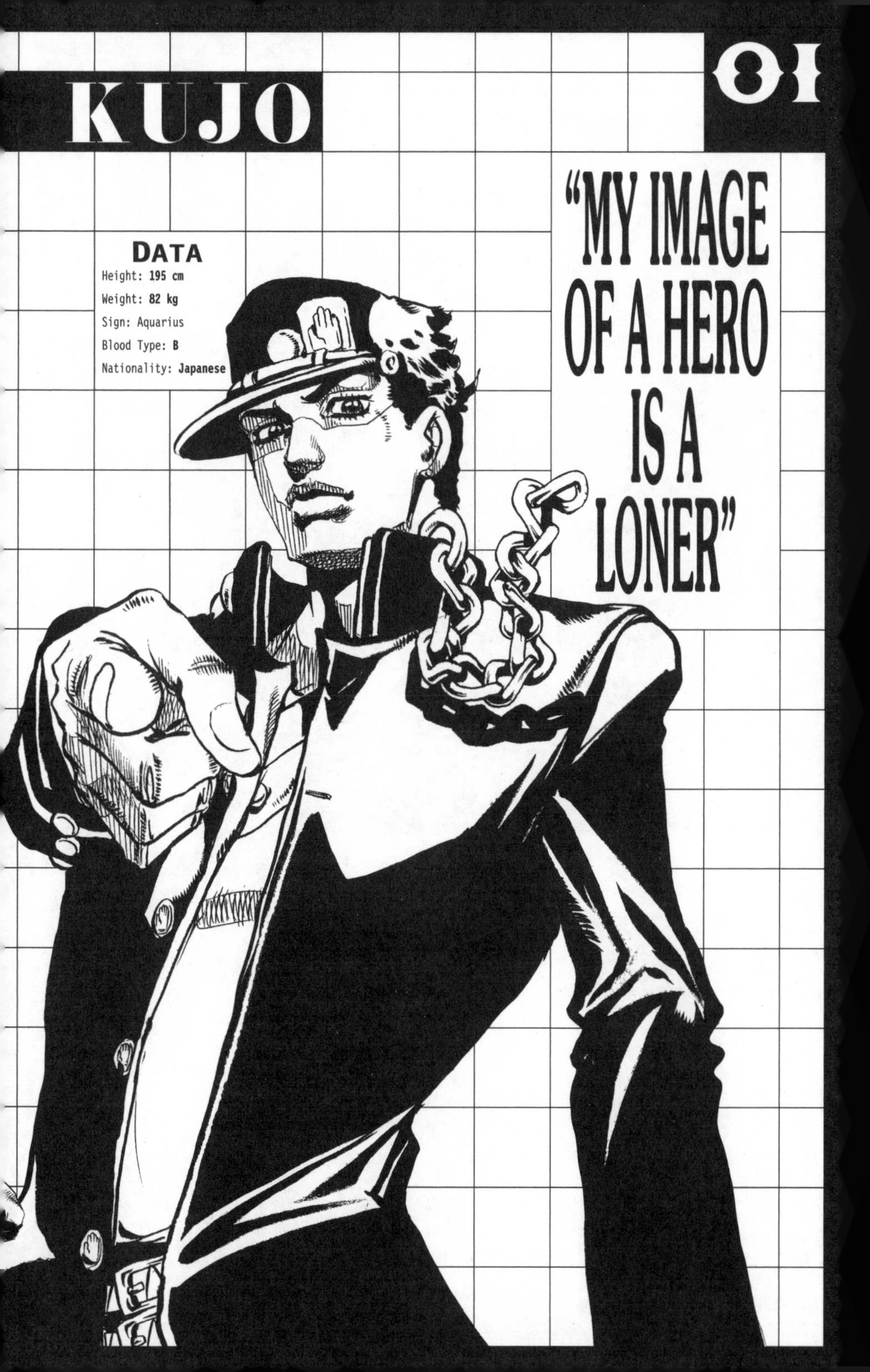
KUJO
01
DATA
Height: 195 cm
Weight: 82 kg
Sign: Aquarius
Blood Type: B
Nationality: Japanese
"MY IMAGE OF A HERO IS A LONER"

JoJo — JOTARO

The idea of making the main character of Part 3 Japanese was something I had thought of doing around the end of Part 1. I had originally planned *JoJo* to be a trilogy, and thought it would be appropriate to have the final, fated confrontation take place in present-day Japan, but I didn't want it to be a tournament-style affair, like what was popular in *Weekly Shonen Jump* at the time. That's when I had the idea of having the characters head for a specific destination, like a road movie, taking inspiration from Jules Verne's *Around the World in Eighty Days*. Years later, a certain TV comedian took a trip across Eurasia along a similar route. Just like with *JoJo's Bizarre Adventure (JoJo no Kimyou na Bouken)* coming out before *Bizarre Stories in This World (Yonimo Kimyou na Monogatari)*, I'll say that for the record, *JoJo* did it first (laughs).

Clint Eastwood, who I love and respect as an actor, served as the model for Jotaro. Jotaro's trademark pose where he points his finger actually was inspired by Eastwood pointing his .44 Magnum. Even details such as Jotaro's catchphrase being "good grief" take inspiration from parts that Eastwood played, where he'd have lines like "A bank robbery? You have to be kidding me…" That's why Jotaro seems a bit "rougher" compared to other *Jump* protagonists. Joseph might be a little easier to get into from a *Weekly Shonen Jump* perspective, but Jotaro actually fits my image of a hero to a tee.

My image of a hero is that of a loner. As opposed to someone who does the right thing looking for compensation or attention from others, my idea of a hero is someone who is an unappreciated symbol of justice.
There are times where taking the correct path leads to loneliness. I also think that heroes shouldn't be in the business of making friends. Jotaro goes on his journey while keeping his feelings bottled up inside because he's a "lone hero." He doesn't celebrate in an over-the-top manner when he defeats an enemy.
For him, a throwaway "good grief" is plenty.

Jotaro has become big enough to function as a synonym for *JoJo* as a whole. I've actually based subsequent JoJos on his visual design and differentiated them from there. My original vision for Jotaro was having him journeying through the desert while wearing his school uniform, and with that, fantastical and bizarre things would happen to him during his day-to-day life. On top of that, it's not your everyday uniform. He's got a chain hooked on to his collar, two belts… I played around with his design quite a bit until I got something that conveyed just the right amount of rebellion. Speaking of teenage rebels, you know how guys used to have chains hanging from their pants, connected to their wallets? I drew Jotaro with his chain on his uniform first (laughs)! Let's add that to the record as well.

The story behind the new illustration for **JoJo Part 3 01**

Q. What is the meaning of Star Platinum's pose?

A. It represents the starting point for Part 3-- the work of Mitsuteru Yokoyama.

The concept of wearing one's school uniform in the desert has its roots in Yokoyama Sensei's *Babel II*. If I were to draw Part 3 all over again, I would have used Yokoyama Sensei's *Tetsujin 28-go* as inspiration for the Stands, representing a return to the basics. ~Hirohiko Araki

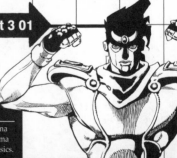

JOJO'S BIZARRE ADVENTURE

PART 3 STARDUST CRUSADERS

BY

HIROHIKO ARAKI

SHONEN JUMP ADVANCED EDITION
Translation ☆ Alexis Kirsch
English Adaptation ☆ Fred Burke
Editor ☆ Jason Thompson

DELUXE HARDCOVER EDITION
Translation ☆ Evan Galloway
Touch-Up Art & Lettering ☆ Mark McMurray
Design ☆ Fawn Lau
Editor ☆ Urian Brown

Original Japanese cover design by
MITSURU KOBAYASHI (GENI A LÒIDE)

Printed in the U.S.A.

Published by VIZ Media, LLC
P.O. Box 77010
San Francisco, CA 94107

10 9 8
First printing, November 2016
Eighth printing, April 2023

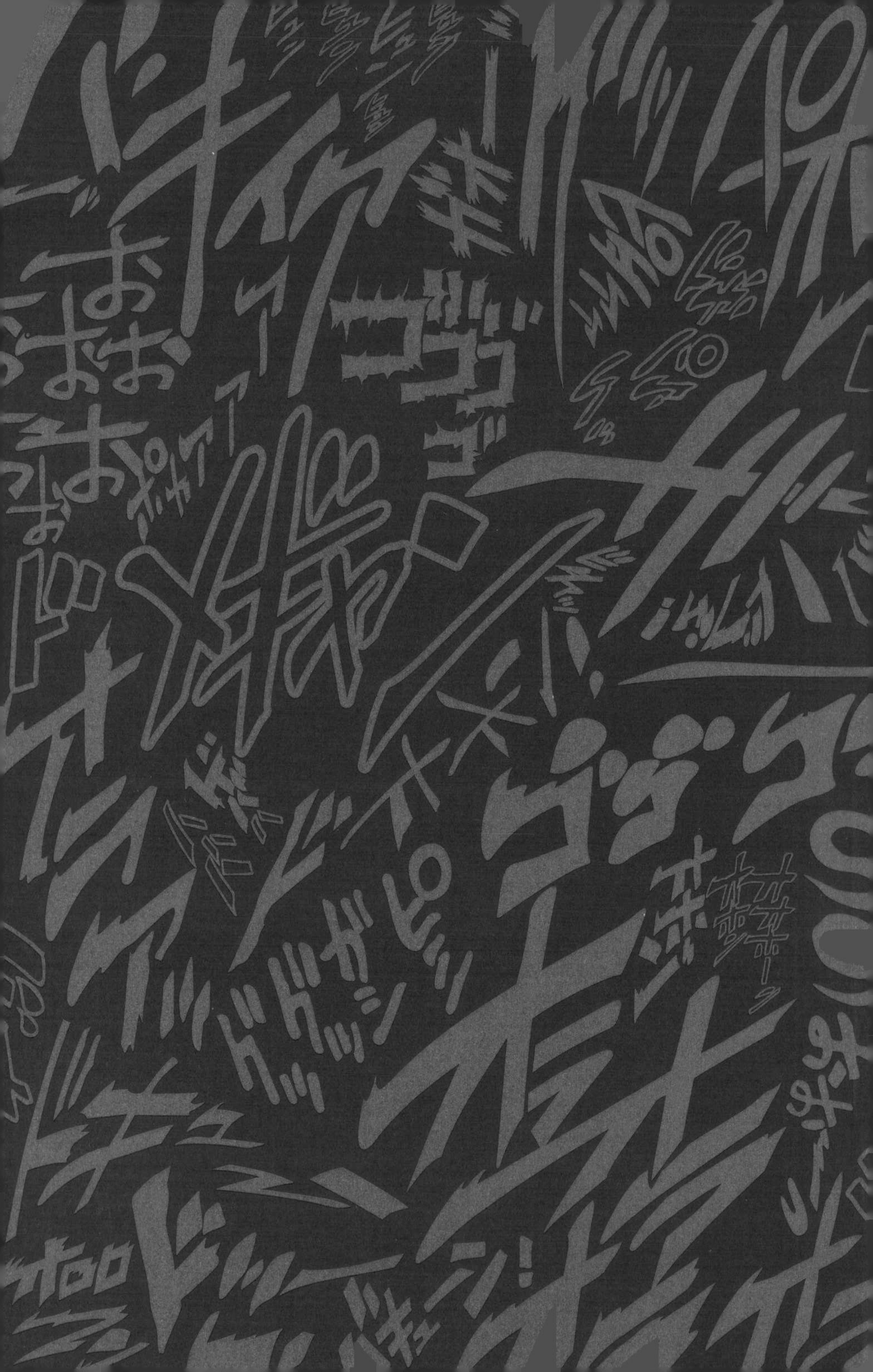

W9-CLC-306

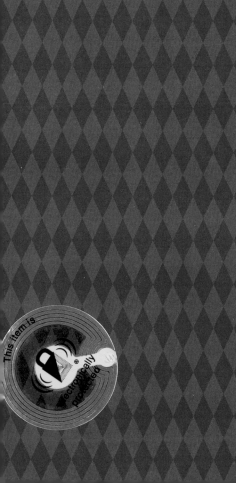